Slutzky equation

$$\eta_t = \eta_s - k\iota$$

Cross-price elasticity of demand

$$\eta_{xy} = \frac{\Delta q_x/q_x}{\Delta P_y/P_y} = \frac{\Delta q_x}{\Delta P_y} \cdot \frac{P_y}{q_x} \quad \text{or}$$

$$\eta_{yx} = \frac{\Delta q_y/q_y}{\Delta P_x/P_x} = \frac{\Delta q_y}{\Delta P_x} \cdot \frac{P_x}{q_y}$$

x **and** y **are substitutes if**

$$\eta_{xy} = \frac{\Delta q_x/q_x}{\Delta P_y/P_y}$$

$\left. \begin{array}{l} \text{Quantity of} \\ x \text{ demanded} \\ \text{increases} \\ \text{Price of } y \\ \text{increases} \end{array} \right\}$ $\dfrac{(+)/q_x}{(+)/P_y} = (+) = \eta_{xy}$

$\left. \begin{array}{l} \text{Quantity of} \\ x \text{ demanded} \\ \text{decreases} \\ \text{Price of } y \\ \text{decreases} \end{array} \right\}$ $\dfrac{(-)/q_x}{(-)/P_y} = (+) = \eta_{xy}$

x **and** y **are complements if**

$\left. \begin{array}{l} \text{Quantity} \\ \text{demanded of} \\ x \text{ increases} \\ \text{Price of} \\ y \text{ decreases} \end{array} \right\}$ $\dfrac{(+)/q_x}{(-)/P_y} = (-) = \eta_{xy}$

Marginal revenue and price elasticity

$$MR = P\left(1 + \frac{1}{\eta}\right)$$

Personal rate of discount

$$= \left(\begin{array}{l} \text{value an individual} \\ \text{places on this year's} \\ \text{goods in terms of } \rho \\ \text{foregone goods of next} \\ \text{year} \end{array} \right) - 1$$

General formula for discounting

$$P_t = \frac{A}{(1+r)^t}$$

The relationship between marginal and average physical product

$$MPP_L = APP_L + (\Delta APP_L)L$$

The law of diminishing marginal returns

Holding technology and all inputs except one constant, as equal increments of the variable input are added, beyond a certain point the resulting rate of increase in product will decrease. Otherwise stated, after a certain point, the marginal physical product of the variable input will diminish.

Slope of the isoquant

$$\text{Slope of isoquant} = \frac{\Delta K}{\Delta L}$$

Marginal rate of technical substitution, (MRTS)

$$MRTS_{L:K} = \frac{MPP_L}{MPP_K}$$

Optimal use of capital and labor for a *given* total cost

$$MRTS_{L:K} = \frac{MPP_L}{MPP_K} = \frac{w}{r}$$

The relationship between AVC and APP

$$AVC = w\,\frac{1}{APP}$$

Cost minimization at a given output level

$$\frac{MPP_{\text{labor}}}{\text{Wage rate/unit}}$$

$$= \frac{MPP_{\text{capital}}}{(\text{implicit rental}) \text{ price/unit of capital}}$$

Relationship between MC and MPP

$$MC = w\left(\frac{1}{MPP}\right)$$

Intermediate Microeconomics

McGraw-Hill Book Company
New York
St. Louis
San Francisco
Auckland
Bogotá
Düsseldorf
Johannesburg
London
Madrid
Mexico
Montreal
New Delhi
Panama
Paris
São Paulo
Singapore
Sydney
Tokyo
Toronto

Intermediate Microeconomics

Theory, Issues, and Applications

Roger LeRoy Miller

Professor of Economics
School of Business
and
Law and Economics Center
School of Law, University of Miami

Intermediate Microeconomics
Theory, Issues, and Applications

34567890 DODO 7832109

This book was set in Palatino and Helvetica by
Textbook Services, Inc. The editors were J. S. Dietrich,
Michael Elia, and Annette Hall; the designer was
Hermann Strohbach; the production supervisor was
Leroy A. Young. The drawings were done by
J & R Services, Inc.
R. R. Donnelley & Sons Company was printer and
binder.

Library of Congress Cataloging in Publication Data

Miller, Roger LeRoy.
   Intermediate microeconomics.

   Bibliography: p.
   Includes index.
    1. Microeconomics. I. Title.
HB171.5.M643   330   77-24761
ISBN 0-07-042150-1

CONTENTS

DETAILED CONTENTS

PREFACE

Microeconomics is exciting and relevant. A textbook for microeconomics should convey this excitement and this relevance. I have attempted in every way possible to do just that, while preserving completeness and thoroughness in the presentation of intermediate price theory.

Some have argued, and I concur, that microeconomics is the basis of virtually all economic analysis. It seems, therefore, especially imperative that students embarking upon a career in economics and/or business be conversant not only with the foundations of microeconomic theory, but also with its application in the real world. At the end of each chapter, I have included a special Issues and Applications section which illustrates theory as a vehicle to clarify social issues and solve social problems. This serves two purposes: It reinforces the student's understanding of the theory and it demonstrates the theory's relevance. These special sections are inserted in such a way as to maintain the continuity of the text. Instructors can use them in a variety of ways or delete all or parts of them when desired.

Traditional materials included

In spite of the above-mentioned innovation, the organization of this book is traditional in nature. There is an introductory chapter; then there are chapters on the theory of consumer behavior, production and costs, the four product market organization possibilities, input markets, and general equilibrium and welfare economics. Thus, instructors used to a traditional text will feel at home with this one.

I should state at the onset that the final decision as to what to include in this text was based in part on the results of an extensive survey undertaken by McGraw-Hill Book Company. A detailed questionnaire was sent to approximately 1,600 professors of intermediate microeconomics. A complicated tabulation technique was used to summarize the information received from the 800-plus respondents. In this manner, I was able to find out whether some of my cherished microeconomic topics were also held in high esteem by my colleagues who might be using this text. (Sometimes the results of the survey were indeed painful.) I also discovered a number of topics that the majority of respondents spent more time on than I had imagined. The outline of my future work was altered accordingly. Thus, I believe that the resultant compromise will be satisfying to the preponderance of intermediate price theory instructors.

Unique chapters

There are, nonetheless, some chapters which I feel are in some ways unique. They are as follows:

Chapter 6—Time, Risk, Speculation, and Hedging. Gives an explanation of the futures market and discusses time as an economic variable.

Chapter 12—The Creation, Destruction, and Regulation of Monopolies. How monopoly profits are generated and the forces which act to dissipate them, at least on the margin.

Chapter 17—Wages, Rents, and Income Differences. Discusses investment in human capital and the distinction between rent and quasi rent.

Chapter 20—Externalities, Public Goods, and Market Failure. Includes social costs and the Coase Theorem.

Distinguishing features of specific chapters

There are certain distinguishing features added to virtually all the chapters in this text. I have included them either because I believe them to be theoretically important or because they add increased student interest in the material. They are:

Chapter 2. Revealed preference; food stamps; fringe benefits.

Chapter 3. Hicks and Slutsky income and substitution effects; Giffen goods; information and searching; effect of guaranteed annual income on work effort.

Chapter 4. Reservation prices and application to prices of stocks; why unions want higher economywide minimum wages.

Chapter 5. An appendix on econometrics; derivation of market elasticity from individual elasticities of demand; relation between price and income elasticities; drug addiction and elasticity; the demand for gasoline.

Chapter 6. Coffee prices and speculation; the used-book market; the New Territories of Hong Kong.

Chapter 7. Why firms exist; technical versus economic efficiency; real world production functions; the blue whale.

Chapter 8. Capacity; technological change; when is a capital resource really fixed; opportunity cost to continued possession.

Chapter 9. Numerous real world illustrations and problems using linear programming.

Chapter 10. Distinction between economic and accounting profit; boundary equilibrium; the cobweb model; competition and the stock market.

Chapter 11. Distinction between short-run and long-run demand and marginal revenue; capitalization of monopoly profits; measuring monopoly power; multipart pricing; economics of youth fares; criminal penalties; IBM machines and IBM cards.

Chapter 12. A market for monopoly power; policing of a cartel; discussion of vertical integration; Averch-Johnson effect; peak-load pricing; tobacco farming.

Chapter 13. Trading stamps; the optimal rate of advertising.

Chapter 14. Limit pricing; the pricing of automobiles; the courts' view of oligopoly.

Chapter 15. Extensions of short-run demand theory; acreage restriction.

Chapter 16. Exploitation; price discrimination; monopsony; what do unions maximize, including property rights materials; monopsony in intercollegiate athletics.

Chapter 17. Investment in human capital; distinction between rent and quasi rent.

Chapter 18. Input-output analysis.

Chapter 19. Distribution criteria; theory of the second best; measuring welfare costs; welfare cost of monopoly; welfare cost of price controls.

Chapter 20. Social costs and benefits; the Coase Theorem; public goods; honeybees and flowers.

The mathematics in this text

Students will find no mathematical "snow" jobs included herein. I attempted to anticipate any difficult mathematical or analytical hurdles that students might have in understanding the development of a concept. I, therefore, reduced the level of mathematics whenever this occurred or returned to very basic ideas and simple language in order to help the student understand what was going on. Thus, readers will find that any proofs given are fully explained, with no intermediate steps left out. There is no calculus anywhere, not even in the footnotes. The delta operator (Δ) is used extensively, though; and, for students unfamiliar with the delta operator, there is an appendix on it following Chapter 3.

Key pedagogical aspects

There are a number of what I consider to be necessary additions to this text to make it pedagogically more appealing to both instructors and students. Specifically, I have added the following:

1. **Self-contained graphs**—all figures contain a detailed legend which obviates the need to refer to the text to understand the graphs. This makes them easier to read the first time around and also allows the student to review more easily for examinations.

2. **Glossary of terms**—each chapter has new terms shown in **bold** the first time they appear. They are again defined at the end of the chapter. There is a special index of terms in the glossary at the end of the book; thus, the student finds reinforcement for new definitions while first reading the

chapter and can also look up a word when needed in the future.

3. **Point-by-point chapter summaries**—these summaries serve as a brief refresher of the first reading of the chapter and also as a test of comprehension during review sessions with the book.

4. **Additional readings**—for those students who wish to do additional work in the area, appropriate references are provided.

5. **Problems**—each chapter has fifteen problems, and answers to even-numbered problems are given in the back of the book. Students can therefore test their understanding of the chapter materials by working through these problems. Professors can assign odd-numbered problems as homework or can use them in examinations. The problems never ask that the student do something the chapter has not prepared him or her to do.

6. **Endpapers**—the endpapers of this text contain a number of important theoretical notions that are developed throughout the book. They can be viewed as a quickie review/refresher/reference section for the student. After reading each chapter, students can glance at the endpapers to see which key theoretical points they should have mastered. They can also use the endpapers for quick reviews for examinations and quizzes.

7. **Supplementary materials**—this text is part of a complete package, which also includes a student's *Study Guide* and an *Instructor's Manual* prepared by my long-time associate, Ronald Reddall. The *Study Guide* includes learning objectives, problems with answers, and other assorted materials which will greatly aid in the student's continued strengthening of his or her understanding of the theoretical materials within each chapter.

   The *Instructor's Manual* has a set of random comments that I have prepared which can be integrated into lectures. These comments range from caveats in the analysis to more detailed theoretical points to areas in the theoretical development that may present problems to some students. You will also find additional selected references relating to the theoretical and/or the applications areas covered in each chapter. These references can be used as a basis for lecture preparation or can be given to more advanced students who wish to do further work in the specific areas under study.

Finally, and perhaps most importantly, the *Instructor's Manual* contains a test bank that has answers to all questions included. Quizzes and examinations can be made using the questions included in the test bank as well as using the odd-numbered text problems for which answers are provided in the *Instructor's Manual*.

Also available to adopters is a complete set of transparency masters of all figures and tables from the textbook.

An alternative short course

It is by no means necessary that the entire book be used in a one-term course. I suggest below the key chapters that might be used when sufficient time is not available for all materials to be covered:

Chapters 1–5
Chapter 7
Chapter 8
Chapter 10
Chapter 11
Chapters 15–17
Chapter 20

If, in a short course, the professor feels that he or she can cover more than this, then Chapters 13 and 19 can be added.

Acknowledgments

There are a number of individuals who, at various stages of this project, offered careful and constructive criticism of the drafts of this manuscript. I list below in alphabetical order those individuals: Michael Behr (University of Wisconsin-Superior), Robert C. Bingham (Kent State University), Thomas Borcherding (Simon Fraser University), Louis De Alessi (University of Miami School of Law), William L. Holahan (University of Wisconsin-Milwaukee), Hugh Nourse (University of Missouri-St. Louis), Charles Shami (American Telephone and Telegraph), Eugene Silberberg (University of Washington), and Raburn Williams (University of Hawaii).

I would like to add a note of special thanks to Professor Robert Bingham, who helped out far in excess of the call of duty. His continued assistance aided appreciably in strengthening both the text and the supplementary materials. I also wish to thank Dr. Roger Meiners for providing Chapter 9 on linear programming.

Finally, I must express appreciation to my editors at McGraw-Hill Book Company, Stephen Dietrich and Michael Elia, both of whom worked more than they should have on this project.

Roger LeRoy Miller

1

INTRODUCTION

One year we have a food shortage, and the next year Congress attempts to pass legislation to prevent the prices of agricultural products from falling too much. One year the price of sugar approaches $3 a pound, and the next year it's selling at 50¢ a pound. A group of scientists tells us that we are definitely running out of oil, and yet another group of people, the American consumers, still buy a large number of gas-hogging automobiles.

The seeming paradoxes in the behavior of prices, markets, and individuals are legion; the three above are only the tip of an iceberg. These problems also form the basis of a multitude of pressing social and economic issues which face us every day; if we don't notice them ourselves, the news media make sure that they are brought to our attention. And if the media are not successful enough in that job, politicians pick up these issues to wage campaigns against equally concerned opponents.

How can an individual with some training in economics understand and, indeed, explain why paradoxes such as those mentioned above are really not paradoxes at all? How can one separate the real issues from the rhetoric when a politician speaks? For many such problems, a bare understanding of the so-called **budget constraint** is sufficient. When you realize that at any moment in time the total amount of resources is fixed, then you are automatically faced with the fact that trade-offs must be made: When the politician asks for more of one thing, it usually means less of something else. But there are many issues which cannot be understood so simply. Rather, a more complete grasp of how markets work is necessary. The knowledge of and ability to apply basic microeconomic theory cannot fail to aid the inquisitive mind's attempt to understand how markets function. A microeconomic model can help to give a better idea of how our entire economic system works and how it can be compared with other economic systems. It can even help to predict what will happen in the world around us when the environment changes.

The market or price system as a form of social organization

The subject matter of economics is the social organization of economic activity. There are numerous ways in which economic activity may be socially organized. When we refer to **organization**, we mean nothing more than the coordination of individuals, each doing different things, in the furtherance of a common end. It does not take much reflection to realize that economic activities in our world are organized. The number of individuals who have contributed in many different ways to supplying the wants of even the poorest citizen in our country is immense. The type of social organization which allows for this coordination of activities among individuals is essentially a **market** or **price system**. In such a system, resources tend to flow where they yield the highest rate of return, or highest profit. Prices generate the signals for such resource movements; they provide information cheaply and quickly; and they affect incentives. These prices are determined in the myriad markets for the myriad goods and services bought and sold every day.

A market system is only one type of social organization for production and distribution.

A political social organization would be another. Within this very broad category of political systems, there are a large number of variants—majority rule, dictatorship, plurality, and so on. Actually, within most countries a combination of market and political systems is used: a hybrid social organization which determines production and distribution. This can be seen in the well-known circular flow of income diagram shown in Figure 1-1. In this simplified economic system, there are individuals, firms, and "the government." The activities, i.e., the flows of goods and resources in the private (i.e., nongovernment) market section of the economy, depend on voluntary exchange. The flows of goods and resources to the government depend on the net result of political activity within the existing institutional framework of laws, precedent, tradition, and custom.

We could depict another social organization in which there was a dictatorship. This is sometimes called a **command economy**. In such a system, flows of goods and resources would be ordered directly by whoever was the dictator. However, in this text we will concern ourselves with the determinants of flows within the private market system of social organization.

Models and methodology

The meaning of the term "microeconomic model" can be inferred from the words themselves. Microeconomics, or price theory, as it is sometimes called, involves, at a minimum, the study of the behavior of households, firms, and the markets in which they operate. It is *micro*economic as opposed to *macro*economic analysis; the latter involves the study of such economywide phenomena as inflation, unemployment, and the like. The term "model" here is meant to be synonymous with theory. Microeconomic models are therefore models

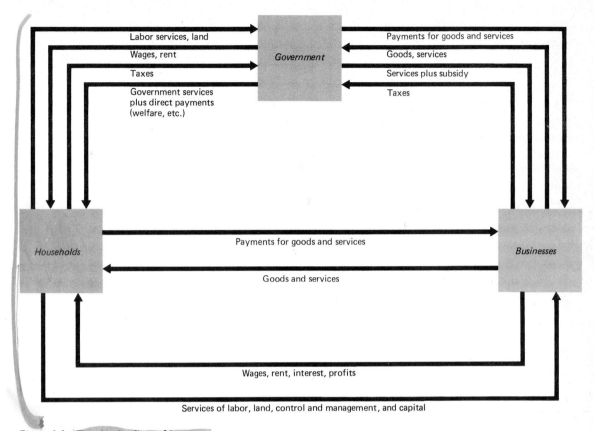

Figure 1-1: The circular flow of income.
This highly simplified diagram shows the circular flows of income within the economy. In this diagram we have left out the foreign sector and the credit and investment markets. What we do show, however, are the basic interrelationships that exist among the different sectors of the economy.

which purport to explain and predict the behavior of consumers and producers.

Models and realism

At the outset, it must be emphasized that no model in any science, and therefore no microeconomic model, is completely realistic in the sense that it captures every detail and interrelationship that exists. Not only is such a model impossible to build, but it would also be impossible to work with. No model of the solar system, for example, could possibly take account of all aspects of the entire system. The nature of scientific model building is such that the model should capture the essential relationships that are sufficient to analyze or answer the particular question at hand. For example, when we attempt to construct a model of consumer behavior in the face of changing prices for a particular commodity, there are at the very least a million determinants of how each consumer will respond to such changes in prices. However, most of those determinants are left out of our model. It is not that they are meaningless; rather, the model that we usually use, which includes the price of the particular commodity, the income of the consumer, the price of substitutes for the commodity in question, and the price of complements for the commodity in question, seems to be adequate. That is, just taking into account the magnitudes of these four determinants of consumer demand works "well," even though the model is "unrealistic" because it does not capture *all* the various determinants of consumer demand. In sum, then, a microeconomic model cannot be faulted merely by stating that it is unrealistic vis-à-vis the real world, for that same model may be very realistic in terms of elucidating the *central* issue at hand or forces at work.

Assumptions

Every model is based on a set of assumptions or axioms. In one sense, we do not directly or explicitly test the assumptions or axioms on which we base our models; that is, we do not try to identify every symbol in the axioms' real world phenomena. To be fruitful, assumptions must be general. On the other hand, assumptions are indeed indirectly tested by comparing their implications with facts in the real world. When facts in the real world refute theories that are based on a certain set of assumptions, the real world facts, or empirical findings, are indirectly refuting those assumptions.

When students undertake the study of chemistry or physics, they often do not question the unrealistic nature of the assumptions used in physical or chemical models. In physics, for example, there is a model of a "perfect gas." Of course, no actual gas in the world meets the requirements of the assumption of a perfect gas, and yet the model that is based on this assumption of perfect gas—called Boyle's law—is well known and accepted. Why? Because it seems to work well. Now, you might be asking, What does work "well" mean?

Deciding on the usefulness of a model

We generally do not attempt to determine the usefulness or "goodness" of a model merely by discussing its realism, i.e., the realism of its assumptions. Rather, if we use scientific methodology, we prefer and consider good the models that yield usable predictions and implications for the real world. The more implications, the better; the more implications not falsified by empirical, real world facts, the better yet. The scientific approach to analysis of the world around us requires that we have a willingness to consider evidence. Evidence is used to test the usefulness of a model. Consider, for example, two competing models that concern themselves with the following phenomenon: Every time I leave paper currency on a table in the student union, it disappears. One model is based on several assumptions, including that of wealth maximization—making oneself as best off as possible. This model predicts that, if the cost of taking possession of the paper currency (which represents general purchasing power over all commodities) is low relative to the benefits, individuals will engage in this activity. The competing model uses some theory of magnetic attraction—paper currency emits a magnetic force which causes people's hands to pick it up.

A testable, i.e., refutable, implication for the first model is that money will disappear faster the larger the denomination of the bills left. This is not an implication of the other competing model. We can run an experiment now to test the predictive capacity of these two models. On some days we randomly leave a dollar bill on a table at different time intervals. Then we keep increasing the possible take, leaving next $5 at a time, then $10, then $50, then $100. If we observe that more individuals hang around the student union as the denomination of the bills gets larger, we have an observed fact that does not refute the implication or prediction of the first model. It does refute the second model, which would predict that the number of students that hang around would be the same no matter what the denomination of the bill was because denomination did not determine magnetic force. In this case, we would choose the first model and tend to reject the second. Note here that we can never *prove* theories, only disprove them.

We also generally use the principle of Occam's razor: If two models are competing with one another and each predicts equally well, the least-complicated model will generally be chosen. For it was William of Occam[1] who once said, "Essentia non sunt multiplicanda praeter necessitatem." In other words, essences shouldn't be multiplied beyond what we need for what we are studying. This is also known as the **principle of parsimony**. The notion of simplicity in model building is worth one further comment. Often the goal of constructing a theory is to have a general model. The more simple the model, the more generalizable it is. The supposed realistic model explains only a single special case and is therefore uninteresting.

The broad class of rational models

Many microtheoretic models are classified under the general heading of rational behavior models. We define **rational behavior** very simply: Alternatives are ranked systematically and consistently and choices are made accordingly, all within real world limitations. A rational behavior model is simply one that uses the assumption of rationality. The reason that economists have continued to use this type of model is because the assumption works in providing refutable implications which ap-

---

[1] A fourteenth-century English scholastic philosopher.

pear to be consistent with real world social phenomena. The definition of rational behavior is that behavior which is purposive and systematic. Nonetheless, a rational behavior model is not necessarily worthless if, when queried, individuals demonstrate thought processes which do not correspond to *our* own ideas of systematic behavior. Our economic models are models of behavior rather than of thought processes.

More importantly, even if specific individuals behave in an unsystematic manner, large groups of individuals taken together will demonstrate collective rationality, which dominates the unsystematic elements of behavior within the group.

Rational individuals and rational analysis

It is useful here to make the distinction between rational individuals and rational analysis. We define rational analysis as a logically consistent theory that enables us to derive empirically testable or refutable implications or predictions about the behavior of groups of people. If these predictions or implications are not refuted by experience, then the rational theory has been found to be consistent with the real world data, or at least not disproved. We make no statements about whether or not individuals really are rational; nothing in a rational theory is dependent upon the premise that individuals are logically consistent in their thought processes. A good example has been given by several researchers doing experiments in mental institutions. Presumably individuals with severe mental illness do not *think* "rationally." Nonetheless, psychologists T. Allyon and N. H. Azrin found that the number of hours that psychotics in a study group were willing to work was a positive function of how much they were paid in the form of tokens which could be exchanged for clothing, toiletries, candy, cigarettes, and such additional hospital privileges as privacy. During one 20-day period, patients were rewarded with tokens when they completed their chosen jobs. In the following 20-day period, they were given tokens whether or not they completed their tasks. After about 5 days of the second 20-day period, the number of hours worked by the experimental group dropped to zero. When again they were paid only if their tasks were completed, the total number of hours worked per day jumped immediately.[2]

Note well, however, that the science of economics is not dependent now and forever upon the rationality postulate. If an alternative comes along that proves more usable in terms of predictive capacity and success, that alternative will undoubtedly be adopted.

The unit of analysis: The individual

All the theories developed in microeconomic analysis are based on propositions about individual behavior in response to changes in environment. Although the point may seem self-evident, many of us are rather loose in our discussions of "society" or "the public." If you were to tell me that the public has decided to clean up the nation's water because that's what is best for society, such a statement would sound somewhat unscientific. There is no such thing as an organized group called "the public" capable of making that decision. Moreover, a reference to "society" is a reference to some sort of entity that presumably is capable of deciding what is good for itself. Individuals can determine whether or not they like the outcome of a particular economic change, and individuals can determine whether they are happy or sad. Society, however, cannot.

*T. Allyon and N. H. Azrin, "The Measurement and Reinforcement of Behavior of Psychotics," *Journal of the Experimental Analysis of Behavior*, vol. 8, November 1965.

Perhaps a more appropriate way of making the same statement would be as follows: Politicians who expressed an interest in passing legislation to clean up the nation's waterways got voters to respond to them because of the increasing level of pollution in those waterways which caused harm to many individual voters. When a sufficiently large percentage of the electorate became sufficiently concerned, those individuals in positions of political power made the decision to pass legislation to reduce the level of polution.

Notice that the analysis here has been in terms of individual behavior. When we look at it this way, we see that the terms "public" and "society" are a bit too broad and vague to have much scientific meaning in rational discourse.

It should not seem particularly unusual that the basic unit of analysis in the science of economics is the individual. The physicist, for example, in the course of scientific investigation, may wish to describe the response of a "typical" molecule of gas when there is an increase in the temperature—even though the behavior of one particular molecule is unpredictable for all practical purposes. The economist may wish to predict the response of consumers in New York to a rise in the relative price of their food even though a particular individual living in a particular condominium near Central Park, perhaps in a response to other stimuli, may actually buy more food when the price goes up.

Although we treat the individual as the basic unit of analysis, we normally apply price theory to the behavior of individuals in groups. From a methodological point of view, we talk in terms of **individualism** because we obtain better predictions about group behavior by identifying and taking into account the diverse and often conflicting objections of the individuals who make up the group. Thus, our understanding of the behavior of groups is not dissimilar to the physicist's understanding of the behavior of a gas by considering the behavior of the molecules involved. In other words, we assert that more accurate predictions about group behavior are derivable from predictions about individual behavior.

Pitfalls in microeconomic analysis

There are a number of points that can be brought out in this introductory chapter that will prevent the student of price theory from making simple analytical errors when applying economic analysis to real world problems. Although the list below is not exhaustive, it does include some important misunderstandings.

Prices

Just about all economic analysis is concerned with prices. We talk about the law of demand, in which the quantity demanded is inversely related to the price. We talk about the law of supply, in which the quantity supplied is directly related to the price. In short, we talk about prices all the time. But today we have to be careful, particularly when we are looking at quantities demanded and supplied in the real world and the prices of the commodities in question.

RELATIVE VERSUS ABSOLUTE PRICES. Lately we have been in a period of rising prices; we are in a period of inflation, which is defined as a sustained rise in an appropriately weighted average of all prices. Inflation is a phenomenon that concerns itself with a rise in absolute prices. Microeconomic theory, on the other hand, concerns itself with what are called relative or real prices. Once the distinction is made between absolute and relative prices, there should be no confusion during a period of inflation. Someone not familiar with the distinction may contend that the law of demand clearly does not hold because, say, the price of washing machines went up last year

by 5 percent, but the quantity demanded did not go down at all. This indeed may have been a possible refutation of the law of demand—assuming that all other things, such as income and taste, are held constant—except for the fact that last year's prices in general, as expressed by the Bureau of Labor Statistics' Consumer Price Index, for example, may have gone up by as much as or more than 5 percent. It is the price of washing machines *relative* to all other prices that is important for determining the relationship between price and quantity demanded.

Unless otherwise specified, all prices mentioned in this book are relative prices. Customarily, we express the relative price of any good as the ratio of its absolute price to the average price of all other goods (except money).[3] For example, if we talk about the relative price of heating oil, we express it in terms of the absolute price of heating oil divided by the average price level which might be represented by the Consumer Price Index. The price of heating oil may have gone up 10 percent last year. If the Consumer Price Index also went up 10 percent, then we would say that the price of heating oil relative to an average of all other prices remained constant.

PRICES AND INFORMATION. A basic hypothesis of price theory is that individuals respond to relative prices rather than absolute prices. It is relative prices which are the conveyors of information in the marketplace. For the buyers, the relative price of a good indicates what the individual consumer must give up in order to purchase that good. In certain cases, it also indicates the amount of resources given up to produce that good. Hence, when the relative price of a commodity goes up, that bit of infor-

---

[3] Under certain conditions, all other goods can be treated as a single (composite) good. This is the composite good theorem. See Abraham Wald, "On a relation between Changes in Demand and Price Changes," *Econometrica*, vol. 20, April 1952, pp. 304–350.

mation tells the buyer and the seller that the good is now relatively scarcer. Note that neither the producer nor the consumer has to know why that particular commodity has become relatively scarcer. It shouldn't really matter to you as a consumer whether the price of gasoline has gone up *because* of a restriction on imports or *because* of a new law which requires gasoline refineries to install more expensive pollution-abatement equipment. The only thing that should definitely matter is the higher relative price, for that is the basis on which you will make a decision about the quantity to purchase. The message is transmitted by the higher relative price. Of course, how you respond to the message is impossible to predict on an individual basis, for the number of ways in which a consumer can "conserve" on a relatively scarcer item is probably infinite.

Changes in relative prices convey this type of information to both buyers and sellers. Of course, buyers respond differently than sellers. Sellers may see a rise in the relative price of a particular commodity as an opportunity to increase profits, and eventually such information may be translated into a larger amount of resources going to the production of that now relatively higher-priced product. It is in this manner that resources are allocated in a system that allows prices to convey the information about relative scarcities. We call this a market system: Prices convey the information to the individuals in the marketplace. There is no need for a central agency to produce information or to allocate resources. This does not mean that problems will not arise and that certain economic activities could not be better handled by other than unrestricted market processes. We will treat such situations on different occasions in this book and in particular detail in Chapter 20.

RELATIVE PRICES: AN EXAMPLE. A few years ago there was much talk of a permanent energy deficit or crisis. Cries of waste on the part of the American consumer were heard on TV and radio and were written in the press. However, it appears that American consumers were at least consistent in their responses not to *absolute* prices but to *relative* prices. Indeed, as the nominal (absolute) prices of electricity and gasoline were rising over a $2^1/_2$-decade period, consumers still consumed more. Part of this increased consumption could be explained by an increase in income, a change in the uses of gasoline, and to some extent, by an increasing population. But if we look at the relative prices of energy from, say, 1950 to the height of the latest so-called energy crisis, we find that the real or relative price of energy was the same in 1974 as it was in 1950! This can be seen in Figure 1-2. It is therefore not surprising that a large quantity of energy was demanded in spite of rising absolute prices for energy sources.

Distinguishing between average and marginal

Since we've been talking about prices, it is important to realize that not everyone need be aware of the relative price of a particular commodity for microeconomic analysis to have meaning and usefulness. This can best be illustrated by two examples.

First, consider a situation of horse trading. We have sets of buyers and sets of sellers of horses. There are "stronger" and "weaker" buyers and sellers. The so-called stronger buyers are willing to pay more for a horse than the weaker buyers. Similarly, the stronger sellers will sell only if they are offered a relatively high price compared with the price at which the weaker sellers would be willing to sell their horses. Look at the situation in Table 1-1.

At a price of $75 or below, all 10 buyers will want to buy a horse; however, from the seller's side, at that price only three sellers are willing to offer horses. Clearly, the price is not high enough. At a price of $150 or more, all the sell-

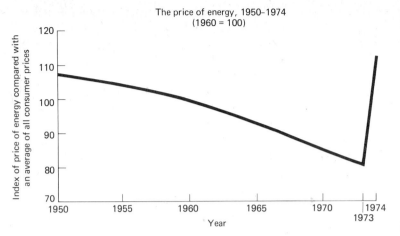

The price of energy, 1950-1974
(1960 = 100)

Index of price of energy compared with an average of all consumer prices (y-axis)

Year (x-axis)

Figure 1-2: The relative price of energy falls.
In this diagram we show what happened to the relative price or the real price of energy for the period 1950-1974. We use an index that compares the price of energy with the price of all other goods in the economy. By 1973, the relative price of energy had fallen almost 20 percent. During the Arab oil embargo of 1973-1974, the relative price of energy rose; however, it was essentially on par with what it was 2½ decades before! Of course, the nominal (absolute) price had risen, but so had the average of nominal prices in the rest of the economy.

ers will want to sell a horse, but none of the buyers will want to buy. Clearly, the price would be too high here.

Now, what would happen if the price were set at $105? We would have five sellers (S_1, S_2, S_3, S_4, S_5), but there would be six willing buyers (B_1, B_2, B_3, B_4, B_5, B_6). If the price were raised from $105 to $110, we would now have six willing sellers ($S_1, \ldots, S_6$), but only five willing buyers ($B_1, \ldots, B_5$). At a price somewhere between $105 and $110, there will be five buyers and five sellers. The price in this horse-trading market is determined by S_5 and B_5. It is the evaluations of the weakest of the successful buyers and of the strongest of the successful sellers that matter. These and these alone matter. Otherwise stated, it is the successful buyer and seller, B_5 and S_5, together with the unsuccessful pair, B_6 and S_6, that matter in determining price. These two sets are the buyers and the sellers on the margin.

Consider another example in which an experiment was carried out. Customers of a large number of gas stations in a given geographic area were quizzed at the end of each purchase of gas. The customers were asked about the price of the gasoline they had just bought. It turned out that most customers did not know the cost of the gasoline. They were vaguely aware of the approximate price but

Buyers	Stronger buyers					Weaker buyers				
	B_1	B_2	B_3	B_4	B_5	B_6	B_7	B_8	B_9	B_{10}
Value per horse	$145	$140	$130	$120	$110	$105	$100	$90	$85	$75
Value per horse	$50	$55	$75	$85	$105	$110	$125	$135	$140	$150
Sellers	S_1	S_2	S_3	S_4	S_5	S_6	S_7	S_8	S_9	S_{10}
	Weaker sellers					Stronger sellers				

Table 1-1: The marginal buyer and seller determine the price. In the upper part of the table, we show how much buyers B_1 through B_{10} would be willing to pay for a horse. In the bottom part of the table, we show how much sellers S_1 through S_{10} would be willing to accept for a horse. At a price between $105 and $110, there will be exactly five buyers and five sellers. The successful buyers and sellers, B_5 and S_5, together with the unsuccessful pair, B_6 and S_6, determine the price. These two sets of buyers and sellers are just on the margin.

not of the exact price, and they were not aware of the possibility of obtaining gasoline at a lower price elsewhere. This would suggest to the casual observer that prices have no meaning in an economic system and that consumers are "irrational" or, at the least, lazy shoppers.

However, at the same time this study was done, a close tab was kept on the quantity of gasoline sold at different gas stations in the area. Lo and behold, it turned out that those gas stations that sold gasoline at a lower price sold more. Now, how can these two facts be reconciled? They can be reconciled by making a distinction between the average consumer and the marginal consumer. The average consumer of gasoline was perhaps unaware of the price of gasoline. However, the fact that the gasoline stations selling gas at a lower price sold more made it clear that *some* consumers were aware. They are the people we call the marginal consumers, the ones who are just on the borderline between buying more and buying less. As the price of gas goes up in one gas station, these marginal consumers switch to a less costly station. They are indeed the determinants of the price of gasoline.[4] This situation shows that information is conveyed by relative prices; but for the price mechanism to work, that information does not need to be known with perfect accuracy by every individual acting in the marketplace.

This is perhaps another reason why critics of the rationality model used in microeconomic theory go astray. They are confusing average with marginal. On average, it may be true that consumers do not have much information about what they buy. (It may not pay them to search for better information.) But on the margin, there are consumers who do care. For example, purchasers of gasoline for, say, fleets of cars or for delivery trucks certainly will take the time, effort, and energy to seek out a supplier offering gasoline at a relatively

lower price. Whenever these marginal buyers find a better deal, they will switch suppliers. It is these marginal buyers who keep suppliers on their toes and tend to cause the price of a given commodity to be uniform within a given geographic area, correcting, of course, for differentials in transportation costs and in quality.

Constant-quality units

All the supply and demand analyses which follow, whether concerned with energy, the labor market, illegal activities, or what have you, must always be expressed in terms of constant-quality units. We know that all shoes are not alike and all automobiles are not alike. Nonetheless, we talk about the market for shoes and the market for automobiles. We also talk about the law of demand as it applies to each of these markets. When we talk about the quantity demanded of these or any other commodities, we must be aware of the fact that we are talking about **constant-quality units**. Hence, the correct way to describe, say, the quantity of shoes demanded is to talk in terms of the *relative price* of shoes and of the quantity of shoes measured in *constant-quality units*. Now that's really a mouthful! Therefore, throughout the rest of this book, the word "price" will be understood to mean the *relative price* of a commodity measured in constant-quality units.

There is a direct relationship between quality and price per constant-quality unit. Often new restaurants start out with relatively high-quality food at a certain set of prices. If the restaurant is very successful, it is not uncommon to see (and experience) a decline in the quality of the food served at the same prices, or alternatively, it is not uncommon to see the size of the portions served get smaller. Thus, the price per constant-quality unit after the restaurant has become more successful rises because of this decline in the quality and/or portion size.

---

[4]Along with the suppliers, of course.

In this text, we don't have to worry about how we would actually measure the quantity demanded or supplied of a particular commodity in constant-quality units. That would be the job of the econometrician, or one trained in the application of mathematics and statistics to the verification of economic theories. Econometricians must worry about adjustments for quality variations in their statistical studies.

Stocks, flows, and the time dimension

Our last point is the distinction between stocks and flows. A **stock** is defined as a quantity of something that exists at a moment in time. One may have a stock of savings, a finished goods inventory stock, a stock of boxes of Kleenex in the closet, and so on. These all essentially involve an instantaneous quantification of an amount available at a particular moment, say, right at this very instant. Much of microeconomic theory does not involve itself with stocks, however.

Rather, we are more inclined to develop theories about **flows**, where flows are quantities received, used, or spent at a particular rate over a specified time period. Defined thus, when we make reference to the law of demand, we are referring to the quantity of a commodity demanded at a particular relative price over a particular time period. Suppose we say that at a price of $1 each, 10 million Big Macs will be purchased. That statement offers little information unless we specify a time period. Ten million Big Macs would be a tremendous quantity demanded at that price if the time period were specified as 1 day. But it may not seem tremendous if the time period specified is 1 year. Thus, for every statement about quantity demanded or supplied, we must also specify or imply a time period. It is generally 1 year, but it can be any other unit of time.

The distinction between stocks and flows is perhaps best illustrated by considering a durable good such as an automobile. Let's say you purchase an automobile for $5,000. You then have a stock—one automobile—valued at $5,000. However, the automobile is generally not purchased for ownership of the stock per se. Rather, the stock of automobile is usually purchased for the flow of services that the stock is expected to render. Thus, when we talk about the consumer demand for services from automobiles, it is generally best to talk in terms of the expected service flow from the stock of an automobile per unit time period, or so much of a given quantity of automobile used per month or per year. This is true for all durable goods, including houses, quadraphonic systems, and golf clubs. The analysis for an automobile can be done in terms of the *service flow per year* measured in, say, constant-quality miles per year. To handle the demand for a *stock* of a durable good, we refer to the services derived (flows) rather than the stock.

Undoubtedly there are other "tricks" of analysis that you will pick up as you read through and apply the theory in this book to issues other than those that have been chosen. And perhaps more importantly, you will see the importance of mastering the analytical fine points just mentioned by applying them to the statements you see in print or hear on the radio, on TV, or in conversation. That is where you may find the greatest reward from the study of microeconomic theory upon which you are about to embark.

Glossary

Budget constraint The resource constraint imposed on individual households, firms, and governments at any point in time. For at any point in time, the total amount of resources is fixed.

Organization The coordination of individuals, each doing different things, in the furtherance of a common end.

Market or price system A social system of organization in which prices direct the use of resources and in which prices are used to allocate resources.

Command economy A social system of organization in which the allocation of resources is carried out by way of centralized political decision making.

Principle of parsimony Sometimes called the Principle of Occam's razor. If given the choice between a less complicated and a more complicated model, the former will be chosen if it works at least as well as the latter.

Rational behavior Individual actions commensurate with the achievement of one's explicit goals.

Individualism A particular type of scientific methodology in which we deduce our understanding of the behavior of groups from the behavior of individuals within the group.

Absolute prices Prices expressed in terms of nominal units. Absolute prices are those prices which are given in a market at any point in time and are to be contrasted with relative or real prices.

Relative or real prices The price of a good expressed in terms of how much of other goods must be given up to purchase a unit of the good in question. To establish relative prices, comparison with other prices must be made.

Constant-quality units Units of commodities for which quality is held constant. To estimate price per constant-quality unit requires that all units of different qualities first be adjusted for differences in quality.

Stock A quantity of anything that exists at a moment in time, such as inventories, savings, houses, and automobiles.

Flow A quantity of anything consumed, earned, produced, etc., per unit time period, i.e., at a specific rate per unit time period.

Summary

1. There are numerous possible social organizations by which individuals coordinate their different activities in the furtherance of a common end. Possible social organization for production and distribution include the market system, majority rule, dictatorship, and so on.

2. Every economic system involves a circular flow of income among firms, households, the government, and other countries.

3. All models are based on assumptions that can never be perfectly realistic. Model building involves simplification by necessity.

4. In one scientific methodology, the usefulness, or goodness, of a model depends on its predictive success record and the number of real world implications that can be drawn from it.

5. Most economic models fall within the broad class of rationality models which assume rational behavior. However, such models are not useful in analyzing individual thought processes.

6. It is important to distinguish between rational analysis and rationality: The former requires a logically consistent theory that allows us to derive empirically testable implications or predictions; the latter has to do with the logically consistent thought processes of individuals.

7. We use methodological individualism in our analysis of groups. In other words, our analyses are based on behavioral hypotheses about individuals.

8. It is important to distinguish between absolute and relative prices when doing microeconomic analysis. During a period of inflation, absolute prices may, for the most part, be rising. However, consumer and producer decisions are based on relative prices.

9. In a market system, prices convey information to buyers and sellers about the relative scarcities of commodities.

10. Prices are determined on the margin. The marginal buyer and the marginal seller determine the price in a market. The confusion between the average and the marginal buyer often leads to the erroneous conclusion that price does not determine quantity demanded and therefore is unimportant.

11. Measurement of the quantity of commodities under study must be made in terms of constant-quality units so that we can talk in terms of the relative price per constant-quality unit of the commodity in question.

12. Generally, in microeconomics we deal with flows, such as the rate of consumption per unit

time period, the rate of production per unit time period, and so on. Hence, whenever we deal with a flow, we must specify a time period.

Selected references

Friedman, Milton, "The Methodology of Positive Economics," in *Essays in Positive Economics* (Chicago: University of Chicago Press, 1953), pp. 1–43.

Lange, O., "The Scope and Method of Economics," *Review of Economic Studies*, vol. 8, 1945–1946, pp. 12–32.

Machlup, Fritz, "The Problem of Verification in Economics," *Southern Economic Journal*, vol. 22, 1955, pp. 1–25.

Robbins, Lionel, *An Essay on the Nature and Significance of Economic Science* (London: Macmillan, 1935).

Wicksteed, Philip H., "The Scope of Method of Political Economy," in G. J. Stigler and K. Boulding, eds., *Readings in Price Theory* (Homewood, Ill.: Irwin, 1952).

Questions

Answers to even-numbered questions are at back of text.

1. What criteria are appropriate in evaluating a scientific model?
2. Does it matter whether all the assumptions are "realistic"? Why, or why not?
3. What is the problem with expressions such as "the health, safety, welfare, and morals of the public" and "the greatest good for the greatest number"?
4. Suppose that in 1970 a liter of beer cost 50¢, while the same quantity of tequila commanded $5. By 1978 the respective nominal prices had risen to 70¢ and $6.30, respectively. What happened to the real or relative price of tequila in relation to beer?
5. Continuing with question 4 above, suppose that the nominal prices of all other consumer goods and services rose by 70 percent over the same 8-year period, so that, on the average, it cost $17 in 1978 to buy the same "basket" of consumer goods and services that could have been bought for $10 in 1970. What has happened to the relative prices of beer and tequila in comparison to all other consumer goods and services?
6. Suppose that by 1985 the current price of electricity has doubled and that of natural gas has tripled. How would this affect consumer purchases of new refrigerators and clothes dryers? Explain.
7. Poor nations typically use "primitive" methods to, say, construct a road. How would the concept of relative prices help to explain this? (Hint: The important relative prices to consider are those of labor and road-building equipment in poor and rich nations.)
8. Suppose you met someone who insisted that "everyone he knew" went right on using sugar at the same rate while the price sextupled. How would you go about explaining to him the unimportance of his observation?
9. It is not unlikely that the same person introduced in question 8 also is aware that a grower of sugar beets or sugarcane who invariably produces the same quantity of sugar each year without reference to changes in the expected wholesale price. What is your response?
10. "When I say *wheat*, I mean U.S. No. 1 Hard Red Winter wheat." Why is it essential that, in measuring quantities of goods, we must deal in constant-quality units?
11. Is the amount of water in a reservoir a stock or a flow? What units are commonly used to express the quantity? Is a city's consumption of water a stock or a flow? In what units might it be measured? Is rainfall a stock or a flow? How is it generally measured?
12. Express the following "stock" phenomena as expected future flows: (*a*) a washing machine, (*b*) a Hobie Cat sailboat, (*c*) a 35-pound cooked turkey, (*d*) a share of common stock, (*e*) a fistful of dollars.
13. Actuaries are statisticians who are commonly employed by insurance companies to *predict* the frequency with which various groups will be involved in, say, traffic accidents. (*a*) To date, what are the factors

which have been most widely used to predict "accident-proneness"?   (b) Would a bigot make a good actuary?   Why, or why not?

14. Suppose you have studied two phenomena, A and B, very carefully and have observed a very close correlation between them: Whenever A increases, B decreases, and vice versa.   (a) Does it matter which one is the cause (independent variable) and which one the effect (dependent variable)?   (b) What if they are both "effects" of some yet undetermined factor C?

15. Over the past decade, first-class mail rates have roughly tripled, while prices of long-distance phone calls, CB radios, televisions, and sound systems have remained fairly stable. (After adjustments for improvements in quality are made, their prices may have even declined.) Over a similar period, it has been reported that there has been a steady decline in the ability of high school graduates to communicate in writing. Do you feel that this increase in the relative price of written communication is related to the alleged decline in writing ability? (For the sake of argument, assume that the latter has in fact occurred.)   If so, what do you feel is the direction of causation?   Which is causing which?

2

PREFERENCES, UTILITY, AND CONSUMER CHOICE

We all have different preferences, or tastes, and we base our choices on our preferences. This truism by itself gives us no useful insights. We must characterize the individual's set of preferences in such a way that we can make refutable predictions about behavior. In this chapter, we will do just that. We will make certain assumptions about consumers' preferences and examine how the consumer makes choices. This will lead us to theoretical tools which enable us to analyze such issues as the food stamp program and employee fringe benefits.

Note that the word "consumer" is used here. We are concerned about consumer decision making. What goes into the decisions that guide the more than $1 trillion of consumer spending each year on goods and services in our economy? Even though the analysis that follows will apply to group behavior, remember from the first chapter that our unit of analysis will always be the individual. That is where we start.

Assumptions relating to consumer preferences

In order to say something scientific about consumer choice, we have to start by making assumptions. The assumptions are straightforward, and they relate to choices of **com-**

modities. We define commodities as all goods and services. Commodities provide a flow of consumption services per unit of time. The objects of choice are then seen as the services that the commodities provide rather than the commodities themselves.[1] The assumptions of our model are the following:

1. *The individual consumer, when faced with a choice between certain amounts of commodities, can decide which he or she prefers or that he or she is indifferent.* In other words, given any set of attainable combinations of satisfaction-yielding commodities, the consumer can determine which combination is preferable or which combinations yield equal satisfaction.
2. *The consumer is consistent in making choices among commodity combinations.* Thus, if the consumer first indicates a definite preference for Fords as opposed to Chevys, and then indicates a definite preference for Chevys as opposed to Toyotas, then, to be consistent, that consumer must also indicate a definite preference for Fords over Toyotas. The consumer's preferences are then said to be *transitive.*
3. *More is preferred to less.* No individual is ever satiated with desired commodities. This is sometimes called the assumption of non-satiety.
4. *The consumer has full knowledge* of the availability of commodities, their technological qualities, and their exact prices.

Go back and reread these four assumptions. You may find yourself disagreeing with one or more of them. How could an individual have full knowledge, even if that were possible? Aren't there some goods with which we become sated, like food or liquor? Aren't there some people who are not consistent in their consumer choices and others who can never make up their minds? Remember, assumptions are used to build models from which theories and predictions are derived. If the predictions based on the model we are building are refuted by the evidence, then the model has failed and another one must be put in its place.

Preference assumptions lead to indifference curves

Much of economic analysis lends itself well to graphic interpretation. That's fortunate because graphical analysis, at a very minimum, allows you to use a language for communicating theoretical analysis that at one and the same time economizes on words and clarifies ideas.

We can translate the four assumptions presented earlier into a geometric device that has been aptly labeled an **indifference curve**. An indifference curve is defined as a curve representing a constant level of satisfaction, or alternatively, as a locus of points representing combinations of two commodities (or baskets of commodities) among which the consumer is indifferent. (Historically such curves were first employed and named by a British economist, Francis Y. Edgeworth, who lived from 1845 to 1926.) Perhaps the easiest way to derive an indifference curve is first to set up an example of an indifference schedule which shows the various combinations of two commodities among which an individual feels indifferent. We see this in Table 2-1, where we have set up a hypothetical indifference schedule for a college student who likes both movies and concerts.

The indifference schedule

In Table 2-1, we look at a hypothetical indifference schedule that relates the different combinations of movies and concerts per month toward which the consumer has declared himself or herself indifferent. Notice that we are

---

[1]This allows us to handle durable goods such as cars and houses.

Movies per month	Concerts per month	Combination
1	7	A
2	5	B
3	4	C
4	$3^1/_2$	D

Table 2-1: Indifference schedule: movies and concerts. This individual consumer has decided that he or she is indifferent to going to one movie and seven concerts per month, or going to three movies and four concerts per month. (Note that we express an explicit time period because we are dealing with a flow concept—consumption of goods and services per unit of time.)

talking about activities which occur over time, and therefore we specify a time period. The activities are the consumption of movies and concerts, and the time period specified is a month. If we were to specify a year, we would have to multiply both columns by 12.

The one thing that we see right away is that in order for the consumer to remain indifferent among various combinations, as less is received of one commodity, more must be received of the other. This follows directly from assumption 3 that more is preferred to less. Since both of these commodities are goods that give satisfaction, if some of one commodity is given up, the only way the consumer can remain equally satisfied is by being compensated with more of the other commodity.

The indifference curve

When we translate combinations A, B, C, and D from Table 2-1 onto a graph showing the commodity space, we end up with an indifference curve. Because of the assumption that more is preferred to less, that indifference curve slopes downward and to the right. This means that more of one good must be consumed to compensate for the reduction in the consumption of another good if the consumer

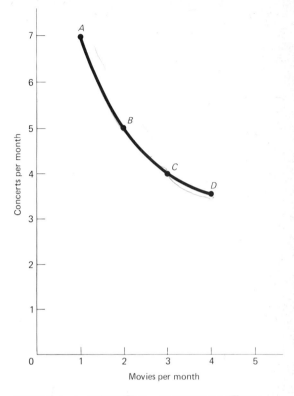

Figure 2-1: An indifference curve for movies and concerts. If we take combinations A, B, C, and D, plot them in the above commodity space, and then connect the points with a smooth line, we come up with an indifference curve for our hypothetical consumer. We note that the indifference curve is downward-sloping.

is to remain indifferent or obtain a constant level of satisfaction. We plot A, B, C, and D onto Figure 2-1.

Let's consider an upward-sloping curve for a moment. This curve implies that as consumers accepted less of x, they would also be quite willing to accept less of y. In Figure 2-2, point L would represent the same level of satisfaction as point N. But no consumer wants (by assumption) to give up a higher level of total consumption for a lower level. That's why indifference curves always slope downward, not upward.

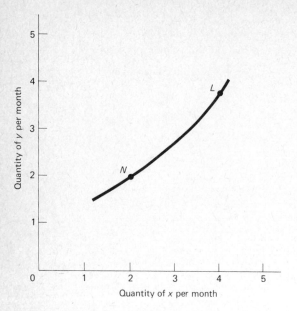

Figure 2-2: Implications of an upward-sloping indifference curve.
If the curve in this diagram represented an individual's indifference curve, it would mean that the individual would accept less of x and less of y and still be indifferent. In other words, points L and N would give equal levels of satisfaction, even though N contains less of both x and y. This would be violative of assumption 3, that more is preferred to less.

Another assumption that we have used in this consumer-choice model guarantees that there are an infinite number of indifference curves in the commodity space. After all, we have assumed that the consumer can compare any two bundles or commodities and decide either a preference for one or indifference between the two. Then no matter what levels of consumption of movies and concerts per month we are talking about, a higher or lower curve similar to ABCD in Figure 2-2 can be constructed.

Different individuals will have different sets of preferences. We expect to see, therefore, different indifference curves. We show four possible ones in Figure 2-3.

The last formal property of indifference curves that comes out of our set of assump-

tions involves assumption 2 of transitivity in choice making. From this assumption, we know that indifference curves logically cannot intersect. This can be easily seen by looking at the intersecting indifference curves I and II in Figure 2-4. The indifference curve taken from Table 2-1 is again presented and labeled here as I. We now see another indifference curve which intersects curve I at point B. It is labeled II. Compare the two points B and C, both on curve I. The consumer is indifferent between them; they yield equal levels of satisfaction. But if indifference curve II is also valid, then the consumer is also indifferent to combination B and combination H; but by our transitivity assumption 2, if our consumer is indifferent between B and C and also between B and H, then the consumer must be indifferent between C and H. However, notice that point H represents both more movies per month and more concerts per month. Since we have also assumed that more is preferred to less, it is impossible for the consumer to be indifferent to combination H and combination C. Thus, it is logically impossible that indifference curves intersect, *given* the assumptions about consumer preferences.

We can now briefly present the properties of indifference curves.

Properties of indifference curves
1. They are negatively sloped.
2. There is an indifference curve which passes through each point in the commodity space.
3. They cannot intersect.

Often, although not implied by the above assumptions about consumer preferences, a fourth characteristic is imputed to indifference curves, and that characteristic has to do with their shape.

The shape of indifference curves

The indifference curves presented in Figures 2-2 and 2-3 are convex to the origin. Those in-

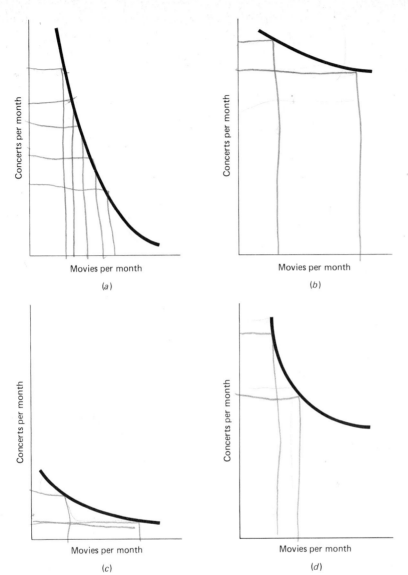

Figure 2-3: Indifference curves for different people.
The four panels in this figure show four possible indifference curves for concerts and movies for different individuals.

(a)

(b)

(c)

(d)

difference curves are convex to the origin because they lie above their tangent at each and every point along any given curve. In Figure 2-5, we show two different indifference curves. One is concave to the origin and the other is convex. The convex indifference curve lies above any representative tangents that are drawn to it; the concave curve lies beneath its tangents. This convex property of in-

difference curves can in no way be derived from the postulates of rational choice and the assumptions given above. Rather, the convexity property is based upon an empirical generalization about the real world. This generalization is called the **principle of diversity in consumption**. That is, consumers do not specialize and consume only one product; instead they diversify and consume a number of dif-

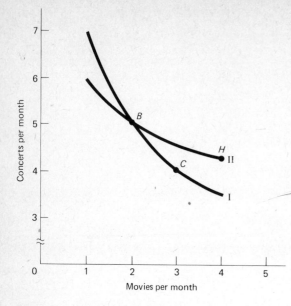

Figure 2-4: Intersecting indifference curves.
Indifference curve I is taken from Figure 2-1. By definition, all combinations of movies and concerts are equally satisfactory along that indifference curve. Now we add indifference curve II, which intersects curve I at combination B. By definition, combinations B and C are equally preferred; i.e., the consumer is indifferent between them. Also by definition, since B and H lie on the same indifference curve, they are equally preferred, and the consumer is indifferent between them. The assumption of transitivity requires, since the consumer is indifferent between B and C and indifferent between B and H, that the consumer must be indifferent between C and H. However, combination H involves both more movies and more concerts than does combination C. Because more is preferred to less, by assumption 3, it is logically impossible for the consumer to be indifferent between H and C. Hence, indifference curves cannot intersect.

ferent products. As we shall see in a later section of this chapter, the implication of indifference curves concave to the origin is specialization in consumption. We reject the concavity assumption because the model based on it does not yield predictions that are supported by empirical observation.

However, we will always be dealing with convex indifference curves because of a basic assumption about consumer preferences. This assumption would be that the more of a particular commodity that a consumer already has, the less that consumer values an additional, or marginal, unit. How the property of convexity results from this assumption will become clear in the following section when we examine the rate at which the consumer is willing to substitute one commodity for another.

Marginal rate of substitution

Because the indifference curve shows something about the individual's subjective evaluations of two different commodities, we should be able to learn something about the rate at which the consumer is willing to substitute one commodity for another by examining an indifference curve in detail. This rate of

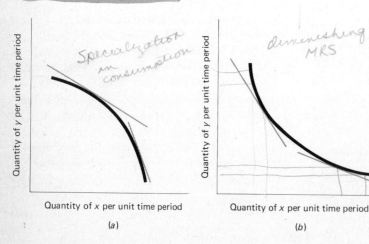

(a)

(b)

Figure 2-5: Concave and convex indifference curves.
Panel (a) shows an indifference curve concave to the origin (the curve is below its tangents). Panel (b) shows an indifference curve convex to the origin, the type we usually use in our analyses. No matter where we draw a tangent to the indifference curve in panel (b), it will always be below that indifference curve. That is the meaning of *convexity*.

substitution is called the **marginal rate of substitution** of x for y, or MRS_{xy}. We can define it as follows:

> MRS_{xy} = the number of units of y that must be given up per unit of x gained if the consumer is to either feel equally well-off or continue to obtain the same level of satisfaction

If we take the example from Table 2-1, we can find the marginal rate of substitution of movies for concerts. We see this in the middle column of Table 2-2. It can also be seen as we move in one-unit steps. For each movie gained per month, the consumer first sacrifices two concerts per month, then one concert per month, then one-half a concert per month. Thus the marginal rate of substitution is first 1:2, then 1:1, then 1:$^1/_2$. This can also be seen in Figure 2-6.

MRS at the limit

If we want to consider only infinitesimal changes in the consumption of one commodity, then instead of measuring discrete changes of x and y to ascertain the MRS between such points as A and B, or B and C, or C and D, we can measure MRS at any one point by finding the *slope* of the indifference curve at that par-

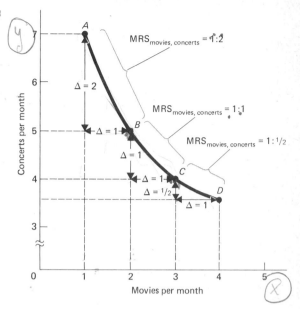

Figure 2-6: MRS graphically.
Each time an additional movie per month is consumed, the individual must sacrifice something in order to remain at the same level of satisfaction. In this case, what is sacrificed is concerts or fractions of concerts per month. We see that, at first, the consumer is more willing to sacrifice concerts to get an additional movie when he or she is consuming a few movies per month than when consuming a larger number of movies (and fewer concerts).

ticular point.[2] As demonstrated in Figure 2-7, this is given by the slope of the tangent drawn at the particular point in question. (Since MRS is positive, we must implicitly multiply the slope, which is negative, by −1.)

All the indifference curves we will be working with will have slopes that get smaller as we move from left to right. Looking at Figure 2-8, we see that as successive tangents are drawn, moving rightward on the indifference curve, their slope gets smaller, i.e., they become flatter. Alternatively, the slope increases as we move leftward. This is a property

Movies per month (1)	MRS (movies for concerts) (2)	Concerts per month (3)
1		7
	1:2	
2		5
	1:1	
3		4
	1:$^1/_2$	
4		3$^1/_2$

Table 2-2: Marginal rate of substitution of movies for concerts. This table is merely Table 2-1 reproduced with an additional column showing the marginal rate of substitution of movies for concerts.

---

[2]Note also that *along* an indifference curve

$$MRS_{xy} = \frac{\text{marginal evaluation of } x}{\text{marginal evaluation of } y} = \frac{\Delta y}{\Delta x}$$

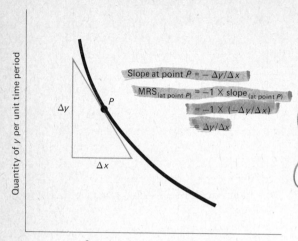

Slope at point $P = -\Delta y/\Delta x$

$MRS_{(at\ point\ P)} = -1 \times slope_{(at\ point\ P)}$

$= -1 \times (-\Delta y/\Delta x)$

$= \Delta y/\Delta x$

Figure 2-7: Measuring the slope of a curve.
The slope at any point on the curve can be measured by drawing the tangent to that point and finding the change in y divided by the change in x (where y is the variable measured on the vertical axis and x is the variable measured on the horizontal axis). Since the indifference curves that we are working with slope down from left to right, the slope at point P is equal to $-\Delta y/\Delta x$. Since our definition of MRS requires a positive number, then MRS at point P is equal to -1 times the slope at point P, or to $\Delta y/\Delta x$.

of all indifference curves that are convex to the origin; hence, it is a property of the indifference curves that will be examined. This property is generally called the **diminishing marginal rate of substitution.**

Diminishing MRS

Notice in Table 2-2 that as more movies were consumed per month, the individual was willing to give up fewer and fewer concerts to obtain successive additional movies. As seen in column 2, the MRS of movies for concerts went from 1:2 to 1:$^{1}/_{2}$. The same thing happens in all convex indifference curves because of the property of diminishing marginal rate of substitution. Either we can simply assume that all indifference curves are convex, and

therefore, the diminishing marginal rate of substitution follows from the assumption of that convexity; or we can attach some additional meaning to our original model of consumer choice by adding the assumption that a person's **marginal evaluation** or feeling of satisfaction from a particular commodity gets smaller as the amount of that commodity increases. This assumption makes all indifference curves convex; diminishing MRS follows from it. The convexity of the indifference curves is another way of saying diminishing MRS.

Or we may add a fifth assumption to our model of consumer choice. This fifth assump-

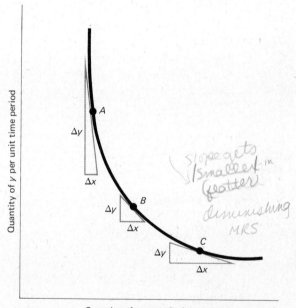

slope gets
smaller in
(flatter)

diminishing
MRS

Quantity of x per unit time period

Figure 2-8: The changing slope along a convex indifference curve.
All indifference curves that are convex to the origin exhibit the property that the slope becomes flatter and flatter as we move from left to right. This can be seen if we compare the changes in $\Delta y/\Delta x$ as we move down the indifference curve from point A to point B to point C. Note that its absolute value gets smaller and smaller.

tion is that a person's marginal evaluation of a particular commodity gets smaller as the consumption of that commodity increases. Then diminishing MRS follows. Again, diminishing MRS does *not* follow from the first four postulates of rational consumer choice. Rather, the opposite of diminishing MRS—increasing MRS—implies that the consumer would spend his or her entire budget on one good. Such an implication is refuted by the facts: Consumers diversify their purchases; they do not specialize in consumption.

A diminishing marginal rate of substitution is also consistent with an earlier analysis of consumer choice, popular for many years, involving assumptions about diminishing marginal utility.

Utility analysis

We have already referred to levels of satisfaction. Another term that can be used for satisfaction is "utility," or want-satisfying power. This is a property that is common to all commodities that are desired. Note, though, that utility is purely subjective. There is no way that you, as an economist, can measure the amount of utility that another consumer might be able to obtain from a particular commodity, for utility does not mean useful or utilitarian or practical. In this sense, there cannot be scientific assessment of the utility that someone may receive by consuming a particular commodity. Thus, in this analysis, illegal activities that many people may consider morally wrong can still be analyzed in terms of the utility that those activities generate for their consumers. Utility, it might be said, is in the perception of the consumer. Nonetheless, economists can analyze consumer choice in terms of utility, just as physicists have analyzed some of their problems in terms of force. No physicist has ever seen a unit of force. No

economist has ever seen a unit of utility. In both cases, however, these constructs have proven useful for analysis.

Cardinal and ordinal utility

Utility theory was first developed in terms of a specific measurement of utility. The term "util" has been used as the unit of measurement. Thus, the first chocolate bar might yield 4 utils of satisfaction, the first peanut cluster, 6 utils. Such utility analysis was called **cardinal**. Numbers such as 1, 2, and 3 are cardinal. We know that 2 is exactly twice as many as 1; 3 is exactly 3 times as many as 1.

However, economists soon found out that it was not necessary in their analyses to make such stringent assumptions about the measurement of utility. (This was particularly helpful in light of the fact that utils were wholly fictional "units.") Rather, it was found that the much weaker notion of merely *ordering* levels of utility was sufficient. Thus, **ordinal utility analysis** came into being. The term "ordinal" means ranked, or ordered. Ordinal numbers are numbers like first, second, and third, and of course, these numbers imply a rank, or order. Nothing can be said about the size relationship of the ordinal numbers; something can be said only about their importance relative to each other. For example, our measurement of temperature is an ordinal ranking. 100°C is "twice" 50°C. However, its Fahrenheit equivalents are 212° F and 122° F. The ordering is the same, but the former is no longer exactly twice the latter.

Modern-day economics is based more on observed facts of choice, not on any psychological interpretation of such choices. What we call utility today therefore reflects only rank ordering of preferences as mentioned above. We will define utility as a variable whose *relative* magnitude indicates the order of preference; therefore, when we talk of a utility-maximizing model, we mean that an individual is indeed maximizing utility in finding his or her most preferred position.

Total and marginal utility in cardinal terms

We now look at the relationship between the quantity consumed and the cardinal utility received. After we do this, we will be able to see how cardinal utility theory can lead to a diminishing marginal rate of substitution and, therefore, to convex indifference curves.

Look at Table 2-3, where we show a measurement of total cardinal utility associated with each particular rate of movie consump-

tion per month. The total utility numbers represent measurement in utils since we are talking in terms of cardinal utility. Total utility, which is represented in column (2), is then transferred in blocks (represented by dashed outlines) to Figure 2-9(*a*). Notice that total

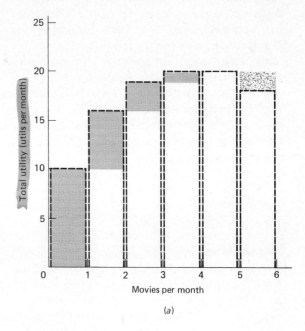

(*a*)

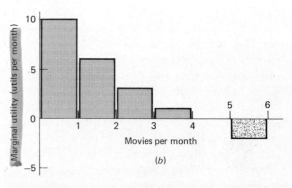

(*b*)

Figure 2-9 (*a*) and (*b*): Total and marginal utility in discrete units.

In panel (*a*), the dashed outline indicates the total utility for each rate of consumption of movies per month. The shaded portion of each dashed box indicates the marginal utility for each additional movie. When we transfer the shaded boxes to panel (*b*), we have a diagram of discrete marginal utility.

Quantity of movies (per month) (1)	Total utility (utils per month) (2)	Marginal utility (utils per month) (3)
0	0	
		10
1	10	
		6
2	16	
		3
3	19	
		1
4	20	
		0
5	20	
		−2
6	18	

Table 2-3: Total and marginal utility in cardinal terms. Column 1 presents the quantity of movies per month. Column 2 shows the associated total utility using a cardinal measure. Marginal utility is represented in column 3 and is defined as the change in total utility due to a one-unit increase in the rate of consumption of the commodity in question. Notice that marginal utility falls to 0 and then becomes negative; this means that after 5 movies per month, the consumer finds an additional movie to be a nuisance.

utility continues to rise until four movies are consumed per month, remains at 20 through the fifth movie, and then falls to 18. If we connect the tops of the total utility blocks by a smooth line, we come up with a representation of the total utility curve associated with the consumption of movies during a period of 1 month. This is shown in Figure 2-10(*a*).

If you look carefully at both parts of Figure 2-9, the notion of marginal utility and what it is can be seen very clearly. In economic theory, marginal always refers to the *rate* at which a total is changing. In this case, the total happens to be utility, but as you will see later when we discuss costs, revenues, output, and so on, we will also make reference to marginal cost, marginal revenue, etc. In this case, the marginal utility of consuming three units of movies per month as opposed to two is the increment in total utility and is equal to 3 utils per month. Marginal utility is represented by the shaded portion of the blocks in Figure 2-9(*a*). We can transfer these shaded portions down to Figure 2-9(*b*) and come up with a graphic representation of marginal utility. When we connect the tops of these marginal utility rectangles in Figure 2-10(*b*), we come up with a smoothly sloping marginal utility curve, which intersects the horizontal axis at the consumption rate of four movies per month. The meaning of zero marginal utility is merely that the consumer would have all he or she wants of the commodity in question, even if its price were zero. When marginal utility becomes negative, such as it does in this example after the consumption of four movies per month, it means that the consumer gets disutility; the consumer is fed up with movies and would require some form of compensation to sit voluntarily through the sixth movie in 1 month.

Choice of scale

We have been dealing with what are called "quantitatively measurable variables," i.e.,

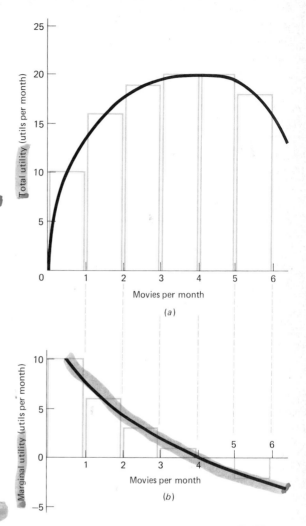

Figure 2-10 (*a*) and (*b*): **Total and marginal utility.** If we take the total cardinal utility units from column (2) in Table 2-3, we obtain rectangles like those presented in Figure 2-9 (*a*). If we connect the tops of those rectangles with a smooth line, we come up with a total utility curve that peaks somewhere between four and five movies per month and then slowly declines [panel (*a*)]. Marginal utility is represented by the increment in total utility, shown as the shaded blocks in Figure 2-9 (*b*). When these blocks are connected by a smooth line in panel (*b*), we obtain the marginal utility curve.

cardinal magnitudes. Such magnitudes are defined as variables whose measurement permits the arbitrary choice of a starting point, i.e., 0, and a unit interval. Figure 2-10 has a starting point of 0, and the unit interval is 1. However, Figure 2-10 can be redrawn as Figure 2-11, where the vertical axis has an alternative "util" scale. The 0 point has been shifted; now, 0 utils on the vertical axis is represented by 4. The unit interval has now tripled; that is, a vertical difference of 1 util on the vertical axis of Figure 2-10(b) is equal to 3 on the vertical axis of Figure 2-11. Note, however, that the two diagrams look exactly the same. This is because we have merely changed the scale of measurement; the relative magnitudes of utility differences remain the same. Now, since marginal utility is defined as the rate of change of total utility, a graph of marginal utility relating to Figure 2-11 would look similar to Figure 2-10(b). After all, comparisons of differences are unaffected by shifts of the 0 point or unit interval. Since marginal quantities are related uniquely to differences of total quantities, scale does not matter.

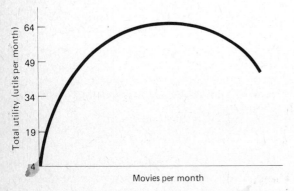

Figure 2-11: Total utility using a different scale.
This figure is exactly the same as Figure 2-10 (a) except that we are using an alternative cardinal scale on the vertical axis. The 0 point has shifted to 4, and the unit interval has tripled in comparison with the vertical axis scale in Figure 2-10 (a). A marginal utility curve for this total utility curve would look exactly the same as the one in Figure 2-10 (b).

Diminishing marginal utility

Notice that in Figure 2-10(b), marginal utility is continuously declining. This is because the total utility of Figure 2-10(b) (and Figure 2-11) is increasing at a *steadily decreasing* rate. This property outlined has been given the name **diminishing marginal utility.** Such a property of a total utility curve will remain valid regardless of the cardinal scale used. There is no way we can *prove* diminishing marginal utility. It does not follow from any postulates of rational consumer decision making; moreover, it would be necessary to be able to measure utility in some cardinal way in order to test such a proposition. Nonetheless, economists and lay persons for years have believed strongly in the assertion of diminishing marginal utility. It has even been called a "law."

Consumer optimum—Indifference curve analysis

While it is possible to develop a theory of consumer choice (decision making) using utility analysis, it is not necessary to do so. We can, however, use the utility analysis when we talk of the position of indifference curves.

The position of indifference curves

If we accept rank ordering of indifference curves, then we can state that a higher total utility value must be given to all indifference curves which are above indifference curve I in Figure 2-12. Thus, indifference curves II and III are both preferred to indifference curve I. They generate a higher level of satisfaction or utility. Why? Merely because it is possible to consume both more movies and more concerts as one moves from lower to higher indifference curves. Thus, with no strings attached (no costs), a consumer in our model must prefer the combinations of goods on higher

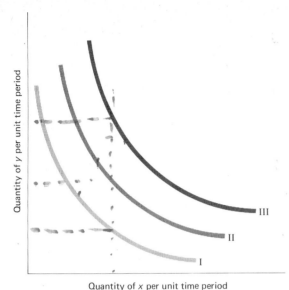

Figure 2-12: Ordering of indifference curves.
Higher indifference curves indicate a higher level of satisfaction or utility; thus, indifference curve III indicates a higher level of satisfaction than indifference curve II, which in turn is indicative of a higher level of satisfaction than indifference curve I.

indifference curves to those on lower indifference curves.

Facing reality: The budget constraint

We impose a constraint on the individual. That constraint has to do with scarcity. It is called the **budget constraint,** which for our purposes will be the amount of income available to the consumer during the time period under study. More sophisticated models would include the amount of assets that the consumer could sell off to obtain additional income, the size of the gifts that the consumer could obtain from philanthropists, and the amount that the consumer could borrow or steal. We will ignore these possible additions to the consumer's available purchasing power during the time period.

We will continue to consider two goods—movies (x) and concerts (y). The nominal prices of those two goods, P_x and P_y, are *given* as far as the individual consumer is concerned (the consumer cannot affect them) and are assumed constant. Money income M will be some fixed amount per month. The budget constraint will therefore be as follows:

$$M = (\text{quantity of movies/month} \times P_x) \\ + (\text{quantity of concerts/month} \quad \text{(2-1)} \\ \times P_y)$$

If we arbitrarily pick some numbers, we can easily see how to graph the budget constraint in the commodity space. Assume that the market price of movies is $3 and the market price of concerts is $2. Assume further that the consumer in question gets $30 per month money income. We draw the budget line in the commodity space given in Figure 2-13. The maximum quantity of concerts per month that can be purchased and consumed is equal to $30 ÷ $2, or 15. This is represented by point B. The maximum number of movies per month that can be consumed is $30 ÷ $3, or 10. This is represented by point B'. When we connect these two points together, we get the budget constraint BB'.

Let's generalize the equation above to any two commodities, y (plotted on the vertical axis) and x (plotted on the horizontal axis), priced at P_y and P_x, respectively. Again, M is the monthly money income available to spend on these commodities; therefore, if all monthly income is spent,

$$M = y \cdot P_y + x \cdot P_x \qquad \text{(2-2)}$$

If we solve this equation for y, we get an equation for the line that represents the budget constraint.

$$y = \frac{M}{P_y} - \frac{P_x}{P_y} \cdot x \qquad \text{(2-3)}$$

The equation intersects the vertical axis (where $x = 0$) at the point M/P_y. In our example, that is the maximum number of con-

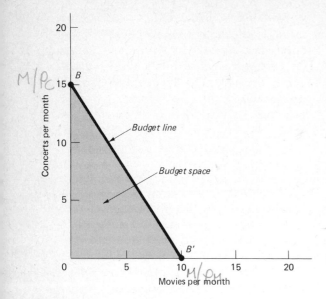

Figure 2-13: The budget constraint.
When all the $30 money income is spent on concerts at
$2 per concert, 15 concerts can be purchased per month.
This gives us one point on the budget constraint, point
B. When all money income is spent on movies at $3 per
movie, 10 movies can be purchased per month. This gives
us point B'. Connecting B and B' gives us the budget
constraint, or *budget line*. The right triangle formed by
that line and the axes is called the *budget space*. It represents the set of combinations of movies and concerts
per month attainable with a fixed money income of $30
per month when the price of each movie is $3 and the
price of each concert is $2.

certs per month (0 movies), which is M
divided by the price of concerts.

The slope of the budget constraint is the
ratio of the prices of the two commodities
under study. In our example, the ratio is
$P_x/P_y = 3/2$. Since the budget constraint is
negatively sloped, the slope of the budget constraint is the *negative* of the price ratio.
Numerically, this slope represents the
marginal rate of market substitution (MRMS)
of the two goods since prices are given to the
consumer. MRMS is the *feasible* or market rate
that the consumer can trade off x for y.

If we fill in the area between the axes and
the budget constraint, or budget line, we get a
graphic representation of the budget space.
The budget line represents the maximum

feasible combinations that can be purchased
with the given income and prices.[3]

Now, in order to obtain the optimal combination of movies and concerts per month, we
must somehow coordinate the *feasible* set of
possibilities with the *subjectively preferred*
possibilities. In other words, we want to combine subjective marginal valuations (or
marginal rates of substitution) represented by
indifference curves, with feasible rates of
market substitution represented numerically
by the slope of the budget constraint. Or, in
still other words, we must impose the set of
combinations allowed by prices and the consumer's money income on the consumer's
preferred set of possibilities to obtain exactly
what combination the consumer will choose.
The position of the budget constraint imposes
the other constraint on the consumer's behavior, for it gives a maximum amount that can be
consumed.

Graphing changes in money income

What happens when there is a change in
money income available to the consumer for
the purchase of goods x and y? The vertical
axis intercept is defined as total amount of
money income divided by the price of good y.
If money income doubles and P_y remains
unchanged, for example, then twice as much y
can be purchased as before. The same is also
true for the intercept of the budget line on the
horizontal axis. If all money income were to
be spent on x, twice as much x could be
purchased if money income doubled and P_x
remained unchanged. We show this in Figure
2-14. An increase in money income, *ceteris
paribus*, shifts the budget line away from the

---

[3]The budget constraint we use here exactly exhausts income. We could use an inequality budget constraint such
as the following: $P_x \cdot x + P_y \cdot y \le M$. If we use this inequality as the budget constraint, it describes the entire
shaded area in Figure 2-13. Note also that if x and y are
the only desired goods, we are excluding the possibility of
saving, which can be defined as the purchase of future
goods.

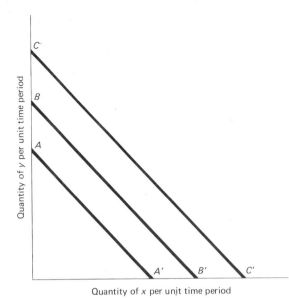

Quantity of y per unit time period

Quantity of x per unit time period

Figure 2-14: Changes in money income.
If nominal and relative prices stay the same, an increase in money income will shift the budget constraint *BB'* outward and upward to *CC'*. These two budget lines are parallel. If money income decreases and nominal and relative prices remain constant, then the budget constraint would shift toward the origin, say, to *AA'*. This budget line is also parallel to the original budget line.

origin and parallel to the original budget line. Similarly, a decrease in money income would shift the budget line toward the origin and parallel to the original line.

Attaining an optimum for the consumer

We are assuming rational behavior. Individual decision making, therefore, consists of comparing *preferences* with *opportunities*. The rational individual arranges his or her affairs to best satisfy given preferences from available opportunities. If we wish to use the utility concept developed in this chapter, we say that the rational individual chooses a consumption basket, or combination, that maximizes his or her utility. The consumption basket that maximizes a consumer's satisfaction, therefore, is the *optimum* for the consumer. It is useful to point out here that the process of **optimization** applies to the *individ-*

ual economic agent's decision-making processes. In later chapters, we will deal with many individuals interacting in the marketplace. Then we will no longer talk about optimization, but rather about the process of attaining **equilibrium** in the marketplace. Generally speaking, equilibrium is a property of markets rather than of individual decision making. Here we can give a short definition of equilibrium as a situation in which the forces acting upon a system (generally a market) are balanced so that there is no net tendency to change. (Note, however, that the terms "optimal" and "equilibrium" are used interchangeably by most economists.)

Consumer optimum will be obtained whenever the consumer maximizes satisfaction within his or her budget constraint. This can be done graphically by drawing in the individual's set of indifference curves on Figure 2-13, so that they are similar to those given in Figure 2-15. The consumer, by assumption, wishes to be on the highest indifference curve possible. Indeed, if it were possible, the consumer would like to be on an indifference curve that is so high that it cannot be represented in this diagram. However, there is a constraint, and that constraint is determined by nominal prices and money income, given by *BB'*. The point at which the consumer maximizes satisfaction is the point on the highest indifference curve that is attainable. This is on indifference curve II. It is tangent to the budget constraint *BB'* at point *E*. Consumer optimum occurs when the consumption rate is nine concerts per month and four movies per month. Point *E* is the point of consumer optimum; and

At the point of consumer optimum, the marginal rate of substitution is equal to the ratio of the price of x to the price of y, or

$$MRS_{xy} = \frac{P_x}{P_y} = MRMS_{xy}$$

Where MRS_{xy} is the marginal rate of (subjective) substitution and $MRMS_{xy}$ is the marginal rate of market substitution.

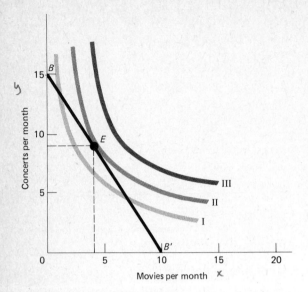

Figure 2-15: Consumer optimum.
Utility maximization requires that the consumer attain the highest indifference curve possible. This occurs only when the rate at which the consumer is *willing* to substitute movies for concerts is equal to the rate at which the consumer can substitute movies for concerts (and where $M = x \cdot P_x + y \cdot P_y$). This occurs at point E on indifference curve II. This is where the highest attainable indifference curve is tangent to the budget constraint. This consumer will purchase nine concerts and four movies per month.

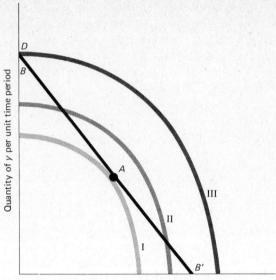

Quantity of x per unit time period

Figure 2-16: Concave indifference curves.
An interior solution to the consumer-optimization problem normally would be at a point such as A where the indifference curve is tangent to the budget line; however, point A represents a position that does not maximize satisfaction. At point A, the consumer is on indifference curve I. This consumer could increase satisfaction by moving to point D, which would put him or her on indifference curve III. Thus the concavity of indifference curves implies specialization in consumption because this consumer would consume only good y.

At the point of consumer optimum, the rate at which the consumer is just *willing* to substitute one commodity for the other is equal to the rate at which he or she *can* substitute one commodity for another; and the latter is determined by the prices of x and y.[4]

Convex and concave indifference curves revisited

Now we can show why indifference curves that are concave to the origin imply specialization in consumption. Look at Figure 2-16. Here we show indifference curves that are

concave to the origin. Ordinarily, the point of consumer optimum is where the highest indifference curve is tangent to the budget line. This would be at point A in Figure 2-16, but point A would not be most preferred by this consumer with these particular indifference curves. By assumption, the consumer prefers to be on a higher rather than a lower indifference curve. This consumer would choose to be at point D on the higher indifference curve III. This would mean that this consumer would specialize in consumption and purchase and consume only good y. This particular equilibrium outcome is also called a **corner solution**; it is to be compared with an **interior solution** of the kind given by point E in Figure 2-15.

---

[4]And, of course, $M = x \cdot P_x + y \cdot P_y$.

Consumers diversify when they consume. They purchase a basket of many different commodities. Only if we used indifference curves which are convex to the origin can we obtain interior solutions which are not contradicted by real world phenomena.

While it is true that we see diversity in consumption, we also see many corner solutions because consumers do not consume the vast majority of goods and services available. We use two goods in our examples, but there are literally thousands of commodities that each consumer purchases and millions, if not trillions, that he or she does not. The reason you and I and everyone else do not consume most commodities in the world is that, given our tastes and income and the prices of other commodities, the price of another commodity which we do not purchase may appear too "high." You might love to have a super-large-screen television with video cassette capacity, but at the current price, you are at the corner solution with respect to such an item. But such a corner solution is consistent with indifference curves which are convex to the origin. Look at Figure 2-17. The preferred position for you is at point D. No x is consumed (you don't buy the services of that large-screen color television). No tangency is involved here. The optimum consumption point, given the budget constraint, is the closest to tangency that you can achieve.

We say, then, that indifference curves which are convex to the origin are capable of explaining not only interior solutions and hence diversity of consumption, but also corner solutions and nonconsumption of many items.

Maximizing behavior: The equal marginal principle

Let's go back to our original model. The consumer is attempting to maximize satisfac-

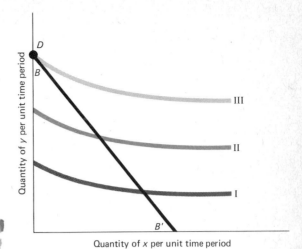

Figure 2-17: Convexity of indifference curves and corner solutions.
The consumer attains his or her highest indifference curve by not consuming any of good x in this example. The highest indifference curve possible is III; the consumer optimum is at point D. No tangency is involved here; but given the budget constraint, point D is the closest to the tangency that can be achieved.

tion. He or she does this by allocating a given income M optimally over the different commodities that can be purchased. In our particular simple example, we consider only two goods x and y.

If we think now in terms of cardinal utility functions, we can talk in terms of units of utils. The consumer optimization problem is now quite simple. The consumer attempts to buy utils from the cheapest source. If we were now to go on to assume diminishing marginal utility, we can come up with a formula for consumer optimization. This formula is as follows:

$$\frac{\text{Marginal utility of } x}{\text{Price of } x} = \frac{\text{marginal utility of } y}{\text{price of } y} \quad (2\text{-}4)$$

What does Eq. (2-4) mean? Simply that the marginal utility per dollar spent on each commodity must be equal if maximum utility is to obtain. In other words, the last dollar spent on

x must yield the same satisfaction as the last dollar spent on y. If such were not the case, then the consumer could increase total utility by shifting his or her consumption pattern. For example (again given the assumption of diminishing marginal utility),[5] assume the marginal utility per dollar spent was lower on x than on y. This consumer could shift some income from expenditures on x to expenditures on y. The marginal utility for the consumption of x would rise, and the marginal utility for the consumption of y would fall. Eq. (2-4) would be satisfied. Let's take a simple example. Suppose that the marginal utility of a dollar spent on restaurant meals was equal to 10 utils and that the marginal utility of a dollar spent on movies was only 5 utils. If the consumer transferred $1 of income from movies to restaurant meals, that individual would give up 5 units of utility, but gain 10. Hence, total utility would increase by (approximately) 5 units of utility. Only when the marginal utility per dollar spent on both restaurant meals and movies is equal will the consumer be obtaining maximum utility, given income and prices.

This optimal consumer situation is sometimes called the **law of equal marginal utilities per dollar** because utility per last dollar spent is equated on the margin for all goods consumed.[6] Another way of stating this "law" is as

$$\frac{\text{Marginal utility of } x}{\text{Marginal utility of } y} = \frac{\text{price of } x}{\text{price of } y} \qquad (2\text{-}5)$$

which is obtained by multiplying *both* sides of Eq. (2-4) by P_x/MU_y.

---

[5] In addition to the assumption of diminishing marginal utility, we must further assume that the marginal utility of x does not depend on the marginal utility of y, or in other words, that there are no cross effects.

[6] Of course, we are only talking here about an interior solution where both x and y are being consumed.

A note on deriving indifference curves by revealed preferences

The model in this chapter has some fairly strict assumptions. Specifically, it requires that individuals can choose between combinations of commodities in terms either of being in favor of one or the other combination or of being indifferent between them. Moreover, the indifference curves that we derive from such a questioning of individuals assumed, at least originally, that utility was of a cardinal nature. We have seen that we analyze consumer choice using ordinal utility, or rank ordering, of indifference curves. Here we show that it is possible to infer the indifference curves of a consumer from observing that consumer's actual behavior. In other words, the model is really quite general.

The method used is called **revealed preference**. In order to develop the revealed preference theory, we must conduct an experiment. In this experiment, we assume that the individual consumer's tastes are constant during the time under study. What we do is see how the individual reacts to various changes in money income and in prices. We know that in such an experiment, the consumer chooses a particular combination of goods over another for one of two reasons. Either the chosen combination is preferred, or the one *not* chosen is outside the budget space. If we vary prices to make the chosen combination *not* cheaper than the alternative combination, we can then categorically state that if the first combination is still chosen over the second, we know that it is chosen because it is preferred to the second combination.

We will again use our simple two-good example. We have a commodity space represented in Figure 2-18. We start with point A. This is the market basket of x and y that this consumer purchases when his or her budget line is BB'. What do we know about every

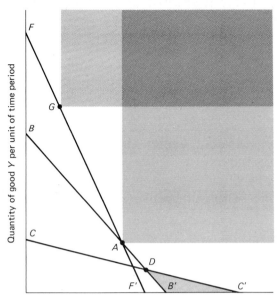

Figure 2-18: Revealed preference—narrowing down the area where the indifference curve must lie.

All points to the immediate right of and above any point chosen on a given budget line are preferred to that point itself. This is true for the shaded area above and to the right of point *A*; it is also true for the shaded area above and to the right of point *G*. In this fashion we can narrow down the preferred areas in the commodity space and come up with an indifference curve. We can also narrow our zone of ignorance, as it were, by picking the unselected points on a budget line that were *not* chosen and finding out what budget line will go through those points such that they *will* be chosen. This gives us areas, such as the shaded one between budget line *BB'* and budget line *CC'*, that are definitely inferior to any of the preferred combinations that were chosen.

other point on or below that budget line *BB'*? We know that because every other point was obtainable with the consumer's money income and that because all other points were not chosen, all the other points were revealed to be inferior to the market basket combination represented by point *A*.

We also know something else. The consumer would prefer to have more of both good *x* and good *y* if it were possible. More of both

good *x* and good *y* is obtainable if the consumer could somehow put himself or herself in the shaded rectangular region drawn to the right and just above *A*. After all, in that shaded region, the market basket that would be consumed would have at least as much of either good *x* or good *y* and more of at least one of them.

We now have some information about where an indifference curve would have to be in this commodity space in Figure 2-18. It would have to be in between the budget line *BB'* and the shaded area directly above and to the right of point *A*.

We can repeat the experiment again and close in on the exact position of the indifference curve for this consumer. Consider another point, such as point *D*, on the budget constraint *BB'*. We know that point *D* is inferior to point *A* because the consumer revealed it to be inferior when he or she did not choose it. However, there must exist a new, lower budget line which would force the consumer to purchase combination *D*. This budget line might be *CC'*. We know then that the shaded area between budget line *BB'* and budget line *CC'* must represent points that are all inferior to both the combination at point *A* and the combination at point *D*. Why? Because no matter whether the budget line was *BB'* or *CC'*, none of those points was chosen. We continue experiments like this to eliminate the areas in the commodity space through which we can categorically say that the indifference curve will *not* go.

We can continue the experiment to points above and to the left of point *A*. We establish a new budget line *FF'*. This budget line goes through the original consumer optimum at point *A*. Consider now that the consumer chooses a new point, say, *G*, for his or her optimum combination of goods *x* and *y*. Given that *A* and *G* are on the same budget line, they are both possible; however, the consumer has revealed his or her preferences to be for combination G rather than A. Thus, by a similar reasoning to the one used when we first started this experiment, all the area immediately to the right and immediately above point G is preferred to point G because it represents combinations which have more of at least one of the goods than does combination G. Moreover, all the points above and to the right of point G are also preferred to point A since they are clearly preferred to point G and G is preferred to combination A.

When we repeat this procedure over and over and over, we narrow down dramatically the area through which an indifference curve could pass; eventually, we come to an indifference curve just like the kind we have been using in this chapter. This theory of revealed preference is useful because it demonstrates that an indifference curve could be derived by means of revealed preference, or what people actually do, rather than by explicitly using the assumptions of our microeconomic model developed in this chapter.

Issues and applications

Providing necessities: the food stamp program in retrospect

The food stamp program is growing by leaps and bounds in the United States. It is estimated that within a few short years, one in every four individuals in this country will be eligible for food stamps. In 1978 alone, it is estimated that 18 million individuals will partake of the food stamp program at a cost of approximately $6 billion. We can represent the food stamp program graphically by using the tools presented in this chapter.

First let's consider a typical consumer who has a budget constraint of BB' before the food stamp program, as seen in Figure 2-19. The choice here is between food and nonfood. If no food were purchased, the quantity of nonfood attainable would be 0B. The slope of BB', the budget constraint, is the negative of the ratio of prices between food and nonfood items. Our typical consumer attains an optimum combination at point E on BB', where his or her marginal rate of substitution is equal to the rate at which food can be substituted for nonfood. The highest attainable indifference curve is I.

Now a food stamp program is instituted. It has a purchase requirement; that is, a certain amount of cash must be handed over to the food stamp officer in order to obtain a specified number of food

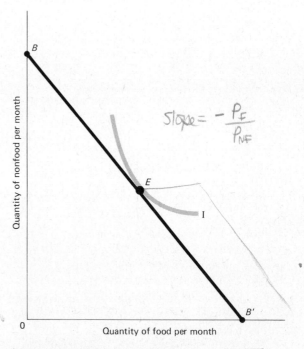

Figure 2-19: The optimal combination of food and nonfood purchases.
Without a food stamp program, our hypothetical consumer reaches an optimum where his or her highest indifference curve is just tangent to the budget line. This occurs at point E where indifference curve I is just tangent to the budget line BB'.

stamps. For example, a household of four persons with a monthly "net income" (defined by an administrative agency) of $300 could obtain $154 worth of food stamps by paying $83 in cash. The purchase requirement is represented by the distance AB in Figure 2-20. The new budget constraint facing this particular family then becomes BB"CD. In other words, it is horizontal between B" and C. The distance B'C (or, alternatively, B'D) represents the food stamp allotment minus the cash that has to be paid to obtain the food stamps. (In the above example it would be $154 − $83 = $71.)

Where does consumer equilibrium occur? It occurs where the consumer attains the highest indifference curve possible. In this particular case, the consumer can attain indifference curve II, for it *just* touches the budget constraint BB'CD at (the discontinuous) point C.

This consumer is clearly better off because a higher indifference curve and hence a higher level of satisfaction is obtained through the food stamp program.

Consider the alternative, however, of a pure cash transfer that is exactly equal to the value of the food stamp allotment minus the purchase requirement. In other words, consider the possibility of the government giving this individual an increase in real income (cash) of the distance B'D ($71) in Figure 2-21 rather than giving that consumer an increase in income of that distance that can only be used for the purchase of food, i.e., an in-kind transfer.

This cash transfer can be represented by a shift in the entire budget constraint from BB' to D'D. If the cash transfer were used, this particular consumer would move from point C to point F because that is where the highest indifference curve is attained; that is where indifference curve III is just tangent to the new budget constraint D'D. Given the in-kind nature of the income transfer to recipients of food stamps, however, attainment of point F and indifference curve III is impossible. From the individual's point of view, therefore, the use of food stamps rather

than cash transfers entails a "waste" of resources in the sense that if cash transfers were used in place of food stamps, the resulting increase in consumer satisfaction would be greater even though less food would be consumed (0F' of food instead of 0C'). The "waste" involved here is represented in terms of nonfood by the (vertical) distance between indifference curves II and III.

Such an analysis of "waste" ignores what might be a very important benefit to society from such an in-kind transfer program. According to testimony of Secretary of Agriculture Freeman before the House Agricultural Committee in 1967,

> But the advantage of the food tie-up is that they use what they had been spending on food, secure the stamps, which then means an additional amount— which means that the money is going for food. It is not going for something else. This is very important, very important.[7]

In other words, transfers of food stamps to recipients may yield utility or satisfaction to nonparticipants—the people who are indeed providing tax dollars to finance such transfers. Thus, all individuals, those who pay for the transfer system and those who benefit from it directly, share in the benefits of the system. Hence, a complete analysis of the food stamp program would have to include the identification and measurement of such benefits to nonrecipients. Taxpayers may derive more satisfaction from knowing that their tax dollars are going specifically for food (particularly if it is food for the children of poor families) than they would obtain if their tax dollars were merely given out in cash to recipients.[8] However, if we are willing to ignore the net benefits that

---

[7] U.S. Congress, House Committee on Agriculture, *Hearings to Extend the Food Stamp Act of 1964 and Amend the Child Nutrition Act of 1966*, 90th Cong., 1st sess., 15 and 16 March, 1967, p. 38.

[8] Further, the analysis of waste assumes that the recipients of food stamps are all sovereign consumers capable of deciding what is best for themselves. The food stamp program, however, might be an efficient way to transfer resources to the children of welfare recipients since it could be argued that they are not sovereign consumers.

nonrecipients might derive from this in-kind transfer program of food, it is possible to come up with an empirical estimate of the size of the so-called waste.

Empirically, the size of this waste depends on the number of individuals whose indifference curves can be represented by those in Figure 2-20, for if most recipients of food stamps had indifference curves which would actually be tangent somewhere along the line CD, such as curve IV in Figure 2-21, no waste would be entailed. Empirically, it has been estimated that the average household receiving food stamps values them at approximately 82 percent of their food-purchasing value. Thus, on average, the waste is 18 percent of the transfer.[9]

---

[9]Kenneth W. Clarkson, "Welfare Benefits of the Food Stamp Program," *Southern Economic Journal*, vol. 43, no. 1, July 1976, pp. 864–878. Clarkson also estimates that is costs $1.09 to transfer $1 of food stamps.

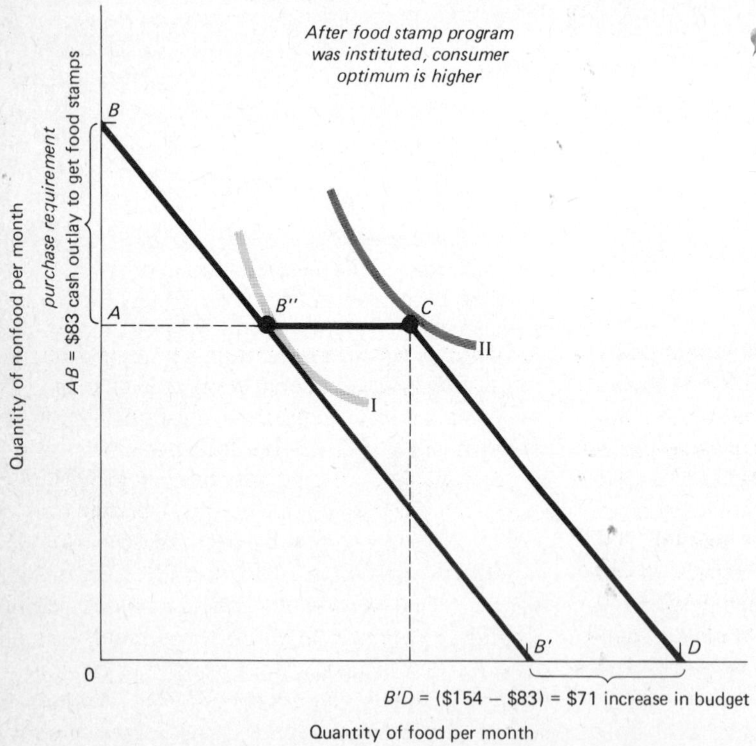

As we will see throughout this text, however, individuals will attempt to reduce waste (because more satisfaction is preferred to less). In this case, they can reduce waste by somehow obtaining nonfood commodities with food stamps. This is done by switching from unprepared food to prepared foods, which embody the purchases of additional preparation. In essence, the consumer is then purchasing less food and more convenience. The same can be said for the increase of service in higher-priced, service-oriented stores. Finally, it has been found that there is a significant amount of illegal trading of food stamps for other goods or for cash.

Fringe benefits: Are they better than more money income?

We can use an analysis very similar to the one presented for food stamps to analyze whether or

After food stamp program was instituted, consumer optimum is higher

Quantity of nonfood per month

AB = $83 cash outlay to get food stamps
purchase requirement

B''D = ($154 − $83) = $71 increase in budget

Quantity of food per month

Figure 2-20: Consumer optimum after the food stamp program.

Food stamps are sold in such a way that the net increase in real income in terms of food shifts the budget line over by the amount B'D on the horizontal axis. However, the new budget line becomes horizontal at point C, moves to B'' on the original budget line, and then takes on the form of the original budget line up the vertical axis. The vertical distance AB represents the purchase requirement, that is, how much money income must be given up in order to obtain food stamps equal to the horizontal distance AC with B''C (or B'D), representing the additional food purchasing power. In this particular example, the highest indifference curve that the consumer can reach is not tangent to the continuous part of the new budget line CD, but is tangent at the discontinuous point C.

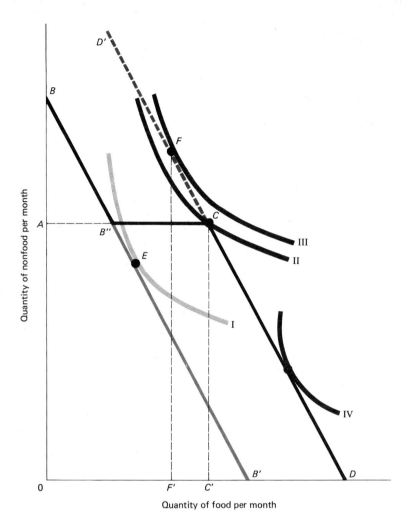

Quantity of nonfood per month

Quantity of food per month

If a cash grant is given, measured in terms of food in the amount of *B'D*, the new budget constraint becomes *DD'*. In this case the cash grant is equivalent in monetary terms to the amount of food offered under the food stamp program only if a consumer could purchase both food and nonfood items with food stamps, but this is not the case. In this particular case, the consumer can be made better off by the cash grant since a higher indifference curve III can be reached. The consumer optimum will be found at point *F* where less food *OF'* would be purchased than the *OC'* bought under the food stamp program. (Note, however, that if the consumer's indifference curve is represented by IV, the consumer is made better off by the full amount of the food stamp program and could not be made better off by a cash grant system instead.)

not employees benefit to the fullest extent possible from fringe benefits offered by employers. Fringe benefits are goods and services made available to employees and paid for by employers. Many employees prefer fringe benefits to higher money income because such benefits are rarely subject to federal and state income taxation. We will ignore for the moment this aspect of the fringe benefit question. What we will do is analyze the offer of the fringe benefit called "dental services" to two representative workers. This is done in Figure 2-22.

The commodity space is now somewhat different from that with which we have been dealing.

The vertical axis is labeled money income (dollars per month) which in ways is similar to the vertical axes in Figures 2-19 through 2-21 that were labeled quantity of nonfood per month. The horizontal axis is dental services, or in-kind income per month. Both workers' budget constraints are represented by *BB'*. We will look at preference patterns of two particular workers: worker 1 and worker 2. Worker 1 will reach consumer optimum at point *E* on indifference curve I₁. Worker 2 will reach consumer optimum at point *F* on indifference curve I₂. Worker 2 clearly prefers more dental services per month than worker 1. In each case, the worker must

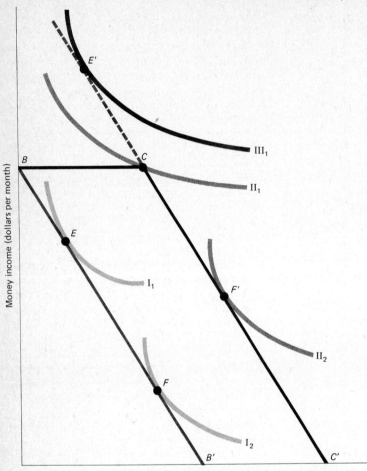

Figure 2-22: Fringe benefits versus additional take-home pay.

In-kind income in the form of dental services is offered to all workers in this company. This moves the budget constraint over from BB' to BCC'; but, unlike the food stamp case, there is no purchase requirement. Worker 2 is definitely made better off by the full amount of the in-kind services offered. He or she shifts from indifference curve I_2 to II_2 and from consumer optimum F to F'. However, worker 1 could be made better off by offering him or her an increase in money income rather than in in-kind dental services, because while the dental services would put him or her on indifference curve II_1, an increase in money income could put him or her on indifference curve III_1.

pay out of his or her pocket for all dental services purchased.

Now the employer offers both worker 1 and worker 2 fringe benefits in the form of dental services. The new budget constraint facing both of these workers is BCC'. The distance B to C or B' to C' represents the actual amount of additional dental services per month that are offered as higher fringe benefits. Worker 1 will move to his or her highest attainable indifference curve, which is II_1. It is tangent to the new budget constraint BCC' at point C. Worker 2, on the other hand, will reach a new optimum at point F'. His or

her highest attainable indifference curve is represented by II_2. Worker 2 is clearly as well-off as possible. So is worker 1, subject to the constraint that the additional income must be received in the form of dental services. However, worker 1, given the preferences as presented in all the indifference curves labeled with the subscript 1, could be made even better off if he or she were given a direct increase in money income equal to the amount of the fringe benefits BC or $B'C'$, instead of the benefits. In other words, worker 1 could move to a higher indifference curve, III_1, and attain consumer optimum point E' if he or she were given the option of having higher money income rather than the fringe benefit in the form of additional dental care.

Thus it would be possible, in principle, for the employer to make worker 1 better-off by withholding the fringe benefit of increased dental care and offering in its place an increase in money income that is *less than* the amount of money that the employer has to spend to provide BC of dental care to worker 1. In other words, worker 1 would be better-off if he or she could attain any indifference curve higher than II$_1$, and that is possible without receiving the full cash equivalent of BC.

Again, we have a situation where waste seems to be appearing even though there is voluntary exchange among individuals. Workers, along with employers, will attempt to minimize such waste. This could help explain, to some extent, the homogeneity of work forces in small firms. If workers all have similar tastes, fringe benefit programs can be tailored to the average worker and not entail any, or very much, waste from the point of view of any of the individual workers in the firm.

Glossary

Commodities A generic term for both goods and services.

Indifference curve A curve along which the level of satisfaction or utility remains unchanged; the locus of points representing combinations of two commodities that all yield equal levels of satisfaction.

Commodity space The x-y plane, or quadrant, that represents all possible combinations of the two commodities in question.

Principle of diversity in consumption A generalization about nonspecialized consumption activity; consumers do not specialize by consuming only one product but diversify their consumption choices and consume more than one.

Marginal rate of substitution (MRS$_{xy}$) The number of units of y that must be given up per unit of x gained in order to maintain a constant level of satisfaction.

Diminishing marginal rate of substitution A MRS$_{xy}$

that declines as more of x (and also less of y) is consumed; a property of convex-to-the-origin indifference curves.

Marginal evaluation The amount of additional satisfaction that an individual obtains from the consumption of one more unit of a commodity; also called marginal valuation and marginal use value.

Cardinal utility analysis The use of cardinal numbers which are quantitatively related to one another in order to measure and compare different levels of utility; such analysis requires the ability to measure utility.

Ordinal utility analysis An analysis which uses rankings, or orderings, of utility levels rather than quantitative numbers on a cardinal scale. Ordinal utility analysis requires only a ranking (first, second, third) of preferences.

Diminishing marginal utility A property of cardinal total utility curves; whenever cardinal total utility increases at a steadily decreasing rate, diminishing marginal utility exists and can be interpreted to mean that the marginal utility derived falls as more units of a good are consumed.

Budget constraint The constraint imposed on consumer decision making by a combination of income and prices. Generally, this is defined as available money income per unit time period and prices in dollars per unit.

Marginal rate of market substitution (MRMS$_{xy}$) The feasible rate at which the consumer can trade off y for x. This rate is usually given by the relative prices of x and of y (= the negative of the slope of the budget line).

Optimization The individual economic agent's decision-making process which leads to a consumer optimum or maximum satisfaction position.

Equilibrium A property of markets rather than individual decision making in which forces acting upon a system are balanced so that there is no net tendency to change.

Corner solution A solution to optimization or equilibrium problems which lies on either the x or the y axis.

Interior solution A solution to either optimization or equilibrium problems which does not lie on either axis.

Law of equal marginal utilities per dollar A

consumer optimum obtains when the marginal utility per dollar spent on a good is the same for all goods consumed.

Revealed preference An approach to consumer demand analysis in which we observe behavior and from it deduce certain properties of taste. The theory of revealed preference is formally independent of utility theory.

Summary

1. There are four assumptions in our model: (*a*) the consumer can determine which combination of commodities is preferable or which combinations yield equal satisfaction; (*b*) the consumer is consistent—preferences are transitive; (*c*) more is preferred to less; and (*d*) the consumer has full knowledge of alternatives.
2. Indifference curves are negatively sloped, pass through each and every point in the commodity space, and cannot intersect.
3. If indifference curves were concave to the origin, they would imply specialization rather than diversity in consumption. We use convex-to-the-origin indifference curves because they are consistent with observed nonspecialized consumption behavior, while not being inconsistent with corner solutions.
4. Any tangent drawn on a convex-to-the origin indifference curve lies below that curve.
5. Indifference curves which are convex to the origin have the property of a diminishing marginal rate of substitution of x for y—as more of x is consumed, the individual is willing to give up less of y in order to get one more unit of x, i.e., the person's marginal evaluation of x falls.
6. Cardinal utility analysis requires measurement of levels of utility, or satisfaction obtained, from consumption. Ordinal utility analysis only requires a rank ordering.
7. The shape of a cardinal total utility curve will remain invariant to the origin and to the unit interval used to measure utility; thus, no matter what scale is used, the resultant cardinal utility curve will look the same.
8. If the cardinal total utility curve is increasing at a steadily decreasing rate, then it has the property of diminishing marginal utility; however,

it is impossible to prove diminishing marginal utility because we have no way to measure utility.

9. A higher indifference curve indicates the consumption of more of both goods in the commodity space or the consumption of enough more of one good to more than compensate for the decreased consumption of the other. Hence, it is preferred to a lower indifference curve.
10. The slope of the budget line is equal to the negative of the price of x over the price of y. It represents the feasible rate at which x can be traded for y.
11. The consumer optimum occurs when the highest indifference curve is tangent to the budget line. At this point, the marginal rate of substitution is equal to the marginal rate of market substitution, or otherwise stated, the MRS_{xy} is equal to the ratio of the prices of x and y, or $MRS_{xy} = P_x/P_y = MRMS_{xy}$.
12. Consumer optimum can also be viewed in marginal utility terms as the combination of commodities which yields equal marginal utility per last dollar spent on each. Otherwise stated, the marginal utility ratio of any two commodities must be equal to the ratio of their prices.
13. Ignoring utility theory altogether, we might derive convex-to-the-orgin indifference curves by using the method of revealed preference which induces properties of consumer tastes from observed behavior.

Selected references

Bowen, Howard R., *Toward Social Economy* (New York: Rinehart, 1948), chap. 19.

Hicks, John R., *Value and Capital*, 2d ed. (Oxford: Clarendon, 1946), chap. 1 and 2.

Marshall, Alfred, *Principles of Economics*, 8th ed. (London: Macmillan, 1920), book 3.

Robertson, D. H., *Utility and All That* (New York: Macmillan, 1952), chap. 1.

Samuelson, Paul A., "Consumption Theory in Terms of Revealed Preference," *Economica*, new ser., vol. 15, November 1948, pp. 243–253.

Scitovsky, Tibor, *Welfare and Competition* (Homewood, Ill.: Irwin, 1951), pp. 65–67.

Stigler, G., "The Development of Utility Theory," *Journal*

Questions

(Answers to even-numbered questions are at back of text.)

1. State the four assumptions which underlie our model of consumer choice.
2. What information is depicted by a single indifference curve?
3. What is the difference between total utility and marginal utility?
4. Suppose a consumer prefers A to B, and B to C, but insists that he or she also prefers C to A. Explain the logical problem here.
5. In the real world, information about alternatives available in the marketplace is a service, the provision of which requires resources and which is therefore not free. What does that say about the omniscience assumption 4?
6. Suppose you are indifferent among the following three combinations of food (f) and drink (d): 1f and 10d, 2f and 7d, 3f and 2d. Calculate the marginal rate of substitution (MRS) in consumption between the two goods. Does the substitution of the third f imply a greater sacrifice of d than did the second? (It should.)
7. What is portrayed by (*a*) a vertical indifference curve, (*b*) a horizontal one, and (*c*) an upward-sloping one?
8. Explain why, if more is preferred to less, indifference curves cannot possibly intersect. In your answer, refer to Figure 2-4, *adding* a point D, directly above point C, to curve II.
9. Construct an indifference curve of the usual convex shape, representing coffee on the *x* axis and tea on the *y* axis. Now add a budget line just tangent to the indifference curve. Next rotate the budget line clockwise, keeping it tangent to the indifference curve as you do so. What do you observe happening, and what is its significance?
10. Construct a budget line from the following information: nominal income of $100 per week, price of beef P_b of $2 per pound, price of shelter P_s of $20 per week; all income is spent on beef and/or shelter. Suppose your money income remains constant, but the price of beef doubles to $4 per pound, while that of housing falls to $10 per week. Draw the new budget line. Are you now better off or worse off? What do we need to know before deciding?
11. Start over again with the initial situation in question 10. Now indicate two separate ways to show an unambiguous decrease in real income (represented by an inward shift of the budget line without any change in its slope).
12. According to the law of diminishing marginal utility, the way to increase the marginal utility of a good is to consume less of it. Explain this seeming paradox.
13. Suppose you are paid your weekly income in kind; you get forty 3-pound chickens (fryers) per week. Only one other good, avocados, is produced, and there is no money at all; goods are bartered by persons not content with their holdings of chickens and avocados. What additional piece of information do you need in order to construct your budget constraint? (Remember, money is out of the picture.)
14. Draw an indifference map containing two indifference curves I and II. How much better off is this consumer when consuming a combination of goods on curve II rather than on curve I? Can you tell? Why, or why not? Explain.
15. Suppose you are standing in the checkout line of a produce market. You have 10 pounds of tangerines and eight ears of corn. Tangerines cost 10¢ a pound; an ear of corn is also a dime. Given the $1.80 which you have to spend, you are satisfied that you have reached the highest attainable level of indifference. Along comes your brother, who tries to convince you that you should put some of the ears of corn back and replace them with additional pounds of tangerines. From what you know about utility analysis, how would you explain the disagreement?

3

CONSUMER DEMAND

The three main goals of this chapter are to extend the indifference curve analysis to find out more precisely how consumers react to changes in their money income; to find out how consumers react to changes in the relative price of a particular commodity, also using the indifference curve analysis; and to examine consumer decision making in the context of positive search and information costs.

The issues and applications treated in this chapter cover the following topics: measuring changes in "the cost of living"; the trade-off between labor and leisure; and an analysis of how a guaranteed annual income program affects a person's labor-leisure decision.

Changes in money income—Deriving the income-consumption curve

We saw in Chapter 2 that an increase in money income (constant prices) shifts the budget constraint, or budget line, outward and to the right to a new position which is parallel to the original budget line. The movement is parallel to the original budget line because the relative prices of the two commodities are assumed to be constant. Remember that the slope of the budget line is equal to the negative of the ratio of the prices of the two commodities. Therefore, if those prices remain constant, the slope of the budget line will be the same no matter how much income increases.

Now we would like to find out how an individual consumer responds to successive increases in money income when nominal and relative prices are constant. We do this in Figure 3-1.

We start out with a money income of M and prices P_x and P_y for the commodities in question, x and y. In what follows, we will use x and y to signify any two desired commodities. The reader can, if he or she wishes, think in terms of movies and concerts from the example in Chapter 2 (or any other pair of goods, for that matter). Remember that the two extreme points of the budget line are found by dividing the nominal price of each commodity into a constant amount of money income. Thus, if all the money income M were spent

on y, an amount $M/P_y = B$ could be purchased. If it were all spent on x, $M/P_x = B'$ could be purchased. Consumer optimum is at point E, where the consumer attains his or her highest indifference level, I, given the budget constraint. At point E, the rate at which the consumer is willing to substitute x for y (the slope of the indifference curve at that point) is equal to the rate at which the consumer is able to substitute x for y in the market (the slope of the budget line). Now let money income be increased from M to M'. The budget line shifts out to CC', which is parallel to BB' because relative prices have not changed. A new consumer optimum is established when the highest attainable indifference curve, II, is reached, and that occurs when that indiffer-

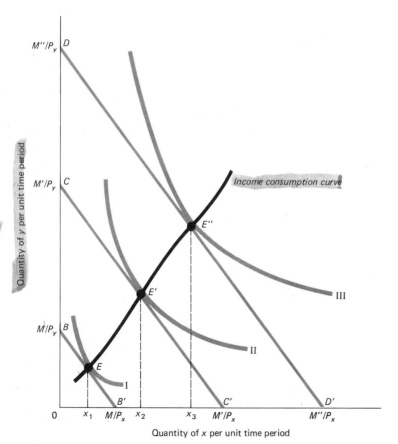

Figure 3-1: Deriving the income-consumption curve.
Nominal and therefore relative prices are constant. Money income initially is M, yielding budget constraint BB'. The consumer optimum occurs at E where indifference curve I is tangent to BB'. Then money income is increased first to M' and then to M''. New consumer optima points are obtained at E' and E''. When we connect these and all other possible consumer optima, we have what is called an income-consumption curve.

ence curve is tangent to the new budget line at point E'. Let's assume once more that money income is increased to M''. A new consumer optimum is obtained at point E''.

If we connect the three consumer optima points E, E', and E'', we have what is called an income-consumption curve. We define an **income-consumption curve** as the locus of the optimum consumption points that would occur if income for that consumer were increased continuously and the nominal and relative prices for the two goods in question remained constant.

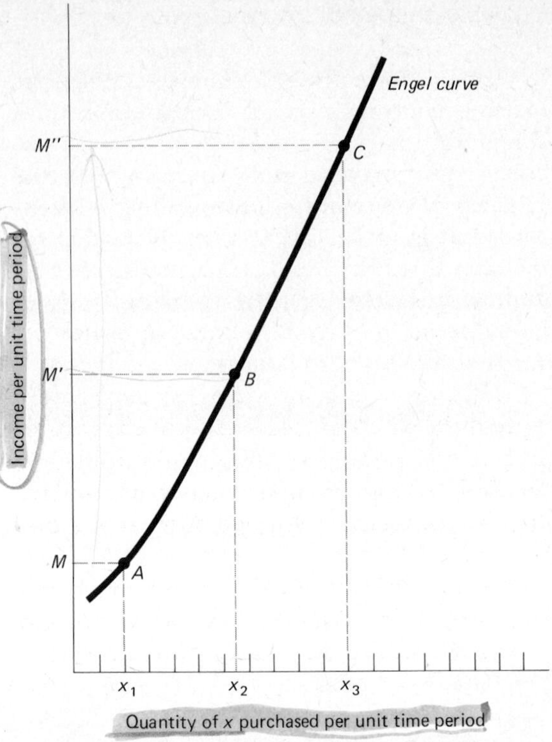

Applying the income-consumption curve—Deriving Engel curves

It is possible to use the income-consumption curve to derive the relationship between the level of income and the equilibrium quantity purchased of each good. A nineteenth-century German economist named Ernst Engel was the first to do empirical work relating expenditures on particular commodities to income. It is fitting, therefore, that curves showing this relationship have often been named after Engel. Here we start out using quantites purchased rather than expenditures.[1]

Let's derive the **Engel curve** for commodity x. We do it by transferring the various combinations of income and quantity of x purchased from Figure 3-1 to Figure 3-2. Thus we get point A, representing income M and the optimal quantity purchased x_1; point B, representing income M' and optimal quantity purchased x_2; and finally, point C, representing income M'' and optimal quantity purchased x_3. When we connect these three

Figure 3-2: Deriving the Engel curve.
We want to relate the optimum quantity of x purchased to various levels of income. We do this by plotting the combinations of money income and quantity of x purchased, holding the nominal and relative prices of x and y constant. Thus, point A is taken from Figure 3-1, where the quantity purchased is x_1 when income is M. Points B and C are obtained similarly. With higher income levels M' and M'', the quantities purchased are higher, equal to x_2 and x_3, respectively.

points, we construct an Engel curve. [Note that the nominal (P_x) and relative (P_x/P_y) price of x remains constant throughout the analysis.] The income-consumption curve in Figure 3-1 and the Engel curve in Figure 3-2 appear identical. However, they are not; the vertical axes on the two diagrams measure different variables. In Figure 3-1, the vertical axis measures the quantity of y per unit time period; in Figure 3-2, it measures income per unit time period.

---

[1] Economists call the relationship between quantity purchased and income an Engel curve, and the relationship between *expenditures* and income an Engel expenditure curve.

Possible shapes of Engel curves

In Figure 3-3, we present two broad categories of Engel curves. In panel (*a*), the quantity of commodity *x* purchased increases with income at a *decreasing* rate. In panel (*b*), the quantity of *x* purchased also increases with income but at an *increasing* rate. Note that for the same amount of increase of money income from *M* to *M'*, the increase in the quantity of *x* purchased is only $2^1/_2$ units in panel (*a*) but it is five units in panel (*b*).

The Engel curve in panel (*a*) supposedly represents what happens to the quantity of groceries purchased as individual incomes go up. Basic foodstuffs, in this sense, are considered a "necessity." A good such as the one represented in panel (*b*) might be a "luxury," such as gourmet restaurant dinners. (However, these labels should not be taken too seriously because they mean different things to different people.) At income *M*, you're probably already purchasing most of the food you think you "need"; increasing your income to *M'* won't cause you to buy much more food. But at income *M*, you probably don't buy too many gourmet dinners; and if your income increased to *M'*, you would probably consume gourmet dinners much more regularly.

Normal and inferior goods

We can classify commodities in terms of how consumers' purchases change when their incomes change. We drew a typical response to a change in income in Figure 3-1 when we drew the income-consumption curve. It shows the quantities of both *x* and *y* consumed as income changes. The resultant Engel curve for a specific commodity *x* was then derived in Figure 3-2, and two general

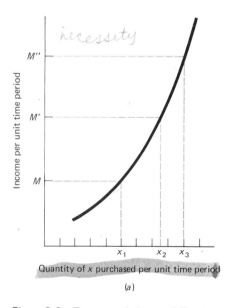

(a)

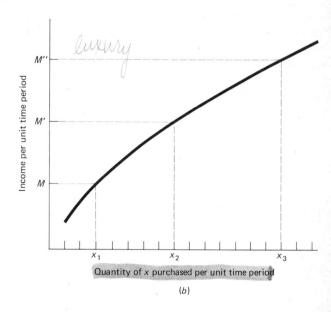

(b)

Figure 3–3: Two general classes of Engel curves.
In panel (*a*), the quantity of *x* purchased increases with income at a decreasing rate; but in panel (*b*), it does so at an increasing rate. Engel curves like the one in panel (*a*) are said to sometimes reflect "necessities," and those like the one in panel (*b*), "luxuries," although such labels leave much to be desired.

classes of Engel curves were presented in Figure 3-3. In each case, the quantity of x purchased went up as income increased. Thus, in each case, x was what we call a normal good. We define a **normal good** as one of which an individual buys more as his or her income increases and buys less as his or her income decreases.

Look at Figure 3-4. Here we have drawn the beginnings of a graph that would show an in-

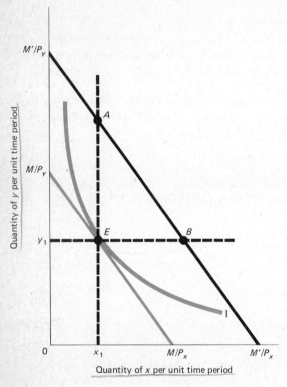

Figure 3-4: Normal and inferior goods.
If income increases to M', we can tell whether x and/or y is normal or inferior by finding out where the new point of consumer optimum lies. If the new point of consumer optimum lies between points A and B, then both x and y are normal goods because as income increases the optimal quantity of these two commodities also increases. If the new point of consumer optimum is to the left of point A, then less of x is purchased, and x is the inferior good. If the point of consumer optimum lies to the right of point B on the new budget line, y is the inferior good.

come-consumption curve. Income starts out at M; the prices are given and are equal to P_x and P_y. The consumer optimum is depicted by point E. Income is then increased to M'. The budget line shifts outward and parallel to the former budget line. We do not know where the consumer will end up unless we draw in additional indifference curves. We can, however, say something about whether or not x and/or y is a normal good. What if a second indifference curve is tangent to the new budget line somewhere between points A and B on that budget line? We know that if this happens, the consumer will purchase more of both x and y. In this situation, both x and y are normal goods. However, if the consumer ends up at a point to the left of A, we know that less of x than x_1 will be purchased after this increase in income. In this situation, we call x an inferior good. An **inferior good** is defined as one of which a consumer purchases less when his or her income rises and more when his or her income falls. TV dinners might be an example of an inferior good for most people. If the new point of consumer optimum is below B, less than y_1 is purchased, and in this case, y is an inferior good. Notice that it is possible for both goods represented in the commodity space to be normal, but it is impossible for both of them to be inferior. (Why?)

Because together they accounts for full income

Engel curves and the classification of goods

We can consider one specific commodity and use the Engel curve to determine whether or not that commodity is an inferior or a normal good. Look at Figure 3-5. We have drawn a hypothetical Engel curve for the commodity x. We find that for increases in income up to income level M_1, the optimum quantity of x purchased per unit time period also increases. However, at income level M_1, the Engel curve starts to bend backward. Thus, above income level M_1, the optimum quantity of x purchased per unit time period falls as income rises.

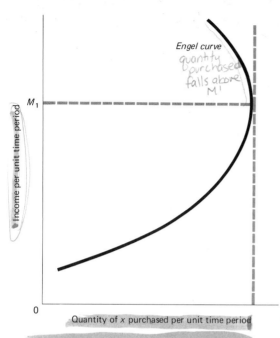

Engel curve

quantity
purchased
falls above
M!

M_1

Income per unit time period

0

Quantity of x purchased per unit time period

Figure 3-5: The Engel curve and classification of goods.
Whenever the optimum quantity of x purchased increases
as income increases, x is called a normal good. Thus,
between income levels 0 and M_1, x is indeed a normal
good. However, above income level M_1, x becomes an
inferior good because less is purchased as income rises.

Thus we say that for incomes from zero to M_1,
good x is superior, or normal; for incomes
above M_1, good x is inferior.

Real world examples

It is not hard to find real world examples of
goods whose Engel curves can be represented
by the one depicted in Figure 3-5. Consider
how a family would react to a rise in income in
its purchases of macaroni dinners. If we assume that the family starts out at a very low
level of income, we can be fairly confident that
as the family's income increases, more macaroni dinner will be bought. However, at some
point as income increases, meat will be introduced into the family's diet as a substitute
for macaroni dinners, resulting in fewer and

fewer of the latter being bought. Thus, the
backward-bending Engel curve would seem
appropriate.

Consider a student's purchase of relatively
low-quality record albums recorded by unknown artists. As the student's income
increases, say, by an increase in part-time
work or by an increase in stipends from the
university, there will (probably) be an increase in the number of low-grade, low-
quality, discounted record albums purchased.
This type of record is a normal good. However, if for some reason the student suddenly has
an increase in income of, say, $1,000 a month
(perhaps an annuity from a rich uncle or aunt),
we could imagine that the amount of low-
quality records purchased would decrease and
that higher-quality records by national record-
ing artists might be substituted. Again, the
backward-bending Engel curve in Figure 3-5
seems appropriate.

Relating changes in the quantity demanded to changes in income—Income elasticity of demand

For any good there is a straightforward way
for us to relate the quantity demanded to
changes in money income (if we assume that
the nominal and relative price of that good is
held constant). This measure of responsiveness to income changes is called income
elasticity. We define it as follows:

Income elasticity of demand = the relative
change in the amount of a commodity purchased ÷ the relative change in money income

Income elasticity of demand can be computed by the following formula:[2]

---

[2]Empirical estimates of the income elasticity of demand
often use expenditures on a product rather than quantity
purchased. Alternatively, these estimates are derived
using expenditures on the product divided by a price
index.

Income elasticity of demand

$$= \mu = \frac{\text{percentage change in optimal amount purchased}}{\text{percentage change in income}} \quad (3\text{-}1)$$

where μ is the Greek letter *mu*.

Sometimes it is useful to define income elasticity of demand in terms of the responsiveness of optimal quantity purchased to changes in *real* as opposed to *money* or *nominal* income. This is particularly relevant when the percentage of total expenditures going to the commodity in question is relatively large so that any change in that commodity's price will greatly affect real income.

A simple example will demonstrate how income elasticity of demand can be computed. In Table 3-1 we give the relevant data. The product in question is stereo records. We assume that the price of stereo records remains constant relative to other prices. In period 1, six records per month are purchased. Income per month is $200. In period 2, monthly income is increased to $300 and the quantity of records demanded per month is increased to eight. We can apply Eq. (3-1) to calculate

Income elasticity of demand $= \mu$

$$= \frac{(8 - 6)/6}{(300 - 200)/200} = \frac{^1/_3}{^1/_2} = 0.667 \quad (3\text{-}2)$$

Hence, measured income elasticity of demand for record albums for the individual represented in this example is 0.667. Note that this holds only for the move from six records to eight records per month purchased. In the move from eight to six records per month, the

number in Eq. (3-2) becomes

$$\frac{(8 - 6)/8}{(300 - 200)/300} = \frac{^1/_4}{^1/_3}$$

with the result that the measured income elasticity of demand is equal to 0.75. Another approximation which is independent of the starting point is

$$\mu = \frac{\Delta x}{x_1 + x_2} \bigg/ \frac{\Delta M}{M_1 + M_2} \quad (3\text{-}3)$$

where $M =$ income.

We can classify goods according to their income elasticity. We have already defined an inferior good as one whose quantity demanded goes down as income goes up, and vice versa. Clearly then, the income elasticity of demand of an inferior good will be negative. Hence we define all goods whose income elasticity of demand is less than 0 as inferior goods.

Similarly, we know that a normal good is one whose quantity demanded goes up as income goes up. Hence, all goods whose income elasticity of demand is greater than 0 but less than 1 are normal goods.

What about the case when the income elasticity of demand exceeds 1? When it exceeds 1, a 1 percent increase in income elicits a *more* than 1 percent increase in quantity demanded. Some economists have adopted the term **ultrasuperior goods** for all those goods whose income elasticity of demand is in excess of 1. The reason "ultra" was added onto superior is because the term "superior good" is often applied to any good which is not inferior. In Table 3-2, we give a summary

Time period	Quantity of record albums demanded per month	Income per month
Period 1	6	$200
Period 2	8	$300

Table 3-1

Income elasticity of demand	Classification
$\mu < 0$	Inferior
μ between 0 and 1	Normal
$\mu > 1$	Ultrasuperior

Table 3-2

of our classification scheme. The ultrasuperior good is the analytical opposite of an inferior good.

The distinction between normal and ultrasuperior goods is actually only one of degree. For a normal good, as income rises, consumers will spend more on that good, but the increases in purchases represent *an equal or reduced* portion of the increased income. For example, if income increases from $200 to $400 per week, the change in money income is 100 percent; if food expenditures increased from $80 to $120 per week, the change is only 50 percent. The approximate income elasticity of demand is 0.5. On the other hand, for ultrasuperior goods, as income rises, consumers will spend a greater portion of the increase in income on that good. Consider, again, income increasing from $200 to $400 per week, or a 100 percent increase. If alcoholic beverages are an ultrasuperior good, purchases will increase from, say, $10 to $25 per week, or a 150 percent increase, yielding an income elasticity of demand of 1.5.

No value judgments made

The use of the terms "ultrasuperior," "normal," and "inferior" is arbitrary. No value judgments are made about particular goods that have income elasticities greater than 1 or less than 1 or are negative. These terms are only descriptive. An ultrasuperior good for one person may be an appalling commodity to someone else. Moreover, one consumer may find a particular commodity to be an inferior good, and another may find it to be a superior good.

Empirical estimates of income elasticities

It is interesting to look at some of the estimated income elasticities of demand for certain groups of commodities that we commonly purchase. In Table 3-3, we do just that. According to our definition of inferior,

Categories of commodities	Coefficient of income elasticity of demand
Alcoholic beverages	1.54
Food	0.51
Tobacco	0.63
Clothing	1.02
Housing	1.04
Furniture	1.48
Electricity, gas	0.50
Fuel	0.38
Drugs (health-oriented)	0.61
Physicians' services	0.75
Dentists' services	1.41
New cars	2.45
Books	1.44
Private education	2.46

Table 3-3: Estimated coefficients of income elasticity of demand. Here we find the estimated income elasticities for selected groups of commodities. Notice that none of them was estimated to be an inferior good, while many were estimated to be normal or ultrasuperior goods. **Source:** H. S. Houthakker, and L. D. Taylor, *Consumer Demand in the United States: Analyses and Projections* (Cambridge, Mass.: Harvard University Press, 1970), pp. 260–263, table 6.5.

normal, and ultrasuperior goods, we can say that if these estimates are correct, food, tobacco, electricity, gas, fuel, drugs, and physicians' services are normal goods; the rest of the commodities listed are ultrasuperior. Note that the categories are broad. Both low-quality and high-quality items have been lumped together.

The relationship between income elasticities of demand for several commodities

Given a change in the budget constraint, a more than proportional change in the consumption of one commodity implies a less than proportional change in the consumption of at least one other commodity. Thus, the income elasticities of demand of several commodities in a consumer's expenditure pattern are related because of the budget constraint. By implication, then, it turns out that there is a relationship between the separate Engel curves for the different commodities that a consumer purchases.

Separate Engel curves are not independent of each other. This becomes clearer if we just look at the proposition that not all Engel curves can have a negative slope at the same income level. After all, not all commodities can be inferior goods at the same time. This was seen in the two-commodity case in Figure 3-4. So we know that all income elasticities of demand cannot be negative. Further, however, we will see that the (weighted) average income elasticity of demand for all goods taken together must be 1, and this leads us to some very interesting implications when we describe a particular good as being strongly inferior. Before we get to the implications, though, we have to prove the above-mentioned theorem.

We do this by first assuming that all money income is spent and that prices are constant. Hence

$$M = (P_x \cdot x) + (P_y \cdot y) \tag{3-4}$$

Now, consider an increase in money income of some small amount. We will signify a small change by the Greek letter delta (Δ). Because we use Δ's so much throughout the text, there is a short appendix at the end of this chapter on Δ analysis techniques. Given our assumption that all money income is spent, an increase in money income by ΔM will lead to a change in the consumption of x by the amount Δx and a change in the consumption of y by the amount Δy. Hence, the increase in income is spent according to the following:

$$\Delta M = P_x \Delta x + P_y \Delta y \tag{3-5}$$

Since an equation is unchanged if both the right-hand and the left-hand sides are multiplied or divided by the same quantity, let us divide both sides of Eq. (3-5) by the change in money income ΔM:

$$\frac{\Delta M}{\Delta M} = P_x \cdot \frac{\Delta x}{\Delta M} + P_y \cdot \frac{\Delta y}{\Delta M} \tag{3-6}$$

We can also multiply either side (or any term for that matter) by 1. What we do here is multiply the first term in the right-hand side of Eq. (3-6) by x/x and M/M, both of which equal 1. We then multiply the second term by y/y and again by M/M, both of which, again, equal 1. The result is

$$1 = \left[P_x \cdot \frac{\Delta x}{\Delta M} \cdot \frac{x}{x} \cdot \frac{M}{M} \right]$$

$$+ \left[P_y \cdot \frac{\Delta y}{\Delta M} \cdot \frac{y}{y} \cdot \frac{M}{M} \right] \tag{3-7}$$

Now, if we rearrange the terms in Eq. (3-7), we come up with a somewhat more interesting equation:

$$1 = \frac{P_x x}{M} \cdot \left(\frac{\Delta x/x}{\Delta M/M} \right) + \frac{P_y y}{M} \cdot \left(\frac{\Delta y/y}{\Delta M/M} \right) \tag{3-8}$$

We can make some sense out of Eq. (3-8) by realizing two things: (1) The term $P_x x/M$ is the percentage of income spent on x and similarly, $P_y y/M$ is the percentage of income spent on y. And remember that the sum of these percentages must equal 1. (2) The expressions in parentheses are merely another way of stating the calculations for the coefficients of income elasticity of demand for x and y. Rather than stating percentage changes, we have merely indicated discrete, small changes by Δ.

Now let

$$k_x = \frac{P_x x}{M} \quad \text{and} \quad k_y = \frac{P_y y}{M} \tag{3-9}$$

and since the sum of the percentages spent on each good must equal 1, therefore $k_x + k_y = 1$, then Eq. (3-8) becomes

$$1 = k_x \mu_x + k_y \mu_y \tag{3-10}$$

Equation (3-10) states that the *weighted* average of income elasticities of demand for all commodities purchased by an individual consumer at a given level of income must be equal to a positive 1 where the weights are the k's. The respective weights are the percent of money income spent on each good. Note that the weights must themselves add up to 1. Equation (3-10) makes sense. If we assume that all income is spent, then *on average*, a 1 percent increase in income will yield a 1 percent increase in purchases. In order to get the appropriate "average," we weigh the income elasticity by the share of total money income spent on each good. In this particular case, we consider only two goods x and y. In the more general case, we would consider the entire array of goods and services that the consumer purchases. Equation (3-10) would become quite long, but the implication would be the same. The weighted average income elasticities for all goods consumed must add up to 1.

The implication of Eq. (3-10) is that whenever one particular commodity is strongly inferior, there must be either (1) an even more strongly ultrasuperior good or (2) a set of fairly strongly ultrasuperior goods. Why? To offset the strongly inferior good so that the average income elasticity of demand equals 1.

Another way of stating this is that whenever there are strongly ultrasuperior goods whose income elasticities exceed 1, they must be offset by other goods with income elasticities that are less than 1.

Finally, Eq. (3-10) allows us to predict that the items that take up a large percentage of a consumer's budget generally have relatively small income elasticities of demand. Consider the budget of a low-income family in which 75 percent of its income is spent on food, or $k_{food} = 0.75$. That means that if the income elasticity of the demand of this family for food exceeded the reciprocal of $^3/_4$ (i.e., was greater than 1.333), then the average income elasticity of demand for all other goods would have to be negative. This is unlikely. Most goods are normal or ultrasuperior. Thus, we surmise that for this particular family, the income elasticity of demand for food is considerably less than 1.333. To illustrate this point with an ex-

aggeration, consider the possibility that $\mu_{food} = 2.00$. By Eq. (3-10), we know that μ_{food} takes up 75 percent of the budget:

$$1 = k_{food} \cdot \mu_{food} + k_{all\ other\ goods} \cdot \mu_{all\ other\ goods} \quad (3\text{-}11)$$

which becomes

$$1 = 0.75 \cdot 2.00 + 0.25\mu_{all\ other\ goods} \quad (3\text{-}12)$$

or

$$1 = 1.5 + 0.25 \cdot \mu_{all\ other\ goods} \quad (3\text{-}13)$$

But for Eq. (3-13) to hold, $\mu_{all\ other\ goods}$ besides food must equal -2! And that is outrageously unlikely.

We now leave the effects of change in income on the quantity of a good purchased and look at the effects of a change in its relative price.

The effects of a change in price—Deriving the price-consumption curve

How do the actual or potential consumers of a commodity react to a change in the relative price of the commodity? In general, they purchase more when the relative price falls and purchase less when the relative price rises. This relationship can be derived by using indifference curve analysis.

The price-consumption curve

Let us hold money income and P_y constant while we change the price of commodity x. This is done in Figure 3-6. What we do in Figure 3-6 is run an experiment in which the price of x falls as money income and the price of y remains constant. Remember that we can find the extreme points for the budget line by asking how much of a particular commodity could be purchased if none of the other commodity were purchased. Consider the horizontal axis. When the price of x is P_x, the amount that can be purchased is derived by dividing P_x into total money income M. That amount is B. When the price of x falls to P'_x,

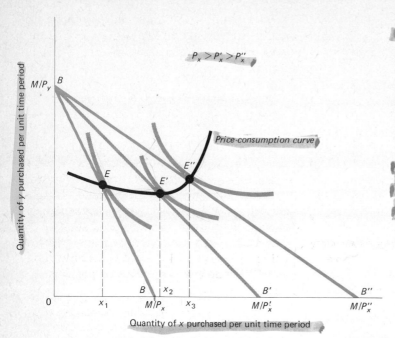

$P_x > P'_x > P''_x$

Quantity of y purchased per unit time period

M/P_y

Price-consumption curve

E E' E''

0 x_1 x_2 x_3

M/P_x M/P'_x M/P''_x

B B' B''

Quantity of x purchased per unit time period

Figure 3-6: Deriving the price-consumption curve.
We start with budget line *BB*. Consumption optimum is at point *E*, where the indifference curve is tangent to the budget line. We now reduce the price of *x* to P'_x. The new budget line rotates out to *BB'*; the new consumption optimum is at point *E'*. We do this again by reducing the price of *x* further to P''_x. The new consumption optimum is at point *E''*. When we connect *E*, *E'*, and *E''*, we have the locus of optimum combinations of *x* and *y* that would be purchased at different relative prices of *x*. This curve is called the *price–consumption curve*.

the amount of *x* that can be purchased with total money income expands to *B'*; and it expands to *B''* when the price falls further to P''_x. Thus, even though money income does not change, the amount of *x* that can be purchased increases.

Each time the budget line changes, there will be a new point of consumer optimum. At first it is at point *E*, then point *E'*, and then point *E''*. If we connect these three points, we obtain a **price-consumption curve**. That curve is defined as the locus of optimum combinations of *x* and *y* that result from a change in relative prices, holding money income constant. [Remember: $-(P_x/P_y) =$ slope of the budget line.] A priori we cannot say anything about the shape or slope of the price-consumption curve.

Obtaining the demand curve from the price-consumption line

Given the way in which we have drawn our indifference curves, we can say something about the relationship between the relative price of a particular commodity and the quan-

tity purchased. We can similarly derive a relationship between the optimum quantity of a good purchased and the relative price of that good by using the diagram showing the price-consumption curve in Figure 3-6. The resultant relationship is a **demand curve**. A general definition of a demand curve is the locus of optimum points relating the various prices of a commodity and the quantity purchased at each price. We must add that other things are held constant. This is the standard *ceteris paribus* assumption. "Other things" in this case are tastes, money income, the prices of other commodities, etc.

To derive the demand curve, we pick from Figure 3-6 and plot the points representing the quantities demanded—x_1, x_2, and x_3—and associated prices, P_x/P_y, P'_x/P_y, and P''_x/P_y. This gives us three points from which to construct the demand curve in Figure 3-7.

The law of demand

The shape of the demand curve depicted in Figure 3-7 is important. It is a graphic representation of the **law of demand**.

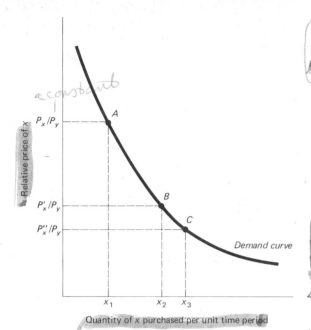

Figure 3-7: Deriving the demand curve from the price-consumption curve.

We have three different relative prices in Figure 3-6: P_x/P_y, P'_x/P_y, and P''_x/P_y. Associated with these progressively lower prices of x are quantities demanded of x_1, x_2, and x_3. We transfer these pairs and obtain points A, B, and C. When these points are connected, they form a demand curve.

Law of demand: The quantity demanded varies inversely with relative price, other things held constant

We will examine applications of the law of demand in much more detail in Chapters 4 and 5.

Here we can point out that a downward-sloping demand curve will follow from convex indifference curves such as those drawn in Figure 3-6 (except in the case of strongly inferior goods, treated later in this chapter). Since the indifference curves are convex, when the budget line is rotated counterclockwise (as a result of a lower price of x, as in Figure 3-6), new tangency points will usually be to the right of the old tangency points. In other words, the new optimum E' in Figure 3-6 will not often be to the left of E if we use convex in-

difference curves. Remember that convex indifference curves will follow from an assumption of diminishing marginal rates of substitution in consumption.

A measurement of price responsiveness —the price elasticity of demand

Earlier we developed the concept of the coefficient of income elasticity of demand, which is a measure of the relative change in optimal quantity demanded when income changes. We can apply a similar concept that relates the change in optimal quantity demanded of a commodity when its relative price changes. This concept is called the **price elasticity of demand.** We define it in a similar manner.

Coefficient of price elasticity of demand = relative change in the quantity demanded of a good ÷ relative change in the relative price of that good

We will treat in detail the concept of price elasticity of demand and how to measure it in Chapter 5. For the moment, we wish to discover first the relationship between price elasticity of demand and total expenditures on the particular good under study. Then we can find how to determine price elasticity of demand by observing the slope of the price-consumption curve.

The relationship between price elasticity of demand and total expenditures on a good

Just as we were able to make classifications according to income elasticity of demand, as in Table 3-2, we can make classifications according to the price elasticity of demand and we do so in Table 3-4. In cases where price elasticity of demand is numerically greater (greater in absolute value) than 1, we call demand price **elastic.** When it is just numerically equal to 1, we have a situation of **unitary** price elasticity of demand. In cases when it is numerically less than 1, we have a situation of price **inelastic demand.**

Consider the simplest case: unitary price elasticity. A 1 percent change in price elicits a 1 percent change in the quantity purchased. Since the total expenditure on any product is equal to the number of units purchased times the price of each unit, consumer expenditures on a good whose price elasticity is numerically equal to 1 will remain constant as price changes in either direction. This is not the case when price elasticity is numerically greater or less than 1. When demand is price-elastic, for example, a reduction in price will lead to a more-than-proportionate increase in quantity demanded, and hence consumer expenditures on that good will rise. You can work through the remaining examples in Table 3-4.

The relationships between the total expenditure by a consumer on a product and the price elasticity of demand will allow us, as we will see, to use the slope of the price-consumption curve to tell us the price elasticity of demand.

Observing the elasticity of demand through the price-consumption curve

In Figure 3-8, we have drawn three different price-consumption curves. The commodity space in each of the panels is somewhat dif-ferent than the one we have been using. The horizontal axis is the same as before. The difference is on the vertical axis, which designates "money for all other goods" rather than the quantity of a specific good. Thus, if no x is purchased at all, M on the vertical axis represents money income available for all other goods. Hence, anytime there is any purchase of x, it reduces money expenditures on all other goods.

Now consider panel (a). Here we have drawn two budget constraints, one for a price of x, P_x, and another for a lower price P'_x. The two points of consumer optimum are E and E'. The price-consumption line connecting those two points is downward-sloping. Notice what happens when the price of x falls to P'_x. The quantity of x demanded goes up, but that is true in most cases when there is a price decrease. However, note that the amount of money available for all other goods has fallen from M_1 to M_2. This can mean only one thing: Total expenditures on x have gone up when the price of x has fallen. Because of the relationship between total expenditures and elasticity, we know that the demand for x over the price range P_x to P'_x, as presented in Figure 3-8(a), is price-elastic.

Now look at panel (b). Here we show that

$\Delta Q / \Delta P$

When price elasticity is numerically	Demand is called	Thus if price changes	Quantity demanded changes (in opposite direction)	So that consumer expenditures on the good ($P_x \cdot x$)
Greater than 1	Price-elastic	$P\uparrow$	More than in proportion	Fall
		$P\downarrow$	More than in proportion	Rise
Equal to 1	Unitary-elastic	$P\uparrow$	In proportion	Remain constant
		$P\downarrow$	In proportion	Remain constant
Less than 1	Price-inelastic	$P\uparrow$	Less than in proportion	Rise
		$P\downarrow$	Less than in proportion	Fall

Table 3-4

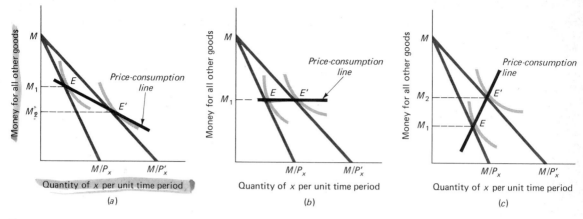

Figure 3-8: Price elasticity of demand and the slope of the price-consumption line.
We can tell the price elasticity of demand by observing the slope of the price-consumption line. In these three commodity spaces, the vertical axis measures money for all other goods instead of "good y." Thus, anytime there is a reduction in money for all other goods, that implies an increase in expenditure on x. In panel (a), as the price of x falls, the amount of money available for all other goods falls, meaning that total expenditure on x increases; hence, the demand over the price range $P_x \rightarrow P'_x$ in panel (a) is price-elastic. In panel (b) the same thing occurs except that the amount of money available for all other goods remains constant. Hence, the demand over the price range $P_x \rightarrow P'_x$ in panel (b) is unit-elastic. Finally, in panel (c) the amount of money available for all other goods rises, and the demand over the price range $P_x \rightarrow P'_x$ is price-inelastic.

after a reduction of P_x to P'_x, the amount of money left over for all other goods remains the same at M_1. Thus, because total expenditure on goods is constant, the demand for x over the price range P_x to P'_x represented in panel (b) must be of unit or unitary elasticity.

And finally, in panel (c), the demand is price-inelastic because, as the price of x falls, the total amount of money left over for all other goods rises, and the total expenditures on x must have fallen. The increase in consumption of x was less than in proportion to the decrease in price.

In summary, the demand for x is price-elastic, unitary-elastic, and price-inelastic when the price-consumption line is downward-sloping (a negative slope), horizontal (zero slope), and upward sloping (a positive slope), respectively.

Income and substitution effects

We have looked at how a change in a consumer's income affects the optimum quantity of a good purchased. We have also looked at how a change in a good's relative price affects the optimum quantity purchased. Now we will consider how a change in the relative price of a good not only affects the rate at which that good can be substituted for another, but at the same time, also affects the consumer's real income, which is analytically defined as a given level of utility. Often, real income is approximated by M/P, where P is an appropriate price index. The meaning of real income, then, is purchasing power, or command over goods and services.

Say your income is $15,000 per year; by itself, that amount of money means little or nothing. But if you think of that amount of money in terms of what it can buy, then you are thinking about what we call *real income*. To illustrate what we mean by an increase or decrease in real income, consider two consumers, Mr. Smith and Ms. Jones, each having income of $20,000 per year. If Mr. Smith spends all his income on food and the price of food goes up, then his real income goes down because his $20,000 will buy less food. If Ms.

Jones spends all her income on opera records and the price of opera records decreases, then her real income has increased because she can buy more records with her $20,000.

When we drew our first price-consumption curve in Figure 3-6, we were dealing with a change in real income. This is obvious if you go back and look at what happens to M/P_x on the horizontal axis when P_x decreases. The budget line rotates outward. Thus, real income measured in terms of good x per unit time period increased, although it remained constant in terms of good y per unit time period because the price of y was held constant. Thus, the person who consumes a lot of x will find his or her real income (expressed in terms of x) increases as the price of x falls. In fact, the increase in real income varies directly with the fraction of money income spent on x. We expect, therefore, that as long as we are dealing with normal or ultrasuperior goods—i.e., goods whose income elasticity of demand is positive—this resultant increase in real income will increase the quantity demanded at each and every price. This is totally separate from the increase in the quantity demanded due to the reduction in the relative price of x.

Now we want to try to isolate each of the two effects that occur when there is a change in the relative price. One effect is due to the substitution of a relatively cheaper good for a good that becomes relatively more expensive. This is called the **substitution effect**. The other effect is the result of the increase in the consumer's real income, expressed in terms of the now cheaper good M/P_x, that comes about as that product becomes cheaper and money income remains unchanged. This is called the **income effect**. For normal and ultrasuperior goods, as income goes up, more is purchased. Therefore, the income effect is positive; i.e., the relationship between changes in income and in quantity demanded is a direct one. For inferior goods, the income effect is negative; i.e., the relationship between changes in income and in quantity demanded is an inverse one. We'll show these effects in the following example.

Example for a reduction in price

Look at Figure 3-9. Here we show the now-familiar indifference curves I and II tangent to two separate budget lines, BB' and BB''. The position from which we start is money income of M and prices P_y and P_x. The initial budget line is therefore BB'. The highest indifference curve attainable is I, which is tangent to that budget line at point A. The quantity of x demanded will be x_1. Now there is a reduction in the price of x to P'_x. The new budget line is BB'' where B'' occurs at the point where money income M is divided by the new lower price of x, P'_x. The budget line has rotated outward to the right. The highest indifference curve attainable is II, which is tangent to BB'' at point C. The new quantity of x purchased will be x_2. The distance from A to C, or from x_1 to x_2, is the total effect of a price change. It includes both the substitution and the income effects.

Now let's ferret out these two different effects. The way we can do it is by constructing a hypothetical budget line that is (1) tangent to the initial indifference curve, curve I, but is (2) parallel to BB''. In this manner, what we are doing is changing the relative prices facing the consumer so that he or she now sees the price ratio P_y/P'_x rather than P_y/P_x. We call the hypothetical budget line HH'; it is tangent to the original indifference curve. Thus we can, in some sense, contend that the consumer still has the same level of satisfaction or "real income." After all, the consumer would still be on the original indifference curve I. In effect, then, in this experiment we are changing relative prices for the consumer such that x becomes cheaper. However, to prevent the consumer's utility from rising, we take away just enough income so that the consumer moves from point C on indifference curve II

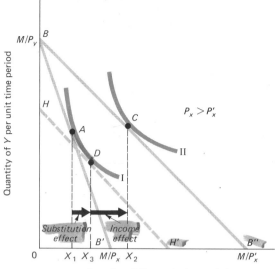

Quantity of Y per unit time period

M/P_y B

H

A

C

$P_x > P'_x$

D

II

I

Substitution effect   Income effect

B'

H' B''

0 X_1 X_3 M/P_x X_2 M/P'_x

Quantity of X per unit time period

Figure 3-9: Substitution and income effect.
The total effect of a lower price of x is comprised of two effects; that is, the consumer buys more of x for two reasons: (1) substitution in favor of the relatively cheaper good and (2) an increase in real income (expressed in terms of good x). The total effect is given by the movement from point A to point C. In order to derive a substitution effect, we hypothetically take away a sufficient amount of this consumer's income so that he or she is forced back to indifference curve I. What is taken away is represented by the vertical distance between H and B, or by the horizontal distance from H' to B''. In other words, we are confronting the consumer with the new relative prices represented by the slope of the new budget line BB'', but not allowing the consumer to have an increase in utility. There is no income effect here. The consumer substitutes x for y and moves from point A to point D, or the horizontal distance from x_1 to x_3. Now we give the consumer back the income that we took away and we find out how much more of x is purchased because of this increase in real income. This is represented by the movement from D to C, or the horizontal distance from x_3 to x_2. In this particular diagram, the income effect is positive for we are dealing with a normal good.

back to point D on indifference curve I. In other words, in this experiment we have taken away BH in income expressed in terms of good y, or what is the same thing, $H'B''$ in terms of good x. Thus we are eliminating any possible income effect. The consumer's

real income has not risen. What will the consumer do? Given the convexity of the indifference curve, the consumer will purchase a larger quantity of x and a lesser quantity of y. In fact, the optimum combination will shift from A to D. This is the substitution effect at work.

Now we allow the consumer to enjoy the increase in real income associated with the reduction in the price of x from P_x to P'_x. We give back the income we just took away in our experiment. The consumer goes back to the new budget line BB'', and the new optimum is at C. The movement from D to C is the income effect because there has been an increase in income from H' to B'' as measured on the x axis in terms of the quantity of x. Since we are dealing with a normal or superior good here, changes in income lead to changes in quantity demanded in the same direction—the income effect is positive. It leads to an even larger increase in the quantity purchased of x when P_x falls.

Derivation of income and substitution effects: An alternative technique

The foregoing derivation of substitution and income effects of a price change was predicated upon altering the consumer's level of real income after the relative price change so that the consumer remains on the original indifference curve. This technique has been called the Hicksian approach, named after Sir John R. Hicks, a British economist. It has been criticized for its lack of real world applicability because it is impossible to know exactly how much real income should be altered in order to keep the individual consumer on the original indifference curve. After all, it is impossible to measure utility. An alternative approach has been developed and is given below. It involves hypothetically altering the consumer's income in such a way that the consumer could purchase the same bundle of commodities as was purchased before the price change. This is the so-called Slutzky technique, named after the Russian economist Eugene Slutzky (1880–1948).

This new procedure for separating the income and substitution effects of a price change is presented in Figure 3-10. The diagram in many respects is exactly the same as in Figure 3-9. The original budget line is BB' with prices P_y and P_x. The price of x falls to P'_x; the new budget line rotates clockwise to BB''. The consumer moves from optimum point A and consumption of x_1 to optimum point B and
D

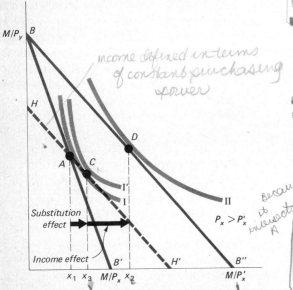

Figure 3-10: Income and substitution effect-the Slutzky method.

Figure 3-10 is essentially the same as Figure 3-9; however instead of taking away income so as to keep the individual on the original indifference curve I, we take away just enough income to allow the consumer to purchase the original combination of x and y. Thus, we hypothetically reduce income after the relative price change so that a consumer is forced back to HH', which goes through point A, the original consumption optimum. Now the consumer faces the new relative price with constant purchasing power. The substitution effect is measured by the movement from A to C, or by the movement of quantity purchased from x_1 to x_3. Now we give back to the consumer the income that we took away, and we move from point C to point D, or from x_3 to x_2. This represents the income effect.

increased consumption of x_2. In order to obtain the substitution effect, the consumer moves from optimum point A and consumption of x_1 at price P_x to optimum point D and consumption of x_2 at price P'_x. In order to obtain the pure substitution effect, we have to find out how much more of x the consumer will buy strictly as a result of the new lower price which attracts him or her to give up some y (which hasn't changed in price) in order to buy more of x, which is now definitely cheaper than y. To do this, we must draw a hypothetical budget line which reflects the new relative price ratio P_y/P'_x within the consumer's original situation (where price ratio was P_y/P_x) and see what happens there. In effect, what we will do with this hypothetical budget line is remove some of the consumer's new income.

Therefore, we draw the hypothetical budget line HH', which is exactly parallel to the new budget line BB'' and intersects point A, the original optimum point. Now we ask ourselves the following question: At its new relative price, how much of x would the consumer purchase? The answer isn't on the original indifference curve I because this hypothetical budget line cannot be tangent to that curve. The answer must be on a higher indifference curve. The answer is given by finding the point of tangency of the highest indifference curve to the new (Slutzky-compensated) budget line HH'. This is at point C. Thus the quantity of x represented by the horizontal distance from x_1 to x_3 represents the substitution effect. The income effect is given by the horizontal distance from x_3 to x_2.

For very small changes in prices, whether we use the Hicks technique or the Slutzky technique to derive the income and substitution effects makes little difference.

Now we look at two cases where the income effect is negative, that is, two cases in which we are dealing with inferior goods. The second case of these is, presumably, the one exception to the law of demand.

Inferior goods

When there is an inferior good involved, the income effect is, by definition, negative—changes in income are associated with changes in quantity demanded in the opposite direction. This can be seen in Figure 3-11,

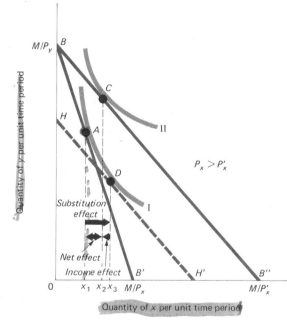

Figure 3-11: Income and substitution effects: the case of an inferior good.
We start off with relative prices and income such that the budget line is BB'. The consumption optimum is at point A, where indifference curve I is just tangent to BB'. The relative price of x falls from P_x to P'_x, so that the new budget line is BB''. The new consumption optimum is at point C. In order to find the substitution effect (using the Hicksian approach), we hypothetically take away income until the consumer finds himself or herself back on the original indifference curve. This hypothetical budget line, then, is HH'. Faced with constant utility and a lower price of x, the consumer moves from point A to point D on indifference curve I. The movement from A to D is the substitution effect, also measured by the change in quantity consumed, from x_1 to x_3. Now we give back the income taken away from the consumer and move to the new consumption optimum on indifference curve II, at point C. The movement from D to C is the income effect. It is measured by the distance inward from x_3 to x_2. This is the case of an inferior good that has, by definition, a negative income elasticity of demand.

which is like Figure 3-9 except that the consumer's preference pattern is somewhat different. We start off at an optimum at point A in Figure 3-11, with a price of P_x and a quantity of x demanded, x_1. As in the prior case, when there is a reduction in the price from P_x to P'_x, there is an increase in the quantity demanded to x_2. Now we wish to sort out how much of that increase is due to the income effect and how much is due to the substitution effect.

First, we obtain the substitution effect by merely rotating the budget constraint around the original indifference curve until it reaches a new point of tangency where it reflects the new price ratio P_y/P'_x. The substitution effect is always negative; i.e., changes in a commodity's own price are associated with changes in quantity demanded in the opposite direction. Therefore, at a lower price, quantity demanded increases; and at a higher price, quantity demanded decreases, *holding real income constant*. A reduction in the relative price of x leads to an increase of consumption from A to D, or from x_1 to x_3.

Now we find the income effect. We increase income by the amount $H'B''$ as measured in terms of good x, or HB as measured in terms of good y. We end up at point C, the new point of consumer optimum on a higher indifference curve. Notice, however, the movement from D to C is a negative one, at least in terms of good x. That is, the increase in real income has caused this consumer to purchase less of x by the distance x_3 to x_2. Thus, the income effect in this example is negative; this is an inferior good. However, the substitution effect is still stronger than the negative income effect, and consequently, the law of demand still holds.

Notice an important point. The substitution effect is always negative. That is, a reduction in price leads to a higher quantity demanded. The income effect, however, can be either positive or negative. In the case of an inferior good, it will be negative. Thus, for all normal and ultrasuperior goods, the law of demand must hold because the income effect serves only to reinforce the substitution effect.

When the law of demand doesn't hold: The Giffen paradox

When we are dealing with a strongly inferior good, it is possible, or at least conceivable, that the negative income effect would not be outweighed by the substitution effect of a decrease in the relative price. Hence, even though the substitution effect would cause more to be purchased when the relative price falls, the negative income effect would more than offset it. The result would be a *positive* rather than the usually negative relationship between price changes and quantities demanded, or an upward-sloping demand curve! This has been labeled the Giffen paradox.[3] Giffen's paradox seems to be the only exception to the law of demand, and it is not clear that there has ever been a case empirically supporting the existence of a **Giffen good**. Intuitively, the possibility of a Giffen good seems quite remote. We usually think that such a good must be a relatively low-priced item like bread or macaroni dinners. A reduction in the price of that good will not have a very big effect on the purchasing power of a given money income. In a more general equilibrium context, i.e., taking account not only of consumers but of producers, the possibility of a Giffen good occurring seems even more remote. If the price of, say, potatoes falls to consumers, it is true that their real purchasing-power income rises because of that price decrease. However, the income of potato producers falls by an equivalent amount because what is consumed must also be produced and sold by producers. Thus the real income gain to those potato consumers who are not potato producers tends to be offset by the income loss to the producers. (On the other hand, if the price of potatoes falls because a new, less expensive potato-production process is developed, then price decreases do not necessarily imply a loss for producers and the above consideration need not apply.)

In any event, look at Figure 3-12. It is similar to Figure 3-11, except that indifference curve II is so far to the left that the consumption of commodity x falls as the price falls.

We note that all Giffen goods must be inferior goods, i.e., have negative income elasticities of demand. However, not all inferior goods are necessarily Giffen goods.

Relaxing the assumption of full knowledge

All the analysis so far has assumed that the consumer has full knowledge about the prices, availability, and qualities of the goods in question. When we relax the assumption of full knowledge, we have a slightly different situation.

Markets and transaction costs

Economic activities take place in markets. We can abstractly define a **market** as the sphere through which price-making forces (the terms of exchange) operate. In other words, supply and demand work themselves out in markets. We can then define **marketplaces** as locations where exchanges occur and where the terms of exchange are registered. In the marketplace, groups of individuals and businesses keep in touch with each other in order to buy or sell some particular good. Finally, market *mechanisms* are aspects of marketplaces and are information networks, for example, to allow individuals to keep in touch with each other. Market mechanisms are often set up to minimize transactions costs.

But what are **transactions costs?** We can define them as all of the costs of enabling

---

[3]See George J. Stigler, "Notes on the History of the Giffen Paradox," *Journal of Political Economy*, vol. 55, 1947, p. 152.

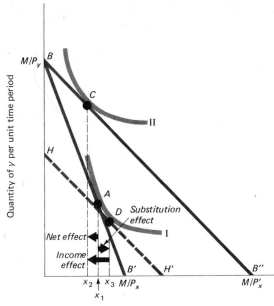

Figure 3–12: The case of the Giffen good.
We start off in consumption optimum at point A, where
indifference curve I is just tangent to the budget line
BB', which is given for money income M and prices
$P'_y P_x$. We now reduce the price of x to P'_x. The budget
line rotates out to BB''. In this case, the new consumption optimum is at point C. The quantity of x demanded
has fallen from x_1 to x_2. In order to ferret out the
income and substitution effects, we hypothetically take
away enough income to keep the consumer on the
original indifference curve I. This new budget line is
HH'. With the same utility or "real income" and lower
relative price of x, the consumer increases his or her
consumption of x. The substitution effect is measured
by the movement from point A to point D, or from
x_1 to x_3. Now we give back to the consumer the
income that we took away, moving from point D to
point C. The income effect is strongly negative and
outweighs the substitution effect, such that the net
effect of a reduction in the price is a *decrease* in the
quantity demanded.

exchanges to take place. Transactions costs
include the cost of being informed about the
qualities of a particular product. The general
nature of a product can include its price, availability, durability record, servicing facilities,
degree of safety, and so on. Consider, for ex-

ample, the transactions costs in shopping for a
10-speed bicycle. Such costs would include
phone calls or actual visits to sellers in order to
learn about product features and prices. These
are transactions costs. In addition to these
costs, we must include the costs of negotiating
a sale. The specification and execution of any
sales contract is thus included, and ultimately,
transactions costs must include the cost of enforcing such contracts.

Without going into a full discussion of the
theory of transactions costs, we can point out
here that they depend on the following:

1. The number of distinct transactions per
   unit time period
2. The volume of goods traded per unit time
   period
3. The number of distinct parties involved
   in each transaction
4. The number of distinct goods per transaction

Information and price dispersion

Ignoring for the moment questions about
quality and availability of a product, let us
dwell only on the fact of life that price dispersion exists even for homogeneous products,
that is, products that have similar qualities.
Even if a product's attributes are well defined,
it is possible to purchase it at different prices
from different sellers. An automobile with exactly the same features may be sold at different
prices by different dealers (even after correcting for possible differentials in service and the
choice of models or brands from which to
choose).

The relaxation of our assumption of full information, in the face of price dispersion, can
be looked at as a situation of consumer choice
with uncertainty. Uncertainty, in this example, is uncertainty about where the product
can be bought at the lowest price. We now can
define the term "information" in the context
of price to mean a change in the consumer's

knowledge of price dispersion or differences. Information generation is an active process. Acquiring information is therefore costly. It uses such resources as time and money income. As such, some information costs are transactions costs. However, Robinson Crusoe (before Friday's arrival on the scene) would have incurred **information costs**, but no transactions costs, because he was alone.

The optimal search for information

Consider now a typical situation in which there is price dispersion and incomplete information about that dispersion. The consumer must engage in a search. In how much searching should he or she engage? Clearly not an infinite amount because searching requires time which is a resource that is scarce and costly. Moreover, a consumer's search for a lower price must eventually run into what must be called diminishing marginal returns. Beyond some point, the expected reduction in unit price is less than the unit cost of the additional search time and effort. After a while, the consumer will find it more difficult to locate a seller who is going to sell the product at a price lower than the lowest price already quoted. Early search efforts are apt to turn up sellers whose prices lie considerably below the average price. After each successive lowest price is found, however, the consumer can expect to encounter more and more firms whose prices are higher. Thus, each time a lower price is found, it is less likely that the consumer in the next search period will encounter a still lower one.[4]

The rational consumer will continue to search for a lower price up to a point where the expected return from one more unit of search will not cover the cost of that activity.

Four propositions regarding the optimal amount of search to undertake can be made.[5]

1. The greater the price dispersion, the greater is the optimal search time, *ceteris paribus*.
2. The greater the percentage of a consumer's total wealth that will be spent on the product in question, the greater is the optimal search time. It may be worth an extended search for a new car bargain, but it is not worth the same time to search for a lower price of common table salt.
3. The more repetitive the purchase in question, the greater is the optimal search time (so long as differential prices among dealers persist).
4. The greater the value of the consumer's time, the smaller the optimal search will be, *ceteris paribus*. Other things being the same, the IBM executive will search less than the lower-salaried IBM filing clerk.

These propositions about search time can explain, for example, why big cities are not so expensive for residents as they are for tourists. Because tourists stay only for a relatively short period of time, it does not pay them to invest much of their relatively scarce time in learning about which are the cheapest-priced restaurants, which are the cheapest-priced bookstores, which are the cheapest-priced department stores, and so on. Rather, we can expect that rational tourists will frequent "tourist spots." The city resident, however, makes repeated purchases and hence will invest a larger amount of time searching for and acquiring information about where the prices of commodities are lowest.

The above argument may also explain the success of franchised fast-food and lodging chains. Although it may appear that the price to tourists is higher than the price to non-tourists for "similar" commodities, such may not be the case. The services offered to

---

[4]This follows from the law of diminishing returns, discussed in Chapter 7:

[5]A detailed discussion can be found in G. Stigler, "The Economics of Information," *Journal of Political Economy*, vol. 69, no. 3, June 1961.

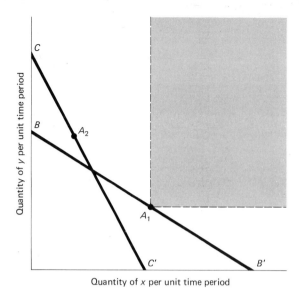

Figure 3-15: Assessing a standard-of-living change—the ambiguous case.

We start off with budget line *BB'*. The consumer finds himself or herself at point A_1. Now prices and income change so that the consumer faces budget line *CC'*. The consumer chooses point A_2. Without knowledge of the consumer's preferences, we cannot unambiguously state that the consumer is better off. Only in situations in which A_2 lies within the quadrant immediately to the right of and immediately above A_1 can we be sure that the combination in the second period dominates the combination in the first period.

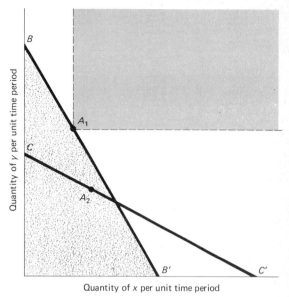

Quantity of x per unit time period

Figure 3-16: An unambiguous reduction in the standard of living—the nondominant case.

The consumer starts off at point A_1. Anywhere within the dotted area is feasible in period 1 because it is to the left of the budget line *BB'*. Prices and income change so that in period 2 the consumer faces budget line *CC'*. The consumer chooses bundle A_2. It does not lie within the dominant area immediately above and to the right of point A_1. Moreover, it was not chosen in period 1 even though it could have been; therefore, it must be inferior to bundle A_1 and the standard of living must have fallen.

a knowledge of the individual consumer's indifference map cannot draw a conclusion from the observation of points A_1 and A_2. In other words, without knowing the indifference curves, one does not know whether A_2 is on a higher or a lower indifference curve than A_1.

In some situations, at first glance it does not seem that we can unambiguously state whether the consumer is better-off or worse off after a change in income and in the relative prices of *x* and *y*. Nonetheless, we can make an unambiguous statement if we are willing to make inferences from the consumer's behavior. Look at Figure 3-16. We start off in period 1, as before, with budget line *BB'*. The consumer chooses bundle of goods A_1. Note that the consumer could have chosen any other bundle of goods along the

budget line *BB'* or anywhere within the entire budget constraint that is the dotted area in Figure 3-16. But since the consumer did not choose any other bundle of goods, it is clear that the consumer is best off with the combination A_1. Now, in period 2, the budget line moves to *CC'*. The consumer chooses combination A_2. A_2 clearly does not lie within the quadrant immediately above and to the right of A_1, as it did not in the previous figure, Figure 3-15. However, A_2 lies within the period 1 budget constraint. Since A_2 was not chosen in period 1, we infer that it is inferior to combination A_1. Hence we can state by inference that if preferences have not changed, the standard of living of this consumer must have *fallen* between period 1 and period 2 as a result of the income and price changes. This can be inferred without any knowledge of the indifference curves of the consumer.

A similar analysis can be applied to show that there has been an unequivocal rise in the standard of living of the consumer even though we are not in the dominant situation. Look at Figure 3-17. In period 1, the preferred combination is A_1. In period 2, the preferred combination is A_2. Clearly, A_2 does not lie within the quadrant immediately above and to the right of first-period combination A_1. Thus we cannot state unambiguously that the period 2 combination dominates the period 1 combination. However, we do know that in period 2 the budget constraint includes the entire shaded area under budget line CC'. Combi-

nation A_1 is therefore possible in period 2. However, by the consumer's revealed preference, we know that combination A_2 is preferred. Thus, we can infer that there has been an increase in the consumer's standard of living.

Devising an index to compare combination A_1 with combination A_2

We would now like to find a way to measure combinations in period 1 and period 2 to derive an index that will show whether or not the standard of living has increased.

The index of quantity that we are looking for should give us an estimate of whether or not the average quantities purchasable have increased between period 1 and period 2. We have to *weight* the individual quantities, however, to obtain this average. The weights that we will use will be prices. Now we have another choice to make: Which prices should be used as weights? Those in period 1 or in period 2? Depending on which we choose, we will obtain either a Laspeyres quantity index or a Paasche quantity index.[6]

In any event, the two different indexes of quantity can be derived by obtaining the *weighted* sums of the quantities of x and y consumable in period 1 and period 2. Let's first use the Laspeyres method and weight the quantities consumable by their base-year prices. Our notation will be as follows:

1. Superscripts indicate the period, either 1 or 2. (Note that these do *not* indicate mathematical operations like squaring a number.)
2. Subscripts indicate the good x or y.
3. q indicates the quantities consumed.
4. P, as always, indicates price.

The **Laspeyeres quantity index** L_Q is then seen

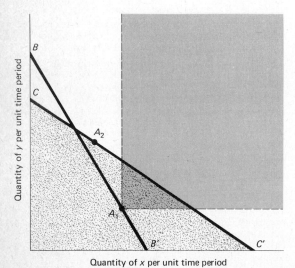

Figure 3-17: A rise in the standard of living—the non-dominant case.

In period 1 the consumer is at point A_1. Anywhere above and to the right of that point represents more of at least one of the goods and is therefore in the dominant area. In period 2, money income and prices change so that the budget line facing the consumer is CC'. The consumer chooses point A_2, which is not in the dominant area. However, in period 2 the consumer could have chosen any point within the dotted area below and to the left of budget line CC'; however, the consumer did not choose A_1. Therefore, the consumer must have preferred A_2 to A_1 and is therefore better off. We infer that the consumer has experienced a rise in his or her standard of living.

---

[6]Etienne Laspeyres was a nineteenth-century economic statistician; Hermann Paasche was one of the earlier proposers of the method used to derive the index named after him.

to be the ratio of the weighted quantities:

$$L_Q = \frac{P_x^1 q_x^2 + P_y^1 q_y^2}{P_x^1 q_x^1 + P_y^1 q_y^1} = \frac{\Sigma P^1 q^2}{\Sigma P^1 q^1} \qquad (3\text{-}14)$$

The capital Greek letter *sigma* (Σ) is a mathematical notation for summation. We do not need to use it in this two-good case, but it is practical to use it when more than two goods are involved. It indicates that the prices times their respective quantities should be added for all the commodities in question. If there were a third commodity—z, for example—then the summation sign would tell us to first multiply the price of x times the quantity of x consumed, then the price of y times the quantity of y consumed, then the price of z times the quantity of z consumed, and then add all those products to get the summation of the three.

We can derive the *Paasche quantity index* P_Q by re-creating Eq. (3-14); but instead of using period 1 prices as the weights, we use period 2 prices and obtain

$$L_Q = \frac{P_x^2 q_x^2 + P_y^2 q_y^2}{P_x^2 q_x^1 + P_y^2 q_y^2} = \frac{\Sigma P^2 q^2}{\Sigma P^2 q^1} \qquad (3\text{-}15)$$

LASPEYRES AND PAASCHE INDEXES IN GRAPHICAL TERMS. In Figure 3-16, we were able to infer that there was an unambiguous decline in the standard of living. Let us recreate that diagram minus the shaded area in Figure 3-18. In period 1, combination A_1 was chosen. In period 2, combination A_2 was chosen. The combination A_1 represents an expenditure of $P_x^1 q_x^1 + P_y^1 q_y^1$. In our *sigma* notation, this becomes $\Sigma P^1 q^1$.

Now, remembering that the Laspeyres index uses prices in the base period (period 1) as weights, but allows for changing quantities in period 2, we draw in a new imaginary budget line, represented by HH' which goes through the period 2 consumer optimum combination A_2 so that the quantities are indeed those that are consumed in period 2; however, the prices that are reflected by the slope of budget line HH' are period 1 prices and the prices that are used in Laspeyres' index for weights. Thus in our Σ no-

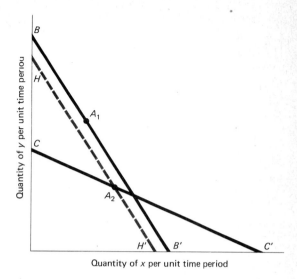

Figure 3-18: **Laspeyres quantity index.**
The Laspeyres index uses prices in period 1 as weights, but allows for change in quantities in period 2. In period 1, the combination chosen is A_1. In period 2, it is A_2. In order to use the weights from period 1, we draw an imaginary budget line HH', which is parallel to BB'. We draw it through point A_2. Clearly, $\Sigma P^1 q^2$ is less than $\Sigma P^1 q^1$ because HH' lies closer to the origin than BB'; thus, the Laspeyres index which is defined as $L_Q = \Sigma P^1 q^2 / \Sigma P^1 q^1$ is less than unity. The consumer has experienced an unambiguous decline in his or her standard of living.

tation for period 2 and combination A_2, con- tion expenditures would be equal to $\Sigma P^1 q^2$; but but clearly this last summation must be a smaller number than the consumption expenditures associated with combination A_1. Why? Because A_2 lies along an imaginary budget line which is totally *within* the budget constraint associated with period 1 prices and income, or budget line BB'. We know, therefore, that

$$\Sigma P^1 q^1 > \Sigma P^1 q^2 \qquad (3\text{-}16)$$

But since the right-hand and left-hand sides of this inequality are the denominator and numerator, respectively, of the Laspeyres index, we know that

$$L_Q = \frac{\Sigma P^1 q^2}{\Sigma P^1 q^1} < 1 \qquad (3\text{-}17)$$

The Laspeyres quantity index is less than 1. The consumer is unambiguously worse off in period 2 than in period 1. The consumer had the opportunity to buy combination A_2 in period 1 but chose not to; therefore, it was not preferred. The consumer must be worse off in the second period if combination A_2 was purchased. The conclusion is that *every time a Laspeyres quantity index is less than 1, the consumer has experienced an unambiguous decline in standard of living since the base period.*

We can take Figure 3-18 and derive a similar statement for the Paasche index. Look at Figure 3-19, where we have merely eliminated the shaded area from Figure 3-17. Remember that we already showed in that situation that there has

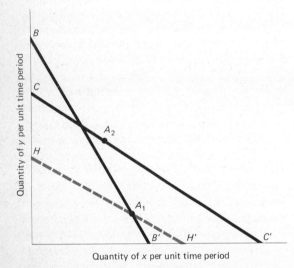

Figure 3-19: The Paasche quantity index.
In the Paasche quantity index, we use the period 2 prices as weights. We start off in period 1 with combination A_1. We move to period 2 with combination A_2 chosen. In order to obtain the Paasche index, we must use period 2 prices as weights; therefore, we draw an imaginary budget line HH' parallel to CC', but passing through point A_1. Clearly, at point A_1, $\Sigma P^2 q^1$ is less than $\Sigma P^2 q^2$. Therefore, the Paasche quantity index exceeds unity since it is equal to $P_Q = \Sigma P^2 q^2 / \Sigma P^2 q^1$. The consumer has unambiguously experienced an improvement in his or her standard of living because the period 2 budget line CC' completely dominates the hypothetical budget line HH'.

been an unambiguous rise in the person's standard of living. The combination A_1 could be chosen in period 2, but nonetheless combination A_2 is chosen and is therefore revealed to be preferred. In Figure 3-19, we draw through optimum point A_1 an imaginary budget line HH' that gives us the quantities of x and y consumed in period 1 at the prices prevalent in period 2. In other words, we are dealing with the Paasche index, where the weights applied to the quantities are prices in period 2. Clearly, the imaginary expenditure on combination A_1, given period 2's prices, is less than the actual expenditure in period 2 on combination A_2. (Why?) Otherwise stated,

$$\Sigma P^2 q^1 < \Sigma P^2 q^2 \qquad (3\text{-}18)$$

But this gives us the denominator and numerator for a Paasche quantity index, and it is necessarily going to exceed 1, or

$$P_Q = \frac{\Sigma P^2 q^2}{\Sigma P^2 q^1} > 1 \qquad (3\text{-}19)$$

We can conclude, then, that *the consumer has unambiguously experienced an improvement in his or her standard of living since period 1 when the Paasche quantity index for period 2 is greater than 1.*

It is possible for the consumer to be worse off without the Laspeyres quantity index being less than 1. It is also possible for the consumer to be better-off without the Paasche index being greater than 1. In such cases, truly unambiguous answer would require knowledge of the consumer's indifference map.

Price indexes

It is possible for us to construct Laspeyres and Paasche indexes of prices. The only difference between the indexes of quantities and the indexes of prices is that instead of weighting quantities by prices, we do the opposite and we weight prices by quantities. And as you might expect, in the Laspeyres index we use period 1, or base-year, quantities as our weights. The definitions follow:

$$L_P = \frac{\Sigma P^2 q^1}{\Sigma P^1 q^1} \qquad (3\text{-}20)$$

$$P_P = \frac{\Sigma P^2 q^2}{\Sigma P^1 q^2} \qquad (3\text{-}21)$$

The Laspeyres price index L_P measures changes in the cost of living as the family lived in the base period, year 1. The Paasche price index P_P measures changes in what it would have cost in year 1 to have lived the way the family lived in year 2.

REAL WORLD PRICE INDEXES AND THEIR PROBLEMS. The Bureau of Labor Statistics uses the Laspeyres method with its fixed base-year weights to estimate the Consumer Price Index. This is a practical index for the government to use because it does not involve obtaining both prices and quantities in each successive period. Only price data need be obtained in a new period. One of the problems with such an index is the possibility that the weights may become obsolete because of changes in tastes, changes in relative quantities purchased, and so on. Moreover, there is an additional problem in calculating price indexes because changes in the *qualities* of goods cannot be fully accounted for. In other words, if a higher price is entirely a reflection of better quality, there has clearly been no increase in the price per constant-quality unit of the product. Nonetheless, price indexes, as normally measured, would not pick up changes in quality, though they would pick up changes in price and would therefore register a change in the "cost of living." Many economists believe that the official price indexes used in the United States overstate the rate of inflation because improvements in quality outweigh decreases in quality and have not been adequately taken into account. We should also note that the most quoted price index, the Consumer Price Index (CPI), is for an average urban family of four. If one's budget allocation differs strongly from that average family's budget, the CPI is not very reliable. For example, an avid skier will find

Florida an expensive place to live even if a specially constructed CPI just for Florida is increasing slower than CPIs in other states.

The effect of income taxes on work effort —What is the supply curve of labor?

We can use indifference curve analysis to analyze the effect of an income tax on the quantity of work effort supplied. At the same time, we can also determine the income and substitution effects of a change in the rate of income taxation.

We will make some simplifying assumptions for this issue: (1) We will assume that we start out in a situation where there are no income taxes; (2) we will assume that the income tax imposed is a proportional one, that is, a constant percentage levied on every dollar earned; and finally, (3) we will assume that there are only two goods, leisure and all other goods, where all other goods refers to money income derived from working.

Look at Figure 3-20. We measure leisure per unit time period on the horizontal axis and all other goods on the vertical axis. The maximum amount of leisure possible is some fixed quantity L. It really doesn't matter at what time period we are looking because we are still faced with a specified physical maximum of leisure that an individual can take. Assuming that the individual lumps together all activities other than work under the rubric of leisure, then if our time period is a day, L equals 24 hours per day. Given that the maximum amount of leisure available is fixed, any reduction in leisure means an increase in work and vice versa.

On the vertical axis we measure "all other goods." But what are all other goods? They are everything besides leisure; in other words, they are all the things that money income can buy. We could alternatively label the vertical axis "money income." The maximum amount of all other goods possible is equal to the total amount of money income that could be earned if zero leisure were consumed. This is the vertical distance 0Y. We now have two extreme points that define the

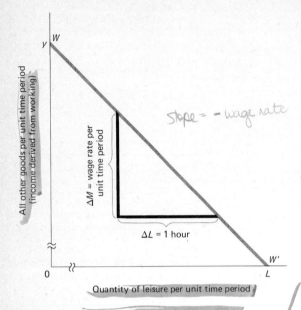

slope = - wage rate

ΔM = wage rate per unit time period

ΔL = 1 hour

Quantity of leisure per unit time period

Figure 3-20: The labor-leisure budget constraint.
On the horizontal axis we measure the quantity of leisure per unit time period. The maximum amount is some time period such as 24 hours per day. On the vertical axis, we measure all other goods per unit time period. This is equivalent to money income earned for working. If there is no leisure, then the maximum amount of income that can be earned is Y. This gives us two points on a labor-leisure budget line that is labeled WW'. Since if leisure is decreased by 1 hour, the increase in money income or income available to purchase all other goods goes up by the wage rate per hour, the slope of the budget line WW', $-w$, or the negative of the wage rate.

budget constraint in our rather peculiar commodity space in Figure 3-20. If only "all other goods" are purchased, the maximum amount that can be purchased is $0Y$. If only leisure is purchased, the maximum amount available is $0L$. When we connect these two points, we get a budget line also labeled WW'. Notice that the negative of the slope of this budget line—(Δ money income/Δ leisure)—is the wage rate. After all, what is the "price" of obtaining one more unit of leisure? It is the wage rate for that time period that has been sacrificed or forfeited. Since the wage rate is positive, the slope of the budget line is equal to the negative of the wage rate $-w$.

In Figure 3-21, the budget line facing the worker

is LW. Given the worker's indifference curve I, the quantity of leisure demanded will be L_1, which is determined at point A, where curve I is tangent to the budget line. Note that if the worker took no leisure and devoted all his or her time to working during the time period, the take-home income would be $0W$ in the no-tax situation.

Now we impose an income tax. What does the income tax do? To answer that, let's first consider that the price of leisure is the opportunity cost of not working. Without a tax, the opportunity cost of not working is exactly equal to a worker's total wages for the period (assuming there are no deductions for other things, e.g., pension, Social Security, etc.). With an income tax, the cost of not working is equal to the net (after-tax), or take-home, wages. Since the income tax reduces the take-home pay, the opportunity cost of not working is lower; this is the same as saying that the income tax lowers the relative price of leisure. Now, if the worker took no leisure and devoted all his or her time to working during the time period, the take-home income would be $0W'$, which is less than $0W$ by the amount of the tax deducted from income. This rotates counterclockwise the budget line LW to LW', the taxed budget line. Effectively, this means that income taxes reduce the price of leisure with respect to all other goods (or income for the period).[7]

What happens when the consumer is faced with a proportional income tax? In our particular example, this consumer will go to a new optimum at point B, where he or she consumes a new quantity of leisure L_2. Since leisure is measured on the horizontal axis, L_2 represents a reduction in the quantity of leisure demanded and therefore an increase in the total number of hours worked. Why does the consumer work more? Because the income effect outweighed the substitution effect. In other words, the income tax reduced the

[7]However, it has been shown that the wage rate is biased upward as a measure of the cost of leisure. We say this because, in general, there is disutility associated with work but not with leisure. See M. Bruce Johnson, "Travel Time and the Price of Leisure," *Western Economic Journal*, Spring 1966, pp. 135–145.

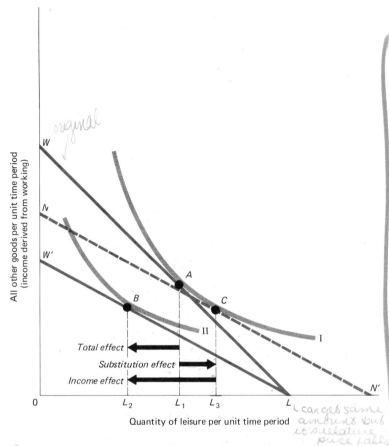

Figure 3-21: The effects of a proportionate income tax on work effort.

The consumer starts out with quantity of leisure demanded L_1, at the consumption optimum point A. A proportionate income tax reduces the amount of money income that is earned per hour of work. If no leisure were consumed, i.e., the individual worked all the time, instead of being able to buy OW of all other goods, the consumer could only buy OW' of all other goods. The budget line rotates counterclockwise to LW'. The new consumption optimum is at point B. The quantity of leisure demanded has fallen from L_1 to L_2. Even though the price of leisure is lower because the take-home pay is lower, the consumer works more to make up for the lost income. To derive the substitution and income effect, we hypothetically increase the consumer's income so that he or she is on the old indifference curve. The hypothetical budget line facing the consumer is now NN'. With the lower price of leisure, the consumer moves from point A to point C and the substitution effect is negative. Now we take away the income that we hypothetically gave the consumer. The consumer moves from point C to point B. The distance from L_3 to L_2 is the income effect.

consumer's income by so much that, even though leisure had become cheaper in this case, the consumer worked more to try to make up some of the lost income that went into taxes.

We can find the substitution effect by drawing in a hypothetical budget constraint that leaves the worker on the same indifference curve I but presents him or her with the new lower relative price of leisure. This is done by drawing in the hypothetical budget line NN', which has the same slope as LW' and is tangent to indifference curve I. The new point of consumer optimum is at C. A larger quantity of leisure L_3 will be bought. The substitution effect is always negative. The lower price of leisure has to lead to a larger quantity demanded; it costs less *not* to work. However, the income effect is measured from the movement from C to B, or L_3 to L_2. It is highly positive

because a reduction in income has led to a dramatic reduction in the quantity of leisure demanded. In other words, leisure is clearly a normal or ultrasuperior good. The normal or ultrasuperior nature of leisure is verified by experience. For example, windfall gains, such as those acquired by winning the Irish Sweepstakes or the New York state lottery, usually result in more rather than less leisure consumed.

We can turn the analysis around and ask what will happen as the take-home wage rate is increased. In other words, what happens to the quantity of work effort, or the quantity of labor supplied, as wage rates rise. One hypothetical example is given in Figure 3-22. We keep raising the take-home wage rate so that the budget constraint rotates upward from $L'L$ to $L''L$ and finally to $L'''L$. The indifference curves are tangent to

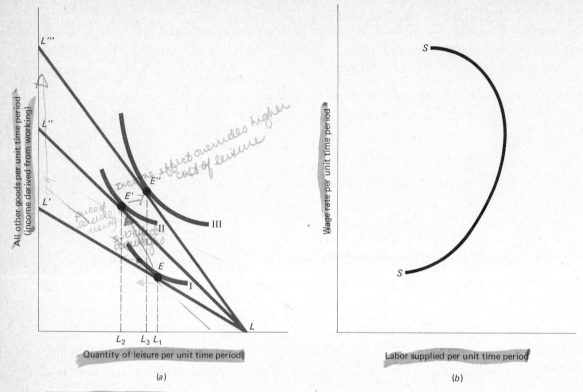

Figure 3-22: Derivation of a labor supply curve.
In panel (a) we progressively increase the wage rate so that the budget line rotates clockwise from L'L to L''L to L'''L. The consumer moves in successively higher indifference curves, from I to II to III. The consumption optimum moves from E to E' to E''. At first, the amount of leisure consumed falls because the substitution effect overrides the income effect, then the quantity of leisure demanded rises as income rises because the income effect overrides the substitution effect. The result, shown in panel (b), is a backward-bending supply curve for labor. After the wage rate where SS starts to turn backward, the income effect is overriding the substitution effect—the individual is so much richer that he or she purchases more leisure in spite of its much higher relative price.

these various budget constraints at E, E', and E''. An increase in wage rates which causes the budget constraint to move from L'L to L''L leads to a reduction in the quantity of leisure demanded from L_1 to L_2. In this case, the substitution effect overrides the income effect. Even though workers are richer, i.e., have more income to spend on all goods, including leisure, they purchase less leisure because the opportunity cost of leisure has risen so much. However, when wage rates rise so that the new budget constraint is LL''', the situation is similar to the one presented in Fig-

ure 3-21 (but in the opposite direction). The new point of consumer optimum is at E''. The new quantity of leisure purchased is L_3. In other words, more leisure is purchased, even though its opportunity cost, or price, has gone up. In this case, the income effect overrides the substitution effect.

If we take the various wage rates and quantity of work effort and plot them on a separate diagram in panel (b), we get a supply curve for labor SS which shows the relationship between the wage rate and the quantity of labor forthcoming per unit time period. (The wage rate can be obtained from panel (a) by measuring the negative slope of the budget constraint.) Note that the supply curve SS is backward-bending. At some point, higher wage rates lead the individual worker to work less rather than more. This begins the point at which the income effect begins to override the substitution effect.[8]

How does a guaranteed annual income affect work effort?

Now that we have used indifference curve analysis to analyze the demand for leisure, as it were, we can undertake an examination of the effect of a guaranteed annual income on work effort.

Consider the consumer depicted in Figure 3-23. Given the wage rate that is equal to the negative of the slope of the budget line $L'L$, this consumer's preferences dictate that he or she buy L_1 of leisure and work the rest of the time earning a money income of M. This occurs because the point of tangency between the budget line and the highest indifference curve attainable is at point E. Now the government comes along and guarantees a minimum money income of M_{min}. This consumer could continue to work the same number of hours as before and merely receive a subsidy equal to the difference between M_{min} and M. The consumer would then be at point G on a higher indifference curve, curve II. However, this would not be the way for this consumer to obtain maximum satisfaction. Rather, all consumers with preferences depicted in this diagram and earning an income below the guaranteed annual income will, in fact, not work at all. These consumers would have both a guaranteed income

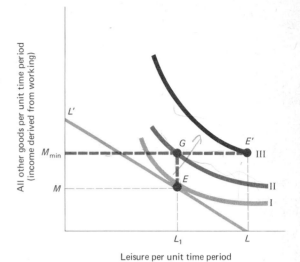

All other goods per unit time period (income derived from working)

Leisure per unit time period

Figure 3-23: Effect on work effort of a guaranteed annual income.
The consumer starts out in consumption optimum at point E, consumes L_1 of leisure, and earns M in money income. The government puts into effect a minimum income M_{min}. Thus, if the consumer is earning only M, he or she will get a subsidy to bring his or her income up to the guaranteed minimum. The consumer could therefore move from point E to point G and thus be on a higher indifference curve, II. However, this consumer can reach an even higher indifference curve if he or she moves to point E' which will put him or her on indifference curve III. This involves 100 percent leisure and receipt of the full guaranteed minimum income.

M_{min} and 100 percent leisure at the same time. And that combination of income and leisure is represented by point E' in the diagram. The guaranteed annual income has put the consumer on a higher indifference curve, deriving a higher level of satisfaction at E', and the consumer doesn't even have to work.

It is even possible for the worker to accept a

---

[8]The backward-bending supply curve of labor is impossible in the aggregate. In the aggregate, there is no net income effect when we hold community opportunities as given or constant. Higher wages mean less return to other nonhuman assets. In turn, this means that an income-compensated supply curve of labor must be of the normal

sort—i.e., as the wage rate rises, more labor is offered. See Yoram Barzel and Richard J. McDonald, "Assets, Subsistence, and the Supply Curve of Labor," *The American Economic Review*, vol. 63, no. 4, September 1973, pp. 621–633.

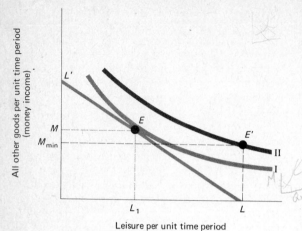

Figure 3-24: Reducing work effort.
In this example, the consumer is originally earning M, more than the guaranteed minimum income M_{min}. The consumption optimum is point E, income earned is M, and leisure purchased is L_1. If a minimum income is put on at M_{min}, the consumer can make himself or herself better off by moving to point E', by "purchasing" 100 percent leisure, and by obtaining a guaranteed minimum income even though it is lower than the income that the individual was earning before.

reduction in money income when there is a guaranteed minimum income. Consider Figure 3-24. Here we show the initial consumer optimum at point E, where money income is M and the amount of leisure consumed is L_1. If a guaranteed minimum income is put on at M_{min}, the consumer can reach a higher indifference curve by not working at all. A consumer optimum is obtained at point E', where work is reduced to zero and income is equal to the guaranteed minimum.

In conclusion, no guaranteed annual income can ever lead to an increase in work effort or labor time. It can only lead to a decrease as long as we assume that leisure is a normal or ultrasuperior good.

Using the same kind of analysis, you should be able to reach similar conclusions concerning unemployment benefits, welfare payments that are partly or wholly eliminated when the recipient earns too high an income, subsidized housing that is no longer available when the recipient's income reaches a certain level, and so on.

Glossary

Income-consumption curve The locus of consumption optimum points that would occur if income were successively increased, nominal and relative prices remaining constant. In other words, it represents the quantities of goods x and y that would be purchased at various levels of income.

Engel curve The locus of points showing the various quantities of a commodity purchased at different levels of income. It is not to be confused with the income-consumption curve, which shows the various combinations of two goods purchased at different levels of income.

Normal good A good of which the consumer purchases more as income increases and whose income elasticity lies between 0 and 1.

Inferior good A good of which a consumer purchases less as income increases and whose income elasticity of demand is negative.

Income elasticity of demand The relative change in the quantity demanded divided by the relative change in money income; the responsiveness of the quantity demanded to changes in income.

Ultrasuperior good A good whose income elasticity of demand exceeds 1; the opposite of an inferior good.

Price-consumption curve The locus of consumption optimum combinations of goods x and y that the consumer would choose as the relative price of the goods changed while money income remained constant.

Demand curve The curve showing the quantities demanded at different relative prices.

Law of demand The quantity demanded varies inversely with relative price, *ceteris paribus*.

Price elasticity of demand The responsiveness of quantity demanded to changes in relative price; defined as the proportional change in the quantity demanded divided by the proportional change in the relative price.

Elastic demand A property of the demand curve; where the quantity demanded changes more than in proportion to the change in price.

Unitary elastic demand A property of the demand curve; where the quantity demanded changes exactly in proportion to the change in price.

Inelastic demand A property of the demand curve; where the quantity demanded changes less than in proportion to the change in price.

Substitution effect Relates to the change in the quantity demanded due to substitution of a relatively cheaper good for a relatively more expensive good while real income is held constant.

Income effect Change in the quantity demanded of a good due to a change in real income while relative prices are held constant.

Giffen good A good that is so strongly inferior that a fall in price induces a reduction in the quantity demanded, i.e., the demand curve slopes upward.

Market Analytically speaking, the sphere through which supply and demand operate.

Marketplace Locations where exchanges take place and where the terms of exchange are registered.

Transactions costs All the costs associated with exchange; they include such costs as the cost of contracting, the cost of enforcing contracts, and the cost of obtaining information.

Information costs Transactions costs, which include the cost of obtaining information on prices, qualities, availability, and service record in the case of durable goods.

Index number of quantity A measure of the relative quantity of commodities consumed that is used to compare quantities consumed in two or more periods.

Index number of prices A weighted average measure of prices of commodities consumed used to compare average prices over two or more periods.

Laspeyres quantity index An index of quantity which uses prices in the base period to weight quantities.

Paasche quantity index An index of quantities which uses prices in period 2 to weight quantities.

Summary

1. If we hold relative and nominal prices constant and increase money income, we shift the budget line outward. If we connect the tangency points between the indifference curves and the budget lines, we derive the income-consumption curve which shows the combinations of x and y that will be chosen as income changes.

2. Engel curves are derived by considering the change in the quantity purchased of only one commodity as relative prices remain constant and income changes. In a diagram with x on the horizontal axis and income on the vertical axis, an upward curvature indicates a less than one-for-one increase in quantity demanded as income goes up; a downward curvature indicates the opposite.

3. When the Engel curve slopes backward, or has a negative slope, the good is inferior.

4. We classify goods according to their income elasticity of demand (μ): an inferior good has a negative μ; a normal good, a positive μ less than 1; and an ultrasuperior good, a μ greater than 1.

5. It is important to remember that the terms "ultrasuperior," "normal," and "inferior" carry with them no value judgment, i.e., they are *not* descriptive of some subjective feeling that all consumers have about a particular commodity.

6. Since the consumer faces a budget constraint, the separate Engel curves for all the commodities in the consumer's market basket of commodities purchased are not independent.

7. The weighted average of income elasticities of demand for all commodities purchased must equal 1. The weights are the relative shares of total expenditures by the consumer.

8. Given that the weighted income elasticities must add up to 1, if a particular commodity is strongly inferior, there must be at least one even more strongly ultrasuperior good in the basket of commodities purchased by the consumer.

9. Items that take up a large percentage of a consumer's budget generally have small income elasticities of demand.

10. We derive the price-consumption curve by connecting the consumption optimum points when the relative price of one good is changed, while holding the price of the other good and money income constant.

11. We can derive a downward-sloping demand curve from the price consumption curve by reading off the price-quantity pairs from the latter curve. That demand curve will be downward-sloping in all cases, except the one in which we have extremely strong inferior goods.

12. Whenever demand is price-elastic, consumer expenditures ($P_x \cdot q_x$) will change in the op-

posite direction of a price change. When demand is unitary-elastic, consumer expenditures will remain constant for any change in price. Finally, when demand is price-inelastic, consumer expenditures will change in the direction of a change in price.

13. If we use a diagram with x on the horizontal axis and money income for all other goods on the vertical axis, we can determine price elasticity of demand by the slope of the price consumption line. When it slopes down, demand for good x is price-elastic; when it is horizontal, demand is unit-elastic; and when it is positively sloped, demand is price-inelastic.

14. Whenever there is a change in the relative price of a commodity, there is also a change in real income, defined as purchasing power. The larger fraction of the total budget spent on the good whose price fell, the greater the increase in real income, and vice versa.

15. When there is a relative price change, we can separate the two parts of the total effect of that price change—the substitution effect and the income effect. We do this by running an experiment in which we change relative prices and then alter income so as to eliminate the income effect. We can then see the substitution effect that is due to the price change. When we reinstate the individual's original income, we find out what the income effect is.

16. For all normal and ultrasuperior goods, the income effect reinforces the substitution effect.

17. Only when the income effect is highly negative—the case of a strongly inferior good—is it possible for the income effect to outweigh the substitution effect and, therefore, for the law of demand not to hold. This is called a Giffen good.

18. Transactions costs are a function of (a) the number of distinct transactions per time period, (b) the volume of goods traded per time period, (c) the number of distinct parties involved, and (d) the number of distinct goods per transaction.

19 The optimal amount of search to undertake depends on (a) the degree of price dispersion, (b) the percentage of the consumer's budget spent on the product, (c) the more repetitive the purchase, and (d) the greater the opportunity cost of the consumer's time.

Questions

(Answers to even-numbered questions are at back of text.)

1. What is the significance of the point of tangency between an indifference curve and a budget constraint? Explain.
2. Define an inferior and a superior good. Can a good be both? How?
3. In deriving a price-consumption curve, which variables are held constant and which ones are allowed to change?
4. How is a demand curve derived from a price-consumption curve?
5. Suppose your money income tripled and so did the prices of both of the goods in your two-good world. Do you now have data revealing an additional point on your income-consumption curve? Why or why not?
6. Suppose that as nominal money income changes, the nominal price of one of the goods also changes. Why will your efforts to trace out the income-consumption curve be thwarted?
7. If it is possible for all goods in a consumer's budget to be superior, why can't they all be inferior?
8. Suppose you were determined to buy a business, and you also expected an economic recession (a decline in real national income) to befall the country. Suppose further that you are the only person on the planet that is bearish (pessimistic) on the nation's economic future. What type of business would you buy: one producing an inferior good, a normal good, or a superior good? Why?
9. Is it possible that the demand for a particular good could be both price-inelastic and also price-elastic? Explain.
10. When a good's price changes, there are two effects, substitution and income. Under what circumstances might one be justified in ignoring the income effect of a change in price? Why?
11. "Rice in Asia" is often asserted to be an example of a Giffen good which defies the "law" of demand. Assuming for the moment that the assertion is correct, what is the reasoning underlying it?

12. In light of the fact that information is a scarce commodity, one must decide how much of it to "consume" (generate) before making a decision. Concerning the purchase of a new car, would you expect a movie star to spend more or less time searching than a police officer? Why?

13. Suppose that last year you spent half of your income on food and half on rent. This year your nominal income has gone up 10 percent, the price of food has increased 20 percent, and rental rates have not changed. Are you able to determine whether your real income has gone up, has gone down, or has remained unchanged? Why, or why not? Explain.

14. Explain why new products and products whose quality has changed cause difficulty for both types of price index. Deal separately with both the Laspeyres and the Paasche indexes.

15. Compare the following three systems of welfare payments:
    System 1: $100 per family per week, regardless of whether any family members earn any income on their own.
    System 2: $100 per family per week, reduced by $1 for every $3 earned by family members on their own.
    System 3: $100 per family per week, reduced

by $1 for every $1 earned by family members on their own.
At what level of weekly earnings would a family get off welfare under each of the three systems? Which system appears to have greater incentives for a family to work and to become at least partially self-supporting?

Selected references

Ferguson, C. E., "Substitution Effect in Value Theory: A Pedagogical Note," *Southern Economic Journal*, vol. 24, 1960, pp. 310–314.

Hicks, J. R., *A Revision of Demand Theory* (Oxford: Oxford University Press, 1956).

Prais, S. J., and H. S. Houthakker, *The Analysis of Family Budgets* (Cambridge: Cambridge University Press, 1955).

Robbins, Lionel, "On the Elasticity of Demand for Income in Terms of Effort," *Economica*, new ser., vol. 10, November 1930, pp. 245–58; also in American Economic Association, *Readings in the Theory of Income Distribution* (Philadelphia: Blakiston, 1946).

Scitovsky, Tibor, *Welfare and Competition* (Homewood, Ill.: Irwin, 1965), pp. 65–69.

Stigler, George, "The Economics of Information," *Journal of Political Economy*, vol. 69, June 1961, pp. 213-225.

———, "Notes on the History of the Giffen Paradox," *Journal of Political Economy*, vol. 40, April 1947.

Appendix to Chapter 3

The use of the Δ operator

In many places in this book the economics makes use of the following proof. Let

$$A = B \cdot C \qquad \text{(A3-1)}$$

Now increase B by a small amount equal to ΔB, and increase C by a small amount equal to ΔC. As a result A will increase by ΔA. We can write

$$(A + \Delta A) = (B + \Delta B)(C + \Delta C)$$

or

$$A + \Delta A = BC + B\Delta C + C\Delta B + \Delta B \Delta C \qquad \text{(A3-2)}$$

From the left side of Eq. (A3-2), we may subtract the left side of Eq. (A3-1); and from the right side

of (A3-2), we subtract the right side of Eq. (A3-1). We then have

$$\Delta A = B\Delta C + C\Delta B + \Delta B \Delta C \qquad \text{(A3-3)}$$

The last term in Eq. (A3-3), $\Delta B \Delta C$, is so small that we can ignore it. Equation (A3-3) is rewritten to express the approximate value of ΔA—the value of ΔA when we treat $\Delta B \Delta C$ as if it were 0.

$$\Delta A = B\Delta C + C\Delta B \qquad \text{(A3-4)}$$

If we now divide both sides of Eq. (A3-4) by ΔB, we obtain

$$\frac{\Delta A}{\Delta B} = B \frac{\Delta C}{\Delta B} + C$$

or, rearranging the terms,

$$\frac{\Delta A}{\Delta B} = C + B\frac{\Delta C}{\Delta B} \qquad \text{(A3-5)}$$

When we multiply the last term on the right side of Eq. (A3-5) by C/C (which is equal to 1) we find that

$$\frac{\Delta A}{\Delta B} = C + B\frac{\Delta C}{\Delta B} \cdot \frac{C}{C}$$

which may be rewritten as

$$\frac{\Delta A}{\Delta B} = C\left(1 + \frac{B\Delta C}{C\Delta B}\right) \qquad \text{(A3-6)}$$

We will see Eq. (A3-6) in a number of different forms throughout the rest of this book.

To illustrate what we have done with the algebra above, suppose A is the area of a rectangle and B and C are the lengths of the sides of this rectangle. The area of any rectangle A is equal to the product of the lengths of the sides BC.

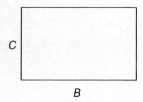

When we increase the lengths of the two sides by ΔB and ΔC, respectively, the area of the rectangle increases by ΔA.

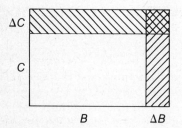

The area of the rectangle is now equal to $(B + \Delta B) \cdot (C + \Delta C)$, or—as we saw in Eq. (A3-2)—to $BC + B\Delta C + \Delta BC + \Delta B\Delta C$. But notice the little rectangle in the upper right portion of the larger rectangle above. Its area is equal to $\Delta B\Delta C$. If ΔB

and ΔC are both very small, the area of this small rectangle is also very small. And if we wish to know the approximate value by which the area of the rectangle has increased when we increase the sides of the rectangle by ΔB and ΔC, we ignore this little rectangle. This approximate *increase* in A, which we have called ΔA, is equal to the small rectangle on the upper left

which has an area equal to $B\Delta C$, *plus* the small rectangle along the right

which has an area equal to ΔBC. The change in A is close to $B\Delta C + C\Delta B$; and this is what Eq. (A3-4) told us.

4

EXCHANGE AND MARKET DEMAND

Until now we have dealt specifically with the individual. Among other things, however, economics is the study of exchange between two or more individuals. Exchanges take place in markets, which we defined in the last chapter. We will continue with our rather loose definition of a market to include all institutions which facilitate the process of exchange. Market mechanisms streamline and regularize channels of communication between potential buyers and potential sellers of a commodity. The term "market," therefore, applies to such very sophisticated and formally structured markets as the New York Stock Exchange, and also to very loose and unorganized markets, such as the one for babysitters.

Exchange takes place because it benefits both parties involved. Exchange occurs because the parties to the exchange expect to gain. We will first examine the basis of exchange using indifference curves. Then we will present an alternative explanation of the gains from exchange. Once we have done that, we can derive a market demand curve for all potential exchangers. Then, after looking at the suppliers' side of the picture, the notion of a market-clearing price is presented. The Issues and Applications section of this chapter will be concerned mainly with exchange theory as it relates to the stock market, minimum wage laws, and national defense.

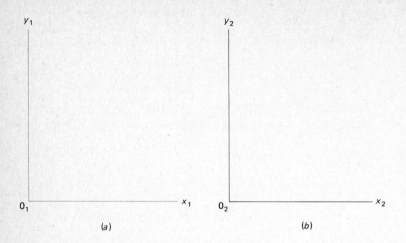

(a)

(b)

Figure 4-1: Two commodity spaces.
Individual 1's commodity space for goods *x* and *y* is given in panel (*a*). Individual 2's commodity space for *x* and *y* is given in panel (*b*).

Exchange and the Edgeworth-Bowley box

To understand the origins of voluntary exchange, we consider a situation where there are two individuals consuming two commodities whose total supply is absolutely fixed. Consider individual 1 and individual 2. Their respective commodity spaces are presented in panel (*a*) and panel (*b*) of Figure 4-1. We label the origin either 0_1 or 0_2, according to whether the commodity space pertains to individual 1 or individual 2.

Now we wish to put these two commodity spaces together. We do this by rotating individual 2's commodity space 180° so that individual 2's origin 0_2 is in the upper right-hand corner. We now see the two commodity spaces in the two panels of Figure 4-2. Panel (*a*) is the same, but panel (*b*) appears to be upside down; actually, it is rotated.

We now wish to fit the two commodity spaces together. At first glance, it might appear that there is a problem involving the lengths of the horizontal and vertical axes. There is no problem, though, when we assume fixed supplies of commodity *x* and commodity *y* that must be shared by individual 1 and individual 2. That is, the amount consumed of *x* by individual 1 plus the amount consumed of *x* by individual 2 must equal the

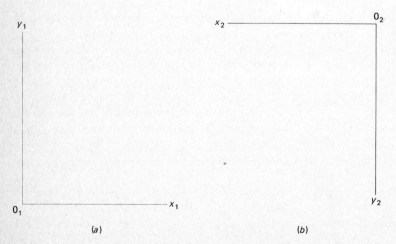

(a)

(b)

Figure 4-2: Rotating individual 2's commodity space.
We duplicate panel (*a*) from Figure 4-1; in panel (*b*), however, we rotate the origin of individual 2's commodity space 180°.

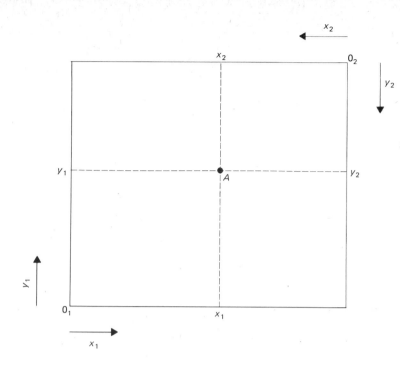

x_2

Figure 4-3: The Edgeworth-Bowley box.

x is measured on the horizontal axis, y on the vertical axis. Individual 1's origin is labeled 0_1; individual 2's origin is labeled 0_2. The dimensions of the box represent the total quantity of x and y available; thus, if we pick point A in the box, the quantity of x consumed by individual 1 is x_1, the quantity of x consumed by individual 2 is x_2, and x_1 plus x_2 is equal to total x available. The same is true for good y.

total available supply of x. The same is true for commodity y. The length of the horizontal and of the vertical axes in panels (a) and (b) must be equal because they measure the fixed available quantity of each commodity. Thus, when we put the two panels together from Figure 4-2, we obtain Figure 4-3. This is called an Edgeworth-Bowley box, named after two English mathematical economists who contributed much to the early neoclassical revolution at the end of the last and the beginning of this century. Any point, such as A, represents specifically how much of the available supply of commodity x and commodity y is consumed by consumer 1 and consumer 2. Thus, from Figure 4-3, we see that $x_1 + x_2 =$ total supply of x, and $y_1 + y_2 =$ total supply of y.

Introducing indifference curves into the box

In Figure 4-4, we add two sets of indifference curves to the Edgeworth-Bowley box. Individual 1's indifference curves are labeled I_1, I_1', and I_1''. Individual 2's indifference curves are labeled I_2, I_2', and I_2''. Remember that the origin for the indifference curves for individual 2 is in the northeast corner (upper right corner). It is labeled 0_2.

As always, the commodity spaces for both individuals 1 and 2 contain an infinite number of indifference curves. We have arbitrarily drawn in three for each individual.

Let us take an initial distribution of x and y allocated between individual 1 and individual 2 at point A in Figure 4-4. Individual 1 has x_1 of x; individual 2 has x_2 of x. Since there is a fixed amount of both x and y, $x_1 + x_2$ must equal the total amount of x available, or the horizontal dimension of the entire box. Similarly, the initial distribution of y is y_1 and y_2, with the sum being equal to the total fixed supply represented by the height of the box.

Gains from trade

At initial distribution point, individual 1 is on indifference curve I_1'. Individual 2 is on indifference curve I_2. Given the definition of an

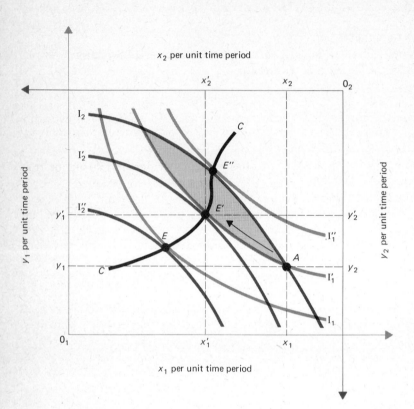

Figure 4-4: The Edgeworth-Bowley box and exchange.
This is Figure 4-3 with indifference curves added. Note that the indifference curves for individual 1 are labeled with a subscript 1. The indifference curves for individual 2 are labeled with a subscript 2 and are convex to the origin at the northeast corner of the box. Thus, they look upside down; however, if you rotate the page 180°, they will appear right side up. Start out at point A, where individual 1 is on indifference curve I'_1. Individual 2 is on indifference curve I_2. Clearly, it is possible to move from point A to point E' without reducing the level of utility of individual 1. However, we will increase the level of utility of individual 2 because we will move him or her to indifference curve I'_2, which is higher (relative to origin 0_2) than is I_2. Anywhere within the shaded area, or region of mutual advantage, one individual can be made better off without harming the other. However, it is impossible to make a movement anywhere along the contract, or conflict, line CC, without harming one individual in order to increase another's level of utility. Along CC, the marginal rate of substitution of x for y (MRS_{xy}) is the same for both individuals.

indifference curve, individual 1 is indifferent among all combinations of x and y which keep him or her on indifference curve I'_1. We have drawn an arrow showing a movement of individual 1 along indifference curve I'_1. The arrow goes from point A to point E'. Since the individual is indifferent, E' is just as good as A. However, notice what has happened to individual 2. Individual 2 was originally on indifference curve I_2. At point E', however, individual 2 is on indifference curve I'_2. Looked at from the origin 0_2 (you can do this by turning the book upside down), it is readily seen that individual 2 is made better-off by a movement from A to E', because E' is on a higher indifference curve.

This is what the gains from trade are all about. Exchange of x and y between individuals 1 and 2 has increased the welfare of individual 2 without decreasing the welfare of individual 1. The new combinations for these two individuals, x'_1 and y'_1, and x'_2 and y'_2, are "preferred" to the original combinations because someone has been moved to a higher indifference curve without anyone else having been moved to a lower one. Assume that the initial position is at point A. Given the indifference curves for individual 1 and individual 2 as drawn, we see that anywhere within the shaded region in Figure 4-4, both individuals can be made better-off relative to the starting position at point A. It is because of this that the shaded region has been called the **region of mutual advantage**, which is specific to starting point A. If we started at some other point, we would shade in a different region of mutual advantage.

Figure 4-4 is sometimes just called an Edgeworth box. We will find further use for this diagram later on in Chapter 18 when we examine in detail what is called general equilibrium analysis.

We can surmise that, with full knowledge and in the absence of transactions costs, two individuals will voluntarily exchange x and y until they reach a point such as E' where their indifference curves are tangent to each other, with the result that no further exchanges of mutual benefit can be made. We have drawn in three such points, E, E', and E'', and have connected them by a curve CC. This curve has been called the **contract curve**. The contract curve is defined as all the possible equilibrium combinations that *might* be obtained. Along the contract curve, one individual cannot be made better-off without reducing the welfare of the other. Whenever the individuals' indifference curves are tangent to each other, we know that their marginal rates of substitution MRS_{xy} are equal. Therefore, we know that an *equilibrium in exchange* will obtain whenever the two individuals have the same marginal rates of substitution. Thus, for equilibrium,

$$\text{MRS}_{xy}^1 = \text{MRS}_{xy}^2 \qquad (4-1)$$

Along the contract curve, the marginal rate of substitution of individual 1 is equal to the marginal rate of substitution of individual 2. The contract curve has also been called the **conflict curve** since movements along it lead to losses in utility by one party and gains in utility by the other. In other words, once two individuals have traded up to the point where they are on the contract, or conflict, curve CC, beyond this point any improvement in one individual's welfare leads to a reduction in the other's; a movement to one individual's higher indifference curve necessarily means a

movement to the other individual's lower indifference curve.

Gains from exchange—Using consumer surplus

There is an alternative way to show the gains from exchange which does not involve indifference curve analysis. Rather, we start with one commodity and two individuals, each of which has a particular demand curve for that commodity. Before we can show geometrically the gains from the exchange of the commodity between these two individuals, we must introduce the notion of **consumer surplus.**

The meaning of consumer surplus

Often when you purchase a quantity of a commodity at a particular market price, you may say to yourself that you really received a "bargain." In some sense, the notion of consumer surplus has a lot to do with the everyday meaning of bargain. Formally, the definition we choose is the following:

> Consumer surplus is the difference between the price a consumer actually pays for some given amount of a good and the price that the consumer would have been willing to pay rather than do without it.

In order to estimate consumer surplus for any of your own purchases, all you need do is carry out this "all or none" experiment. Say that you buy about 40 gallons of gas a month for your car. Ask yourself how much you would be willing to pay for that quantity of gas rather than do without it completely. That gives the *total valuation* that you place on that quantity of the commodity. Then compare that total valuation with the actual total price that you must pay for 40 gallons per month (price per unit times quantity purchased). The difference is the consumer surplus that you derive from the purchase of 40 gallons of gas each month.

DIMINISHING MARGINAL VALUATION.　Consumer surplus exists because the prevailing price of a product is an indication of the marginal valuation of or **marginal use value** received from the commodity in question. Marginal valuation is the marginal rate of substitution between x and y expressed in money terms, where y represents all other goods. In other words, marginal valuation is MRS_{xy} in money terms. Marginal valuation can also be called marginal use value. They mean the same thing. If we assume diminishing marginal valuation, we know that the marginal valuation placed on the last unit of a commodity purchased will be less than the marginal valuation placed on prior units purchased. This can be seen in Figure 4-5.

In this situation, if the individual is asked for the maximum he or she would pay for one Coke per day, it might be $1. The marginal use value of the first Coke is therefore $1 times 1, or the first shaded rectangle. Next, after the individual has already purchased and consumed one Coke, the following question is asked: How much would he or she be willing to pay for a second Coke per day? In this experiment the amount is 75¢.　Thus the marginal use value of the second Coke, given that the first Coke has been purchased and consumed, is 75¢ per Coke times one Coke, or the second shaded rectangle. We also do this for the purchase of three and four Cokes per day.　Now we know that adding up the rectangles gives us the total valuation derived from the consumption of a particular number of Cokes per day.　In other words, if four Cokes per day were purchased, the marginal use value, added up together, would be $1 (for the first Coke) plus 75¢ (for the second) plus 50¢ (for the third) plus 25¢ (for the fourth), or $2.50; and this is equal to the entire shaded area in Figure 4-5.

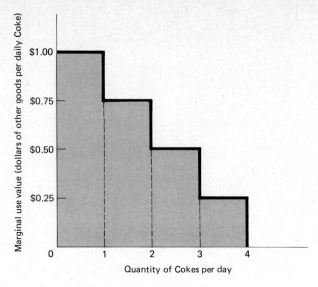

Figure 4-5: Declining marginal use value.
On the horizontal axis, we measure quantity of Cokes per day. On the vertical axis, we measure marginal use value expressed in terms of dollars of other goods given up in order to purchase Cokes. We run an experiment in which an individual is offered one Coke. The individual is willing to give up $1 of all other goods to purchase this Coke and, therefore, that is a monetary measure of his or her marginal use value of one Coke. Now, after one Coke has been consumed, the individual is offered a second. Assume that he or she is willing to give up 75¢ of all other goods; thus, the marginal valuation, or marginal use value, of the second Coke is 75¢. We continue this experiment to show diminishing marginal valuation of Cokes.

What would happen if this individual were offered Cokes at 25¢ apiece for as many Cokes as he or she wanted to buy? The individual would continue purchasing Cokes until the marginal valuation was equal to that price of 25¢ each. Thus, this individual would purchase four Cokes per day. The *total* valuation or use value derived from the purchase of four Cokes has just been calculated as $2.50. However, the total price that had to be paid for the four Cokes was 25¢ times 4, or $1.00. Thus, the difference between the total valuation of four Cokes and the total price paid was $2.50 minus $1.00, or $1.50 per day. This figure, $1.50 per day, represents the consumer surplus from purchasing four Cokes per day at a constant price of 25¢ apiece.

USING A DEMAND CURVE TO MEASURE CON-
SUMER SURPLUS. We can generalize this discussion by assuming infinite divisibility of
Cokes, i.e., that one can buy *fractions* of a Coke
also. We come up, therefore, with the demand
curve *dd* in Figure 4-6. At any point along that
demand curve, we can find the individual's
marginal valuation of a daily Coke. For a
quantity of two Cokes per day, the marginal
valuation is found at E, or P_1. That is the
marginal use value received from purchasing
and consuming two Cokes per day. When
viewed in this manner, the area under the demand curve out to the vertical line at the quantity of Cokes purchased per day is the total
valuation received from the consumption of
that quantity.[1]

Now assume a particular fixed price, say, P_1,
per Coke. The quantity demanded will be 2.
The total use value derived from the consumption of two cokes would be the area under the
demand curve down to E, or $0dE2$. However,
the price that had to be paid for two Cokes is
P_1 times 2, or the rectangular area $0P_1E2$. The
difference, then, between the dollar measure
of total valuation and what had to be paid for
the Cokes is the shaded triangle, P_1dE. That
is labeled consumer surplus; it is a geometric
presentation of the amount of money income
that a consumer would pay in addition to
what he or she already paid, rather than go
without two Cokes per day.

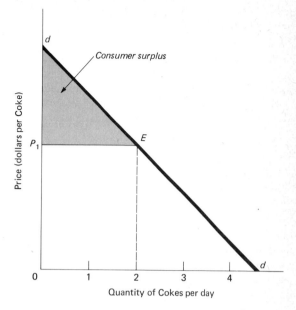

Figure 4-6: The demand curve and consumer surplus.
If we assume that the demand curve represents the
individual's marginal valuation or marginal use value, then
we can derive a graphical interpretation of consumer
surplus. Assume that the price in the market is given as
P_1. Two Cokes per day will be chosen. The marginal
valuation of the last Coke is equal to P_1, expressed as
dollars of other goods given up. The total amount paid
for the Cokes is therefore equal to price times quantity,
or $0P_1E2$. However, the total valuation is the entire area
under the demand curve to E or quantity 2 ($0dE2$). The
difference is the shaded triangle, which represents consumer surplus—the excess of total valuation over what
was actually paid for the particular quantity purchased.

Seeing the gains from trade

Let's start off with a simple situation in which
there are two individuals who both like

---

[1]The above argument is strictly correct only in the situation where the consumer's demand price for any quantity
of the good in question is independent of income, which
would be the case if the demand has been derived holding
real income (utility) constant. For normal or ultrasuperior
goods this is clearly not the case, and the area under the
demand curve exaggerates the aggregate willingness to
pay. (The converse occurs for inferior goods.) Only when
the income elasticity is zero is our argument strictly valid.

Alternatively, if we were dealing with what is called an
income-compensated demand curve (a demand curve
which shows only substitution effects), then we need not
worry about the income effects on the demand for the
good in question. In our discussion we will abstract from
the income effects by making, as a first approximation,
the assumption that the summation of marginal valuations equals total valuation.

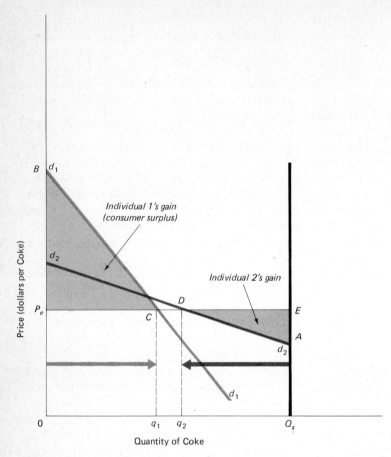

Figure 4-7: The gains from trade.
The total quantity of Coke outstanding is represented by the horizontal distance from 0 to Q_s. Individual 2 owns all the Coke. Individual 1 and individual 2 have demand curves d_1d_1 and d_2d_2, respectively. Individual 1 in the preexchange situation has zero Coke; therefore, his or her marginal valuation of Coke would be at point B on the lefthand vertical axis. Individual 2 has Q_s Cokes and, therefore, his or her marginal valuation of Cokes is given at point A. Clearly $0B$ exceeds Q_sA. If individual 2 sells Coke to individual 1 for anything greater than a price of Q_sA, that individual will be better off. If individual 1 buys Coke at a price less than $0B$, that individual will be better off. These two individuals will continue exchanging until a price is reached that causes individual 1's marginal use value to equal individual 2's marginal use value. This will be at price P_e. The amount q_2Q_s will have been sold by individual 2 to individual 1; thus, individual 1 will have bought $0q_1$ from individual 2 and will have paid price P_e. The gain to individual 1 is represented by the consumer surplus he or she obtains; likewise, the gain to individual 2 is represented by the corresponding shaded area. (We assume Coke is sold at a single equilibrium price.)

Cokes, but only one of them has any Coke. This can be seen in Figure 4-7.[2] The fixed stock of Cokes is a vertical line starting at Q_s. That is the stock of Cokes, denoting that the total quantity of Cokes available is Q_s, no matter what the price.[3] Individual 2 has all the Coke, but both individuals 1 and 2 want Coke. Their wants are expressed in demand curves d_1d_1 and d_2d_2, respectively.

What do we know about the marginal valuation of the quantity of Coke possessed by individual 2? We know that the marginal use

value or marginal valuation is equal to the vertical distance from Q_s to A. What about the marginal use value of Coke for individual 1? Initially, individual 1 has no Coke at all, and his or her marginal use value is therefore at the upper extreme of his or her demand curve, or the distance between 0 and point B. Individual 1 would be willing to pay any price below B in order to obtain some Coke. Individual 2, who owns all the Cokes, would be willing to exchange some Coke, provided that the price received is a price in excess of his or her marginal valuation Q_sA. There is room for mutually beneficial exchange because the two individuals' marginal valuations of the good differ.

We can imagine individual 2 selling more

---

[2]This analysis is due to Professor S. N. S. Cheung of the University of Washington.

[3]The price elasticity of supply is zero.

and more Coke and thus moving up his or her demand curve d_2d_2. As individual 1 buys the Coke, he or she moves down the demand curve d_1d_1. Exchange is taking place, and both individuals are making themselves better off. Eventually an equilibrium will be reached. Trading will stop when the marginal use value of Coke for individuals 1 and 2 is equal and, hence, equal to the price of Coke. Thus, trading stops when marginal valuation of Coke for individual 1 equals marginal valuation of Coke for individual 2 and both are equal to P_e. And clearly, since the quantity of Cokes in existence remains fixed, the amount of Coke sold by individual 2 must equal the amount of Coke purchased by individual 1. Thus we know that, in equilibrium, the quantity of Coke given up by individual 2 equals the quantity of Coke purchased by individual 1. That is exactly what we have shown by drawing two arrows of equal length in Figure 4-7. The quantity of Coke given up by individual 2 is the distance from q_2 to Q_s. The quantity of Coke obtained by individual 1 is equal to the distance 0 to q_1. Those two distances are necessarily and identically equal. Thus, in equilibrium, individual 1 owns quantity q_1 and individual 2 owns quantity q_2 (plus money at least equal to q_2DEQ_s, received in exchange for the Coke sold to individual 1).

WHAT ARE THE GAINS FROM EXCHANGE? The gains from exchange can be seen in Figure 4-7. Individual 1 is better-off by the amount of consumer surplus that he or she obtained after exchange took place. After all, the demand curve d_1d_1 is a representation of the different *marginal* valuations in money terms of the purchase of different quantities of Coke. The entire area under the demand curve for any specific quantity is a representation of *total* valuation. Individual 1 was able to purchase $0q_1$ of Coke at a price of P_e. Total valuation, however, exceeded the price times the quantity by an amount equal to the shaded triangu-

lar amount P_eBC. Another way of expressing this is that the consumer surplus for individual 1 is the total valuation of the quantity $0q_1$ of Coke minus the total price which individual 1 must pay to individual 2 to receive that quantity of Coke, or area $P_eBC =$ area $0BCq_1 -$ area $0P_eCq_1$.

Individual 2 clearly gains also. Total valuation of the quantity of Coke *sold* to individual 1 is represented by the area under the demand curve d_2d_2 from Q_s to q_2, or q_2DAQ_s. However, the amount of money received from individual 1 is equal to the price of Coke. (P_e) times the quantity sold (q_1), or the rectangle q_2DEQ_s. The difference is the shaded triangle DEA, which is a geometrical representation of individual 2's gain from selling $(Q_s - q_2)$ Coke to individual 1.

Another way of looking at the gains from trade

Now that we have established that the area under the demand curve represents the total valuation of the commodity in question, we can show the gains from trade very simply by combining two demand curves on one diagram. This is done in Figure 4-8. There is a total supply of good x in existence. It is represented by the length of the horizontal axis. Individual 1's origin starts in the lower left-hand corner and is labeled 0_1. Individual 2's origin starts in the lower right-hand corner and is labeled 0_2. Individual 1's demand curve slopes downward from left to right and is labeled d_1d_1. Individual 2's demand curve starts from the right and slopes downward to the left; it is labeled d_2d_2. Let us start out with an initial distribution of good x between individuals 1 and 2 at point G. That means that individual 1 is consuming 0_1G and individual 2 is consuming 0_2G.

Now we can find out the total valuation that individual 1 and individual 2 put on the amount of good x they each currently con-

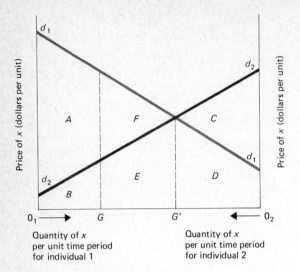

Figure 4-8: The gains from trade revisited.
Individual 1's origin starts in the lower lefthand corner and is labeled 0_1; individual 2's origin starts in the lower righthand corner and is labeled 0_2. Individual 1's demand curve is $d_1 d_1$. Individual 2's demand curve is $d_2 d_2$; it slopes from right to left. Assume that the initial position is at G. Individual 1 is consuming $0_1 G$; individual 2 is consuming $0_2 G$. Total valuation for individual 1 is equal to the areas designated $A + B$. Total valuation for individual 2 is equal to $C + D + E$. Now, exchange takes place such that the marginal valuations are equal. This occurs at G'. Individual 1 is now consuming more; individual 2 is consuming less. Total valuation for individual 1 is $A + B + E + F$; individual 2's total valuation is equal to $C + D$. The gains to trade are therefore represented by F. That was not part of the total valuation of either individual before exchange.

sume. For individual 1, the total valuation is the area under his or her demand curve to quantity $0_1 G$; that area is represented by $A + B$. For individual 2, the total valuation is the area under the demand curve to quantity $0_2 G$ which consists of three parts: $C + D + E$.

Now, move to a trading equilibrium where the marginal valuations or marginal use values expressed in money terms are equal for both individual 1 and individual 2. This would be where their two demand curves intersect. Individual 1 would now consume quantity $0_1 G'$; individual 2 would consume $0_2 G'$. The total valuation for individual 1 would be $A + B + F + E$. The total valuation for indi-

vidual 2 would be $C + D$. The gains from trade in this example are represented by the triangle labeled F. F was not part of the total valuation of either individual before exchange took place. Notice that total valuation for individual 1 has increased by the area $(F + E)$. Individual 2's total valuation for this particular commodity has been *reduced* by only the area labeled E. Individual 1 paid individual 2 money income that was *at least equal* to the area E. What is more likely is that individual 2 was more than compensated for his or her loss in total valuation equal to area E. In the limit, individual 1 would be willing to pay up to the entire area $F + E$ for the additional quantity of good x. The actual distribution of the gains from exchange F depends upon the bargaining skill of the respective parties.

Market demand

Every beginning course in economics states that the equilibrium price is determined by the intersection of the market demand and market supply curves. However, in Figure 4-7, we came up with an equilibrium price P_e without ever showing an intersection of a demand curve with a supply curve at that particular price. There was no *market demand curve* or summation of all individual demand curves in Figure 4-7. Rather, there were only individual demand curves for individuals 1 and 2. The supply curve, which was the vertical line at Q_s, was, in some sense, the market supply curve for these two individuals who constituted the entire market for Coke.

It is possible for us to redo the analysis given in Figure 4-7 in such a way that we can obtain the market-clearing, or equilibrium, price P_e at the intersection of a market demand curve and a market supply curve. Before we can do that, however, we have to derive the market demand curve. We do this by summing the individual demand curves. We engage in *horizontal* summation of individual demand curves. At *each price* we add together the corresponding *quantities* of Coke demanded by each individual in the market. Thus, we add up the demand curves from panel (*a*) and panel (*b*) in Figure 4-9. The horizontal summation of the two demand curves d_1d_1 and d_2d_2 is presented in panel (*c*). The aggregate or market demand curve is DD. The market demand curve presented in panel (*c*) is identically equal to individual 1's demand

curve in panel (*a*), down to the price at which individual 2's demand curve intersects the vertical axis in panel (*b*). This is where the kink appears to the demand curve DD in panel (*c*).

Price determination

Price is determined by the intersection of market demand and market supply. It is only at the intersection of the market demand and market supply curves that an equilibrium exists. Remember that we defined a system as being in equilibrium whenever the forces acting upon it are balanced and there is no tendency to change. Clearly, when the market price is such that the quantity demanded equals the quantity supplied, conditions are in balance and there is no tendency for either the quantity or the price to change. We say that the market is in equilibrium.

Market demand is DD in Figure 4-9. It intersects the market supply, which is the vertical line at quantity Q_s at E. The market-clearing, or equilibrium, price P_e is exactly the same equilibrium price in Figure 4-7, where we did not have a market demand schedule. (In Figure 4-9 (*c*), at price P_e the marginal valuation of Coke for individual 1 is equal to the price of Coke, which is also equal to the marginal valuation of Coke for individual 2. This condition is *not* explicit in panel (*c*), however. It is inferred from the fact that DD is a horizontal summation of the individual marginal valuation or demand curves for those in this particular market.)

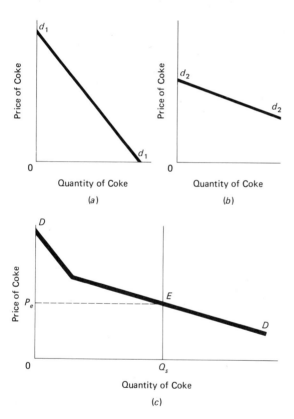

(a)

(b)

(c)

Figure 4-9: Deriving the market demand curve.
Assume that there are only two individuals in the entire market. Individual 1's demand curve is given in panel (*a*); individual 2's demand curve is in panel (*b*). We obtain the market demand curve by horizontally summing d_1d_1 and d_2d_2. The result is given as DD in panel (*c*). If we draw in supply (a vertical line), the market-clearing or equilibrium price will equal P_e. It will be exactly the same price as that given in Figure 4-7. At that price, the quantity demanded equals the quantity supplied. There are no further gains from exchange possible.

The meaning of price on the vertical axis

When demand (and supply) curves are derived, the vertical axis should measure *relative* price. We have referred to relative prices often, but we have not explicitly put down the term "relative price" on the vertical axis. One way out of this is to assume that the price of the commodity under study is relative to the price of, say, all manufactured goods. If we are willing to define the units of all manufactured goods so that each of their respective prices is equal to $1, then the price axis on all our demand (and supply) diagrams can be labeled in dollars and cents without showing the relative price. For example, if ballpoint pens have a price of 50¢ apiece, we will refer to a unit of ballpoint pen as equal to two pens so that each unit of ballpoint pen has a price of $1. If a lawn mower has a price of $149, we will refer to lawn mowers in units equal to 1/149th of a lawn mower so that each unit of lawn mower has a price of $1. We do this for all manufactured goods. Henceforth, we will assume that this convention has been, in fact, utilized.

Competition and transactions costs

A price such as P_e in our example is said to be an equilibrium price that clears the market because at that price the quantity supplied equals the quantity demanded. We predict that such a price will prevail and will be an equilibrium price. However, this statement rests on two additional assumptions: One concerns the number of potential buyers and sellers; the other, the ease with which exchanges can take place.

In our example of two individuals in Figure 4-7 and 4-8, it could have been possible for individual 2 to "take advantage" of individual 1 and to acquire some of individual 1's consumer surplus. Individual 2 could have, for example, threatened *not* to sell any Coke to individual 1. Alternatively, since individual 1 was the sole buyer, individual 1 could have tried to extract some of individual 2's gains from trade by threatening *not* to trade at all. In order for such "extortion" situations not to occur, we have to make the assumption that there are a substantial number of potential and actual buyers and sellers. Where there is a substantial number, the process of bidding and asking will operate smoothly and, in the

limit, instantaneously, and a single price will result. The market-clearing price P_e would obtain *as if* all the information about potential suppliers and demanders were put into a computer that handled all the transactions.

The second assumption we need make is that transactions costs are zero. For when they are not zero, it is possible that information concerning prices and quantities will not be readily available. It is possible that a single market-clearing price, as expressed in our diagram, will not prevail because our diagrams and analyses have ignored, for the most part, the possibility of positive transactions costs.

In sum, the quantity supplied will equal the quantity demanded at the market-clearing, or equilibrium, price. In this equilibrium situation, no further gains from trade are possible. This should not come as a surprise since the market-clearing price P_e in Figure 4-9 is exactly the same as the price at which individual 1 and individual 2 will no longer wish to trade in Figure 4-7. That price was P_e also; no further gains from trade were possible. When we say that no further gains from trade can be derived from any change in the situation, we mean that it is impossible to make one individual better-off without making the other individual worse off. In the language of our first example, which related to the Edgeworth-Bowley box in Figure 4-4, we have arrived at a point on the contract, or conflict, curve.

The determinants of demand

In Figure 4-10, we have drawn three possible market demand schedules; DD, $D'D'$, and $D''D''$. Each of these market demand curves represent the horizontal summation of individual demand curves. We know that any change in the price of the commodity in question results in a movement *along* a fixed or given market demand curve. A change in the

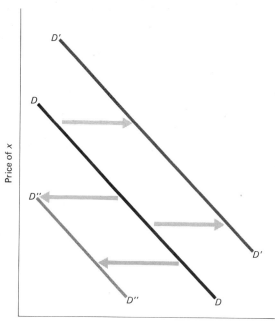

Figure 4-10: Shifts in the demand curve.
If demand is positively related to income, an increase in
real income will shift the demand curve *DD* outward to
the right to *D'D'*. If demand is positively related to
expected future relative prices, and it is expected that
relative price will decrease in the future, this will cause
the current demand curve *DD* to shift inward to the left
to *D''D''*. Only variables other than a commodity's own
price can shift the demand curve inward or outward. A
change in a commodity's own price, however, leads to a
movement along a given demand curve.

quantity demanded results from a change in a
commodity's own price. The change in price
causes an opposite change in the quantity
demanded, according to the law of demand.

The position of any demand curve in the
price-quantity quadrant, however, will be a
function of other determinants of demand that
are not shown in the diagram. Some of those
determinants are (1) real income; (2) tastes and
preferences; (3) the price of related goods
(substitutes and complements); (4) changes in
expectation of future relative prices; and (5)
population. To be sure, you can probably
come up with other determinants of demand.

The point to remember is that only variables
other than price can *shift* the demand curve. A
change in *price* always leads to a movement
along a given demand curve.

Real income

Unless we are dealing with inferior goods, an
increase in real income will lead to an increase
in demand. Notice that the phrase "increase
in demand" always refers to a comparison between two different demand curves. Thus, an
increase in real income for a normal or ultrasuperior good will lead to a rightward *shift*
in the position of the demand curve from, say,
DD to *D'D'* in Figure 4-10. If we are dealing
with an inferior good, an increase in real income would lead to a leftward shift in the demand curve from, say, *DD* to *D''D''* in Figure
4-10. The reader can avoid confusion about
shifts in curves by always relating an *increase*
in demand to a *rightward* shift in the demand
curve and a *decrease* in demand to a *leftward*
shift in the demand curve. (As we will see in
Chapter 10, the same terminology is also appropriate for increases and decreases in supply.)

Tastes and preferences

Tastes and preferences determine the degree
of convexity and the position of indifference
curves in a commodity space. There is no way
of determining what is a taste or a preference.
Economists have little to say about the determination of tastes, so not much is mentioned
about what causes consumers' tastes to be
what they are.

If one observes an increase in the demand
for a product from, say, *DD* to *D'D'* in Figure
4-10, it is not very helpful to indicate that the
reason the demand curve shifted was a change
in tastes. Indeed, it is possible to explain *everything* on the basis of asserted changes in
tastes and preferences. Thus, if we use

changes in tastes to explain changes in behavior of individuals, we end up with mere truisms or tautologies. Economists do not have a theory of taste change. Moreover, we have no measure of alleged taste changes. A theory requires approximations in order to measure or check out predictions. Thus, theories that are based on supposed changes in tastes are generally not satisfactory for our purposes. For this reason, we assume constant tastes and look for other characteristics that may affect consumer behavior.[4]

Prices of related goods: Substitutes and complements

Demand schedules are always drawn with the prices of all other commodities given. That is to say, we assume that only the price of the good under study changes. Actually, we need only concern ourselves with making sure that the prices of *related* commodities remain constant when we draw a particular commodity's demand curve. For example, when we draw the demand curve for butter, we assume that the price of margarine is held constant. When we draw the demand curve for tennis rackets, we assume that the price of tennis balls is held constant. The general term "related goods" refers to any goods for which a change in price will change the demand of other goods.

There are two types of related goods: **substitutes** and **complements**. We can define and distinguish between substitutes and complements in terms of how the change in price of one commodity affects the demand for its related commodity.

Consider two goods x and y out of many possible goods, x, y, z, etc. If x and y are substitutes, when the price of y falls, the demand

curve for x shifts to the left. If the price of y rises, the demand curve will shift to the right. Butter and margarine would be an example. In other words, the relationship is positive: An increase in the price of y leads to an increase in the demand for x and vice versa. With complementary goods, the situation is reversed. If a decrease in the price of y leads to an increase in the demand for x, and an increase in the price of y leads to a decrease in the demand for x, x and y are said to be complementary. Tennis rackets and tennis balls would be an example.[5]

Changes in expectations of future relative prices

Expectations about future relative prices play an important role in determining the position of a demand curve. If all of a sudden there is an expectation of a rise in the future relative price of x, then we might predict, *ceteris paribus*, that the present demand curve will shift from DD to $D'D'$ in Figure 4-10. If, on the other hand, there is a new expectation of a future decrease in the price of x, the present demand curve would shift instead to $D''D''$ in Figure 4-10.

Note that we are talking about changes in expectations of future *relative* rather than *absolute* prices. If all prices are rising at 10 percent a year, year in and year out, this fully anticipated inflation has no effect on the position of the demand curve for a particular commodity (if the price is measured in relative terms on the vertical axis). Consider, for example, what would happen to the demand curve for new automobiles if it were known that their price would rise by 10 percent next year. If it were anticipated that all prices would rise by 10

---

[4]Clearly, however, we cannot assume tastes are constant if we want to allow the introduction of new products into the marketplace.

[5]We can define substitutes and complements in terms of marginal utility. The marginal utility of the good rises when the quantity of a complement increases and falls when the quantity of a substitute increases.

percent, then the price of new cars relative to an average of all other prices would not be any different next year than it is this year. Thus, the demand curve for new cars this year would not increase just because of the *anticipated* 10 percent price rise.

Population

It is usually correct to predict that an increase in the population (holding per capita income constant) in an economy will shift the market demand curve outward for every product. Conversely, a reduction in the population would shift those demand curves inward. For example, as birth rates dropped in the United States, the firms dealing in baby food started to diversify and moved into other fields because they anticipated a shift inward in the market demand curve for baby food because of the reduction in the infant population.

Reservation demand and reservation supply

We were somewhat loose in dealing with the demand for a commodity when we talked about the gains from exchange. We failed to point out that, depending on the price of that same commodity, suppliers of a particular commodity may become demanders. If, for example, you own an automobile that you are trying to sell for $500, you are a supplier of used automobiles. However, at a sufficiently low price for alternative automobiles of exactly the same kind, quality, etc., you may not only be induced to take your automobile off the market but, indeed, to buy one or more others just like it. That might be the case if you could get another automobile for, say, $100. We call such a demand for automobiles on the part of a seller of automobiles the **reservation demand**.

Similarly, there is a concept called the **reser-**

vation supply of demanders. A person looking for a second car may, at a sufficiently high enough price, change from being a demander of automobiles to a supplier of automobiles. Suppose that you are looking for a second car; something happens in the economy; and the market price for the car you already own increases by 300 percent. You may decide that rather than be a demander for a second car, you should be a supplier of the car you now own. You may wish to sell it and use part of the proceeds to purchase a cheaper form of transportation and the remainder to purchase other goods and services. The combined valuation that you will put on the cheaper form of transportation plus the goods and services purchased with the remainder of the proceeds will exceed the valuation that you put on the car that you were driving.

For each individual, there is a **reservation price** for a particular commodity, below which the person becomes a demander of more and above which the person becomes a supplier.

This can best be illustrated by looking at two individuals who have particular allotments of, say, commodity x. Look at panel (*a*) in Figure 4-11. Here the consumer has a demand curve for this commodity represented by d_1d_1. The consumer starts out owning the amount q_1. If the price is P_1, this particular consumer will neither demand more nor supply x. P_1 is this consumer's reservation price for commodity x. However, at prices *below* P_1, this consumer becomes a demander of x, even though he or she already has q_1 of that commodity. The horizontally gridded area, therefore, constitutes this consumer's reservation demand. At prices *above* P_1, the consumer would be better-off by selling part of what he or she owns of x. In fact, at price P_2, this consumer will sell all q_1 of x. The vertically gridded area, therefore, represents the reservation supply of commodity x by individual 1.

Similarly, we have another individual represented in panel (*b*). This individual's res-

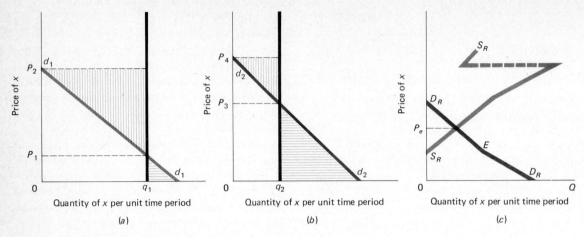

Figure 4-11: Deriving the reservation supply and demand curve.
Individual 1's supply and demand are given in panel (a); individual 2's in panel (b). The supply that the first individual owns is q_1; the second individual's is q_2. The first individual's reservation price is given at the intersection of $d_1 d_1$ and the vertical supply curve and is equal to P_1. If the price falls, the individual will demand more; if the price rises, the individual will sell or supply some of what he or she owns. In panel (b), the reservation price is P_3. Below that price, this individual will buy; above that price, the individual will sell. We horizontally add the reservation demands represented by the horizontally crossed triangles in panels (a) and (b) to obtain the reservation demand curve in panel (c), $D_R D_R$. We horizontally add the reservation supplies from panel (a) and panel (b), which are the vertically crossed triangles. This gives us reservation supply curve $S_R S_R$. The intersection of reservation supply and reservation demand yields a market-clearing price of P_e.

ervation price is P_3, with demand schedule $d_2 d_2$ and an initial supply of q_2 of commodity x. Again, the horizontally gridded area represents reservation demand; the vertically gridded area represents reservation supply.

To analyze further the relationship between these two individuals, it is possible to derive both a reservation demand curve and a reservation supply curve. We do this in panel (c). The reservation demand curve $D_R D_R$ is merely the horizontal summation of the two horizontally gridded areas in panels (a) and (b). The reservation demand curve starts at price P_3, where individual 2's reservation demand starts; it has a kink at price P_1, where we now add in individual 1's reservation demand. The reservation supply curve is also the horizontal summation of the two reservation supplies in panels (a) and (b), or the vertically shaded areas. It starts at price P_1 and has a kink at price P_3 where individual 2's reservation supply is added to individual 1's. It is discontinuous at price P_2 when individual 1

no longer has any supply to offer. That is why there is that long, perfectly horizontal stretch at the upper end of the reservation supply curve $S_R S_R$. Note, however, that as we add more people to the market, the curves don't have kinks or discontinuities in them. When they refer to the reservation demand and supply for many individuals aggregated together, the kinks are gone.

The market-clearing price of commodity x can now be obtained by looking at the intersection of the reservation demand and supply curves at point E in panel (c) of Figure 4-7. The equilibrium price is P_e. This is merely another method by which we can find the market-clearing price. You should also be able to find the market-clearing price by adding together horizontally the two demand curves $d_1 d_1$ and $d_2 d_2$, and adding together the two initial supplies q_1 and q_2. The intersection of the market demand curve with the perfectly inelastic market supply curve must be at the same equilibrium market-clearing price P_e.

Issues and Applications

Is the "true" price of a stock the price at which it trades?

We can put to good use the last section on reservation demand and supply to dispel a common myth about the price that stocks sell for in the stock market. It is often contended that a stock that sells for, say, $100 is not really worth $100. That is, the "true" price is not the trading price because only a very small proportion of the number of outstanding shares are traded on a given day. After all, if a huge block of shares had been thrown onto the market, the price of the stock would have been lower.

It is true, certainly, that for most stocks on any one day, only a fraction of 1 percent of the total number of shares owned is traded; but this does not mean that the bulk of the holders of a particular stock do not influence the price of the stock at any moment in time. Those who trade a particular stock on a particular day may or may not have experienced a shift in their particular demand curves for the stock. Some decide to sell their shares at the current price. Some decide to buy at its current price because they have had an increase in their wealth and want to invest it in the stock market. The market demand curve for a particular stock is the horizontal summation of all individual demand curves. If more individual demand curves have shifted inward on average than have shifted outward on average, there will be a *net* decline in the demand for the particular stock. With a fixed supply, the price will fall. If, on the other hand, more individual demand curves have shifted outward than have shifted in *on average,* there will be a *net* increase in demand, and the price will rise.

Remember our discussion of reservation demand and supply? Current owners of shares of a particular stock will sell, at sufficiently high prices, some or all of their shares. On the other hand, at sufficiently low prices they will buy more shares. In other words, current owners who have a stable demand curve for the stocks that they own act as stabilizers on any change in price. Thus, if there is a *net* shift inward or outward in the demand for a stock, the price will indeed change. But the existence of current owners with stable demand curves will lessen that price change.

The mass of individuals who do not trade in a stock nonetheless influence its ultimate equilibrium price. The reason the stock didn't go up more in price, if it was rising in price, is because of the reservation supplies of all those who weren't trading. The reason that the price did not go down by more, if the price of the stock was falling, is because of the reservation demands of all those who were not trading.

In sum, those who sell are those with reservation supply prices (including transactions costs) that are below the market price. Those who buy are those with reservation demand prices above the market price. Nonetheless, the market for shares of stocks would still be efficiently operating. The market corrects disequilibrium situations, and such corrections need not be of immense magnitudes. In other words, one does not have to observe a tremendous volume of shares of stocks being traded on the New York Stock Exchange to obtain proof that the New York Stock Exchange is a market in which disequilibrium situations are continuously being corrected.

Substitutes, or why unions want higher economywide minimum wages

We pointed out that one of the determinants of the position of a demand curve was the price of substitutes and complements. We defined substitutes as those commodities whose demand curves shift outward when the price of the other commodity goes up. There is an interesting application of this analysis to the question of minimum wages. Ignoring for the moment the arguments concerning the desire for workers to have "decent" or "living" wages—a topic which we will get to later on in the text—why would we predict that unions would want legislation which raised the minimum wage?

To the extent that workers working at the minimum wage are substitutes for union workers, we would expect unions, in their own self-interest, to lobby in favor of increases in the minimum wage. This can be seen in Figure 4-12. The demand curve for union labor is *DD* when the price of the substitute— nonunion labor—is held constant at the minimum wage of $2.80 an hour. Now, if the minimum wage is raised to $3.50 an hour, the demand curve for union workers will shift to the right to *D'D'*. Thus, we can see in Figure 4-12 that for any given union wage rate, the quantity of union labor demanded per time period will be greater, the higher is the wage rate of the nonunion alternative. In other words, more union labor will be hired.

It is not surprising that the record shows that union leaders and senators and members of Congress from heavily unionized states have been consistent advocates for raising minimum wages. Over a decade ago, Senator Jacob Javits of New York was reported in the *Congressional Record* of February 23, 1966, p. 2692, to have said:

> I point [out] to Senators from industrial states like my own that a minimum wage increase would also give industry in our states some measure of protection as we have too long suffered from the unfair competition based on substandard wages and other labor conditions in effect in certain areas of the country—primarily in the South.

In other words, the demand for industrial workers who are mostly unionized in the North is adversely affected by lower wages in the South; conversely, an increase in the minimum wage reduces the competition from the South. It shifts the demand schedule for union workers (primarily in the North) outward.

Why are diamonds more expensive than water?

For many years economists and interested lay persons tried to solve the so-called diamond-water paradox. Water is necessary for life; without it we cannot live. Diamonds, although they are pretty and useful in certain industrial processes, are not essential for life. How can it be, then, that diamonds are more expensive than water? Some observers concluded that the market or price system had gone awry. Commodities which were less "vital" were selling much more expensively than commodities which were more "vital." If this be the case, then prices are not a reflection of value but are arbitrary.

One relatively straightforward way to explain the diamond-water paradox is to assume that the demand curves for both diamonds and water are both downward-sloping. Given a relatively much larger supply of water than of diamonds, the market-clearing price for the latter is less than for the former. But we can approach the paradox another way.

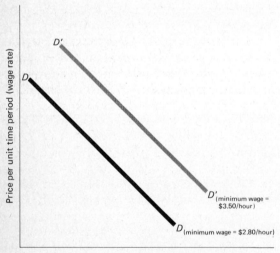

Quantity of union labor per unit time period

Figure 4-12: The effect on the demand for union labor of an increase in the minimum wage.
The demand curve for union labor is drawn with the price of substitutes held constant. It is first given as *DD* with the minimum hourly wage equal to $2.80. If legislation increases the minimum hourly wage to, say, $3.50, the demand curve for union labor will shift to the right to *D'D'*.

We can understand the diamond-water paradox by using the notion of consumer surplus and marginal valuation or marginal use value. Look at Figure 4-13. Here we plot quantity in kilograms per unit time period on the horizontal axis and the price in dollars per kilogram on the vertical axis. We use kilograms as our common unit of measurement for water and for diamonds. We could have just as well used gallons, acre-feet, or liters. In any event, we can be fairly certain that the demand curve for water, labeled $D_{water} D_{water}$, is

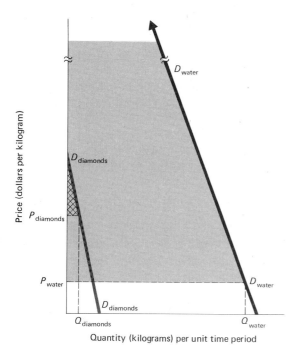

Figure 4-13: The diamond-water paradox.
We use a common unit of measurement of quantity for both diamonds and water in this diagram—kilograms per unit time period. The demand curve for water is given as $D_{water} D_{water}$. The quantity supplied of water is assumed to be Q_{water}. The market-clearing price is, therefore, P_{water}. The consumer surplus is the shaded area under the demand curve down to the horizontal price line at P_{water}. The demand curve for diamonds is $D_{diamonds} D_{diamonds}$. The supply is given as $Q_{diamonds}$. The market-clearing price is $P_{diamonds}$. The consumer surplus is the crosshatched area. The *marginal* valuation of diamonds is greater than the *marginal* valuation of water; however, the *total* valuation of water greatly exceeds the *total* valuation of diamonds.

way to the right of the demand curve for diamonds, which is labeled $D_{diamonds} D_{diamonds}$. We draw in the supply of water as Q_{water} and the supply of diamonds as $Q_{diamonds}$. The shaded area under the demand curve for water represents the consumer surplus from consuming the quantity Q_{water} of water. Note that the upper end of the area of consumer surplus is not shown on the diagram because the demand curve goes up much higher, in relation to that of diamonds, than we could show. In other words, consumer surplus is much greater than is shown here in Figure 4-13. Remember that consumer surplus represents the amount over and above what is actually paid for the quantity Q_{water} of water that would be paid rather than go without water completely. For simplicity, we are assuming that the market price of water is P_{water} and it is the same to everyone.

If we look at the demand curve for diamonds, we find that with a given supply, $Q_{diamonds}$, the market-clearing price will be $P_{diamonds}$. The consumer surplus associated with diamonds is equal to the crosshatched area. Clearly, the consumer surplus associated with diamonds is much smaller than that associated with water. Remember that any point along a demand curve measures marginal valuation or marginal use value of that particular quantity of the good. Marginal valuation or marginal use value is the marginal rate of substitution between the good and the monetary representation of all other goods. In other words, it's the consumer's monetary valuation of the last unit consumed. We see in Figure 4-13 that the marginal valuation or marginal use value of diamonds exceeds the marginal use value of water, i.e., $P_{diamonds}$ is greater than P_{water}. The confusion here lies between the price and, hence, the *marginal* use value of the product and the *total* value in use of the product. The total value in use of water is exceedingly large compared with its market price. The difference, consumer surplus, is immense. For diamonds the opposite is true. The total value in use of diamonds, i.e., willingness to pay, is quite small relative to their value in exchange, i.e., the market price for diamonds. The difference is also comparatively small; that is, the consumer surplus for diamonds is relatively insignificant compared with the consumer surplus for water.

In sum, the total valuation of water consumed is much greater than that of diamonds, but *on the margin* the reverse is true.

What does the demand curve for national defense look like?

When we wanted to derive the market demand curve for a particular commodity, we added the individual demand curves horizontally. That is, at each price we found out the quantities desired. However, such a horizontal summation is appropriate only when we are talking about goods which have attached to them the characteristic of *exclusivity*. An apple has this characteristic. If I eat the apple, you cannot eat it. My use of the apple excludes your use of the apple. Thus, if at a price of 15¢ apiece, I demand and get 10 apples per week, that means that there will be 10 less apples for anyone else to consume that week. If you demand and get 20 apples per week at that price, then altogether we will consume 30 apples per week that no one else will be able to consume. If we want to find out the total number of apples that all individuals will demand at a specific price, we add up all the quantities demanded by each of the individuals at that price. In such situations, horizontal summation of individual demand curves is indeed appropriate. Each price therefore indicates the marginal valuation in the entire market of the total quantity of apples demanded at each price.

However, there is a whole class of commodities for which the **principle of exclusivity** does *not* apply. Consider that when I turn on my television set, I do not detract from your ability to watch the same television program at exactly the same time on your own set. In other words, when I buy (if I could) a particular television signal and consume it fully, I do not prevent you from buying and consuming that exact same television signal. The same is true for national defense. My consump-

tion of national defense does not in any way interfere with your consumption. National defense can be consumed simultaneously by individuals without decreasing anyone else's consumption of it. Like it or not, we each get the same level of protection.

In panels (*a*) and (*b*) in Figure 4-14, two individual demand curves for national defense are drawn. Assume that these individuals value differently any given level of protection. Consider the purchase of two units of national defense. The marginal valuation of two units of national defense is equal to P_1 for individual 1 and equal to P_2 for individual 2.

The total market demand curve for national defense should, in principle, represent the marginal valuations of all individuals. Thus, for two units of national defense, the marginal valuation for the total market of two persons would be $P_1 + P_2$. We have, therefore, one point, labeled *A*, on the market demand curve in panel (*c*). We can obtain similar points by summing *vertically* the respective demand curves of individual 1 and individual 2. This gives us the market demand curve labeled *DD* in panel (*c*). Thus, the market demand curve for goods such as national defense is different from the market demand curve for most of the commodities that we study. The class of commodities like national defense, for which individual demand curves must be summed vertically, is called **public** or **collective goods**. We will treat public goods in more detail in Chapter 20.

Glossary

Edgeworth-Bowley box A rectangular graph that has two individual commodity spaces superimposed on each other and has each individual's origin at opposite corners (catercorner) of the box. Within the box we can draw two sets of indifference curves. The length of the box is the total quantity of *x* available, and the height of the box is the total quantity of *y* available. It is used to analyze exchange between two individuals.

Region of mutual advantage A region in the Edgeworth-Bowley box. An initial distribution

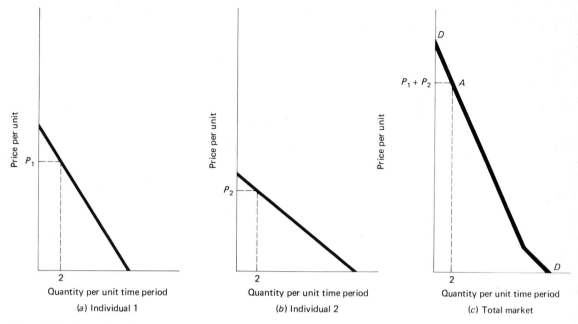

Figure 4-14: The market demand for a public good.
In panel (a), we show the demand curve for, say, national defense for one consumer; and panel (b) is the demand curve of another consumer. Since a public good is defined as one that can be consumed simultaneously by more than one individual without decreasing anyone else's consumption of that good, to derive the market demand curve for a public good, we sum *vertically*. Thus, to obtain one point on the market demand curve DD in panel (c), we look at the marginal valuation or price that two units of the public good could fetch in the market. For the consumer represented in panel (a), it would be P_1, for the one in panel (b), P_2. Thus in panel (c), the market marginal valuation of two units of a public good is $P_1 + P_2$.

of goods x and y is given. The indifference curves of the two individuals that intersect at that point form a "banana." Within this region, movements (exchanges) can be made which benefit at least one of the parties without harming the other party, all within the context of the initial *endowments*.

Contract curve In an Edgeworth-Bowley box, the locus of all possible equilibrium combinations and at which the marginal rate of substitution of one individual equals the marginal rate of substitution of the other individual. Any movement along the contract curve benefits one party and must necessarily reduce the welfare of the other party.

Conflict curve Another name for the contract curve; once on the curve, the two parties are in conflict with each other.

Consumer surplus The difference between what was actually paid for a particular quantity of a commodity and that which would have been willingly paid rather than do without the product entirely.

Marginal valuation (marginal use value) The marginal rate of substitution between x and y expressed in money terms where y represents all other goods. It is the consumer's personal value placed on the last unit of a commodity purchased expressed in terms of general purchasing power; how much the consumer would be willing to give up of all other goods in order to purchase an additional unit of the commodity in question. Marginal valuation is sometimes called marginal evaluation.

Market demand curve The horizontal summation of all individual demand curves (public goods being the sole exception to this technique).

Substitute A commodity whose quantity demanded varies directly, *ceteris paribus*, with the price of another commodity.

Complement A commodity whose quantity demanded varies inversely, *ceteris parbus*, with the price of another commodity.

Reservation demand The demand of a seller or supplier of a good which becomes effective when the "going" price of the good falls far enough.

Reservation supply The supply of a buyer or demander which becomes effective when the price of the good rises sufficiently.

Reservation price The price of a particular commodity below which an individual will become a demander and above which the same individual will become a supplier.

Principle of exclusivity The enjoyment by one person of a commodity precludes its enjoyment by another. If you use the services of an auto mechanic, I cannot use those services at exactly the same time.

Public or collective goods Goods for which the principle of exclusivity does not apply. Once a public good is produced, the additional cost that an additional user of the good imposes on society is effectively zero.

Summary

1. Voluntary exchange must, by definition, make both parties to the exchange better-off.
2. When we consider two-person exchange, if the two parties find themselves at a point in the combined commodity space (Edgeworth-Bowley box) where their respective indifference curves cross, gains from trade are possible. A movement along either's indifference curve does not harm that party and does move the other party onto a higher indifference curve.
3. No further gains from exchange can be obtained once the two parties reach the contract, or conflict, curve along which their respective indifference curves are tangent, i.e., along which the marginal rates of substitution for the two goods, x and y, are equal for both persons. Along the contract, or conflict, curve, there is an equilibrium in exchange.
4. The area under a demand curve represents the total valuation of a commodity (when real income is held constant). The area under the "going" price line represents the amount that had to be paid for the particular quantity that is purchased at that price. The difference is called consumer surplus.
5. The market demand curve is derived by the horizontal summation of individual demand curves, except for public goods.
6. Prices are determined by the interaction of market demand and market supply. The resultant equilibrium price is also called the market-clearing price.
7. Implicit in the prices presented on the vertical axes of all supply and demand diagrams is the relative nature of price. Supply and demand curves are derived on the basis of relative rather than absolute prices.
8. It is important to distinguish between a movement along a given demand curve and a shift in that curve. The former refers to changes in the quantity demanded when there is a change in relative price of that commodity. The latter occurs when some other variable changes.
9. The position of a demand curve is a function of (a) real income, (b) tastes and preferences, (c) the prices of substitutes and complements, (d) expectations of future prices, and (e) population. Any change in one or more of these variables will shift the demand curve to the left or to the right. There are, of course, other determinants of demand.
10. When we think of an increase in demand, we refer to a rightward shift in the demand curve rather than an upward shift. When we think of a decrease in demand, we think of a leftward shift in the demand curve rather than a downward shift.
11. At a sufficiently high price, a demander of a commodity will become a supplier if he or she owns any of that commodity; conversely, at a sufficiently low price, a supplier will become a demander. The price at which the demander becomes a supplier and vice versa is called the reservation price; hence, each supplier has a reservation demand and each demander has a reservation supply.
12. The existence of reservation supplies and demands lessens the price changes necessary to bring nonclearing markets into equilibrium.

Selected references

Buchanan, J. M., *The Demand and Supply of Public Goods* (Chicago: Rand-McNally, 1969).

Edgeworth, Francis Y., *Mathematical Psychics* (London: C. K. Paul, 1881).

Hicks, J. R., *Value and Capital*, 2d ed. (Oxford: Clarendon, 1946), chap. 3.

Schultz, H., *The Theory and Measurement of Demand* (Chicago: University of Chicago Press, 1938), chap. 1.

Tarascio, V. J., "A Correction: On the Genealogy of the So-called Edgeworth-Bowley Diagram," *Western Economic Journal*, vol. 10, June 1972, pp. 193–197.

Questions

(Answers to even-numbered questions are at back of text)

1. What do the dimensions of an Edgeworth-Bowley box portray? How many origins are there and where are they located? If the point representing the distribution of the goods is on the contract curve, what can be said about the benefits to be had by exchange?

2. Define consumer surplus. In a two-person world, could one astute trader "capture" part or all of another's consumer surplus? How? (*Hint*: Look at Figure 4-6 again.)

3. List five determinants of demand, the change in any one of which will shift the entire demand curve.

4. From what you have read about "reservation price," what would you imagine is meant by the term "auction without reserve"?

5. Suppose you "exchange" goods with someone holding a gun at your head. The person with the gun sets both the terms of trade (relative prices) and the absolute amounts "exchanged." After the trade, what can be said about the welfare of both of you?

6. Look at the Edgeworth-Bowley box in Figure 4-4. The initial endowments are shown by point *A*. When voluntary exchange commences, which good will individual 1 be offering? Individual 2?

7. Look at Figure 4-5. The horizontal axis measures the daily rate of Coke consumption. The vertical axis is labeled marginal use value of Coke; however, the units are in dollars per Coke. How can this be?

8. Explain why a person who pays a single unit price for his or her purchases of a good inevitably realizes some consumer surplus.

9. How are the gains from exchange shown in the two separate techniques given?

10. In the consumer surplus analysis of Figures 4-7 and 4-8, does it make any difference in the final outcome which individual had the stock of goods at the outset?

11. Five factors, other than its price, affecting the demand for a good were discussed in the chapter. Place each of the following events in its proper category and state how it would shift the demand curve in question.

    (*a*) New information is disclosed that large doses of vitamin C prevent common colds. (The demand for vitamin C.)

    (*b*) A drop in the price of tape recorders occurs. (The demand for stenographic services.)

    (*c*) A fall in the price of pretzels occurs. (The demand for beer.)

12. National defense is an often cited example of a "public good." Now that Alaska and Hawaii are part of the United States, is the example still valid? Is local police protection a public good? Explain.

13. When you carry your own baggage, sell your own home, or buy eggs directly from an egg rancher on the edge of town, are you cutting out the intervening broker (used to be called the "middleman")? Do these examples prove that such persons are parasites who don't deserve their "cut"?

14. Have you ever heard the allegation that the negotiating rooms of car dealers are sometimes bugged? In light of what you now know about gains from exchange, why might a car dealer engage in such a practice?

15. Why doesn't an ounce of gold of the exact same quality always sell for the identical dollar price in New York, London, Paris, Zurich, and Hong Kong? Explain.

5

PRICE ELASTICITY OF DEMAND

We introduced the concept of the price elasticity of demand in Chapter 2. There we showed that elasticity was related to changes in total expenditures. Then we showed that price elasticity of demand could be gleaned from the slope of the price-consumption curve. In this chapter, we want to look at how coefficients of the price elasticity of demand are computed, the changing nature of elasticity along straight-line demand curves, the difference between slope and elasticity, the relationship between revenues and elasticity, the determinants of the price elasticity of demand, and finally, real world examples of price elasticities. The Issues and Applications section of this chapter will cover the demand for physiologically addicting drugs, capital punishment, and energy.

Definition of price elasticity

We formally defined price elasticity of demand as

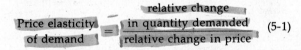

$$\frac{\text{Price elasticity}}{\text{of demand}} = \frac{\text{relative change in quantity demanded}}{\text{relative change in price}} \quad (5\text{-}1)$$

Price elasticity of demand is a measure of the relative responsiveness of quantity demanded to a change in price. The term "relative" is important in this definition. In terms of percentage changes, the definition would become (denoting elasticity now with the Greek letter η, or *eta*):

$$\eta = \frac{\text{numerical percentage change in quantity demanded}}{\text{numerical percentage change in price}} \quad (5\text{-}2)$$

η will always be a negative number because of the inverse relationship between a change in price and the resulting change in quantity demanded. That is why you see minus signs in Eq. (5-1) and Eq. (5-2).

When we assume the changes both in the quantity demanded and in the price are quite small, then we can define the coefficient of price elasticity of demand as

$$\eta = -\frac{\dfrac{\Delta q}{q}}{\dfrac{\Delta P}{P}} = -\frac{\Delta q}{\Delta P} \cdot \frac{P}{q} \quad (5\text{-}3)$$

As stated before, the Greek letter *delta* (Δ) signifies small change in; P is price and q is quantity.

This definition of price elasticity leads to a measure which is completely independent of the units in which quantities and prices are measured. Elasticity is also a pure number; it has no dimensions. This makes it easy for us to compare the price elasticities of various commodities. Consider a purely hypothetical example for wheat

where $P = \$5/\text{bushel}$
$q = 100 \text{ bushels}$
$\Delta P = \$1/\text{bushel}$
$\Delta q = 5 \text{ bushels}$

Then Eq. (5-3) becomes

$$-\frac{\dfrac{5 \text{ bushels}}{100 \text{ bushels}}}{\dfrac{\$1/\text{bushel}}{\$5/\text{bushel}}} = -\frac{0.05}{0.20} = -0.25$$

This number has no dimensions; they all were canceled out.

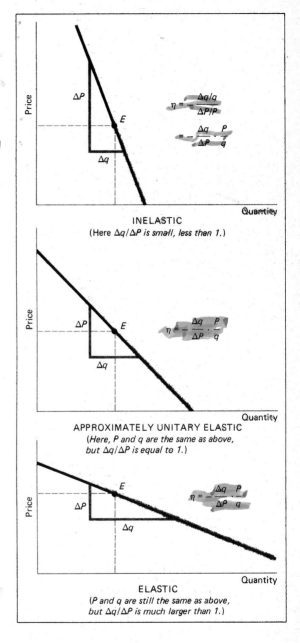

INELASTIC
(Here $\Delta q/\Delta P$ is small, less than 1.)

$$\eta = -\frac{\Delta q/q}{\Delta P/P}$$

$$= -\frac{\Delta q}{\Delta P} \cdot \frac{P}{q}$$

APPROXIMATELY UNITARY ELASTIC
(*Here, P and q are the same as above, but $\Delta q/\Delta P$ is equal to 1.*)

$$\eta = -\frac{\Delta q}{\Delta P} \cdot \frac{P}{q}$$

ELASTIC
(*P and q are still the same as above, but $\Delta q/\Delta P$ is much larger than 1.*)

$$\eta = -\frac{\Delta q}{\Delta P} \cdot \frac{P}{q}$$

Individual and market elasticities of demand

We looked at the derivation of individual demand curves and then derived the market demand curve by summing horizontally all individual demand curves (except in the case of public goods, where we summed vertically). As might be expected, there is a definite relationship between the individual price elasticities of demand and the market price elasticity of demand. The market price elasticity of demand is equal to the weighted average of all the individual price elasticities of demand. The weights are equal to the relative quantities purchased by each individual buyer at any given price. This can be seen in the following exercise. Let

$$X \equiv x_1 + x_2 \qquad (5\text{-}4)$$

where X is the market quantity demanded and x_1 and x_2 are the individual quantities demanded. Then with a small change, Δ, Eq. (5-4) becomes

$$\Delta X = \Delta x_1 + \Delta x_2 \qquad (5\text{-}5)$$

Divide both sides of Eq. (5-5) by ΔP, the small change in market price,

$$\frac{\Delta X}{\Delta P} = \frac{\Delta x_1}{\Delta P} + \frac{\Delta x_2}{\Delta P} \qquad (5\text{-}6)$$

Multiply both sides of Eq. (5-6) by P/X:

$$\frac{\Delta X}{\Delta P} \cdot \frac{P}{X} = \left(\frac{\Delta x_1}{\Delta P} \cdot \frac{P}{X} \right) + \left(\frac{\Delta x_2}{\Delta P} \cdot \frac{P}{X} \right) \qquad (5\text{-}7)$$

Then multiply each term on the right-hand side of Eq. (5-7) by x_1/x_1 and x_2/x_2, respectively.

$$\begin{aligned} \frac{\Delta X}{\Delta P} \cdot \frac{P}{X} &= \left(\frac{\Delta x_1}{\Delta P} \cdot \frac{P}{X} \cdot \frac{x_1}{x_1} \right) + \left(\frac{\Delta x_2}{\Delta P} \cdot \frac{P}{X} \cdot \frac{x_2}{x_2} \right) \\ &= \left(\frac{\Delta x_1}{\Delta P} \cdot \frac{P}{x_1} \cdot \frac{x_1}{X} \right) + \left(\frac{\Delta x_2}{\Delta P} \cdot \frac{P}{x_2} \cdot \frac{x_2}{X} \right) \end{aligned} \qquad (5\text{-}8)$$

Rearranging Eq. (5-8) into some recognizable terms,

$$\frac{\Delta X / X}{\Delta P / P} = \left(\frac{\Delta x_1 / x_1}{\Delta P / P} \cdot \frac{x_1}{X} \right) + \left(\frac{\Delta x_2 / x_2}{\Delta P / P} \cdot \frac{x_2}{X} \right) \qquad (5\text{-}9)$$

In Eq. (5-9), we recognize three terms representing price elasticity of demand; and we can

also recognize that the terms x_1/X and x_2/X merely represent the proportion of the total market demand that is accounted for by individuals 1 and 2, respectively. If we let each share be denoted by g_1 and g_2, respectively, we get

$$\eta_{\text{total market}} = g_1 \cdot \eta_{\text{individual 1}} + g_2 \cdot \eta_{\text{individual 2}} \qquad (5\text{-}10)$$

$\left(x_1 \text{ amt. bought by 1} \over X \text{ total} \right)$

The relationship between price elasticity and income elasticity

We showed in Chapter 3 that a change in the quantity demanded of a commodity is composed of two different effects—substitution and income. The substitution effect is always negative. The income effect can be negative or positive, depending on whether the good is inferior, normal, or ultrasuperior. Since price elasticity of demand relates the change in the quantity demanded to the change in price, it would seem to follow that there is some relationship between price elasticity of demand and the income elasticity of demand.

Remember that the definition of income elasticity of demand (μ) is the relative change in the quantity demanded divided by the relative change in income. Let us be specific here and refer to *real income*. Thus the coefficient of **real income elasticity of demand** is defined as

$$\iota = \frac{\Delta q / q}{\Delta R / R} = \frac{\Delta q}{\Delta R} \cdot \frac{R}{q} \qquad (5\text{-}11)$$

where ι is the Greek *iota* and R is real income (defined as money income divided by the price level, or M/P).

Now let us divide up the change in the quantity demanded due to a change in the relative price of x into its two parts, the substitution effect and the income effect. Thus we will have

$$\Delta q_t = \Delta q_s + \Delta q_i \qquad (5\text{-}12)$$

where the subscript t refers to the total effect, the subscript s refers to the substitution effect, and the subscript i refers to the real income effect. Thus the total change in the quantity demanded is equal to the change due to the substitution effect (the relative price of x has fallen) plus the income effect (due to a change in real income). Note that real income rises, even though money income doesn't, when the relative price of one good in the market basket of goods falls. After all, if the nominal and relative price of one particular good that is being purchased falls, no other prices change, and money income is constant, it becomes possible to buy more of the now cheaper good and still purchase the same quantity of all other goods. Hence, real income goes up.

We maintain the equality of the relationship given by Eq. (5-12) when we divide both sides of it by ΔP, which gives us

$$\frac{\Delta q_t}{\Delta P} = \frac{\Delta q_s}{\Delta P} + \frac{\Delta q_i}{\Delta P} \qquad (5\text{-}13)$$

Now we multiply the last term in Eq. (5-13) by the quantity $\Delta R/\Delta R \cdot R/R$ (which is equal to 1). When we do this, we obtain

$$\frac{\Delta q_t}{\Delta P} = \frac{\Delta q_s}{\Delta P} + \frac{\Delta q_i}{\Delta P} \cdot \frac{\Delta R}{\Delta R} \cdot \frac{R}{R} \qquad (5\text{-}14)$$

Now we multiply both sides of Eq. (5-14) by the same quantity P/q. This does not alter the equality, and we obtain

$$\frac{\Delta q_t}{\Delta P} \cdot \frac{P}{q} = \frac{\Delta q_s}{\Delta P} \cdot \frac{P}{q} + \frac{\Delta q_i}{\Delta P} \cdot \frac{\Delta R}{\Delta R} \cdot \frac{R}{R} \cdot \frac{P}{q} \qquad (5\text{-}15)$$

In order to simplify this rather messy equation, we have to find an equivalent expression for ΔR, the change in real income. It turns out that

$$\Delta R = -q\Delta P \qquad (5\text{-}16)$$

Why? Because the change in real income is equal to the amount of income that is released for the purchase of other goods when the relative price of the commodity in question falls and the nominal price of all other goods remains constant.

If, for example, a consumer were buying 100 Big Macs a year at \$1 apiece and their price fell by 10¢, that consumer could still buy 100 a year and pay only \$90. The increase in real income, or money income, released for the purchase of other goods, is \$10 {or $[-100 \cdot (-\$0.10)] = +\$10$}.

Now by substituting the right side of this identity for ΔR in the numerator of the last term in Eq. (5-15), we obtain

$$\frac{\Delta q_t}{\Delta P} \cdot \frac{P}{q} = \frac{\Delta q_s}{\Delta P} \cdot \frac{P}{q}$$

$$+ \frac{\Delta q_i}{\Delta P} \cdot \frac{(-q\Delta P)}{\Delta R} \cdot \frac{R}{R} \cdot \frac{P}{q} \qquad (5\text{-}17)$$

In the last term we can "cancel out" the ΔP's and rearrange the equation so that it becomes

$$\frac{\Delta q_t/q}{\Delta P/P} = \frac{\Delta q_s/q}{\Delta P/P} - \left(\frac{Pq}{R}\right)\left(\frac{\Delta q_i/q}{\Delta R/R}\right) \qquad (5\text{-}18)$$

Now we can define two different price elasticities of demand.

The normally defined price elasticity of demand (that is, what we will call the total price elasticity of demand), we will denote with the symbol η_t. The total price elasticity of demand is computed with a constant money income but a changed real income. Thus, the left-hand term of Eq. (5-18) is the total price elasticity of demand η_t.

The price elasticity of demand associated with the substitution effect is computed by holding real income constant. We will denote the price elasticity of demand associated with the substitution effect as η_s. The first term on the right-hand side is the substitution effect price elasticity of demand η_s; and the second term on the right is the percentage of real income[1] originally spent on the commodity. The second expression in the second term on the right-hand side of the equation is our definition of the coefficient of the real income elasticity of demand, ι. Hence, Eq. (5-18) can be

---

[1] And money income, too, since the initial situation is our base period.

written as follows:

$$\eta_t = \eta_s - k\iota \qquad (5\text{-}19)$$

where we denote the percentage of income spent on the commodity as $k \; (= Pq/R)$.

This equation (due to E. E. Slutzky) indicates that the price elasticity of demand, as normally measured, is a combination of two things: the price elasticity of demand only with respect to a relative price change, plus some fraction of the income elasticity of demand. That fraction is the share of total expenditures taken up by the good in question.

Implications of the Slutzky equation

Equation (5-19) allows us to generate some hypotheses about price elasticities of demand. First, we repeat that the substitution effect η_s is always negative because it follows the law of demand. k is always positive because it represents the percentage of income spent on the commodity. We can now determine that when the good in question is a normal or ultrasuperior good (i.e., ι is positive), (1) the total price elasticity of demand η_t will be negative, and (2) η_t will be larger in absolute value (numerically) than η_s.[2] This means that income effect reinforces the substitution effect.

When x is an inferior good, the income elasticity of demand (ι) is negative. The income effect works counter to the substitution effect; η_s will be smaller numerically than η_t. In the case of a Giffen good, the second term on the right-hand side of Eq. (5-19) is larger than the first term; the total price elasticity of demand η_t is a positive number; and the demand curve slopes upward.

Cross elasticities: Substitutes and complements revisited

We have already talked about the effect of a change in the price of one good on the quantity demanded of a related good. We defined substitutes and complements in terms of whether or not a reduction in the price of one good caused a shift leftward or rightward, respectively, in the demand curve of the other.

Now we can also use a definition of elasticity to define substitutability and complementarity. Up to this point, we have discussed what happens to the quantity demanded of a good when its *own* price changes; we have been referring to the **own price elasticity of demand**. Now we examine the **cross-price elasticity of demand**, which is defined as

$$\eta_{xy} = \frac{\Delta q_x / q_x}{\Delta P_y / P_y} = \frac{\Delta q_x}{\Delta P_y} \cdot \frac{P_y}{q_x} \quad \text{or}$$

$$\eta_{yx} = \frac{\Delta q_y / q_y}{\Delta P_x / P_x} = \frac{\Delta q_y}{\Delta P_x} \cdot \frac{P_x}{q_y} \qquad (5\text{-}20)$$

The subscripts refer to two commodities x and y. Whenever η_{xy} or η_{yx} is positive, we classify the two commodities as substitutes. When it is negative, we classify them as complements.[3] Another way of looking at this is given in Figure 5-1.

The numerical computation of price elasticity of demand

Equation (5-2) gives us a definition of the coefficient of the price elasticity of demand. However, it is given in terms of small, but discrete, changes in both price and quantity. That is

---

[2]When we refer to the absolute or numerical value of a number, we disregard the sign. Thus, if $\eta_1 = -100$ and $\eta_2 = -10$, then the former is greater numerically than the latter, i.e., η_1 is greater in absolute value than η_2, or $|\eta_1| > |\eta_2|$ since 100 is a larger number than 10. Of course, in real values $\eta_1 < \eta_2$ since -100 is less than -10.
[3]The definition of complementarity or substitutability as implied in Eq. (5-20) is a gross definition. We are refer-

ring to gross substitutes and gross complements since there is no way to take account of compensating changes in the level of real income. In other words, we might want to relabel the cross elasticity of demand, as defined in Eq. (5-20), as the *total* cross-price elasticity of demand, similar to the total price elasticity of demand we dissected in deriving the Slutzky Eq. (5-19).

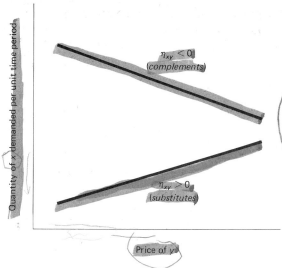

Figure 5-1: Complementarity and substitutability. Here we show the relationship between the quantity of x demanded per unit time period and the price of y. If that relationship is positive, the commodities are substitutes; if it is negative, they are complements.

$$\eta_{xy} = \frac{\Delta q_x / q_x}{\Delta P_y / P_y}$$

Quantity of
x demanded
increases
Price of y
increases
$\left.\right\}$ $\dfrac{(+)/q_x}{(+)/P_y} = (+) = \eta_{xy}$

Quantity of
x demanded
decreases
Price of y
decreases
$\left.\right\}$ $\dfrac{(-)/q_x}{(-)/P_y} = (+) = \eta_{xy}$

x and y are substitutes

Quantity
demanded of
x increases
Price of
y decreases
$\left.\right\}$ $\dfrac{(+)/q_x}{(-)/P_y} = (-) = \eta_{xy}$

x and y are complements

not what the real world presents to us. Rather, we observe discrete changes that are sometimes rather large. Even if we think in terms of percentage changes in both price and quantity, we still have trouble.

Inherent in the definition given in Eq. (5-3) is the notion that elasticity is measured at a *point* along the demand curve. This is so, because we are talking about a ratio of a very small relative change in quantity to a very small relative change in price. When the price range is made as small as possible, that is, shrunk to a point, the relative changes must also be made as small as possible. We get the term **point elasticity** when we use a formula such as the one in Eq. (5-3).

Arc elasticity

If, instead of trying to measure price elasticity of demand at a point on the demand curve, we measure it over a price range, or arc, we can come up with a workable definition of price elasticity that actually allows us to approximate it numerically. However, there are problems.

It's not enough just to say that we will measure **arc** price **elasticity** of demand by comparing percentage changes in price. The percentage change in price, for example, will depend critically on whether we are talking about an increase or a decrease in the price. For example, consider the percentage change associated with a price change of 25¢, or $\Delta P = 25$¢. If we start off with $1 as the initial price and reduce it by 25¢, the percentage change is −25 percent. However, if we consider an increase in the price by the same amount (25¢), from 75¢ to $1, then the percentage price change is +33$^1/_3$ percent. Clearly, then, the percentage change in price will depend upon whether we talk about an increase or a decrease in price. You can easily verify this for yourself by taking a couple of numerical examples.

USING AVERAGE VALUES. One way out of this difficulty is to take the average of the two prices and of the two quantities. In this manner, the estimate of price elasticity of demand is at the midpoint of the arc on the demand curve. The formula for computing arc elasticity then becomes

$$\eta = \frac{\dfrac{\Delta q}{\frac{1}{2}(q_1 + q_2)}}{\dfrac{\Delta P}{\frac{1}{2}(P_1 + P_2)}} \qquad (5\text{-}21)$$

where the subscripts refer to the quantities and prices which establish the dimensions of the "arc" in question. We see the meaning of the midpoint formula in Figure 5-2.

The geometric computation of elasticity

It is possible to obtain a formula for the point price elasticity of demand for a particular demand curve such as the one in Figure 5-3. It turns out that there are two ways of doing this. There is a horizontal axis formula and a vertical axis formula. Both were developed by Alfred Marshall, a British economist in the late nineteenth and early twentieth centuries.

Horizontal axis formula

Look back at Eq. (5-3). It consists of two parts, $\Delta q/\Delta P$ and P/q. The first part of the formula

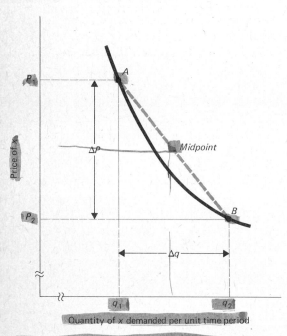

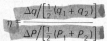

Quantity of x demanded per unit time period

Figure 5-2: Using the midpoint formula for arc elasticity. The percentage change in both price and quantity will be different if we go from point A to point B on the demand curve than if we go from point B to point A. As a compromise, we compute price elasticity of demand at the midpoint of a straight line between points A and B. Our formula is then

$$\eta = \frac{\Delta q \big/ \left[\frac{1}{2}(q_1 + q_2)\right]}{\Delta P \big/ \left[\frac{1}{2}(P_1 + P_2)\right]}$$

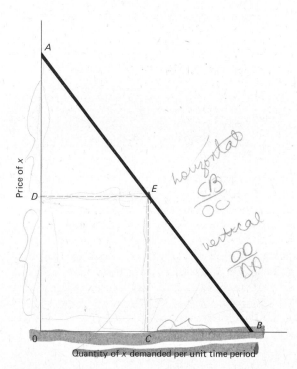

Quantity of x demanded per unit time period

Figure 5-3: Geometric computation of price elasticity of demand.

We wish to measure price elasticity of demand at point E on demand curve AB. The slope of AB is equal to $\Delta P/\Delta q$. To derive the horizontal axis formula, consider the slope at point E. $\Delta P/\Delta q$ is equal to CE/CB. If we insert this into the formula $\eta = -(\Delta q/\Delta P)(P/q)$, then we obtain $-(CB/CE)(CE/OC)$, which is equal to $-CB/OC$. We can derive the vertical axis formula similarly. It is equal to $-OD/DA$.

for price elasticity of demand ($\Delta q/\Delta P$) is approximately equal to the reciprocal of the slope of a demand curve for small changes in P around some price.[4] Of course, it is an exact expression of the slope of a demand curve at any point, if we consider the Δ's to mean infinitesimally small changes. In any event, the formula for price elasticity consists of the reciprocal of the slope of the demand curve multiplied by the ratio P/q.

Look at the straight line curve AB in Figure 5-3. Let us see if we can translate our price elasticity of demand formula, Eq. (5-3), into geometric terms. The slope at point E on the demand curve AB is equal to CE/CB:

$$\frac{\Delta P}{\Delta q} = \frac{CE}{CB} \tag{5-22}$$

We can invert this to CB/CE and obtain the first part of the expression in Eq. (5-3). The second part is just price and quantity; but price is equal to the vertical distance of CE and the quantity is equal to $0C$. Thus

$$\eta = -\left(\frac{\Delta q}{\Delta P} \cdot \frac{P}{q}\right) = -\left(\frac{CB}{CE} \cdot \frac{CE}{0C}\right) = -\frac{CB}{0C} \tag{5-23}$$

This horizontal axis formula for the price elasticity of demand tells us that to compute price elasticity of demand for a straight line or linear demand curve, we drop a line from the point we are interested in perpendicular to the horizontal axis. The ratio of distance from that point to the intersection of the demand curve with the horizontal axis and the distance from the origin to the point where the perpendicular hits the horizontal axis gives us the price elasticity of demand.

Vertical axis formula

A similar formula for η can be derived involving the ratio of the two distances on the vertical axis. We do this by obtaining another expression of the slope of the demand curve AB. Starting from point A, $\Delta P/\Delta q$ is equal to DA/DE. Hence, our formula becomes

$$\eta = -\left(\frac{\Delta q}{\Delta P} \cdot \frac{P}{q}\right) = -\left(\frac{DE}{DA} \cdot \frac{0D}{DE}\right) = \frac{0D}{DA} \tag{5-24}$$

Point elasticity for a nonlinear demand curve

We can apply either the horizontal or the vertical axis formula to obtain the point elasticity of demand for a nonlinear demand curve, such as the one shown in Figure 5-4. Our task is to compute the price elasticity of demand for point E. This is easily done by drawing a tangent AB at point E. Then we construct a perpendicular to either the horizontal axis or the vertical axis. When we have done this, we can compute the price elasticity of demand. Using the horizontal axis formula, Eq. (5-3),

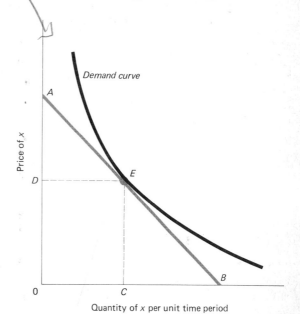

Figure 5-4: Point elasticity of demand for a nonlinear curve.

If we wish to derive the price elasticity of demand at point E on the nonlinear demand curve shown above, we draw the tangent at that point and extend it to both the horizontal and vertical axes. That tangent is labeled AB. We can then apply either the horizontal or the vertical axis formula.

---

[4] $\Delta q/\Delta P$ is equal to the *reciprocal* of the slope of the demand curve because economists put quantity on the horizontal axis instead of on the vertical axis.

price elasticity of demand at point E in Figure 5-4 is $-CB/0C$; using the vertical axis formula from Eq. (5-24), the price elasticity of demand is $-0D/DA$.

Elasticity and the class of linear demand curves

We can use either the horizontal or the vertical axis formula to demonstrate that the price elasticity of demand changes continuously along any straight-line or linear demand curve.

We can find, first of all, the price at which the elasticity of demand is -1. This is where the perpendicular, dropped from a point on the demand curve, bisects (cuts in half) the distance $0B$ in Figure 5-5. The horizontal axis formula will give us elasticity of $CB/0C$, and since those two distances are equal, the result will be 1. (Since we are accepting the law of demand which asserts an inverse relationship between P and q, we must introduce the negative sign. Negative changes in price are associated with positive changes in quantity demanded and vice versa. The negative sign is labeled accordingly in Figure 5-5.) Above price P_1, the midpoint on demand curve AB in Figure 5-5, price elasticity of demand is numerically greater than 1 ("elastic"). For prices less than P_1, it is numerically less than 1 ("inelastic").[5] Thus, we have two regions in a straight-line demand curve: above price P_1, where demand is elastic; and below price P_1, where demand is inelastic. At price P_1 there is unitary elasticity.

The two extremes are prices $0A$ and $0B$. At price $0A$ ($q = 0$), demand is infinitely elastic. At quantity $0B$ ($P = 0$), demand has zero elasticity. [Can you use Eq. (5-3) to prove this?] In sum, a straight-line demand curve has a

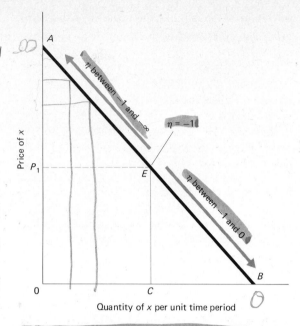

Figure 5-5: Changing price elasticity of demand along a linear demand curve.

We draw a perpendicular line midway between the origin and where the demand curve AB intersects the horizontal axis. We will hit point E on the demand curve AB where $\eta = -1$. At prices above P_1, price elasticity of demand is numerically greater than 1; at prices below P_1, it is numerically less than 1. At point A, it is equal to $-\infty$, and at point B, it is equal to 0.

price elasticity of demand that ranges from $-\infty$ to 0 as we move down the curve.

Slope does not equal elasticity

The last statement should suggest to you the inadvisability of looking at the slope of a linear demand curve as being indicative of its elasticity. Let's go back to our original formula for price elasticity of demand

$$\eta = -\left(\frac{\Delta q}{\Delta P} \cdot \frac{P}{q} \right) \tag{5-25}$$

The first part of this formula is the reciprocal of the slope, and the second part is the ratio of the price to the quantity. The slope of a demand curve, i.e., its flatness or steepness, is

---

[5]Numerically greater or lesser refers to absolute value; i.e., it disregards the sign of the number.

based on the *absolute* changes in price and quantity; in other words

$$\text{Slope} = \frac{\Delta P}{\Delta q} = \frac{1}{\Delta q / \Delta P}$$

absolute change

However, price elasticity of demand has to do with *relative* changes in price and quantity, that is, the change in quantity relative to the original quantity and the change in price relative to the original price; or in other words

$$\eta = -\frac{\Delta q / q}{\Delta P / P}$$

relative change

Therefore, the reason why the slope of the demand curve does not equal price elasticity of demand is because

$$\frac{1}{\Delta q / \Delta P} \neq \frac{\Delta q / q}{\Delta P / P}$$

Furthermore, by definition, the slope of a straight line or linear demand curve, such as the one presented in Figure 5-5, is constant, whereas the price elasticity of demand varies from $-\infty$ to 0. It is important, therefore, that one not confuse flatness or steepness in a demand curve with its price elasticity. This caveat can be illustrated by comparing the price elasticities or two or more demand curves.

Comparing elasticities

In Figure 5-6, we have drawn two demand curves *AB* and *A'B'*. If you were asked to figure out, just by inspection, which demand curve was more elastic than the other, you probably would say *A'B'*. After all, it is flatter, so it looks more price-responsive. But you would be wrong.

This can be seen by using the vertical axis formula for price elasticity of demand. According to this formula, price elasticity of demand is equal to the ratio of the vertical distance from the origin to a horizontal price line drawn from the point on the demand curve

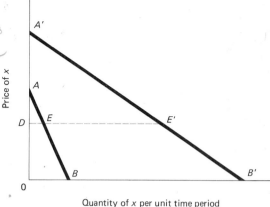

Figure 5-6: Comparing the price elasticity of demand of two demand curves.

Even though demand curve *AB* is steeper than demand curve *A'B'*, at each and every price it is more price-elastic. You can prove this by using the vertical axis formula where $\eta = -0D/DA$ at point *E* on demand curve *AB*. Elasticity is numerically greater than 1 at that point for demand curve *AB*; however, using the same formula but substituting *DA'* for the denominator, we see, by inspection, that price elasticity of demand is numerically less than 1 at point *E'* on demand curve *A'B'*.

where elasticity is to be measured to the vertical distance from that point to where the demand curve intersects the vertical axis. Take any particular price, say, price *D*, where we wish to compare the elasticities of the two demand curves in Figure 5-6. This will be at points *E* and *E'*. The dashed line drawn from *E'* goes through *E* to *D* on the vertical axis. The price elasticity of demand for the steeper demand curve, *AB*, is $-(0D/DA)$, which is, by inspection, numerically greater than unity. However, the price elasticity of demand for the flatter demand curve *A'B'* is $-(0D/DA')$ and is observably numerically less than unity. Hence, at price *D* (and all other prices as well), demand curve *AB* is more elastic than demand curve *A'B'*. The moral of the story? You can't usually look at the slope of two demand curves to determine which is more elastic.

However, when *P* and *q* are identical, you

can look at the relative flatness or steepness of the two intersecting demand curves to determine which one is less or more elastic. This can be seen in Figure 5-7. Here we show two demand curves AB and $A'B'$, which intersect at point E. If we wish to make a statement about the relative price elasticities of demand of the two different curves at price P_1, where they intersect, we can unambiguously state that the flatter curve is the more elastic one. In other words, if we rotate a demand curve at a point, as that demand curve gets flatter, its elasticity increases at that particular price around which the curve is being rotated. This can be understood by remembering Eq. (5-3). Elasticity is the negative of the reciprocal of the slope of the demand curve times P/q. If we are rotating the demand curve at a particular point, P and q do not change; however, the slope of the demand curve does. As the de-

mand curve gets flatter, the slope decreases. Therefore, the reciprocal of the slope, or $\Delta q/\Delta P$, becomes greater. Thus the elasticity becomes greater in numerical terms.

Another way of proving that the flatter demand curve is more elastic at price P_1 in Figure 5-7 is by remembering the vertical axis formula. In fact, we can make a general statement: *Whichever linear demand curve intersects the vertical axis closer to the origin will be more elastic than the other at any given price.* Thus even two parallel demand curves will have different relative elasticities at each and every price. In Figure 5-8, the one closer to the origin will be the more elastic of the two.

Finally, you should be able to see immediately from the vertical axis formula, Eq. (5-24), that demand curves AB and AB' in Figure 5-9 have exactly equal elasticities at every single price!

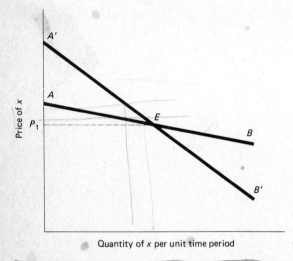

Figure 5-7: Comparing elasticities at a point where two demand curves intersect.

It is possible to deduce the relative price elasticities of two demand curves at the point where they intersect by their relative steepness or flatness. Demand curve AB is more elastic at price P_1 (point E) than is demand curve $A'B'$. You can prove this using the vertical axis formula. Whichever demand curve intersects the vertical axis closest to the origin is more elastic at each and every price.

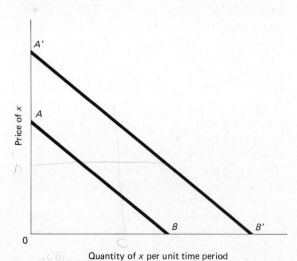

Figure 5-8: Price elasticity of demand for parallel demand curves.

Demand curve AB and demand curve $A'B'$ are parallel; they have exactly the same slope. However, demand curve AB is more elastic than demand curve $A'B'$ at any given price. Use the vertical or horizontal axis formula to show why.

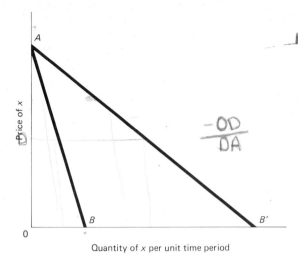

Figure 5-9: Comparing price elasticities again.
Even though demand curve *AB'* is considerably flatter than
demand curve *AB* at each and every price, they have
exactly the same price elasticity of demand because they
intersect the vertical axis at the same point, *A*.

The sellers' side of the story: The relationship between price elasticity of demand and revenues

When we introduced elasticity, we noticed a relationship between price elasticity of demand and the total expenditures of buyers. Briefly, total consumer expenditures vary inversely with price changes when demand is elastic and directly with price changes when demand is inelastic, and are invariant to price changes when demand is unit-elastic. It turns out that if we look at the sellers' side of the picture, we find the same relationship between price elasticity of demand and the total revenues of the sellers of the product. Their revenues are the mirror image of buyers' expenditures.

Computing total and marginal revenue

We define **total revenue** (TR) as price per unit times quantity demanded because that is the amount of revenues received by any seller of a

product who charges a single price for all units sold. **Marginal revenue** (MR) is defined as the change in total revenue due to a one-unit change in the quantity sold. **Average revenue** (AR) is defined as total revenues divided by quantity demanded, or $AR = (P \cdot Q)/Q \equiv P$, assuming that the same price is charged to everyone. And in fact, the demand curve is sometimes called the **average revenue curve**, because any point on the demand curve gives the average revenue realizable from the sale of that particular quantity per unit time period (again, assuming that a single price is charged for all units sold).

Look at Table 5-1. Here we have shown a hypothetical demand schedule. In column (1) is the price of *x*. In column (2) is the number of units demanded. Thus, columns (1) and (2)

Price of *x* ($ per unit) (1)	Units demanded (per time period) (2)	Total revenue $TR = P_x \cdot Q$ [(1) × (2)] (3)	Marginal revenue $MR = \dfrac{\Delta TR}{\Delta Q} = \dfrac{\Delta TR}{1} = \Delta TR$ (4)
11	0	0	
			$10
10	1	$10	
			8
9	2	18	
			6
8	3	24	
			4
7	4	28	
			2
6	5	30	
			0
5	6	30	
			−2
4	7	28	
			−4
3	8	24	
			−6
2	9	18	
			−8
1	10	10	

Table 5-1

constitute the demand schedule for product x. Column (3) is total revenue, or the price of x times the quantity demanded. Column (4) is marginal revenue, defined as the change in total revenues due to a one-unit change in the quantity sold. Marginal revenue is equal to the difference in the total revenue of each row (as long as $\Delta Q = 1$).

Note that total revenue reaches its maximum at 5 units sold, stays constant for one more unit, and then starts to fall. Marginal revenue, therefore, becomes 0 for quantities between 5 and 6 and thereafter becomes negative. We can plot all the information in the four columns in Table 5-1 on two diagrams in Figure 5-10. The top of the figure shows total revenue. It starts at 0, peaks at 5 units, remains constant at $30 through the sixth unit, and then falls thereafter. The bottom diagram in Figure 5-10 shows the demand curve, or average revenue curve, plotted as DD. It represents the price-quantity pairs of columns (1) and (2) in Table 5-1. Marginal revenue is a stepladder-type function because we are dealing in discrete units. The marginal revenue curve, if we can call it a curve, starts at $10 and falls to 0 at 5 units and then becomes negative after 6 units sold.

Notice that there is a relationship between marginal revenue and total revenue. Marginal revenue becomes 0 when total revenue reaches its maximum. This is shown by the shaded area between 5 and 6 units. Beyond 6 units, MR becomes negative.

The marginal revenue curve always lies below a downward-sloping demand curve. This is because price, which is identically equal to average revenue, is not the same thing as marginal revenue. Marginal revenue is always less than price for a downward-sloping demand curve. This can perhaps be better understood by looking at Figure 5-11. Here we show a unit increase in sales due to a reduction in the price of product x from P_1 to P_2. After all, the only way that sales can increase, given a downward-sloping demand

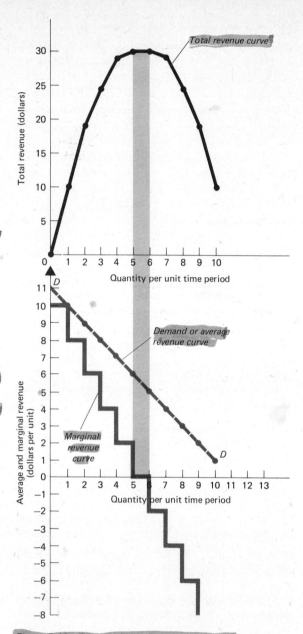

Figure 5-10: Total and marginal revenue curves.
Data from Table 5-1 are transferred to this figure. The top diagram shows the total revenue curve; the bottom diagram shows the marginal revenue curve, which is the change in total revenue. Note that when total revenue reaches its maximum between five and six units, marginal revenue is equal to zero. Thereafter, it becomes negative.

curve is for price to fall. The price P_2 is the price received for the last unit. Thus that price P_2 times the last unit sold represents what is received from the last unit sold. That would be equal to the horizontally gridded column showing the effects of a one-unit increase in sales. The area of that horizontally gridded column is one unit wide times P_2 high.

But the price times the last unit sold is not the addition to total revenues received from selling that last unit. Why? Because price was reduced on all other units sold ($0Q$) in order to sell the larger quantity ($0Q_1$). The reduction in price is represented by the vertical distance from P_1 to P_2 on the vertical axis. We must subtract, therefore, the vertically gridded row from the horizontally gridded column in order to come up with the *change* in total revenues due to a one-unit increase in sales. Clearly, the change in total revenues, i.e., marginal revenue, must be less than price because marginal revenue is always the difference between the two gridded areas in Figure 5-11.

The relationship between marginal revenue and price elasticity

There is a definite relationship between marginal revenue and the price elasticity of demand. If we look at the definition of marginal revenue, we can find this relationship. Marginal revenue is equal to the change in total revenue due to a one-unit change in unit sales. In the case of a price decrease, it is identically equal, therefore, to the lower price at the higher unit-sales rate minus the change in price times all of the initial quantity sold. To see this, consider Figure 5-11 again. To make the proof easier, let the initial quantity Q be called Q_1 and the other quantity ($Q + 1$) be called Q_2. Then

Total revenue at price $P_1 = TR_1 = P_1 \cdot Q_1$
Total revenue at price $P_2 = TR_2 = P_2 \cdot Q_2$

Marginal revenue from selling Q_2 is then

$$MR_{1-2} = TR_2 - TR_1$$

$$= P_2 Q_2 - P_1 Q_1$$

But we let $Q + 1 = Q_2$, so if we substitute, we get

$$MR_{1-2} = P_2 (Q_1 + 1) - P_1 Q_1$$

$$= P_2 Q_1 + (P_2 \cdot 1) - P_1 Q_1$$

$$= (P_2 \cdot 1) + Q_1 (P_2 - P_1)$$

This is exactly what we see in Figure 5-11. P_2 is less than P_1, so $(P_2 - P_1)$ is a negative number. Hence, MR will be the new lower price P_2 minus some number; ergo $MR_{1-2} < P_2$.

We can generalize the above:

$$MR = P + \Delta P \cdot q \qquad \text{for price decreases} \qquad (5\text{-}26)$$

always negative for price decrease

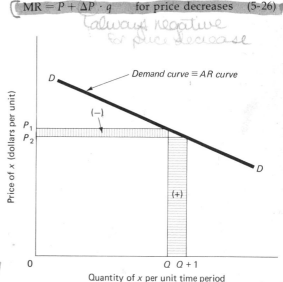

Figure 5-11: Marginal revenue is always less than price. The only way to sell one more unit when facing a downward-sloping demand curve is by lowering the price. The price received for the last unit is equal to P_2. The revenues received from selling this last unit are equal to P_2 times one unit, or the area of the horizontally crosshatched vertical column. However, if a single price is being charged for all units, total revenues do not go up by the amount of the area represented by that column. The price had to be reduced on all the previous units $0Q$ which were being sold at price P_1. Thus, we must subtract the vertically lined area from the horizontally lined area in order to derive marginal revenue. Marginal revenue is, therefore, always less than price.

$$MR = P - \overset{+}{\Delta P} \cdot \overset{+}{q} \quad \text{for price increases} \quad (5\text{-}27)$$

Here we are dealing with one-unit discrete changes in q, and when we consider other arbitrary changes in q in the amount of Δq, we must write as a general statement[6]

$$MR = P + \frac{\Delta P \cdot q}{\Delta q} \quad (5\text{-}28)$$

Now we do a little algebraic manipulation. We multiply the right-hand side of Eq. (5-28) by P/P, which does not change the equality. This gives us

$$MR = P + \left(\frac{\Delta P}{\Delta q}\right)\left(\frac{q}{P}\right)\left(\frac{P}{1}\right) \quad (5\text{-}29)$$

Now we factor out P:

$$MR = P\left(1 + \frac{\Delta P}{\Delta q} \cdot \frac{q}{P}\right) \quad (5\text{-}30)$$

But the second term in the parentheses is merely the reciprocal of the elasticity of demand, so that

$$MR = P\left(1 + \frac{1}{\eta}\right) \quad (5\text{-}31)$$

Since we are always dealing with downward-sloping demand curves, the price elasticity of demand η will always be negative. Hence, Eq. (5-31) is consistent with the notion that marginal revenue is always less than price, since as long as the term $1/\eta$ does not equal 0, it will be negative and therefore reduce the entire term in parentheses in Eq. (5-31) to be less than unity.

Using Eq. (5-31), we see that when η is numerically greater than 1, MR must be positive; when η is numerically less than 1, MR must be negative. (Why?)

From Eq. (5-31) we can find out the geometric relationship between marginal revenue and the demand curve.

[6]Actually, Eq. (5-28) holds only at the limit ($\Delta q \to 0$ and $\Delta P \to 0$).

Total revenue and elasticity

Look at the demand curve AB in Figure 5-12. It is a linear demand curve, and therefore we can use the horizontal axis formula to find out where along that curve the elasticity of demand is unitary (technically, -1). All we have to do is find the midpoint of the distance $0B$. That midpoint is at C. If we draw a perpendicular line from C up to E on the demand curve, we know at point E, $\eta = -1$. We have some information about point E in terms of marginal revenue. Substitute -1 for η in Eq. (5-31). Marginal revenue then becomes equal

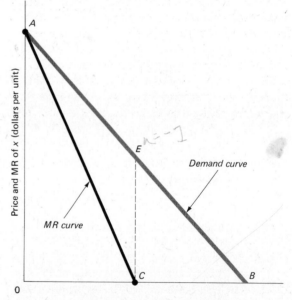

Figure 5-12: Deriving the marginal revenue curve.
By using the formula $MR = P(1 + 1/\eta)$, we know that marginal revenue will equal zero only when $\eta = -1$. But this is exactly at the midpoint between the origin and where the demand curve AB intersects the horizontal axis at point B. This gives us point C below E on demand curve AB. Using the same formula, we know that $MR = P$ when $\eta = -\infty$. This gives us point A. We now have two points and can draw the marginal revenue curve, which always bisects a line drawn parallel to the horizontal axis from the vertical axis outward to any linear demand curve.

to 0 for the quantity-price combination denoted by E on the demand curve AB. Thus, where demand is unitary-elastic at point E, marginal revenue is equal to 0.

Let's see if we can find another point. We do this by using the vertical axis formula for price elasticity of demand. Using the vertical axis formula, we know that where the demand curve cuts the vertical axis, the price elasticity of demand is $-\infty$. (Why?) Thus we have some information about the marginal revenue at price A. From Eq. (5-31), marginal revenue $= P\ (1 + 1/-\infty)$. Since anything divided by infinity is equal to 0, marginal revenue equals price (MR $= P$) where the linear demand curve AB cuts the vertical axis. Thus marginal revenue equals price A. We now have two points to connect for our marginal revenue curve. Those two points are A and C, and we have therefore drawn in that curve.

All straight-line demand curves have straight-line marginal revenue curves which bisect the horizontal axis between the origin and where the demand curve intersects the horizontal axis. In fact, any point on the marginal revenue curve always bisects any horizontal line (parallel to the horizontal axis) drawn from the demand curve to the vertical axis.

The relationship between price elasticity and total revenue

There is a relationship between price elasticity of demand and total revenue that should be quite clear by now. It is a relationship similar to the one we discussed in Chapter 3 when we talked about total expenditures. This relationship is shown in Table 5-2, where we note that an elastic demand implies a negative relationship between changes in price and total revenue and that an inelastic demand yields a positive relationship. When demand is of unitary elasticity, total revenue is invariant to price changes. This occurs everywhere along a

	Price elastic demand	Unitary price elasticity	Price inelastic demand
Price decrease	TR ↑	TR constant	TR ↓
Price increase	TR ↓	TR constant	TR ↑

Table 5-2

demand curve that is a rectangular hyperbola, shown in Figure 5-13. Note that the formula for a rectangular hyperbola is $x \cdot y =$ constant, or $P \cdot q =$ constant. The demand curve DD is a rectangular hyperbola. It has the property that, at any point along the demand curve, the area enclosed by the rectangle which is formed is always the same. Take point A. Here the price is P_1 and the quantity demanded is q_1. Total revenues are P_1 times q_1 or $8 times 4 equals $32. At point B, the total revenues are P_2 times q_2, or $4 times 8, which again equals $32.

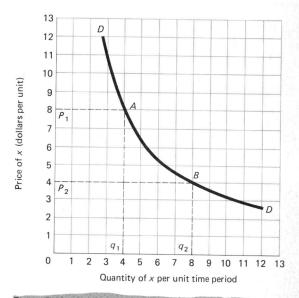

Figure 5-13: A rectangular hyperbola demand curve. DD is a rectangular hyperbola. At any point along it, price elasticity of demand equals -1. You can prove this by finding out total revenues at point A and at point B. In other words, $(P_1 q_1) = (P_2 q_2)$.

Determinants of the price elasticity of demand

On page 91 we gave five determinants of the position of the demand schedule. It is possible for us to come up with a similar list for the determinants of the price elasticity of demand. The price elasticity of demand depends on:

1. The existence and closeness of substitutes
2. The "importance" of the commodity in the total budget of the consumer
3. The length of time allowed for adjustment to changes in price

Existence of substitutes

The strongest statement we can make about what determines the price elasticity of demand is that the more substitutes there are, the greater will be η. In the limit, if there is a perfect substitute—if indifference curves are straight lines—the price elasticity of demand for the commodity will be $-\infty$. We're really talking about two goods that the consumer believes are exactly alike and desirable, like a half-dollar and two quarters. We can predict that the more narrowly and more specifically a commodity is defined, the more close substitutes there will be for that commodity and hence the more price-elastic will be the demand. Thus, the price elasticity of demand for a particular brand of tea will be greater than the price elasticity of demand for all tea. In turn, the price elasticity of demand for all tea will be greater than the price elasticity of demand for all beverages.

The importance of the commodity in the consumer's budget

If we mean by "importance" the percentage of total expenditures that the individual allocates

to a particular commodity, we can speculate that the greater the percentage of total real income spent on the commodity, the greater the person's price elasticity of demand for that commodity. This can be seen by looking at the Slutzky equation, derived on pages 104–106. We will restate it here:

$$\eta_t = \eta_s - k\iota \qquad (5\text{-}23)$$

The total price elasticity of demand η_t is equal to the price elasticity associated with the substitution effect (η_s) minus the percentage of real (and money) income spent on the good (k) times the real income elasticity of demand ι. Thus, for all normal and ultrasuperior goods, the income effect reinforces the substitution effect because the term $(-k\iota)$ is always negative. Hence, the larger k, *ceteris paribus*, the greater will be η_t (in absolute value).

This argument, however, is not totally compelling. To be sure, if a commodity constitutes a large fraction of the consumer's total expenditures, a drop in the price of that commodity will entail a relatively large increase in real income, and thus not only for that commodity but for all others—whether normal or ultrasuperior—there will be an increase in purchases. But here we are talking about an *absolute* (i.e., *not* about percentage terms) increase in the purchase of the commodity in question due to an increase in real income because of a drop in that commodity's price. When we refer to the notion of elasticity, however, we are talking about *relative* changes in consumption. If the absolute quantity of the good in question is already large, there is no reason to think that the relative increase in the quantity demanded of the commodity will be greater because of any given drop in its price, just because it constitutes a large portion of the budget. In the extreme case, when the commodity in question constitutes 100 percent of the budget, the total price elasticity of demand (η_t) cannot be large. It must, in fact, be exactly equal to -1. (Why?)

The time for adjustment in rate of purchase

When the price of a commodity changes and that price change persists, the greater will be the information flow about that price change; i.e., more people will learn about it. Second, consumers will be better able to revise their consumption patterns, the longer the time they have to do so. And in fact, the longer the time they do take, the less costly it will be for them to engage in this revision of consumption patterns. Consider a price decrease. The longer the time that that price decrease persists, the greater will be the number of new *uses* that consumers will "discover" for the particular commodity, and the greater will be the number of new *users* of that particular commodity.

It is possible to make a very strong statement about the relationship between the price elasticity of demand and the time allowed for adjustment: *The longer any price change persists, the greater the price elasticity of demand.* Otherwise stated, price elasticity of demand is greater in the long run than in the short run.

We can think of an entire family of demand curves, such as those depicted in Figure 5-14. The immediate-run (or market period) demand curve may be D_1D_1. The immediate, or market, period is defined as one in which there is *no* time for adjustment. As more time is allowed, the demand curve becomes flatter, going first to D_2D_2 and then all the way to D_4D_4. We know that the flatness or steepness of a demand curve is not an indication of its elasticity. However, if we are comparing straight-line demand curves that intersect at a particular price, we know from the vertical axis formula for calculating the price elasticity of demand that those curves which intersect

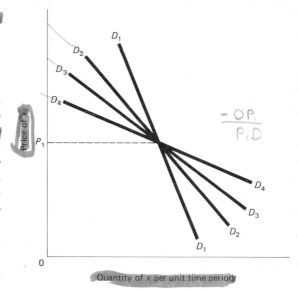

Figure 5-14: Long- and short-run price elasticity of demand.

The longer the time allowed for adjustment, the greater the price elasticity of demand. We, therefore, have a whole family of demand curves depending on the time allowed for adjustment. D_1D_1 is a demand curve for a shorter adjustment period than D_4D_4.

the vertical axis at lower and lower levels are more and more elastic. (Can you prove this?)

The estimation of elasticities

When physicists want to find out the relationship between two variables, they can often construct experiments to measure the relationship. Chemists can do so as well. However, economists generally cannot run similar types of experiments. If an economist wants to find out the price responsiveness that one or more consumers exhibit for a particular commodity, it is generally not possible to set up an experiment in which a set of consumers is faced with different prices for the same commodity and is asked to purchase accordingly. Moreover, it is generally useless to engage in interviews to ask individuals how much they would buy of a particular commodity at various prices because consumers often do not know how much they will buy until actually faced with the prices. Of course, this is not to say that some researchers have not gone this route. For example, in one study a group of duck hunters was sent a detailed questionnaire in which each was asked to indicate how many ducks he or she would want to shoot each hunting season at various prices charged per bagged bird.

Such interview techniques cannot guarantee satisfactory estimates of the price responsiveness of an individual for a particular commodity. We do not find out how consumers *will* react to something by asking them how they think they *would* react. We have to have some evidence of what they actually do in a real world situation. Consumers are very fickle individuals. It is generally safest to infer their preferences from their actual buying behavior.

What the economic researcher has to do to estimate price elasticities of demand is to look at what consumers did when relative prices changed. However, we know that relative price is not the only thing that determines the demand curve for a commodity. In our particular model, it has generally been the only variable shown on the diagrams. We did point out, however, that there were other determinants of changes in demand. These were changes in such things as real income, tastes and preferences, the prices of related goods, expectations of future price changes, and population. Thus we know that if we were to attribute changes in quantity demanded solely to changes in the relative price of that particular good, we would probably be introducing a serious error into our estimates of price elasticity of demand. The error would be due to the fact that we had not held constant the other variables that affect the position of the demand curve.

Category	Estimated η	
	Short run	Long run
Food		
Potatoes	−0.3	
Peas, fresh	−2.8	
Peas, canned	−1.6	
Tomatoes, fresh	−4.6	
Tomatoes, canned	−2.5	
Nondurable goods		
Shoes	−0.9	
Newspapers and magazines	−0.4	
Tires and related items	−0.8	−1.2
Services		
Auto repair and related services	−1.4	
Radio and television repair	−0.5	−3.8
Travel and entertainment		
Legitimate theater and opera	−0.2	−0.31
Motion pictures	−0.87	−3.7
Foreign travel by United States residents	−0.1	−1.8
Public transportation		
Taxicabs	−0.6	
Local public transportation	−0.6	−1.2
Intercity bus	−0.2	−2.2
Utility services		
Electricity	−0.1	−1.8
Telephone	−0.25	
Miscellaneous		
Jewelry and watches	−0.4	−0.6

Table 5-3: Selected estimates of price elasticity of demand.

Source: For the food category, D. M. Shuffett, *The Demand and Price Structure for Selected Vegetables* (Washington, D.C.: U.S. Department of Agriculture, 1954; Technical Bulletin no. 1105); for all other categories, H. S. Houthakker and L. D. Taylor, *Consumer Demand in the United States: Analyses and Projections* (Cambridge, Mass.: Harvard University Press, 1970). Fractions have been rounded.

By using what are called multiple-regression econometric techniques, it is possible to hold constant, in effect, these other important demand-determining variables. In multiple-regression analysis, an equation is set up relating the quantity demanded to the relative price, real income, the price of related commodities—complements and substitutes—and so on. Data are collected on all these variables over a certain period of time during which the relative price for the commodity in question changed often enough to generate statistically significant estimates of the price elasticity of demand. We present an appendix on econometric techniques at the end of this chapter.

Some estimates of price elasticities

In Table 5-3, we are presented with some estimated price elasticities of demand for some food items, nondurable goods, services, travel and entertainment, and public transportation. For a number of these items, there are separate short- and long-run estimates of the price elasticity of demand. All the elasticities are negative. In all cases, the estimated long-run price elasticity of demand was numerically greater than the short-run figure. Therefore, these estimates do not refute our hypothesis that the longer the time for adjustment, the greater the price elasticity of demand.

Issues and applications

Drug addiction and elasticity

Law enforcement agencies around the world are concerned with the problem of drug abuse. More specifically, the sale and use of so-called hard or physiologically addictive drugs is usually a felony punishable by imprisonment and/or fines. Clearly, the more resources that are used in enforcing the laws against drug use, the higher the implicit price to the drug user; the total price of illegal drug use is the actual out-of-pocket cost to purchase the drug, plus the anticipated or expected cost associated with getting caught, jailed, fined, harassed, and so on. If drug laws are not enforced at all, then this expected cost is effectively equal to 0. However, the more resources that go into enforcement, the greater the probability of being caught becomes and the greater the total expected cost of using the drug.

What is at issue here is the price elasticity of demand for hard drugs. Take the case of heroin. If indeed the individual heroin user's demand curve is dd in Figure 5-15, then the quantity demanded will be q_1 "no matter what the price." In other words, no matter how expensive the

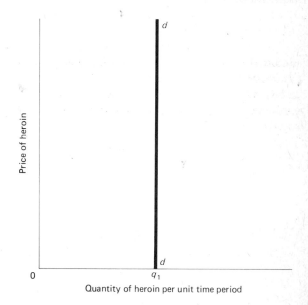

Figure 5-15: Hypothetical individual demand curve for heroin.

If an individual is willing to pay "any price" for a given quantity of heroin, that individual's demand curve is represented by vertical line dd, at quantity q_1. The price elasticity of demand is equal to zero.

drug becomes because of increased law enforcement against sellers and users, the same quantity will be demanded. If every individual has a demand curve such as *dd and no budget constraint*, then the market demand curve will also be a vertical line. Here the price elasticity of demand is 0; that is, we have a completely inelastic demand curve. Those who contend that users of hard drugs become not only psychologically but physiologically addicted as well, contend that the demand curve is perfectly inelastic, as in Figure 5-15. According to one researcher, "... for the heroin user jail sentences cease to be a deterrent...."[7] Since the quantity of heroin demanded is the same, irrespective of the implicit price charged, researchers in this area often suggest that emphasis must be given to therapeutic programs directed toward altering the addict's life-style (moving his or her demand curve to the left), as opposed to raising the implicit price of the illegal drug.

On a more fundamental level, the entire discussion of the price elasticity of the demand for heroin may often be based on a confusion of averages with margins. The demand curve for heroin may be relatively inelastic. However, there certainly exist marginal heroin users, such as curious teenagers deciding whether to try the drug once or a few more times, who have a relatively elastic demand curve for the drug. Thus the *market* demand curve will not exhibit a zero price elasticity of demand.

Does capital punishment have an impact on the murder rate?

While we are talking about the area of criminal activities, it is interesting to question whether or not capital punishment has any effect on criminal activities, such as murder. Sociologists, psycholo-

gists, and others have numerous theories relating the number of murders committed to various psychological, sociological, and demographic variables. For example, some researchers contend that, *ceteris paribus,* the higher the density of population, the more murders there will be. Others contend that as the family unit becomes less and less viable, there will be more murders.

An economist comes along, however, and considers these factors important but wants to test an economic model based on the assumptions given in Chapter 2. In other words, we attempt to use a utility- or wealth-maximizing model in which the individual attempts to maximize utility, subject to constraints. These constraints are the budget constraint as well as institutional constraints, such as laws and customs. When we make the further assumption that the marginal rate of substitution is diminishing, we can derive a downward-sloping curve (except for Giffen goods) in which quantity demanded is negatively related to the relative price.

Now we start out with a commodity that happens to be called the act of murder. If the act of murder is like any other commodity, the quantity "demanded" (by perpetrators, of course, not victims) will be negatively related to the relative price. But what is the price of murder? Ignoring now all the sociological, psychological, or psychic costs of murder, we have to consider the cost to the murderer when he or she is caught. We have to consider the probability of being caught and, then, once caught, the possible jail sentence or capital punishment that may be called for. But here again, we have to look at the probability of a particular jail sentence and the probability of going to the gas chamber or the guillotine or the four winds. Thus it would do little good to observe the difference in murder rates between states that had capital punishment and states that did not. Rather, it would be necessary to look at the probability of a convicted murderer going to the gas chamber in those states that had capital punishment compared with what happened in states where there was a

[7]Raul A. Fernandez, "The Clandestine Distribution of Heroin, Its Discovery and Suppression: A Comment," *Journal of Political Economy*, vol. 77, no. 4, part 1, July/August 1969, p. 487.

zero probability. In fact, there are some states with capital punishment where the probability of going to the gas chamber is effectively zero for a convicted murderer. We find, for example, that states with the death penalty for first-degree murder often change the charge to second-degree murder. But states with life maximums for first-degree murder seldom lower the charge.

Now, critics of such analysis immediately point to the "fact" that the murderer, either in a moment of unreasoned passion or when confronted with an unanticipated situation during an armed robbery, does not take into account the expected probability of going to the gas chamber at the moment of the murder. That is to say, murderers are not acting rationally when they murder. Is this a valid criticism of the economic model of the demand for murder? No, it is not. If the model predicts poorly, then the assumptions must be changed or the model changed in some other way. Indeed, if one contends that the expected "price" of committing a murder has no effect on the quantity of murders, one is implicitly negating the law of demand or stating that the price elasticity of the demand for murder is 0. In other words, the demand curve for murders is similar to the one shown for heroin in Figure 5-15. One is also confusing the average murderer with the marginal murderer. All potential murderers do not have to be aware of or react to the change in the expected "price" of committing a murder for the theory to be useful. If there are a sufficient number of marginal murderers who act as if they were responding to the higher expected "price" of murdering, then the demand curve for murders by perpetrators will be downward-sloping.

Actual estimates

A few economists have actually worked through economic models of the demand for murder and other crimes. One of the variables they put in was the objective conditional risk of execution—in other words, the risk of being executed if caught and convicted of murder. Two elasticities that

were given in one study were −0.06 and −0.065.[8] While these elasticities are relatively small, they are not 0. The implication of these elasticities, given the number of murders and executions over the period of study in question, which was 1935–1969, was striking. The implied trade-off between murders and executions was between 7 and 8. "Put differently, an additional execution per year over the period in question may have resulted, on average, in 7 or 8 fewer murders."[9] Similar evidence for felonies, such as burglary, robbery, etc., has also been compiled.[10]

One final note. In the case of capital punishment, the execution must be thought to fall on the guilty parties, rather than randomly applied. History tells us that under the emperors in China, executions were frequent. However, the emperors were not always quite so good at getting the right person. This system of "punishment" does little good for society in terms of combating crime, not to mention the loss suffered by the innocent victim and his or her family due to such injustice.

Is the demand for gasoline price-inelastic?

Many items in the consumer's budget are considered "necessities." One such item that has been called a necessity, at least recently, is gasoline. It has been posited by a number of observers of the gasoline market that indeed the price elasticity of demand for that product is 0, or close to it. Hence, a change of the price within the relevant range—that is, a small change—will not lead to a change in the total quantity demanded after correcting for changes in other variables that may shift the demand curve. Some of these other variables include real income and population.

[8]Isaac Ehrlich, "The Deterrent Effect of Capital Punishment: A Question of Life and Death." *The American Economic Review*, vol. 65, no. 3, June 1973, p. 414.

[9]Ibid.

[10]See, for example, Arleen Smigel, "Does Crime Pay? An Economic Analysis," unpublished M.A. thesis, Columbia University, 1965.

Indeed, not too many years ago there was an embargo on the exportation of oil from Persian Gulf countries to the United States. This reduction in the available supply of oil would, in the absence of restrictions, lead to an increase in the relative price of oil products. However, the exact shape of the demand curve was, at that time, in question. Oil company executives and some economists outside the industry contended that the price elasticity of demand for petroleum or, at the very least, for gasoline was 0.[11]

If, in fact, the demand for gasoline were completely price-inelastic, the resultant gasoline price increases after the Arab oil embargo on the United States would not have caused motorists to "conserve" gasoline. What actually happened, according to a number of researchers' accounts, was that the quantity of gasoline demanded per vehicle dropped by 8 percent at the end of the period during which gasoline prices rose by 40 percent. Thus, the price elasticity of demand can be roughly calculated as the negative value of 8 percent divided by 40 percent, or −0.2.[12] Now, −0.2 is small, but it is clearly not 0. Thus, it is one thing to say that the demand is inelastic; it is quite another to say that it is completely inelastic.

The reduction in the quantity of gasoline demanded, due in the main to an increase in the relative price of gasoline, probably did not come as a surprise to those of you who understand the economic problem, that is, the allocation of scarce resources. Each family with a limited budget must allocate its limited means among competing uses. Gasoline for an automobile is only one possible outlet for spending As the relative price of gasoline rises, the amount of other goods that must be given up in order to continue purchasing fixed quantities of gasoline becomes "excessive."

Hence the consumer moves, in degrees, away from gasoline toward additional consumption of other goods.

Glossary

Real income elasticity of demand The relative change in quantity demanded of a commodity divided by the relative change in real income (defined as money income divided by the price level).

Own price elasticity of demand The relative change in the quantity demanded divided by the relative change in the price of the commodity; to be contrasted with cross-price elasticity of demand.

Cross-price elasticity of demand The relative change in the quantity demanded of good x divided by the relative change in the price of good y; to be contrasted with own price elasticity of demand.

Point elasticity Price elasticity of demand measured at a single point on a demand curve; to be contrasted with arc elasticity.

Arc elasticity Price elasticity of demand measured along a section of a demand curve rather than at a single point.

Total revenue Price per unit times quantity sold.

Marginal revenue Change in total revenue due to a one-unit change in the quantity sold.

Average revenue Total revenue divided by quantity; the result is price per unit.

Average revenue curve Another name for the demand curve because at any point along the demand curve the price represents the average revenue (if all units are being sold at that same price).

Summary

1. The coefficient of price elasticity of demand is

$$\eta = -\frac{\Delta P/P}{\Delta q/q} = -\frac{\Delta P}{\Delta q}\frac{q}{P}$$

2. For other than Giffen goods, η is always negative, holding *money* income constant.

3. The market elasticity of demand is equal to the

---

[11]"Don't Fill'er Up," *The Wall Street Journal*, vol. 184, no. 23, Aug. 23, 1974, p. 1.

[12] $\dfrac{\Delta P}{P} \approx 40$ percent; $\dfrac{\Delta Q}{Q} \approx 8$ percent; $\eta = -\dfrac{\Delta P/P}{\Delta Q/Q}$

$= -\left|\dfrac{0.08}{0.40}\right| = -0.2.$

weighted sum of individual demand elasticities, where the weights are equal to the share of total market demand accounted for by each individual.

4. We can calculate real income elasticity of demand just as we calculated money income elasticity of demand, except now we utilize real income, or money income divided by the price level.

5. The change in the quantity demanded due to a relative price change can be broken up into a substitution and an income effect.

6. The gross, or total, price elasticity of demand is equal to the price elasticity of demand due to the substitution effect minus the weighted real income elasticity of demand where the weight is the percentage of income spent on the commodity. This is called the Slutzky equation and is written as $\eta_t = \bar{\eta}_s - k\iota$.

7. From the Slutzky equation, we see that the income effect always reinforces the substitution effect whenever we are dealing with normal or ultrasuperior goods.

8. The cross-price elasticity of demand is defined as $\eta_{xy} = (\Delta q_x / \Delta P_y)(P_y / q_x)$. When η_{xy} is positive, the goods are substitutes; when it is negative, they are complements.

9. If we wish to compute the arc elasticity, we must use a compromise formula; in one of these we estimate price elasticity at the midpoint of the arc.

10. We can derive the point price elasticity of demand by using the horizontal or the vertical axis formula. In the horizontal axis formula, we draw from the horizontal axis a perpendicular to the point on the demand curve where we wish to measure price elasticity of demand. The ratio of the distance from that line to the intersection of the demand curve on the horizontal axis over the distance from the origin to that line on the horizontal axis is our measure of price elasticity of demand at that point on the demand curve. A similar procedure is used with the vertical axis formula: A line is drawn horizontally from the point on the demand curve to the vertical axis.

11. Price elasticity of demand along the linear demand curve varies from $-\infty$ to 0 as we move from the upper-left extreme of the demand curve down to the lower right where the demand curve terminates on the horizontal axis.

12. It is important to distinguish between the slope of the demand curve and its price elasticity. Since η is equal to the negative value of the reciprocal of the slope of the demand curve times the fraction P/q, the slope does not uniquely determine price elasticity.

13. When comparing any two straight-line demand curves on the same diagram, the one that intersects the vertical axis closer to the origin is the more elastic at each and every price.

14. Producers' revenues are the mirror image of consumers' expenditures.

15. Marginal revenue becomes zero at the quantity where total revenue reaches its maximum.

16. Marginal revenue is always less than price and is given by the formula $\text{MR} = P\left(1 + \dfrac{1}{\eta}\right)$. always negative

17. A vertical line drawn from the point where the marginal revenue curve intersects the horizontal axis will hit the demand curve where $\eta = -1$.

18. When demand is elastic, total revenues change in the opposite direction of a price change. When demand is unitary-elastic, total revenues remain constant when there is a price change. When demand is price-inelastic, total revenues change in the same direction as a price change.

19. Price elasticity of demand depends on (1) the existence and closeness of substitutes, (2) the "importance" of the commodity in total expenditures, and (3) the length of time allowed for adjustment to price changes.

20. Long-run demand curves are more elastic than short-run demand curves.

Selected references

Allen, R. G. D., "The Concept of Arc Elasticity of Demand," *Review of Economic Studies*, vol. 1, June 1934, pp. 226–229.

Baumol, W., *Economic Theory and Operations Analysis* (Englewood Cliffs, N. J.: Prentice-Hall, 1965), pp. 211–214.

Dean, J., "Estimating the Price Elasticity of Demand," in E. Mansfield (ed.), *Managerial Economics and Operations Research*, 3d ed. (New York: Norton, 1975).

Lerner, A. P., "Geometrical Comparisons of Elasticities," *American Economic Review*, vol. 37, March 1947, p. 191.

Marshall, Alfred, *Principles of Economics*, 8th ed. (London: Macmillan, 1920), book 3, chap. 4.

Norris, Ruby T., *The Theory of Consumer's Demand*, rev. ed. (New Haven: Yale University Press, 1952), chap. 9.

Robinson, Joan, *The Economics of Imperfect Competition* (London: Macmillan, 1933), pp. 29–40.

Schultz, Henry, *The Theory and Measurement of Demand* (Chicago: University of Chicago Press, 1938).

Working, E. J., "What Do Statistical 'Demand Curves' Show?" *Quarterly Journal of Economics*, vol. 41, 1927, pp. 212–235; reprinted in American Economic Association, *Readings in Price Theory* (Chicago: Irwin, 1952).

Questions

(Answers to even-numbered questions are at back of text.)

1. Define price elasticity of demand, income elasticity of demand, and cross elasticity of demand.

2. Looking at the formula $\eta = (\Delta q/\Delta P)\ (P/q)$, how can you tell that when the demand curve is a straight line, the price elasticity of demand must be different at every price?

3. Construct on the same graph two straight-line demand curves with the same y intercept, with one flatter than the other. Can you make a general statement about which one is the more elastic demand curve? If so, what is it?

4. Now construct on the same graph two straight-line demand curves with the same x intercept, with one flatter than the other. Answer the same question which was posed in question 3 above.

5. Draw the Seven-Up Bottling Company's demand curve for 1-liter returnable 7-Up bottles. What is its price elasticity of demand?

6. Can any demand curve possibly be perfectly inelastic ($\eta = 0$) regardless of price? Explain.

7. Like the perfectly (infinitely) elastic and perfectly (zero) inelastic demand curves, the *unitary elastic* demand curve is somewhat of a curiosity. Give its equation. What is the geometric name for such a curve? Looking at that equation, why is it impossible for the curve ever to "cut" (intercept) either axis? Suppose you were the only owner in the world of a perishable good, the demand for which was unitary-elastic at all prices. How much would you charge, per unit, if you wanted to make the most money possible?

8. Explain how you would calculate the point elasticity of a nonlinear demand curve at some price p.

9. What is the difficulty inherent in estimating arc elasticity $(\%\ \Delta q)/(\%\ \Delta P)$? How was it suggested that you deal with it?

10. Which of the following cross elasticities of demand would you expect to be positive and which to be negative?
    a. Tennis balls and tennis racquets
    b. Tennis balls and golf balls
    c. Dental services and toothpaste
    d. Dental services and candy
    e. Liquor and ice cubes
    f. Liquor and marijuana

11. For any given relative price, would you think that the demand for canal transportation was more or less elastic in 1840 than in 1880? How about the demand for Pony Express messengers before and after the transcontinental telegraph? The demand for rail transportation before and after the Model T Ford? Before and after the Ford Tri-Motor? The demand for transatlantic cables before and after Telstar? The demand for slide rules before and after introduction of the pocket-sized electronic calculator? Why?

12. A new mobile-home park makes no charge whatsoever for water used by its inhabitants. Consumption is 100,000 gallons per month. Then the decision is made to charge according to how much each mobile-home owner uses, at a rate of $10 per thousand gallons. Consumption declines to 50,000 gallons per month. Try to measure the demand elasticity. Can you?

13. "A harsh winter in Florida, by wiping out much of the orange crop, will certainly decrease the revenues of citrus growers." Is this statement true or false, and why?

14. "The demand curves of wealthy persons are consistently less elastic than those of the less affluent." Is this statement true or false?

15. "The demand for sodium chloride (salt) must be pretty inelastic. Even if the price did change, surely this wouldn't affect the amount people use on hard-boiled eggs, french fries, and the like." Is this statement true or false, and why?

Appendix to Chapter 5

Introduction to econometrics

In Table 5-3 of this chapter, we gave some estimates of the price elasticity of demand for various commodities. It was indicated that an econometric technique called multiple-regression analysis was used to derive the estimates. In this Appendix, we present a brief introduction to the most widely used of such techniques, linear-regression analysis.* The term "linear" has already been used with reference to straight-line demand curves. The term "regression" has its origin in a study done of the relationship between the height of sons and the height of their fathers. Researchers contended that they observed a regressive relationship, and the term stuck. It now is a general term for causal relationships, such as that between quantity demanded and relative price.

The regression equation

The starting point for econometric research is a regression equation model which postulates a causal relationship between a dependent variable and one or more independent variables. A variable is called dependent because it is supposed to be functionally dependent on the other variables. In the classic demand model, the quantity demanded is the dependent variable and price, real income, population, the prices of substitutes and complements, etc., are the independent variables. The regression model attempts to explain observed changes in a dependent variable as caused by changes in the independent variables (or explanatory variables). Conceptually, at least, the changes in the independent variables are observed independently of the causal relation expressed by the model.

The causal relation between the dependent variable (Y) and the independent variables (X_1, X_2, ..., X_N) may be of any implicit functional form. Consider, for example, the relation

$$Y = f(X_1, X_2, \ldots, X_N) \qquad \text{(A5-1)}$$

where $f(\ )$ is any implicit functional form. If we are dealing with a demand function, we would let $Y =$ quantity demanded, $X_1 =$ relative price, and so on.

If we wish to find an estimate of the functional form which might give us, for example, the price elasticity of demand, the income elasticity of demand, and so on, then we must specify what the functional form is. In other words, $f(\ )$ has to be made into an explicit function; it cannot be left implicit.

The linear function form

An explicit functional form widely used to express the causal relationship between a dependent variable and an independent variable is the linear form. Even in the relationship is not linear, when the relevant range of operation is small, the linear form may adequately represent the true functional form. The linear relationship between the dependent and independent variables may be expressed as

$$Y = \beta_1 X_1 + \beta_2 X_2 + \cdots + \beta_N X_N + \Psi \qquad \text{(A5-2)}$$

where Ψ is the error due to the linear approximation of some other implicit functional form.

---

*This appendix is adapted from Chapter 1 in Potluri Rao and Roger LeRoy Miller, *Applied Econometrics* (Belmont, Calif.: Wadsworth Publishing Company, 1971).

When the true relationship is linear, then of course the error term Ψ is zero. The β's are the parameters of the function. They are what we will want to estimate and what ultimately allows us to give an estimate of an important parameter, such as the price elasticity of demand.

When the list of X's exhausts the sources of variation in Y, then all observed sets of (Y,X) satisfy the relationship in Eq. (A5-2). When there are several observations, distinguished by t, we may rewrite Eq. (A5-2) as

$$Y_t = \beta_1 X_{1t} + \beta_2 X_{2t} + \cdots + \beta_N X_{Nt} + \Psi_t \quad \text{(A5-3)}$$

Keeping the same example, the t's could refer to years. We might have observations on quantities demanded, prices, and income from 1950 through 1977 for a specific commodity, say, movies.

In a real life situation, Eq. (A5-3) is not strictly true. Because of the randomness of the observed phenomena, even when we completely control all independent variables and the functional form, we still observe some "unaccounted for" variation in the dependent variable. All biological and natural data exhibit this characteristic. Some of it is inherent in the phenomenon, and some of it is due to errors in measurement. After all, it is usually impossible to measure exactly the number of movies that people purchased in each year over the last $2\frac{1}{2}$ decades; and sometimes it is extremely difficult to even approximate some of the variables necessary to complete our regression study.

If the random variation in the dependent variable has no systematic explanation or reason, it is generally called "pure noise" and is denoted as η. (This η has nothing to do with the η used in the chapter to denote price elasticity of demand.) Thus, all real world situations, Eq. (A5-3) may be expressed as

$$Y_t = \beta_1 X_{1t} + \beta_2 X_{2t} + \cdots + \beta_N X_{Nt} + \Psi_t + \eta_t \quad \text{(A5-4)}$$

Equation (A5-4) specifies the causal relationship between the dependent variable and all *conceivable* variables that could have caused a change in it. The list that we might think up for all conceivable variables that could have caused a change in the quantity demanded of, say, movies per year is certainly very long. In a practical situation, however, not all such variables are observable or quantifiable or important. In empirical research, only the measured independent variables may be used in estimating a causal relationship. For example, let us make it easy and suppose that we have data only on the price of movies and the income of the population, X_1 and X_2. There is no information on X_3 through X_N. Equation (A5-4) expressed in terms of the two measured variables alone may be written as

$$Y_t = \beta_1 X_{1t} + \beta_2 X_{2t} + Z_t + \Psi_t + \eta_t \quad \text{(A5-5)}$$

where Z stands for the combined influence of all the nonmeasurable variables. The value of Z depends on the values of X_3 to X_N; and a change in the values of these variables results in a change in Z.

For convenience of presentation, we may express the variable Z and the error of approximation Ψ as deviations from their respective means and rewrite Eq. (A5-5) as

$$Y_t = \beta_1 X_{1t} + \beta_2 X_{2t} + (\overline{Z} + z_t) + (\overline{\Psi} + \psi_t) + \eta_t \quad \text{(A5-6)}$$

with
$$Z_t = \overline{Z} + z_t \quad \text{(A5-7)}$$

and
$$\Psi_t = \overline{\Psi} + \psi_t \quad \text{(A5-8)}$$

In this case, z and ψ are deviations of Z and Ψ from their respective means. Since the pure noise term η does not have any systematic fluctuations, its mean is 0. By rearrangement of terms we may write Eq. (A5-6) as

$$Y_t = \beta_0 + \beta_1 X_{1t} + \beta_2 X_{2t} + \epsilon_t \quad \text{(A5-9)}$$

where
$$\beta_0 = \overline{Z} + \overline{\Psi}$$

and
$$\epsilon_t = z_t + \psi_t + \eta_t \quad \text{(A5-10)}$$

Equation (A5-9) is what has come to be called the standard linear regression equation with two independent variables. The β's are the regression parameters and the ϵ's are the so-called error terms.

In applied econometrics, the researcher has data on the dependent and independent variables and wants to find the values of the parameters (β's). When no errors are present (that is, when ε's are 0), then of course, the problem of finding the values of parameters is easy. For example, to find the values of the parameters (β's) in Eq. (A5-9) when ε's are 0, the researcher needs only three observations. Since all these satisfy Eq. (5-9), he or she has three linear equations in three unknowns (β's). By solving these three equations for the three unknowns, the values of the β's can be obtained. But the case is rarely so simple in econometrics because error terms are always present. Since the values of these error terms are generally unknown, we have to look for alternative ways of solving for the unknowns (β's). An exact mathematical solution is unattainable, and any values of the parameters that are obtained from statistical estimation procedures depend on the sample data; therefore, we shall refer to the values of the parameters obtained from any data as estimates of the parameters.

What is the best procedure for obtaining these estimates? This is a difficult question, and its answer depends on what the researcher wants to do with the estimates of the parameters. There are three major reasons why a researcher may be interested in obtaining the values of the parameters of Eq. (A5-9): (1) to verify empirically a theoretical proposition; (2) to make a decision upon which profits and losses will depend; and (3) to predict values of a specified variable for planning purposes. His or her primary objective will dictate the best way of estimating the parameters and the estimate will depend on how the error terms are distributed. If the researcher can specify, at least in some minimum way, the nature of the behavior of the error terms in Eq. (A5-9), then he or she can derive the best method of estimating the parameters according to a given criterion. The subject of econometrics deals, *inter alia,* with these decisions.

A simple case of estimation

Look at Figure A5-1. Here we have shown a typical price-quantity quadrant. We have also put in a bunch of dots that represent hypothetical observations on the prices and quantities demanded of

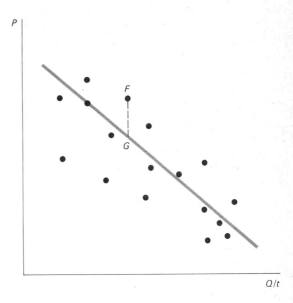

a particular commodity. The equation we wish to estimate from these observations is

$$Q_t^d = \beta_0 + \beta_1 P_t + \epsilon_t \qquad \text{(A5-11)}$$

The most popular technique used is to fit a line through the dots in Figure A5-1 so that the sum of the squares of the distances from the observed points to the fitted line is minimized. Take point F in Figure A5-1, for example. If we drop a line perpendicular to the horizontal axis, we get the distance F to G. This represents the difference between the fitted or estimated line and the actual observation or what happened in the real world. This is the error term from the estimated equation. The technique used to fit that equation is called least squares, where we square the error terms (such as the distance between F and G) for all observations, sum them up, and minimize that sum when we fit the line.

Problems in estimation

We have already given a hint as to some of the problems encountered in estimatiing causal relationships. There are sometimes immense data problems; it is difficult to get good data on the variables necessary to estimate the correct relationship. There are problems of not specifying the function correctly. Here in our example above, we used a linear demand function. But what if it is not linear? If we are too far off, the estimates of price elasticity of demand, for example, may be seriously biased. There is also another problem which has to do with the simultaneous nature of most of the relationships that we observe. It may be true that the quantity demanded is a function of price; but so, too, is the quantity supplied. Those dots in Figure A5-1, therefore, represent the simultaneous workings of *both* supply and demand. If we estimate what we think to be a demand relationship from the observations given in Figure A5-1, how can we be certain that we are not getting things confused with the supply function? This is sometimes called the identification problem in econometrics, where we have difficulty in identifying which causal relationship we are actually estimating.

In spite of the problems inherent in econometric research, it offers one of the few avenues of possible empirical refutation of our economic theories. Accordingly, the interest in econometric work continues to grow, techniques get more sophisticated, and some of the problems mentioned above are lending themselves to better and more precise solutions.

6

TIME, RISK, SPECULATION, AND HEDGING

Time duration is a scarce economic resource; it has a positive economic value. Up until now we have ignored time in our analysis. We have not considered (1) that there is a **time cost** involved in the purchase and consumption of goods; and (2) that consumers place different values on the consumption of items at different points in time.

We have also ignored, to a large extent, uncertainty. In so doing, we have left out the crucial fact that decision makers will pay for increased certainty and also for reduction in risk. Thus, we have left out the markets dealing in risk reduction, where some individuals are able to pay others to take on risk.

In this chapter, we will extend our basic analysis to include the economics of time, the economics of time preference, markets dealing with risk, and especially the markets dealing with the *current* buying and selling of *future* rights to commodities.

The economics of time

Clearly, time is required for work effort. There is a time constraint imposed on each individual. We showed that in our analysis of the labor-leisure choice (pages 69–73). However, consider the fact that the consumption of commodities requires time too. A haircut is not purchased and consumed instantaneously. The purchase of the haircut involves the explicit monetary cost plus the time involved waiting to be serviced plus the time consumed sitting in the barber's chair. The consumption of a meal includes the time involved in sitting at the table while the meal is being eaten. A vacation trip, which uses up time, by definition has a time cost. Hence, the cost of a trip is not merely the monetary outlay—the reduction in wealth available for other consumption activities—but also the value placed on the reduction in time available to engage in other activities.

In this context, rather than separate the notions of consumption and production, we can consider the cost of all facets of the process of satisfying human wants. Thus, the production of a meal will require all the inputs, including groceries, fuel, shopping time, preparation time, and so forth, as well as the time required to eat the meal.

Total cost of consumption

When viewed in this fashion, the total price of consuming any good is the sum of its market price and the opportunity cost of the time required to consume the good, where opportunity cost is the value of that time in its best alternative use.

Market price (explicit cost)	Opportunity cost (implicit cost)

Total cost of consumption

Thus, it is possible to say that the total price of consuming a product selling for a fixed monetary price varies with the opportunity cost of the individual consuming the product. Hence, a 15-minute haircut that "costs" $4 is more expensive to an individual whose opportunity cost of time is higher than it is to some other individual. This example leads to an interesting hypothesis.

If we include in the time cost of haircuts the cost of waiting to be serviced by a barber, an increase in the relative money cost of a haircut will lead to a decrease in the total cost of consumption for certain individuals. How can that be? If the price elasticity of demand for haircuts is sufficiently high in numerical value, then an increase in the relative money price of haircuts will reduce significantly the quantity demanded at a given barber shop. Some people just won't get haircuts, or not as often. The amount of time one must wait for a barber will therefore fall. Thus, the relatively more highly paid individual whose opportunity cost of time (by definition) is higher may find that the total cost of a haircut has fallen, even though he or she must now pay a higher money price.

Using this approach, we can explain, at least in part, much of the behavior of certain (income) groups of individuals who are willing to spend relatively larger amounts of time to consume particular goods. Teenagers, by and large, are more willing than are adults to wait in line for tickets to sporting events. This follows from the law of demand. At a lower price, a larger quantity will be demanded. The price to teenagers of purchasing a ticket to an important sporting event plus watching the sporting event will be lower than to an adult who typically has a higher opportunity cost of time. Hence, most teenagers will demand a larger quantity of the product than will most adults.

Similarly, there is a fairly obvious negative correlation or relationship between the salaries of married people who work and the number of children they choose to have. If we consider children as a consumption item, then the demand for children should be inversely related to the relative price. But the relative price of children includes the time necessary to take care of them. The more a person earns in the marketplace, the higher this opportunity cost; hence, the higher the total cost or price of a child and the fewer children demanded.

Lastly, using this approach, we can point out what might occur as real wages rise. As after-tax wages increase, the time cost of consuming all items goes up in proportion to that increase in wages. However, for those goods for which time cost represents a larger fraction of total costs, their (total) relative price will rise as wages rise. Hence, we predict that the consumption of these time-intensive goods—those that require relatively large amounts of time to consume—will fall, *ceteris paribus*, with a rise in the wage rate. Strictly speaking, of course, for such a prediction to prove correct for these reasons for normal or ultrasuperior goods, the income effect must be outweighed by the substitution effect.

Computing the time elasticity of demand

We can combine the time constraint with the budget constraint to derive the elasticity of demand with respect to time. First we must consider the usual budget constraint

$$P_x x + P_y y = M \qquad (6\text{-}1)$$

which is equal to Eq. (2-2) from Chapter 2. Now we add the time constraint

$$t_x x + t_y y = T \qquad (6\text{-}2)$$

where t_x = time cost per unit of good x
t_y = time cost per unit of good y
T = total time devoted to the consumption of x and y

Since time can be converted into income, we can combine the two constraints, Eqs. (6-1) and (6-2), into one. After all, a consumer can engage in household activities that use time but reduce the need to earn income. In other words, time can be used to clean the house rather than hire a housekeeper. Also, the consumer can reduce the time in consumption and use this time for income-earning activities in the job market.

We make the assumption that on the margin, the opportunity cost of an hour used for consumption activities is equal to the hourly wage rate w. In other words, we assume that every hour used in the process of consumption could have been used in an income-earning activity in the job market at the going after-tax wage rate w. Thus, time cost of consumption will be equal to the number of hours used in consumption times the wage rate. If we let T_c equal the total number of hours used in all consumption, then consumption time is worth $(w \cdot T_c) = w(t_x x + t_y y)$ from Eq. (6-2). We have here a dollar estimate. Now we can add Eqs. (6-1) and (6-2) to obtain

$$(P_x x + P_y y) + w(t_x x + t_y y) = M + wT_c \quad (6\text{-}3)$$

or

$$(P_x + wt_x)x + (P_y + wt_y)y = M + wT_c$$

The total unit price for good x, for example, is equal to $P_x + wt_x$, since this is the money price plus the monetary value of the time required to consume it. Equation (6-3) tells us that the effective price of x times the quantity of x plus the effective price of y times the quantity of y cannot exceed money income plus the monetary value of the total number of hours spent in consumption. In other words, we now have a time and money budget constraint.

We can now present the elasticity of demand with respect to the money price of a product and the elasticity of demand with respect to the time price. We define them in the normal way:

$$\eta_{MP} = \frac{\Delta q/q}{\Delta P/P} = \frac{\Delta q}{\Delta P} \cdot \frac{P}{q} \qquad (6\text{-}4)$$

$$\eta_{\text{time}} = \frac{\Delta q/q}{\Delta wt/wt} = \frac{\Delta q}{\Delta wt} \cdot \frac{wt}{q} \qquad (6\text{-}5)$$

where η_{MP} is the normal price elasticity of demand and η_{time} is the time price elasticity of demand. We can simplify Eq. (6-5). If we assume that the wage rate w is constant,

$\Delta wt = w \Delta t$; and

$$\eta_{time} = \frac{\Delta q}{w \Delta t} \cdot \frac{wt}{q} \qquad (6\text{-}6)$$

But the w's cancel out so that

$$\eta_{time} = \frac{\Delta q}{\Delta t} \cdot \frac{t}{q} \qquad (6\text{-}7)$$

There has been very little work done in estimating real world time elasticities of demand. Undoubtedly, however, there will be an increased interest in such work as the time element of consumption becomes more important as a result of higher real incomes and, hence, higher time opportunity costs. We might surmise, for example, that the present successes of fast-food chains in countries that in the past scorned American hamburger stands is in part due to the rising opportunity cost of time (the wage rate) in those countries. This has been particularly evident in France.

Now that we have dealt with the time cost of consumption in our analysis, we can turn to time preference, or choosing between consuming now and consuming later.

Time preference

When we started our formal analysis, the choice confronting the consumer was between two goods, movies and concerts, or more abstractly, between commodity x and commodity y. The two goods were to be consumed "today." It was a choice of concurrent consumption of either one of the goods or a combination of the two. We carried out that analysis using indifference curves.

Similarly, we can consider consumers making choices today between consuming commodities "today" and consuming them "tomorrow." Clearly, it is possible to forego spending some of one's income today in order to be able to spend it tomorrow or the next day. Moreover, it is possible for individuals to borrow in order to consume today and to repay tomorrow, thereby reducing tomorrow's consumption. Thus we see that there is a choice between consumption today and consumption tomorrow. This is generally called the **theory of time preference**. How much does the individual prefer current consumption to future consumption? There is a market which deals with time preference. It is the credit market which permits individuals to satisfy their time preferences.

Indifference curve analysis

In order to obtain consumer equilibrium with respect to the two commodities, present goods and future goods, we have to deal with the budget constraint facing the consumer and the consumer's preferences. In order to derive a budget constraint, we have to introduce a special price. This special price is the price of time preference and, more specifically, is the **interest rate** r which we will define as the rate of exchange between goods today and goods tomorrow. We can derive the interest rate by looking at the market for credit.

DERIVING THE INTEREST RATE. One way to view the credit market is to consider it a market in which persons are exchanging present and future consumption. In other words, the *suppliers* of credit are willing to trade present consumption (command over current purchasing power) for the promise of higher future consumption. On the other hand, *demanders* of credit are willing to exchange claims to future consumption for present consumption.

In Figure 6-1, we show a simple supply and demand model for the credit market. The intersection of the supply curve with the demand curve determines the market rate of interest. In this example, we assume that we live in a world of no expectation of future inflation. It would be relatively simple to take account of inflation by adding on an inflationary factor to the interest rate r in our model, but we choose

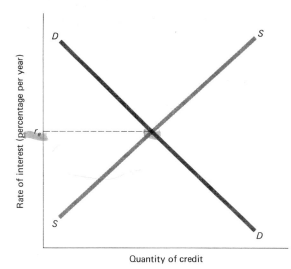

Figure 6-1: Determination of the interest rate.
The credit market is essentially a market in which debtors purchase the rights to current consumption and creditors sell these rights in expectation of higher future consumption. The demand curve DD slopes down; the supply curve SS slopes up. The intersection yields a market rate of interest r_e. In this model we assume no expectation of future inflation.

not to do so in order to keep the analysis less complicated.

The budget constraint

We assume that the consumer is a very small part of the entire credit market, and therefore the consumer can either borrow or lend at the prevailing market rate of interest. The market rate of interest gives us the price of future consumption and the return for *not* consuming today. If the market rate of interest is 10 percent, an individual can save (not consume), say, $100 today and have $110 one year from now. Assuming no inflation, the consumer can purchase $110 worth of consumption a year from now, or 10 percent more, by waiting 1 year rather than consuming the $100 today. Otherwise stated, with a market interest rate of 10 percent, a commodity which costs $110 can be purchased a year from now by setting

aside $100 today. Assuming that all income is received at the *start* of each period, we have numerically

$$(1 + 0.10)\ \$100 = \$110 \qquad (6\text{-}8)$$

Looked at another way, if the consumer's income is $100 in period 1 and $0 in period 2, the consumer can save all $100 in period 1 and have a wealth position of $110 in period 2.

Let's reverse the situation. Let's assume that the individual makes no income in period 1 and is certain of making $110 in period 2. A bank may decide to use the certain $110 (to be earned in period 2) as collateral for a $100 loan to this individual and charge an interest rate of 10 percent. At the beginning of period 2, the principal of $100 plus $10 interest must be paid.

In these two extreme examples, the individual can consume in the period in which income is not received.

A general formula can be developed from this analysis to give us the budget constraint that the individual has over the two periods. In period 1, the individual can consume everything earned in period 1 plus the amount that can be borrowed on the basis of income that is expected to be earned in period 2. If we let M_1 equal the income in period 1 and M_2 equal the income in period 2 and call r the interest rate, then our formula for the maximum amount of consumption in period 1 will be

$$M_1 + \frac{M_2}{1 + r} = \text{maximum period 1 consumption} \qquad (6\text{-}9)$$

In the last example, M_1 was zero, M_2 was $110, and the interest rate was 10 percent. Thus, the equation would become

$$0 + \$110/1.10 = \$100 \qquad (6\text{-}10)$$

Now, what about the budget constraint for period 2? The maximum consumable in period 2 is clearly the total amount of money income in period 2 plus the amount of money income made in period 1 plus the interest earned from saving that, or

$$M_2 + M_1(1 + r) = \text{maximum period} \atop \text{2 consumption} \qquad (6\text{-}11)$$

We now have two extreme points from which we may construct the budget constraint. This is done in Figure 6-2. The budget constraint is BB'. Just as the slope of the budget constraint for two commodities purchased concurrently and consumed today was the negative of the ratio of their prices, the same is true in this case. However, the marginal rate of market substitution (MRMS) between one commodity, goods today, and another commodity, goods tomorrow, is 1 plus the interest rate, or $1 + r$. Thus the slope of BB' is $-(1 + r)$. That is the feasible or market rate at which individuals can substitute present consumption into future consumption, or future consumption into present con-

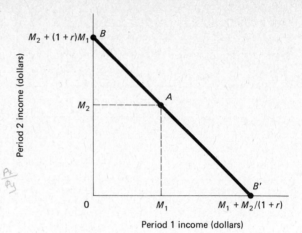

Figure 6-3: The slope of the budget constraint.
For point $A(M_1, M_2)$, the slope will equal $-M_2B/M_2A$. If we substitute the values for B and A, then we obtain a formula for slope which is equal to

$$\text{Slope} = -\frac{M_2 + (1 + r)M_1 - M_2}{M_1}$$

which, upon simplification, becomes $-(1 + r)$.

sumption. We can better see how we derive the slope of the budget constraint BB' by considering Figure 6-3. We take an arbitrary point labeled A which is for income in period 1 of M_1 and income in period 2 of M_2. The slope at that point will equal the negative of the vertical distance between M_2 and point B divided by the horizontal distance between M_2 and point A, or slope $= -M_2B/M_2A$. But we have given the exact value at point B. It is equal to $M_2 + (1 + r) M_1$. So the distance between M_2 and B is equal to $M_2 + (1 + r)M_1 - M_2$. Moreover, the horizontal distance between M_2 and A is merely income in period 1, M_1. Thus, our formula becomes

$$\text{Slope} = -\frac{M_2 + (1 + r) M_1 - M_2}{M_1}$$

$$= -\frac{(1 + r) M_1}{M_1}$$

$$= -(1 + r)$$

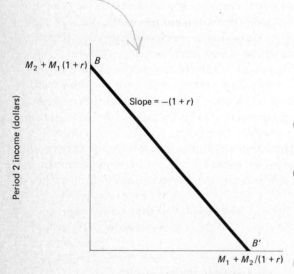

Figure 6-2: The time preference budget constraint.
If all income is consumed in period 1, total consumption is equal to $M_1 + M_2/(1 + r)$. If, on the other hand, all income is saved in period 1, total income available in period 2 is $M_2 + M_1(1 + r)$, or period 2 income plus income from period 1 plus accrued interest from the saving during period 1. This gives us two points for our budget constraint. The resultant budget line is labeled BB'. Its slope is equal to $-(1 + r)$.

The individual time preference mapping

Now that we have dealt with the budget constraint, let us try to understand the individual's (subjective) marginal valuation of goods today compared with goods tomorrow. In other words, we wish to come up with an indication of the time preference of an individual.

First of all, assume that present consumption is generally preferred to future consumption, *ceteris paribus.* If I am offered a commodity, say, a book, with a choice of either having it today or having it next year, assuming there are no storage or insurance costs, I generally will prefer to possess the book today, if merely for the reason that I have the option of using it over the next year. That option is not available if I have to wait until next year to get the book. Thus, if the book is offered to me today or next year, I generally will be willing to pay a higher price for immediate possession rather than to wait a year. This is, of course, the analogue of why individuals generally must be rewarded by a market interest rate in order to induce them to save. Saving is nonconsumption in the current period. If someone else wishes to obtain current command over resources that I presently own, I cannot be induced voluntarily to give up that command unless I am rewarded. That reward will be the interest received.

Assuming that present consumption is preferred to future consumption, *ceteris paribus,* we can define an individual's personal valuation of consumption today compared with consumption tomorrow. This is called an individual's **personal rate of discount**, and it is defined as follows:

$$\text{Personal rate of discount} = \left(\begin{array}{c} \text{value an individual} \\ \text{places on this year's} \\ \text{goods in terms of the} \\ \text{foregone goods of} \\ \text{next year} \end{array} \right) - 1 \quad (6\text{-}12)$$

Another way we can express the individual's personal rate of discount is by considering his or her marginal rate of substitution between consumption in period 1 and consumption in period 2. The rate at which the individual is willing to give up some of this year's consumption C_1 to get more of next year's consumption C_2 is $MRS_{1:2} = \Delta C_2 / \Delta C_1$. Equation (6-12) can now be restated as

$$\text{Personal rate of discount} = \frac{\Delta C_2}{\Delta C_1} - 1 \quad (6\text{-}13)$$

This definition can be best understood by an example. An individual enjoys drinking 7-Up. The individual is offered a choice: 100 7-Ups this year or 110 7-Ups next year. Assume that the individual is indifferent. If so, the individual's personal valuation of this year's 7-Ups, in terms of next year's, is 110/100, or 1.1. He or she values today's 7-Up at 1.1 7-Ups of 1 year hence. Thus, this individual's personal rate of discount is $(1.1 - 1)$ per year, or 10 percent per year. We will label the individual's personal rate of discount with the Greek letter *rho* (ρ).

It is the individual's personal rate of discount that determines the shape of the indifference curve between consumption today and consumption next year. We have drawn a typical indifference curve, I, in Figure 6-4. Here the two goods in question are consumption in period 1, C_1, and consumption in period 2, C_2. At any point along the indifference curve I, the slope, as measured by the slope of the tangent to that point, represents the marginal (subjective) rate of substitution between future and present consumption, $MRS_{1:2}$. Remember that $MRS_{1:2} = \Delta C_2 / \Delta C_1$. Using Eq. (6-13), $\rho = (\Delta C_2 / \Delta C_1) - 1$. Then, $\Delta C_2 / \Delta C_1 = 1 + \rho$. But because the indifference curve has a negative slope, $\Delta C_2 / \Delta C_1 = -(1 + \rho)$. Therefore, the slope of the indifference curve I in Figure 6-4 is $-(1 + \rho)$. We have drawn the indifference curve convex to the origin, reflecting diminishing marginal valuation of present consumption in terms of future consumption.

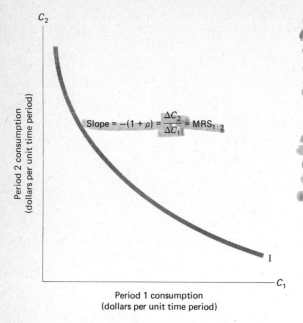

$$\text{Slope} = -(1 + \rho) = \frac{\Delta C_2}{\Delta C_1} = \text{MRS}_{1:2}$$

Figure 6-4: The individual's personal time preference.
If the individual values current consumption over future consumption, then the indifference curve between consumption today and consumption tomorrow will be convex to the origin. This follows from diminishing marginal rate of valuation between the two commodities—consumption today and consumption tomorrow. The individual's personal discount rate is *rho* (ρ). Therefore, the slope at any point on the indifference curve is equal to the negative of $1 + \rho$, or $-(1 + \rho)$.

Consumer optimum

We can put together the indifference curve in Figure 6-4 with the budget constraint in Figure 6-2 to find out where consumer optimum will be. This is done in Figure 6-5. The budget constraint is BB', and the highest indifference curve attainable is indifference curve I. It is tangent to the budget constraint at point E. Thus, consumer optimum dictates period 1 consumption of C_1 and period 2 consumption of C_2. Note that the horizontal axis depicts period 1 income, consumption, and **saving** (or borrowing, for that matter, because borrowing means present consumption). In fact, we see that with hypothetical income levels of M_1 in period 1 and M_2 in period 2,

there will be saving equal to the distance between M_1 and C_1. In period 2, income is M_2, but consumption is greater because of the saving in the first period and the interest earned. The distance between M_2 and C_2 represents that principal ($M_1 - C_1$) plus interest.

At the individual point of consumer optimum, point E, the rate at which the individual *can* save or borrow (the marginal rate of market substitution, or MRMS) is equal to the rate at which the individual *wants* to save or borrow (marginal rate of substitution, or MRS). In other words, at point E there is

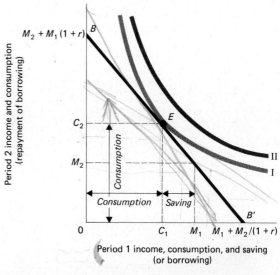

Figure 6-5: Consumption optimum between two periods.
The horizontal axis measures income, consumption, and saving or borrowing during period 1. The vertical axis measures income, consumption, and saving or borrowing during period 2. A consumption optimum between the two periods will occur when the marginal rate of substitution between consumption today and consumption tomorrow ($\text{MRS}_{1:2}$) equals the marginal rate of market substitution (MRMS) between the two. The latter is given by the slope of the budget line and the former by the slope of the indifference curve. In this figure, the optimum occurs at the tangency point E. Assume that income is M_1 in period 1. The optimum consumption rate is C_1; saving will be equal to the difference $M_1 - C_1$. Assume income is M_2 in period 2: consumption will be C_2, and the difference $C_2 - M_2$ will be equal to $M_1 - C_1$ plus the interest accrued.

consumer optimum, the slope of the budget line being equal to the slope of the indifference curve, or

$$-(1+r) = -(1+\rho) \qquad (6\text{-}14)$$

Thus, a consumption optimum requires that $r = \rho$; the market rate of interest must equal the personal rate of discount. We should note that, psychologically, nothing precludes a negative personal rate of discount. That is, some individuals might be willing to pay someone else to save for them or to make them save. After all, individuals do join Christmas clubs, which impose a penalty (interest is withheld) if they make withdrawals before December. Additionally, on many of these Christmas club accounts, no interest whatsoever is paid. We also observe individuals putting away their savings at a $5\frac{1}{2}$ percent rate of interest in a savings account, while the rate of inflation is greater than $5\frac{1}{2}$ percent. This gives them *less* rather than more purchasing power at the end of their saving period. What we observe then is a demand to consume tomorrow—that is, a demand for saving outlets—and banks provide "safe" storage of wealth that can be consumed in the future. On average, however, individuals usually demand positive rates of interest in order to get them to give up present consumption.

Discounting and present value

In our analysis of time preference, we employed the notion of a personal rate of discount. We also *implicitly* used it with the present value of the sum of future purchasing power. The two are intimately related. In the example where the individual is indifferent between 100 bottles of 7-Up this year and 110 bottles next year, the personal rate of discount was calculated to be 10 percent per year. The **present value** of 110 bottles of 7-Up 1 year hence, given the personal rate of discount of 10 percent, is 100 bottles.

Think now of the present value of money in terms of a market rate of interest. What is the present value of $110 to be received 1 year from now? That depends on the market rate of interest. If the market rate of interest is 5 percent, we can figure out the present value by answering the question, How much money must I put aside today in a bank, for example, at a market rate of interest that will give me $110 1 year from now? Or

$$(1 + 0.05)P_1 = \$110 \qquad (6\text{-}15)$$

where P_1 is the sum I must set aside now. Solving this, we get

$$P_1 = \frac{\$110}{1.05} = \$104.76 \qquad (6\text{-}16)$$

That is to say, $104.76 will accumulate to $110 at the end of 1 year with a market rate of interest of 5 percent. Thus, the present value of $110 1 year from now, using a rate of interest of 5 percent, is $104.76. The formula for present value thus becomes

$$P_1 = \frac{A}{1+r} \qquad (6\text{-}17)$$

where P_1 = present value for a sum 1 year hence

A = future sum of money paid or received 1 year hence

r = market rate of interest

Present values for more distant periods

The present-value formula for figuring out today's worth of dollars to be received at a future date can now be easily seen. How much would have to be put in a savings account today if the account pays a rate of 5 percent per year, compounded annually, to have $110 two years from now? After 1 year, the sum that would have to be set aside, P_2, would have grown to $P_2 (\$1.05)$. This amount during the *second* year would increase to $[P_2 (\$1.05)]\$1.05$ or to $P_2 (\$1.05)^2$. To find the P_2 that would grow to $110 over 2 years, set

$$P_2 \,(\$1.05)^2 = \$110 \qquad (6\text{-}18)$$

and solve for P_2

$$P_2 = \frac{\$110}{(1.05)^2} \quad \text{or} \quad P_2 = \$99.77 \qquad (6\text{-}19)$$

Thus the present value of $110 to be paid or received 2 years hence discounted at an interest rate of 5 percent per year compounded annually is equal to $99.77. In other words, $99.77 put into a savings account yielding 5 percent per annum compound interest would accumulate to $110 in 2 years.

The general formula for discounting becomes

$$P_t = \frac{A}{(1+r)^t} \qquad (6\text{-}20)$$

where the exponent t refers to the number of years in the future the money is to be paid or received. Table 6-1 gives the present value of $1 to be received t years hence for various interest rates. These interest rates which were

Year	3%	4%	5%	6%	8%	10%	20%	Year
1	.971	.962	.952	.943	.926	.909	.833	1
2	.943	.925	.907	.890	.857	.826	.694	2
3	.915	.890	.864	.839	.794	.751	.578	3
4	.889	.855	.823	.792	.735	.683	.482	4
5	.863	.823	.784	.747	.681	.620	.402	5
6	.838	.790	.746	.705	.630	.564	.335	6
7	.813	.760	.711	.665	.583	.513	.279	7
8	.789	.731	.677	.627	.540	.466	.233	8
9	.766	.703	.645	.591	.500	.424	.194	9
10	.744	.676	.614	.558	.463	.385	.162	10
11	.722	.650	.585	.526	.429	.350	.134	11
12	.701	.625	.557	.497	.397	.318	.112	12
13	.681	.601	.530	.468	.368	.289	.0935	13
14	.661	.577	.505	.442	.340	.263	.0779	14
15	.642	.555	.481	.417	.315	.239	.0649	15
16	.623	.534	.458	.393	.292	.217	.0541	16
17	.605	.513	.436	.371	.270	.197	.0451	17
18	.587	.494	.416	.350	.250	.179	.0376	18
19	.570	.475	.396	.330	.232	.163	.0313	19
20	.554	.456	.377	.311	.215	.148	.0261	20
25	.478	.375	.295	.232	.146	.0923	.0105	25
30	.412	.308	.231	.174	.0994	.0573	.00421	30
40	.307	.208	.142	.0972	.0460	.0221	.000680	40
50	.228	.141	.087	.0543	.0213	.00852	.000109	50

Table 6-1: Present value table: Present values of a future dollar. Each column shows how much a dollar received at the end of a certain number of years in the future (identified on the extreme left-hand or right-hand column) is worth today. For example, at 5 percent a year, a dollar to be received 20 years in the future is only worth 37.7¢. At the end of 50 years, it isn't even worth a dime today. To find out how much $10,000 would be worth a certain number of years from now, just multiply the figures in the columns by 10,000. For example, $10,000 received at the end of 10 years discounted at a 5 percent rate of interest would have a present value of $6,140.

used to derive the present value are sometimes called the rate of discount, or the **discount rate**. We have specified the rate of discount in our examples as the market rate of interest available on savings. (That particular rate may not always be appropriate.) We note two important conclusions: (1) *The farther in the future a sum of money is to be paid or received, the lower is its present value for any given discount rate.* (2) *The higher the interest rate used, the lower is the present value of any given sum of money to be spent or received at a particular future time.*

The present value of an annuity (a sequence of periodic future amounts)

We can use the above formula for present value to derive the present value (also called capitalized value and discounted value) of an expected future stream of monies. For example, in the simplest case, we might want to know the present or capitalized value of an **annuity** of $1 per year for 20 years. We are looking at a stream of payments in the future. What we want to obtain is that amount of

money that must be set aside today at a specified interest rate so that the payments will flow at the intervals and for the period required, just exhausting the original "account" with the last payment. To find this amount, i.e., present value, we have to discount each dollar for each year it is to be received in the future. This would be done using the following formula, where A_1 would be a dollar to be received at the end of year 1, A_2 a dollar to be received at the end of year 2, and A_{20} a dollar to be received at the end of year 20:

$$P_{20} = \frac{A_1}{(1+r)} + \frac{A_2}{(1+r)^2} + \frac{A_3}{(1+r)^3} + \cdots + \frac{A_{20}}{(1+r)^{20}} \tag{6-21}$$

The formula in Eq. (6-20) is usually called a **capital value** formula rather than a present value formula to indicate the computation of the current price of the rights to a series of receipts (or obligation of a series of costs) in the future.

When the stream of receipts or costs is to last forever, or to infinity, Eq. (6-21) becomes simplified to[1]

---

[1] The proof goes as follows:
Let $S = 1 + R + R^2 + \ldots + R^t$, where R is any number. Multiply by R to obtain

(a) $R \cdot S = R + R^2 + R^3 + \cdots + R^t + R^{t+1}$

Now subtract this last equation from the first equation:

(b) $S - RS = 1 - R^{t+1}$

which becomes

(c) $S(1 - R) = 1 - R^{t+1}$

or

(d) $S = \dfrac{1}{1-R} - \dfrac{R^{t+1}}{1-R}$

If R is less than 1, as t approaches infinity (∞) the numerator in the last term approaches 0 and so does the entire term; and $S = 1/(1-R)$.

Now let $R = 1/(1+r)$, where r is less than 1. Assume A_1 to A_t are all equal and $t = \infty$. Then

(e) $P = \dfrac{A}{1+r} + \dfrac{A}{(1+r)^2} + \cdots + \dfrac{A}{(1+r)^\infty}$

If we add and subtract A on the right-hand side, Eq.

(e) becomes

(f) $P = -A + A + \dfrac{A}{1+r} + \dfrac{A}{(1+r)^2} + \cdots + \dfrac{A}{(1+r)^\infty}$

Factoring out an A,

(g) $P = -A + A\left[1 + \dfrac{1}{1+r} + \left(\dfrac{1}{1+r}\right)^2 + \cdots + \left(\dfrac{1}{1+r}\right)^\infty\right]$

But the expression in brackets is equal to

(h) $\dfrac{1}{1-R} = \dfrac{1}{1-\{[1/(1+r)]\}}$

so that

(i) $P = -A + A\left\{\dfrac{1}{1-[1/(1+r)]}\right\}$

$= -A + \dfrac{A}{r/(1+r)}$

$= -A + \dfrac{A}{r} + \dfrac{Ar}{r} = -A + \dfrac{A}{r} + A = \dfrac{A}{r}$

$$P = \frac{A}{r} \qquad (6\text{-}22)$$

where A in this case represents the sum to be received or spent once per year, in perpetuity. For the formula to be correct, that annual sum must be a fixed one. This formula is a good approximation of present value at higher interest rates for periods greater than 20 years. Look at Table 6-2. There we show the present capitalized value of an annuity of $1 that is received at the *end* of each year. Take a relatively high rate of interest, say 20 percent. The present value becomes indistinguishably close at 40 years to what it is at in-

finity, $5. Thus Equation (6-22) is a good approximation, even though the series of $1 payments stops well short of infinity.

The present value of future streams of income or costs turns out to be important for understanding the price that people are willing to pay for goods that last for more than a year.

The demand for durable goods

Now that we have the tools of discounting and present value behind us, we can properly analyze the demand for **durable goods**

Year	3%	4%	5%	6%	8%	10%	20%	Year
1	0.971	0.960	0.952	0.943	0.926	0.909	0.833	1
2	1.91	1.89	1.86	1.83	1.78	1.73	1.53	2
3	2.83	2.78	2.72	2.67	2.58	2.48	2.11	3
4	3.72	3.63	3.55	3.46	3.31	31.6	2.59	4
5	4.58	4.45	4.33	4.21	3.99	3.79	2.99	5
6	5.42	5.24	5.08	4.91	4.62	4.35	3.33	6
7	6.23	6.00	5.79	5.58	5.21	4.86	3.60	7
8	7.02	6.73	6.46	6.20	5.75	5.33	3.84	8
9	7.79	7.44	7.11	6.80	6.25	5.75	4.03	9
10	8.53	8.11	7.72	7.36	6.71	6.14	4.19	10
11	9.25	8.76	8.31	7.88	7.14	6.49	4.33	11
12	9.95	9.39	8.86	8.38	7.54	6.81	4.44	12
13	10.6	9.99	9.39	8.85	7.90	7.10	4.53	13
14	11.3	10.6	9.90	9.29	8.24	7.36	4.61	14
15	11.9	11.1	10.4	9.71	8.56	7.60	4.68	15
16	12.6	11.6	10.8	10.1	8.85	7.82	4.73	16
17	13.2	12.2	11.3	10.4	9.12	8.02	4.77	17
18	13.8	12.7	11.7	10.8	9.37	8.20	4.81	18
19	14.3	13.1	12.1	11.1	9.60	8.36	4.84	19
20	14.9	13.6	12.5	11.4	9.82	8.51	4.87	20
25	17.4	15.6	14.1	12.8	10.7	9.08	4.95	25
30	19.6	17.3	15.4	13.8	11.3	9.43	4.98	30
40	23.1	19.8	17.2	15.0	11.9	9.78	5.00	40
50	25.7	21.5	18.3	15.8	12.2	9.91	5.00	50
∞	33.3	25.0	20.0	16.7	12.5	10.00	5.00	∞

Table 6-2: Present value of $1 per year for various periods at different discount rates. Here we show the present value of $1 received at the end of each year for a specified number of years. For example, the present value of a dollar received at the end of each year for 10 years at an interest rate of 5 percent would be $7.72. If it were received for 50 years, it would have a present value of $18.30.

—goods that last.   We treat the demand for a durable good as a demand not for the good itself, but rather for the net stream of services that the good yields.   "Net" means after taking account of all costs associated with the use of the durable. Hence, the demand for an automobile is not treated as the demand for the car per se, but rather the demand for the right to use the car day in, day out over a specified period of time.   We are dealing with an *expected* flow of services to which the consumer will attach some monetary valuation.

For example, take an automobile. Let's let A equal the monetary valuation of the stream of future services (net of operating costs) expected from the automobile each year; as usual, the interest rate is r. Thus, the present value of the stream of services from the automobile will equal

$$P_t = \frac{A_1}{1 + r} + \frac{A_2}{(1 + r)^2} + \cdots + \frac{R_t}{(1 + r)^t} \qquad (6\text{-}23)$$

where R_t is the resale value or the scrap value of the automobile when it is no longer desired. The denominator of the last term on the right-hand side of Eq. (6-23) is $1 + r$ taken to the power t, where t is the expected number of years that the individual will keep the automobile.

Clearly, the larger the expected flow of services per year, the greater the present value. Moreover, the larger the expected scrap value, *ceteris paribus*, the larger the present value. And finally, the lower the rate of interest used in discounting, the greater the present value of the durable asset. (Why?)

Assets in general

Instead of talking solely in terms of durable consumer goods, we can talk in terms of assets in general. **Assets** are defined as anything expected to give a stream of utility in the future. Assets include stocks, bonds, automobiles, stereos, a college degree, and so on.   The present value of any asset is the discounted expected future income stream or monetary value of the anticipated flow of service from that asset. Thus we expect the price of an asset to reflect its present value. In fact, we say that the price of any asset is the discounted present value of the anticipated flow of future services or income from that asset. Equation (6-23) is thus applicable to explaining the price at which a share of common stock sells at any moment.   Equation (6-23) is useful for describing the price of a house at a moment in time.   Indeed, the equation can be used to explain the price of any asset.

The market for risk assumption

Security is a scarce good. It has a positive value. Individuals are willing to pay to have more security in their lives, in their income streams, and hence in their consumption streams. Markets have arisen to take care of individual quests for a reduction in risk. One of those markets is the insurance market, in which individuals "pool" their individual risks so that when disaster hits any one of them, the pool of funds provided by all of them will take care of the disaster without altering the wealth position of the insured. Take a simple numerical example. There are 100 families. On the average, we assume that one house burns down to the ground a year. Each house is worth $50,000. The total annual loss sustained by the group of 100 families is $50,000. The mathematical probability for any one individual family of a loss in any 1 year is 1 percent times $50,000, or $500 per year. If all families get together and agree to pool their risks by paying $500 per year into a common reserve fund, then when the one house burns down per year, the family affected is paid $50,000 out of the reserve fund.

The above is insurance based on the **mutual principle**. When the profit incentive and the costs of administering the program are added, the risk-pooling aspect of insurance remains the same, but the annual premium for insurance exceeds the mathematical expectation of the annual loss.

Risk and time: The futures market

We have talked about markets dealing in time—the credit market—and we have talked very briefly about a market dealing with risk elimination—the insurance market. There is a market in which both elements, time and uncertainty, are found. This is the **futures market,** in which economic agents agree in the present to the sale or purchase of a particular commodity for delivery at a particular date in the future at a particular price. Those economic agents who participate in futures trading are generally called *speculators.* Before we analyze **speculation** and its effect on the allocation of resources over time and on the degree of risk taking by separate groups of individuals, we will explain briefly the market for futures.

The futures market

Many of us engage in contracting where a product is to be delivered at a future date. I may order next year's model of a Chevrolet from my local Chevrolet dealer 2 months before the car is scheduled to arrive on the premises. You may order a book from the bookstore that will not be delivered to you for 3 weeks. A farmer may make a contract to deliver a million bushels of grain to a grain elevator operator at a specific month in the future at a price that is agreed upon by both parties today. All such contracts are called forward contracts.

A **forward contract** is not, strictly speaking, the same as a **futures contract;** the latter applies only to those commodities executed in *formal* commodities exchange markets. There are a number of such markets: the Chicago

Board of Trade, the Chicago Mercantile Exchange, the New York Coffee and Sugar Exchange, and others throughout the world. In the United States there are organized open futures markets for frozen orange juice concentrate, oats, soybeans, wheat, corn, cotton, sorghum, sugar, barley, lard, hides, soybean oil, eggs (frozen, powdered, and shelled), frozen chickens, potatoes, silver, rubber, cocoa, pepper, flax seed, copper, wool, pork bellies, platinum, foreign exchange, and government-insured mortgages. Moreover, futures contracts are made for standard qualities and quantities of a commodity. As an example, in the futures market for frozen orange juice concentrate, a standard contract is for 15,000 pounds of concentrate. It is also necessary for the futures contract to call for delivery at a standard time during the year. And finally, futures contracts can be entered into only through a broker.

The difference between a forward and a futures contract is more profound than the simple explanation above indicates. In a futures market, the dealings are strictly impersonal; buyers and sellers know nothing but the price, the time, a few attributes of the product, and the place of delivery. In other words, in a futures contract it might be stated that 40,000 bushels of Minnesota No. 2 Red wheat will be delivered in Winnipeg between November 3 and November 10, 1979. Clearly, there are lots of economies of transactions here. In other words, the transactions costs are relatively low in a futures market. But it turns out that comparatively speaking, few futures markets actually exist; there are many more unorganized forward markets. The reason may be due to the fact that forward markets, in contrast to futures markets, permit more "custom-made" contracting. The buyer and seller engage in a personal rather than impersonal dealing and can specify many more aspects of the transaction than is possible in an organized futures market.

If you *buy* a futures contract today, you

agree to accept delivery of a specified amount of, say, wheat at a specified date in the future at a specified place. You also agree to pay the price specified in the futures contract. The price that is specified in the futures contract is called the **futures price**. You might look in the newspaper today and find out that the futures price of wheat to be delivered 3 months from now is so many dollars per bushel. You can compare the futures price with today's **spot price**, which is the price of wheat bought "on the spot." It is also called today's *cash* price. People who trade in the spot, or cash, market are the actual producers, processors, and distributors of the commodity.

On the other side of the exchange, it is possible to *sell* a futures contract. When you sell one, you agree to deliver a specified amount of a commodity on a specified date at a specified price. Those who have agreed to deliver commodities in the future at a stated price are said to have a **short position**, or to be or to have gone short. They have sold futures contracts. Those who agree to buy a certain quantity at a stated price in the future have a **long position**, or they are or have gone long. They have bought futures contracts; they have some commodities coming to them.

Note that futures contracts are not generally settled at maturity by actual physical delivery of the commodity to a warehouse, for which the purchaser obtains the warehouse receipt. Rather, most futures contracts are either closed out before their maturity date or settled by payment of the difference between the price stipulated in the contract and the spot price of the commodity at the date of maturity. Hence, if the futures price for a bushel of wheat were $5 when the contract was written, and at the date of maturity the spot price were $5.10, the seller of the futures contract would merely pay the purchaser of the futures contract 10¢ times the number of bushels specified.[2]

---

[2]Note that the volume of futures contracts is not tied to the volume of physical product or even constrained by it.

Transferring risk—Hedging and speculation

A crucial function of the futures market is that it allows individuals to eliminate risk. The process of using the futures market to eliminate risk is called **hedging**. Those who engage in this activity are called *hedgers*. Consider the operator of a grain elevator (a storage place) who buys corn from farmers at harvest time. The grain elevator operator stores the corn and sells it to processors (millers) over the period between each corn harvest. The grain elevator operator wants to specialize in storing corn. He or she does not want to specialize in predicting future spot prices of corn. Knowing that there are fluctuations in the spot, or cash, price of corn, this grain elevator operator may wish to reduce the possibility of loss (or profit) due to a reduction (increase) in the spot price of corn later on. This loss (profit) would occur, for example, if the elevator operator bought corn today at $5 a bushel and 2 months from now would get $3 ($7) a bushel when it was sold to processors.

Using the futures market, it is possible for the grain elevator operator to transfer some of the risk of any reduction in the value of the corn that he or she holds to someone else in exchange for transferring the gains realizable if in fact the spot price of corn rises. What the elevator operator does is sell futures contracts in corn at the same time he or she buys the corn.

A numerical example

Let's take a simple example which ignores such things as buying on margin (credit). Assume the elevator operator has just paid $2 a bushel for 10,000 bushels of corn. The elevator operator plans on selling this corn 6 months from now. During that 6 month period, the operator estimates inventory costs—insurance, opportunity cost of capital invested, etc.—will be 5¢ per bushel. Thus, for 10,000 bushels, the storage cost will be $500. Assume market conditions are such that the operator can sell a futures contract for 10,000 bushels of corn to be delivered in 6 months for the sum of $20,500, which is a price of $2.05 per bushel. We have assumed that the futures contract has been sold at a price that is just equal to the spot price of corn today ($2) plus the storage costs ($0.05) for 6 months. (Normally, the futures price will be higher than the spot or cash price by the cost of insurance, storage, and interest for the period of time from today to the delivery date.) Given that assumption, the elevator operator is indifferent to the price of corn remaining the same, going up, or going down over the 6-month waiting period.

The arithmetic is quite simple. Consider the three cases.

PRICE IS UNCHANGED. If the spot price 6 months from now is exactly the same as the current spot price, the value of 10,000 bushels of stored corn will have remained the same. The elevator operator will sell it for exactly the same amount that he or she paid for it. However, the futures contract was sold at a specified price of $2.05 per bushel. (Selling a futures contract is not the same thing as actually selling the physical commodity corn.) At maturity, the buyer of the futures contract, generally called a speculator, will settle the account by paying our elevator operator $500; but this just equals the cost of storing the corn for 6 months.

PRICE GOES UP. When the spot price of corn goes up by, say, 20¢, the elevator operator has an increase in the value of his or her stored corn of 20¢ times 10,000 bushels, or $2,000. But there are costs involved too. The futures contract specified a price of $2.05 per bushel. The difference, 15¢ per bushel, must be paid to the speculator, or the owner, of the futures contract. The cost, then, is $1,500. Added to that is the other cost of storage, $500. On net, then, a 20¢ rise in the spot price of corn after 6 months yields the elevator operator zero additional profits.

PRICE GOES DOWN. Now, you should be able to work through the example when the spot price of corn falls to, say, $1.85 at the end of 6 months. Again, you will find that the net worth position of the elevator operator remains constant.

A selling hedge

What has occurred here? The holder of corn, the elevator operator, has shifted the risk inherent in the ownership of the asset called corn to another class of individuals who are typically speculators. The "hedge" that was effected in the transaction mentioned above is called a selling hedge. The elevator operator has a long position in corn because he or she actually purchased the corn. To eliminate the risk of the change in the value of that long position, the elevator operator established an equal short position by selling futures contracts. The storage operator gets $2.05 per bushel in 6 months from the speculator (the owner of the contract) no matter what the spot price is at that time. If the spot is higher than $2.05 per bushel, the speculator gets to keep the difference; if the price is lower than $2.05 per bushel, the speculator must pay the difference.

A buying hedge

A buying hedge is also possible. A pork farmer may make a forward contract (forward since there is no organized market in fresh pork) with a meat processor to sell so many pounds of fresh pork at a predetermined price per pound at a future date. However, the pork farmer, until that future date, must feed grain to the pigs. The price established in the forward contract with the same meat processor is based perhaps on the assumption that the cost of grain that goes into fattening the pigs will remain constant. If, however, the price of grain rises, the pork farmer will suffer because the price of the product he or she has agreed to sell at some future date is already agreed upon in the forward contract. As protection, the pork farmer will buy grain in the futures market by buying futures contracts which guarantee delivery of grain at a specified time at a price agreed upon today. That is the price which the pork farmer would put into his or her cost calculations in arriving at the price to charge the meat processor in the forward contract that guarantees delivery of so many pounds of pork. You should be able to work through an example similar to the one just mentioned, in which you can show that after entering the two separate contracts, the pork farmer's wealth position will not change due to a change in either the price of feed or that of fattened hogs.

Speculation

Those who do not enter simultaneously into long and short cash and futures positions in a particular commodity are not hedgers, but rather, speculators. Speculators are betting that the future spot price of a commodity will be different than the price specified in a futures contract today. In the case of the grain operator, the purchaser of a futures contract from the grain operator at $2.05 per bushel of corn is betting that in 6 months the spot price of corn will not be $2.05, but will be something greater. If it is selling for $2.15 per bushel in 6 months, the speculator who has purchased the futures contract makes a profit of 10¢ per bushel. Speculators also sell futures contracts. When they sell a futures contract, they are betting that the spot price of the commodity on the date of maturity of the contract in the future will be lower than the current futures

price (i.e., the price specified on futures contracts sold today). The difference is their profit on each unit of the commodity sold. They are betting that there will be a difference between the actual *future* price and the current *futures* price. The future price is the actual market price at some specified date in the future; the futures price is the anticipated or expected future price that is put into the futures contract.

Speculation and allocation of nonperishable goods over time

The futures market is more than just a market to provide the transfer of risk from hedgers to speculators (or to other hedgers). It is also a market which generates signals that alter the consumption pattern of commodities over time from what it would be in the absence of a futures market.

Consider the two periods, 1 and 2, depicted in Figure 6-6. We assume that it is known with certainty in this example that the corn crop in period 1 will yield a supply of S_1S_1, illustrated in panel (*a*). It is also known with certainty that in period 2 there will be a smaller crop, as represented by the supply curve S_2S_2 in panel (*b*). The demand curve, in the absence of speculation, is D_1D_1 in panel (*a*) for period 1. It represents the demand curve for corn by period 1 users only. In the absence of speculation, the intersection of D_1D_1 with S_1S_1 would yield a market-clearing price of P_1 at which $0S_1$ would be consumed. In period 2, the demand curve also represents the demand by period 2 users only. It is drawn as D_2D_2. It intersects the supply curve of corn S_2S_2 at a price P_2. Notice here that in the absence of speculators, a larger quantity of corn will be consumed in period 1 because of the relatively low price, and a smaller quantity will be consumed in period 2 because of the higher relative price.

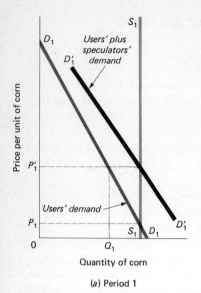

(a) Period 1

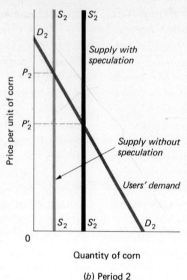

(b) Period 2

Figure 6-6: Speculation smooths out the rate of consumption.
In the absence of speculation, period 1 supply is $S_1 S_1$, period 2 supply is $S_2 S_2$. The demand curves for period 1 and 2 are $D_1 D_1$ and $D_2 D_2$, respectively. The price without speculation, would therefore be P_1 in period 1 and P_2 in period 2. If speculators enter the market, they add to the current demand in period 1. The new demand curve becomes $D_1' D_1'$, and is user's plus speculators' demand. The market-clearing price in period 1 rises to P_1'. The period 1 quantity demanded by users falls to Q_1, and the difference $S_1 - Q_1$ goes into the inventories held by speculators. In period 2, the supply curve shifts out by the amount of these inventories to $S_2' S_2'$. The price in period 2 falls to P_2', which is less than P_2.

Now speculators enter the market. They foresee the possibility of a profit because of a smaller crop next year. If they can purchase futures contracts for corn somewhere near period 1's spot price, they will make a profit when period 2's spot price exceeds that futures price. Their demand is represented by the horizontal distance between $D_1 D_1$ and $D_1' D_1'$. With a given supply $S_1 S_1$, the price of corn in period 1 will not be P_1, but rather P_1', because this is the intersection of $S_1 S_1$ with $D_1' D_1'$. The quantity demanded by current users will now be Q_1, less than the $0S_1$ without speculative demand. The difference will be held in storage to deliver to purchasers of futures contracts at maturity in period 2. Now go to panel (b), which represents period 2. The supply curve shifts out to the right by the amount of corn that has been stored from period 1 to period 2. The market-clearing price in period 2 ends up being P_2' rather than P_2 because this is where the then-current demand curve of current users, $D_2 D_2$, intersects the supply curve $S_2' S_2'$. In an idealized setting with perfect information, the difference between P_1' in panel (a) and P_2'

in panel (b) will be equal to the cost of storage plus a normal risk-corrected profit sufficient to induce speculators to tie up their capital in the futures market during the period of time under study.

Thus, what do speculators do? They induce current owners of inventories of commodities to withhold sale until future periods. Current owners anticipate that the supply of the commodity in the future will be sufficiently low relative to the demand to cause its future spot price to be greater than it is in the present. You should be able to redo panels (a) and (b) under the assumption that speculators anticipate a "bumper" crop of corn in period 2. How would that affect the futures price of corn, and how would that alter the quantity of corn consumed in the present period?

Now you can see why the current price of a nonperishable commodity can rise without any change in the current demand by current users. A premature frost in coffee-growing countries in Latin America may signal to speculators that the future supply of coffee will be lower than anticipated and, hence, that the price of coffee in the future will be higher than had been anticipated. Speculators will bid up the price of futures contracts. As they do this, current owners of inventories of coffee will withhold coffee from the market in order to benefit from higher expected future prices, and this will mean that today's spot price will also go up. The rise in today's price has not been caused by speculation; it has been caused by the premature frost and the expectation that the future crop of coffee will be smaller. Speculators had nothing to do with that premature frost. If their anticipations prove to be incorrect, they will be the ones to suffer a wealth loss.

The above example also serves to show the service that speculators can provide to consumers. The former indirectly even out the latter's consumption of a storeable commodity over time. By reducing current supply, speculators are necessarily increasing future supply. Steady consumption, as opposed to famine-feast cycles, is usually preferred by consumers. Moreover, the total value of the corn in the above example has been raised by speculation. Why? Because of the law of demand. Without speculation, the marginal use value of corn in period 1 would have been relatively much less than its marginal use value in period 2. Speculation allows these marginal use values in the two periods to come closer together and thereby raised the *total* use value of corn.

Speculation and risk taking

To be sure, it is possible for hedgers to shift risk onto speculators. However, speculation is not limited to futures markets. Anyone who has any assets or liabilities is by definition a speculator. The value of assets can go up or down, depending on shifts in the supply and demand curves of the assets in question. Owners usually have nothing to do with the shifts in supply and demand; unanticipated inflation, for example, can alter the burden of liabilities. Hence, owners of assets or liabilities are at the mercy of "the market." To the extent that you have a short or long interest in any asset, you are by definition a speculator. You can reduce speculation by renting and leasing assets rather than by owning them, because by leasing, you don't go short or long. But even then you still cannot completely eliminate speculation. A long-term lease involves speculation because you could be "locked into" a high monthly lease fee during a period in which the value of the asset you are leasing falls in the open market. When this happens, new leases that are written will be at a lower rate. You will suffer a reduction in your wealth in comparison to what your wealth would have been had you not signed the long-term lease but rather signed a series of short-term leases through time.

Issues and applications

Should the project be built?

Businesses and governments are constantly faced with choices about which capital investment projects should be undertaken. We can use present value calculations for deciding on the desirability of a capital investment project.

Every capital investment project will have a present and future stream of costs and a future stream of benefits. It is not appropriate to look at the stream of costs, add them all up, and compare them with the stream of benefits all added up. The reason it is not appropriate is because a dollar in cost tomorrow is worth less than a dollar in cost today. Also, a dollar in benefits tomorrow has less value than a dollar in benefits today. We calculate the present value of future costs and benefits by using the following formula:

Present value of net benefits =

$$B_0 - C_0 + \frac{B_1 - C_1}{1 + r} + \frac{B_2 - C_2}{(1 + r)^2} \cdots + \frac{B_t - C_t}{(1 + r)^t} \quad (6\text{-}24)$$

where B refers to benefits and C refers to costs. The subscript refers to the year in which the benefit is received or the cost incurred (the subscript 0 refers to the current year).

The r chosen for this benefit-cost calculation is crucial. For an individual company, the r is fairly obvious. It is the opportunity cost of capital to that company, or, it is the rate of return that the company could earn by taking a dollar and investing it in the next-best alternative project. It could be either the borrowing or the lending rate, depending upon which would be applicable to the next-best alternative. At a minimum, the company could purchase bonds with a specified rate of return over a specified period.

If, when using appropriate opportunity cost of capital, the present value of net benefits does not exceed zero, the project should definitely not be undertaken.

Government agencies have a tougher time figuring out the appropriate r. The capital used in the construction of a government project could have been used not only in some other govern-

ment project but also in the private sector. Thus, the social opportunity cost of capital might be the appropriate r, and of course, the social opportunity cost of capital includes the taxes on their profits that private firms pay to the government. If too low a discount rate r is used, projects with benefits too far in the future will be undertaken when it is inappropriate. On the other hand, if too high an r is used, not enough projects with future benefits will be undertaken.

To understand in detail how costs and benefits are compared, consider the following example in which a simple investment cost of $5,000 is incurred at the end of the "zero-th" year. The investment "lives" for 5 more years. We will use a discount rate of 5 percent. Table 6-3 shows all the appropriate calculations. Column (1) shows the year; column (2), the costs; column (3), the benefits or revenues; and column (4), the difference between benefits and costs, or net benefits. Column (5) is the discount factor taken from Table 6-1, and finally, column (6) is the present value of net benefits. Notice that the total present value exceeds 0, and hence, this project has a positive discounted net benefits stream. However, if a higher discount rate were used, this would no longer be the case. Go back and redo the calculations, using an interest rate of 10 percent to discount the net benefits stream. Would you want to undertake this project?

End of year (1)	Investment and operating costs C (2)	Revenue B (3)	Net Benefits $B - C$ (4)	Discount factor for $r = 5$ (5)	Present value of $B - C$ (6)
0	5,000 (C_0)	—	−5,000 $(B_0 - C_0)$	1.000	−$5,000.00
1	500 (C_1)	3,500 (B_1)	3,000 $(B_1 - C_1)$	.952	$2,856.00
2	1,500 (C_2)	4,000 (B_2)	2,500 $(B_2 - C_2)$	.907	$2,267.50
3	3,500 (C_3)	3,000 (B_3)	−500 $(B_3 - C_3)$	.864	−$ 432.00
4	1,500 (C_4)	3,000 (B_4)	1,500 $(B_4 - C_4)$	.823	$1,234.50
5	2,000 (C_5)	2,000 (B_5)	0 $(B_5 - C_5)$	.784	0
Total					$ 926.00

Table 6-3

Planned obsolescence, or the waste makers revisited

Having developed the tools of present value calculations and their relationship to the demand for durable goods, we can analyze the notion of planned obsolescence. This means that the manufacturer of a commodity that is durable, allegedly builds into the commodity a reduction in its serviceable life. The easiest example we can take is planned obsolescence by way of style change. An automobile has a planned reduction in resale value after, say, 3 years, attributable to the introduction of a different style which will render the old-style automobile model "obsolete," if only because it looks different. Another notion of planned obsolescence involves making the product in such a way that it will become useless sooner than it would have otherwise. Implicit in this notion of planned obsolescence is the dubious notion that the cost to the manufacturer of having the product last longer is minimal, or in the extreme case, zero.

Remember the formula for the present value of an asset, Eq. (6-21) on p. 141? Let us modify that formula slightly and assume that the resale or scrap value of the durable asset in question is 0 at the end of 3 years. The present value of the asset is therefore

$$PV = \frac{A_1}{(1+r)} + \frac{A_2}{(1+r)^2} + \frac{A_3}{(1+r)^3} \qquad (6\text{-}25)$$

Now consider what happens to the present value when planned obsolescence is effected by way of altering the production of the durable asset so that it only lasts 2 years. Now the present value is

$$PV' = \frac{A_1}{(1+r)} + \frac{A_2}{(1+r)^2} + \frac{0}{(1+r)^3} \qquad (6\text{-}26)$$

But clearly $PV > PV'$. For a given nominal price of the durable good, the price per constant-quality unit will be higher in the second case than in the first case. If the good cost $100 in both cases, its cost *per year of service* will certainly be higher when the good lasts only 2 years than when it lasts 3 years. If the unit of constant quality is 1 year of service, the price per constant-quality unit will have increased with planned obsolescence. Assuming the law of demand still holds, the quantity demanded of the durable asset for which planned obsolescence makes it worthless at the end of 2 years will be less than the quantity demanded of a durable asset that will last 3 years. You can work through the same arithmetic in the case of style changes. Style changes implicitly reduce the monetary value placed on the service flow per year. Thus A_1, A_2, and A_3 will be smaller. At any particular price, when the present value is smaller, the price per constant-quality unit will be larger and the quantity demanded will be less.

At this point, the most we can say about planned obsolescence is that a manufacturer engaging in this process will find the quantity demanded reduced at any given price.

Would publishing firms and authors be better off if the used-book market were abolished?

A related problem deals with new and used textbooks. Superficially, it would appear that the elimination of the used-book market would benefit the sale of new books by eliminating a substitute. Thus, if the publisher of this book wants to maximize revenues from the sale of this edition, presumably it should not aid in any way the smooth functioning of a used-book market for this text. After all, used Miller price theory books are substitutes for new ones. When someone purchases a used text from a college bookstore, that person does not purchase a new one. The publisher (and the author) get paid only when a new book is sold.

Present value falls

This analysis is incomplete, however. If you as a student purchased this text new and cannot resell it because a used-book market does not exist, then the present value of this book is smaller. In terms of Eq. (6-23), there is no last term that includes R_t, or resale value. Thus, the present value is lower by that amount. At any given nominal price for this textbook, the *price per constant-quality unit* would therefore be higher. Assume that the textbook costs $10. If normally you are able to resell the textbook at the end of the term for 50 percent of its new-book price, then you anticipate that the cost for one term's use of the book wil be $5; however, if the bookstore absolutely refuses to buy the book back, then the cost for one term's use of that same book has doubled to $10. A lower quantity would be demanded.

If one continues this analysis to its ultimate extreme, one would expect individual textbook manufacturers to *aid* in increasing the efficacy of used-book markets so long as their aid was relatively cheap; increasing the efficacy of used-book markets would increase the present value of their textbooks. At the same price, a larger quantity would be demanded, or alternatively, a higher price could be charged for the textbook and the same quantity would be demanded. This is what has actually happened in the market for used IBM typewriters. IBM acts as the intermediary in this market, first buying the used typewriters, then reconditioning them, and then reselling them. Some textbook publishers also engage in this type of behavior. But there are other publishing houses that instruct their sales staff to dissuade bookstores from acting as intermediaries for used versions of the textbooks sold. Presumably these publishers believe that they will have higher profits by reducing the substitutes for new books.

Other effects need to be considered

It turns out that the above analyses are not so simple as outlined there because they focused only on increasing the benefits stream from the ownership of a durable good. However, there is a substitution effect at work. Used versions of durable goods are indeed substitutes for newly produced durable goods. The elimination of part or all of the available supply of substitute used durables leads to a shift outward to the right in the demand curve for the new durable good.

A case for the elimination of used versions of the durable good can be seen in Figure 6-7. The original demand curve is DD. It is drawn by assuming a given availability of substitutes. Assume that the market price per constant-quality unit is P_1. It is the nominal price, let us say, for each unit of the durable good. Now consider the elimination of the used-version market of the durable good. The demand curve for the new dura-

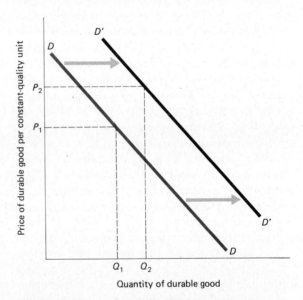

Figure 6-7: The case for eliminating the used-durable-good market.
The demand curve DD is drawn by assuming the existence of a market for the used durable good. The price expressed in present value constant-quality units is, we assume, P_1. Now, the used market is eliminated. This leads to a substitution effect in which the demand curve for the new version of the durable good shifts to the right, outward to D'D', since a substitute has been eliminated. However, the elimination of the used-durable-good market reduces the present value of the good, thus raising its price per present value constant-quality unit from P_1 to P_2. Nonetheless, even at this higher price, the quantity demanded increases from Q_1 to Q_2 because of the shift outward in the demand schedule that resulted from the elimination of the substitute.

ble shifts from *DD* to *D'D'*. However, the present value of the durable good has fallen because its resale value is no longer as great as it was when the market for the used version of the durable good existed. In other words, we have cut off a part of the future expected income stream from owning this durable good. We have cut off the possibility of selling the asset after it has been used awhile. If this is the case, at a constant nominal price per nominal unit P_1, the effective price per constant-quality unit must rise. After all, the purchaser of the durable good is purchasing fewer *present-value* units with the same amount of dollars. In our example in Figure 6-7, the price rises from P_1 to P_2. However, even at the higher price P_2, the quantity demanded along the new demand curve *D'D'* increases from Q_1 to Q_2. In this case, the substitution effect outweighed the present-value reduction effect.

A case against the elimination of the used version of the durable good can be seen in Figure 6-8. Everything is the same as in Figure 6-7 except that the shift in the demand curve for the new durable good is not as great. At the higher implicit price per constant-quality unit of the durable good, P_2, the quantity demanded Q_2 is less than the original quantity demanded Q_1 when the market for the used version of the durable good was in existence.

What one has to compare in these situations is the own price elasticity of demand and the cross-price elasticity of demand.[3] This, of course, is an empirical question. From casual observation, however, we can surmise that the IBM Corporation believes that it is better to encourage a used market for its equipment. Specifically, IBM

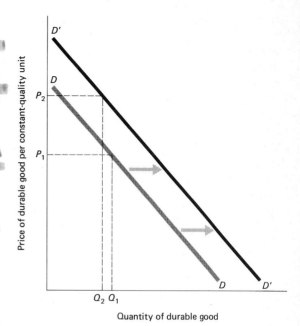

Figure 6-8: The case against elimination of the used-durable-good market.
This diagram is similar to Figure 6-7; but the shift outward in the demand curve from *DD* to *D'D'* was not sufficient to overcome the implicit increase in the price per present value constant-quality unit of the durable good when the used market was eliminated. Thus, the quantity demanded falls from Q_1 to Q_2.

operates an extensive used-IBM-typewriter market, where one can purchase a reconditioned IBM electric typewriter. Clearly, there is no attempt on the part of IBM to destroy "competition" for new IBM electric typewriters with used IBM electric typewriters.

Throwing money down the drain: The case of the New Territories

Visitors to the New Territories of Hong Kong marvel at the amount of construction that has been undertaken in the last decade or so. These visitors may even become incredulous when told that the land is leased from the People's Republic of China and must be turned back about the end of this century. Assume for the moment that, in fact,

---

[3]Students interested in a more elaborate examination of this problem are referred to Daniel K. Benjamin and Roger C. Kormendi, "The Interrelationship between Markets for New and Used Durable Goods," *The Journal of Law and Economics*, vol. 17, no. 2, October 1974, pp. 381–401. Also see H. Larry Miller, "On Killing Off the Market for Used Textbooks and the Relationship between Markets for New and Secondhand Goods," *Journal of Political Economy*, vol. 82, no. 3, May/June 1974.

the land will return to the mainland Chinese on the stroke of midnight, December 31, 1999. Was it irrational for entrepreneurs to build large hotels, apartment buildings, and so on in the New Territories?

Think of the benefit-cost analysis just presented in the previous section. Here, benefits were subtracted from costs in every year into the future for the life of the project. In essence, the net income stream obtained was discounted back to today. Look at Table 6-1 again. Look at some present values of a dollar in future net income 25 years from now. If the appropriate opportunity cost of capital for the entrepreneur investing in a building in the New Territories is, say, 12 percent, the value of a dollar in net profits in 25 years is only $.0588! Thus, it is not so foolish for an entrepreneur to invest in New Territories real estate. Those discounted potential profits in the year 2000 and beyond will not alter significantly the present value of net benefits from engaging in the project. All the entrepreneur need do to carry out the correct profitability calculation is cut off the $(B - C)$'s after the year 1999. If, when using the appropriate rate of discount, the present value of net benefits is still positive, it will be appropriate to invest in the New Territories.

We can speculate about some other aspects of the New Territories. If the lessees were certain that they would not only lose the territory but would obtain no compensation whatsoever for the buildings that they put up on the territory owned by the mainland Chinese, we would predict that they would construct those buildings in such a way that they would have minimal value by the year 2000. In other words, the average durability of assets that were fixed to the land in the New Territories should always be equal to the number of years remaining on the lease. It would not pay to make assets any more durable if there is no anticipation of compensation or scrap value for those assets in the year 2000.

Presumably, however, the Chinese will not want these assets to be completely neglected and, hence, have a relatively small value when they are taken over in the year 2000. If mainland China wants, for example, to maintain the New Territories as a tourist area after the year 2000, it may decide to arrange for appropriate compensation to the current lessees of its land for the durable assets that they are constructing and/or using on it. Our prediction would be that the lessees in the New Territories would treat their durable assets fixed to the land in a less "destructive" manner if the mainland Chinese government set up a system of promised compensations based on, for example, the quality of the buildings that they were going to take over in the year 2000.

Glossary

Time cost The time required for the purchase and/or consumption of a commodity.

Theory of time preference Hypothesis relating to the individual's preference for current consumption over future consumption, i.e., that the individual prefers current over later consumption.

Interest rate The rate of exchange between goods today and goods in the future.

Personal rate of discount A measure of the individual's personal time preference or degree of preference for current consumption over future consumption.

Saving Nonconsumption of income and/or wealth in the current period.

Present value The current value expressed in terms of today's dollars of any sum to be received or to be paid in the future. Sometimes called the discounted value or discounted present value because future sums are discounted back to today.

Discount rate The interest rate used to compute present value, or the interest rate used in discounting future sums.

Annuity A sequence of future amounts to be received at regular calendar intervals for a specified period of time.

Capital value The present value or discounted value of a sequence of future amounts or of an annuity.

Durable goods Goods which are expected to yield a stream of services or satisfaction for more than just the current period, e.g., stereos, TVs, machines, and automobiles.

Asset Anything expected to give a stream of utility in the future; includes durable goods, contracts, stocks, bonds, etc.

Mutual principle A principle used in insurance whereby individuals pool their individual risks so as to reduce the risk faced by any one individual in the group. That risk is thereby converted into a *certain* payment or liability of a specified insurance premium.

Futures market The market in which futures contracts are traded. Such contracts specify the future date of delivery of a certain amount of a commodity and specify the particular price to be paid on that date. This term refers only to organized markets.

Speculation The buying and selling of assets and liabilities in the hope of making a profit on their price fluctuations. Both long and short positions are possible. Actually, any ownership of assets or obligations to pay (liabilities) involves speculation.

Forward contract A contract for the delivery of a specified quantity of a good on a specified date at a specified price and with specified qualities; refers to contracts on goods that are traded in other than organized markets.

Future contract Like a forward contract, except that it refers to standardized contracts traded on organized exchanges.

Futures price The price that is specified in a futures contract and that must be paid upon expiration of the contract for the specified commodity.

Spot price The current or cash price of a commodity. The price "on the spot."

Short position This is the position of anyone who has agreed to *deliver* a specified quantity of a commodity at a specified time in the future at a stated price.

Long position This is the position of anyone who has agreed to *receive* a specified quantity of a commodity at a specified price in the future at a stated price.

Hedging The process of using the futures market to reduce risk. In hedging, the individual simultaneously enters into short and long cash and futures positions or simultaneously into long and short cash and futures positions in a commodity.

Summary

1. The total cost of consuming a commodity equals the money cost plus the opportunity cost for the time expended purchasing and/or consuming it. Thus, *ceteris paribus*, as the opportunity cost of time rises, the consumption of time-intensive goods will fall relatively.

2. In a theory of time preference, individuals are assumed to prefer current consumption to future consumption.

3. The market rate of interest can be derived from the demand for and the supply of credit, or present as opposed to future consumption.

4. In a world of no inflation, the interest rate represents the rate of exchange between goods today and goods in the future. However, if there is an expectation of inflation, the market rate of interest represents the rate of exchange between dollars today and dollars in the future. A correction then must be made for that expected rate of inflation to arrive at the real interest rate.

5. The slope of the budget line facing the individual in his or her choice between consumption today and consumption tomorrow is equal to $-(1 + r)$, where r represents the rate of transformation between consumption today and consumption tomorrow and is determined in the credit market.

6. The individual's time preference is expressed by his or her personal rate of discount and is labeled *rho*, ρ. The slope of the indifference curve between consumption today and consumption tomorrow is equal to $-(1 + \rho)$.

7. Consumer optimum occurs where the budget constraint is tangent to the indifference curve, or where the rate at which the consumer can transform future consumption into current consumption is equal to the rate at which the consumer desires to make this transformation, or when $r = \rho$.

8. All future values must be discounted to obtain their present value, or their value in terms of today's dollars and today's consumption. The general formula for present value is

$$P_t = \frac{A}{(1 + r)^t}$$

interest rate goes down

PV ↑

9. We see that the farther in the future a sum of money is paid or received, the lower is its present value; and the higher the interest rate used, the lower is the present value of any future sum of money.

10. The demand for durable goods is not a demand for the stock per se, but rather for the expected stream of useful services from the durable good.

11. The price of a durable good, or any asset for that matter, is equal to the present value of the net future stream of services.

12. Individuals seek ways of reducing risk; they are willing to pay for increased certainty. One of these ways is by purchasing insurance at a *certain* premium cost.

13. The futures market allows individuals to hedge against future fluctuations in prices. It also provides the mechanism by which speculators, in anticipating consumer wants, smooth out the consumption of nonperishable goods over time.

14. In a futures market, futures contracts are bought and sold by both hedgers and speculators. The former engage in both buying and selling of futures contracts; the latter are defined as those who deliberately take either a short position or a long position in the expectation of profit.

15. Sellers of futures contracts (those agreeing to deliver the goods) are betting that the spot price in the future will be lower than the futures price specified in the contract. Purchasers of such contracts (those agreeing to accept delivery of the goods) are betting the opposite.

16. Speculation leads to a smoothing out of consumption over time by forcing up the futures price of the commodity when a lower supply is anticipated and thus causing current owners of the commodity to withhold more from the spot market. This raises the current spot price and discourages present consumption. The opposite occurs if a relatively larger supply is anticipated in the future.

17. It is virtually impossible to avoid speculation. Any owner of assets or liabilities implicitly incurs risk. The value of any asset can change in an unexpected manner, and so can the relative burden of a liability. Leasing is one way to reduce speculation, but it does not eliminate speculation completely.

Selected references

Bailey, Martin, "Saving and the Rate of Interest," *Journal of Political Economy*, vol. 65, 1957, pp. 279–305.

Becker, Gary S., *Economic Theory* (New York: Knopf, 1971), lecture 10, pp. 45–47.

DeHaven, J. C., and J. Hirshleifer, "Feather River Water for Southern California," *Land Economics*, vol. 33, August 1957.

Fisher, Irving, *The Theory of Interest* (New York: Macmillan, 1930), chaps. 4–11.

Hieronymus, Thomas A., *Economics of Futures Trading* (New York: Commodity Research Bureau, Inc., 1971).

Jones, C. E., "Theory of Hedging on the Beef Futures Market," *American Journal of Agricultural Economics*, vol. 50, December 1968, pp. 1760–1766.

Sandor, Richard I., *Speculating in Futures* (Chicago: Board of Trade of the City of Chicago, 1973).

Stevens, Neil A., "The Futures Market for Farm Commodities—What It Can Mean to Farmers," *Federal Reserve Bank of St. Louis Review*, August 1974, pp. 10–15.

Stigler, George, *The Theory of Price*, 3d ed. (New York: Macmillan, 1966) chap. 17.

Questions

(Answers to even-numbered questions are at back of text.)

1. Food, clothing, and paper towels are examples of so-called nondurable goods. How can a good be nondurable and still be a good? (*Hint:* Is a service durable?)

2. "My wages have increased so much in recent years that I can hardly afford to play golf anymore!" On its face, this is a paradox; explain what the person really means.

3. Suppose you know someone whose time preference is such that they are indifferent between 110 fresh peaches now and 100 a year from now. Does this prove that the interest rate must be negative? Explain.

4. "I can't understand people who will fork over $5 or $10 to see a first-run movie when they could see it for about half that price a few months later, or even watch it on TV for free a few years later." What does time-preference theory say about this?

5. If you have a positive personal rate of dis-

count and the interest rate you face falls, *ceteris paribus*, how would our theory predict that you would respond?

6. Explain, in words, why an absolutely certain contractual right to receive a dollar in the future is less valuable than having the dollar right now. Assume, as we have throughout the text, that no inflation is expected.

7. How is it possible that an absolutely certain annuity of $1 per year to be paid or received for 20 years has a present value of less than $20?

8. A perpetuity is a perpetual annuity. Note that its present value formula $(P = A/r)$ is much simpler than those of annuities for a finite number of years. If you were able to invest your money at 5 percent per year without risk, how much would you be willing to pay for an absolutely certain perpetuity of $1 per year? Why? If, after you bought it, the no-risk interest rate fell to 2 percent per year, what would your perpetuity now be worth? Why?

9. Looking at the present value equation, Eq. (6-23), how would you expect an increase in the price of new Honda motorcycles to affect the market price of your used one. Explain.

10. Suppose you buy a United States government bond which entitles you, as the holder, to the following: You will receive $100 per year in interest starting 1 year from today, for the next 10 years. Ten years from today, when the bond matures, you will also receive, in addition to the tenth interest payment, the bond's face value of $1,000. If you are to earn 10 percent per year on your investment, what is the maximum price you will be willing to pay for the bond? What would you be willing to pay if your targeted rate of return were 8 percent per year? Twelve percent per year?

11. Suppose you own a bar in Las Vegas near the University of Nevada. Every time the local college basketball team wins a home game, business is brisk and you clear $200 for the day. When it loses, business is slow and on those days you clear only $50. The problem is, you don't like risk; you would prefer a certain income to an uncertain one. Fortunately for you, gambling is legal in Nevada and there are hoards of people who like to shoulder risk, among other ways, by wagering on athletic events. Assuming you can get even odds, how much should you bet on each game and on which team, in order that you will be "hedged" against the team's having a bad (or good) season?

12. Suppose a group of 100 women, all age twenty-five, decide to "cut out the middle people" by forming a mutual pregnancy-insurance league. From statistics they ascertain that for every 100 women of age twenty-five, an average of 15 conceptions occur per year. Medical expenses in their area average $1,000 per pregnancy. Based upon these figures, what annual "insurance premium" would they assess one another to take care of the expected pregnancies? Can you anticipate any potential problems with their scheme to beat the insurance companies out of some business?

13. In present value terms, what two financial rights do you buy when you purchase a share of common stock? Does the past performance (earnings, etc.) of the firm have any bearing on either of these two rights?

14. Why might a speculator in commodities futures want to have instantaneous reports on changes in weather throughout the world? How much should a speculator spend generating weather information? Should he or she go as far as to have an in-house weather service generating its own reports?

15. Is it possible for someone to eliminate all financial risk by investing properly? Discuss.

7

THE FIRM AND PRODUCTION

Until now we have been concerned essentially with the household sector of the economy. But there is another broad sector that consists of business firms. We want to analyze business behavior now to see how firms choose inputs and outputs and set prices (where this is possible). We will first define production and then discuss the reasons why firms exist and their possible goals. Then an analysis of production is undertaken; this includes many of the aspects of the relationship between inputs and outputs.

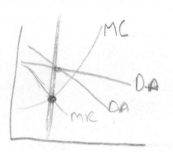

Defining production

We can define **production** as any use of resources that converts or transforms a commodity into a different commodity over time and/or space. Production, in this fairly broad sense, therefore includes not only manufacturing, but storing, wholesaling, transporting, retailing, repackaging, attempting to alter regulatory agency rulings, using lawyers and accountants to find tax loopholes, and so on.

Production includes both goods and services because the term "commodity" refers to both. However, we will simplify the analysis in the following pages by considering only the production of goods. Services, such as cleaning, repairing, etc., could be handled in a similar manner.

Production is a flow concept. It is an activity that is measured as a *rate of output per unit time period*, where output is expressed in constant-quality units. Thus, when we talk of increasing production, we mean increasing the rate of output, with all other dimensions of production held constant.

Why do firms exist?

Commodities are produced by firms. Here we will limit our definition of a **firm** to any **organization** in which there is an employer and one or more employees.[1] The employees are paid a contractual wage that they receive for a specified period, no matter what the rate of output and no matter what the rate of sales. On the other hand, the employer, who is also defined as an **entrepreneur**—the organizer and undertaker of business risks—does not receive a contractual wage rate in the capacity of entrepreneur. Rather, the employer receives what revenue is left over, if any, after all contractual payments are made. In accounting, "what is left over" from each year's revenues is called *profit*, or *net income*. It is also called the *residual*, or *net revenues*, by economists. We will have occasion to examine the concept of profit in more detail in Chapter 8.

Firms do exist. In principle, an individual could, for example, make automobiles, but automobile *firms* in fact produce most automobiles. Many of the production activities that go into the final product called an automobile are carried out within an automobile manufacturing firm.

Much can be learned about the reasons firms exist merely by recognizing that economic transactions are not costless. Exchange between two individuals has its costs, gener-

ally called *transactions costs*. Given the existence of transactions costs, it may be cheaper to organize production in such a way that some market transactions are eliminated and replaced instead by an entrepreneur who both monitors and directs the production process.

However, such an organization does have its bad points. Production by a group of individuals who are not the **residual claimants** to any profits—"what's left over"—increases the cost of monitoring, metering, directing, and renegotiating contracts. If 10 Haitian basket weavers operate separately as individual entities in which each one is an entrepreneur, each one will feel the full brunt of "not doing his or her job." Income and profits will fall for each individual who slacks off in proportion to how much the individual slows down. However, if all 10 are put into one firm in which they work together as a coordinated group, each specializing, say, in one aspect of production, the cost of any one individual member's not doing the job will be spread out equally among all members. Hence, if a firm is used to organize production, the cost to an individual of slacking off on the job is less than in a situation where the worker is also the residual claimant to any profits. Moreover, in a firm, it is more difficult to meter the output of each individual in the group because they are all working together. Thus, it is more difficult to work out a proper incentive system to reward a worker who generates a higher output by way of a greater work effort. The above are factors working *against* organizing firms.

What we observe in firms, however, are monitors. These monitors make sure that workers perform. Monitors also attempt to meter the output of workers. The ultimate monitor in a firm is the entrepreneur or employer. If the entrepreneur or employer doesn't monitor effectively, his or her net wealth position is reduced. Employees, in choosing to work for a firm, implicitly agree to being monitored by the entrepreneur.

---

[1] More generally, we could define a firm as an organization that buys and hires resources and sells goods and services. A single-person proprietorship would fall under this broader definition.

All this leads us to the prediction that *firms will exist whenever cooperative group effort results in a larger product than the sum of the products of individual efforts*. The difference, of course, must be at least as great as the costs of organizing, monitoring, metering,[2] and enforcing contracts with employees less the transactions costs associated with the subcontracting alternative.

The goal of the firm

Lurking behind the explanation of why firms exist was an implicit assumption about the goal or goals of the firm. It was stated that the buck stopped at the ultimate monitor—the owner-entrepreneur or employer who had a residual claim on whatever was left over after all expenses were paid. This residual claim is called **profit**. Underlying our assertion that the entrepreneur as monitor will slack off less in his or her duties because of the immediate impact on net worth is an assumption of net worth maximization (in the present value sense). The theory of the firm as we present it in this book is built around this hypothesis.

Profit maximization

In demand theory, utility or satisfaction maximization provided the basis for the analysis. In the theory of the firm and production, at least initially, profit or wealth maximization is the underlying hypothesis of our predictive theory.

Is this assumption of profit maximization realistic? If we are trying to explain business behavior, we don't actually have to assume that entrepreneurs consciously try to maximize profits. We hypothesize that their behavior is consistent with the maximization of profits. If a physicist wants to predict where a billiard player will hit the cue ball in order to cause a particular ball to go into a pocket on the billiard table, the physicist predicts the billiard player's behavior by hypothesizing that the player knows the laws of physics, even though this may be an "unrealistic" assumption. Remember from our discussion in Chapter 1 that it is not necessary that assumptions be directly testable—indeed, normally they are indirectly tested by the refutable predictions of the model. If the real world consistently refutes a model's predictions, then the assumptions of the model may be inappropriate.

Theories of managerial discretion

Nonetheless, other goals of the firm can be presented, and we examine several of them below. However, we will use the profit-maximizing assumption throughout the remainder of this text.

Staff maximization

Whenever there is a separation of the ownership of a business from its control, the possibility arises that the managers will not act in the best interests of the owners.[3] Since monitoring is not a costless activity, owners would not be expected to eliminate completely managerial activities which benefit the managers but harm the owners. Given the separation of ownership and control, it is possible that man-

---

[2]A detailed discussion of the notion of monitoring and metering and of the existence of firms can be found in A. A. Alchian and H. Demsetz, "Production, Information Costs, and Economic Organization," *American Economic Review*, December 1972, pp. 777–795. See also R. H. Coase, "The Nature of the Firm," *Economica*, new ser., vol.

4, November 1937, pp. 386–408. The article is also reprinted in G. Stigler and K. Boulding, *Reading in Price Theory* (Homewood, Ill.: Irwin, 1952), pp. 332–335.

[3]See, for example, Adolph A. Berle and Gardiner C. Means, *The Modern Corporation and Private Property* (New York: Macmillan, 1948).

agers may seek to satisfy their own utility by having a larger staff than is necessary to achieve maximum profit or wealth for the owners. The manager is willing to trade off some of the owners' profit for an increase in his or her staff, particularly when it is difficult for the managers to "get caught" at not acting 100 percent in the owners' interest. We can represent the trade-off in terms of indifference curves. Three of these we show in Figure 7-1.

We see in Figure 7-1 that the horizontal axis measures staff hours per unit time period and the vertical axis measures profit per unit time period. Assume that the indifference curves for a manager are convex to the origin. There is a profit curve showing the relationship be-

tween profit and staff size. *Ceteris paribus*, as more staff members are added, profit rises to a maximum of B associated with a staff size of S_2 and then falls; reaching zero with a staff size of S_0. To maximize the utility of the manager, the staff size would be set at S_1, for that is where the indifference curve II is tangent to the "budget constraint" or trade-off line between profit and staff size (point E). If there were no separation of ownership and control, or if monitoring by owners were costless, the size of the staff would be set at S_2 and profits would be at their maximum of B. In other words, managers would act *as if* they were owners in setting the optimal staff size.

This is a utility-maximizing theory of managerial behavior. It requires the existence of imperfect information among the owners-stockholders. It also requires that the firm have some degree of market power.[4] If the firm were in a completely competitive market, a topic we will discuss in Chapter 10, it would have to maximize profits merely to survive.

Sales maximization[5]

Another type of model that has been offered for the firm is based on sales maximization. Managers may pursue sales maximization if they think that their own compensation and/or their professional prestige depends more on sales than on profits. We must insert the constraint here that there be a minimum rate of return on investment that stockholders require. (Note that we are referring now to the *rate* of profit—profits/investment per year—rather than to absolute profits.)

We present the model of sales maximization in Figure 7-2. Profit, expressed as a rate of return on investment, is represented on the ver-

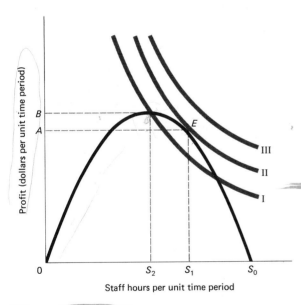

Figure 7-1: Staff maximization.
Staff hours per unit time period are measured on the horizontal axis. Profit is expressed as dollars per unit time period on the vertical axis. Up to S_2 as staff is added, profits increase. After that point, profits decrease. Thus, the profit-maximizing size of staff is at S_2; however, the managers are assumed to obtain utility from a larger staff size. Thus, they hire staff up to the point where they can reach their highest indifference curve, II, or at point E. Staff hired will be equal to S_1, which is greater than S_2. The corresponding profit A will be less than the maximum profit B.

[4]Oliver E. Williamson, *The Economics of Discretionary Behavior* (Englewood Cliffs, N.J.: Prentice-Hall, 1964).

[5]William J. Baumol, *Business Behavior, Value and Growth*, rev. ed. (New York: Harcourt Brace Jovanovich, 1967).

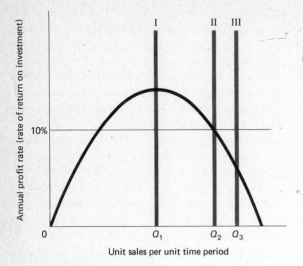

Figure 7-2: Sales maximization.
Assume that profitability, expressed as a rate of return on investment, is an increasing function of unit sales up to rate of unit sales Q_1, after that profitability diminishes. Assume, also, that there is a minimum annual rate of return that managers must meet and that it is 10 percent. The indifference curves for the managers are I, II, and III. They are vertical, indicating the managers receive no utility from profitability per se. The highest indifference curve that managers can reach is not III, with the rate of unit sales at Q_3 because that rate of unit sales yields a rate of profitability below 10 percent per year. Therefore, the rate of unit sales that managers will strive for is Q_2, which puts them on indifference curve II. Note that this rate exceeds the profitability maximizing rate of unit sales Q_1.

tical axis, and unit sales per unit time period on the horizontal axis. The relationship between the profit rate and unit sales is given by the curve; the profit rate reaches a maximum at a rate of sales Q_1. However, assume that the point of maximum revenues (price times quantity) occurs at a quantity of sales Q_3. Even if management wishes to maximize sales revenues, it will not be able to produce at the quantity Q_3. This is because there is a constraint imposed upon it. That constraint is the minimum profit rate which we have drawn in arbitrarily at 10 percent per year. Thus the managers will set sales at Q_2 rather than at the profitability-maximizing rate of Q_1.

We have drawn indifference curves I, II, and

III vertically. The reason they are drawn vertically is because we assume that management obtains no utility at all from profitability; thus, a higher utility curve is merely a vertical line that is farther to the right. How can managers increase unit sales and hence revenues? Provided they are operating in the elastic portion of their demand curve, they can lower the price of the product and increase total revenues. (Why?) Further, they can engage in more advertising to increase sales by shifting the demand curve outward to the right.

Growth maximization

A similar model of the firm involves managers attempting to maximize the rate of growth of sales revenues. Presumably this would explain why managers are so amenable to mergers with other firms. If they see that their salaries are related to the rate of growth of their firm and to having larger organizations under their influence, they will engage in activities to make the firm larger. However, they are still constrained by a minimum profitability requirement. This minimum profitability requirement exists, in principle, because if profitability becomes too low, there exists the possibility that some group of stockholders will attempt to take over the firm (and fire some or all of the current managers).

A combination of managerial utility maximization, sales maximization, and growth-rate maximization is inherent in the view of the firm presented in J. K. Galbraith's *New Industrial State* and *Economics and the Public Purpose*. Additionally, Galbraith points to the managerial drive for prestige and technical virtuosity. He further suggests that the managers can carry out their plans because they are able to influence the behavior of consumers, primarily by advertising. Since the corporation is run by managers who wish to have an easy life for themselves, Galbraith emphasizes that large corporations will try to avoid risks and engage in extensive planning to produce stability. This is his so-called planning sector of the economy, and it is run by corporate technocrats—*technically* skilled individuals who, in Galbraith's view, make all the important business planning decisions.

Satisficing behavior[6]

According to the satisficing theory of firm behavior, the firm sets for itself a minimum standard for performance. It aims at a "satisfactory" rate of profit; presumably, once this rate of profit is obtained, the firm will slack off. An implication of the satisficing theory of firm behavior is that within the firm there is no consistent attempt to minimize costs for any given level of output, provided, of course, that a satisfactory rate of return is being earned. In other words, there is "internal slack."

Criticisms of non-profit-maximizing assumptions

Aside from the question of the role of assumption in economic theory, there have been criticisms leveled against the alternative models presented above. One is that there is indeed a market in managers. Every management team of every firm faces the possibility that some other management team may convince the stockholders that the latter will increase the profitability of the firm if allowed to take control. Given the existence of a market for corporate control, behavior that deviates dramatically from profit maximization presumably will not be allowed to continue indefinitely. (Although clearly the more impediments there are to controlling corporate management, the more likely is the firm to operate in a non-profit-maximizing dimension.)

Additionally, critics of non-profit-maximizing models of the firm point out that not only

existing stockholders but *potential* stockholders must be considered. Remember in the last chapter when we said that the price of an asset is the discounted stream of its anticipated future net income? If the asset in question is the common stock of a firm, then its value or price in the marketplace will be the present value of the expected stream of future net profits. Thus, to the extent that current management decisions are not maximizing long-run profits, the current market price of the firm's stock will be less than it otherwise would be. Some outsiders might take note of this, making the corporation a sitting duck for a takeover bid. A group of investors would attempt to take over the corporation by buying a large block of its stock at its current low price, kicking out the current managers, and installing a new set, thereby increasing anticipated future profitability. The market value of the stock will then rise. Those who took over would experience an increase in their net worth—a capital gain—since the stock they owned in the company could now be sold for more than they paid for it. Thus, to the extent that there exists a market for corporate takeovers, non-profit-maximizing behavior has some limits set on it.

Accepting for the moment, then, the assumption of profit maximization, we can now proceed to examine the determinants of the way in which a firm organizes production. Specifically, we will look at the optimal use of inputs.

Production inputs

What goes into the production of a commodity? Broadly speaking, inputs, by definition. These inputs include managerial talent, entrepreneurial risk taking, raw materials, various types of labor, and so on.

Classification of inputs

In order to simplify our analysis, we will group all inputs into either of two categories:

---

[6]Herbert Simon, "Theories of Decision-making in Economics and Behavioral Science," *American Economic Review*, June 1959.

labor and capital. Once the analysis has been done with this simplified division of production inputs, the reader can expand the analysis by any refinements in the classifying inputs he or she wishes to undertake.

A further classification that we will use is the division of inputs into those that are fixed and those that are variable. Complying with tradition and ease of exposition, we will treat capital as fixed and labor as variable. The distinction between fixed and variable factors of production is clearly an arbitrary one and one that is dependent upon the time period for which the firm has to make decisions.

Short versus long run

Commonly, a fixed factor of production is one that cannot be altered in the short run but can in the long run. But, then, what is the meaning of short run and long run here and what is meant by "cannot be altered"? Certainly, you would agree that a steam generator already in place must be classified as a fixed factor of production in the short run because it is hard to expand the firm's stock of steam generators in a short period of time. That, however, is an incomplete statement of reality. At a high enough cost, an electrical utility can have a steam generator installed in a relatively short period of time. For enough money, it can purchase an additional steam generator from another utility and have it delivered on short order.

Again, we will have to make a rather arbitrary distinction between short and long run as applied to our way of defining fixed and variable factors of production. What we will have to say is that a fixed factor of production is one whose quantity cannot be expanded in a short period of time without substantially increasing the cost per unit of the fixed factor; it can, however, be altered in the long run without an increase in cost per unit.

The definition of the long run is a time period during which all factors of production are variable. Within the context of the above

reasoning, the long run is a time period during which all factors can be varied without causing their per-unit cost to rise. The long run is an investment-decision framework. In the long run, a decision is made whether to invest, to reinvest, or to scrap a production process.

Relating output to inputs

The firm brings together certain types of inputs and combines them in such a way that an output results. The output is what the firm sells. Our theory implies that the way in which the firm uses inputs to produce output is technologically efficient.

Economic versus technical efficiency

Efficiency has to do with the relationship of inputs to output. Let us first consider the technological aspects of this relationship. At any moment in time, the total list of all known productive processes for a society is its available technology. We will assume in our economic analysis of production that there is perfect transmission of technological information across firms; thus the available technology will be the same for all firms. As time goes on, new technologies are discovered, new ways in which inputs can be used together to produce outputs. As new processes are discovered, old ones of course remain known. Thus the list of available technology becomes longer and longer.

Now consider the situation in which a new process has been discovered. Assume further that it uses the same types of input and produces the same type of output as an existing process. However, the new process uses less of one or more of the inputs and no more of any one input in producing a given rate of output. Alternatively, it can produce more output with the same amounts of each input. In such a situation, the old process has now become technically inefficient. Clearly, no profit-maximizing producer would use more inputs than need be used for a given level of output. It is, therefore, not unreasonable for us to assume that once a process has become technically inefficient, it will never be used.

By definition, then, **technical efficiency** requires using a production process which uses no more inputs than is necessary for a *given* output.

Now let us consider a technological change where a new process is discovered that uses the same inputs to produce the same output as did the old process. However, it uses less of some inputs and more of others to produce any given quantity of output. We cannot automatically call the old process technologically inefficient. In fact, the old process may continue to be used in some situations, the new process in others. Which one is used in each case will depend on the prices of the inputs. We currently have a "new" process for building highways. We use workers and sophisticated machinery. The old process uses workers with picks and shovels. The old process uses more labor and less capital, the new process less labor and more capital. In a society where there is lots of labor, the old process will continue to be used in spite of the fact that firms in that society know of the existence of the new process. The choice of processes now becomes an *economic* rather than a purely *technical* one. The engineer must step aside; the economist enters the scene.

The notion of **economic efficiency** implicit in the above paragraph rests on a comparison of the value of output to the value of inputs. Economic efficiency requires that the dollar value of output per dollar's worth of resource input be maximized. The use of resources is economically efficient only when the resulting output maximizes the total or aggregate satisfaction of wants for all individuals in society.

In the discussion that follows, we take for granted technological efficiency on the part of the firm. The profit-maximizing firm will never voluntarily select a production process that physically "wastes" inputs. If 10 units of output can be produced with 10 units of labor and 10 units of capital, then the firm will never use 10 units of labor and 12 units of capital in the production of 10 units of output. Once we derive this implication of technical efficiency, we will find that the optimal choice of inputs on the part of the firm corresponds to our notion of economic efficiency.

The production function

We label the relationship between physical output and physical inputs the **production function**. It is defined as the schedule or mathematical equation that gives the *maximum* quantity of output that can be produced from specified sets of inputs, *ceteris paribus*.[7]

In its broadest form, a production function is described by the equation

$$Q = f(K, L) \qquad (7\text{-}1)$$

where Q is the rate of output per unit time period, K is the service flow from the stock of capital per unit time period, and L is the service flow from the firm's laborers per unit time period. All that this equation tells us is that output is some function of the inputs, capital and labor. We haven't specified the exact relationship. Rather, we have left it as an unspecified function.

Perhaps it is easiest to understand the notion of a production function by working through a hypothetical numerical example. We will deal with only one variable factor of production in this example and work it through in its entirety. Then we will deal with two variable inputs.

The production relationship with one variable factor

We present a production-function relationship in Table 7-1.

---

[7]A more formal definition is the envelope of the attainable set of technically efficient combinations of inputs.

Number of workers per year	Total physical output (pounds of corn per year)
1	100
2	210
3	330
4	405
5	475
6	500
7	490

Table 7-1

The production function can be written as

$$Q = f(L, \bar{K}) \qquad (7\text{-}2)$$

where K is constant.

Here we are assuming that there is only one variable factor of production, and that is labor. Capital is held constant. As more workers are added, total output increases. The **total physical product** curve that results is presented in Figure 7-3. We have joined the successive points taken off Table 7-1 to form that curve. It reaches a maximum at six workers per year. After that point, total physical product actually declines.

If we examine **average physical product** and **marginal physical product**, we will be able to explain why the total product curve is shaped the way it is.

AVERAGE PHYSICAL PRODUCT. Average physical product (APP) is defined as the total product divided by the quantity of the variable input employed. We present average physical product in column (3) of Table 7-2. It is total output per year divided by the number of workers per year. Column (3) combined with column (1) can be transferred to Figure 7-4. Here we show the average physical product curve, which first rises, then reaches a peak at three workers, and then falls.

MARGINAL PHYSICAL PRODUCT. Marginal physical product (MPP) is defined as the change in total output due to a one-unit

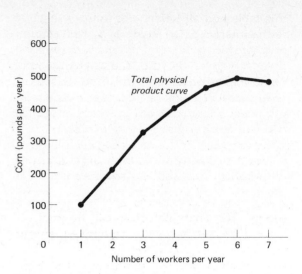

Figure 7-3: Total physical product.
The production function of Table 7-1 is transferred to this graph. Total physical product rises until six workers per year are employed and then falls.

increment or decrement in the variable input. In this example, we are talking about labor; therefore, we refer to the marginal physical product of labor, which is presented in Table 7-2. It is basically the change in total output in column (2). Note that we follow the standard convention that all marginal figures in

Number of workers (1)	Total output (2)	Average physical product of labor [(2) ÷ (1)] (3)	Marginal physical product of labor* (Δ total output/ Δ labor input) (4)
1	100	100	100
2	210	105	110
3	330	110	120
4	405	101.25	75
5	475	95	70
6	500	83.33	25
7	490	70	−10

Table 7-2
*All marginal figures refer to an interval between the indicated amount of the variable input and one unit less than that indicated amount. This convention will be used in all tables showing marginal quantities.

this table and all others that follow will refer to the interval between the indicated amount of whatever is under study and one unit less than whatever is the indicated amount. Thus, the marginal physical product for the second row refers to the change in total output when going from one worker per year to two workers per year (or vice versa).

We can transfer the data from column (4) to Figure 7-4. The result is the marginal physical product curve and it is so labeled.

WHAT MARGINAL PHYSICAL PRODUCT OF LABOR MEANS. The marginal physical product of labor does not mean the amount of output produced by an additional or last unit of labor. Rather, it refers to the change in total output when the labor input is changed by one unit. It is a comparison, as it were, between total output associated with a particular size of labor input and total output when that size of labor input is increased or decreased by one unit, keeping capital fixed. Thus, marginal physical product of labor never means the amount produced by the last unit of labor. This can be seen by examining the exact relationship between marginal product and average product.

THE RELATIONSHIP BETWEEN MARGINAL AND AVERAGE PHYSICAL PRODUCT. One way of looking at marginal physical product is to see that it represents the average physical product corrected for any change in the average physi-

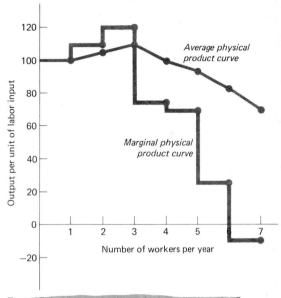

Figure 7-4: Average and marginal physical product. The average physical product curve is taken from the third column in Table 7-2. It rises up to three workers per year and then falls thereafter. Marginal physical product is taken from the last column in Table 7-2.

cal product due to adding or subtracting one worker. In other words, marginal physical product is average physical product plus the change in average product times the number of workers. Or

$$MPP_L = APP_L + (\Delta APP_L)L \qquad (7\text{-}3)$$

where the subscript L refers to labor.[8] The term ΔMPP_L is negative in cases where

---

[8]To prove this, start with average physical product Q/L, where $Q =$ output; then

(a) $\qquad Q = L\left(\dfrac{Q}{L}\right)$

For simplicity, let $Q/L = X$.

(a') $\qquad\qquad Q = L \cdot X$

(b) $\qquad Q + \Delta Q = (L + \Delta L)(X + \Delta X)$

$\qquad\qquad\qquad = LX + L\Delta X + \Delta LX + \Delta L\Delta X$

(c) $\qquad\qquad \Delta Q = L\Delta X + \Delta LX + \Delta L\Delta X$

(d) $\qquad \dfrac{\Delta Q}{\Delta L} = L\dfrac{\Delta X}{\Delta L} + X + \Delta X$

As $\Delta L \to 0$, ΔX also approaches 0, since $X = \dfrac{Q}{L}$, then (d) becomes

(e) $\qquad \dfrac{\Delta Q}{\Delta L} = L\dfrac{\Delta X}{\Delta L} + X$

(f) $\qquad \dfrac{\Delta Q}{\Delta L} = L\dfrac{\Delta(Q/L)}{\Delta L} + \dfrac{Q}{L}$

(g) $\qquad MPP_L = APP_L + L\dfrac{\Delta APP_L}{\Delta L}$

which is Eq. (7-3) when ΔL is assumed equal to one unit.

a one-worker change reduces the average productivity of all workers. In the example we have been dealing with, this occurs when the seventh worker is added or subtracted. The workers get in each other's way so much that total physical product actually falls when the seventh worker is put on the labor force and rises with the seventh worker's removal. We can use Eq. (7-3) to determine the marginal physical product when seven laborers are working. The average physical product of seven workers is 70. The change in average physical product when we go from six to seven workers is $-13^{1}/_{3}$. We multiply $-13^{1}/_{3}$ by 6, and we get -80. $70 + (-80) = -10$, which is exactly equal to the marginal physical product of labor when seven workers are working.

We can also use Eq. (7-3) to figure out the relationship between average and marginal physical product on a graph. Marginal physical product will exceed average physical product only when average physical product is rising. Marginal physical product will be less than average physical product only when average physical product is falling. Thus we know that whenever the average physical product curve is rising, the marginal physical product curve must be somewhere above it; when the average physical product curve is falling, the marginal physical product curve must be somewhere below it. This is as we have drawn it in Figure 7-4. We also know from Eq. (7-3) that the only time marginal physical product equals average physical product is when average physical product is constant, for that is when the last term in Eq. (7-3) becomes 0. This occurs at the maximum point on the average physical product curve.

(Note that all these relationships apply only when it is possible to produce different levels of output with different proportions of capital and labor inputs. It would be impossible for us to draw the curves that we have drawn if capital and labor had to be used in fixed proportions. Thus we say that the above relations apply only to variable-proportion production functions.)

The law of diminishing marginal returns

The shape of the total physical product curve in Figure 7-3 and the resulting average and marginal physical product curves in Figure 7-4 was not accidental. The way we have drawn these curves is consistent with the so-called **law of diminishing marginal returns**, or of diminishing marginal *physical* product. Actually, in the way we have set up our example, the marginal physical product from adding one more worker per year first rises, going from 100 to 110 to 120, and then falls. At the point at which the marginal physical product of labor falls, we say that diminishing marginal returns have set in. It is relatively easy to understand why the so-called law of diminishing marginal physical product (or returns) would be operative in just about all production functions. After all, we are holding the amount of capital constant and merely adding more workers. Each worker is thus working with a smaller and smaller capital stock. Think of it in terms of the capital stock consisting of hoes for a bunch of workers who are going to weed an acre of cotton. After some point, there will be more workers than hoes, and the hoes will have to be shared. At least at that point, and perhaps even before, diminishing marginal physical returns will probably set in.

Let us formally state the law of diminishing marginal returns:

Holding technology and all inputs except one constant, as equal increments of the variable input are added, beyond a certain point the resulting rate of increase in product will decrease. Otherwise stated, after a certain point, the marginal physical product of the variable input will diminish.

The law of diminishing returns holds if: (1) only one variable input is varied and all others are held strictly constant; (2) the "state of the arts" is fixed—i.e., technology does not change; and (3) the coefficients of production are variable—i.e., we are not dealing with fixed-proportions function in which one unit of labor has to be used with, say, two units of capital. For example, we rule out a road-building production process which requires that only one laborer with one pick be used. We assume that it is possible to substitute more sophisticated machinery in order to use fewer workers.

The law of diminishing returns is an empirical assertion about reality. It is not a theorem derived from a set of assumptions or an axiomatic system. It is not a logical proposition and hence is not susceptible to mathematical proof or refutation. Rather, it is merely a statement concerning physical relationships that have been observed to hold in the real world. One of the reasons that we accept this "law" is that we would otherwise find it difficult to explain why firms *stopped* hiring additional labor (or any other input) at some point.

The geometry of total, average, and marginal physical product

There is a definite relationship between total, average, and marginal physical product curves. We will see this when we work out their geometry. Look at Figure 7-5. Here we have shown a smoothly drawn total physical product curve. In order to figure out average physical product, pick any amount of the variable input, say, L_1. The amount of output produced is Q_1. The definition of average physical product tells us that it is measured by the vertical distance $0Q_1$, which is also equal to L_1A, divided by the horizontal distance $0L_1$. Thus, average physical product of $0L_1$ units of the variable inputs equals

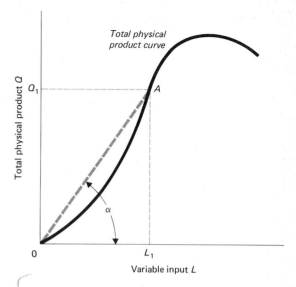

Figure 7-5: Deriving average physical product from total physical product.

We draw in a smooth total physical product curve here. Pick a point, such as A, where L_1 of workers are hired. Their total physical product is measured on the vertical axis as Q_1. Average physical product is, therefore, Q_1/L_1; but this is equal to the numerical value of the slope of the line connecting point A with the origin, or with the tangent of angle α.

$L_1A/0L_1$. But $L_1A/0L_1$ is identically equal to the slope of the line, or ray, connecting point A with the origin. Otherwise stated, APP is the slope of the straight line that connects point A with the origin and is equal to the tangent of angle α.

We now have a geometric way to figure out what happens to average physical product as we increase the use of the variable input. It is shown in Figure 7-6. Consider first quantity A of the variable input, then B, then C, all the way through H. We see that the slope of the straight lines from the origin to the input-output combination quantities in question gets steeper and steeper, reaches its maximum at E, and then gets less steep. Thus average physical product increases up to the amount of E units of the variable input and thereafter decreases. Quantity E would corre-

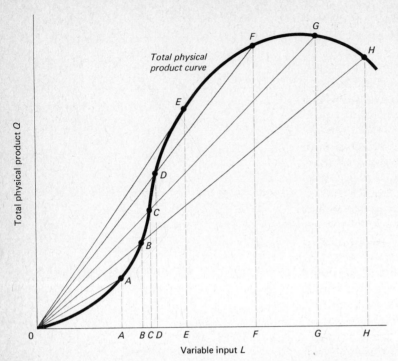

Figure 7-6: Changing APP.
As we increase the variable input from quantity A to quantity B, we see that the lines connecting those quantities with the origin have an increasing slope up to E and then have a decreasing slope. Thus, APP of the variable input increases up to E and decreases thereafter.

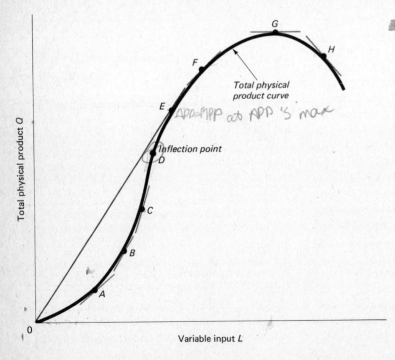

Figure 7-7: Deriving MPP from the total physical product curve.
Marginal physical product is defined as the change in total physical product due to a one-unit change in the variable input. Thus, it is equal to the slope of a tangent drawn to any point on the total physical product curve. We see, then, that marginal physical product increases as it moves from point A to points B and C, then decreases after the inflection point D through points E and F, finally becomes zero at point G, and is negative thereafter.

spond to three workers in Table 7-2 in our previous example.

Marginal physical product

Marginal physical product is defined as the change in total physical product due to a unit change in the variable input. When we are dealing with infinitesimally small changes in the variable input, marginal physical product can be defined as the slope of the total physical product curve at the point in question. It is important to make the distinction between average physical product and marginal physical product. Average physical product is determined by the slope of the line from the origin to the point in question on the total physical product curve; marginal physical product is determined by the slope of the tangent line drawn at the point in question on the total physical product curve. This is shown in Figure 7-7, where eight amounts, A through H of the variable input, are pinpointed on the total physical product curve. A tangent is drawn at each of these points. The slope of the tangent first rises and then falls and eventually becomes negative after point G. Notice two things about the slope of these tangent lines. At some point D, the slope of the tangent line stops getting steeper and starts getting less steep. This is the *inflection point* on the total physical product curve. Note also that the tangent line at point E intersects the origin. Thus, at point E, average and marginal physical product are equal. Furthermore, from the last section, we know that at point E average physical product is at its maximum. Finally, at point G, the slope of the tangent is 0 and marginal physical product is 0.

Putting it all together

In Figure 7-8, we have put all the above geometric information together. We show a total physical product curve in the top half of the

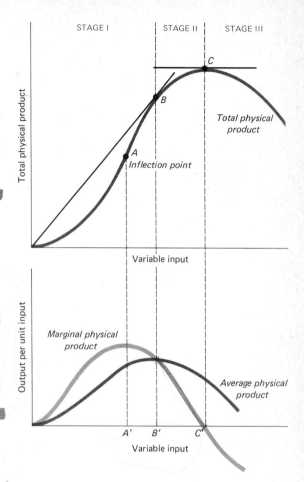

Figure 7-8: The relationship between total, average, and marginal physical product.

In the top panel, we draw a smooth total physical product curve. Its inflection point is at point A, where marginal physical product changes from increasing to decreasing, i.e., reaches its maximum at variable input level A' in the lower panel. At point B in the top panel on the total physical product curve, marginal physical product is equal to average physical product, i.e., the two curves intersect; this is seen in the bottom panel at quantity of variable input B'. Thereafter, average physical product declines. At point C, total physical product has reached its maximum; marginal physical product is zero, and thereafter it is negative. In the top panel, we have shown stages I, II, and III. Stage II is called the *economic region of production.*

diagram. From information in this total physical product curve, we can derive various points on the average and marginal physical product curves and learn the exact relationships between them. These are shown in the bottom half of the diagram. First of all, point A is the inflection point on the total physical product curve. At the inflection point, marginal physical product reaches its maximum. This is shown in the marginal physical product curve in the bottom part of the diagram. At point B, we know two things: Average physical product is at its maximum, and average physical product equals marginal physical product. Thus, in the bottom half of the diagram, we see that the average physical product curve has reached its maximum at B' and that the average physical product curve intersects the marginal physical product curve here. Finally, at point C, we know that marginal physical product is equal to 0. Thus we show the marginal physical product curve intersecting the vertical axis in the bottom half of Figure 7-8 becoming negative for levels of variable input greater than C'.

The three stages of production

The top part of Figure 7-8 has also been partitioned into three regions: stage I, stage II, and stage III. These are the so-called three stages of production. The first stage of production is a stage in which the average physical product of the variable input is increasing. In stage II, its average physical product is decreasing, as is its marginal physical product, but the marginal physical product is still positive. In stage III, the average physical product continues to decrease and so, too, does the total physical product because the marginal physical product is now negative.

Clearly, no producer would want to produce in stage III. It is definitely disadvantageous to use more of the variable input. Why? Because a higher total physical product could be obtained by reducing the amount of the variable input.

The case of two variable inputs

Perhaps a more interesting production decision involves not the choice of how much of one variable input to use, but rather what combination of two variable inputs to use. We will now assume that the capital and labor available to the firm are both variable, and that very small increments of capital and labor are available to the firm. Certain combinations of capital and labor will therefore produce certain levels of output. We can use a geometric device in our theory of production that is similar to the geometric device that we used in the theory of consumer demand. Remember the indifference curve which gave the combination of two commodities which yielded a constant level of satisfaction? If we now consider that we are talking about a constant level of output, then we have a geometric device showing the various combinations of labor and capital that yield a constant output.

Production isoquants

The technical term for this geometric device is a **production**, or **output**, **isoquant**. It is defined as a curve in an **input space** (rather than a commodity space) that shows all the possible combinations of two inputs (capital and labor, in our example) that are physically capable of producing a given rate of output. We show a hypothetical isoquant in Figure 7-9. The horizontal axis measures labor, expressed in service flow per unit time period; capital, expressed in units of service flow per time period, is depicted on the vertical axis. The isoquant is drawn for a particular production rate Q_1. Thus any combination of capital and labor given by a point along the isoquant will yield exactly Q_1 in product. As we move along Q_1, we simultaneously vary the amounts and the proportions in which capital and labor are used.

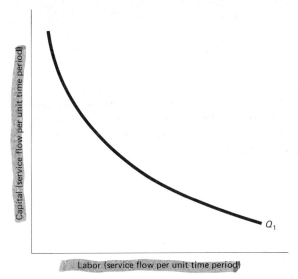

Figure 7-9: An output isoquant.
When we are dealing with a variable-proportion production function, we can vary labor and capital input so as to produce a constant level of output. This is shown by a constant output curve called an *isoquant* and labeled Q_1.

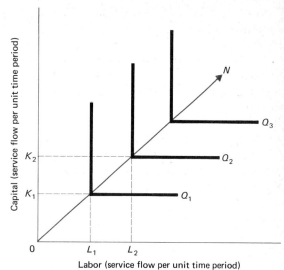

Figure 7-10: Fixed-proportion production function.
The ratio of capital to labor is physically fixed in this particular production function. That ratio is given by the slope of the ray $0N$. For output Q_1, it is necessary to use L_1 of labor and K_1 of capital. It does not matter if more capital is used, holding the quantity of labor constant; that will not increase output. It does not matter if more labor is used, holding the quantity of capital constant—it will not increase output. In other words, the MPP of either input is zero.

Fixed-proportion production functions

Up until now we have implicitly or explicitly been dealing with variable-proportion production functions—any combination of capital and labor can be used in production. It is possible, however, that two inputs, such as cars and wheels, must be used in fixed proportions. We demonstrate what the isoquants would look like in the case of a fixed-proportion production function. The ratio of capital to labor is fixed physically and immutably in the particular example illustrated in Figure 7-10. The ratio is given by the slope of the ray $0N$. The isoquants are necessarily right angles. For output Q_1, it is necessary to use labor and capital in the proportion $L_1:K_1$. In other words, given the amount of labor L_1, it does not matter if more capital than K_1 is used. In fact, more than K_1 would be technically inefficient. The only output available is Q_1. Conversely, given the amount of capital K_1, it

does not matter if more labor than L_1 is used. More than L_1 would be technically inefficient. Go on to the next output level, Q_2. Here the amount of labor necessary is L_2 and the amount of capital K_2. The proportion $L_2:K_2$ is equal to the proportion $L_1:K_1$. That is the nature of the fixed-proportion production functions. In Chapter 9, we take up this case in more detail when we deal with linear programming. Suffice it to say here that the real world does not exhibit a great number of fixed-proportion production functions. When the isoquants are perpendicular, as in Figure 7-10, we say that the inputs are either joint or perfectly complementary; i.e., they must be used in fixed proportions. For such cases, it is useful to speak of the demand for bundles of the two inputs in their fixed proportion.

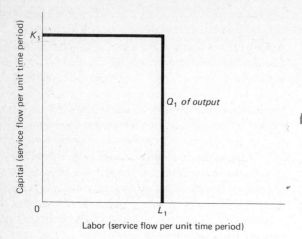

Figure 7-11: A non-real-world isoquant mapping.
In this inside-out isoquant, only one of the inputs is necessary to produce a particular level of output. This isoquant would lead to complete specialization in inputs.

A non—real world isoquant mapping

It is possible, in principle at least, to reverse the above example. This is shown in Figure 7-11. Here we show an isoquant in which the two "sides" are perpendicular to the vertical and horizontal axes. In this particular production relationship, only one of the inputs is necessary to produce a particular level of output. In Figure 7-11, in order to produce Q_1 of output, it is necessary to have L_1 of labor. But no capital is necessary. Or alternatively, to produce Q_1 of output, the amount of capital necessary is K_1, and it is of no consequence how much labor (even zero) is used. This sort of production relationship is definitely not observed in the real world.

Distinguishing between movements along and among isoquants

Look at Figure 7-12. Each isoquant represents the combinations of capital and labor that may be used to produce given outputs Q_1, Q_2, and Q_3, where $Q_1 < Q_2 < Q_3$. Now, what happens when we move from A to B along the isoquant corresponding with output level Q_1? We merely change the combination of labor and capital—both the proportion *and* the absolute amounts—but we do not change the output level. We see the change in the proportion of labor to capital by the change in the angle of the ray (straight line) from the origin to points A and B. At point B, there is more capital used and less labor; i.e., the ratio of capital to labor is greater, and clearly the slope of the ray $0B$ is greater than the slope of the ray $0A$, for at A there is less capital and more labor used.

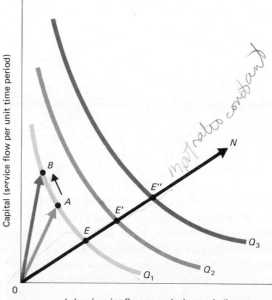

Figure 7-12: Distinguishing between a movement along a single isoquant and a movement among isoquants.
As we move along isoquant Q_1, with the quantity of output held constant at Q_1, we change the proportions of the two inputs. In other words, the movement from A to B involves an increase in the capital to labor ratio. However, a movement along any ray, such as $0N$, entails a movement among isoquants where output is changing while the factor proportion remains fixed at points E, E', and E''. The capital-labor ratio is the same, but output has increased.

Movements out along a particular ray, such as $0N$, guarantee that the proportion of capital and labor will remain constant, but the output level associated with each will rise because more of both capital and labor is being used. Thus, for movements along any ray (which is a straight line from the origin) we will find the level of output changing continuously but the input ratio (K/L or L/K) remaining constant. The input ratio at E, E', and E'' is constant in Figure 7-12.

Substitution among inputs

We have assumed that substitution among inputs is feasible. It turns out that the shape of an isoquant indicates the amount of substitution that is *technically* feasible. We can better understand the slope of an isoquant by relating it to the marginal physical product of the input.

The slope of an isoquant

When we move along an isoquant, we increase the usage of one input and decrease the usage of the other input, all the while keeping output constant. The degree to which the usage of one input is increased while the other is decreased is given by the slope of the isoquant. The slope of the isoquant is clearly the change in capital divided by the change in labor as output is held constant, or

$$\text{Slope of isoquant} = \frac{\Delta K}{\Delta L}$$

$$Q_1 = Q \quad \text{i.e., output held constant}$$

(7-4)

The slope of the isoquants that we have drawn is negative—the direction of a change in capital will always be opposite of a change in labor.

We can relate the slope of a convex isoquant, which is always changing, to the marginal physical product of labor and of capital. Remember that MPP_L is defined as the change in output resulting from a one-unit change in the amount of labor used, *keeping the capital input fixed*. The marginal physical product of capital MPP_K is the change in output resulting from a one-unit change in the amount of capital used, *holding the labor input constant*. Let us begin the analysis on the isoquant relating to a level of output Q_1 in Figure 7-13 at point A. We increase the amount of labor used by ΔL, which lands us at point B. The movement from A to B is the result of a ΔL change in the amount of labor. The movement from B to C is caused by a ΔK change in the use of capital. Now, along the Q_1 isoquant, output is held

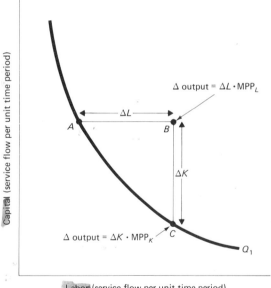

Figure 7-13: The slope of an isoquant.
The slope of an isoquant is given by the negative of the ratio of the change in capital to the change in labor. A change in labor from point A to point B will change output by $\Delta L \cdot \text{MPP}_L$. In order to keep output constant, we must reduce it by reducing capital. Capital must be reduced by the amount ΔK, and output will then fall by $\Delta K \cdot \text{MPP}_K$. These two quantities must be equal to keep output constant; hence, $-\Delta K / \Delta L$, the slope of the output isoquant must be equal to $\text{MPP}_L / \text{MPP}_K$.

constant at Q_1. So for any movement along the isoquant, $\Delta L \cdot MPP_L + \Delta K \cdot MPP_K = 0$. In words, if one input, say, labor, is increased, output will increase by that change in labor times labor's marginal physical product. But along an isoquant, output does not change, by definition. Therefore, there must be a corresponding reduction in the other input—capital. That reduction must reduce output back down to where it was before. Another way of stating this is that along any isoquant, $\Delta L \cdot MPP_L = -\Delta K \cdot MPP_K$. When we rearrange this last relationship we see that $-(\Delta K/\Delta L) = MPP_L/MPP_K$.

Hence the numerical value of the slope at any point on the isoquant is going to be equal to MPP_L/MPP_K. There is a special name for this ratio.

Marginal rate of technical substitution

The ratio MPP_L/MPP_K is the numerical value of the slope of the isoquant and is called the **marginal rate of technical substitution**, or MRTS. Formally, then,

$$MRTS_{L:K} = \frac{MPP_L}{MPP_K} \qquad (7\text{-}5)$$

Diminishing MRTS

With convex isoquants, the marginal rate of technical substitution diminishes as L increases (and K decreases). In other words, the consequence of moving down a convex-to-the-origin isoquant is diminishing MRTS. The analysis here is analogous to what we did in the theory of consumer demand. There we talked about convex indifference curves and diminishing marginal rates of substitution in consumption. Now we are talking about convex isoquants and diminishing marginal rates of technical substitution in production.

Presumably, we could talk about a law of diminishing MRTS in which we would state

that as labor was substituted for capital along an isoquant, the marginal rate of technical substitution declines. The only time this is true, however, is where isoquants are convex—have negative slopes.

Uneconomic regions of production

Consider the lowest isoquant Q_1 in Figure 7-14. Look at point D. Here Q_1 of output can be produced with L_1 of labor and K_1 of capital. What if more labor, that is, a quantity in excess of L_1, is used? In order to use more than L_1 of labor, more than K_1 of capital would have

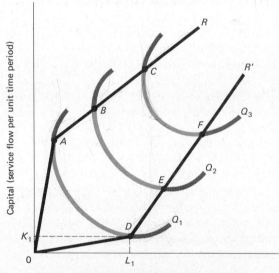

Figure 7-14: Ridge lines.
Points A, B, C, D, E, and F all occur where the slopes of the isoquants become positive. These are noneconomic regions of production because they require an increase in the use of both inputs with no corresponding increase in output. These points are connected by ridge lines. Everywhere along ridge line OR, the marginal physical product of capital is zero. Above the ridge line OR, marginal physical product of capital is negative. Everywhere along the ridge line OR', the marginal physical product of labor is equal to zero. Everywhere below OR', the marginal physical product of labor is negative.

to be used in order to maintain Q_1 of output. That is going to be uneconomic for any producer. After all, both capital and labor have a positive price. Thus, why would any entrepreneur want to hire more labor to produce the same quantity of output if doing so required the hiring of more capital services as well? Clearly, it would never pay to use more than L_1 of labor to produce Q_1 of output. This would be technically inefficient. A symmetrical analysis can be done for point A. It would never pay to use more capital services to produce Q_1 than the amount indicated at point A; doing so would require the use of more labor services just to keep output from falling below Q_1. All the points A, B, C, D, E, and F have this same property. They are points beyond which the isoquant turns back on itself. It is never economic to use the factors of production indicated by the section of the isoquants past points A, B, C, D, E, and F. If we connect these points with the lines $0R$ and $0R'$, we have sectioned off the economic area of production. The lines $0R$ and $0R'$ are called the **ridge lines**. On one side of the ridge line, the input ratios are economic; on the other side they are not. The area enclosed by the two ridge lines is stage II, similar to stage II in the top half of Figure 7-8.[9]

Now that we understand that the numerical value of the slope of the isoquant is given by the numerical value of the ratio of the marginal physical product of labor to the marginal physical product of capital, we can understand even better why the area outside the ridge lines in Figure 7-14 is noneconomic. (Actually, that area corresponds to stages I and III in Figure 7-8.)

Look again at Figure 7-14. Notice that the slope of the isoquants changes at points A, B, C, D, E, and F. At point A, for example, as we move along the isoquant upward, we now have an increasing marginal rate of technical substitution, but the only way we can have an increasing marginal rate of technical substitution is for one of the marginal physical products to be negative. This is exactly what occurs outside the ridge lines. In the case of moving along the first isoquant past point A in Figure 7-14, the marginal physical product of capital becomes negative. This is true anywhere above the ridge line $0R$. At any point below the ridge line $0R'$, the marginal physical product of labor becomes negative.[10]

Input combination of optimum—adding costs

In order to find out the optimum input combination for a firm working to produce a given level of output, we must add some cost data. This is what we had to do with consumer theory when we wanted to find the consumption optimum. We added price and income data. There we drew a budget line; now we draw what is called an **isocost curve**.

Isocost curve

We assume that input prices are taken as given as far as any one producer is concerned and determined by the forces of supply and demand in the input market. The producer is a small part of that market and can buy as much or as little as he or she wants at the market price.

We will call the unit price of labor services w and the unit price of capital services r, where r is *not* an interest rate. Sometimes r is called the implicit rental value per unit of capital. If, for example, a firm is able to rent a dump truck for $500 a week, then the weekly price for the services of the dump truck, r, is equal to $500.

---

[9]This symmetry holds only for linear homogeneous production functions.

[10]Along $0R'$, $\text{MPP}_L = 0$; and along $0R$, $\text{MPP}_K = 0$. Below $0R'$ is stage III for labor; above $0R$ is stage III for capital.

If the firm owns the dump truck which it paid $130,000 for, the unit price of services from the dump truck does not change to $130,000. Rather, it implicitly would stay the same —$500 per week, if that continues to be the going weekly price at which dump trucks can be rented. Thus the total cost for any volume of labor and capital will equal

$$TC = wL + rK \qquad (7\text{-}6)$$

where TC equals total cost.

A line along which total costs are constant is called an *isocost curve* or *isocost line*. It is similar to the budget line along which total consumer expenditures are constant. Look at Figure 7-15. We can find the extreme point on the horizontal axis for a particular constant amount of total costs TC by dividing total costs by the wage rate. This gives us the max-

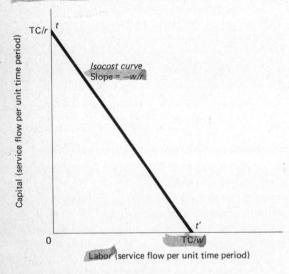

Figure 7-15: An isocost curve.
If we divide total cost by the wage rate, we obtain the maximum quantity of labor that can be hired t'. If we divide total cost by the price per unit of capital, we obtain the maximum amount of capital that can be purchased t. When we connect these two points, we obtain the firm's isocost curve. It represents the combinations of capital and labor that can be purchased with a particular outlay TC. Its slope is equal to $-w/r$.

imum quantity of labor t' that could be purchased with total costs equal to TC. With the other extreme point on the vertical axis, we do the same thing for capital. We divide total costs TC by the implicit rental price per unit of capital, or TC/r, and get a maximum quantity of capital t. The resultant isocost line is tt'.

THE SLOPE OF THE ISOCOST CURVE. The slope of the isocost curve tt' in Figure 7-15 will be equal to $-0t/0t'$. But $t = TC/r$ and $t' = TC/w$, so that

$$\text{Slope of } tt' = -\frac{TC/r}{TC/w} \qquad (7\text{-}7)$$

The TCs cancel out, leaving

$$\text{Slope of isocost curve} = -\frac{w}{r} \qquad (7\text{-}8)$$

CHANGING TOTAL COSTS. If input prices remain constant, an increase in total cost will shift the isocost curve tt' in Figure 7-15 to the right without changing its slope. With input prices fixed, an infinite number of isocost curves can be drawn in the input space in Figure 7-15.

Attaining productive optimum

It is now possible to combine isocost curves with isoquants to find the input combination that would maximize output obtained from a given "budgeted" cost. In other words, the entrepreneur takes as given input prices w and r. For a given total cost TC, there is one and only one combination of labor and capital that will maximize total product. (Note that maximizing output for a given TC is *not* equivalent to maximizing profits.)

Output is maximized for a given TC only when the highest isoquant is attained. In Figure 7-16, the highest attainable isoquant is the one which is just tangent to the isocost line tt'. That isoquant corresponds to an output level of Q_2, which is clearly greater than Q_1. The tangency occurs at point E. The optimal quantity of labor used will be L_e, and the optimal quantity of capital used will be K_e. (For simplicity, we have drawn in only the portion of each isoquant that is contained within the ridge lines.)

At the point where the isoquant is tangent to the isocost line tt', their slopes are, by definition, equal: At point E, the slope of the isoquant is equal both to the marginal rate of technical substitution and to the marginal physical product of labor divided by the marginal physical product of capital. The slope of the isocost curve is equal to the ratio of the wage rate per unit of labor and the implicit rental rate per unit of capital. Thus, optimal use of capital and labor for a *given* total cost requires that[11]

$$\text{MRTS} = \frac{\text{MPP}_L}{\text{MPP}_K} = \frac{w}{r} \qquad (7\text{-}9)$$

In other words, the optimal combination of labor and capital occurs when the ratio of the prices of labor and capital is equal to the marginal rate of technical substitution of labor for capital. From Eq. (7-9), we also know that the optimal combination occurs when the price ratio of labor and capital equals the ratio of the marginal physical product of labor to the marginal physical product of capital.

At this point, we could show why a diminishing MRTS is important. If isoquants were not convex to the origin but rather concave to the origin, we would end up with a corner rather than an interior solution. In Figure 7-16, the optimal combination would be at either the vertical intercept of tt' or the horizontal intercept. In other words, concave-to-the-origin isoquants (increasing MRTS) imply specialization in input usage. Since we do not observe such specialization in the real world, we use convex- rather than concave-to-the-origin isoquants. This analysis is similar to the one presented in Chapter 2 when we talked about convex- versus concave-to-the-origin indifference curves in the theory of consumer demand.

---

[11]The proof is as follows: If capital is decreased by ΔK, the resulting change in Q will be $-\text{MPP}_K \Delta K$. Capital costs will change by $-r\Delta K$. But we want TC to remain a constant, so we must somehow increase labor costs by an equal amount, or

(a) $+w\Delta L = -r\Delta K$

We can divide (a) by w to get

(b) $\Delta L = -\dfrac{r}{w}\Delta K$

Now we ask what the change in output will be if labor is changed by ΔL. We can find out by multiplying ΔL by its marginal physical product MPP_L; so our answer is (b) multiplied by MPP_L or

(c) $\text{MPP}_L \Delta L = -\dfrac{r}{w}\text{MPP}_L \Delta K$

The net change in output is

$$\Delta Q = \text{MPP}_K \Delta K + \text{MPP}_L \Delta L$$

Substituting the right side of (b) for ΔL, we get

$$\Delta Q = \text{MPP}_K \Delta K + \text{MPP}_L \left(-\frac{r}{w}\Delta K\right)$$

(d) $= \Delta K \left(\text{MPP}_K - \dfrac{r}{w}\text{MPP}_L\right)$

But along an isoquant, $\Delta Q = 0$ so that (d) becomes

(e) $0 = \Delta K \left(\text{MPP}_K - \dfrac{r}{w}\text{MPP}_L\right)$

Dividing (e) by ΔK we get

(f) $0 = \text{MPP}_K - \dfrac{r}{w}\text{MPP}_L$

or

$$-\text{MPP}_K = -\frac{r}{w}\text{MPP}_L$$

$$\frac{\text{MPP}_K}{\text{MPP}_L} = \frac{r}{w}$$

which we must invert to arrive at

(g) $\dfrac{\text{MPP}_L}{\text{MPP}_K} = \dfrac{w}{r}$

QED.

Warning   Warning   Warning

Superficially, it would appear that the theory of production as presented above is identical with the theory of consumer demand. Isoquants look like indifference curves, and isocost curves look like budget lines. However, the similarity ends there. The theory of consumer behavior does indeed explain the nature of the consumer's optimum. However, the optimum presented in Figure 7-16 and in Eq. (7-9) is incomplete. It does not represent a final optimum. It tells us how the producer will combine inputs to maximize output *for a given total cost.* Alternatively, it tells us how a producer would combine inputs to minimize costs *of producing a given output.* But we have yet to show which output rate is the profit-maximizing one. We will answer that question in Chapter 10.

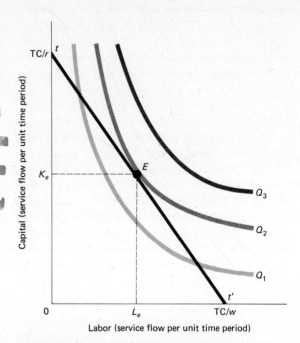

Figure 7-16: Optimal combination of inputs.
The firm's optimal combination of inputs for a given outlay TC is obtained when an isoquant is tangent to the isocost curve, or at point E. The optimum combination of capital and labor would be K_e and L_e.

Issues and applications

What do real world production functions look like?

Many researchers have investigated the nature of real world production functions. A variety of techniques have been developed to estimate these functions. Researchers have analyzed data from a long time period to show the various inputs used in each period in the past and the amount of output that resulted in each period. For example, one could obtain information on the amount of labor and capital used in the primary aluminum industry during each year from, say, 1950 to 1978. The researcher would then have 29 observations, and from these observations, an estimate of the

relationship between inputs and the resulting output could be obtained.

An alternative technique involves analyzing statistically data either from a large number of firms or from different sectors of the industry at a particular point in time. Information on the amount of capital and labor used by firms in the tire manufacturing industry could be obtained for a particular year, say, 1977. The number of observations would be equal to the number of firms from which data were obtained. From such data, an estimate of the relationship between inputs and the resulting output could be obtained.

Statisticians dealing with the data used to estimate production functions run into many problems. It is often difficult to measure the capital input since at any point in time the stock of capital is composed of equipment that is not of the same type or of the same age and productivity. Even the measurement of the labor input is difficult because the labor in any one firm is of varying quality. A complete list of the problems in the measurement of production functions could fill an entire book.

The exact mathematical form of the production function must also be chosen. If you'll go back to Eq. (7-1), you will see that we did not specify the form, but rather left it implicit. Researchers in this area have often used, or rather assumed, that the production function was of the Cobb-Douglas nature. This broad class of production functions has the following appearance:

$$Q = AL^\alpha K^\beta \qquad (7\text{-}10)$$

where Q = output

L = the quantity of labor services

K = the quantity of capital services

A, α, and β are parameters that vary from firm to firm and from industry to industry.

This type of production function is multiplicative. An additive type of production function would look like the following:

$$Q = A + \alpha L + \beta K$$

To give you an idea of some of the estimates of the coefficients of labor and capital, α and β, we present in Table 7-3 a variety of estimates for different industries in different countries.

The coefficient of labor α from the Cobb-Douglas production function [Eq. (7-10)] is the percentage increase in output that would result from a 1 percent increase in labor, the quantity of capital held constant. Similarly, β is the percentage increase in output that would result from a 1 percent increase in capital, the quantity of labor held constant. In other words, α and β are elasticities; they are the elasticity of output with respect to each input. So we see, for example, that the estimate for α in the cotton industry in India in 1951 is 0.92. We would predict, therefore, that

Industry	Country	Year	α	β
Metals and machinery	United States	1909	.71	.26
Cotton	India	1951	.92	.12
Coal	United Kingdom	1950	.79	.29
Jute	India	1951	.84	.14
Food	United States	1909	.72	.35
Sugar	India	1951	.59	.33
Coal	India	1951	.71	.44
Telephone	Canada	1972	.70	.41
Paper	India	1951	.64	.45
Chemicals	India	1951	.80	.37
Gas	France	1945	.83	.10
Electricity	India	1951	.20	.67

Table 7-3: Estimates of α and β for selected industries.

Source: A. Dobell, L. Taylor, L. Waverman, T. Liu, and M. Copland, "Communications in Canada," *Bell Journal of Economics and Management Science,* 1972; A. A. Walters, "Production and Cost Functions," *Econometrica,* January, 1963; J. Moroney, "Cobb-Douglas Production Functions and Returns to Scale in U.S. Manufacturing," *Western Economic Journal,* 1967.

a 1 percent increase in the labor input would result in a 0.92 percent increase in the output of cotton. Similarly, given a β of 0.12, a 1 percent increase in the capital input would increase output by 0.12 percent.

What happened to the blue whale?

Many problems concerned with the destruction and extinction of specific species lend themselves to an analysis of marginal and average physical product. Let us set up a hypothetical situation in which whale-harvesting rights in the world's oceans are well defined. We depict the situation in Figure 7-17. On the horizontal axis we show the number of whalers per unit time period and on the vertical axis the whales caught per whaler (individuals who hunt whales, not whaling ships). Implicitly we are assuming that we are dealing with constant-quality units of whalers and constant-quality units of whales.

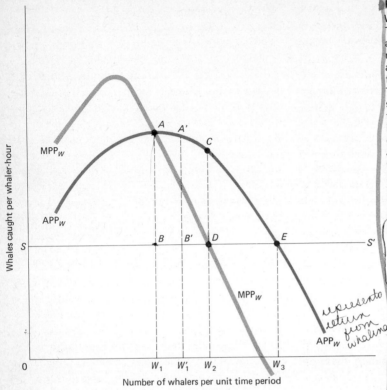

Figure 7-17: Productivity and whaling.
We assume that all whalers are the same. They are represented on the horizontal axis. The whales caught per whaler are represented on the vertical axis. The average physical product curve APP_w first increases and then decreases. The curve marginal to it, MPP_w, intersects APP_w at point A. The opportunity cost of each whaler is expressed in terms of whales and is $0S$. The opportunity cost line is, therefore, SS'. It is also the supply curve of whalers. Without property rights in whales, entry into the industry would continue until there were W_3 whalers, each earning his or her opportunity cost of $0S$. However, at that point the marginal physical product of whalers is negative. If someone were to own all the whales, the maximum fee that could be charged would be the distance from A to B. If this were the fee expressed in terms of whales, W_1 whalers would be in the industry. That, however, is not the wealth-maximizing solution for the owners of whales. They would do better by charging CD. The number of whalers in the industry would be W_2, and each would be earning only $0S$, his or her opportunity cost.

We have drawn the average physical product curve of whalers APP_w and marginal physical product curve MPP_w. Remember that the marginal physical product curve intersects the maximum point of the average physical product curve. Whenever the average physical curve is rising, the marginal product curve is above it; whenever the average physical product curve is falling, the marginal physical product curve is below it. The relationship between the marginal physical product of whalers and the average physical product of whalers is identical with the general case we provided previously in Eq. (7-3). That is to say[12]

$$MPP_w = APP_w + \Delta APP_w \cdot W \qquad (7-11)$$

where W = whalers.

Let us add the opportunity cost of whaling to

each whaler expressed in terms of whales caught per unit time expended. This opportunity cost is the alternative wage rate that whalers could earn if they exited from the whaling industry. We will assume that it is the same for all whalers because they are measured in constant-quality units. This wage rate, or opportunity cost of whaling, is represented by the vertical distance $0S$. In other words, it is a wage rate expressed in whales per unit time. The horizontal line SS', therefore, represents the opportunity cost of whalers. In some sense it can be considered the supply curve of the whalers also because they are presumably indifferent to whaling or not whaling at their opportunity cost.

When no one owns the whales

When no one owns blue whales, we have a situation in theory that is very similar to what the facts

---

[12]Assuming that $\Delta W = 1$.

have been in the whaling industry: We expect individuals to enter the whaling industry up to the point where it is no longer worthwhile. That occurs when the return from whaling just equals the opportunity cost of whaling. But the return from whaling is represented by the average physical product curve APP_W. In other words, a potential whaler assumes that it is possible to earn the industry average, but the industry average is merely the total physical product divided by the number of whalers, of APP_W. Therefore, we know that in the absence of property rights in blue whales, the number of whalers working per unit time period will be set at the intersection of the average physical product curve APP_W and the opportunity cost line SS', or point E. The number of individuals who will be whaling will be at W_3. The number of whales caught per whaler will be equal to the vertical distance from the origin 0, to S. The total number would be equal to $0W_3ES$.

Notice one thing important here. In the absence of property rights in blue whales, there are so many whalers engaging in whaling that the marginal physical product in Figure 7-17 is negative.[13] In other words, we are operating in stage III, and this would never occur if an individual entrepreneur were "running the show." Why does it occur in this situation? Simply because no individual whaler can, even if he or she wants to, take account of his or her actions on productivity. If one whaler decides not to whale because this might lead to the extinction of the species, some other whaler will come in and kill those whales that our previous whaler decided not to kill. No individual whaler has any effect whatsoever on the total number of whales harvested. There will be whaling up to the point where the average wage rate, given in terms of whales, is equal to the opportunity cost.[14]

When the whales are owned

We now examine the situation when the whales are owned by, let us say, one individual. That individual has the right to charge anyone who wishes to harvest the whales. The maximum fee that the owner of the whales could charge to each whaler is the difference between the opportunity cost of the whaler's time $0S$ and the monetary value of the whales caught. Assume for a moment that the owner of the whales charges a price of AB for any and every person who engages in whaling. At this price, the maximum number of whalers would be $0W_1$. Why? Because given that number, the APP_W is equal to the vertical distance between W_1 and A. The owner of the whales takes away as a fee the vertical distance between B and A. What is left over is exactly equal to $0S$, or the opportunity cost to the whalers. No more than $0W_1$ individuals will enter this industry unless, however, the owner of the whales reduces the fee charged each whaler.

It turns out that the maximum fee chargeable is AB because this is the distance between the maximum average physical product curve and the opportunity cost to whalers. If $1 more were charged, no one would engage in whaling.

The other extreme would be to charge nothing. Then we are right back to the case we began with when no one owned the whales. We would end up with $0W_3$ of whalers, and they would each earn their opportunity cost.

In between these two extremes lies the optimal fee that the owner of the whales should charge each whaler. Let's start from the high end with a fee of AB.

We lower it a little bit to $A'B'$. More whalers would want to enter the industry than when the fee was AB because with only $0W_1$ whalers, they would be earning higher than their opportunity

---

[13]Though this is not necessary.

[14]Contrary to what follows from this model, lack of property rights in blue whales—or any other hunted species—may not imply that all whalers earn exactly their opportunity cost. Some whalers are more efficient than others. See Stephen N. S. Cheung, "The Structure of a Contract and the Theory of a Non-Exclusive Resource," *The Journal of Law and Economics,* vol. 13 (1), April 1970, pp. 49–70, and compare it with H. Scott Gordon, "The Economic Theory of a Common Property Resource: The Fishery," *Journal of Political Economy,* vol. 62, no. 1, 1954, pp. 124ff. Both are reprinted in H. G. Manne, *The Economics of Legal Relationships: Readings in the Theory of Property Rights* (St. Paul, Minn.: West, 1975).

cost. So more whalers enter the industry. As they do, average physical product falls because we are in the downward sloping portion of that curve. The number of whalers that would ultimately stay in the industry at a fee of $A'B'$ (expressed in whales) would be W_1'.

From the point of view of the owner of the whales, his or her total receipts have increased by the number of the additional whalers harvesting whales times the new fee $A'B'$ *less* the reduction in receipts due to the fact that the fee has been lowered to all those whalers, $0W_1$, who were previously paying AB. (We are assuming here that everyone is charged the same fee.) Thus, the owner of the whales must compare the additional revenues collected from the new whalers with the revenues lost from charging the old whalers a lower fee. It will be worthwhile for the owner of whales to continue lowering his or her fee and therefore attracting more whalers up to the point where the increase in revenues due to the collection of fees from new whalers is just equaled by the reduction in revenues that results from the lower fees charged to all the original whalers. This reduction in fees charged to all the original whalers is equivalent to the change in average physical product, or ΔAPP_W. As can be seen by comparing the fee AB with the fee $A'B'$, since we are in the negatively sloped portion of the APP_W curve, this change will be negative. The cost to the owner of the whalers of lowering the fee is therefore

$$\Delta APP_W \cdot W \qquad (7\text{-}12)$$

Since ΔAPP_W is negative in the case under study, we must put a negative sign in front of Eq. (7-12) in order to come out with the positive cost. Now, to obtain the optimal fee, we set the benefits equal to the cost of lowering the fee. We have given the cost in Eq. (7-12), and the benefit is merely the fee $APP_W - 0S$ obtainable from the new whalers, or

$$APP_W - 0S = -\Delta APP_W \cdot W \qquad (7\text{-}13)$$

We now add $0S$ to each side of Eq. (7-13) and also add $(\Delta APP_W \cdot W)$ to each side so that we get

$$APP_W + (\Delta APP_W \cdot W) = 0S \qquad (7\text{-}14)$$

but the left-hand side of this equation is also the right-hand side of Eq. (7-11), and therefore it is equal to MPP_W; so we can say that $MPP_W = 0S$.

Thus, the owner will want to lower his or her fee up to the point where $MPP_W = 0S$. To reach that point, the owner will charge a fee of CD in Figure 7-17. There will be $0W_2$ whalers harvesting whales.

Notice that at point D, marginal physical product and the opportunity cost to whalers are equal. In the situation where the whales are owned by an individual, that individual will force every whaler to take account of the impact that he or she has on the catch of the other whalers. What is that impact? It is the reduction in average physical product brought about by the addition of one whaler. We can find it by looking at the MPP_W curve in Figure 7-17, for that is the meaning of a marginal physical product curve—the change in total product brought about the addition of one more unit of the variable factor of production. When there are W_2 whalers harvesting whales, on the margin a whaler reduces the aggregate amount of physical product to everyone else by the distance between C and D. The owner of the whales charges each whaler this amount. The net income of each whaler, then, becomes equal to his or her marginal physical product. Total whale production equals $W_2 \cdot W_2C$ and this is less than the $0W_3ES$ total whales that are harvested when no one owns whales.

Our conclusion is that under private ownership, blue whales would not be harvested so intensively as when there is no ownership of whales.

Glossary

Production Any use of resources that converts one commodity into a different commodity; production, therefore, includes storage, wholesaling, transportation, repackaging, and manufacturing.

Firm An organization in which there is an employer and one or more employees.

Organization A group of individuals engaged jointly in production.

Entrepreneur The organizer and undertaker of risk in a business whose income is the residual after all expenses are subtracted from revenues.

Residual claimants Individuals who have a right to that which is left over after all contractual expenses in a business are paid. They claim the residual, if any.

Profit The residual that is left over after all expenses are paid in a business; the difference between total revenues and total costs, including the opportunity cost of all resources used.

Technical efficiency The technical relationship between output and inputs; measured in terms of physical units of output compared with physical units of inputs.

Economic efficiency The ratio of value of output to value of input. A production process which yields the greater dollar value of output per dollar's worth of resource input is economically more efficient.

Production function The technical relationship between output and inputs; the relationship which yields all of the attainable and technically efficient combinations of inputs.

Total physical product The physical output that results from production.

Average physical product Total physical product divided by the number of units of the variable input used.

Marginal physical product The change in total physical product due to a one-unit change in the single variable factor of production, all other factors of production held constant.

Law of diminishing marginal returns With a given technology and all inputs except one fixed, as equal increments of that one input are added, beyond a certain point the *rate* of increase in output will decrease.

Production or output isoquant The locus of points showing all the combinations of capital and labor that will yield a constant amount of output.

Input space In our two-dimensional production situation, a quadrant representing combinations of capital and labor; similar to a commodity space.

Marginal rate of technical substitution The rate at which labor can be substituted for capital holding output constant; or the ratio of marginal physical product of labor to marginal physical product of capital, i.e., $MRTS = MPP_L/MPP_K$.

Ridge lines The lines connecting the points on isoquants where those isoquants turn back on themselves. To the left of the upward ridge line and to the right of the rightward ridge line lie the uneconomic areas of production. Along the ridge line either MPP_L or MPP_K is zero.

Isocost curve Also called an isocost line; the business firm's "budget constraint" that gives the different combinations of capital and labor that can be purchased with a fixed outlay and with the nominal and relative prices of capital and labor fixed. The line along which total costs are constant in an input space.

Summary

1. Production includes all uses of resources that transform a commodity into a different commodity. It is a flow concept and is measured as a rate of output per unit time period.

2. Firms exist whenever cooperative (or team) effort results in a larger product than the sum of the products of individual efforts.

3. The assumption of profit maximization is the one we use in this text; however, there are alternative theories of managerial behavior, such as staff maximization, sales maximization, growth maximization, and satisficing.

4. To the extent that a market for corporate control exists, there is a limit to the non-profit-maximizing behavior of managers.

5. Whenever average physical product is rising, marginal physical product will be above it; whenever average physical product is falling, marginal physical product will be below it. Marginal physical product equals average physical product at the latter's maximum.

6. The law of diminishing marginal returns does not follow from a set of assumptions; it is an assertion about reality that seems to be true.

7. There are three stages of production. In stage I, the average physical product of the variable factor is rising since the marginal physical product is above it. In stage II, both average and

marginal physical product are falling, but MPP is positive. In stage III, both APP and MPP are decreasing, but MPP has become negative. No producer would knowingly produce in stage I or stage III.

8. When dealing with two variable inputs, we find the optimal combination of the two inputs where an isoquant is tangent to the isocost curve. At this point, the marginal rate of technical substitution is equal to the ratio of the price of labor to the price of capital.

9. It is important to distinguish between movements along and among isoquants. The former refers to changes along an isoquant where both the ratio and the absolute amount of the inputs change. The latter refers to a northeastward movement along a line from the origin from one isoquant to the next. The ratio of capital to labor is constant, but output increases.

10. The uneconomic regions of production in a capital-labor input space are bounded by so-called ridge lines. Above the upper ridge line, the marginal physical product of capital is negative; below the bottom ridge line, the marginal physical product of labor is negative.

11. In that area where isoquants are convex to the origin, the firm is experiencing a diminishing marginal rate of technical substitution of labor for capital.

12. The production optimum is not strictly analogous to the consumption optimum. All it tells us is how the producer will combine inputs to maximize output for a given total cost or, alternatively, how the producer would combine inputs to minimize costs of a given output. We have not yet dealt with the determination of the profit-maximizing rate of output.

Selected references

Cassels, John M., "On the Law of Variable Proportions," in American Economic Association *Readings in The Theory of Income Distribution* (Philadelphia: P. Blakiston's Sons & Company, 1946), pp. 103–118.

Douglas, Paul, "Are There Laws of Production?" *American Economic Review*, March 1948.

Hicks, J. R., *Value and Capital*, 2d ed. (Oxford: Clarendon Press, 1946) chaps. 6 and 7.

Knight, Frank H., *Risk, Uncertainty, and Profit* (Boston: Houghton Mifflin, 1921), pp. 94–104.

Machlup, Fritz, "Theories of the Firm: Marginalist, Behavioral Managerial," *American Economic Review*, March 1967.

Reder, Melvin W., "A Reconsideration of the Marginal Productivity Theory," *Journal of Political Economy*, vol. 55, October 1947, pp. 450–58.

Scitovsky, Tibor, "A Note on Profit Maximization and Its Implications," *Review of Economic Studies*, vol. 2, no. 1, 1943, pp. 56–60.

Questions

(Answers to even-numbered questions are at back of text.)

1. Using this chapter's definition of production, examine each of the following two statements to determine if any production took place:

   a. Five minutes after buying a used car for $500, and without so much as washing it, the dealer turns around and sells it to someone else for $600.

   b. A ton of pitted apricots, with a market value of $300, is exposed to the sun's rays for a week and then sold (only a half ton now that much of the water has evaporated) for $400.

2. Can you think of a good or service that is produced solely with labor and without the use of any capital equipment whatsoever?

3. If production is a flow concept measured with reference to a period of time, how would you describe the "output" of a speculator who merely buys, say, an ounce of gold, holds it a year, and then resells it?

4. Is it possible to be in the freight delivery business without owning any trucks, and if so, who in their right mind would do so? How? Why?

5. "The way to have the best of both worlds (low transactions costs and low costs of supervision) is to have all your employees working on piecework and pay them according to just how much they produce." If this statement were accurate, we would expect to see few, if any, workers paid according to their time input. Yet the vast majority of peo-

ple are paid by the hour, week, or month. The theory must be rejected. What do you think has been overlooked here?

6. By definition, an entrepreneur must be willing to take risks. Aside from such a willingness to shoulder risks, what quality would you expect a good entrepreneur to possess? (*Hint:* Turn back to Figure 4-4 and study the Edgeworth-Bowley box for a while.)

7. "Since 'proxy fights' (the attempted takeover of a corporation by a united block of stockholders) rarely occur, they obviously cannot be a very important factor in keeping inefficient managements in line." Is this statement true or false? Why?

8. Why is is difficult to give a concrete definition of when a firm's short run "ends" and its long run "begins"?

9. What is meant by technical efficiency, and how does it differ from economic efficiency?

10. Suppose you are an industrial engineer charged with keeping your firm's production costs at a minimum. (You are *not* asked to make decisions as to the rate of output of the firm; such decisions are made for you by the marketing division on the basis of orders obtained by salespeople in the field.) In order to do your job well, what information do you need to know besides that given by the production function? Why? (*Hint:* Look at Figure 7-16.)

11. Why, if average physical product is falling, must marginal physical product be less than average physical product? Also, explain why total physical product can only be declining if marginal physical product is negative.

12. Why would a firm never operate in either stage I or stage III of its production function?

13. What information is shown by a single production isoquant? What is signified by a move to the northwest along an isoquant, and what might induce a firm to make such a move?

14. Look at Figure 7-16. Suppose a firm is producing output Q_2 at point E and using K_e of capital and L_e of labor; r and w are the respective input prices, and total cost is TC. If the firm is to expand output to Q_3, clearly more resources must be employed (assuming no change in the underlying production function). Focusing now on the isocost curve, what are the three variables that, with a sufficient change in any one of them, would enable the firm to expand output to Q_3?

15. "Our union represents all the city's garbage collection engineers. The city-owned trash company is a monopoly requiring all residents to pay for trash collection even if they don't generate any trash. Consequently, even a 50 percent increase in our hourly wages will have no adverse effect on how many hours of our labor will be hired per week." Is the statement true or false? Why?

8

THE COSTS OF PRODUCTION

When a firm produces a commodity, costs are incurred. Some of the costs of production include interest costs, wages for workers, the prices paid for raw materials, rent for land, and so on. For purposes of analysis, we must, at one and the same time, broaden our notion of the meaning of costs in general and place costs into a number of subclassifications.

Opportunity cost

Cost has a very special meaning in economics, not only when we are referring to the theory of the firm but also when we are referring to consumer decision making. Cost in economics means one and only one thing—**opportunity cost**. Opportunity cost is defined as the value of a resource in its next best alternative use. Note that in this definition opportunity cost does not depend on who is using the resource. For example, the opportunity cost of a piece of machinery to a firm is not just its best alternative use *within* the firm but the value of its highest alternative use anywhere in the world. Thus, if we define capital as a machine in place, we can define a cost of the use of the machine by its owner as equal to the price that could be fetched if the services of the machine were sold to the highest bidder. This could be accomplished in several ways, the most obvious being leasing or renting of the machine. Indeed, the owner of a machine has the option not only of leasing the machine but also of selling it and earning interest on the money previously "tied up" in the machine.

What is the opportunity cost of having that machine? It is its highest alternative use value. That may be the value obtained by renting the machine, or it may be the value in selling it to someone else and putting the proceeds in certificates of deposit yielding 8 percent per annum.

Another way to look at cost is that it is a currently available alternative *that is sacrificed.* With a machine in place, the alternative that is sacrificed is leasing the machine or selling it and investing the proceeds. Strictly speaking, when there is no currently available alternative that is being sacrificed, there is no cost involved in using the resource. For example, if a machine in place is so highly specialized to a particular production process that no one else will lease it or buy it even at a zero price, then there is no alternative that is sacrificed. The opportunity cost of the machine is effectively zero.

Private versus social costs

For the firm, the cost of any action is the opportunity cost, or the most valued opportunity foregone. However, it is conceivable, perhaps obvious, that many firms' decisions are based on costs which are incurred by the firm but entail additional costs of which the firm does not take account. The costs incurred by the firm or the individual decision maker are called **private costs**. These are indeed the costs that affect the decisions of the firm owners. However, the production activities of the firm (or the consumption activities of consumers for that matter) can visit economic benefit or harm upon others. A firm producing paper pulp incurs the cost of raw materials, of labor, and of capital. These are the private costs of producing pulp. However, in the process of production, such by-products as foul odors

and liquid and solid effluents are emitted. Foul odors visit economic damages or costs upon those in the vicinity of the paper mill. Effluents visit damages on those who use the waters into which the effluents flow. If we add together the private costs of production of paper pulp and the economic damage visited upon others, we come up with what are called **social costs**.[1]

We will deal with this distinction between private and social costs in the last chapter of this book when we examine the concept of market failure or externalities. Suffice it to say here that the costs of any activity are the social opportunity costs and not just the private ones.

Explicit versus implicit costs

Perhaps another way to look at costs will bring us a better understanding of the true nature of costs for the firm. Firms can usually present to the public a set of **explicit costs**. These are generally the costs that the accountant will be able to measure and put down in some previously agreed upon accounting system. However, these explicit costs leave out a lot of the implicit costs that go into the production of a particular product. Remember that cost is defined as the best alternative use of the resources at hand. Thus the **implicit cost** of having a machine in place is the possible rental rate that could be obtained if the machine were leased out or, alternatively, the returns from investing the proceeds realized from the sale of the machine.

When an entrepreneur looks at the explicit costs of raw materials that go into the production process, there can often be a difference between the explicit costs and the implicit costs of those materials. Consider two batches

---

[1]The terms private and social costs were first employed by A. C. Pigou, *The Economics of Welfare,* 4th ed. (London: Macmillan, 1932), part II, chap. 9.

of copper that were purchased at different times. The first batch was purchased at a price lower than was the second. The explicit costs of the two batches of copper are different. However, *all productive resources that are identical necessarily have the same opportunity or alternative cost irrespective of the differences in their actual or "historical" costs.* If an automobile manufacturer has an inventory of steel, half of which was purchased 6 months ago at $200 a ton and the other half yesterday at $300 a ton, the opportunity cost of *all* the steel is the current market price of $300 per ton for *every* ton in inventory. Thus we see the distinction that must be made between historical costs and opportunity or alternative costs. **Historical costs** are the explicit costs incurred by the producer in obtaining specific resources.

To take another example, consider the standard accounting practice of treating the interest payments on borrowed capital as an explicit cost to a firm but ignoring the implicit cost of obtaining equity capital by the issuance of shares of common stock. A firm can obtain additional capital by selling additional shares of common stock. This is the process by which the firm assigns part of the ownership, or equity, of the firm in exchange for the money that purchasers of the new shares pay for those shares. Thus, the distinction between equity financing and debt financing is the difference between assigning part of the ownership of the business by selling common stock (equity) and borrowing money that the firm's owners promise to repay (debt financing). Firms that borrow money from banks or other financial institutions are allowed to show interest costs as an expense on their annual profit-and-loss statement. If the exact same quantity of funds were obtained by selling new shares in the company, under current tax laws no interest cost is entered on the firm's ledger. However, there is an implicit cost of obtaining equity financing. That im-

plicit cost is the rate of return that potential shareholders must expect to earn if they are to be induced to invest in that company. In other words, the firm selling common stock must anticipate not only being able to cover all its explicit costs but also having adequate after-tax revenues left over to compensate stockholders. The implicit cost of equity financing of investment is called the opportunity cost of equity capital.

Consider a final example of the difference between explicit and implicit costs. Take a farmer who has paid off all his or her debts for all the resources used in farming, such as land, tractors, fertilizer, etc. Let's say that this farmer works the land without anyone else's help. In this particular example, explicit costs of farming approach zero. However, implicit costs clearly do not. All the resources that the farmer owns have an alternative use which is sacrificed; thus, each has an opportunity cost, even though it is only implicit.

Short and long runs

We introduced the concept of the short and the long run in the last chapter when we made the arbitrary distinction between fixed and variable factors of production. We defined the short run as a period during which some inputs could not be increased without appreciably increasing their cost per unit. We defined the long run as the period during which all factors of production became variable. Short run and long run do not refer to specific clock or calendar time, but rather to the time required for individuals to adapt to new conditions.

Obviously, our definition of short run has to be loose because at a sufficiently high cost entrepreneurs can adjust rapidly to a change in economic conditions. (It also depends on the industry and the production techniques used.) In a world with zero transactions costs and complete nonspecialization of production inputs, there would be no distinction between long and short run. However, there are costs of renegotiating long-run contracts, for example, and there are resources that are specialized in the production of particular goods and, therefore, have negligible value in producing other goods. Hence, it is meaningful to make the distinction between long- and short-run cost curves.

We could talk in terms of short runs of varying lengths, intermediate runs, and then the long run. We will stick with the standard division of short and long run, and therefore we will have short-run costs and long-run costs. We will constantly keep in mind that the alternative uses of a particular resource will be different and fewer in the short run compared with what they are in the long run. In other words, the opportunity cost of a given resource changes when a longer time is allowed for adjustment.

The family of short-run total cost curves

The concept of total costs used in this section is all costs associated with the production of a commodity. We have divided total cost (TC) into two components: total fixed costs (TFC) and total variable costs (TVC).

Total fixed cost

Fixed costs are often defined as those costs which are "sunk," i.e., cannot be reduced no matter what the rate of output. In other words, fixed costs are those costs that are invariant to the rate of production.[2]

We should be careful here because *fixed*, or

sunk, costs are not costs at all in the sense that we have described them above when we talked about opportunity costs. Sunk costs do not represent a currently available alternative that must be sacrificed. The true meaning of the word "cost," then, does not really relate to fixed costs, even though the standard analysis we use in this chapter will refer to this cost element. Remember that the cost of producing output is the outlay that could be avoided if that rate of output were not undertaken at all.

Consider the following example. You buy a new automobile for $10,000. If you went to sell it the same day you bought it, you might be able to get, say, $8,000. Already we have something to think about. The difference between the purchase price and the immediate resale price is $2,000. That $2,000 has been used up, or sunk. There is no way you can do anything about that $2,000. That is the true/actual **cost of acquisition** of the machine. You now have an option. You can do something with the resale value of the machine, the $8,000 that you could get. What you could get if you sold the machine is the opportunity cost of that car as soon as you own it. This is called the **cost of continued possession**. It is the alternative income that could be earned if the car were sold and the proceeds invested. To get a complete idea of the cost of continued possession, we must add any expected depreciation of the car over the time period it is going to be held. Notice that the cost of continued possession is invariant to the rate of output.

If you have already purchased the car and if you have definitely made the decision to keep the car for 1 year, then the *fixed* cost associated with that car for owning it 1 year is the (sunk) cost of acquisition plus the opportunity cost of continued possession.

In what follows, total fixed costs are the costs of all fixed inputs of production, although we will show in the Issues and Application section how important the cost of con-

---

[2] A sunk investment is one that cannot be transferred to some other *profitable* use. Its true opportunity cost equals 0 (e.g., a stamping machine which makes only grilles for Ford's Edsel!).

tinued possession can become when we wish to compute the rate of return on investment in different industries.

Total variable costs

In their most simplified form, total **variable costs** are those costs incurred by the use of variable inputs in the production process. In other words, variable costs, by definition, are a function of the rate of output. Variable costs would then include the wage bill, the raw materials bill, and so on.

We present a hypothetical set of total cost schedules in Table 8-1. The resultant cost curves are presented in Figure 8-1.

THE RELATIONSHIP BETWEEN TOTAL VARIABLE COST AND TOTAL PHYSICAL PRODUCT. It turns out that there is an important relationship between the production function with one variable input (all other inputs fixed) and the total variable cost curve TVC, as presented in Fig-

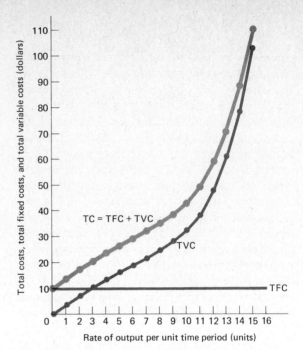

Figure 8-1: Total cost curves.
From columns (1) and (2) in Table 8-1, we obtain total fixed costs which are invariant to the rate of output at $10. Total variable costs are taken from columns (1) and (3) in Table 8-1. Total costs are total variable costs plus the total fixed costs ($10 in this case).

Rate of output per unit time period (units) (1)	Total fixed costs (TFC) ($) (2)	Total variable costs (TVC) ($) (3)	Total costs (TC) ($) (4)	Marginal costs ($/unit) ΔTC (= ΔTVC) Δ output (5)	Average total costs (ATC) ($/unit) [(4) ÷ (1)] (6)	Average variable costs (AVC) ($/unit) [(3) ÷ (1)] (7)	Average fixed costs (AFC) ($/unit) [(2) ÷ (1)] (8)
0	10.00	0	10.00	—	0	0	—
1	10.00	4.00	14.00	4.00	14.00	4.00	10.00
2	10.00	7.50	17.50	3.50	8.75	3.75	5.00
3	10.00	10.75	20.75	3.25	6.92	3.58	3.33
4	10.00	13.80	23.80	3.05	5.95	3.45	2.50
5	10.00	16.70	26.70	2.90	5.34	3.34	2.00
6	10.00	19.50	29.50	2.80	4.92	3.25	1.67
7	10.00	22.25	32.25	2.75	4.61	3.18	1.43
8	10.00	25.10	35.10	2.85	4.39	3.14	1.25
9	10.00	28.30	38.30	3.20	4.26	3.14	1.11
10	10.00	32.30	42.30	4.00	4.23	3.23	1.00
11	10.00	38.30	48.30	6.00	4.39	3.48	.91
12	10.00	47.30	57.30	9.00	4.78	3.94	.83
13	10.00	60.30	70.30	13.00	5.41	4.64	.77
14	10.00	78.30	88.30	18.00	6.31	5.59	.71
15	10.00	102.30	112.30	24.00	7.49	6.82	.67

Table 8-1

ure 8-1. In order to convert the known total physical product curve of a variable factor of production (all others held constant) into a total variable cost curve, all we need know is the price of the variable input. Take the example in Figure 8-2. We have drawn a total physical product curve for labor in panel (a) of the diagram. The horizontal axis measures labor in hours per unit time period leftward from the origin 0. The vertical axis measures the rate of output per unit time period. We see that Q_1 of the output requires L_1 of labor input. Assume a wage rate $= w_1$. Then, the total variable cost at rate of output $Q_1 = w_1 \cdot L_1$, which is C_1 on the horizontal axis in panel (b). The horizontal axis of panel (b) measures total variable cost, which in this simplified case is the wage rate times the amount of labor required to produce any given rate of output measured on the vertical axis. When we do this for all different rates of output, we obtain the total variable cost curve, $TVC_{|w=w_1}$, in panel (b). The total variable cost curve is the mirror image of the total product curve in panel (b) for one variable factor of production and wage rate w_1. Thus, the total variable cost curve in this simplified case reflects the same properties of the total product curve (marginal product at first increases and then diminishes). If the wage rate were to increase to w_2, then we would get the second curve in panel (b) of Figure 8-2, labeled $TVC_{|w=w_2}$. If w increased again to w_3, we would get the third curve, labeled $TVC_{|w=w_3}$.

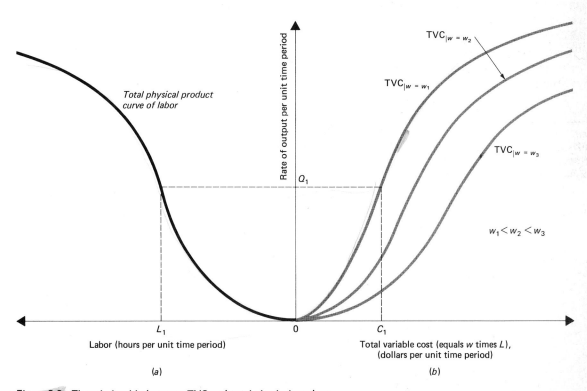

Figure 8-2: The relationship between TVC and total physical product.
We assume that the only variable factor of production is labor. It is measured from the origin, 0, to the left. The resultant total physical product curve is given in panel (a). To obtain total variable cost, we multiply the wage rate times the amount of labor used at each rate of output (measured on the vertical axis). When the wage rate is equal to w_1, we get the top TVC curve. When it is equal to w_2, we get the middle TVC curve. When it is equal to w_3, we get the bottom TVC curve. Note that $w_1 < w_2 < w_3$.

Total cost

Total cost is defined as the summation of total variable cost and total fixed cost. We show total cost in column (4) in Table 8-1. It is translated into the TC curve in Figure 8-1. The only difference between the total cost curve and the total variable cost curve in that figure is that the TC curve is vertically $10 higher than the TVC curve. Notice that the TFC curve is merely a horizontal line at $10.

Short-run average cost curves

The three short-run total cost curves presented above can be converted to average cost curves. In the following sections, we will look at average fixed costs, average variable costs, average total costs, and marginal costs.

Average fixed costs

An average is the total divided by the number of units over which the total is spread; thus, **average fixed costs (AFC)** equal total fixed costs divided by the number of units of output, or AFC = TFC/Q. We find average fixed costs for a hypothetical cost situation in column (8) of Table 8-1. It is transferred to the continuously downward-sloping AFC curve in Figure 8-3. The AFC curve, a rectangular hyperbola, never meets the horizontal or vertical axes (which are its asymptotes).[3]

Average variable costs

Average variable costs (AVC) are merely defined as average total costs divided by output, or AVC = TVC/Q. We find AVC in our example in column (7) of Table 8-1. When we transfer these data to Figure 8-3, they become

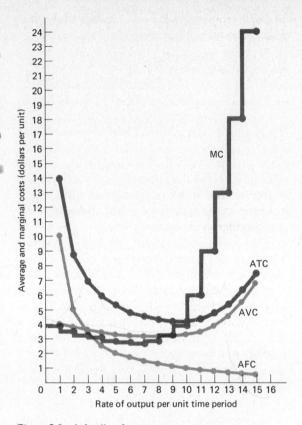

Figure 8-3: A family of cost curves.
These curves are taken from columns (1) and (5) through (8) in Table 8-1. Note that the AFC curve is a rectangular hyperbola. Further, the MC curve intersects both the ATC and the AVC curves at their respective minimum points.

the AVC curve which is first downward-sloping and then upward-sloping.

The relationship between AVC and APP

Just as we showed a relationship between the total variable cost curve and the total physical product curve, we can show a relationship between the average variable cost curve and the average physical product curve. Again, we will assume that there is only one variable factor of production. Total variable costs then equal the price per unit of the variable factor of production times the number of units used.

---

[3] It's a rectangular hyperbola with the algebraic form: $y = $ constant/x, or $xy = $ constant. So output times AFC equals TFC.

In our example, where labor is the only variable factor of production, $TVC = w \cdot L$.

But AVC is defined as

$$AVC = \frac{TVC}{Q} \qquad (8\text{-}1)$$

If we substitute wL for TVC in Eq. (8-1), we get

$$AVC = \frac{wL}{Q} = w\frac{L}{Q} \qquad (8\text{-}2)$$

We can see, however, that the term in parentheses is the reciprocal of the average physical product of labor:

$$AVC = w\frac{1}{APP} \qquad (8\text{-}3)$$

Assuming a production function like the one shown in panel (*a*) of Figure 8-2, we know that average physical product first rises and then falls. Thus average variable costs must first fall and then rise. This has to do with increasing and then diminishing marginal physical returns.

COMBINATIONS OF VARIABLE RESOURCES. When there are several variable resources that can be used, each one must be considered in relation to the other. Let us consider two variable resources: labor and capital. We suppose that the cost curves in Figure 8-3 are based on different ratios of uses and costs of these two variable resources. We also now assume that there is a given market price for each resource. It turns out that there is a way in which the resources should be combined in order to minimize costs for a given level of output.

COST MINIMIZATION AT A GIVEN OUTPUT LEVEL. From Chapter 7 we know that the way in which a firm can minimize the costs of producing a given level of output is by distributing expenditures among various inputs so that the marginal physical product of the last

dollar spent on any input is equal to the marginal physical product of the last dollar spent on any other input used. The formula for cost minimization, given output, is therefore

$$\frac{MPP_{labor}}{Wage\ rate/unit} = \frac{MPP_{capital}}{(implicit\ rental)\ price/unit\ of\ capital} \qquad (8\text{-}4)$$

MPP refers to the marginal physical product. Notice that since we are concerned with opportunity costs, we do not talk about the price of capital, but about the implicit rental value which is the implicit opportunity cost of this factor of production. This formula is given in Chapter 7, page 179. We obtained that formula by finding out where the optimal combination of inputs would be for a given total cost. That occurred when the isocost curve was tangent to an isoquant.

Average total costs

Average total costs (ATC) are defined as total costs divided by output, or $ATC \equiv TC/Q$. We show average total costs in column 6 of Table 8-1. This is also shown as ATC in Figure 8-3. The vertical distance between the ATC curve and the AVC curve is, of course, AFC. Average total costs have the same property as average variable costs: They first fall and then rise. This is a consequence of the shape of the production function that we are implicitly assuming.

Marginal costs

Marginal costs are defined as the change in total costs when there is a one-unit change in the rate of production. Otherwise stated, marginal cost is equal to the change in total cost per unit change in output, i.e.,

$$MC = \frac{\Delta TC}{\Delta Q} \qquad (8\text{-}5a)$$

where $\Delta Q = 1$. We present marginal cost for our example in column (5) of Table 8-1. Columns (1) and (5) are transferred to Figure 8-3, and the resulting curve is labeled MC. Since we are working in discrete unit changes, the curve is a stepladder rather than a smooth line.

RELATIONSHIP BETWEEN MC AND MPP. There is a relationship between marginal cost and marginal physical product, just as there was a relationship between average variable cost and average physical product and a relationship between total variable cost and total physical product. Consider the example where we have only one variable input, and that input is labor. Thus, any change in total costs is due to a change in labor input:

$$\Delta TC = w\Delta L \qquad (8\text{-}6)$$

where w is the given wage rate and L is the quantity of labor per unit time period. If we substitute Eq. (8-6) into Eq. (8-5a), we come up with

$$MC = \frac{w\Delta L}{\Delta Q} = w\left(\frac{1}{\Delta Q/\Delta L}\right) \qquad (8\text{-}5b)$$

But $\Delta Q/\Delta L$ is the marginal physical product of labor. Therefore

$$MC = w\left(\frac{1}{MPP_L}\right) \qquad (8\text{-}7)$$

The marginal cost curve will be the mirror image of the marginal physical product curve. And *for any given wage rate w, a diminishing marginal physical product will result in an increasing marginal cost.* In other words, whenever we have diminishing marginal physical product or diminishing marginal returns, we will have an increasing marginal cost.

The geometry of short-run cost curves

We can go through the geometry of the relationships between the various short-run cost curves just as we did when we showed the relationships between the various physical product curves in the last chapter.

Total costs and average total costs

Average total costs are total cost divided by the rate of output. In Figure 8-4, panel (a), we have shown a total cost curve. Pick any output

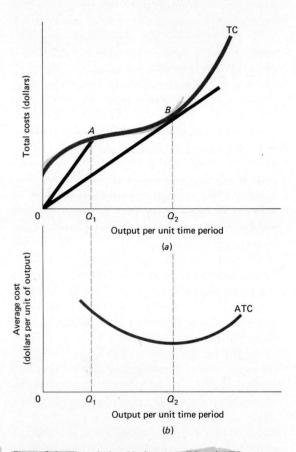

Figure 8-4: The relationship between TC and ATC.
For any output rate such as Q_1 or Q_2, we can obtain the ATC curve by measuring the slope of the ray drawn to the respective point on the TC curve. This is exactly the way we derived the average physical product curve from the total physical product curve in the last chapter. At output rate Q_2 we know that average total costs reached their minimum because before that point B, the slope of any ray drawn to the TC curve was decreasing and after B the slope was increasing. The resultant ATC curve is shown in panel (b).

level, say, Q_1; total costs will equal the vertical distance from Q_1 to A. Output is the horizontal distance 0 to Q_1. Therefore, average total cost ATC = $Q_1A/0Q_1$, but this is merely the slope of the straight line drawn from the origin 0 to point A on the total cost curve. Therefore, we know that average variable cost is the slope of the straight line from the origin drawn to the corresponding point on the total cost curve for any given level of output. We also know that at output Q_2, then, average total costs reach a minimum, for here the slope of the ray is as small as it is going to get; after output Q_2 the slope of that ray will be greater. The ATC curve generated in panel (b) below panel (a) therefore reaches its minimum point at output Q_2.

It is now relatively easy to derive geometrically the average variable cost curve. All we need do is move the total cost curve down until it starts at the origin in panel (a) of Figure 8-4. The same procedure would then be used. The slope of the rays to various points on the total variable cost curve would give average variable cost.

Relationship between total cost and marginal cost

Marginal cost is defined as the change in total costs due to a one-unit change in output. If we think in terms of very small changes in output, then marginal cost is defined as the slope of a tangent drawn to any particular point on the total cost curve. Remember that the slope of a curve is equal to $\Delta y/\Delta x$, where y is the variable measured on the vertical axis and x is the variable measured on the horizontal axis. If total costs are on the vertical axis and the rate of output is on the horizontal axis, the slope of a total cost curve at any point will give the change in total cost due to a change in the rate of output. The way we find the slope of a nonlinear curve is by drawing a tangent at any point and finding the slope of that tangent; hence, marginal cost is measured at any point

along the total cost curve by finding the slope of the tangent to that point.

We draw tangents to various points on the total cost curve in panel (a) of Figure 8-5. Points A, B, C, and D correspond to rates of output of Q_1, Q_2, Q_3, and Q_4. Notice that the slope of the tangent at A is greater than the slope of the tangent at B. The way we have drawn the total cost curve, the slope of the

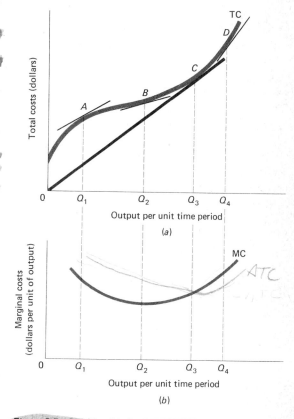

Figure 8-5: Relationship between TC and MC.
Just as we derived marginal physical product from total physical product by measuring the angle of the tangents at five points on the total physical product curve, we can derive the marginal cost curve in panel (b) from the respective slopes of tangents drawn to the total cost curve at various output rates such as Q_1, Q_2, Q_3, and Q_4. Marginal costs reach their minimum point in panel (a) at the inflection point B on the TC curve, or at output rate Q_2. Note that at output rate Q_3, the tangent to the TC curve at point C is also the ray to the origin; thus, MC and ATC would be equal at this output rate. Beyond output Q_4, MC > ATC.

tangent corresponding to output Q_2 is the smallest (MC is the lowest) that it will be. Notice the special nature of the output rate Q_3. The tangent at point C on the total cost curve also is the ray from the origin. Thus, at output rate Q_3, we know that marginal cost and average total cost will be equal. The resulting marginal cost curve is shown in panel (b) of Figure 8-5.

The relationship between marginal cost curves and average cost curves

It should be clear now from Figures 8-4 and 8-5 that there is a distinct relationship between marginal and average cost curves. We noted that when the ray to the origin was tangent to the total cost curve, average costs were at their minimum. But when this ray is tangent to the total cost curve, its slope also indicates marginal cost. Hence, just from the geometry, we know that marginal costs and average costs are equal at the latter's minimum. Examine Figure 8-3. Note that the marginal cost curve MC intersects both the AVC curve and the ATC curve at their minimum points.

We can see that MC must equal AC when AC is at its minimum by writing down the formula for marginal cost.

$$MC = AC + \frac{\Delta AC \cdot Q}{\Delta Q} = AC + \Delta AC \cdot Q \quad (8\text{-}8)$$

where $\Delta Q = 1$.[4]

Marginal cost is defined as the change in total costs that is brought about when there is a one-unit change in the rate of production. Taking the case where $\Delta Q = 1$, we can explain Eq. (8-8) in exactly the way we explained Eq.

(7-3) when we related marginal physical product to average physical product. In fact, the relationships between marginals and averages are the same no matter what we are talking about. Consider the cost of increasing output by one unit. It will equal the average cost of producing all units plus a correction factor. That correction factor will be the change in average cost for all the previously produced units. If marginal cost is rising, this correction factor will be positive; if marginal cost is falling, this correction factor will be negative. We see this in Eq. (8-8). Whenever average cost is increasing, it will be greater than marginal cost; whenever marginal cost is decreasing, it will be less than average costs.

Now, when will marginal costs equal average costs? When the average costs are constant. Where are average costs constant on a continuous average cost curve? Only where the slope of the tangent drawn to a point on the curve is 0. This occurs at the minimum point of the average cost curve. An infinitesimal change in output involves no change in average costs. Hence, marginal cost equals average cost at the average cost curve's minimum point.[5] This holds for either average total cost or average variable cost. (Why?)

Furthermore, we can deduce from either the geometry of the relationship between marginal and average costs or Eq. (8-8) that when average costs are falling, marginal costs must be below average costs, and when average costs are rising, marginal costs must be above average costs. This can be seen by rearranging Eq. (8-8) into

$$AC = MC - \frac{\Delta AC \cdot Q}{\Delta Q} = MC - \Delta AC \cdot Q \quad (8\text{-}9)$$

---

[4]The proof has been given for the relationship between marginal physical product and average physical product in footnote[8], p. 167. Also note that AC can be either ATC or AVC, since $ATC - AVC = AFC$; but AFC does not change with output changes. Therefore $\Delta ATC/\Delta Q = \Delta AVC/\Delta Q$.

[5]Note, Eq. (8-8): $MC = AC + [(\Delta AC \cdot Q)/\Delta Q]$ becomes $MC - AC = (\Delta AC \cdot Q)/\Delta Q$. When $MC = AC$, then $(\Delta AC/\Delta Q) \cdot Q = 0$. Dividing by Q, we obtain $\Delta AC/\Delta Q$. Ergo, AC is at its minimum point—where its slope $= 0$.

where $\Delta Q = 1$.

When average costs are falling, ΔAC is negative. Thus, $-[(\Delta AC \cdot Q)/\Delta Q]$ is positive, and for the equality to hold, marginal costs must be less than average costs. When average costs are rising, ΔAC is positive; thus the term $-[(\Delta AC \cdot Q)/\Delta Q]$ is negative. For the equality to hold in Eq. (8-9), marginal costs must be greater than average costs.

Long-run cost curves

The long run, as you will remember, is defined as a time period during which full adjustment can be made to any change in the economic environment. Thus, in the long run, all factors of production are variable. Long-run curves are sometimes called planning curves, and the long run is sometimes called the **planning horizon**.

We start out our analysis of long-run cost curves by considering a single firm with a single plant. The firm has, let us say, three alternative plant sizes from which to choose on the planning horizon. Each particular plant size generates its own short-run average total cost curve. Now that we are talking about the difference between long- and short-run cost curves, we will label all short-run curves with an S; short-run average (total) costs will be labeled by SAC, and all long-run curves will have an L before them.

Look at Figure 8-6. Here we have shown three short-run average cost curves for three plant sizes which are successively larger. Which is the optimal plant size to build? That depends on the anticipated permanent rate of output per unit time period, which in turn hinges on the firm's expected demand. Assume for a moment that the anticipated permanent rate is Q_1. If plant size 1 is built, the average costs will be given C_1. If plant size 2 is built, we see on SAC$_2$ that the average costs will be C_2 which is greater than C_1. Thus, if

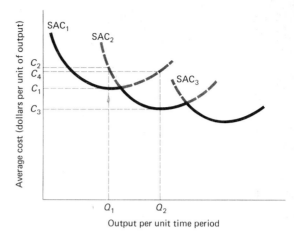

Figure 8-6: The optimal plant size.
If the anticipated permanent rate of output per unit time period is Q_1, the optimal plant to build would be the one corresponding to SAC$_1$, because average costs are lowest. However, if the permanent rate of output increases to Q_2, it will be most profitable to have a plant size corresponding to SAC$_2$. Unit costs fall to C_3.

the anticipated rate of output is Q_1, the appropriate plant size is the one from which SAC$_1$ was derived.

Note, however, that if the anticipated permanent rate of output per unit time period goes from Q_1 to Q_2, and plant 1 had been decided upon, average costs would be C_4. However, if plant 2 had been decided upon, average costs would be C_3, which are clearly less than C_4.

In choosing the appropriate plant size for a single plant firm during the planning horizon, the firm will pick that plant size whose short-run average cost curve generates an average cost which is lowest for the expected rate of output.

Long-run average cost curve

If we make the further assumption that the entrepreneur is faced with an infinite number of choices of plant sizes in the long run, then we can conceive of an infinite number of SAC curves similar to the three in Figure 8-6. We

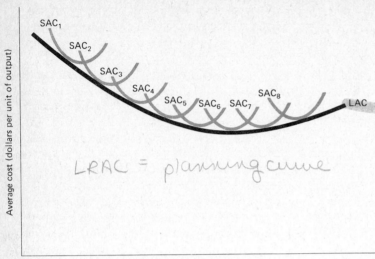

Figure 8-7: Deriving the long-run average cost curve.

If we draw all the possible short-run average cost curves that correspond to different plant sizes, and then draw the envelope to these various curves, SAC$_1$, . . . , SAC$_8$, we obtain the long-run average cost curve, or the planning curve.

LRAC = planning curve

are not able, of course, to draw an infinite number; we draw quite a few, however, in Figure 8-7. We then draw the "envelope" to all these various short-run average cost curves. The result is the **long-run average cost curve LAC**. This long-run average cost curve is sometimes called the **planning curve**, for it represents the various average costs attainable at the planning stage of the firm's decision making. It represents the locus of points giving the least unit cost of producing any given rate of output. Note that the LAC curve is *not* tangent to each individual SAC curve at the latter's minimum point. This is only true at the minimum point of the LAC curve. Then and only then are minimum long-run average costs equal to minimum short-run average costs.[6]

Long-run marginal cost

We can draw a long-run marginal cost curve using methods similar to those used to draw the short-run marginal cost curve. We show a long-run marginal cost curve LMC in Figure 8-8. It is marginal to the long-run planning curve LAC. As with all marginal curves, it intersects the average curve at the latter's minimum point. To reemphasize the discussion in the last paragraph, we have drawn in two short-run average cost curves SAC$_1$ and SAC$_2$. SAC$_1$ is tangent to LAC at point *B*. The curve marginal to SAC$_1$ is labeled SMC$_1$. SMC$_1$ intersects SAC$_1$ at its minimum point, which is point *C*. Point *A* represents the point where SMC$_1$ is equal to LMC. At point *A* the rate of output is such that SAC$_1$ is tangent to LAC.

[6]In preparing a classic article on the short- and long-run cost curves, an economist named Jacob Viner had given instructions to a draftsperson which were literally impossible to execute. Viner had told the draftsperson to construct the LAC curve so that it was tangent to the minimum point on every single SAC curve. Apparently, it was only after a considerable amount of argument from the draftsperson, who was not an economist, that Viner finally realized that it was physically impossible to have all SAC curves tangent to the LAC curve at the former's minimum points. See Jacob Viner, "Cost Curves and Supply Curves," *Zeitschrift für Nationalökonomie*, vol. 3, 1931, pp. 23–46. Also reprinted in George J. Stigler and Kenneth E. Boulding (eds.) *Readings in Price Theory*, American Economic Association (Homewood, Ill.: Irwin, 1952), pp. 198–232.

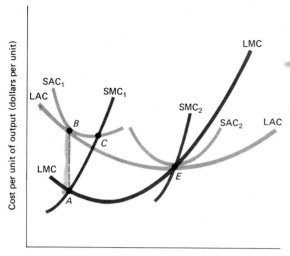

Cost per unit of output (dollars per unit)

Rate of output per unit time period

Figure 8-8: Long-run marginal costs.

The long-run marginal cost curve intersects the minimum point of the long-run average cost curve. Since at the minimum point of LAC the short-run average cost curve is also tangent at its minimum point, then we know that at point E, LMC = LAC = SAC_2 = SMC_2. Every short-run marginal cost curve (such as SMC_1) intersects its respective short-run average cost curve at the latter's minimum point (such as point C). LMC will always intersect a short-run marginal cost curve (such as SMC_1 at point A) at the rate of output where SAC_1 is tangent to LAC (point B).

This follows from the definition of the long-run average cost curve as the locus of points representing the minimum unit cost of producing any given rate of output. The curve marginal to LAC, i.e., **the long-run marginal cost curve LMC**, is defined as the locus of points showing the minimum amount by which total cost is increased when the rate of output is expanded. Thus, *short-run marginal costs and long-run marginal costs will only be equal when short-run average costs and long-run average costs are equal.* Hence, this is why we expect the intersection of any short-run marginal cost curve with the long-run marginal cost curve to be at a rate of output which corresponds to the point of tangency of

the respective short-run average cost curve with the long-run average cost curve.

LMC will intersect LAC at its minimum point. This point will also necessarily be at the minimum point on the short-run average cost curve which is tangent to the long-run average cost curve at the SAC minimum point. This SAC is labeled SAC_2 in Figure 8-8. Thus, at point E, short-run marginal costs $SMC_2 = SAC_2 = LMC = LAC$. Why? Because long-run marginal cost is defined as the *minimum* amount by which total cost is increased when the rate of output is expanded. Thus, LMC will equal short-run average costs when they are at their minimum. But when they are at their minimum, the short-run marginal cost curve intersects the short-run average cost curve and, therefore, must also intersect LMC (and LAC too).

Long-run total costs and the expansion path

We can derive the long-run total cost curve and from it the long-run marginal cost curve and the long-run average cost curve from the isoquant-isocost apparatus presented in the last chapter. We can obtain the LAC by determining the expansion path.

The expansion path

A profit-maximizing entrepreneur combines capital and labor so that the ratio of their marginal physical products is equal to the ratio of their prices. This occurs at the tangency point between an isocost curve and an isoquant. What happens to the capital/labor ratio when output expands? We do this in Figure 8-9. We pick three successively higher rates of output, Q_1, Q_2, and Q_3. Then we ask what will be the cost-minimizing ratio of capital to labor and hence the minimum total costs necessary to produce at these three

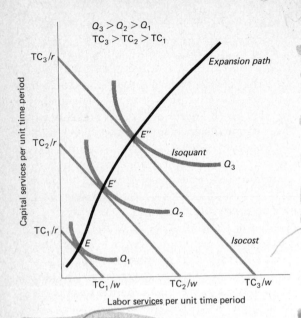

$Q_3 > Q_2 > Q_1$
$TC_3 > TC_2 > TC_1$

Capital services per unit time period

TC_3/r

Expansion path

TC_2/r E''

Isoquant

Q_3

E'

Q_2

TC_1/r E

Isocost

Q_1

TC_1/w TC_2/w TC_3/w

Labor services per unit time period

Figure 8-9: The expansion path.
To find the expansion path, we increase output from Q_1 to Q_2 to Q_3. We then draw in the minimum isocost curves (all of slope $-w/r$), i.e., the ones that are tangent to the isoquants corresponding to those three rates of output. When we connect the tangency points E, E', and E'', we obtain the expansion path.

different rates of output. This is done by drawing in isocost lines that are tangent to the isoquant curves. The resulting isocost lines are labeled by their respective total costs TC_1, TC_2, and TC_3. The extreme points on the vertical and horizontal axes are obtained by dividing each successive total cost by the implicit rental rate of capital and the wage rate of labor, respectively. The tangency points E, E', and E'' are then connected by a line called the **expansion path**. This is the line along which output will expand when input factor prices remain constant. It is the expansion path which depicts how input factor proportions change when output changes while relative input prices remain constant.[7]

When we ask for each successively higher total cost, what the maximum output will be, we get exactly the same diagram as in Figure 8-9; but now the expansion path is given the name of **isocline**, which is defined as the locus of points along which the marginal rate of technical substitution (MRTS) is constant. Remember that the slope of the isoquant is equal to the negative of the marginal rate of technical substitution. Otherwise stated, the isocline is the locus of points along which the ratio of the marginal physical product of capital to the marginal physical product of labor is constant.

Deriving the long-run total cost curve

It is easy to derive the long-run total cost curve from the expansion path. We merely ask the following question: For each rate of output, given the relative price of L and K, what are the minimum total costs given by the expansion path? We see from Figure 8-9 that for the rate of output Q_1 total costs would be TC_1. This gives us one point on the long-run total cost schedule presented in Figure 8-10; it gives us point A. The combination of rate of output Q_2 and total costs TC_2 gives us point B, and finally, the rate of output Q_3 and total costs TC_3 gives us point C. In the input space of Figure 8-9, there are an infinite number of combinations of rates of output and total costs. This infinite number of combinations gives us an infinite number of points which will become our LTC curve in Figure 8-10.

It would now be relatively simple to obtain the long-run marginal cost curve and the long-run average cost curve. The former would be obtained by getting the slopes of the tangents to different points along LTC; the latter would be obtained by getting the slopes of the rays to different points along the LTC curve. There is no difference between the LTC curve, the LAC curve, and the LMC curve derived in this manner and those derived in the previous sections.

---

[7]Note that there can never be a vertical or horizontal section in an expansion path, because this would indicate that output could be increased without increasing the use of one of the inputs.

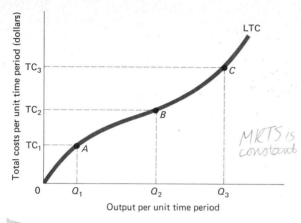

Figure 8-10: Deriving the long-run total cost curve.
The LTC curve can be derived from the expansion path.
The total outlays for each rate of output can be read
from Figure 8-11.

MRTS is constant

Capacity

One often reads about the fact that manufacturing capacity is being used only 70 percent, or 60 percent, or 80 percent. One often hears the phrase "at full capacity." The notion of full capacity for a firm is an elusive one. Clearly, it must be short-run concept, because in the long run the size of the plant and the number of plants are variable. Hence, the term "capacity" must refer to the use of a given capital stock. But it cannot refer to some physical notion of using plant and equipment to its ultimate limit. At a high enough price, just a little bit more output can always be obtained from a plant already running 24 hours a day; but the marginal cost of obtaining that additional "bit" may be astronomical. Thus, the notion of capacity must in some way relate to unit cost.

Indeed, it is possible, but not appropriate, as we will see, to define capacity in terms of minimum average cost. In fact, one suggested definition of capacity is the output at which short-run average costs are at a minimum. Then if this definition were used in Figure 8-11, for plant size 1, which yields short-run

average cost curve SAC_1 (intercepted at its minimum point by SMC_1), capacity would be Q_1. But something seems wrong here. The long-run average cost curve is defined as the minimum unit cost of producing at every feasible rate of output. Average costs for output rate Q_1 in Figure 8-11 are represented by the vertical distance from point A, the minimum point on SAC_1, to the horizontal axis. However, if the firm expected to produce this rate of output indefinitely, it would not build so large a plant; it would build a smaller plant whose short-run average cost curve would be tangent to the LAC curve at point B. Average costs per unit would drop from AQ_1 to BQ_1.

This gives a hint of what the appropriate definition for capacity for a given size of plant might be. **Capacity** will be defined as the rate of output at which there is no incentive to alter the size of the plant, if that rate of output is expected to be permanent. Thus, for plant size 1,

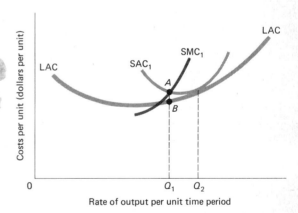

Figure 8-11: Defining capacity.
Capacity is often defined as the rate of output at which short-run average costs are at a minimum. One such output rate is Q_1, but, at that output rate, the difference between short-run average costs and long-run average costs is the vertical distance between A and B. The firm would not, in the long run, keep that plant size if the expected output rate were permanently Q_1. If capacity is defined as the rate of output at which there is no incentive to alter the size of the plant, then output rate Q_2 is the measure of capacity because, at that output rate, short-run average costs are equal to long-run average costs.

as represented by SAC$_1$, the capacity would have to be at output rate Q_2 because here long-run average costs and short-run average costs are equal.

Thus our notion of capacity, even though short run in nature, relates to long-run considerations.

Returns to scale

We would now like to be able to answer the question of how output responds in the long run to changes in the scale of the firm. This topic is generally referred to as **returns to scale**. What is the payoff, if any, from increasing the scale of the firm in the long run? It is also possible to talk about returns to scale at the plant level.

There are three possibilities for the returns to scale: Output may increase by a larger proportion than each of the inputs; output may

increase by the same proportion; output may increase by a smaller proportion than each of the inputs. Accordingly, we talk about **increasing**, **constant**, and **decreasing returns to scale**. Remember now, we are talking about altering all inputs by the same proportion. Thus, when we say a doubling of scale, we mean doubling all labor inputs and all capital inputs.

The isoquant approach

Increasing, constant, and decreasing returns to scale can be shown by using the isoquant approach.

Look at Figure 8-12. Here we have three panels. Panel (*a*) represents increasing returns to scale; panel (*b*), constant returns to scale; and panel (*c*), decreasing returns to scale. We start off with a given rate of output of 1 in each of the three panels. We also start out with a given capital/labor ratio, K_1/L_1,

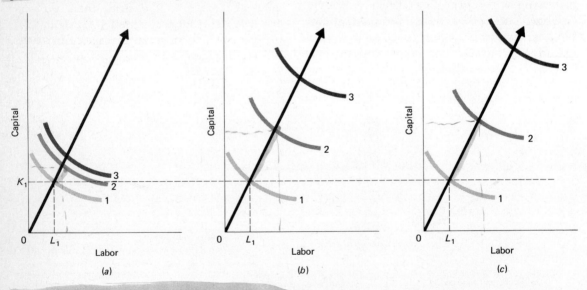

(a)   (b)   (c)

Figure 8-12: Increasing, constant, and decreasing returns to scale.
We wish to increase output by proportional changes in both capital and labor. Along any ray from the origin, the capital-labor ratio remains the same. In other words, K_1/L_1 will be equal along all the rays shown in panels (*a*), (*b*), and (*c*). In panel (*a*) we see increasing returns to scale. An increase in the output from 1 to 2 requires a less-than-proportional increase in capital and labor. In panel (*b*), we see constant returns to scale. An increase in output from 1 to 2 requires a proportional increase in both inputs. Finally, in panel (*c*), we show decreasing returns to scale. An increase in output from 1 to 2 requires a more-than-proportional increase in both inputs.

which is the same in each of the three panels. Now we ask the question, How much do we have to increase capital and labor, while keeping their ratios constant, in order to increase the rate of output from 1 to 2? Isoquant 2 represents exactly twice the output of isoquant 1. We see in panel (a) that when there are increasing returns, the increase in capital and labor inputs is less than in proportion to the increase in output. We can see this by looking at the respective distances along the ray from the origin. Remember that along any (straight-line) ray from the origin in an input space, the capital/labor ratio remains the same. Since we are dealing with proportional changes in all inputs, we can only look at what happens along any given ray. The rays drawn in panels (a), (b), and (c) all have equal slopes. In any event, in panel (a), the length of the ray between zero and where it intersects the isoquant associated with the rate of output of 1 is less than the length of the portion of the ray between the isoquant labeled 1 and the isoquant labeled 2. Otherwise stated, a doubling of output is achieved by less than a doubling of inputs. The same experiment is

even more persuasive when we increase output from a rate of 2 to a rate of 3, where isoquant 3 represents exactly three times the output of isoquant 1. (Thus the numbers 1, 2, and 3 are cardinal as opposed to ordinal.)

In panel (b), we show constant returns to scale. Here the length of the distance measured along the ray is the same between output rates of 0–1, 1–2, and 2–3. A doubling of inputs results in an exact doubling of output.

Finally, in panel (c), we show decreasing returns to scale. The distance between the isoquants gets larger for equal increments in output. Hence it requires more than proportionate increases in inputs to increase output. Otherwise stated, a doubling of output requires more than a doubling of inputs.

The long-run average cost approach

If we assume constant input prices no matter what the scale of the firm, then we can translate the results of panels (a), (b), and (c) in Figure 8-12 to long-run average cost curves. We see in Figure 8-13 panels (a), (b), and (c).

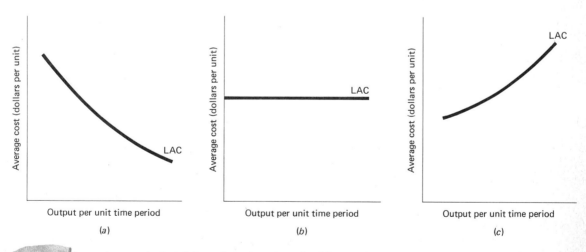

Figure 8-13: Increasing, constant, and decreasing returns to scale with cost curves.

The implication of Figure 8-12 is that long-run average costs will fall when there are increasing returns to scale [panel (a)], will be constant when there are constant returns to scale [panel (b)], and will rise when there are decreasing returns to scale [panel (c)].

In panel (a), the long-run average cost curve falls over the relevant range of outputs; in panel (b), it is horizontal; and in panel (c), it rises.

The distinction between returns to scale and economies of scale

We have just referred to increasing, constant, and decreasing returns to scale. These phenomena are related to the *technological* relationship between a proportionate change in all inputs and the resultant change in output. In other words, returns to scale refer only to the *technological* phenomena that occur *within* a firm. The ability to combine inputs in a more efficient manner as the output rate increases would be an example of a technological phenomenon within a firm. When we consider the possibility of things changing *exterior* to the firm, we are then considering the possibility of changes in such things as the prices of factors. These are external to the firm. If all firms are expanding production and, therefore, demanding more factors of production at each and every price, this may cause the prices of those factors to change. When we allow for such external changes, we are considering what have been called **economies** and **diseconomies of scale.** A firm may possibly enjoy the effects of industry economies of scale because the industry is expanding; this leads to lower prices of inputs to *all* firms, since the inputs are now purchased in larger quantities by the industry. On the other hand, diseconomies of scale might occur when input prices rose as the industry expanded production.

Thus, economies of scale and increasing returns to scale are related but are not all exactly the same. The latter is the technological basis for the former. However, economies of scale can come about solely from price effects on inputs. Hence, it is possible for there to be increasing returns to scale but no economies of scale if the firm must buy its inputs at a price that rises when the industry (or firm) expands production.

Increasing returns to scale

Here we list several reasons why a firm might be expected to experience *increasing* returns to scale.

SPECIALIZATION. As a firm's scale of operation increases, the opportunities for specialization in the use of resource inputs also increase. This is sometimes called increased division of tasks, or operations. Gains from such division of labor or increased specialization are well known; see, for example, Adam Smith's famous pin factory case.[8] When we consider managerial staffs, we also find that larger enterprises may be able to put together more highly specialized staffs. Larger enterprises may have the ability to tap better managerial technology.

DIMENSIONAL FACTOR. Large-scale firms often require proportionately less input per unit of output simply because certain inputs do not have to be physically doubled in order to double the output. Consider the cost of storage of, say, oil. The cost of storage is basically related to the cost of steel that goes into building the storage container; however, the amount of steel required goes up less than in proportion to the volume of the container.

TRANSPORTATION FACTOR. The transportation cost per unit will fall as the market area increases. The market size increase by πr^2, which is the formula for the area of a circle where r is the radius. However, transportation distance from the center of the circle is equal to r, the radius. For example, transportation distance only doubles when market area quadruples.

---

[8]Adam Smith, *The Wealth of Nations* (1776), book I, chap. 1, pp. 4–5.

IMPROVED PRODUCTIVE EQUIPMENT. The larger the scale of the enterprise, the more it is able to take advantage of larger-volume types of machinery. Small-scale operations may not lend themselves to machines that require a large volume of output to be profitably used.

Decreasing returns to scale

One of the basic reasons we can eventually expect to observe decreasing returns to scale at the firm level is that there are limits to the efficient functioning of management. Moreover, as more workers are hired, a more than proportionate increase in managers may be needed, and this could cause increased costs per unit. For example, it might be possible to hire from 0 to 10 workers and give them each a shovel to dig ditches; however, as soon as 10 workers are hired, it may also be necessary to hire an overseer to coordinate their ditch-digging efforts. Thus, perhaps constant returns to scale will obtain until 10 workers and 10 shovels are employed; then decreasing returns to scale set in. As the layers of supervision grow, the cost of information and communication grows more than in proportion.

Returns to scale at the plant level

We have already talked about some of the implicit reasons why we might observe decreasing or increasing returns to scale at the plant level. Rather than go into detail here, we merely point out that at the plant level, increasing returns to scale basically are a result of production economies. A larger plant lends itself to greater specialization in the use of resource inputs and a greater subdivision of the productive tasks.

The multiplant firm

If a firm has more than one plant producing the same thing, how should it allocate produc-

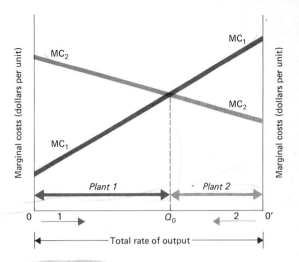

Figure 8-14: The multiplant firm.
This firm is operating two plants. Assume that output has been chosen and is equal to the horizontal dimension of the diagram $00'$. The marginal cost curve for plant 1 is measured from the left-hand axis; the marginal cost curve for plant 2 from the right-hand axis. The optimal allocation of output between the two plants will occur when $MC_1 = MC_2$, or at output rate Q_0.

tion among the plants? It should allocate production so that marginal cost is equal at all plants.[9] This is illustrated in Figure 8-14. We start out with an output that is represented by the horizontal distance between the two vertical axes. We measure marginal cost of plant 1 starting on the left-hand axis; we measure marginal cost for plant 2 starting on the right-hand axis. The origin for plant 1 is on the left-hand side of the diagram; the origin for plant 2 is on the right-hand side. The optimal allocation of output between the two plants is such that $MC_1 = MC_2$. This occurs where the two marginal cost curves intersect, or at quantity Q_0. Thus the allocation would be represented by the horizontal distance, labeled plant 1, and the horizontal distance, labeled plant 2; the sum of these two distances is the total output.

---

[9]And equal to marginal revenue (as we shall see in Chapter 10), as well as being greater than AVC.

If the allocation of output were anything else, total costs would rise. (Why?)

Technological change

Throughout the last three chapters, we have taken as given the production function of the firm. In other words, we have been concerned with the optimal choice of inputs under stationary conditions with no changes in technology. We have taken as given the "state of the arts." In other words, technology has been considered fixed. However, technology is not fixed; over time it changes. Technological change consists of discovering new methods of producing old products, of developing new products, and of introducing new techniques of marketing, organization, and management. Technological change is synonymous with a change in the production function. In this sec-

tion, we are assuming that factor prices remain constant. Technological change is motivated by the desire to produce the same quantity at a lower average cost. We can examine technological change by using the isoquant technique that we have used so much already. We will examine three types of **technological change: neutral, labor-saving,** and **capital-saving.**

Neutral technological change occurs when there is an improvement in technology that allows for the production of the same amount of output as before, but with equal reductions in both capital and labor inputs. Panel (a) in Figure 8-15 depicts a situation of *neutral* technological change. We start off on the isoquant labeled $Q = 1$. The rate of output per unit time period is 1. As a result of technological change to obtain the same output, we now have to use less of both labor and capital. We move from isoquant labeled $Q = 1$ to the lower

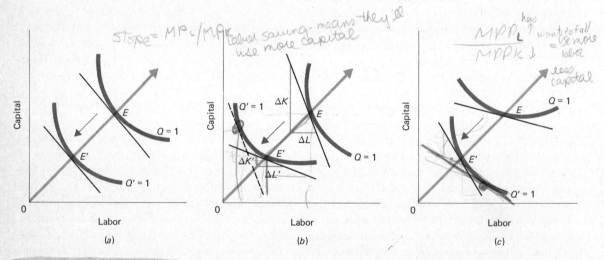

Figure 8-15: Technological change.
In panel (a), we show neutral technological change. Output equal to 1 can be attained using less capital and less labor. This is shown by movement from isoquant Q to isoquant Q', both of which have an output rate equal to 1. The reduction in capital and labor is proportionate as we move from point E to point E'. In panel (b) we show labor-saving technological change. There is a movement similar to the one in panel (a) from isoquant $Q = 1$ to isoquant $Q' = 1$; however, with constant factor prices, the firm would not stay at point E' because at that point $\Delta K/\Delta L = \text{MPP}_K/\text{MPP}_L$ is no longer equal to the ratio of the price of capital to the price of labor. The firm would have to use more capital and less labor. In panel (c), we show a capital-saving technological change.

isoquant labeled $Q' = 1$. The tangency along a particular ray drawn from the origin [which has the same slope as the rays drawn from the origin in panels (b) and (c)] is given at points E and E'. The slope of the tangents along that ray are equal. That means that the marginal rate of technical substitution (MRTS) is constant before and after technological change. That means that the marginal physical product of labor and the marginal physical product of capital have not changed (since $\text{MRTS} = \text{MPP}_L/\text{MPP}_K$). In this sense, the technological change is neutral. It does not induce the firm to change the capital/labor ratio because the ratio of their marginal physical products has not changed, or otherwise stated, because the marginal rate of technical substitution has not changed.

Labor-saving technological change

Panel (b) in Figure 8-15 represents labor-saving technological change. The original position is given by isoquant labeled $Q = 1$, where output is at the rate of 1 per unit time period. Now technological change takes place. The isoquant shifts downward so that an output of 1 per unit time period can be obtained with less labor and less capital. However, there is a difference between what has happened in this situation and what happened in the previous situation. Look at the respective slopes of the tangents drawn at point E and point E'. The slope is much steeper at point E than it is at point E'. This means that for any given ratio of capital to labor, such as the one represented along the ray drawn from the origin in panel (b), the marginal rate of technical substitution has changed; or otherwise stated, the ratio of the marginal physical product of labor to the marginal physical product of capital has changed. In fact, in this situation it is clear that the marginal physical product of capital has risen relative to the marginal physical product of labor. Thus, given the relative price of labor and capital, w/r, less labor will be used per unit of output than before. In this sense, technological change is labor-saving.

Clearly, if, for example, E were an optimum position, then E' is *not* an optimum position for the firm if factor prices are constant. For given constant factor prices, the optimum position will require less labor be used and more capital be used. Why? Because of the law of diminishing marginal physical returns. At point E', the marginal product of capital has increased relative to the marginal product of labor. At firm optimum, however, we know that the ratio of the two marginal physical products must be equal to the ratio of their respective prices. But the price of capital and labor is given. The only way to decrease the marginal physical product of capital is to increase the amount of capital used relative to labor. Conversely, the only way to increase the marginal physical product of labor is to decrease the amount of labor used relative to capital. Hence, this is why the technological change depicted in panel (b) is called labor-saving. (It could also be called capital-*using*.)

Capital-saving technological change

We could go through a similar analysis to describe the capital-saving technological change which is depicted in panel (c) of Figure 8-15. The marginal physical product of labor increases relative to capital in such a situation. Hence, less capital need be used per unit of output with a given quantity of labor. The only way to get to the firm optimum will be to increase the amount of labor used and decrease the amount of capital, thereby affecting their relative marginal physical products. This is why it is called capital-saving. (It could also be called a labor-*using* technological change.)

Issues and applications

When is fixed capital really fixed?

We tend to think of fixed costs as being associated with fixed capital. When a machine is in place, particularly a big one, we don't generally consider the possibility of moving it. However, General Motors Corporation found out that what may seem like fixed capital to some can in fact be moved.

In 1974, after the problems of gasoline availability, there was an attempt made by automobile manufacturers to come up with smaller, gas-saving automobiles. General Motors wanted to put six-cylinder engines into more of its cars. In order to tool up to make a six-cylinder engine, it would have then required about $15 million and 2 or 3 years. The immediate dilemma could not be solved in this manner.

In the past, GM had owned a six-cylinder-engine manufacturing assembly line that it had been using for 12 years. However, in 1968 it sold the assembly line, i.e., the fixed capital to American Motors Corporation. This engine manufacturing assembly line had been idle in an AMC plant since late 1971.

What did GM do? It bought back the six-cylinder production line from the Jeep Corporation, a subsidiary of AMC. It paid more than the $5 million that it had received when it sold the fixed capital in 1968. GM also incurred several million dollars in additional expenses in moving, refurbishing, and making other changes in the equipment so that the resultant engine would conform with the performance and pollution-control requirements of 1974 and later years.

Thus we have an example of fixed capital, that is, capital which an outsider might consider fixed, that can in fact be moved. And clearly, the capital equipment in question was cheaper to purchase from someone else than it would have been to build from scratch, particularly when the time factor is considered.

When does the opportunity cost of continued possession matter?

At the beginning of this chapter, we discussed the different costs associated with production. One of the costs that was discussed was the *opportunity cost of continued possession* of such assets as machines, equipment, buildings, and the like. It turns out that an accurate measure of total costs and, hence, profitability on an investment, requires careful consideration of the opportunity cost of the continued possession of all assets that the firm owns. Many of the assets that the firm owns are intangible. These are called **intangible capital**. Examples of intangible capital include, but are not limited to, goodwill established in the market, trademarks, patents, and trade secrets.

If we wish to determine the rate of return earned by a firm, we have to examine the relationship between net revenues and *the investment that would be required to currently replicate the existing firm capacity.* That investment would most certainly include intangible capital. If a firm has spent an amount of money in the past on a nationwide advertising campaign to make the community aware of its existence and the quality of its products, the intangible capital, e.g., brand recognition, resulting from that advertising outlay forms part of the investment that someone else would have to make to replicate the existing firm's capacity.

Research and development

Clearly, then, to understand the profit, if any, that a company is earning requires us to have a complete accounting of all the costs involved in selling the firm's product. The costs include the opportunity cost of continued possession of not only tangible capital such as machines and buildings, but also intangible capital such as the results of past research and development expenditures (R&D) which have not yet been applied to actual production. For example, if a pharmaceutical company has spent $10 million this year in R&D on a drug that will not be marketed until 3 years from now, during those 3 years that drug company is implicitly foregoing a return on $10 million over the 3-year period. In other words, it is incurring a cost of continued possession of R&D. After all, it could have taken that $10 million and invested it in, say, government bonds yielding 8 percent. For the 3 years in question, then, the pharmaceutical company could receive 8 percent of $10 million, or $800,000, per year. This $800,000 per year is an opportunity cost of continued possession of $10 million worth of R&D.

Depreciation of advertising outlays

Not only must we take account of the cost of continued possession of R&D, for example, but we should also take account of the fact that an expenditure such as that on advertising is not really the same as an expenditure on labor. Wages paid to workers represent a current expense related to the current use of an input that yields its output immediately; however, advertising does not yield its output immediately. Rather, it has a longer-run effect. Companies typically do not consider 100 percent of their outlay on a machine as a current expense in the year that the machine is purchased. For one thing tax laws prevent this; but also, from an economic point of view, if the machine lasts for, say, 5 years, the true cost of the services from the machine are, in the most simple example, equal to one-fifth of its purchase price each year.[10] From an accounting point of view, the firm depreciates the machine each year by an

amount based on its expected service life and the rules that the Internal Revenue Service has set up for depreciation. However, the IRS allows firms to deduct as a current expense all costs associated with advertising in the year that they are made. From an economic point of view (not to be confused with sound *tax* accounting), these costs should be treated similarly to those associated with the purchase of tangible capital; just because advertising represents intangible capital does not mean its cost is appropriately charged to the year in which it is spent.[11]

Correcting accounting rates of profit

In order to correct standard accounting rates of profit for a firm that engages in advertising and research and development, we have to do two things: (1) Depreciate intangible assets resulting from expenditures on advertising and research and development over their expected lifetimes rather than expensing them in the year in which they are incurred; and (2) take account of the opportunity cost (i.e., foregone interest) of continued possession of such intangible capital as that embodied in research and development.

A study taking account of these corrections has been completed by K. W. Clarkson.[12] We present here some of the results of Clarkson's study. In Table 8-2, we show advertising and promotion expenditures expressed as a percentage of net sales for different industries. We note that there is a dramatic difference in those industries in terms of their promotional expenditures. Pharmaceuticals and chemicals spend (relatively) approximately 10 times more on advertising and promotion than do ferrous metals and aerospace industries.

---

[10]This is called straight-line depreciation.

[11]From a firm's point of view, however, it is always best to expense any costs in the year that they are incurred and to depreciate capital expenditures as fast as the law allows. The reason has to do with present-value calculations. Any expenses that the IRS allows to be deducted from revenues reduces current operating profit and therefore in-

come taxes owed. Thus, the present value (see Chapter 6) of any tax savings is greater the sooner that savings is obtained.

[12]K. W. Clarkson, *Intangible Capital and Rates of Return: Effects of Research and Promotion,* American Enterprise Institute for Public Policy Research, Washington, D.C., 1977.

Industry	Advertising and promotion (percentage of net sales)
Pharmaceuticals	3.7
Chemicals	3.7
Foods	2.3
Electrical machinery	1.6
Rubber products	1.5
Office machinery	1.0
Motor vehicles	0.8
Paper	0.7
Petroleum	0.5
Ferrous metals	0.3
Aerospace	0.3

Table 8-2: Advertising and promotion expenditures.
Source: Industry average for 1949–1971, U.S. Bureau of the Census, *Statistical Abstract of the United States, 1951–1971*, and U.S. Treasury, *Statistics of Income: Corporate Income Tax Reforms, 1949–1951*.

In Table 8-3, we show research and development expenditures both in absolute terms and as a percentage of sales. Again, there is a marked difference among industries. The pharmaceutical industry spends (relatively) almost 8 times more on R&D than does the ferrous metals industry.

Moreover, there is a different average expected research and development pay-out for different industries. This can be seen in Table 8-4. Pharmaceuticals have an average pay-out period of 6 years; food has an average pay-out period of 3 years. In other words, an investment of $1 million in R&D in pharmaceuticals won't come to fruition for 6 years, whereas the same investment will come to fruition in 3 years in the foods industry. That means that there is a greater opportunity cost of continued possession of R&D in the pharmaceuticals industry than in the foods industry.

Clarkson takes account of the necessity of depreciating intangible capital—advertising and R&D—and also of adding the opportunity cost of continued possession to that intangible capital. In Table 8-5, the average rate of return on net worth for different industries with and without these corrections on the cost side are shown.

Industry	Research and development expenditures (millions of constant dollars)	R&D as a percentage of sales
Pharmaceuticals	4,167	5.3
Electrical machinery	21,376	3.6
Aerospace	12,025	3.5
Chemicals	13,560	3.1
Office machinery	14,210	3.1
Motor vehicles	14,704	2.5
Rubber products	2,201	1.7
Paper products	1,702	0.9
Petroleum	5,431	0.9
Ferrous metals	1,819	0.7
Foods*	2,293	0.4

Table 8-3: Company research and development expenditures, 1961–1971.
*Data not available for 1963.
Source: Calculated from statistics reported in *Research and Development in Industry, 1971*, National Science Foundation, NSF 73-305.

Industry	Average years
Pharmaceuticals	6
Petroleum	5
Aerospace	4
Chemicals	4
Rubber products	4
Paper products	4
Ferrous metals	4
Electrical machinery	3
Office machinery	3
Motor vehicles	3
Foods	3

Table 8-4: Average expected research and development payout periods.
Sources: Pharmaceutical average payout period was estimated from various sources reported in D. Schwartzman, "Pharmaceutical R and D Expenditures and Rates of Return," in R. Helms (ed.), *Drug Development and Marketing* (Washington, D.C.: American Enterprise Institute for Public Policy Research, 1975), pp. 63–80. Average payout periods for all other industries were computed from data reported in E. Mansfield, et al., *Research and Innovation in the Modern Corporation* (New York: Norton, 1971), p. 7.

Industry	No depreciation of intangible or capital accumulation	With advertising and research capitalization and depreciation
Pharmaceuticals	18.29	12.89
Electrical machinery	13.33	10.10
Foods	11.81	10.64
Petroleum	11.23	10.77
Chemicals	10.59	9.14
Motor vehicles	10.46	9.22
Paper	10.49	10.12
Rubber products	10.11	8.69
Office machinery	10.48	9.90
Aerospace	9.23	7.38
Ferrous metals	7.55	7.28
All above:		
Average	11.2	9.6
Variance	7.5	2.5

Table 8-5: Average rate of return, 1959–1973.
K. W. Clarkson, *Intangible Capital and Rates of Return: Effects of Research and Promotion on Profitability,* American Enterprise Institute for Public Policy Research, Washington, D.C., 1977. Table 16.

There are some remarkable differences. The pharmaceuticals industry, which is the most intangible capital-intensive of the industries studied, and the one that has the longest expected pay-out period for investment in R&D, has a dramatic drop in its rate of return from 18 percent to a little less than 13 percent. As would be expected, where there is little advertising and promotion, little R&D, and a fast pay-out period for investment in R&D, there is almost no change in the computed rate of return. Ferrous metals had an uncorrected rate of return of 7.55 percent and a corrected rate of return of almost the same, 7.28 percent.

Social versus private costs: The case of two roads

The apparent originator of the terms "social costs" and "private costs," British economist A. C. Pigou, presented what has become a classic case illustrating what can happen when there is a divergency between social and private costs. This case was written up in Pigou's first edition of *The Economics of Welfare,* published in 1918. Pigou contended that in situations where social costs exceeded private costs, individuals freely left to their own initiative will end up overinvesting and overconsuming, from "society's" point of view, in such activities. He demonstrated his point by comparing two roads.

Road 1 was a well-paved but narrow road that, when uncrowded, could get motorists to their destination faster than the alternative road. The alternative was unpaved, and hence, relatively slow speeds had to be observed on it. It had the virtue, however, of being very broad, and was capable of handling (in Pigou's hypothetical example) any volume of traffic without congestion.

When making a choice between road 1 and road 2, motorists would choose road 1 as long as it did not become crowded, for they could get to their destination cheaper in terms of time. However, after road 1 became crowded, the decision was not so easy. After some point, the increased congestion on road 1 would slow traffic down so much that it would be as cheap in terms of time to use road 2.

We can illustrate the situation in Figure 8-16. Panel (*a*) represents the situation on road 1 and panel (*b*) the situation on road 2. Panel (*b*) is easier to understand. By assumption, in Pigou's example, no matter how many cars used road 2, the time cost of travel remained the same. If we measure time on the vertical axis and cars per unit time period on the horizontal axis, the average cost curve expressed in terms of time will be a horizontal line at T_2. On road 2, average costs are constant, and therefore marginal time cost must equal average time cost and also be constant, i.e., $0T_2 = AC_2 = MC_2$.

In panel (*a*), the time-cost situation is depicted for road 1. Until the quantity of cars per unit time period Q_1 is reached, the time cost remains at T_1. Thus, from T_1 to point A, average cost equals marginal cost, or $AC_1 = MC_1$. After Q_1, when cars enter road 1, congestion arises and the time cost

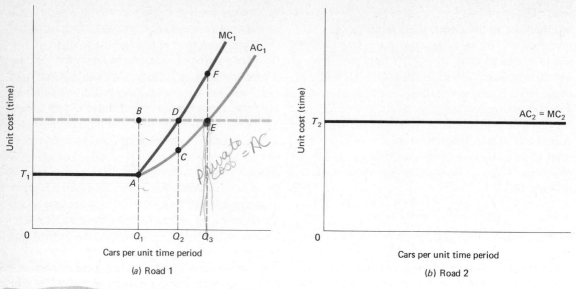

(a) Road 1

(b) Road 2

Figure 8-16: Private versus social costs—the case of two roads.
In panel (b), we show road 2 which can accommodate any volume of cars at a constant time cost of T_2; therefore, $AC_2 = MC_2$. In panel (a), we show a constant time cost for road 1 at T_1 up to volume Q_1. Thereafter, average cost rises, and marginal cost MC_1 is above it. If no one owns the better road, 1, cars will enter the road until the time costs are equated or until volume Q_3, when the time cost will equal the vertical distance from Q_3 to point E, which is also equal to T_2 in panel (b). However, at that volume, the social cost of the last driver entering the road is equal to the vertical distance Q_3 to F, since that driver imposes a cost on all other drivers by slowing them down. If someone owns the road, a toll can be charged. It will equal the monetary value of the reduction in time saved by using road 1 instead of road 2. The maximum toll that can be charged, therefore, is BA. The optimum toll is equal to DC. In this case, social costs equal private costs to the individual driver because that driver will pay marginal costs rather than average costs.

increases. Average cost rises after point A; marginal cost, therefore, is above average cost. Remember, we are expressing cost in terms of travel time.

Until what volume of traffic would motorists continue to enter road 1? According to Pigou, motorists would continue entering road 1 until the total travel time was equal to what it would be on road 2. This occurs at quantity Q_3 of cars per unit time period. Here, total travel time is equalized between the two roads and is equal to T_2. Motorists would not enter road 1 at a rate in excess of Q_3 because it would be cheaper in time cost to switch to road 2.

Divergency of social and private costs

The private time cost of using road 1 is equal to the vertical distance between point E and Q_3,

which is equal to T_2. In other words, the private cost to the individual motorist is equal to the average cost or average total travel time spent on road 1. The marginal social cost, however, is greater. It is equal to the vertical distance between point F and Q_3. Why? Because all Q_3 motorists using road 1 are not only incurring a private total time cost of EQ_3, but each is also slowing down every other motorist on road 1. The amount that any given user slows down every other motorist is given by the distance between F and E. The delay per motorist might be trivial, but the total is large. For example, consider 100 motorists who each take 60 minutes to travel the road. When the 101st driver enters, he or she causes congestion, slowing down all 100 other drivers. They each require 61 minutes to drive the road. He or she, therefore, adds 1 minute times 100 drivers or 100 minutes of driving time for that road. The social marginal cost of his or her entering the road in time units is 61 minutes plus 100 minutes, or 161 minutes. In other words, the social marginal cost of the last motorist's entrance onto road 1 is given by the marginal cost curve MC_1. Social cost is defined as all costs associated with an activity. These social costs must include not only the total private time cost incurred by the last motorist on road 1, but also the total additional time costs incurred by all other motorists. If you will remember Eq. (8-8), this can be stated as

$$MC_1 = AC_1 + \Delta AC_1 \cdot Q \qquad (8\text{-}10)$$

where Q equals the cars per unit time period on road 1.

According to Pigou's original analysis, road 1 is used too much and road 2 is used too little. The individual undertaking the decision to enter road 1 is not forced to take into account the greater travel time cost that he or she imposes on all other drivers on road 1. In such a free entry onto a highway situation, he or she does not have to consider social costs, only private costs.

The effects of charging a toll

In a rebuttal to Pigou's analysis, Professor F. H. Knight[13] pointed out that Pigou's prediction would only hold true if both roads were free to all comers. Knight then went on to demonstrate that if road 1 charged the proper toll, there would be the optimal number of cars per unit time on road 1 and there would be no overuse of the resource (that road).

Suppose that there were private property rights in road 1 or that the state operated in a profit-maximizing manner. Then suppose that the owner of road 1 would like to make some income from that road. Let's assume for the moment that there are no costs of collecting tolls or of physical use of the road. Clearly, the owner of road 1 could

---

[13]F. H. Knight "Some Fallacies in the Interpretation of Social Costs," *Quarterly Journal of Economics*, vol. 38, 1924, pp. 582–606.

not charge a toll in excess of the monetary value of the time cost between *A* and *B*. This distance represents the time saving by using road 1 rather than road 2 when the former is uncongested. No motorist would be willing to pay a toll that was higher in monetary terms than the value placed on the time saving between road 1 and road 2. Thus we have the maximum toll that could be charged, and it is equal to the monetary value of the time saving and is represented by the distance between *A* and *B*. If this toll were charged, quantity Q_1 of cars per unit time period would use road 1. If the minimum toll, i.e., no toll at all, were charged, we would be back in the first situation discussed by Pigou. The quantity Q_3 of cars per unit time would use road 1.

We now have two extreme points between which the owner of the road must set the toll in order to maximize revenues collected. Let's start from the maximum toll and keep decreasing it until we find the optimal toll. We must realize that as the toll is decreased from (in monetary terms) *AB*, more motorists will enter road 1. Thus, the owner of the road will have a larger volume of traffic. However, this is only obtained by reducing the toll to all who come on the road. Note that the toll is equal to the difference between average costs on road 2 and average costs on road 1, or $AC_2 - AC_1$. The maximum toll *AB* is equal to $T_2 - T_1$.

The owner of the road will want to continue lowering the toll as long as the amount collected on the marginal motorist, $AC_2 - AC_1$, exceeds the reduction in revenue collected from the other motorists. This reduction in revenue from other motorists is equal to $\Delta AC_1 \cdot Q$. Rearranging this we obtain the optimum toll when $AC_1 + \Delta AC_1 \cdot Q = AC_2$. Notice that the left-hand side of this expression is exactly equal to our definition of MC_1 given in Eq. (8-10). In other words, the optimal toll is charged so as to make the marginal cost on road 1 equal to the average cost (which is equal to the MC of road 2 by assumption) on road 2. This occurs in panel (*a*) when the toll is equal to *CD* and the quantity of cars per unit time period on the road is Q_2. The owner of road 1 would make all those who used road 1 take account of the full social cost of their actions; and the social cost is represented by the marginal cost curve in panel (a). In other words, motorists on road 1 would be forced to pay for the additional time cost that they impose on other motorists.

Knight's qualification of Pigou's argument is based on road 1 being privately owned and operated for a profit. The charging of a price in the form of a toll forces the individual motorists to recognize the full social cost of their actions.

Glossary

Opportunity cost The foregone value of resources used in their best alternative use; a currently available alternative that is sacrificed.

Private costs All costs explicitly or implicitly incurred by individuals or firms.

Social costs Private costs plus costs imposed on other members of society who are not parties to the transaction (third parties).

Explicit costs The costs that firms explicitly incur and write down on their books (accounting costs).

Implicit costs Opportunity costs incurred by firms but not explicitly recognized (e.g., foregone rent on land owned and used by a firm).

Historical costs The explicit outlays made by a producer in obtaining a specific resource at the time that the resource was purchased.

Fixed costs (FC) Costs which are "sunk"; costs which are invariant to the rate of output.

Cost of acquisition The difference between the purchase price of an asset and its immediate resale price.

Cost of continued possession The opportunity cost of holding the asset plus the cost of depreciation of the asset if it is not used.

Variable cost The cost that is related to the rate of output, i.e., it varies as output varies.

Average fixed costs (AFC) Total fixed costs divided by output.

Average variable costs (AVC) Total variable costs divided by output.

Average total costs (ATC) Total of all fixed and variable costs divided by output.

Marginal cost The change in total cost (or in variable cost) due to a one-unit change in the rate of production.

Planning horizon Another name for long-run cost curves. All inputs are variable during the planning period.

Long-run average cost curve The locus of points representing the minimum unit cost of producing any given rate of output, given current technology and resource prices.

Planning curve Another name for the long-run average cost curve.

Long-run marginal cost curve (LMC) The locus of points showing the minimum amount by which total cost is increased as the rate of output is expanded by one unit.

Expansion path The line along which output will expand while relative factor prices remain constant; shows how factor proportions change when output changes and relative input prices are constant.

Isocline The locus of points along which the marginal rate of technical substitution is constant; shows us how output changes as successively higher total outlays are incurred while holding relative price of inputs constant.

Capacity That permanent rate of output at which there is no incentive for the firm to alter plant size in the long run.

Returns to scale The relationship between changes in output and proportionate changes in all factors of production.

Increasing returns to scale Output increases more than in proportion to the change in inputs due to technological changes within the firm.

Constant returns to scale Output increases by the same proportion that all inputs increase.

Decreasing returns to scale Output increases less than in proportion to the increase in inputs.

Economies of scale Output increases more than in proportion to the change in inputs; may result from both increasing returns to scale or such external-to-the-firm changes as falling factor prices.

Diseconomies of scale Output rises less than in proportion to a change in inputs; may result from either decreasing returns to scale or such external changes as an increase in the price of inputs.

Neutral technological change A change in the production function such that the same output can be produced with equal reductions in both the capital and labor inputs; the ratio of the marginal physical products of the inputs remains the same.

Labor-saving technological change A change in the production function such that the same rate of output can be obtained with a reduction in both capital and labor; but the percentage reduction in labor is, however, greater.

Capital-saving technological change A change in the production function such that the same rate of output can be obtained by using less capital and labor; but the percentage reduction in capital, however, is ~~less~~ greater.

Intangible capital Assets that are not physically in existence; to be contrasted with tangible capital such as machines and equipment. Examples are goodwill created by years of selling high-quality products, advertising, trademarks and patents, and trade secrets.

Summary

1. The cost of any action is the best currently available alternative that is sacrificed.
2. Firms and consumers generally take account of private costs rather than social costs; the latter includes all costs of any activity.
3. Firms often take account of the explicit costs and ignore the implicit costs. For example, two identical inputs may have been purchased at different historical costs. From an economic point of view, they have the same opportunity cost; but the firm's accountant may treat one as being less expensive than the other. However, all productive resources that are identical have the same opportunity cost.
4. Fixed costs are usually defined as those that are invariant to the rate of output; however, a true fixed, or sunk, cost, which is the cost of assets that cannot be transferred to some other profitable use, actually has an opportunity cost equal to zero.
5. If a machine is highly specialized and, therefore, has no alternative use and also no scrap value, its cost of acquisition is equal to its price and its cost of continued possession is effectively zero.
6. The total physical product curve is a mirror image of the total variable cost curve when the units of the single variable input are altered so that the input price is equal to $1 unit. Whenever the input price changes, the total variable cost curve pivots; but it is still related to the total product curve.
7. Average fixed costs can be represented by a rectangular hyperbola; the axes are the aysmptotes.
8. The marginal cost curve intersects both the average variable cost curve and the average total cost curve at their minimum points.
9. Whenever AVC and/or ATC are falling, marginal cost is below them; whenever they are rising, marginal cost is above them.
10. Cost minimization for a given output level requires that the ratio of marginal physical product of an input to its price be equal across all inputs.
11. Average variable cost is equal to the input price divided by the average physical product of the input.
12. Marginal cost is equal to the input price divided by the marginal physical product of the input.
13. In the long run, the firm is able to alter all inputs. It therefore faces a planning horizon.
14. The appropriate plant size for a single-plant firm during the planning horizon is the one that minimizes the short-run average cost at the expected rate of output.
15. The long-run average cost curve is obtained by drawing the envelope of all the short-run average cost curves. Only at the minimum point on the LAC curve is the LAC curve tangent to the minimum point of a short-run average cost curve. The long-run marginal cost curve will always intersect each short-run marginal cost curve at the output rate at which the respective short-run average cost curve is tangent to the long-run average cost curve.
16. If we connect the points of tangency between successively higher isoquants and parallel isocost curves, we obtain the expansion path; it shows us how factor proportions change when

output increases while input prices remain constant.

17. Capacity in the short run is the output at which the firm has no incentive to alter the size of plant when that rate of output is expected to be permanent. Thus, capacity must be at a point on a short-run average cost curve where it is tangent to the long-run average cost curve; only at that tangency point will the firm keep that size of plant if that output is considered permanent.

18. Returns to scale relate to the change in output due to a proportionate change in all inputs. Returns to scale are a technological phenomenon *within* the firm.

19. Economies of scale can result from returns to scale, but can also be caused by such changes outside the firm's control as a change in the input price due to a change in the *industry's* rate of output.

20. Increasing returns to scale may be due to: (*a*) specialization, (*b*) dimensional factors, (*c*) transportational factors, and (*d*) improved productive equipment.

21. Decreasing returns to scale may be due to the managerial limits in a firm.

22. Technological change is a change in the production function. If the same output can be obtained with less of at least one input, and if such a change induces the firm to keep constant, increase, or decrease its capital/labor ratio, then the technological change is said to be neutral, labor-saving, or capital-saving, respectively.

Selected references

Chamberlin, Edward H., "Proportionality, Divisibility, and Economies of Scale," *Quarterly Journal of Economics*, vol. 62, February 1948, pp. 229–262.

Clark, J. M., *The Economics of Overhead Costs* (Chicago: University of Chicago Press, 1923), chaps. 4–6.

Liebhafsky, H. H., *The Nature of Price Theory*, rev. ed. (Homewood, Ill.: Dorsey and Irwin, 1968), chap. 7.

Mansfield, Edwin, *The Economics of Technological Change* (New York: Norton, 1968).

Moore, Frederick T., "Economies of Scale: Some Statistical Evidence," *Quarterly Journal of Economics*, May 1959.

Stigler, George J., "The Economies of Scale," *Journal of Law and Economics*, vol. 1, October 1958, pp. 54–71.

Questions

(Answers to even-numbered questions are at back of book.)

1. How would you go about determining the opportunity cost of going to college from September until June? Who bears this cost?

2. "We seldom use that old machine, but it doesn't cost us anything to keep it because it's been completely depreciated on the company books." Criticize this statement.

3. "We demand that Riskyroad Market be investigated by the state consumer ombudsperson. It is widely known that their meats are centrally butchered and that the better cuts are trucked out to the affluent suburban stores and only the fat- and bone-laden meat (chuck steak, ham hocks, chicken wings, and the like) are left for the inner-city stores. This discrimination must be brought to a halt." What does the opportunity cost of preparing food at home have to do with the above situation?

4. The concept of social costs was introduced in this chapter. Its counterpart is social benefits. Suppose an X-rated film at a drive-in movie is visible from an adjacent highway. Is this an example of an external cost or an external benefit?

5. Suppose that Congress changed the tax laws so that stock dividends became a tax-deductible "expense" for corporations. What impact would such a move have on the relative attractiveness of debt financing (issuing new bonds or borrowing from a bank to raise capital) and equity financing (issuing new shares of stock to raise capital)? Why?

6. "I know that the 'short run' for my gas station won't end for at least 10 more years, since that's how long my lease runs." Criticize this statement.

7. Is a fixed cost ever a function of output in the short run? Why or why not? What is the formula for average fixed cost? What is a curve of that sort called?

8. Suppose you were producing a rate of output Q, employing a combination of inputs such that the marginal physical product of capital was 8 times that of labor. If the implicit rental

value per unit of capital were 10 times as much as the wage rate per unit of labor, are you minimizing your costs for that output? Why or why not? What change in inputs will lower your cost of producing output Q? Explain.

9. Define marginal cost. Does your definition refer to a change in total cost or in variable cost? Does it matter? Why or why not?

10. Define long-run average total cost. In light of the fact that businesses are operated day to day in the short run, of what use is the concept of long-run average total cost to an entrepreneur?

11. "Despite all of the developments in power gardening equipment which have occurred in recent years, the typical home gardening service consists of a single gardener, sometimes two, and a pickup truck full of equipment. One of these days, one of them is going to get smart and increase the scale of operations to six or eight workers and operate with a very large truck full of highly specialized equipment. The result will be lower costs and the small traditional operators will be driven out of business." Criticize this statement.

12. Consider a three-plant firm. At present output Q, each plant is producing one-third ($Q/3$) of the total. You are hired as the company's new industrial engineer. The first thing you do is ascertain the marginal cost of each plant at the present output rate of $Q/3$. Your figures show plant 1's marginal cost to be $10 and that of plants 2 and 3 to be $8. Assuming that you wish to continue output at the same level Q, how should you rearrange production shares so as to decrease costs?

13. Why is it that a significant expansion of an entire industry will often shift the marginal cost curve of each individual firm leftward?

14. What is the relationship between the "commerce clause" ("Congress shall have power ... to regulate commerce with foreign nations, and among the several states ....") of the United States Constitution and the LAC concept?

15. Why do you think that the federal government allows taxpayers using their own personal cars in their work (other than just to and from) to deduct as an expense an amount (15¢ per mile at this writing) which is approximately equal to the ATC of the vast majority of car owners? Why doesn't Congress limit the deduction to one's marginal cost?

9

LINEAR PROGRAMMING

Unlike most tools of mathematics, linear programming is relatively new in design and application.[1] Like all other mathematical tools employed in economics, linear programming has no inherent economic content; it is simply a mathematical technique which helps in problem solving. By itself, it can never tell us anything about the operation of the economy; it can only help produce answers to questions based on available information and the necessary assumptions.

Since it is only a manipulative device, if incorrect assumptions are made or misinformation is injected into the system, *the mathematical technique will not magically eliminate these errors and produce correct answers.* As anyone the least bit familiar with the use of computers knows, any logical or numerical errors made by the user will not be corrected; the machine either will refuse to perform the requested task or will produce incorrect answers.

Students taking microeconomics and business people observing economists are sometimes critical of what they believe to be a lack of applicability of economic theory to the so-called real world. Linear programming is one area where the critics might be placated by witnessing economic principles in action in concrete situations. This form of analysis is

---

[1]The winners of the 1975 Nobel Prize for economic science, T. C. Koopmans and L. V. Kantorovich, are among the scholars who developed linear programming techniques.

much closer to the view that business people have of day-to-day production. Linear programming enables the analyst to isolate individual inputs in the production process and to study the outputs of a production process, individually or in combinations. The economist usually studies the production process in a generalized, theoretical manner. Linear programming is merely a more particularized view of the production process.

A simple illustration

To get a rough idea of the type of problem that can be handled by linear programming, consider a simple example. Upon graduation, you are unable to bear leaving your alma mater, and you accept a position as head of food services for the school dormitories. Your instructions are simple: You must meet the minimum daily nutrition requirements of the students, you must do this with the foods available for this purpose, and you must minimize costs. There are three minimum daily nutrition requirements to be met: calories, protein, and vitamins. These three requirements must be met simultaneously, or the students may develop scurvy and other unpleasant diseases for which you will be held responsible. Not only must these minimum standards be met, but they have to be met with only two ingredients: meat and potatoes. This situation is pictured in Figure 9-1. There the axes represent the quantities of the two foods you can order for the number of students you have to feed on a daily basis.

The lines within the quadrant display the alternative combinations of meat and potatoes that will fulfill the students' nutrition requirements, as defined by a dietetics handbook. *AB* shows that to provide the minimum number of calories required would take at least *A* pounds of meat or *B* pounds of potatoes, or any combination of the two along that line. Similarly, *CD* displays the minimum quanti-

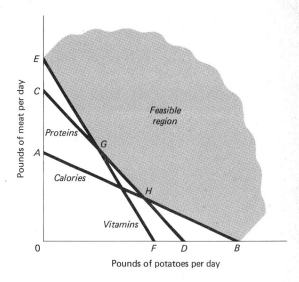

Figure 9-1: Obtaining the feasible region.
We assume that there are three nutritional requirements given in nutritional handbooks; vitamins, calories, and proteins. The lines *EF*, *AB*, and *CD*, respectively, represent those requirements. In order to meet all those requirements simultaneously, you must be along or above the line *EGHB*; it is labeled the *feasible region.*

ties that will just meet the protein requirement; and *EF* shows those combinations satisfying the minimum vitamin requirements.

To meet the three nutritional requirements simultaneously, your menu must lie somewhere along the *EGHB* or at some point above or to the right of that line. There is likely to be only one point, among the multitude that have been revealed acceptable, that will also satisfy your other instruction, to minimize costs. To meet that restriction, the relative prices of the foods purchased must be considered.

Contacting various food wholesalers reveals the best prices at which you can purchase meat and potatoes. Taking the two prices together, you can compute the price ratio; this ratio, when considered with the other restrictions, yields the solution to your problems. In Figure 9-2, the price ratio has been added to the diagram to show the "lowest" (least costly) combination on the nutrition requirement boundary. Remember that the price ratio is

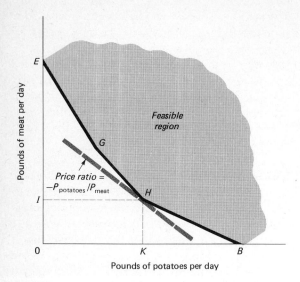

Figure 9-2: Determining the least-cost solution.
If we add a price line given by the relative price of the
two foods, potatoes and meat, we can find where it
just touches the feasible region boundary *EGHB*. This
occurs at point *H*, so that *I* pounds of meat per day
and *K* pounds of potatoes per day would be chosen.

posed of linear segments rather than being a smooth curve.[3]   The line displays different input combinations that can be used to produce a desired level of output, which is defined here with reference to three criteria. The price ratio line is like an isocost line and displays the various combinations of the inputs that may be purchased for a given level of expenditure.   The point of tangency between an isoquant and an isocost yields the unique cost-minimizing point, just as here the junction of the segmented line and the price ratio yields the only cost-minimizing combination of the inputs.[4]

Basic concepts

The preceding example illustrated most of the major aspects of linear programming.   This form of analysis concentrates on short-run choices of **production processes** and outputs.

A production process is a specific method of achieving a given output.   There are always alternative processes which will produce the same result.   In some instances, there are a very large number of alternative processes available, but usually there are a small number of practical alternatives to be considered.

For example, in the production of a book such as this one, the alternatives might be having ten people set type by hand or having two people use an electronic typesetter.   Such a trade-off would be between capital (the use of an electronic typesetter) and labor (eight typesetters' time).   This is an example of a fundamental choice which was considered in more general terms in Chapter 7.   The more production alternatives that are available, the closer the linear segment isoquant will come

the negative of the price of the good on the horizontal axis divided by the price of the good on the vertical axis. By shifting this line down through the quadrant until it just touches (is tangent to) the lowest point on the boundary of the feasible region (the point closest to the origin but still in the feasible region), the least-cost combination of meat and potatoes has been established. Thus you have determined that *I* pounds of meat per day and *K* pounds of potatoes per day will feed the students at the least cost and satisfy their nutritional needs.[2]

Some readers may have noticed the similarities between some parts of the example and some more general economic concepts.   The line *EGBH* is like an isoquant; but it is com-

---

[2]The rash assumption is made here that the students will in fact eat the food.

[3]This differs from the usual isoquant because it does not measure a specific volume or level of a product. However-

er, since it "produces" a minimum nutrition requirement, it can be treated as effectively the same.

[4]The same would be true, of course, if this were a profit-maximizing example rather than a cost-minimizing one.

to looking like the smooth curve used to illustrate isoquants.

The production process alternatives considered in linear programming are usually short-run decisions and distinguish between fixed factors of production and variable factors of production. Fixed factors, such as the size of an existing factory building, are treated mathematically as having zero variable cost. The variable factors are treated as available in any desired amount at a constant unit cost, because each firm's decision makers assume that their short-run production decisions will not change input prices.

As the name suggests, the programming is linear. This is the simplest form of a more general analysis. **Linearity** is a simplifying assumption that keeps the problem in a form that can be easily handled and still illustrate the basic process. Linearity is the name of the mathematical relationship between variables when variations in one variable are matched by proportional variations in another variable, the factor of proportions remaining constant. ($Y = aX$ is an example.) In economic terms, linearity means constant returns and constant prices for inputs and outputs; that is, marginal and average products are identical and price lines are horizontal. This has the advantage of keeping the analysis manageable, yet does not significantly affect the logic of the results.

Frequently, linear programming is used to solve for the minimization of costs or for the maximization of profits in a particular production situation. Technically, there is an **objective function** to solve. This function is merely an expression formalizing the basic problem at hand. For instance, in the meat-and-potatoes example just covered, the food-service manager was required to minimize food costs (his objective was cost minimization). Soon we will consider how such objectives can be formally expressed.

The objective function is subject to **constraints** which state certain conditions that must be surpassed or cannot be surpassed. For example, if a given machine requires at least four operators to function properly, there must be at least four operators, but there may be more (in mathematical notation, ≥ 4). The machine is subject to the limitation that it cannot be operated more than 24 hours in a day, but it can always be run less than that (≤ 24).

After the constraints have been established, the range of **feasible solutions** can be considered. In the preceding example, there were many feasible solutions, but only one was revealed to be the **optimal solution**; it was the best, given the criterion of cost minimization, in the feasible region. This is usually the case, but occasionally there will be a number of optimal solutions. Then it is irrelevant which of those positions is chosen. For example, consider what would have happened in the example given above if the price ratio had been parallel to and coincident with the line segment GH in Figure 9-2. In that case, any of the points from G to H (including those two points) would have been equally acceptable and all would be optimal solutions.

Profit maximization

Using the concepts we've covered, let us now consider an example of profit maximization employing some simple algebra.

After a food riot in the dining hall, you discreetly changed your occupation. You went into business for yourself producing sailboats. After hiring some workers, producing some boats, and discovering the prices at which they would sell, you make the following observations. Each Swiftsail model (S) yields a profit of $520; and there is a $450 profit on each sale of a Rapidsail model (R). A Swiftsail requires 40 hours for assembly and 24 hours for finishing; each Rapidsail requires 25 hours for assembly and 30 hours for finishing. You have paid your workers for 1 month's labor.

Given the specialization of the persons hired, there will be available 400 hours of labor for assembly work and 360 hours for finishing work. Considering the data summarized in Table 9-1, how many of each boat should you produce, or should you produce only one of the two models?

	Hours required for each Swiftsail	Hours required for each Rapidsail	Hours available each month
Assembly hours	40	25	400
Finishing hours	24	30	360

Table 9-1

Remembering your food-service days, you can solve the problem. Your objective function is the maximization of total profits (Z) in the upcoming month. The function is stated like this:

$$Z = \$520S + \$450R$$

Multiplying the number of boats of each type to be produced by their respective profits yields total monthly profits. How many boats will be produced will be determined by the physical constraints you face. The following are the linear constraints confronting you:

$$40S + 25R \leq 400 \text{ (assembly)} \qquad (9\text{-}1a)$$

$$24S + 30R \leq 360 \text{ (finishing)} \qquad (9\text{-}2a)$$

You will have no more than 400 hours assembly time available to be used in assembling the boats. Swiftsails and Rapidsails require 40 and 25 hours, respectively, for assembly. Similarly, you have up to 360 hours of finishing time. For that operation, Swiftsails and Rapidsails require 24 and 30 hours, respectively. For mathematical exactness there is also a nonnegativity condition that must be expressed; this condition does not enter into the calculations, but you cannot produce fewer than zero Rapidsails or Swiftsails: $R \geq 0$, $S \geq 0$.

The constraints can be graphed to show the feasible solutions by expressing the linear constraints in the form of equalities:

$$40S = 400 - 25R \qquad (9\text{-}1b)$$

$$S = 10 - 5/8R \qquad (9\text{-}1c)$$

$$30R = 360 - 24S \qquad (9\text{-}2b)$$

$$R = 12 - 4/5S \qquad (9\text{-}2c)$$

Let's plot the linear constraints, Eqs. (9-1b) and (9-2c). Remember that in each equation the first number on the right-hand side is the vertical axis intercept and the second number is the slope. For Rapidsail, Eq. (9-2c), plot 12 as the intercept on the vertical axis (the R axis in this case). From that point, draw a line with the slope of $-4/5$ to the S axis, which will lead to an intercept at $S = 15$. To make Eq. (9-1c) consistent with Eq. (9-2c), solve that constraint for R:

$$\begin{aligned} S &= 10 - 5/8R \\ 5/8R &= 10 - S \\ R &= 8/5 (10) - 8/5S \\ R &= 16 - 8/5S \end{aligned} \qquad (9\text{-}1c)$$

Now draw Eq. (9-1c) in the same manner as Eq. (9-2c) is drawn. The result is seen in Figure 9-3, where the constraints have outlined the feasible solutions, which are contained on the borders of and inside the shaded polygon.

It is of no particular interest that zero output is within the feasible set of solutions. Our sole interest is in the profit-maximizing solution. This is obtained by the simultaneous solution of the two constraints in the following manner. There are two equations and two unknowns:

$$40S + 25R = 400 \qquad (9\text{-}3a)$$

$$24S + 30R = 360 \qquad (9\text{-}4a)$$

We can find a common base for one of the variables so that it is eliminated, and we can solve for the other variable. This can be done by multiplying Eq. (9-3a) by 3 and Eq. (9-4a) by

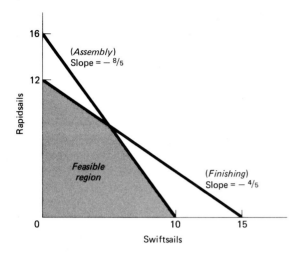

Figure 9-3: Solving a production problem.
The two straight lines represent the technological production constraints for assembling and finishing Swiftsails and Rapidsails. We then find the feasible region.

Therefore this solution yields the maximum profit possible, $Z = 5(\$520) + 8(\$450) = \$2{,}600 + \$3{,}600 = \$6{,}200$ per month, when the production constraints that exist in the short run are given. Figure 9-4 displays the optimum solution.

In this framework, the only feasible solutions are at the corners (except for the origin) of the polygon. To test if the solution derived is superior to the other possibilities [combinations ($S = 0$, $R = 12$) and ($S = 10$, $R = 0$)], those values should also be substituted in the objective function to assure profit is at its maximum.[6] Occasionally, the optimum point does not lie at one of the intercepts and not at a corner inside the quadrant as it did in this case.

−5 (−5 rather than 5 so the equations can be added and one variable eliminated)[5]. (Remember, multiplying through any equation by a constant does not change its equality.)

$$
\begin{array}{ll}
120S + 75R = 1200 & (9\text{-}3b) \\
-120S - 150R = -1800 & (9\text{-}4b) \\
\hline
-75R = -600 & \\
R = 8 &
\end{array}
$$

Algebraically adding the equations yields one variable and its unique solution. Substituting this value into either of the constraints [that is, into either Eq. (9-3a) or (9-4a)] yields the unique value for the other variable for the optimum solution.

$$
\begin{array}{ll}
40S + 25(8) = 400 & \\
40S = 200 & (9\text{-}3c) \\
S = 5 &
\end{array}
$$

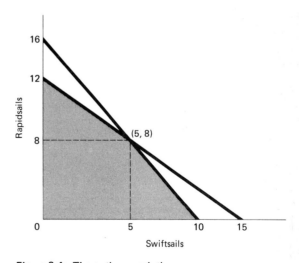

Figure 9-4: The optimum solution.
We now subject Figure 9-3 to profit maximization. In this particular problem, it occurs at a corner where the output rate is five Rapidsails and eight Swiftsails.

[5]This is not a unique solution. You can multiply the constraints by any numbers you can think of to help get one of the variables to the same value in each equation. For instance, if Eq. (9-3a) had been multiplied by −3/5 [the ratio of the S's in Eq. (9-3a) and Eq. (9-4a)], it would have also made possible the elimination of S, so we could solve for R.

[6]Profits of $6,200 per month are achieved with combination (8, 5). Compare that amount to the profits achieved with combinations (0, 12) or (10, 0).

Applying linear programming

It is not difficult to imagine that linear programming problems can quickly become large and complicated. When alternative methods of production are considered for a multiproduct firm which has many possible input combinations, the need for computers to solve the equation is obvious. Students interested in the more advanced aspects of linear programming are referred to the references listed at the end of the chapter. The purpose here is merely to give an overview of the use of linear programming in economics so that future encounters with the topic will not be totally mystifying.

The most productive applications of linear programming have been in the areas of welfare economics and advice to business people. Both of these applications attempt to reveal to the party concerned the most efficient manner of working toward his or her objectives. The following discussion examines the areas in which linear programming is frequently applied.

Meeting minimum requirements

Like the first example considered in this chapter, contracts often include certain minimum specifications which a product must meet. Such requirements are often self-imposed by manufacturers so that their products maintain a certain level of quality. Feed lots often use linear programming to calculate which diet will provide animals with certain nutrient requirements for optimal growth as the least cost. As relative feed prices change, so will the least-cost diet. If the price of feed becomes too high relative to the market value of additional flesh on the animal, feeding will be stopped and the animals slaughtered. This happened following a year of poor crops and the Russian grain deal in 1973. If the market

value of the animal is high and is expected to remain so, the diet may be increased to make the animal grow faster. Hence, not only must relative input prices be considered, but also current and expected output prices.

Least-cost problems solved by linear programming have also included gasoline blending, optimal inventory levels, assignment of personnel to jobs, and minimizing waste of raw materials.

Optimal production processes

Firms are frequently constrained, in the short run, by things such as plant size, the number of trained employees, and machine capacity. Given such short-run constraints, the firm must decide on the most efficient use of its scarce resources by considering the alternative outputs and their prices. The trade-offs that arise there are not difficult to imagine. One product might entail minimal use of personnel but require relatively large amounts of machine capacity. The other product might require much more labor input but less machine time. Coordination of all inputs in the most efficient manner, considering the relative profitability of alternative outputs, is the role of linear programming.

A building contractor may be faced with the problem of how to use men and machines most efficiently in erecting the walls of a brick building. Suppose all the bricks and bricklayers are at the construction site (and have already been paid for) and that the contractor's problem is to decide how many machines to rent by the hour to hoist bricks and how many brick carriers to hire at a given hourly wage. This is a traditional labor-capital trade-off problem.

By experience the contractor knows it is efficient to use certain ratios of men to machines. These alternative ratios are displayed graphically as process rays in Figure 9-5. The

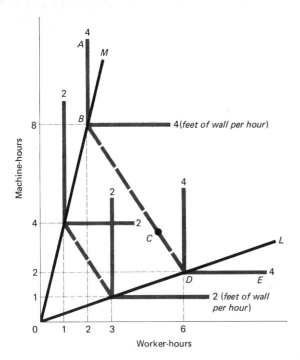

Figure 9-5: Choosing between capital- and labor-intensive processes.

Along ray 0L more labor relative to capital will be used than along ray 0M. Line ABDE is a typical constant-output isoquant. The profit-maximizing point in this figure depends on the relative prices of capital and labor.

capital-intensive process is ray $0M$. This process would use more machines per laborer, and the bricks would be delivered by machine close to each bricklayer. The labor-intensive process, ray $0L$, would use fewer machines per laborer, and there would be more hand-carrying of bricks to the bricklayers.

Assume a tall building is under construction. The building is being constructed with bricks and is 100 feet long on each side. Progress is measured by the number of vertical feet per hour at which the 100-foot wall sections are built up. If there are enough bricks and bricklayers to build walls at the rate of 4 feet per hour, process $0M$ would require 2 human hours for every 8 machine hours.

Process $0L$ requires 6 human hours for every 2 machine hours. Joining the same production level points on the two rays yields a kinked isoquant (one such isoquant is $ABDE$). The same can be done at the other production points on the process rays for isoquants displaying input combinations possible at different levels of output.

One can measure output along the process rays because the production function is assumed to be homogeneous of degree one. This type of production function exists when an increase of all inputs by some proportion increases the output by the same proportion. Hence, to increase the rate at which the wall is built from 2 to 4 feet per hour, the number of workers and machines used per hour must double (for example, from 4 machines and 1 worker to 8 machines and 2 workers when the machine-intensive process is used).

The process that will be chosen will depend upon the relative cost of workers and machines per hour. As in the food-service example, the lowest point of tangency of the ratio of the input prices to the line $ABDE$ will determine the minimum cost process for 4 feet of wall per hour. It is possible that an input combination as described by point C could emerge. For this to happen, the ratio of the prices of the inputs would parallel and be tangent to segment BD of the isoquant. Point C would have to be a technologically feasible combination for it to be chosen (which it is not here), otherwise, points B and D would do the same job at the same price, since any point from B to D would cost the same. The more processes that are available, the more kinks there will be in the production isoquant and the curve would begin to look more like the usual smooth isoquant. Such smooth isoquants, however, assume continuous substitutability between inputs; this rarely happens in the world faced by decision makers.

As in the food-service problem considered previously, the applicability of the linear programming technique was displayed here. This tool permits complicated practical problems to be formulated and solved.

Transportation

Almost all goods produced and used by humans have to be transported, and the shipment alone can be a major factor in the cost of production. A firm typically must ship inputs and outputs and maintain inventories of both. Careful planning of commodity shipments can produce important savings. A trucking firm must coordinate the use of trucks and the capacity of its transport facilities (warehouse space and truck service) and also plan the most efficient routing of the trucks in their pickup and delivery schedules. The complex minimum rate structures established for transportation by the Interstate Commerce Commission and state public utilities commissions further complicate transportation decisions.

Suppose a television manufacturer assembled television sets at plants in Atlanta and Chicago. To market the product, five distribution centers were maintained in Atlanta, Chicago, Dallas, New York, and San Francisco. The plants could produce the televisions for their own market areas but would have to ship by truck to the other three distribution centers. The manufacturer would have to determine how many sets to ship from the two plants to the other three distribution centers to meet the given demands and, at the same time, minimize total shipping costs. This spatial problem is diagrammed in Figure 9-6.

Linear programming could solve such a problem by taking account of various constraints (the respective production rates at the two plants, the demand for television sets in the separate market areas, seasonal variations

SHIPPING ROUTES: TWO PLANTS, FIVE DISTRIBUTION CENTERS

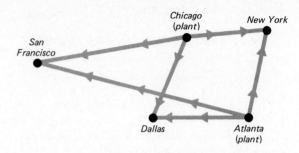

Figure 9-6: A transportation problem: minimizing total shipping costs.
A television manufacturer assembles TV sets in both Atlanta and Chicago. It markets its product in both cities, plus New York, Dallas, and San Francisco. Its problem is to decide which plants should ship to which markets.

in demand, and shipping costs). It may seem like common sense that the plant closest to a distribution center would supply it, but this may not be so. The result obtained by linear programming may confirm this notion or may reveal some other shipping pattern to be the cheapest. Instead of relying on seat-of-the-pants judgments or gut feelings, the linear programming technique involves the application of specific rules which guarantee that an optimal shipping pattern will be utilized, based on the information used in the calculations.

The preceding introduction to some of the applications of linear programming is not intended to leave the impression that business decisions are based on the answers produced by programmed analyses. Just as economists use mathematics as a tool, linear programming is one of a number of tools used by decision makers in business. Often there are considerations which linear programming simply cannot handle that have to be taken into account. In such cases, linear programming analysis provides only one of the inputs into the decision-making process.

Issues and applications

Solving linear programming problems

Readers interested in more than the rudiments of linear programming provided in the previous section can work through some specific problems which are designed to illustrate the method of solution and the types of problems common to linear programming. Students are urged to diagram the problems and to solve them mathematically before reading the answers.

1. *The oil refinery mix*   The petroleum industry has made extensive use of linear programming in many phases of its complex operations to enhance efficiency. Consider the application of linear programming to a simplified refinery operation.

    Assume the following information is known. The refinery can store up to 5,000 barrels of gasoline, G, and up to 10,000 barrels of fuel oil, F, in each production period. The refining process uses 24,000 barrels of crude oil each period. Each barrel of gasoline produced requires 3 barrels of crude oil. Each barrel of fuel oil produced requires 2 barrels of crude oil. The profit from each barrel of gasoline is \$8; each barrel of fuel oil yields a profit of \$4.

    The refinery operators must decide how much of its crude oil to devote to the production of gasoline and how much to fuel oil. The firm's objective is to maximize profits, P. To solve, write the problem as follows:

$$\text{Maximize } P = 8G + 4F$$

$$\text{subject to } 3G + 2F \leq 24{,}000$$
$$G \leq 5{,}000 \qquad F \leq 10{,}000$$
$$G \geq 0 \qquad F \geq 0$$

    In Figure 9-7, the problem can be visualized by defining the feasible region. The storage capacity constraints form two boundaries to the feasible region. The other

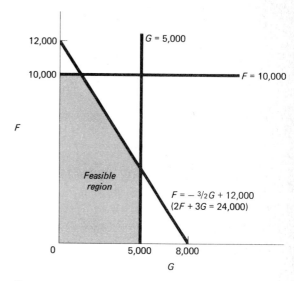

Figure 9-7: A production problem.

boundary is determined by the technological constraints of the production process. The solution must be within the feasible region or lie on the boundary.

To determine the profit-maximizing solution, it is easiest to rewrite the profit function, $P = 8G + 4F$, in the form $F = P/4 + (-8/4)G = 1/4P - 2G$. If profits were 0, the line defined by this equation would pass through the origin of Figure 9-8 and have a slope of -2 (which equals $-8/4$, the ratio of the two products' profits.) Since the highest profits possible are desired, move the line, called the isoprofit line, out from the origin to the farthest point still in the feasible region to which the isoprofit line is just tangent. This solution yields a value of $G = 5{,}000$. Substituting this value into the constraint yields the value of the other variable:

$$3G + 2F = 24{,}000$$
$$3(5{,}000) + 2F = 24{,}000$$
$$F = 4{,}500$$

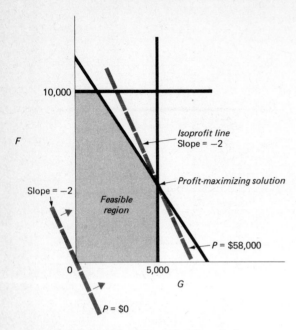

Figure 9-8: Finding the profit-maximizing solution.

The profit-maximizing production mix yields

$$P = 8(5,000) = 4(4,500)$$
$$P = 40,000 + 18,000$$
$$P = \$58,000$$

2. *The shipping crates* A company manufactures two types of wooden shipping crates. The profit on each type 1 crate is $20, and the profit on each type 2 crate is $12. Each crate must go through two production processes. In each production period, a total of 100 hours are available on production line A and a total of 120 hours are available on production line B. Type 1 crates, T_1, require 2 hours on line A and 4 hours on line B. Type 2 crates, T_2, require 5 hours on line A and 3 hours on line B. Determine the number of crates of each type that should be produced in order to maximize profits. Solve, rounding to the nearest whole number. Remember that when you have two unknowns and two equations, you can solve for the variable by adding the equations algebraically once you

have equated one of the variables in both equations. (The diagram is left to the student to draw; it is similar to the boat-building example given previously.)

Set up the problem in this manner:

$$\text{Maximize } P = 20T_1 + 12T_2$$

$$\text{subject to } 2T_1 + 5T_2 \le 100$$
$$4T_1 + 3T_2 \le 120$$
$$T_1 \ge 0 \qquad T_2 \ge 0$$

Solve for one variable. If

$$2T_1 + 5T_2 = 100$$

then multiplying by -2 yields

$$-4T_1 - 10T_2 = -200$$

Now add the other constraint

$$+4T_1 + 3T_2 = 120$$

which leaves one variable

$$-7T_2 = -80$$

$$T_2 = 11 \qquad \text{(approximately)}$$

Solve for the other variable by substitution

$$2T_1 + 5T_2 = 100$$

$$2T_1 + 5(11) = 100$$

$$2T_1 = 100 - 55$$

$$T_1 = 22 \qquad \text{(approximately)}$$

Solve the objective function for maximum profits

$$P = 20T_1 + 12T_2$$

$$P = 20(22) + 12(11)$$

$$P = \$572$$

3. *Labor contract restrictions* Suppose the manager of a widget-producing plant was told to manufacture 1,000 widgets of a certain quality a day at the lowest cost possible. With the existing machinery a widget can be produced by either $1/5$ unit of higher-skilled labor H, or $1/2$ unit of lower-skilled labor L.

This is expressed as $5H + 2L \geq 1,000$ to eliminate the fractions. Since 5 units of higher-skilled labor produces the same number of widgets as does 2 units of lower-skilled labor, the labor productivity trade-off can be written in this manner. The plant has negotiated a contract with the labor union to pay the higher-skilled workers $80 per day and the lower-skilled workers $45 per day. The contract specifies that the plant must employ at least 300 lower-skilled workers, except that two higher-skilled workers can be substituted for every 1 lower skilled worker released (expressed as $^{1}/_{2}H + L \geq 300$).

At the union hall there are 160 higher-skilled laborers available and 400 lower-skilled workers. Solve.

Costs (the total wage bill, in this case) are to be minimized so the objective function is

$$\text{Minimize } W = 80H + 45L$$

$$\begin{aligned}
\text{subject to } & ^{1}/_{2}H + L \geq 300 \\
& 5H + 2L \geq 1,000 \\
& H \leq 160 \quad L \leq 400 \\
& H \geq 2 \quad L \geq 1
\end{aligned}$$

This set of constraints is diagrammed in Figure 9-9. The feasible region is defined by both the labor union and technological constraints.

The optimal solution, where costs are minimized, is where the isocost line is just tangent to the feasible region. This line has a slope equal to the ratio of the wages $(-80/45)$. Mathematically, the optimal values can be derived as follows. First, solve for one variable. If

$$^{1}/_{2}H + L = 300$$

multiplying by -10 yields

$$-5H - 10L = -3,000$$

adding the other constraint

$$+5H + 2L = 1,000$$

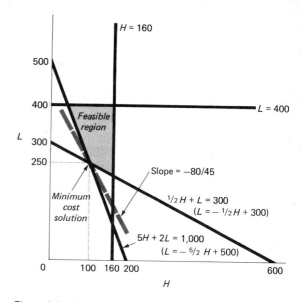

Figure 9-9: A hiring problem.

yields one variable

$$-8L = -2,000$$
$$L = 250$$

Solve for the other variable by substitution

$$\begin{aligned}
5H + 2L &= 1,000 \\
5H + 2(250) &= 1,000 \\
5H &= 1,000 - 500 \\
H &= 100
\end{aligned}$$

Solve the objective function for minimum cost

$$\begin{aligned}
W &= 80H + 45L \\
W &= 80(100) + 45(250) \\
W &= \$19,250
\end{aligned}$$

Consider the change in solution that would emerge if the union were voted out by its members and the plant manager were free to hire whomever he or she wished. The constraint that the plant must hire at least 300 laborers, or 2 higher-skilled workers for every released lower-skilled worker would no longer exist. The relative wages of the two classes of workers might change such that higher-skilled workers earned $75 per day and lower-skilled workers $25. In the short run, the number of higher-skilled laborers may be assumed to remain about the same as before with 160 still available. The number of lower-skilled laborers would probably expand (there was presumably an excess quantity supplied at $W = \$45/day$) and consequently there would be no constraint in the range of operation under consideration. (All changes are purely hypothetical.) Again, costs are to be minimized, taking into account the wages of the workers and the technological (i.e., labor productivity) constraints. The problem now looks like this:

$$\text{Minimize } W = 75H + 25L$$

$$\text{subject to } 5H + 2L \geq 1,000$$
$$160 \geq H \geq 0 \quad L \geq 0$$

This situation is illustrated in Figure 9-10, which displays the change in constraints and the broadened feasible range of positions.

As before, the optimal solution is where the isocost line just reaches the feasible region. In this case, the slope of the line (the ratio of the wage rates) is $-75/25 = -3$, and the solution happens to be 500 lower-skilled workers and no higher-skilled workers. Solving the objective function for minimum costs yields

$$W = 75(0) + 25(500)$$
$$W = \$12,500$$

This figure is considerably less than the $19,250 figure arrived at previously. Note that if the lower-skilled workers' wages were to rise and/or the higher-skilled workers' wages were to fall so that the ratio of the relative wages fell below 5/2, then only higher-skilled workers would be hired.

Glossary

Production process Uses inputs to produce one or more outputs. In linear programming, each process is presumed to use inputs in fixed proportions.

Linearity A simplifying assumption that requires constant returns to scale and fixed prices for inputs and outputs.

Objective function A linear function to be maximized (or minimized) subject to certain constraints on the values of the variables.

Constraints Also called conditions, are inequalities describing structural (capacity) limits.

Feasible solutions All possible combinations of the commodities that can be purchased, used, or produced, given the existing constraints.

Optimum solution The best of the feasible solutions; may be more than one.

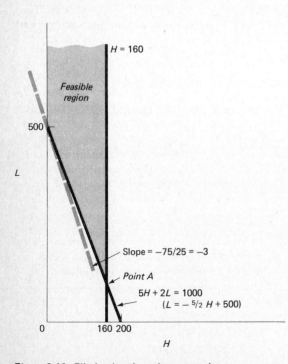

Figure 9-10: Eliminating the union constraint.

Summary

1. Linear programming has developed since World War II and, to date, has been the most successful

mathematical programming method. It enables consumers and business firms to plan more effectively.

2. This technique allows decision makers to solve complex mathematical problems and to maximize or minimize key variables subject to existing or forecasted constraints.

3. The most common applications involve the maximization of profits subject to certain technical cost and revenue constraints, the maximization of output subject to the constraint of limited resources, and the minimization of the costs of producing a predetermined rate of output.

4. As a purely mathematical tool, linear programming can never do more than it is set up to do, nor can it be more accurate than the data and assumptions used in formulating the problem.

5. Feasible solutions are derived after the constraints have been established. Usually only one of the feasible solutions will be optimal when the objective function (which expresses whatever is required in mathematical terms) is maximized or minimized.

6. When linear programming analyses are portrayed geometrically, isoquants become kinked curves. When a corner on the isoquant is just touched by the isocost or price ratio line, a unique solution has been obtained.

7. The change in the value of a constraint or the addition of another constraint may or may not change the optimal solution.

8. In production, common linear programming applications are the minimum requirements which are frequently imposed to minimize costs by choosing the optimal production process from the set available and by determining the most efficient transportation structure.

Selected references

Baumol, William J., "Activity Analysis in One Lesson," *American Economic Review,* vol. 48, December 1958, pp. 837–873.

—— *Economic Theory and Operations Analysis* (Englewood Cliffs, N.J.: Prentice-Hall, 1972).

Dorfman, Robert, "Mathematical, or 'Linear,' Programming: A Nonmathematical Exposition," *American Economic Review,* December 1953, pp. 797–825.

—— Paul Samuelson, and Robert Solow, *Linear Pro-*

gramming and Economic Analysis (New York: McGraw-Hill, 1958).

Samuelson, Paul, "Professor Knight's Theorem on Linear Programming," *Zeitschrift für Nationalökonomie,* vol. 18, 1958, pp. 310–317.

Wagner, Harvey, *Principles of Operations Research, with Applications to Managerial Decisions* (Englewood Cliffs, N.J.: Prentice-Hall, 1969).

Questions

(Answers to even numbered questions are found at back of book.)

1. Describe briefly the decision process of an analyst concerned with maximizing a firm's profits by using the linear programming method.

2. Construct a quadrant which shows labor and capital as inputs; draw three alternative process rays and connect them at the same output level, forming a kinked isoquant. Identify the most labor-intensive process ray and the most capital-intensive process ray.

For questions 3, 4, and 5, use the following information: Suppose you are having a party and the only two inputs to go into producing drinks are 1,000 ounces of cola and 100 ounces of rum.

3. In a quadrant with the inputs measured on the two axes, graphically display the limits you face and the corresponding feasible region.

4. Suppose your guests mix their drinks in three different proportions: 20 ounces of cola to 1 ounce of rum; 10 ounces of cola to 1 ounce of rum; and 1 ounce of cola to 1 ounce of rum. Display these production process rays in the quadrant drawn for question 3.

5. In the quadrant drawn for question 3, graph an isoquant corresponding to 75 drinks. If 75 drinks are to be consumed at the party, what do you know from the completed graph?

Use the following information for questions 6, 7, and 8:

$$Z = 5X_1 + 2X_2$$
$$3X_1 + 2X_2 \leq 10$$
$$6X_1 + X_2 \leq 8$$
$$X_1 \geq 0 \qquad X_2 \geq 0$$

6. What equation is the objective function? What equations are the constraints?

7. Diagram the constraints and define the feasible region.

8. Maximize the objective function subject to the constraints given.

9. Noisy Records plans to use one of its record-making units to produce two different records. The profit is $2 for record 1 and $3 for record 2. Record 1 requires 4 minutes for pressing and 6 minutes for packaging. Record 2 requires 5 minutes for pressing and 3 minutes for packaging. There are 200 minutes per time period available for pressing and 210 minutes available for packaging. What is the profit-maximizing number of each record to produce in one time period, and what is the resultant profit?

10. From the following information, diagram the constraints in a quadrant and define the feasible region. A beer factory makes cases of beer and kegs of beer. Each case has 300 ounces of beer, while each keg has 3,000 ounces of beer. The factory can produce only 200,000 ounces of beer per 24-hour day. The factory's packaging facility can handle 16 cases or 4 kegs per hour, or any combination of the two. The factory's transportation facility can handle 36 cases or 3 kegs per hour, or any combination of the two. Assume the factory runs 24 hours per day. Do not write the equations, but in drawing the diagram, be sure all values are on a 24-hour basis.

11. Given the diagram in the solution to question 10, if the profit from a case is $1 and the profit from a keg is $6, what will be the output of the factory? What if the profit from a case and from a keg are both $1? (Draw in the profit ratios to determine the answers; do not solve mathematically for the exact numbers.)

Appendix to Chapter 9

Dual linear programming

In the general linear programming problem there is an objective function to solve. Typically, this *primal* problem is the maximization of profits. However, as noted before, the primal problem could be the minimization of costs or some other objective. Whatever the primal problem, there is always a *dual* problem. At times it is simpler to solve the dual problem than it is to solve the primal problem, and the dual may produce valuable information, so one should be aware of this option.

Recall the example in this chapter which concerned the maximization of profits in the production of the sailboats, Rapidsail and Swiftsail. The same problem can be set-up in the form of its dual:

The dual, it can be seen, is the converse of the primal. The signs of the constraints are reversed and the number of variables and inequalities are reversed. The information provided by this dual enables the decision maker to *impute* the profits from production to the resources used in production. These imputed profits are artificial accounting values which reveal the relative value of the inputs in the production process. For a complete development of this notion, the reader is urged to consult the reference material.

Primal Problem

Maximize

$$Z = 520S + 450R$$

Subject to

$$40S + 25R \leq 400$$
$$24S + 30R \leq 360$$
$$S \geq 0, R \geq 0$$

Dual Problem

Minimize

$$Y = 400M + 360N$$

Subject to

$$40M + 24N \geq 520$$
$$25M + 30N \geq 450$$
$$M \geq 0, N \geq 0$$

10

COMPETITIVE PRICING AND OUTPUT

We presented the theory of demand and the theory of the firm in the last nine chapters. We have not yet, however, devoted much space to finding out how much will actually be produced and sold and at what prices. In order to do so, we must specify the market organization or structure in which the firm operates. In this chapter, we will analyze a perfectly competitive situation. In the chapters that follow, we will analyze market organizations which deviate from the model of **perfect competition**.

The meaning of competition

At the outset, a distinction should be made between a fairly relaxed notion of competition and a model of perfect competition. The more relaxed view of the competitive process focuses on the concept of rivalry among economic transactors.

Rivalry

In a world of scarce resources, there will perforce be **rivalry among sellers and rivalry among buyers**. Rivalrous behavior among sellers takes on many forms: advertising, improvement in the quality of the product, sales promotion, development of new products, modification of old products, and so on. Rivalry among buyers also takes on many forms:

finding better deals, figuring out ways to take advantage of quantity discounts, offering a higher price to obtain a product which is in fixed supply, and so on.

Competition and survivorship

In the last three chapters, we examined the total, average, and marginal product curves; however, exact knowledge of these curves and of the demand curve is not necessary for rivalry to exist. In a world of scarce resources, consumers will opt for the lower-priced product, other things held constant. That the firm has exact information on its costs and on demand is immaterial. For the firm that chooses the best combination of output qualities, quantities, and price will ultimately survive, forcing other firms to at least imitate if they also wish to survive. This is sometimes called the **survivor principle**. It helps us to understand the nature of real world rivalry.

However, the more commonsense notion of rivalry outlined here will not be particularly evident in the analysis of a competitive market. We now specify the model of perfect competition.

Perfect competition

Basically, a market characterized by perfect competition is one in which no individual buyer or seller influences the price by his or her purchases or sales. The conditions under which a perfectly competitive market arises are five in number, and the presence of all five is essential. We list them here.

HOMOGENEITY OF PRODUCT. If we aren't dealing with a homogeneous product, it is meaningless to talk about a large number of sellers because each product is different from the others. Buyers must be able to choose from a large number of sellers of a product that the buyers believe to be the same.

COSTLESS RESOURCE MOBILITY. Firms must be able to enter any industry; resources must be able to move without friction among alternative uses; and goods and services must be salable wherever the price is highest.

LARGE NUMBER OF BUYERS OR SELLERS.[1] In order that each economic agent have no influence upon price, there must be a large number of them and they must act independently. In addition, the largest buyer or the largest seller must provide only a small fraction of the total quantities bought and sold.[2]

PRODUCT DIVISIBILITY. The product must be such that small quantities of it can be purchased or at least rented.

PERFECT INFORMATION. All buyers and sellers must have perfect information about their demand curves and their cost curves. Thus there is perfect information about the prices at which commodities can be bought and sold. This guarantees that the price per constant-quality unit, corrected for transportation charges, will be uniform.

Perfect competition and rivalry

The definition of perfect competition might have added the additional attribute of a complete *lack* of rivalry. For once we assume perfect information, there is really no market

---

[1] Under certain reasonable conditions in a general equilibrium model, it is correct to state that in a perfectly competitive market, no producer has any effect on market price. See E. Fama and A. Laffer, "The Number of Firms in Competition," *American Economic Review*, vol. 63, 1972, pp. 670–674.

[2] Strictly speaking, perfect competition does not require large numbers of sellers if there is free entry into the industry and all actual or potential firms face constant costs (linear homogeneous production function).

rivalry and therefore no market process to analyze. Indeed, in a perfectly competitive market, all the signs of rivalry will be absent and there will be no motivation to advertise, no need for market research, and certainly no differentiation because the product is homogeneous. On the buyer's side, no buyer ever need search for a more favorable deal, no buyer will ever regret having made a purchase, and certainly no buyer will ever bother to look at brand names. In short, no activity on the part of individuals can be classified as rivalry in a perfectly competitive market.

In some ways, however, this contradicts the analytical usefulness of the model that will follow. For example, we will undertake in the Issues and Applications section the analyses of situations in which surpluses or shortages might exist. We will see that an equilibrium will occur at some price different than that currently existing in the market. However, the only way the equilibrium can come about is through a dynamic process that works through rivalry among economic transactors. In the case of a surplus, for example, economic transactors may want to advertise a lower price for their product in order to get rid of unwanted inventories. Thus, the perfectly competitive market can really only have meaning at an equilibrium price (or in a world with instantaneous movements from one equilibrium to another).

The point to be made here is not that the perfectly competitive model has no value. Indeed, we will find that it allows us to understand the consequences of a number of common restrictions on economic behavior. Rather, we must realize that in dealing with a perfectly competitive model, we will have to relax, to some extent, the assumptions in order to apply it to real world phenomena. The static equilibria that follow in this chapter are useful in understanding perfect competition. Assertions of the model's inapplicability to the real world because one or more of the assumptions is violated do not reduce the mod-

el's usefulness any more than such criticisms lessened the usefulness of the rationality model used to explain consumer demand behavior. Keeping this in mind, we will proceed to an analysis of firm and industry equilibrium situations in both the short and the long run.

Industry pricing in the immediate run

In the last few chapters, we have introduced the concept of the short and the long run. Indeed, in what follows, we will reintroduce those concepts and talk about equilibrium in the short and the long run. For the moment, let us consider a situation that we will call the **immediate run**, or **market period**.[3] This is a situation in which there is no time allowed for adjustment on the part of suppliers of a product. We then ask what the price will be in an industry in such a situation. We define an **industry** as any group of firms that produces a homogeneous product.

Industry equilibrium price

We see in Figure 10-1 the situation described above. The supply curve is vertical (perfectly inelastic), indicating that there is no possibility for an increase in the quantity supplied by firms in the industry beyond Q_0. The industry supply curve is SS. What will the equilibrium price be? First remember that we derive the market demand curve by horizontally summing all the individual demand curves. Thus if the market demand curve is DD, the intersection with the industry supply curve SS is at E. The market-clearing price will be P_e. If, however, the market demand curve is $D'D'$, then the intersection with SS is at E' and the industry equilibrium price will be P'_e.

SS might represent the amount of fresh fish available after all the fishing boats come in

---

[3] Or very short run.

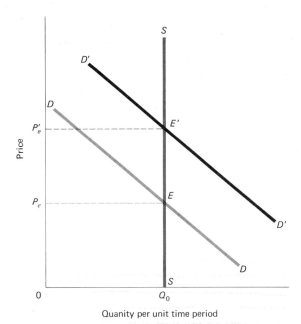

Figure 10-1: Rationing a fixed supply in the immediate period.

In the immediate run (market period), the supply curve is vertical. The equilibrium quantity Q_0 is uniquely determined by supply. The market-clearing, or equilibrium, price is determined by the intersection of market demand curve DD with SS (at price P_e). If demand increases to $D'D'$, the market-clearing price will increase to P'_e, but the equilibrium quantity will remain at Q_0.

some early morning. If the demand curve for fish that day is DD, then the market clearing price will be P_e. However, if the demand curve for fish that day is $D'D'$, then the market-clearing price will be higher at P'_e.

Rationing the fixed supply in the immediate run

Clearly, the price in the situation shown in Figure 10-1 serves a rationing function. Supply in that figure bore no relation to the cost of production. The price in the immediate run that obtains in the industry is such that the quantity demanded equals the quantity supplied. The price rations the fixed supply of goods among actual and potential demanders.

Do not get the impression that in other situations price does not also serve as a rationing device. Rather, this immediate-run situation demonstrates to an extreme degree the manner in which price rations scarce resources.

Note that price as a rationing system, or as a way in which resources are allocated, is discriminatory. Those who are discriminated against are those who are unwilling to pay the going price. Those who are being discriminated in favor of are those who are willing to pay the price in order to obtain their desired quantity. Thus, we can categorically state that the price system is discriminatory in the way in which it rations scarce resources. However, this same statement is true no matter what system is used to allocate scarce resources. Given scarcity, any system, whether via market prices, a centralized allocation system, or a system based on "need," that results in some division of resources among economic agents will of necessity employ discriminatory criteria.

The demand curve facing the perfectly competitive firm

A firm in a perfectly competitive industry does not influence the price of the commodity sold and must take price as given. The firm is such a small part of the market that by itself it is insignificant. How is this given (market-clearing or equilibrium) price determined? By the interaction of *market* demand and *market* supply. Later on in the chapter, we will derive the market supply curve; the market demand curve has already been derived in Chapter 4.

If the individual firm in a perfectly competitive market must take the price as given, then the demand curve facing that firm will look like dd in Figure 10-2, which is a line parallel to the horizontal axis at the vertical distance $0P_e$, where P_e is the "going" (equilibrium) price determined by the intersection of the market demand curve and the market supply curve. It

Figure 10-2: The demand curve facing a perfect competitor.
A firm providing a very small part of the total market demand will face a horizontal demand curve that has a price elasticity of demand of $-\infty$ at the market-clearing price P_e.

has a price elasticity $\eta = -\infty$; i.e., it is perfectly elastic. The reason that the demand curve dd facing the individual perfect competitor raises his or her price for the product above the equilibrium price in the market, his or her quantity demanded will fall to zero. In other words, a perfect competitor will sell zero units at a price that is even slightly above price P_e. The perfect competitor would never set a price below P_e because he or she can sell, by assumption, any and all output at that price. Therefore, selling at a price below P_e would not be profit-maximizing.

The demand curve depicted in Figure 10-1 represents total or market demand facing the entire industry composed of numerous perfect competitors. The demand curve labeled with lower case d's in Figure 10-2 represents the demand curve facing only one perfect competitor in that industry.

Price elasticity of demand

Remember that the formula for the price elasticity of demand is the relative change in quantity demanded divided by the relative change in price. However, by definition, the individual seller in a perfectly competitive industry cannot influence the price. Price must be taken as given. Thus, we see that the de-

mand curve dd in Figure 10-2 exhibits a price elasticity of demand of $-\infty$. An infinitesimally small increase in the price leads to a very large reduction in the quantity demanded. Alternatively, an infinitesimally small percentage decrease in the price leads to an infinitely large percentage increase in the quantity demanded. Hence again, the price elasticity of demand is $-\infty$. Another way of seeing this is by remembering the formula for price elasticity of demand $\eta = -(\Delta q/\Delta P)(P/q)$. As the demand curve dd facing the individual firm gets flatter and flatter, its slope $\Delta P/\Delta q$ gets closer and closer to 0. Thus, the reciprocal of the slope, $\Delta q/\Delta P$, gets bigger and bigger. In the limit, η becomes $[-\infty(P/q)] = -\infty$, and that's what it is for dd in Figure 10-2.

Marginal revenue for the perfect competitor

Remember that we defined marginal revenue as the change in total revenues due to an increase in sales of one unit.

We came up with an alternative definition of marginal revenue which related it to the price elasticity of demand. From Chapter 5, page 116, we repeat this formula:

$$MR = P(1 + \frac{1}{\eta}) \qquad (10\text{-}1)$$

However, we have just indicated that price elasticity of demand for the firm in a perfectly competitve industry is $-\infty$. Thus, Eq. (10-1) becomes

$$MR = P(1 + \frac{1}{-\infty}) = P(1 + 0) = P \qquad (10\text{-}2)$$

Hence, for the perfectly competitive firm, marginal revenue is equal to price. This should come as no surprise. After all, the marginal revenue received for any incremental unit of sales is equal to the market price, since the individual perfect competitor has no influence on price.

Real world approximations

In the real world, when there are less than an infinite number of firms, there is, of course, an effect on price when the quantity supplied by an individual firm changes; but the effect will not be much if that firm is "small." We can see this by finding out the approximate price elasticity of demand facing the individual firm. First, we define Q_i as the amount of output supplied by the ith firm and Q_S as the total quantity supplied by all firms. Thus, the ith firm's share of the market (k_i) is given by

$$k_i = \frac{Q_i}{Q_s} \qquad (10\text{-}3)$$

If the ith firm takes the output of all other firms as given, we can find the elasticity, η^i, of the ith firm. We start by using our familiar elasticity formula and realizing that, in equilibrium,

$$\eta = \frac{\Delta Q}{\Delta P} \cdot \frac{P}{Q} = \frac{\Delta Q}{\Delta P} \cdot \frac{P}{Q_S} \qquad (10\text{-}4)$$

Now we multiply the right-hand side of Eq. (10-4) by $\dfrac{Q_i}{Q_i}$ to obtain

$$\eta = \frac{\Delta Q}{\Delta P} \cdot \frac{P}{Q_S} \cdot \frac{Q_i}{Q_i}$$
$$\eta = \frac{\Delta Q}{\Delta P} \cdot \frac{P}{Q_i} \cdot \frac{Q_i}{Q_S} \qquad (10\text{-}5)$$

or

But this is just equal to

$$\eta = \eta^i k_i \qquad (10\text{-}6)$$

so that

$$\eta^i = \frac{\eta}{k_i} \qquad (10\text{-}7)$$

Therefore, as k_i approaches 0 (i.e., as the individual firm becomes an insignificant part of the market), the price elasticity of demand facing that individual firm, η^i, approaches $-\infty$.

Now that we have characterized the demand situation facing the individual perfect competitor, we can add some cost information

to determine the rate of output of an individual producer in the short run.

Profit maximization for the firm in the short run

We continue to assume that the firm's goal is profit maximization. Profits are defined here as the difference between total revenues and total costs.

The profit-maximizing rate of output— TR − TC approach

Since profits are defined as TR − TC, the profit-maximizing firm in a perfectly competitive industry (or any industry, for that matter) will produce the output at which the difference between TR and TC is largest.

We have taken the cost data used in Chapter 8 and presented some of them in Table 10-1. We have also added some revenue information. The price per unit is in column (2) and is assumed to be $9. Column (3) represents total revenues and is equal to price per unit times rate of output (all of which is sold). Total profits, then, are given in column (5) and are the difference between total revenues and total costs. We see that total profits are maximized at a rate of output of either 11 or 12 per unit time period. The reason there are two rates of output which maximize profit is that we are working with discrete units. In the continuous case, there would be only one profit-maximizing rate of output. To simplify matters, we can arbitrarily say that the firm will always choose the larger of the two profit-maximizing rates of output.

Column (3) and column (4) from Table 10-1 are transferred to Figure 10-3. The total revenue curve TR is a straight line from the origin and has a slope of +9 (since the firm can sell all that it wants at a constant price of $9). The total cost curve is taken from column (4) of

Rate of output (1)	Price ($ per unit) (2)	Total revenues ($) [(2) × (1)] (3)	Total costs ($) (4)	Total profits ($) [(3) − (4)] (5)	Marginal costs ($/unit) (6)	Marginal revenue ($/unit) (7)
0	9.00	0	10.00	−10.00	—	—
1	9.00	9.00	14.00	− 5.00	4.00	9.00
2	9.00	18.00	17.50	0.50	3.50	9.00
3	9.00	27.00	20.75	6.25	3.25	9.00
4	9.00	36.00	23.80	12.20	3.05	9.00
5	9.00	45.00	26.70	18.30	2.90	9.00
6	9.00	54.00	29.50	24.50	2.80	9.00
7	9.00	63.00	32.25	30.75	2.75	9.00
8	9.00	72.00	35.10	36.90	2.85	9.00
9	9.00	81.00	38.30	42.70	3.20	9.00
10	9.00	90.00	42.30	47.70	4.00	9.00
11	9.00	99.00	48.30	50.70	6.00	9.00
12	9.00	108.00	57.30	50.70	9.00	9.00
13	9.00	117.00	70.30	46.70	13.00	9.00
14	9.00	126.00	88.30	37.70	18.00	9.00
15	9.00	135.00	112.30	22.70	24.00	9.00

Table 10-1

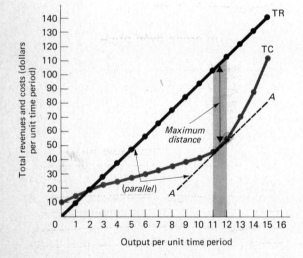

Output per unit time period

Figure 10-3: _Profit maximization for the perfect_ competitor—TR-TC approach.
Profit maximization dictates that the rate of output be set such that the difference between TR and TC (if TR > TC) is maximized. This occurs at an output rate of either 11 or 12. We know that the firm is a perfect competitor because the total revenue curve is a ray from the origin. Any quantity can be sold at $9 per unit. Note also that a tangent to the total cost curve, which has the same slope as the total revenue curve, gives the profit-maximizing rate of output. That tangent is labeled AA. It is parallel to TR.

Table 10-1. The profit-maximizing rate of output is that rate which maximizes the vertical distance between the TR curve and the TC curve (when TR > TC). This is shown to be an output rate of either 11 or 12 per unit time period.

Short-run firm profit maximizing— The marginal approach

We can do exactly the same thing we did in the previous section by looking at marginal quantities rather than total quantities.

In Figure 10-4, we have drawn in the marginal revenue curve horizontally at $9 per unit. This marginal revenue curve is the same as the demand curve dd facing each individual firm in a perfectly competitive market. It is given in column (7), Table 10-1. The marginal cost curve is obtained by plotting the data from column (6) of Table 10-1.

Now we ask the question, What is the rate of output per unit time period that will maximize profits? The answer is the rate of output

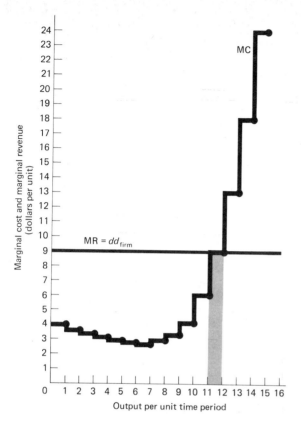

Figure 10-4: Profit maximization—MR-MC approach.
Profits are maximized when marginal revenue equals marginal cost. For the perfectly competitive firm, marginal revenue is the same as its demand curve dd. It is the horizontal line at $9 per unit. The marginal cost curve is taken from column (6) of Table 10-1. The profit-maximizing rate of output is either 11 or 12.

nue and total profits would be less. If the output rate were less that 11 units per unit time period, marginal revenue would exceed marginal cost and total profits could be increased by expanding production. Again, the profit-maximizing rate of output is either 11 or 12 per unit time period because we are dealing in discrete units.

Short-run shutdown and break-even prices

If we add some of the other average cost curves to the marginal diagram presented in Figure 10-4, we can indicate (1) the price at which a perfectly competitive firm will just break even, i.e., make zero profits, and (2) the price at which the perfectly competitive firm will shut down operations, i.e., produce no output in the short run.

The short-run break-even price

Rather than continuing to deal in discrete units, we will generalize our diagrammatic analysis and deal with smooth curves that still retain the essence of cost and revenue conditions facing the firm. We no longer use the specific data contained in Table 10-1.

Look at Figure 10-5. Here we have shown a marginal cost curve, an average total cost curve, and an average variable cost curve. At any price above P_1, the firm will find that each unit it sells fetches a price that exceeds average total cost and hence generates positive profits. However, at price P_1, the price line is just tangent to the minimum point on the average total cost curve; the firm will find that there is no difference between price per unit and average total cost. This is, of course, the output at which the marginal cost curve intersects the average total cost curve at its minimum. We call point E the short-run break-even point, and we call price P_1 the **short-run break-even price**.

at which marginal revenue equals marginal cost.[4] That rate is indicated in the diagram, Figure 10-4, by the shaded area below the marginal revenue curve between the output rates of 11 and 12 per unit time period. If the rate of output were in excess of 12 units, marginal costs would exceed marginal reve-

---

[4] We must further specify that the marginal cost curve cut the marginal revenue curve from below. If the marginal cost curve cuts the marginal revenue curve from above, then we have loss maximization.

The short-run shutdown price

Will the firm automatically shut down if the price at which it can sell its output falls below P_1? The answer is no, not necessarily. It is true that at a price below P_1, average total costs are not being covered. However, at prices below P_1 but above average variable cost, the firm is covering some of its fixed costs. It is clear, though, that the firm will never want to produce at a price below average variable cost, for in so doing it is actually lowering the net worth position of the owners by continuing to produce. Price P_2, which is obtained by finding the intersection of the marginal cost curve with the (minimum point on the) average variable cost curve, is a price below which this firm will not continue production in the short run. This intersection is labeled E'. It is marked the short-run shutdown point. The price P_2 is the **short-run shutdown price**. Another way of looking at this is to consider any price between P_1 and P_2; consider a price midway between P_1 and P_2. Such a price yields a rate of return on invested capital of, say, only 4 percent when the rate of return on capital elsewhere in the economy is, say, 8 percent. In other words, the rate of profitability in this firm is one-half what it could be elsewhere. However, where there are fixed (or sunk) costs, bygones are bygones. A 4 percent rate of return on invested capital is certainly better than negative rate of return. As long as the market price exceeds the shutdown price, the investor gets something back on the original investment, even though he or she may not be earning very much on it. If, however, the market price falls *permanently* below the shutdown price, the investor loses everything that was invested forever.

Even if the market price falls below the shutdown price P_2, the firm may shut down only temporarily. The shutdown point is defined only at a moment in time. The firm might want to wait out a downturn in the industry by stopping current production and then starting it again if and when the market price moves up in the future. If we take this consideration into account, average variable costs ought to include the opportunity cost of closing down and starting up again.

Total costs and profits

Perhaps the fact that we labeled E in Figure 10-5 the break-even point may have disturbed you. At E and price P_1, price is just equal to average total costs. If this is the case, why would a firm continue to produce if it were making no profits whatsoever? If we make the distinction between **accounting profits** and **economic profits**, at price P_1 the firm has zero economic profits but positive accounting profits.

Accounting versus economic profits

Remember back in Chapter 8 when we made the distinction between explicit and implicit costs? It turned out that much of what is accounting profit is an implicit cost of doing business and must be included in average total costs. A firm requires assets. Those who invest in the firm, whether they be proprietors or stockholders, must anticipate a rate of return that is at least as great as could be earned in similar investments of equal risk. Looking at capital alone, we know that the cost of capital is its opportunity cost. Accountants, however, in conforming with tax laws, do not enter as a cost of doing business the opportunity cost of **equity capital** and are content with entering as a cost the interest payments on **debt capital**. In our analysis, the average total cost curve includes both the explicit and implicit opportunity costs of capital. Indeed, the average total cost curve includes the opportunity cost of *all* factors of production used in

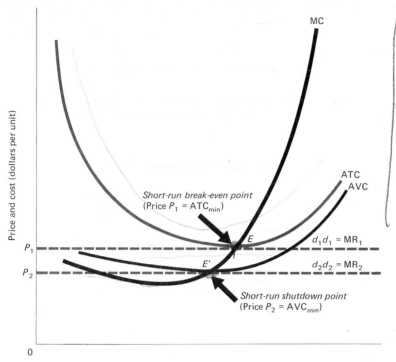

MC

ATC
AVC

P_1

P_2

E

E'

$d_1d_1 = MR_1$

$d_2d_2 = MR_2$

Short-run break-even point
(Price P_1 = ATC$_{min}$)

Short-run shutdown point
(Price P_2 = AVC$_{min}$)

Price and cost (dollars per unit)

0

Output per unit time period

Figure 10-5: The firm's short-run break-even and shutdown points. Any price line represents a marginal revenue curve for the perfect competitor, and the profit-maximizing rate of output is always the output at which the price line intersects the marginal cost curve. The short-run break-even point is at E; the short-run break-even price is P_1, the price that just covers average total costs. The short-run shutdown point is at E'; the short-run shutdown price is P_2 and is equal to the minimum average variable cost. It does not pay the firm to continue production if it cannot at least cover variable costs.

the production process. We define *economic profits* as those profits over and above what is required to keep capital in the firm. At price P_1 in Figure 10-5, economic profits are, by definition, zero. However, accounting profits at price P_1 are not equal to zero; they're positive. Consider an example. A baseball bat manufacturer sells bats at price P_1. The owners of the firm have just invested their own equity capital in the business; they have borrowed no money from anyone. Moreover, assume that they explicitly pay the full opportunity cost to all factors of production, including any labor that they contribute to the business. In other words, they pay themselves salaries which show up as a cost on the books and those salaries are equal to what they could have earned in the next-best alternative occupation. At the end of the year, the owners find that after they subtract all explicit costs from total revenues that they have earned

$100,000. Their investment we will say was $1 million; thus, the rate of return to that investment is 10 percent per year. This turns out to be, we will assume, equal to the rate of return that, on average, all other baseball bat manufacturers make in the industry.

Now, this $100,000, or 10 percent rate of return, is actually then a competitive or normal rate of return on invested capital in that industry. If the owners had only made $50,000, or 5 percent, on investment, they would have been able to make higher profits by leaving the industry. Thus, we say that the 10 percent rate of return was the opportunity cost of capital. The accountants showed it as a profit; we call it a cost. We also include that cost in the average total cost curve shown in Figure 10-5. Thus, at price P_1, average total costs, including this opportunity cost of capital, just equaled price. The firm is making zero economic profits, but a 10 percent accounting rate of return.

Another case in which accounting profits exceed economic profits is the owner-run business in which the owner is an employee who does not pay himself or herself at the market wage rate. In the typical "mom and pop" grocery store, the proprietors may not explicitly pay themselves any wages at all. They do, however, work a combined total of 140 hours a week. Had they rented out their labor services, they would have received wages. In order to obtain economic profits, the hourly wage rate that they could have earned in their next-best alternative job times the number of hours they actually worked in the grocery store must be added to total costs. Then, if there is an excess of total revenues over total costs (assuming, of course, that the opportunity cost of all other factors of production were correctly entered into the books), the couple has an economic or *pure* profit. It is not inconceivable to find an owner-run enterprise in which economic profit is actually negative although the accountant reports a $10,000 profit. The fact is that many persons pay a price for their self-employed status.

The break-even point in the long run

The reason we labeled the break-even point in Figure 10-5 the short-run break-even point is that, in the long run, point E is the going-out-of-business point; this is because below P_1, the opportunity cost of capital invested would not be covered by revenues. In the long run, capital would be withdrawn and would go somewhere else.

The position of the SATC curve

While it is true in the short run that minimum short-run ATC can be below or above the price line, we should be aware that the ATC curve can move up or down in the long run. Assume for a moment that at some outputs short-run ATC is below the price line. That means that the firm receives positive econom-

ic profits. What would happen now if the owner of this firm sold the firm to someone else? With competition in the market for assets, the selling price of the firm would be a price that would just yield the new owner a *normal* rate of return. This is a rate of return that would just equal the opportunity cost of the owner's invested capital. Otherwise stated, the future stream of positive economic profits would be capitalized and included in the sale price of the firm (see Chapter 6). Now, what would the average total cost curve for the new owner look like? It would rise to take account of the price that was paid for the firm. In fact, it would rise so that it became tangent to the price line and the new owner would be making zero economic profits and "normal" accounting profits.

In the opposite situation, if a firm were suffering economic losses and potential buyers anticipated that these losses would persist into the future, the sale price of the firm would be reduced from what it was previously by the present discounted value of the economic losses. Thus, the average total cost curve for the new owner would be lower than for the previous owner. It would move down until it was just tangent to the price line, and the new owner would make a normal rate of return—nothing more, nothing less. (Note that if the price fell below P_2 and was expected to stay there, the firm would only be worth the scrap value of its assets.) Moreover, if the industry rate of return is not sufficiently high compared with other industries, then no new plants will be built in the industry. Investment decisions are made on the basis of comparisons among alternative possibilities.

The firm's short-run supply curve

We saw in the last sections that the firm would never produce at a price below average variable cost. The firm will, however, produce at prices above the average variable cost curve.

The price line, however, coincides with the marginal revenue line, which in turn coincides with the individual firm's demand curve. We know, then, that we can draw an infinite number of price lines above the intersection of the marginal cost curve with the average variable cost curve, and that we can then find the resultant quantities that will be supplied at each of these prices. Those quantities can be found at each of the points of intersection between successively higher price lines and the marginal cost curve. Therefore, a part of the firm's short-run supply curve is coincident with the marginal cost curve above the average variable cost curve. We have drawn this part of the firm's supply curve as the heavily shaded portion of the marginal cost curve in Figure 10-6.

The short-run industry supply curve

The industry short-run supply curve can be found by horizontally summing the individual firms' short-run supply curves. In other words, we add together the quantities supplied by each firm at each price. We do this for a simple example of two firms in Figure 10-7. We have shown the marginal cost curves for two separate firms, MC_1 and MC_2. We have also pointed out that the minimum average variable costs for firm 1 is at price P_1 and the minimum average variable costs for firm 2 is at P_2. Thus, the **industry supply curve** SS does not include any of the section of the marginal cost curve for firm 2 below the price P_2. We see that the industry supply curve is the heavily shaded line SS, which coincides with the marginal cost curve for firm 2 up to the relevant section of the marginal cost curve for firm 1, which is at price P_1 and above. Thus SS has a discontinuity at price P_1 which would disappear if there were a large number of firms in the industry with different minimum AVC points.

Often you will see the industry supply curve denoted by ΣMC to denote that we are summing across *quantities* supplied at each price (marginal cost); that is, we are summing *horizontally* just as we did with individual demand curves to derive the market demand curve.

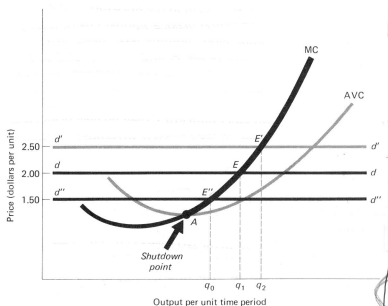

Price (dollars per unit)

2.50 — d' .... E' .... d'

2.00 — d .... E .... d

1.50 — d'' .... E'' .... d''

MC

AVC

A

Shutdown point

q_0 q_1 q_2

Output per unit time period

Figure 10-6: The individual firm's supply curve.
Here we show the marginal cost curve MC and three different individual demand curves. The first one is *dd*. If the demand curve is *dd*, the equilibrium, or profit-maximizing, point for the firm will be at the intersection of *dd* and MC, or at *E*. It will produce q_1. If the firm's demand curve shifts up to *d'd'*, the new intersection will be at *E'* and output will be q_2. If the demand curve falls to *d''d''*, the new intersection is at *E''*. The firm will produce only q_0. The supply curve, then, for the individual firm is its marginal cost curve. Actually, though, it is only that portion of its marginal cost curve above the shutdown point, or point *A*. That is at the point of the intersection of the average variable cost curve and the marginal cost curve. Thus, the supply curve is only the heavily shaded portion of the MC curve.

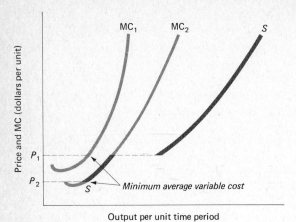

Figure 10-7: The industry supply curve.
The industry supply curve is the horizontal summation of those portions of the individual firm's marginal cost curves above their respective minimum average variable cost points. This is indicated at price P_1 for firm 1 and at price P_2 for firm 2.

We note also that the short-run industry supply curve is the horizontal summation of each individual firm's marginal cost curve only so long as input prices remain constant. It is possible that the simultaneous increase in the output of *all* firms in an industry may cause input prices to rise. In such cases, the industry supply curve will be more steeply sloped (and less-price elastic) than if input prices remain constant.

Determinants of supply

When supply curves or demand curves are drawn, it is assumed that other things remain constant. The other things assumed constant when drawing a demand curve were such variables as tastes, income, and the prices of related goods. The "other things" that are assumed constant when a supply curve is drawn are as follows.

THE PRICES OF RESOURCES USED TO PRODUCE THE PRODUCT. If one or more input prices fall, the supply curve will shift outward to the right; that is, more will be supplied at each and every price. The opposite will be true if one or more inputs become more expensive. In other words, when we draw the supply curve of wool, we are holding the price of lamb constant.

TECHNOLOGY. Supply curves are drawn by assuming a given technology or "state of the art." When the range of production techniques available changes, the supply curve will shift. If a better production technique becomes available, the supply curve will shift to the right. A larger quantity will be forthcoming at each and every price.

Short-run industry or market equilibrium

Now we can find out where we obtain the "going" or market-clearing price that was used to determine the vertical height of the individual firm's demand curve *dd* in previous sections in this chapter. The market-clearing price is determined by market demand and the market supply curves.

In Figure 10-8, panel (*a*), we have drawn a market demand curve and a market supply curve, *DD* and *SS*. Their intersection occurs at point *E*. The market-clearing price is P_e. The short-run rate of output for the industry will be Q_e. For the individual firm represented in panel (*b*) of Figure 10-8, the demand curve is *dd* at price P_e. The profit-maximizing rate of output is the output at which the marginal cost curve MC intersects the firm's demand curve *dd* (which is also its marginal revenue curve) at *e*, giving the rate of output, q_e.

The meaning of equilibrium

P_e and Q_e are called the equilibrium price and equilibrium (total market) quantity. The equilibrium price is the price from which there is no tendency to deviate and the price toward which any other price will gravitate.[5]

---

[5]For the class of stable equilibria.

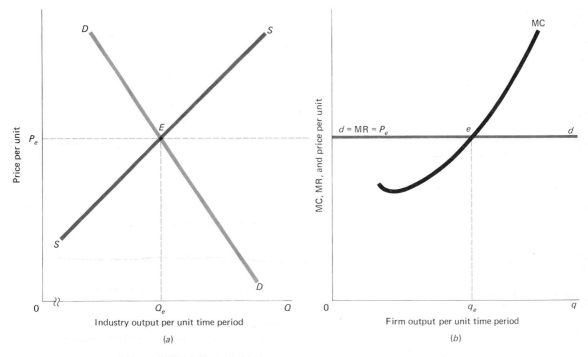

Figure 10-8: Market equilibrium and firm optimization.
In panel (a), we show the market demand as DD and the market supply as SS. Their intersection is at point E. The market-clearing price is P_e, and the market-clearing quantity is Q_e. Then P_e gives the demand curve dd facing the perfect competitor in panel (b). That firm's marginal cost curve intersects dd (= MR = P_e) at point e. The profit-maximizing quantity produced by the perfect competitor is q_e.

Look at Figure 10-9. Here we show an equilibrium price of P_e. What if the price were P_1, which is more than P_e? Then the quantity supplied will exceed the quantity demanded at that price. The result will be an excess quantity supplied at price P_1, or a "surplus." However, given DD and SS, there will be forces pushing the price back down toward P_1. Suppliers will attempt to reduce their inventories by cutting prices, and/or demanders will offer to purchase more at lower prices. The reason that suppliers will want to reduce inventories is because they will be above their optimal level for the firm; that is, there will be an excess over what the firm believes to be the profit-maximizing stock of inventories. After all, inventories are costly to hold. Their cost is, at minimum, the opportunity cost of the capital tied up in them. On the other hand, demanders may find out about such excess inventories and see the possibility of obtaining increased quantities of the good in question at a reduced price. It behooves demanders to attempt to obtain a good at a lower price; they will therefore try. If not prevented from moving, the price will eventually reach its equilibrium at P_e again.

What if the price is, for some reason, at P_2? At this price, the quantity demanded exceeds the quantity supplied. There is an excess quantity demanded at P_2, or a "shortage." Forces will cause the price to rise. Demanders will bid up the price, and/or suppliers will raise the price. Note that in the situation depicted at P_2, the individual firms are temporarily no longer **price takers** because they

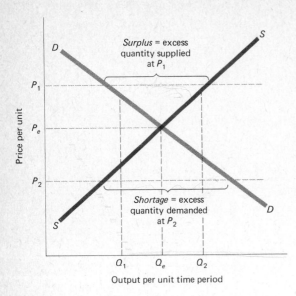

Figure 10-9: Equilibrium price, shortages, and surpluses.
At a price of P_e, the quantity demanded equals the quantity
supplied. At price P_1, the quantity supplied exceeds the
quantity demanded. The difference is the excess quantity
supplied at price P_1. It is sometimes called a *surplus*. At
price P_2, the quantity demanded exceeds the quantity
supplied. There is an excess quantity demanded at P_2. It
is sometimes called a *shortage*. In both cases, forces will
push the price toward P_e.
The equilibrium quantity is Q_e. If quantity is Q_1, the
demand price exceeds the supply price. If quantity is Q_2,
the supply price exceeds the demand price. In both
cases, the quantity will move toward Q_e.

do not take the price as given. The individual
firm can raise the price even if other competitors do not and still sell all of his or her output.
Thus, the usual assertion that a perfect competitor cannot charge a price higher than the
existing price without losing all its customers
is correct only if the existing price is not lower
than the equilibrium price.

Quantity adjustments

Let's look at it another way now. Let's assume
that the quantity were not at the equilibrium
rate of output at Q_e. If the quantity were at Q_1,
the demand price (the price at which that

quantity will be demanded) would exceed the
supply price (the price at which that quantity
will be supplied). This would induce more
exchange among suppliers and demanders so
that quantity would rise toward Q_e. If the
quantity were somehow Q_2, this would indicate that the supply price would be greater
than the demand price. Less exchange would
take place. The quantity exchanged would fall
to Q_e.

The point of this analysis is that any disequilibrium situation automatically brings
into action correcting forces which will cause a
movement back toward equilibrium. The
equilibrium price and quantity will be maintained so long as demand and supply do not
change.

When we refer to a *stable* equilibrium, we
mean that if there is a movement away from
the equilibrium price or quantity, there will
be forces pushing price or quantity back to the
equilibrium level or rate. An *unstable* equilibrium is one in which, if there is a movement
away from the equilibrium, there are forces
that push price and/or quantity further away
from equilibrium (or at least do not push price
and quantity back toward the equilibrium
level or rate). The difference between a stable
and an unstable equilibrium can be illustrated
by looking at two balls: one made of hard rubber, the other made of soft, moist Play-Doh. If
you were to squeeze the rubber ball out of
shape, it would bounce back to its original
shape. However, if you were to squeeze the
Play-Doh ball out of shape, it would remain
out of shape. With respect to the shape of the
two balls made out of different materials, the
former illustrates a stable and the latter an unstable equilibrium.

Boundary equilibria

We do not see any solid-gold Mercedes being
produced. Is this an equilibrium situation?
Yes, it is. It is a boundary equilibrium, which
can be seen in panel (*a*) of Figure 10-10. The

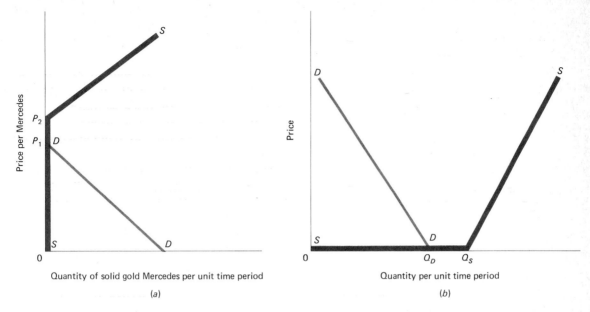

Figure 10-10: Boundary equilibria.

In panel (a) the supply of solid-gold Mercedes is SS and is the vertical axis from 0 to price P_2 and then out along a normally sloped supply curve. The demand curve is DD, which actually coincides with the vertical axis at any price above price P_1. The equilibrium quantity of solid-gold Mercedes is 0 at an equilibrium price somewhere between P_2 and P_1. In panel (b) we show another boundary equilibrium for a good whose supply curve is DD. The equilibrium is at a zero price with quantity demanded of Q_D.

demand curve for solid-gold Mercedes is represented by DD. The supply curve is, however, somewhat different than we are used to seeing. It is represented by SS. This supply curve starts at the origin, rises along the vertical axis to point P_2, and then takes on the familiar upward slope. The reason the supply curve has this shape is that no quantity of gold Mercedes will be forthcoming between the prices of 0 and P_2. However, the most that anyone would pay for a gold Mercedes is P_1, which is less than P_2. In a sense, we can say that the equilibrium quantity is 0 and the price is indefinite but lies somewhere in the range between P_1 and P_2. This is called a **boundary equilibrium**; sometimes it is called a corner solution. The equilibria that we have been shown prior to this diagram are called **interior equilibria** or **interior solutions**.

Another boundary situation occurs in panel (b) of Figure 10-10. The demand curve DD intersects the supply curve SS, where the latter coincides with the horizontal axis. In other words, there is a supply Q_s forthcoming at a zero price. To obtain more than Q_s requires a positive price. However, the quantity demanded at a zero price is Q_D. The boundary equilibrium in this situation is at a zero price and quantity Q_D. Goods represented by these curves in panel (b) are generally called free goods or noneconomic resources.

Movements in prices and quantities— The cobweb theorem

The prices and outputs of many commodities show cyclical movements over long periods of time.   As prices moved up and down in waves, quantities produced seemed to move up and down in counterwaves. One explanation for such cycles in commodity prices and outputs is the so-called **cobweb theorem.** The name "cobweb" comes from the way in which the diagrams look. It turns out that the cobweb theorem is one of the simplest models of the dynamics of supply, demand, and price.

We divide the periods with which we are dealing into discrete units. For the sake of simplicity, they will be 1-year periods. We further assume that the quantity produced this year is a function of the price of the product last year, or

$$Q_{t+1}^S = f(P_t) \qquad (10\text{-}8)$$

where the superscript S refers to supply and the subscript t refers to time. Thus, the quan-

tity supplied next year will be a function of this year's price, or alternatively, the quantity supplied this year is a function of last year's price.   On the demand side, the quantity demanded this year is the function of the price this year, as always, or $Q_t^D = f(P_t)$. The equilibrium price in any 1 year is, of course, the price of which the quantity supplied equals the quantity demanded, or $Q_t^S = Q_t^D$. Finally, in any 1 year we assume that there is a perfectly inelastic supply which is equal to the quantity that has been produced. In the case of agricultural commodities, no more is forthcoming until after the next growing season.

We can see perpetually oscillating prices and quantities in panels (a) and (b) of Figure 10-11. Let us assume that the price in year 1 is P_1. Thus the quantity supplied in year 2 is going to be Q_2 in panel (a). But in order to sell Q_2 in year 2, the price that will be fetched in

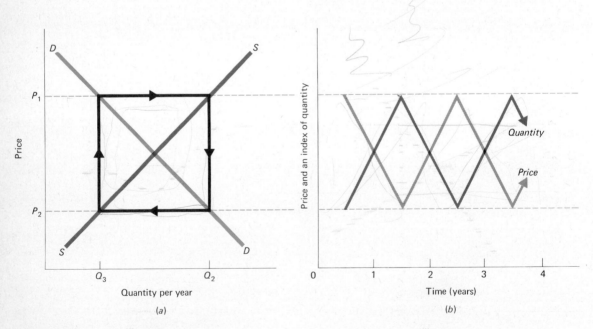

(a)

(b)

Figure 10-11: A cobweb model.
The quantity supplied next period is a function of this period's price. Assume that this year's price is P_1. The quantity supplied next year will be Q_2, but Q_2 can be sold only at price P_2. Thus, the quantity supplied the following year will be Q_3; however, that quantity can be sold at price P_1. In panel (b) we show the continuous oscillation of price and quantity.

the marketplace is going to be P_2. In year 3, the quantity supplied will be a function of P_2 or Q_3, which will command a price P_1. This will continue. We see in panel (*b*) that price and quantity will oscillate between P_1 and P_2 and that quantity will oscillate between Q_2 and Q_3.

In the next example we see *damped* oscillation and the familiar cobweb appearance of the diagram. In a situation of damped oscillation, whatever is oscillating eventually "homes in" on some value rather than continuously moving up and down. A good example of damped oscillation is what happens when a perfectly balanced pendulum is pushed. The pendulum moves back and forth but eventually oscillates less and less until it ends up in its original position. Look at Figure 10-12. In panel (*a*), we have drawn the supply curve with a numerically greater slope than the slope of the demand curve.[6] We start out in year 1 with price P_1. That calls forth in year 2 the

quantity Q_2 which is sold at a price P_2; but P_2 calls forth in year 3 a quantity of Q_3, which is sold at the price P_3. This price calls forth in year 4 the quantity Q_4. We can see that eventually the oscillation will dampen to zero so that the price, year in and year out, will be P_0 at the intersection of DD and SS; and the quantity will be Q_0. In panel (*b*) we show that the oscillation damps over time. If we were to draw the demand curve with a slope numerically greater than the slope of the supply curve, we would get an explosive oscillation.

The real applicability of the cobweb model is dubious. Economic agents would eventually learn; these changes would be anticipated and smoothed out through speculation.

---

[6]The absolute value of the slope of the supply curve is greater than the absolute value of the slope of the demand curve.

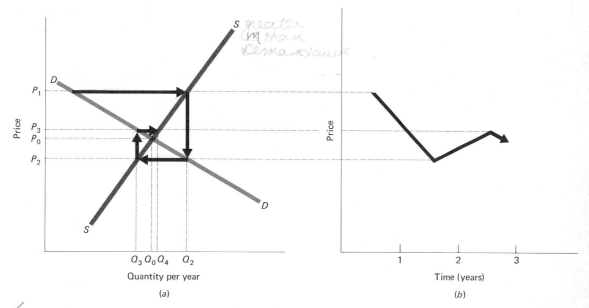

Figure 10-12: The cobweb model—damped oscillation.
If the slope of the supply curve in panel (*a*) is numerically greater (in absolute value) than the slope of the demand curve, the cobweb model leads to damped oscillation, as shown in panel (*b*).

Short-run industry adjustments to shifts in demand

We can easily use the apparatus already developed to find out what will happen in the short run to price and output in a competitive industry when there is a shift in demand caused by a change in tastes, a change in the prices of related goods, a change in real income, a change in population, or a change in expectations about future relative prices. With a market supply curve SS in Figure 10-13, the market-clearing price will be P_e and the market equilibrium quantity will be Q_e when the market demand curve is DD. If for some reason the market demand curve shifts outward to $D'D'$, the equilibrium price will rise to P'_e and the equilibrium quantity will rise to Q'_e. On the other hand, if the market demand curve shifts to the left to $D''D''$, then the equilibrium price will fall in the industry to P''_e and the equilibrium quantity will fall to Q''_e.

Firm profits and losses

For the firm in a perfectly competitive industry, the price of the commodity is given. The economic profits or losses of the firm depend in the short run on the position of its average total cost curve in relation to the price of the commodity.

In panels (a) and (b) in Figure 10-14, we depict the situation facing two firms in a competitive industry. Both firms face a horizontal demand curve at price P_e. In panel (a), the profit-maximizing rate of output is found at the intersection of the marginal cost curve with the demand (or marginal revenue) curve. In panel (a), this is at point e; the equilibrium rate of output for firm 1 is q_1. The average total cost curve is ATC_1. At the rate of output of q_1, firm 1 makes a profit per unit equal to the vertical distance between point e and point A. When we multiply the per-unit profit times the quantity, we get the shaded-in rectangle labeled profits, which represents pure economic profits—revenues over and above all opportunity costs, including that of capital. In panel (b), we show a situation where pure economic losses are being incurred. The only difference between firm 2 in panel (b) and firm 1 in panel (a) is that firm 2 has a higher average total cost curve. Its losses per unit are given by the vertical distance between A' and e'. Total losses are represented by the shaded-in rectangle.

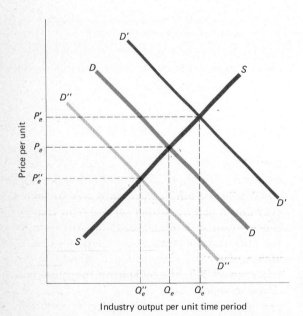

Figure 10-13: Short-run industry adjustments to shifts in demand.
If demand shifts outward from DD to $D'D'$, the industry market-clearing price will move up to P'_e and the quantity produced will increase to Q'_e. If industry demand shifts inward to $D''D''$, price will fall to P''_e and industry output will fall to Q''_e

The adjustment process in the industry

In the long run, the existence of economic profits or losses is a signal to the owners of capital within and outside of the industry. If

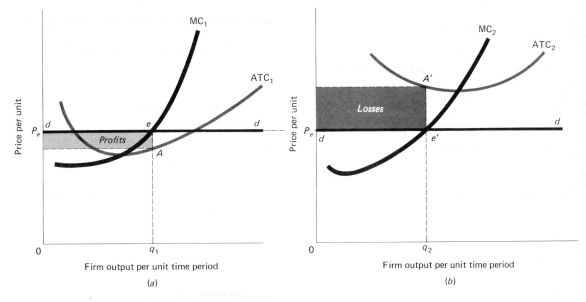

Figure 10-14: Economic profits and losses.
In panel (a) we show a situation where the marginal cost curve MC_1 intersects the marginal revenue curve (= dd) at point e. At the profit-maximizing rate of output q_1, average total costs are A. Economic profits are represented by the shaded area. In panel (b) we show economic losses; the difference between price P_e and average total cost is the vertical distance between A' and e'. When we multiply that by quantity sold, we obtain the shaded rectangle labeled "losses."

the industry is characterized by a large number of firms showing pure economic profits, as in panel (a) of Figure 10-14, this will signal to owners of capital elsewhere in the economy that they, too, should enter this industry. If, on the other hand, there are a large number of firms in the industry that are like those represented by panel (b) in Figure 10-14, this signals to resource owners outside the industry not to enter; it also signals to resource owners within the industry not to reinvest. It is in this sense that we say that profits direct resources to their highest-valued use. Capital and labor will flow into industries where profitability, adjusted for differential risk, is highest and will flow out of industries in the economy where profitability is lowest. In a price system, the allocation of capital is therefore directed by relative rates of return on investment.

In addition to generating signals for potential entrants, economic profits and losses will also cause expansion and contraction of the scale of established firms.

Long-run equilibrium for the firm

In the long run the firm can change the scale of its plant. We should assume that in the long run the firm would adjust plant size in such a way that it had no further incentive to change. Since we are assuming profit maximization, in the long run the firm should be producing in such a way that profit is maximized. In the short run it did this by setting marginal cost equal to price. This will be true in the long run also. Long-run marginal cost will also equal price, and as we shall see, long-run marginal cost will also equal short-run marginal cost at the profit-maximizing rate of output and equilibrium scale of plant.

Consider the firm depicted in Figure 10-15. Assume that the anticipated long-run equilib-

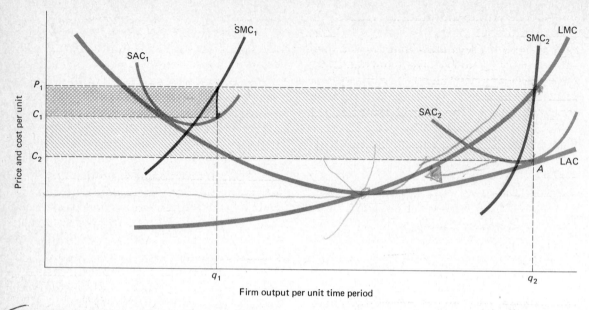

Figure 10-15: Long-run equilibrium for a competitive firm.
If the long-run equilibrium price is P_1, the optimal plant is not given by the cost curves SAC$_1$ and SMC$_1$, for, at the profit-maximizing rate of output with that plant, q_1, the firm is not operating on the long-run average cost curve LAC. The firm would want to expand its plant until its cost curves were given by SAC$_2$ and SMC$_2$. The profit-maximizing rate of output is q_2; the firm is operating on LAC. Profits per unit have increased from the vertical distance between P_1 and C_1 to the vertical distance between P_1 and C_2.

rium price of the the commodity in question is P_1. Assume that the firm is starting out with a plant scale whose short-run cost curves are given by SAC$_1$ and SMC$_1$. The firm will produce quantity q_1 because this is the output at which the short-run marginal cost curve for plant size 1 intersects the price line (which is the firm's demand curve and marginal revenue curve). Given costs represented by SAC$_1$, the firm will make a per-unit profit equal to the vertical distance between P_1 and C_1.

However, this is not a long-run profit-maximizing equilibrium position for the firm. It can expand the scale of plant and increase its profit. First of all, we note that at output rate q_1, the firm was not "on" its long-run average cost curve. However, at output rate q_2, the firm is on its long-run average cost curve. It will utilize plant size 2, whose short-run average cost curve is represented by SAC$_2$, which is just tangent to the long-run average

cost curve at point A. Profit per unit will increase from the vertical distance P_1 to C_1 to the vertical distance between P_1 and C_2. Note also that at the long-run profit-maximizing equilibrium rate of output, the firm's short-run marginal cost = long-run marginal cost = the price of the product:

$$SMC = LMC = P$$

However, even though this may be the long-run desired equilibrium position of the firm with respect to plant size, or otherwise stated, the firm's optimal plant size, the firm does not operate in a vacuum. The area of $(P_1C_2 \cdot q_2)$ represents economic profits per unit time period. Such economic profits will induce entry of other firms into the industry. But entry into the industry will cause the industry supply curve to shift outward, as seen in panel (a) of Figure 10-16. But the shifting outward of the supply curve from SS to $S'S'$

due to entry into the industry reduces the equilibrium price from P_e to P'_e. The industry rate of output per unit time period will increase from Q_e to Q'_e. The reduction in the price will clearly have an effect on the optimal plant size in the long run for the perfectly competitive firm. The optimal plant size will no longer be represented by plant size 2 in Figure 10-15. It will be a smaller plant. There will be a movement down the long-run average cost curve LAC.

When does this process stop? It stops when the perfectly competitive firm is making zero economic profits in the long run. This is represented by panel (b) in Figure 10-16. The long-run equilibrium of a perfectly competitive firm occurs when the price, or dd curve, is equal to the minimum long-run average cost which necessarily corresponds with the minimum short-run average cost; and, necessarily, to both the short-run marginal cost and long-run marginal cost.

This point is marked E in panel (b), where $SMC = SAC = LAC = LMC = P'_e$. The long-run equilibrium rate of output for the perfectly competitive firm is rate q_e.

Note again that zero economic profits means positive accounting profits. Zero economic profits means that all factors of production, including equity capital, are paid their opportunity cost. Moreover, just because the long-run equilibrium position of the competitive firm is one of zero economic profits, this does not mean that certain resource owners in highly competitve industries cannot earn positive economic profits. A person with superior entrepreneurial talents may be able to generate economic profits in a competitive industry (although such superior talent then has a higher opportunity cost). This profit will persist because no other firm has that specialized resource, and if any capitalist wished to buy that firm, he or she would have to pay that person a salary reflecting the present dis-

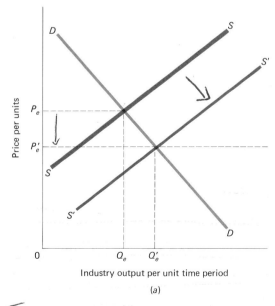

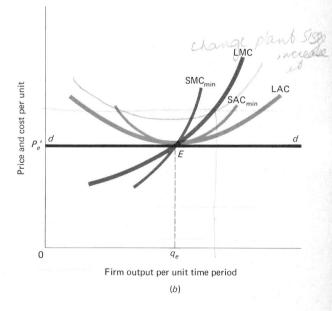

Industry output per unit time period

(a)

Firm output per unit time period

(b)

Figure 10-16: Long-run competitive equilibrium.
If economic profits such as those depicted in Figure 10-15 are being made, there will be entry into the industry. The supply curve will shift rightward in panel (a) from SS to $S'S'$. The industry output will increase from Q_e to Q'_e; the market-clearing price will fall from P_e to P'_e. The firm eventually will find itself in the situation depicted in panel (b) where, at the profit-maximizing rate of output Q_e, LAC = LMC = P'_e = SMC = SAC. No economic profits or losses are being made.

counted value of the future stream of economic profits generated by that specialized resource. Hence, the average cost curve would rise so that the new owner would earn only a normal rate of return and hence zero economic profits. Take as an example the small-boat industry. Assume for the moment that all firms except one are making a 10 percent rate of return on investment. That one firm is making a 15 percent rate of return because it has an entrepreneur with talents that far exceed anyone else's in the industry. No other firm will be able to duplicate that 15 percent rate of return, because no other firm has the same entrepreneurial talents with which to work. However, if you were to buy that one firm making 15 percent rate of return on investment, you would have to pay that person a salary that would reflect the present discounted value of that extra 5 percent return on investment per year generated by the specialized resource. You would end up making, in the long run, only a 10 percent accounting rate of return and, since 10 percent is the average rate of return in the industry, zero economic profits. (Why?)

Constant-, increasing-, and decreasing-cost industries

We have generally assumed that price remained constant when the entire industry increases its rate of production. If this is the case, then the industry is a **constant-cost industry**. If, however, the average unit cost curve rises, we are dealing with an **increasing-cost industry**. And finally, if the unit cost curve falls when the industry expands output, it is a **decreasing-cost industry**. These three possibilities are shown by the slope of the long-run supply curve presented in panels (a), (b), and (c) in Figure 10-17.

We can work through the case in which constant costs prevail. We start out in panel (a) with demand curve DD and supply curve SS. The equilibrium price is P_e. There is a shift in market demand to $D'D'$. In the short run the supply curve remains stable. The equilibrium price rises to P'_e. This generates positive economic profits for those in the industry. Such economic profits induce capital to flow into the industry. The existing firms expand and/or new firms enter. The supply curve

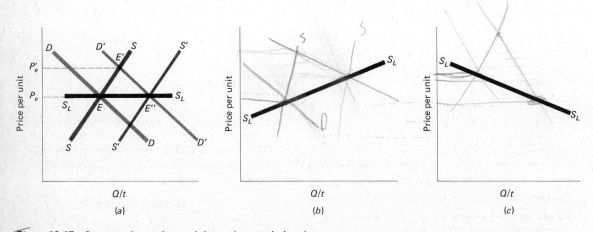

Figure 10-17: Constant, increasing, and decreasing cost industries.
In panel (a) we show a situation where the demand curve shifts from DD to D'D'. Price increases to P'_e; however, in time the supply curve shifts out to S'S', and the new equilibrium shifts from E' to E''. The market-clearing price is, again, P_e. If we connect points such as E and E'', we come up with the long-run supply curve $S_L S_L$. This is a constant-cost industry. In panel (b) costs are increasing for the industry and, therefore, the supply curve is upward-sloping; in panel (c) costs are decreasing for the industry as it expands and, therefore, the supply curve is downward-sloping.

shifts out to $S'S'$. The new intersection with the new demand curve is at E''. The new equilibrium price is again P_e. The long-run supply curve is obtained by connecting the intersections of the various demand and supply curves, E and E''. It is labeled $S_L S_L$. It is horizontal. Its slope is zero. Long-run supply is perfectly elastic. Any shift in demand is eventually met by an equal shift in supply so that the long-run price is constant at P_e. This is a constant-cost industry.

An increasing-cost industry is shown by the supply curve $S_L S_L$ in panel (b); it is upward-sloping. A decreasing-cost industry is shown in panel (c). To test your understanding of the derivation of $S_L S_L$, draw in the appropriate sets of short-run market demand and industry supply curves in panels (b) and (c)

Diseconomies and economies of scale

One of the reasons that an industry can be other than a constant-cost industry is the presence of external economies and diseconomies of scale. The former could generate the long-run supply curve in panel (c) and the latter the long-run supply curve in panel (b) in Figure 10-17.

External diseconomies of scale

External diseconomies of scale are the factors which increase costs and over which the individual firm has no control (as we briefly noted in Chapter 8). The most obvious external diseconomy of scale is the impact of the industry's expanding production on resource prices. If all firms expanding production simultaneously caused the price of one or more inputs to rise, *ceteris paribus*, then this is an increasing-cost industry. The external diseconomy to increasing output is not controllable by the individual firm and does not occur within the firm itself. Another possible external diseconomy of scale is increased conges-

tion in a manufacturing area that results from an expansion of all plants together.

External economies of scale

External economies of scale can occur when an increase in the output of the entire industry allows suppliers to engage in increased specialization and to lower their unit costs. This would cause the downward-sloping long-run supply curve shown in panel (c) in Figure 10-17. Consider, for example, one or two firms who start business in a small residential area. They have photocopying needs, but not enough to justify the purchase or lease of their own equipment. They must take their originals to be photocopied. If many firms move into the same area, it may become profitable for a photocopying firm to start in business. There will at least be a reduction for the original two firms in the time cost of having their photocopying done. Additionally, it may turn out that larger and hence lower-per-unit-cost photocopying machines may be used by the photocopying firm and that the actual monetary price per unit of photocopying falls. This would be another case of economies of scale which are external to the firm and over which the firm has no control.

The price elasticity of supply

We can define the **price elasticity of supply** in the same manner as we defined the price elasticity of demand. We use the Greek letter ϵ to denote the coeffieicent of the price elasticity of supply. It will be equal to

$$\epsilon = \frac{\Delta Q/Q}{\Delta P/P} = \frac{\Delta Q}{\Delta P} \cdot \frac{P}{Q} \qquad (10\text{-}9)$$

It is similar to the formula for the coefficient of the price elasticity of demand. However, supply curves are generally upward-sloping: ϵ will, except in cases of decreasing-cost industries, be positive. We denote supply curves as elastic, unit-elastic, or inelastic, according to whether ϵ exceeds 1, is equal to 1, or is less than 1. A vertical supply curve has an elasticity ϵ equal to 0; a horizontal supply curve has an elasticity ϵ equal to ∞. Thus, the long-run supply curve at $S_L S_L$ in panel (a) of Figure 10-17 has $\epsilon = \infty$. The immediate period supply curve SS in Figure 10-1 has an elasticity equal to 0.

As with a linear demand curve, we cannot determine the price elasticity of demand by looking at its slope. Consider supply curves $S''S''$ and $S'''S'''$ in Figure 10-18. They have different slopes, yet both of them have a price elasticity of supply equal to 1. Look at Eq. (10-9) again. It is equal to the reciprocal of the slope of the supply curve times P/Q. In other words, it is equal to P/Q divided by the slope of the supply curve. However, for any supply curve that passes through 0, the origin, $\Delta P/\Delta Q$, will always equal P/Q. Thus, any linear supply curve passing through the origin has unitary elasticity at each and every price.

Two linear supply curves with the same slope will have different elasticities, depending on whether they intersect the vertical or the horizontal axis. Supply curve SS in Figure 10-18 is elastic at all prices. Supply curve $S'S'$ in Figure 10-18 is inelastic at all prices. To see why, consider again the formula for price elasticity of supply:

$$\epsilon = \frac{\Delta Q/Q}{\Delta P/P}$$

For supply curve SS, pick any price. The numerator in the formula for price elasticity of supply $\Delta Q/Q$ will always equal 1. The denominator $\Delta P/P$ will always be less than 1. Hence, ϵ will always be greater than unity. The converse occurs for supply curve $S'S'$ in Figure 10-18. The numerator $\Delta Q/Q$ will always be less than 1, and the denominator $\Delta P/P$ will always equal 1. Hence, ϵ will always be less than 1, i.e., $S'S'$ is inelastic at all prices.

Elasticity of supply and length of time for adjustment

Very early in this book, we pointed out that the longer the time allowed for adjustment, the more price-elastic is the demand curve. It turns out that the same proposition applies to supply. The longer the time for adjustment, the more price-elastic is the supply curve. Thus, in Figure 10-19, we could hypothesize that the immediate-run (market period) supply curve would be $S_1 S_1$. However, as more time were allowed for adjustment, the supply curve would rotate to $S_2 S_2$, then $S_3 S_3$, then $S_4 S_4$. Otherwise stated, long-run supply curves will be more price-elastic than short-run supply curves, other things being equal.

The longer the time allowed for adjustment, the more are actual and potential firms able to

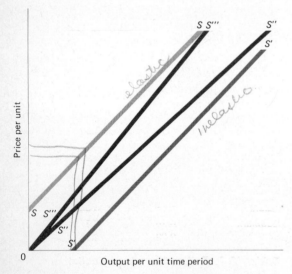

Figure 10-18: The price elasticity of supply.
One cannot tell by the slope of a supply curve whether it is elastic or inelastic. Any supply curve such as $S''S''$ or S''' S''' that forms a ray from the origin has an elasticity of unity. Any supply curve such as $S'S'$ that cuts the horizontal axis is inelastic. Any one such as SS that cuts the vertical axis is elastic.

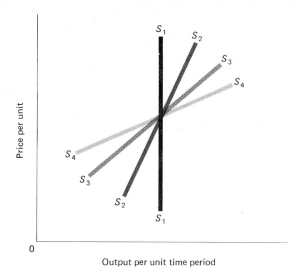

Figure 10-19: **Allowing for the time of adjustment.**
The immediate-run (market period) supply curve $S_1 S_1$
is vertical. Its price elasticity is equal to zero. As more
time is allowed for adjustment, it becomes less inelastic
(or more elastic).

Second, more apartment buildings, con-
dominiums, co-ops, duplexes, and single-
family dwellings will be built so that eventually the housing stock will grow and so, too,
ceteris paribus, will the quantity of housing
services supplied.

We can also think in terms of how the individual firm responds to a change in the price
of its output. If an increase in price, for example, is expected to be short-lived, the firm
will increase its variable factors; i.e., it will use
its variable factors more intensively—running
its machines longer and paying overtime rates
to workers. If, on the other hand, the price is
expected to be permanent, fixed factors of
production would be increased more and variable factors less. Presumably, per-unit cost
will fall in the long run as the firm readapts to
the optimal scale of plant. Thus, we can generate the set of supply curves depicted in Figure
10-19 in this manner.

figure out ways to increase production in an
industry. Moreover, the longer the time
allowed, the more resources can flow into the
industry. As an example, consider the amount
of housing services offered for rent or sale in a
particular city. Note now that we are referring
to housing *services* rather than the *stock* of
housing available. In the immediate run, it is
conceivable that the supply curve of housing
services offered for rent or sale is relatively
inelastic. However, as more time is allowed
for adjustment, two things can happen. First,
current owners of the housing stock can find
ways to increase the amount of housing services they will offer for rent from that given
stock. This is done, for example, by the owner
of a large house who decides to have two of
his or her children move into one room and
rent out the "new" extra bedroom. This can
also be done by the owner of a large house
who decides to move out into an apartment
and rent each floor of the house to a family.

Commodity	Elasticity (ϵ)	
	Short run	Long run
Cabbage	0.36	1.20
Carrots	0.14	1.00
Cucumbers	0.29	2.20
Onions	0.34	1.00
Green peas	0.31	4.40
Tomatoes	0.16	0.90
Watermelons	0.23	0.48
Beets	0.13	1.00
Cauliflower	0.14	1.10
Celery	0.14	0.95
Eggplant	0.16	0.34
Spinach	0.20	4.70

Table 10-2: **Estimated price elasticities of supply.**

Source: M. Nerlove and W. Addison, "Statis-
tical Estimation of Long-Run Elasticities of
Supply and Demand," *American Journal of
Agricultural Economics* (formerly *Journal of
Farm Economics*), vol. 40, November 1958,
pp. 861–880.

Real world estimates of the price elasticity of supply

There are problems in obtaining empirical estimates of supply elasticities. They are similar to the estimation problems for price elasticity of demand discussed in Chapter 5. In Table 10-2, we present some estimates of short- and long-run elasticities of supply for fresh vegetables in the United States. In estimating these elasticities, the short run was defined as one "production period." We note that most short-run elasticities are considerably less than their long-run counterpart.

Issues and applications

What is the meaning of competition in the stock market?

The market for shares of stock approximates as closely as possible the perfectly competitive situation, at least for shares of stock traded on the major stock exchanges. Information concerning prices and quantities and transactions is readily available at very small per-unit costs. All you need do is telephone or go to a brokerage firm, and it can find the latest price and quantity sold of any stock on a major exchange within seconds. We are dealing with homogeneous products within each particular company category. Moreover, there is mobility of resources—people buy and sell all the time. And finally, in most cases the individual buyer or seller represents an insignificant part of the total market. Therefore, the individual buyer or seller of shares of stock must take prices as given. (However, when there is institutional trading, which involves the purchase or sale of large blocks of shares by institutions such as pension and mutual funds and insurance companies, these traders are not an insignificant part of the total market and hence do have some influence over price. This influence, however, will be diminished when the institutional large-quantity or block trading is done through a computerized system which will break up the block into many small transactions.)

The price for an individual share of stock in a company traded on a major exchange is determined by the supply of and demand for that stock.

(The total number of outstanding shares of that stock is fixed at any moment in time.) We have actually already treated part of this issue when we examined the reservation demand and supply of shares of stock in Chapter 4.

Information costly to obtain

Here we are more interested in how far we can push the competitive model to understand pricing of shares of stock on major stock exchanges. First, we know that a share of stock is an asset. Its price reflects the discounted present value of the expected future stream of net income. What determines the expectations of future net income for a particular stock? To a large extent, knowledge of the current and expected future profits of the company in question. Here is where the notion of competition continues in our analysis. There is certainly no such thing as free information, even about prices and quantities of stocks sold. This is a fortiori correct when we talk about information concerning the future profitability of a company, an industry, or all industries within the nation. Information about companies is costly to obtain.

Nonetheless, there is rivalry among those who buy and sell shares of stock. This rivalry causes many of them to expend resources to obtain information about the future profitability of companies or industries. They engage in research or analysis. But since there is rivalry among literally millions of individuals, all wishing to get rich, we know that lots of resources are spent to obtain this valuable information. In fact, resources for each individual researcher are expended up to the point where marginal cost equals expected marginal revenue. When we add all the results of these researchers together, we come up with a tremendous amount of information on individual companies.

The value of public information

Now, this is the question: Given that we are dealing with a very competitive market (even though it may not be *perfectly* competitive), can we say anything about the value of research information? Yes, we can. The value of research information that is publicly known is zero, for such information has already been "used" by the time it reaches the public. In other words, be it bullish (good) or bearish (bad), all public information is discounted very quickly by a change in the stock's prices. Those who first find out about the increased present or future profitability of a company will bid up the price of the shares of stock in that company, and those who first find out that the company is going to be less profitable in the future will, by their selling, cause the price of the stock to fall. Actually, what is involved is many individuals doing this simultaneously. That is why we say that the current price of a stock reflects all presently available information, properly discounted, concerning the future profitability of the firm, the industry, or the economy. This is also known as the **efficient-market hypothesis**. In a highly efficient market, such as the stock market, rates of return to investment will tend toward equality on the margin (when these rates of return are corrected for risk).

The dynamic competitive process

This is no different from the dynamic process outlined in this chapter when we showed what would happen in an industry making positive economic profits or negative economic profits (losses). In any highly competitive, efficient

market, capital flows to wherever rates of return corrected for risk are highest. When we say "corrected for risk," we mean that even with perfect competition, the rate of return necessary to induce capital into a risky venture will be higher than the rate of return necessary to induce capital into a less risky venture. As capital moves around to where rates of return are anticipated to be highest (corrected for risk), this shuffling around tends to drive down expected high rates of return (corrected for risk). If one area of potential investment has an extremely high risk-corrected expected rate of return, the capital that will flow in will constitute an additional supply. With a given demand for capital, the additional supply (shifting the supply curve outward to the right) will drive down that high anticipated risk-corrected rate of return to capital. The reverse will occur when there is a relatively low risk-corrected expected rate of return to capital somewhere in the economy.

In a highly competitive investment market, it therefore usually does little good to obtain public information, that is, information which is known to more than a relatively small number of individuals who can make timely use of that information to make capital gains or avoid capital losses. Public information includes not only research service results, presented free of charge by stockbrokerage firms, but also schemes on how to get rich quick that are printed in magazines, newspapers, and books, and investment services offered by the numerous investment firms in this country and elsewhere.

The conclusion to be reached is perhaps best summed up in the words of Paul Samuelson:

> Even the best investors seem to find it hard to do better than the comprehensive common-stock averages, or better on the average than random selection among stocks of comparable variability.[7]

---

[7]P. A. Samuelson, "Proof That Properly Discounted Present Values of Assets Vibrate Randomly," *The Bell Journal of Economics and Management Science*, vol. 4, no. 2, Autumn 1973, pp. 369–374.

We must point out one caveat in the above discussion. If you as an investor are better at interpreting public information than the market in general, then you can make higher-than-normal rates of return using this public information. In other words, if you are the sole possessor of a truly superior theory that allows you to use public information to predict the future course of a stock market, then as long as you are able to keep your theory secret from everyone else, you can "make a killing" in the market.

The effect of a per unit tax on relative prices

Consider a commodity that is sold in various *quality* bundles. Take the example of cigarettes. A package of cigarettes can contain cigarettes using higher-quality tobacco or lower-quality tobacco. What happens to the relative price of higher-quality tobacco cigarettes when a per-unit (specific) tax of, say, 10¢ is put on each package of cigarettes? It falls. This can be seen in the following numerical example.

In Table 10-3, we see that prior to the 10¢ tax on a pack of cigarettes, the relative price of higher quality to lower quality is 2 to 1. That is, lower-quality cigarettes cost 50 percent of what higher-quality cigarettes cost. After the per unit tax of 10¢, however, the relative price changes from 5 to 3. Now, lower-quality cigarettes cost 60 percent of the price of higher-quality cigarettes. Their relative price has gone up. A smaller quantity will be demanded after the tax than before, relative to higher-quality cigarettes.[8] Indeed, this actually happened in the United States, and as the theory would predict, lower-quality cigarettes gradually disappeared from the market. Had an equal *percentage* tax been put on all brands of cigarettes, the situation would have been different. An equal

	Higher quality	Lower quality	Relative prices
Price before tax	40¢	20¢	2:1
Price after tax	50¢	30¢	5:3

Table 10-3: Effect of a specific tax on relative price of differing qualities of cigarettes.

percentage tax per pack of cigarettes, based on the selling price of each pack, would not have affected the relative price of the various qualities of cigarettes. That is to say, high-quality- and low-quality-tobacco products would have maintained their relative price even after the equal percentage tax was put on.

Can price controls work?

We can use the analysis of the competitive industry to predict the effects of price controls. When the maximum price that is imposed by law is below the market-clearing price (or the price that would prevail in the absence of any centralized coercion), the results can be predicted.

Price controls in their simplest form

Let us take a simple case where a maximum price is put on the product of an industry that sells its product directly to the consumer. We represent this situation in Figure 10-20. The market-clearing price is P_e, and the equilibrium quantity supplied and demanded at that price is Q_e. The government sets the maximum price at P_{max}. At that price, however, the quantity demanded increases to Q_D but the quantity supplied falls to Q_S. The difference is an excess quantity demanded (or "shortage") at price P_{max}. If the only amount available remained at Q_S, consumers would be willing to pay P_e'. If indeed it is legally impossible for consumers to pay a higher price, then the excess quantity demanded will manifest itself in queues. More realistically, ways around price

---

[8]This discussion ignores income effects and certain other problems. See John P. Gould and Joel Segall, "The Substitution Effects of Transportation Costs," *Journal of Political Economy*, January/February 1968, pp. 130–137.

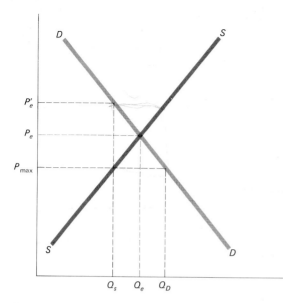

Figure 10-20: Price controls–no black markets.
If an effective price control is put on at price P_{max}, the quantity demanded Q_D will exceed the quantity supplied Q_S. For that quantity supplied, the difference will be called a *shortage*. That quantity Q_S could be sold at price P'_e.

Taking account of black markets

The analysis given for Figure 10-20 is incomplete because it does not take account of the possibility of black markets arising. We define a **black market** as a market in which the product in question is sold at a price above the legal maximum. We will consider three separate cases in order to analyze the effect on the total quantity produced and sold as well as the price at which the product is sold in the black market.

SANCTIONS IMPOSED ON SUPPLIERS ONLY. In this situation, we assume that there are no sanctions imposed whatsoever on demanders, and moreover, that demanders find no distastefulness in using a black market. Hence, we are assuming no legal or moral costs involved in black market

transactions on the demander's side. On the supplier's side, however, we will assume added risk and added cost because of the possibility of sanctions which may include public chastisement, fines, and jail terms.

In Figure 10-21, we draw in the unrestricted supply and demand curves SS and DD. The market-clearing price without restrictions would be P_e, and the equilibrium quantity would be Q_e. A price maximum is imposed at P_{max}. At such a price, without a black market, the quantity demanded is given by Q_D and the quantity supplied is given by Q_S. Now, producers enter the black market. The supply curve becomes SCS_B. It pivots at the intersection of the maximum price with the original supply curve. The reason it pivots counterclockwise is because suppliers

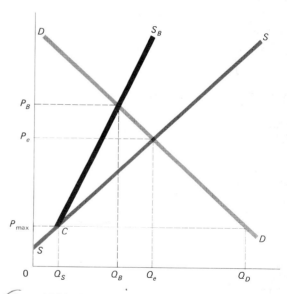

Figure 10-21: Price controls–black-market sanctions on suppliers only.
It is assumed that demanders run no risk when engaging in black-market dealings and also incur no moral costs. The supply curve SS now becomes SCS_B. It pivots at the intersection of P_{max} with the original supply curve. This is because firms engaging in illegal black-market dealings incur higher costs and must be compensated. The intersection of the black-market supply curve with the demand curve DD is at P_B. The black-market quantity supplied and demanded will be Q_B at that price.

controls—black markets and decreases in quality—will be devised.

willing to offer the product in the black market at a price in excess of the legal maximum incur additional costs equal to the risks of penalty. Thus, the only way that they will offer more of the product is by being compensated for this additional expected cost.

In this situation, the black market supply curve, SCS_B, intersects the original demand curve DD at price P_B. Consumers will purchase the quantity Q_B at price P_B.

In this particular case, the black market price exceeds the original unregulated market-clearing price.

PENALTIES IMPOSED ONLY ON CONSUMERS. In this case, we assume that suppliers incur no legal or moral penalty when engaging in black market transactions—selling the product at higher than the legal maximum price. However, the consumer does incur a legal and/or moral penalty when buying in the black market. In Figure 10-22, we show the original supply and demand curves SS and DD. The legal maximum price is P_{max}. At that price, without a black market, the quantity demanded is Q_D, but the quantity supplied is the smaller quantity Q_S. Suppliers are willing to sell varying quantities of the product at prices exceeding P_{max}. The supply curve thus remains at SS. However, the black market demand curve is to the left of DD. Because of the additional costs associated with legal and/or moral penalties for those who purchase goods in the black market, the black market demand curve is given in this hypothetical example as $D_B D_B$. Progressively lesser quantities will be demanded at black market prices exceeding P_{max} until point A, where the black market price reaches P_1 and a zero quantity is demanded in the black market.

The black market–clearing price will be at the intersection of the black market demand curve $D_B D_B$ with the original supply curve SS. This is given as price P_B. The quantity sold at price P_B is equal to Q_B. In this particular example, the black market price is *less* than the price that prevailed prior to the imposition of a legal maximum price.

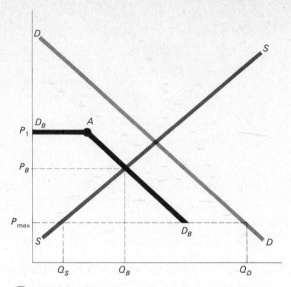

Figure 10-22: The black market—penalties imposed on consumers only.

The supply curve remains the same as before price control. The demand curve in the black market is $D_B D_B$. It tells us that at prices above P_{max}, consumers will purchase less and less in the black market. Finally, at price P_1, they will purchase nothing in the black market. The black-market price will be P_B; the quantity supplied and demanded will be Q_B.

PENALTIES ASSOCIATED WITH BOTH SUPPLYING AND PURCHASING GOODS IN THE BLACK MARKET. When we combine the possibility of penalties, both moral and legal, on the demander's side and the supplier's side, we come up with the situation depicted in Figure 10-23. What we have done in that figure is combine Figures 10-21 and 10-22. The intersection of the black market supply and the black market demand curves yields a black market–clearing price of P_B. In this particular example, the black market price P_B is slightly less than the price that prevailed without price controls. In other words, the black market price can be less than the unrestricted market-clearing price that existed prior to the price control. On the other hand, to the extent that the black market demand curve $D_B D_B$ is significantly greater, i.e., is positioned outward to the right of where it is in Figure 10-23, the black market price for the good

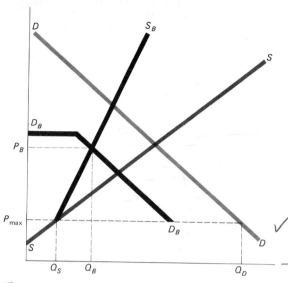

Figure 10-23: The black market—sanctions imposed on both consumers and suppliers.
We combine Figure 10-22 and Figure 10-23 to arrive at a black-market clearing price of P_B with quantity Q_B. In this particular example, P_B is less than the original unrestricted market-clearing price; however, this is just a hypothetical case. Empirically, P_B has typically exceeded the unrestricted market price.

in question will exceed the prior unrestricted market-clearing price. Casual observation of black market prices throughout the world suggests the empirical validity of the latter.[9] Since the *relative* legal penalties and moral sanction are usually heavier on sellers than on buyers, the SS pivots more westward than does DD.

The "farm problem"

Since the 1930s, the United States government has engaged in a number of agricultural programs to solve the "farm problem." For many years, the solution was defined as keeping the price of farm products higher than the market-

[9] See A. F. W. Plumtre, "The Theory of the Black Market: Further Considerations," *Canadian Journal of Economics and Political Science*, vol. 13, no. 2, May 1947, p. 280.

clearing price. This was done by way of a price-support program.

The effects of price supports

In Figure 10-24 we present the analysis of a price-support or minimum-price program. The equilibrium price is P_e; the equilibrium quantity is Q_e. The government sets the support price for a particular commodity at P_{min}. This increases the quantity supplied to Q_S and decreases the quantity demanded to Q_D. The difference is the excess quantity supplied at price P_{min}. This is called a surplus. The only way for the price P_{min} to continue is for the surplus to be continuously bought up by the government. For many years prior to 1973 (and for some commodities since 1973), the surplus, in effect, was purchased by the Commodity Credit Corporation (CCC). The CCC made nonrecourse loans at the support price for however much farmers wanted to "borrow." A

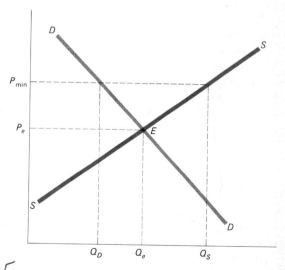

Figure 10-24: The farm program—price supports.
We show the analysis of the effect of price supports. The market-clearing price is P_e; the equilibrium quantity is Q_e. A price support greater than P_e is put on at P_{min}. The quantity demanded will be Q_D; the quantity supplied will be Q_S. The difference between Q_D and Q_S is the excess quantity supplied at the support price.

nonrecourse loan works as follows: The farmer puts up as collateral some price-supported commodity, say, corn. The CCC loans the farmer a sum of money equal to the support price per unit of the commodity times the number of units put up as collateral. At no time in the future is the farmer required to ever pay off the loan. This is the nonrecourse nature of it. The CCC will be stuck with the collateral so long as the equilibrium price stays below the support price.

The soil bank program

In order to eliminate surpluses, the government has at times engaged in "conservation" or soil bank programs in which a certain amount of arable land had to be left unused in order for the owners of the land to participate in the price-support program. The results of the soil bank program can be seen in Figure 10-25. We start off in equilibrium with DD and SS intersecting at point E, an equilibrium price of P_e, and an equilibrium quantity of Q_e. A price support is put into effect at the price P_{min}. The government knows that at that price there will be surpluses, so it restricts the amount of land available. However, when it restricts the amount of land available, it changes the shape of the supply curve. Eventually, the supply curve rotates to SS'. Each individual producer now has one fixed factor of production, even in the long run, and that is land. However, other factors of production such as fertilizer, labor, seed, etc., are not fixed. Each individual producer, therefore, uses more of all of these other variable inputs. In a sense, then, the unrestricted land that is used for production is farmed more intensively. The cost per unit of production goes up so that the new supply curve is to the left of the old supply curve.

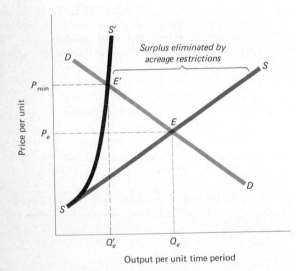

Figure 10-25: Soil bank program.
If price controls are set at P_{min}, there will be a "surplus" at that price. In order to eliminate the surplus, the government imposes restrictions on the use of one input—land. All other inputs are increased. The supply curve pivots to SS'. If the soil bank program is perfectly "effective," all surpluses will be eliminated. The market-clearing price with the now-constrained supply schedule will be P_{min}; the equilibrium quantity will be Q'_e.

Glossary

Perfect competition A model of industrial or market organization that requires (1) homogeneity of product, (2) costless resource mobility, (3) large numbers of buyers and sellers, (4) product divisibility, and (5) perfect information.

Rivalry The more commonsense notion of competition in which economic agents attempt to improve their net worth position by advertising, marketing, developing new products, and so on.

Survivor principle In a world of scarce resources, firms which make the "right" decisions survive—and others imitate them.

Immediate run or market period That period of time in which the stock (supply) is given and cannot be increased.

Industry A group of firms that produces a homogeneous product.

Short-run break-even price That price which just covers short-run average total costs.

Short-run shutdown price A price equal to minimum short-run AVC; the price below which the firm will shut down production in the short run.

Accounting profits The profits shown on an accountant's books which may not have taken full account of *all* costs of production, including the opportunity cost of capital; to be contrasted with the broader notion of economic profits.

Economic profits The pure profit left over when all costs, including the full opportunity cost of all inputs, are subtracted from total revenues.

Equity capital Capital in a business that has been raised by selling shares of common stock in that business; to be contrasted with debt capital.

Debt capital Capital that has been raised for a business by issuing bonds or borrowing from a commercial bank.

Industry supply curve The locus of points showing the minimum prices at which given quantities will be forthcoming; also called the market supply curve.

Price taker A firm which must accept as given the market price for its product; a price taker cannot influence the price of the product.

Boundary equilibrium An equilibrium that occurs on the horizontal or on the vertical axis; sometimes called a corner solution.

Interior equilibrium An equilibrium that occurs somewhere inside the price-quantity quadrant rather than on the axes; sometimes called an interior solution.

Cobweb theorem A simple dynamic model in which the quantities supplied in one period are a function of the price which prevailed in the previous period.

Constant-cost industry An industry whose long-run supply curve is horizontal.

Increasing-cost industry An industry whose long-run supply curve is upward-sloping.

Decreasing-cost industry An industry whose long-run supply curve is downward-sloping.

Price elasticity of supply The relative change in the quantity supplied divided by the relative change in the price.

Efficient-market hypothesis In a highly competitive market that is working efficiently, the value of any asset completely reflects the discounted present value of all information about the future income stream derivable from the asset.

Black market A market in which goods are sold at prices which exceed the legally stipulated maximum.

Summary

1. Scarcity usually implies rivalry and/or competition.

2. The definition of perfect competition implies a complete lack of rivalry because the product is homogeneous and there is perfect information. Thus, in order to analyze real world issues, we must relax some of the assumptions in the model of perfect competition.

3. Price acts as a rationing system and this is discriminatory; however, all systems of rationing are, by necessity, discriminatory by virtue of the criteria established for distribution of commodities.

4. The demand curve facing a perfectly competitive firm is horizontal. Its elasticity is $-\infty$

5. The marginal revenue for a perfect competitor is equal to price.

6. The profit-maximizing rate of output for the perfect competitor is the output at which marginal revenue equals marginal cost. Since marginal revenue equals price in a perfectly competitive industry, the firm produces the output at which marginal cost equals price.

7. In the short run, the firm makes no economic profits at a price which just covers average *total* costs. In the short run, the firm will shut down below the price which just covers minimum average *variable* costs.

8. The industry supply curve is the horizontal summation of the firms' marginal cost curves above their respective average variable cost curves.

9. It is important to distinguish between accounting and economic profits; the latter refers to those profits that are left over after the opportunity cost of all inputs is subtracted from total revenues.

10. In the long run, the short-run break-even point is actually the going-out-of-business point; if price falls below that point, the opportunity cost of capital will not be covered; the firm will not stay in the industry (at least not with that set of facilities).

11. The position of the supply curve depends, *inter alia*, on (a) the prices of resources used to produce the product, and (b) technology.

12. Equilibria can occur inside the price-quantity quadrant, in which case they are called interior equilibria, or on the axes, in which case they are called boundary equilibria. Generally, we are interested only in interior equilibria.

13. A cobweb model of dynamic adjustment has the quantity supplied in the current period as a function of the price in the previous period. If the supply curve has a numerically greater slope than the demand curve, we get damped oscillations that look like cobwebs on the demand and supply diagram.

14. In a price system, resources flow to industries that are making higher-than-average, risk-adjusted rates of return (economic profits) and resources flow out of industries, or are not reinvested in industries that are making economic losses.

15. In the long run, the competitive firm produces an output at which $LMC = LAC = SMC = SAC = P_e$.

16. Economies of scale in an industry can cause the market-clearing price to fall as the industry expands. In this case, the long-run supply curve is downward-sloping, and the industry is called a decreasing-cost industry. The opposite occurs if there are industrywide diseconomies of scale; then the industry is called an increasing-cost industry.

17. The longer the time for adjustment, the greater the price elasticity of supply.

Selected references

Knight, Frank H., *Risk, Uncertainty and Profit* (New York: Harper & Row, 1921; reprint edition, 1965), chaps. 1, 5, and 6.

Machlup, Fritz, *Economics of Sellers' Competition* (Baltimore: Johns Hopkins, 1952), pp. 79–85, 116–125.

Marshall, Alfred, *Principles of Economics*, 8th ed. (London: Macmillan, 1920), book 5, chaps. 4–5.

Samuelson, Paul A., "Dynamic Process Analysis," in H. S. Ellis (ed.), *A Survey of Contemporary Economics* (Philadelphia: Blakiston, 1948), chap. 10.

———,"Dynamics, Statics,. and the Stationary States," *Review of Economics and Statistics*, vol. 25, February 1943, pp. 58–68.

Smith, Vernon, "An Experimental Study of Competitive Market Behavior," *Journal of Political Economy*, vol. 70, April 1962, pp. 111–137.

Stigler, George, "Perfect Competition, Historically Contemplated," *Journal of Political Economy*, vol. 65, February 1957, pp. 1–17.

Wicksteed, P. H., *The Common Sense of Political Economy* (London: Routledge, 1934), vol. 2, book 3.

Questions

(Answers to even-numbered questions are found at back of book.)

1. In our model of a perfectly competitive market, does an individual firm compete with others? If so, how?

2. In a perfectly competitive market, what is the difference between the demand facing the industry and the demand facing an individual firm?

3. Explain how goods are rationed in the immediate run (market period) in a perfectly competitive market.

4. List five criteria, other than price, which might be used to ration a scarce good.

5. Look at Figure 10-3. Geometrically speaking, how would MC and MR be portrayed? What then would be the geometric solution, using Figure 10-3, for profit maximization?

6. Why might a firm continue to produce in the short run, even though the going price was less than its average total cost?

7. Why would the perfectly competitive model predict that if price is above ATC and is expected to remain there, new firms will enter the industry?

8. You have a friend who earns $10,000 per year working for a collection agency. She quits her job, takes $100,000 out of the savings and loan where it was earning 8 percent per year, and buys a car wash. She shows you her tax return after a year of operations, and it shows the car wash had a pretax "profit" of $16,000. "What do you think about that?" she remarks. What is your answer?

9. What is one possible danger in deriving an industry's short-run supply curve by summing the MC curves (above AVC) of the individual firms?

10. "When a good's price is 'clearing the market' (at equilibrium), everybody is happy, but disequilibrium prices are bound to make somebody mad." Criticize this statement.

11. "If there's anything I can't stand, its a bar or restaurant that sets its prices too low." Complete this person's statement.

12. Construct a supply and demand diagram for a "free" good (one which is not scarce).

13. In long-run equilibrium, what is the relationship between the various per unit cost and revenue variables? Why must these equalities hold?

14. Suppose you know someone who is very good at making economic profits in perfectly competitive industries in which everyone else is barely covering all their costs. How would you explain (or explain away) this phenomenon?

15. Do you see any inconsistency between a federal "farm program" and a federal "wage-price control program"? If so, what is it?

11

MONOPOLY
PRICING
AND OUTPUT

We have just studied perfect competition. It is one of the two polar opposite market structures. We will now analyze the other polar extreme—pure monopoly. Just as the conditions for perfect competition are rarely met in the real world, the conditions for pure monopoly are also rarely met. Nonetheless, we find the model useful for analyzing and predicting price and output changes in less than perfectly competitive industries. In this chapter, we will analyze pure monopoly where there is only one firm in an industry. Indeed, we will define the **monopolist** as a single seller, or supplier, of a well-defined commodity. (Entry by would-be competitors is somehow prevented.) In this chapter, we will take as given the fact that a monopoly can arise and the methods by which individuals attempt to gain and maintain monopoly power.

The demand curve facing a monopoly

The monopoly is the only firm in the industry; the demand curve facing the monopoly is the industry, or market, demand curve. Assuming that the law of demand holds, the industry demand curve will be downward-sloping with an elasticity between $-\infty$ and 0. We draw such a curve in Figure 11-1, panel (a).

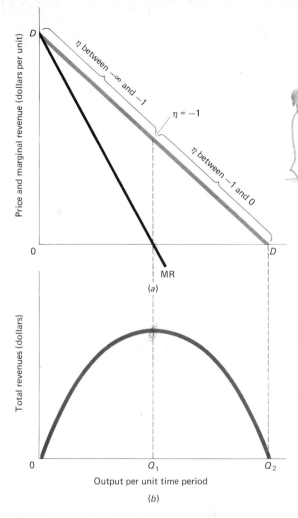

(a)

(b)

Output per unit time period

Figure 11-1: Elasticity and total revenues.
In panel (a) we show a linear demand curve along which the price elasticity of demand decreases as we increase quantity. At the midpoint on the demand curve, price elasticity of demand is equal to −1 and marginal revenue is equal to 0. In panel (b) we can see that total revenues start at 0, reach a peak at output rate Q_1, and then fall to 0 when price reaches 0 at output Q_2. Total revenues are maximized at the output rate at which $\eta = -1$.

Price elasticity of demand

It is often thought that a monopolist faces an inelastic demand curve. However, this does not follow from the definition of monopoly. The demand curve shown in Figure 11-1 (a) is

linear and hence has a price elasticity of demand which goes from $-\infty$ to 0 as we move rightward along the curve. (Why?)

A priori, there is very little we can say about the elasticity of the monopolist's demand curve. About the only thing we can say is that the demand facing a monopolist will be more elastic the cheaper and more numerous are the available substitutes for the monopolist's commodity; furthermore, there is a trade-off between the number of substitutes and closeness of substitutability. Thus the demand curve facing the monopolist may be relatively elastic, even if there are no close substitutes for his or her commodity, provided that there are a substantial number of poor substitutes. On the other hand, the demand curve facing a monopolist may be relatively elastic if there is only one substitute, but that substitute is very close in price and has similar attributes.

Monopoly marginal revenue

You will remember that marginal revenue is defined as the change in total revenue due to a one-unit change in volume sold. We also saw in Chapter 5 that marginal revenue was related to price and elasticity of demand. The formula showing this relationship was

$$MR = P\left(1 + \frac{1}{\eta}\right) \qquad (11\text{-}1)$$

In the case of a perfect competitor, $\eta = -\infty$ by definition; therefore, marginal revenue equals price because Eq. (11-1) becomes $MR = P(1 + 1/-\infty) = P(1 - 0) = P$. The monopolist, however, does not face a horizontal demand schedule with η always equal to $-\infty$. The monopolist would never willingly operate where marginal revenue is less than 0, even if there were zero costs of production, for it could always reduce output and thereby increase revenues, and consequently profits. MR becomes 0 in Eq. (11-1) when $\eta = -1$ [then $MR = P(1 + 1/-1) = P(1 - 1) = 0$]. When η is between -1 and 0, MR is negative.

That means that the monopolist will never operate on that portion of the demand curve where demand is inelastic. This can be better seen by looking at the relationship between marginal revenue, total revenue, and elasticity of demand. We developed the technique for drawing the marginal revenue curve back in Chapter 5.

Marginal revenue, total revenue, and elasticity of demand

We have drawn panel (b) in Figure 11-1 to show the relationship between total revenue, marginal revenue, and elasticity of demand. Total revenue is clearly 0 when unit sales are zero; thus, in panel (b), the total revenue curve starts at the origin. Total revenues are also 0 when the price is 0, so that total revenues are equal to 0 at the rate of output Q_2, at which demand curve DD intersects the horizontal axis in panel (a) of Figure 11-1. In between the output of 0 and that output Q_2, total revenue first rises and then falls. It reaches a peak at the rate of output Q_1 where marginal revenue is equal to 0, i.e., where elasticity of demand must be -1. It is clear from panel (a) that the monopolist would never operate at a rate of output larger than Q_1 because marginal revenue is negative. This is equivalent to saying that the monopolist will never operate in the inelastic region of the demand curve DD.

It should be noted here that this entire discussion of monopoly assumes that the monopolist charges the same price to all purchasers of his or her product. This is the case of a **non-discriminating monopoly**. Later in this chapter, we consider the possibility of a **discriminating monopoly**, where different purchasers are charged different prices for the same product.

Marginal revenue in the short and the long run

The perfect competitor has no effect on the price of its product; the marginal revenue of the perfect competitor is equal to price which is taken as given. For planning purposes, the short-run and the long-run price and marginal revenue are the same for the perfect competitor. This follows from the assumption that the current market price is the long-run equilibrium price.

Such is not the case with monopolists who cannot ignore the fact that the price that they set today may influence tomorrow's sales. Specifically, a reduction in price this year may lead to an increase in sales next year. That would occur whenever buyers have delayed responses to price changes. Indeed, the responsiveness of consumers to changes in prices is greater the longer the price change has been in effect. That is to say, long-run price elasticities of demand are greater than short-run price elasticities of demand. The perfect competitor does not worry about this distinction because, by definition, its demand curve always has $\eta = -\infty$.

That means that if a monopolist computes marginal revenue from the *current* changes in quantity demanded that result from a current change in price, that monopolist will understate the long-run marginal revenue. The short-run marginal revenue will be less than the long-run marginal revenue.

The monopolist's costs

Just because a firm is a pure monopoly in the product market implies nothing about its position in the input markets. To simplify our analysis, we will assume that our pure monopolist has to buy all his or her inputs in purely competitive input markets. Thus, the cost curves for a monopolist can be derived in the same manner that we used to obtain the cost curves of a perfectly competitive firm. (In Chapter 16, we examine the case of monopoly in the *buying* of inputs.)

However, monopolists (and competitors too) face higher future costs when there is a temporary reduction in output today. A reduction in output that results in a laying off of employees means that when output is increased in the future, those workers must be rehired. There are certainly costs associated with rehiring or retraining. Hence the reduction in costs resulting from a decline in current output is an incomplete measure of the actual reduction in costs. That is to say, short-run marginal costs understate long-run marginal costs. Assume for the moment that the only variable input is labor, that output is curtailed, and that the wage bill is reduced by 20 percent. When we take into account the additional costs of increasing production in the future because of the cost of rehiring, marginal costs have been reduced by *less* than 20 percent. This explains why some firms will reduce inputs by *less* than the optimal amount indicated by purely short-run considerations.

When we take account of future effects on both costs and demand, we can state that the price elasticity of demand and cost curves will both be higher in the long run than in the short run.

Short-run equilibrium

We assume profit maximization is the goal of the pure monopolist, just as we assumed it was the goal of the perfect competitor. With the perfect competitor, however, we had only to decide on the profit-maximizing rate of output because price was given. For the pure monopolist we must seek a profit-maximizing *price-output combination.* We can determine this in either of two ways: the total revenue – total cost approach or the marginal revenue–marginal cost approach. Both approaches will be demonstrated. We present some hypothetical data which, for the sake of simplicity, are the same as the cost data we used for the perfect competitor.

Total revenue–total cost approach

Column (3) of Table 11-1 shows total revenues for our hypothetical monopolist, and column (4) of Table 11-1 shows total costs. We can transfer these two columns to Figure 11-2. The

Rate of output (1)	Price per unit (2)	Total revenues [(2) × (1)] (3)	Total costs (4)	Total profit [(3) − (4)] (5)	Marginal cost (6)	Marginal revenue (7)
0	8.00	0	10.00	−10.00	—	—
1	7.80	7.80	14.00	− 6.20	4.00	7.80
2	7.60	15.20	17.50	− 2.30	3.50	7.40
3	7.40	22.20	20.75	− 1.45	3.25	7.00
4	7.20	28.80	23.80	5.00	3.05	6.60
5	7.00	35.00	26.70	8.30	2.90	6.20
6	6.80	40.80	29.50	11.30	2.80	5.80
7	6.60	46.20	32.25	13.95	2.75	5.40
8	6.40	51.20	35.10	16.10	2.85	5.00
9	6.20	55.80	38.30	17.50	3.20	4.60
10	6.00	60.00	42.30	17.70	4.00	4.20
11	5.80	63.80	48.30	15.50	6.00	3.80
12	5.60	67.20	57.30	9.90	9.00	3.40
13	5.40	70.20	70.30	− 0.10	13.00	3.00
14	5.20	72.80	88.30	−15.50	18.00	2.60
15	5.00	75.00	112.30	−37.30	24.00	2.20

Table 11-1: Monopoly Costs, Revenues, and Profits

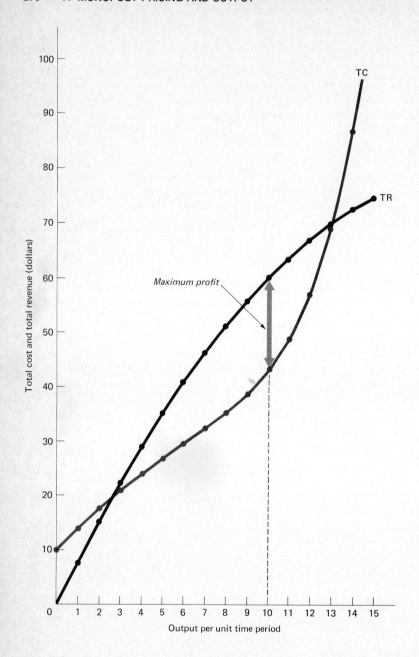

Maximum profit

only difference between Figure 11-2 and the similar figure (Figure 10-3) we drew for a perfect competitor is that the total revenue line is no longer a linear ray from the origin. Rather, it is a nonlinear curve. For any given demand curve, in order to sell more, the monopolist must lower the price; and after a certain point (where elasticity of demand equals −1), a further lowering of price causes total revenues to fall. [Refer back to Figure 11-1 panel (b).]

Profit maximization involves maximizing the difference between total revenues and total costs. This occurs at a rate of output of 10. We must be careful to be maximizing the *positive* difference between total revenues and total costs; otherwise, we could end up maximizing losses rather than profits. Thus, we are only interested in that range of outputs (if it exists) of Figure 11-2, where the total revenue line is *above* the total cost line. Consequently, in this case we won't consider output rates below 3.

Marginal revenue–marginal cost approach

Profit maximization also occurs where marginal revenue equals marginal cost. This is as true for a monopolist as it is for a perfect competitor. If the firm goes past the output at which marginal revenue equals marginal cost, total profits will be less than they could have been, because for each additional unit sold, costs have increased more than revenues. If the firm does not produce up to the output at which marginal revenue equals marginal cost, again total profits are less than they could be, because an additional unit sold would increase revenues by more than it would increase costs.

We transfer the marginal revenue and marginal cost curves from columns (6) and (7) in Table 11-1 to Figure 11-3. Marginal revenue equals marginal cost at an output rate of about 10. This is the profit-maximizing rate of output for a pure monopolist; and the optimal output rate is the same as in Figure 11-2.[1]

What price to charge for output?

The monopolist must set the price. He or she is said to be a **price searcher**. What price will be set? The profit-maximizing price, of course, but this is related to the profit-maximizing rate of output. Indeed, these two variables are determined simultaneously. At a profit-maximizing rate of output of 10 in Figure 11-3, the firm can charge a maximum price of $6 and still sell all the goods produced. The maximum price that can be charged for this output is discovered by drawing a vertical line from the profit-maximizing rate of output to the demand curve *DD*. This vertical distance from the horizontal axis to the demand curve gives the profit-maximizing monopoly price.

The procedure for finding the profit-maximizing short-run price-quantity combination for the monopolist is first to determine the profit-maximizing rate of output, either by the total revenue–total cost method or the marginal revenue–marginal cost method, and then to determine by use of the demand schedule *DD* the maximum price that can be charged in order to sell all that output.

What about a monopolist's supply curve?

We were able to derive the single firm's supply curve in a perfectly competitive industry from the firm's marginal cost curve. We were able to derive an industry supply curve by the horizontal summation of all individual firms' marginal cost curves above average variable cost. It would seem, then, that the monopolist's supply curve would be its marginal cost curve because this is how the perfectly competitive supply curve was found.

Even though it would seem so, it turns out *not* to be so. *The monopolist has no supply curve.* A supply curve is defined as the locus of points showing the minimum price at which a given quantity will be forthcoming. There is *no* unique relationship between price and quantity supplied by a monopolist. This can be seen by looking at Figure 11-4. We draw one marginal cost curve MC. The

---

[1]Note that the MC curve must cut the MR curve from *below*.

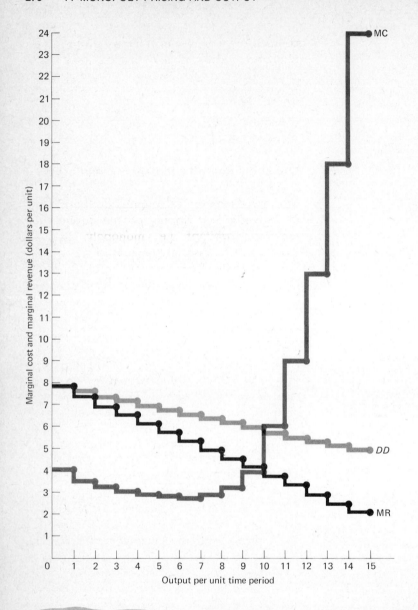

Figure 11-3: Profit maximization: the MR-MC approach.
Profit maximization occurs where marginal revenue equals marginal cost. This is at an output rate of approximately 10. (Also, the MC curve must be cutting the MR curve from *below*.)

first demand curve is D_1D_1. It has a marginal revenue curve MR$_1$. The intersection of marginal revenue and marginal cost curves is at a rate of output per unit time period of Q_1. The monopolist facing this demand curve D_1D_1 will charge a price of P_1.

Now consider another demand situation with the same marginal cost curve. Demand has now shifted to D_2D_2. The marginal reve-

nue curve that results from that is MR$_2$. It intersects the marginal cost curve at a profit-maximizing rate of output per unit time period of Q_2. But as you can see, this rate of output will be sold at the same price P_1 as before. Thus we find that price P_1 is associated with two different rates of output—Q_1 and Q_2. Any particular monopoly price can result in a wide variety of rates of

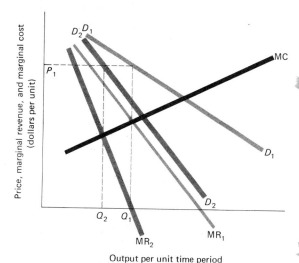

Output per unit time period

Figure 11-4: No supply curve for a monopolist.
Since a supply curve is defined as the locus of points
showing the minimum prices at which given quantities
will be forthcoming, a monopolist does not have a supply
curve. We show two different demand curves D_1D_1 and
D_2D_2 that yield exactly the same profit-maximizing
price but two different quantities supplied by the
monopolist. Hence, there is no unique relationship
between price and quantity supplied by a monopoly.

output, depending on the price elasticity of
demand and the position of the demand
curve. Thus, for a monopolist there is no
unique relationship between price and quantity forthcoming — no supply curve.

Monopoly short-run profit

We have talked about the monopolist maximizing profit, but we have yet to indicate
how much profit the monopolist makes. We
can do this by putting a short-run average
total cost curve (SATC) into Figure 11-3. We
do this in Figure 11-5. When we add the
average total cost curve, we find that the profit
that a monopolist makes is equal to the shaded
area (whose dimensions are P–SATC high
and Q long). In figure 11-5, the monopolist
earns a pure profit in the short run. Perfect

competitors may also earn a pure profit in the
short run. Thus, in the short run, the main
difference between monopoly and perfect
competition is in the slope of the demand
curve. Both types of firms may earn pure
economic profit, and of course, either may
incur a loss.

Monopoly doesn't necessarily mean profits

The term "monopoly" conjures up the notion
of a greedy firm ripping off the public and
making exorbitant, i.e., monopoly, profits.
However, the mere existence of a monopoly
does not guarantee monopoly profits. Look at
Figure 11-6. Here we show the demand curve
facing the monopolist as DD and the resultant
marginal revenue curve as MR. It does not
matter at what rate of output this particular
monopolist operates; total costs cannot be covered. Look at the position of the average total
cost curve. It lies everywhere above DD (the
average revenue curve). Thus, there is no
price-output combination that will allow the
monopolist to earn monopoly profits. This
monopolist will always suffer economic losses.
The diagram in Figure 11-6 depicts a situation
for millions upon millions of typical monopolies that exist; they are called inventions. The owner of a patented invention or
discovery has a pure legal monopoly, but the
demand and cost curves may be such that it is
not profitable to produce. Every year there are
inventors' conventions where one can see
many inventions that have never been put
into production or innovated, having been
deemed "uneconomic" by potential users.

Multiplant short-run equilibrium

Consider for a moment how a firm should
operate two plants so as to maximize profits in
the short run. We examined this problem in
the last chapter. It was easily solved when
we realized that the plants should be

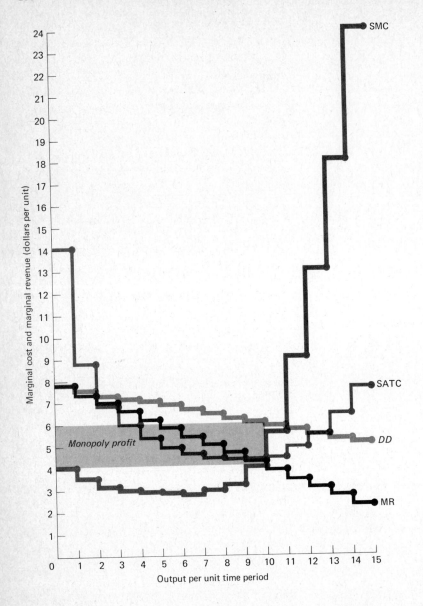

Figure 11-5: Monopoly profit.
We find monopoly profit by subtracting total costs from total revenues at an output rate of 10, which is approximately the profit-maximizing rate of output for the monopolist. Monopoly profit is given by the shaded area. This diagram is similar to Figure 11-3, except that we have added the short-run average total cost curve SATC.

operated at an output rate such that marginal cost in plant 1 is equal to marginal cost in plant 2, both being equal to price. The monopolist would act similarly; the rule would be changed to

$$MC_1 = MC_2 = MC = MR$$

With two plants that have different marginal cost curves, the monopolist's marginal cost curve for operating both plants can be derived by running both plants in different combinations of rates such that *total* cost is minimized at each output rate. This can be seen by looking at an example in Table 11-2. The first column is the rate of output, the second column is the marginal cost in plant 1,

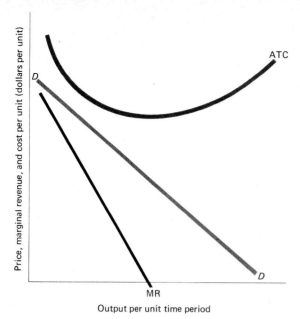

Price, marginal revenue, and cost per unit (dollars per unit)

Output per unit time period

Figure 11-6: Monopolies aren't always profitable.
This diagram depicts the situation confronting some monopolists. The average total cost curve ATC is everywhere above the average revenue or demand curve DD.

Now, what about a rate of output of 2 per unit time period? If both units are produced in plant 1, marginal cost is $5. However, if 1 unit is produced in plant 1 and 1 unit in plant 2, marginal cost is $4. Thus, marginal cost for the firm at a rate of output of 2 is $4. For a rate of output of 3 per unit time period, if all 3 are produced in plant 1, marginal cost is $6. However, if 2 are produced in plant 1, marginal cost is $5, and the one produced in plant 2 will yield the marginal cost of $4. Finally, at a rate of output of 4, the firm can minimize total cost by producing 3 units per unit time period in plant 1 at a marginal cost of $6 and 1 unit per unit time period in plant 2 at a cost of $4; the firm's marginal cost at a rate of output of 4 is $6 per unit.

We have transferred the information from Table 11-2 onto Figure 11-7. MC_1 is the marginal cost curve for plant 1. MC_2 is the marginal cost curve for plant 2. Their horizontal summation is labeled ΣMC. In other words, we have added the horizontal distance between the vertical axis and any point on MC_1 to the horizontal distance between the vertical axis and MC_2 to derive the points that we connect for ΣMC. We then draw in a hypothetical demand curve with its resultant marginal revenue curve MR. Profits are maximized where marginal revenue equals marginal cost or where the MR curve intersects ΣMC. This is at a rate of output of 3 units per unit time period for which the monopolist can charge a charge P_m per unit (which is approximately equal to $10.40).

The monopolist will operate each plant so that marginal cost in each plant is equal to the marginal revenue from selling the combined outputs. Marginal revenue and marginal cost at the profit-maximizing rate of output is given by C_1 on the vertical axis in Figure 11-7 and is approximately equal to $4.80. In order to produce 3 units per unit time period, the monopolist will produce approximately 1.2 units in plant 2, which is q_2 on the horizontal

and the third column is the marginal cost in plant 2. Now we derive the sixth column, which is the marginal cost for the monopoly firm (both plants taken together). At a rate of output of 1 per unit time period, it is clear that the firm would operate plant 1 at that rate and not operate plant 2 at all. The marginal cost for the firm, therefore, at that rate of output is $3.

Output	MC_1 ($/unit)	MC_2 ($/unit)	Output Plant 1	Plant 2	MC ($/unit)
1	3	4	1	0	3
2	5	7	1	1	4
3	6	9	2	1	5
4	8	10	3	1	6
5	.	.	.	.	.
6	.	.	.	.	.
7	.	.	.	.	.

Table 11-2: Multiplant Monopoly

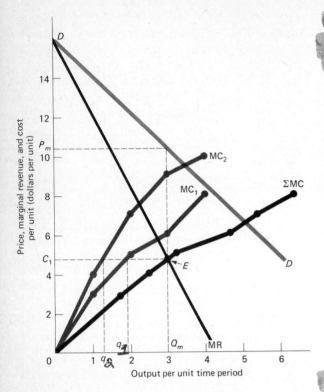

Figure 11-7: Profit maximization for the multiplant monopolist.

The multiplant monopolist with two plants faces marginal cost curves MC_1 and MC_2. The horizontal summation of these two cost curves gives ΣMC. The profit-maximizing rate of output is at the intersection of ΣMC with MR. Now the firm produces such that $MC_1 = MC_2 = MC$. Plant 1 will operate at an output rate of approximately 1.8; plant 2 will operate at an output rate of approximately 1.2.

axis, and 1.8 units in plant 1, which is q_1 on the horizontal axis. Notice that there is a slight difference between the marginal cost per unit for a rate of output of 3 in Table 11-2 and C_1 in Figure 11-7. In Table 11-2, we see in the last column that the marginal cost per unit per 3 units of output per unit time period is equal to $5; however, in this table we do not allow for continuous production rates where fractions of a unit can be produced. In other words,

production is depicted in discrete units. In Figure 11-7, however, we allow for the possibility that fractions of a unit can be produced per unit time period. Thus, the marginal cost at the rate of output of 3 is slightly less than $5, as is given in Table 11-2.

On the existence of long-run monopoly profits

Can monopoly profits persist in the long run? Some economists will answer no to this question not because the monopoly loses its monopoly power, but because any monopoly (economic) profits will be capitalized and thus included in the average total cost curve. We have referred to this when we talked about the suspicious nature of the ATC curve back on page 246. In other words, if a monopoly is really making monopoly profits and you were to purchase the monopoly firm, you would have to pay a price that reflected the (discounted) present value of those monopoly profits forever after. The average total cost curve that you would face would therefore be higher than the average total cost curve that the original owner of the monopoly faced.[2] Consider the situation where one firm somehow obtained the legal right to be the only food concession on your campus. That firm would have a monopoly in selling food *on* campus. Assume that the company is making monopoly profits every year it is in operation and is expected to continue to do so. How much do you think you would have to pay for that firm to take over its entire business on campus? Most likely, you would have to pay a price that reflected the expectation that it would make monopoly profits into the future as long as no other firm were allowed to compete with it on

---

[2]The analysis of losses is symmetric; they are capitalized into the market value of the monopoly. The ATC curve would shift down.

campus. You would expect, therefore, to end up making a normal, or competitive, rate of return on your investment, given that you had to pay a price which reflected the expectation of future monopoly profits. Only the original owner of the firm would benefit directly from the monopoly position bestowed upon that firm by the school administration. But a sale does not have to take place for the implicit price of a resource to change. The opportunity cost to the monopolist remains the same whether or not the monopoly firm is actually sold.

We can compare a long-run average cost curve for a monopolist with and without the capitalization of the monopoly profits included in the costs.

This is shown in Figure 11-8. The standard long-run average cost curve (an "envelope" of all the short-run average cost curves) is given by LAC. Assume for the moment that at rates of output Q_1 and Q_2, a normal competitive rate of return is earned on investment (TR = TC). In other words, at output rates of Q_1 and Q_2, the monopolist earns a rate of return equivalent to what could be earned in a competitive industry (with the same amount of risk). Thus at output rates less than Q_1 and more than Q_2, the monopolist will incur pure economic losses. Between those two points the monopolist receives monopoly profits. Thus we can come up with a new long-run average cost curve labeled LAC'. It includes in it *capitalized* monopoly profits (both positive and negative). It clearly lies below LAC to the left and to the right of rates of output Q_1 and Q_2, but in between those two rates of output it lies above LAC.

Measuring monopoly market power

It is one thing to say that a monopoly exists; it is quite another to measure the *degree* to which it exists. There are several methods that

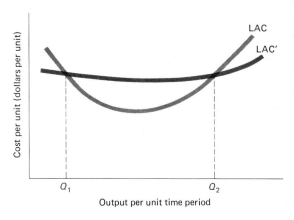

Figure 11-8: Including capitalized monopoly profits in the long-run average cost curve.
LAC is a typical long-run average cost curve for a monopolist. Assume that to the left of output rate Q_1, the monopoly would earn economic losses. This is also true to the right of output rate Q_2. In between those two output rates, the monopoly would earn economic profit; however, if the firm were sold, the losses or profits would be capitalized into the sale price and thus included in the new owner's total cost. If we include the capitalized value of monopoly profits (positive and negative) as a cost, we come up with the long-run average cost curve LAC', which is flatter than LAC.

have been used by economists in an attempt to measure monopoly market power that arises from the negative slope of the demand curve. None of these measures is completely satisfactory.

Industry concentration

Sometimes the measure of monopoly power is given by the amount of industry concentration. Industry concentration can be measured in a number of ways. The most popular is the percentage of total sales or production accounted for by, say, the top four or top eight firms. Thus, a four-firm **concentration ratio**, as it is called, of 80 percent implies more monopoly power than a four-firm concentration ratio of 50 percent. An example of an industry with 25 firms is given below.

	Sales	
Firm 1	$150,000,000	
Firm 2	100,000,000	
Firm 3	80,000,000	= $400,000,000
Firm 4	70,000,000	
Firms 5–25	50,000,000	
Total	$450,000,000	

$$\text{4-firm concentration ratio} = \frac{\$400,000,000}{\$450,000,000} = 88.9\%$$

Although at first glance the concentration ratio seems to be a useful measure of monopoly power, it has a serious shortcoming: Monopoly power is a function not only of a firm's market share but of potential supply from either existing firms or firms that could enter the industry. As Paul Samuelson pointed out,[3] an industry concentration ratio could be 100 percent—i.e., one firm—and yet the monopoly power of that one firm could be zero if the potential supply elasticity is great enough. In other words, a price which yields monopoly profits in this situation will cause the existing monopoly to be deluged by new entrants into the industry.

The Lerner Index

An economist named Abba Lerner has given us another measure of monopoly power that skirts the necessity of inferring the degree of monopoly power from sales data. This index is

Lerner Index of monopoly power $= \dfrac{P - MC}{P}$ (11-2)

where P = the price of the product and MC = marginal cost of production of the product. In essence, this index looks at the per-

---

[3]Paul A. Samuelson, *Foundations of Economic Analysis* (New York: Atheneum, 1965), p. 79.

Concentration ratios (Percent)

| | Share of value of shipments accounted for by the: | | | |
	Largest four companies		Largest eight companies	
	1967	1972	1967	1972
Motor vehicles	92	93	98	99
Primary copper	77	72	98	*
Aircraft	69	66	89	86
Synthetic rubber	61	62	82	81
Blast furnaces and steel mills	48	45	66	65
Industrial trucks and tractors	48	50	62	66
Construction machinery	41	43	53	54
Petroleum	33	31	57	56
Papermills	26	24	43	40
Meatpacking	26	22	38	37
Newspapers	16	17	25	28
Fluid milk	22	18	30	26

*Withheld by Commerce Department to avoid disclosing figures for individual companies.
Source: U.S. Department of Commerce

formance of a monopolist. This index measures the degree to which price deviates from marginal cost. For example, if MC = $5 and monopoly price = $10, then the Lerner Index =

$$\frac{\$10 - \$5}{\$10} = 0.5,$$

or 50 percent.

The Lerner Index of monopoly power requires the ability to measure marginal cost. This is not an easy task, to say the least. Moreover, price must refer to a constant-quality unit. Thus the researcher attempting to compute the Lerner Index of monopoly power in order to compare firms in an industry has to be sure that he or she has quantified all qualitative aspects of the product.

Comparing pure monopoly with perfect competition

We can compare competition and monopoly from two perspectives—costs and output rates. Strictly speaking, in order to compare monopoly with competition, we must first obtain the long-run equilibrium of the pure monopolist. We know that in the long run, if the monopolist can find no plant size that at least results in a competitive rate of return, the monopolist will go out of business. If, on the other hand, the monopolist is making a profit in the short run with one plant size, that monopolist must determine if an even greater profit can be obtained with a larger or a smaller plant size. As with the long-run equilibrium of a competitive firm, the monopolist will adjust plant size so that he or she is operating on the long-run average cost curve.

The long-run profit-maximizing rate of output will be such that long-run marginal cost equals marginal revenue. (See Figure 10-15 in Chapter 10. The only difference will be in the downward slope of the demand curve and the resultant marginal revenue curve which is below the demand curve.)

Comparing costs

Conceptually, in the long run, a perfectly competitive firm operates with an optimal plant size such that short-run average cost = long-run average cost = marginal revenue = price (= average revenue) = long-run marginal cost = short-run marginal cost. This is seen in Figure 11-9 (*a*). However, compare this situation with the long-run equilibrium for the single-plant monopolist depicted in panel (*b*) of Figure 11-9. The profit-maximizing

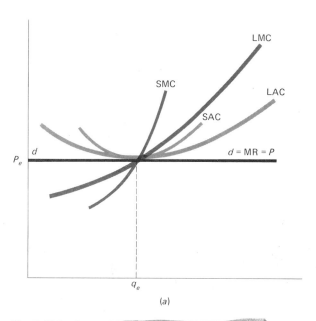

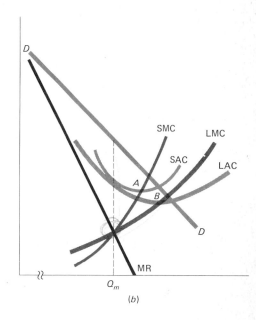

(*a*) (*b*)

Figure 11-9: Comparing monopoly and competitive costs.
In panel (*a*) we show long-run equilibrium for a perfectly competitive firm. Its rate of output q_e is such that SMC = SAC = LAC = LMC = MR = P. Moreover, average total cost is at a minimum. In panel (*b*) we show the situation for a monopolist. At the profit-maximizing rate of output Q_m, the monopolist is not operating at the minimum point A on its short-run average cost curve SAC, nor at the minimum point B on its LAC curve.

rate of output is Q_m. It is the output at which long-run marginal cost = marginal revenue = short-run marginal cost. But at that rate of output, neither short-run average cost nor LAC is at a minimum. The minimum SAC occurs at point A, where SMC intersects SAC. The scale of plant will not be such that either short-run and/or long-run average costs are a minimum at the rate of output chosen to maximize profits. Thus, in comparing monopoly with competition, some observers infer from a comparison of panels (*a*) and (*b*) that monopoly is inefficient because average costs are not at a minimum. Note that the only way this statement could have any possible meaning is if the cost curves facing a monopoly and the set of pure competitors would be exactly the same if we switched from one market structure to the other market structure; this is a heroic assumption. Let us keep the assumption for the moment and compare the long-run price and output combinations in the two extreme market structures.

Comparing price and output under the two market structures

In Figure 11-10, we have drawn an industry demand schedule DD. Assume now that the industry is perfectly competitive and that each competitor has a horizontal marginal cost curve depicted by the horizontal line MC. Thus the horizontal summation of each firm's marginal cost curve is going to be the horizontal line at price P_c. The intersection, then, of the industry supply curve, which is MC, will be at E; the market-clearing price will be P_c and an equilibrium quantity will be Q_c. Now we assume that overnight the industry is fully monopolized—say, by government fiat—and owned by one person, and further that all cost curves remain exactly the same. The monopolist sets the rate of output where marginal cost = marginal revenue. (Perfect competitors do also, but for them MR = P.) The monopolist, then, sets the rate of output at Q_m. The

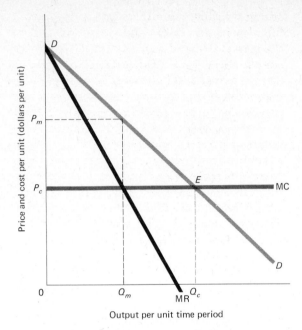

Figure 11-10: Comparing price and output for monopoly in competition.

Assume constant marginal cost for the industry. Given an industry demand curve DD, and assuming that the industry supply curve is MC, the competitive industry output would be Q_c; the industry price would be P_c. Now consider the possibility that all firms become a single-monopoly firm overnight and that there are no changes in costs. The profit-maximizing rate of output will now fall to Q_m; the price will go up to P_m. The conclusion is that monopolization of a perfectly competitive industry restricts production and increases price, *ceteris paribus.*

monopolist can sell this rate of output at a price of P_m. Thus, under the assumption that the cost curves remain the same when the industry goes from competition to monopoly, we can state that the monopolist restricts production and raises price.

Competition and monopoly with strong cost advantages

If there are strong cost advantages at the firm level, then it is conceivable that a monopoly could be selling more output at a lower price than a group of numerous competitors selling the same product. Consider this possibility in Figure 11-11. Here we have shown the market demand curve as DD. The market supply curve under competition is, for numerous firms, ΣMC. It is the horizontal summation of all individual firms' marginal cost curves above the minimum point of their average variable cost curves. Equilibrium occurs at price P_c and quantity at Q_c. Now assume that the firms are monopolized. If there are really substantial cost advantages, the new marginal cost curve will be everywhere below the old industry supply curve. This new marginal cost curve is labeled MC for a monopolist. The monopolist will set the rate of output where marginal revenue = marginal cost. This rate of output will be Q_m. The monopolist will be able to sell that rate of output at a price of P_m. In this case, monopoly leads to an increase in the rate of output sold at a lower price.

Price discrimination

In a perfectly competitive market, each buyer is charged the same price for the particular commodity (corrected, of course, for quality differences and differential transportation charges). Since the product is homogeneous and since we also assume full knowledge on the part of the buyers, a difference in price per constant-quality unit could not exist. Any seller of the product who tried to charge a price higher than the going market price would find that no one would purchase from him or her. In this chapter, we have assumed up until now that the monopolist charged all consumers the same price. A monopolist, however, may be able to charge different people different prices and/or different unit prices for successive units sought by a given buyer. This is called **price discrimination**. It must be made clear at the outset that different prices charged to different people which reflect differences in the cost of service to those particular people is *not* price discrimination. This is **price differentiation**, or differences in prices which reflect differences in marginal cost.

We can turn this around to say that a uniform price does not necessarily indicate an absence of price discrimination. If costs are different and different people are charged the same price, then this is also a case of price discrimination.

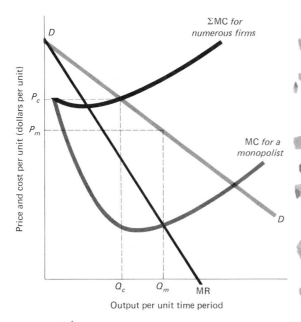

Figure 11-11: Monopoly with strong cost advantage.
Assume that the horizontally summed marginal cost curve ΣMC for a competitive situation is given as drawn. Now the firm is monopolized, and it experiences tremendous cost advantages such that the marginal cost curve for the monopolist falls dramatically as drawn. Profit-maximizing rate of output goes from Q_c out to Q_m and, price falls from P_c to P_m.

Necessary conditions for price discrimination to exist

For price discrimination to be possible, there must first of all be at least two identifiable classes of buyers whose price elasticities of demand for the product are different; and the monopolist must know the relative price elasticities. Further, it is necessary that these two or more identifiable classes of buyers can be separated at a reasonable cost. Additionally, the monopolist must be able to prevent, at least partially, the resale by those buyers who paid a low price to those buyers who would be charged a higher price. Charging students a

lower price for a movie than nonstudents can be done relatively easily. The cost of checking out student IDs is apparently not significant. Also, it is fairly easy to make sure that students do not resell their tickets to nonstudents.

We know that for profit to be at a maximum, marginal revenue must equal marginal cost. For the monopolist who is able to discriminate

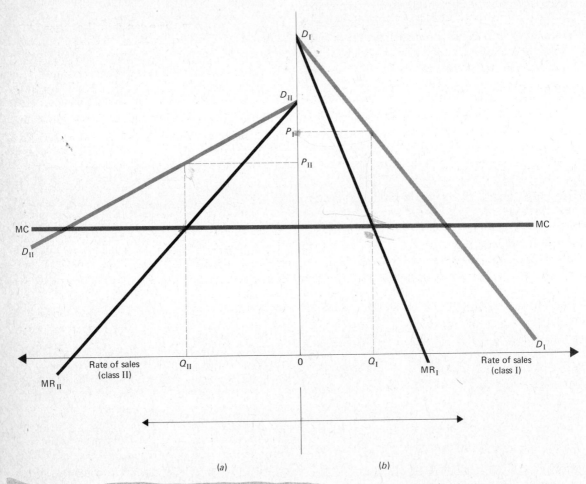

(a)   (b)

Figure 11-12: Price discrimination with constant marginal cost.
Assume that the monopolist has been able to separate two classes of demanders, I and II. The profit-maximizing rate of output for each class will be given by the respective intersection of MR_I amd MR_{II} with the common marginal cost MC. The output rate for class I demanders will be Q_I; the price charged will be P_I. For class II demanders the price will be lower, P_{II}. The demand curve for class II consumers is more elastic at any given P because it cuts the vertical axis closer to the origin.

between two classes of buyers, I and II, for profit to be a maximum, $MR_I = MR_{II} = MC$. It is as if the goods sold to class I and class II were two *different* goods having exactly the same marginal cost of production. In other words, to maximize total profits, the monopolist wants to set marginal revenue equal to marginal cost in all markets in which he or she is selling. If marginal revenue in market I exceeded marginal cost, profits could be increased by expanding sales (lowering price) in market I. The same holds for market II. On the other hand, if marginal revenue in market I (or market II) were less than marginal cost, profit could be increased by reducing sales (raising price) in market I (or II).

We show this in Figure 11-12. Class I buyers are presented in panel (*b*), class II buyers in panel (*a*). Note that in panel (*a*), the rate of sales to class II buyers gets larger as we move from right to left. We assume for simplicity's sake that the marginal cost for servicing both classes of consumers is both equal and constant. Marginal cost equals marginal revenue for class I at quantity Q_I. The price at which this quantity can be sold is P_I. On the other hand, for buyers in class II who have a more elastic demand curve (at any given P) than in class I buyers, the intersection of marginal cost with MR_{II} is at quantity Q_{II}. The price at which this quantity is sold is P_{II}, which is lower than P_I. In other words, the price-discriminating monopolist will sell that same product to the class of buyers with a relatively less elastic demand curve at a higher price than that charged to the other class of buyers who have a relatively higher elasticity of demand.

This can be seen by using the formula in Eq. (11-1) and equating the two marginal revenues:

$$MR_I = P_I(1 + \frac{1}{\eta_I})$$

$$MR_{II} = P_{II}(1 + \frac{1}{\eta_{II}})$$

(11-3)

When we make these two equal (since $MR_I = MR_{II} = MC$), we get

$$P_I(1 + \frac{1}{\eta_I}) = P_{II}(1 + \frac{1}{\eta_{II}})$$

(11-4)

We know, however, that class I buyers have a market demand schedule that is more inelastic than that of class II buyers. In order for the two sides of Eq. (11-4) to be equal, P_I must be greater than P_{II}.

THE GENERAL CASE. We can take the more general case with an upward-sloping marginal cost curve to show the profit-maximizing prices that a price-discriminating monopolist will charge to two identifiably different classes of demanders. In Figure 11-13, we have shown a demand curve for class I as $D_I D_I$. Its marginal revenue curve is labeled MR_I. Class II demanders have a demand curve represented by $D_{II} D_{II}$ and a marginal revenue curve of MR_{II}. In this case, the relative elasticity of demand is numerically greater for class II demanders than for class I demanders. (This is so even though $D_{II} D_{II}$ at first glance looks more inelastic than $D_I D_I$ because it is steeper; however, remember from Chapter 5 that we cannot determine the elasticity of demand by the *slope* of the demand curve. Using the vertical axis formula for elasticity, we found in Chapter 5 that whichever demand curve intersects the vertical axis closer to the origin will be the relatively more elastic.)

We now derive the summed marginal revenue curve labeled $MR_I + MR_{II}$ in Figure 11-13. Here we are horizontally summing the two separate marginal revenue curves. The horizontally summed marginal revenue curve intersects the common marginal cost curve at point E; thus, the profit-maximizing quantity to be produced and sold is Q_m. We now have a specific marginal cost labeled C_1 on the vertical axis. To satisfy the profit maximization criterion, which requires that marginal revenue be equal to marginal cost, a monopolist

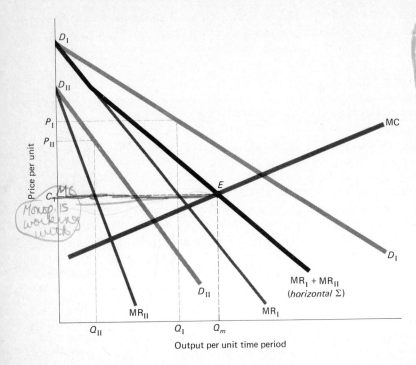

Figure 11-13: Price discrimination—the general case.
We horizontally sum the marginal revenue curves to derive $MR_I + MR_{II}$. The summed marginal revenue curve intersects the common marginal cost curve at point E. The total output rate will be Q_m. It will be distributed between the two classes so that the first receives Q_I and the second receives Q_{II}. We find the prices that the monopolist can charge for those rates of output on their respective demand curves: class I buyers will pay a higher price P_I than the P_{II} charged class II buyers.

will allocate quantity Q_I to class I and Q_{II} to class II, their sum being equal to Q_m. These quantities are given by the respective intersections of specific marginal cost C_I with marginal revenue in each separate market. The prices that will be charged are P_I and P_{II} or the price at which the profit-maximizing quantities can be sold in each individual market. As in the previous example, in the market with the more elastic demand curve, the price will be lower than in the market with the less elastic demand curve, i.e., $P_{II} < P_I$.

The different types of price discrimination

Economists define three different types of price discrimination (there are more if one wishes to stretch the point). They are labeled first, second, and third degree. What we have just talked about is third-degree price discrimination.

THIRD-DEGREE PRICE DISCRIMINATION. **Third-degree price discrimination** occurs when a monopolist charges different prices in different markets for the same product. That is exactly what we have shown above. There were two different markets for the product. A higher price was charged in the market with the less elastic demand. Charging students a lower price than nonstudents for movies, magazines, and professional journals is a common example of third-degree price discrimination. Charging senior citizens a lower price than other buyers for movies and spectator events is another common example.

SECOND-DEGREE PRICE DISCRIMINATION **Second-degree price discrimination** is found when there are many markets and many buyers within each market. A declining rate schedule embodying "quantity discounts" is an example of this type of discrimination. Some electric utilities charge lower prices for each additional "block" of electricity used. Anybody who uses a certain amount of electricity can buy the next block at a lower price. Second-degree price discrimination induces greater consumption by offering quantity discounts that are made in a stepladder fashion. This is also called **multipart pricing.**

FIRST-DEGREE PRICE DISCRIMINATION. In **first-degree, or perfect, price discrimination** the monopolist is able to charge each buyer the maximum amount that that person will pay rather than do without the specified quantity of the commodity being offered. Consider, for example, a situation in which you are a diamond purchaser. You go into a small room in which a sack of diamonds is presented to you. You are faced with the choice of "take it or leave it." If the seller of the diamonds can figure out exactly the shape of your demand curve, you can be charged a price which leaves you indifferent to buying or not buying the sack of diamonds. You will then be the "victim" of perfect price discrimination.

Perfect price discrimination allows the monopolist to extract every last bit of consumer surplus from each buyer. Remember that consumer surplus was defined in Chapter 4 as the difference between what the consumer would have paid for a particular quantity of a commodity rather than do without it completely and what the consumer had actually to pay. Here that difference is zero.

Multipart pricing

Multipart pricing involves charging successively lower prices for the marginal unit of a commodity as more of the commodity is purchased. Multipart pricing occurs, for example, in supermarkets when you are allowed to buy one can for 20¢ and two cans for 39¢. In other words, the first can is 20¢ and the marginal cost of the second can is 19¢. A uniform price of 19.5¢ is charged to all those who buy two cans, and so on.[4]

There is a difference between multipart pricing, which is second-degree price discrimination, and first-degree, or perfect, price discrimination. Multipart pricing is an imperfect way to extract as much money as possible from each consumer. It is a way of dealing with broad, discrete intervals of quantity

---

Forms of price discrimination

Type of price discrimination	Attributes	Examples
Third-degree	Different classes of buyers charged different prices for same product.	Student and senior citizen discounts at entertainment events and on public transportation.
Second-degree	Declining rate schedules; lower price per unit as larger quantities purchased.	Electricity pricing; quantity discounts at supermarkets.
First-degree (perfect)	Each buyer charged exactly that price which leaves him or her indifferent between buying and not buying.	Wholesale diamond sales; haggling over prices of souvenirs in "tourist traps."

---

[4]Some economists contend that multipart pricing in supermarkets is not a form of price discrimination, but rather a classic case of price *differentiation*. They point out that supermarkets are highly competitive and that multipart pricing is merely a method by which they economize on transactions costs; e.g., it takes less cashier time per unit sold when larger quantities are purchased. This saving in cashier time is, in essence, "passed on" to the consumer who buys in larger quantities. (A way to reconcile these two hypotheses is to point out that the competitors must use multipart pricing to merely survive.)

purchased and charging appropriate revenue-maximizing prices for each additional unit purchased, without ever selling any unit below MC.

We expect to observe second-degree price discrimination, or multipart pricing, rather than first-degree price discrimination because of the costs of negotiation, monitoring, and enforcing exchanges. It is difficult to determine what the actual price elasticity of demand is for different classes of buyers; it is even more difficult to prevent the resale of goods by buyers who bought the product at a lower price to those who would be charged a higher price if they purchased it from the monopolist.

When price discrimination is required for "existence" of an industry

Sometimes price discrimination is necessary if an industry is to continue to exist (or to begin in the first place.) Consider the situation depicted in Figure 11-14. We have drawn the demand curves for two different classes of buyers of the product in question. Those curves are labeled D_1D_1 and D_2D_2. We know that demand curve D_2D_2 is relatively more price-elastic than D_1D_1 because it cuts the vertical axis closer to the origin. We now horizontally sum these two demand curves in order to derive the total or market demand curve that would face a monopolist in this industry. This demand curve is the heavily shaded line labeled D_1D_T. This market demand curve coincides with the demand curve D_1D_1 until the price at which D_2D_2 begins.

We have drawn in a long-run average cost curve LAC, which is *everywhere* above the market demand curve D_1D_T. Thus, if a single price had to be charged in this market, there is no single price that would allow the monopolist to cover long-run average costs. The industry would not exist.

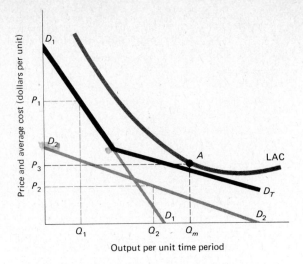

Figure 11-14: Price discrimination necessary for industry's existence.

If the long-run average cost curve is everywhere above the market demand curve D_1D_T, the firm cannot exist without price discrimination. If, however, the monopolist is allowed to charge P_1 to those with less elastic demand and P_2 to those with more elastic demand, then the weighted price P_3 would just equal long-run average cost at point A. The industry can and will exist.

Now consider the possibility of third-degree price discrimination. The profit-maximizing prices for the two different classes of demanders are given as P_1 and P_2. They are derived in the same manner employed in Figure 11-13. We have, for the sake of simplicity, drawn in neither the separate marginal revenue curves nor the horizontally summed marginal revenue curve. The profit-maximizing quantity that would be sold to class 1 demanders is given as Q_1 and to class 2 demanders as Q_2. The total quantity that the price-discriminating monopolist would provide is given as Q_m $(= Q_1 + Q_2)$. It is sold at a (weighted) average price of P_3 which, in this particular example, is just equal to long-run average costs at rate of output Q_m, or point A. The weighted average is

$$P_3 = \frac{Q_1P_1 + Q_2P_2}{Q_m}$$

In this instance, unless price discrimination is both feasible and permitted, the industry will not exist, i.e., the product will not be offered for sale.

A final note—Business pricing behavior

It is not unrealistic to assume that most businesses face downward-sloping demand curves. Although they are not pure monopolists, they are certainly not perfect competitors. A common method of business pricing is called **markup pricing**. It involves tacking a markup of, say, 20 percent or 40 percent onto the unit cost of production. Is such behavior consistent with anything we have said in this chapter? It turns out that it is.

Remember that profit maximization requires in every instance that marginal cost equal marginal revenue. Using the formula for marginal revenue given in Eq. (11-1), if $MC = MR$ and $MR = P(1 + 1/\eta)$, to maximize profits, it is necessary that

$$MC = P\left(1 + \frac{1}{\eta}\right) \qquad (11\text{-}5)$$

Dividing both sides of Eq. (11-5) by $\left(1 + \frac{1}{\eta}\right)$, we find that price equals

$$P = MC\left(\frac{1}{1 + 1/\eta}\right) \qquad (11\text{-}6)$$

which becomes

$$P = MC\left(\frac{1}{\eta/\eta + 1/\eta}\right) = MC\frac{1}{([\eta + 1]/\eta)} \qquad (11\text{-}7)$$

which becomes

$$P = MC\left(\frac{\eta}{\eta + 1}\right) \qquad (11\text{-}8)$$

Now consider the case where there are constant returns to scale over a very wide range of output. With constant returns to scale, long-run average cost equals long-run marginal cost. We also know that LAC is the same as long-run variable cost (in the long run all costs are variable). Thus Eq. (11-8) becomes

$$P = AVC\left(\frac{\eta}{\eta + 1}\right) \qquad (11\text{-}9)$$

Assume, as an example, that $\eta = -4$. Using Eq. (11-9), we obtain

$$\text{Price} = AVC\left(\frac{-4}{-3}\right) = AVC(1.33^{1}/_{3}) \qquad (11\text{-}10)$$

Hence, if $\eta = -4$, then price should be set equal to average costs plus a one-third markup. In other words, markup pricing, based on average costs, may be an attempt by a business to guess at the coefficient of price elasticity of demand.

Issues and applications

Price controls for a monopoly

It turns out that a price control put on a monopolist can result in not only a lower price but a larger quantity supplied. This can be seen in Figure 11-15. The monopolist's demand curve is *DD*, and the resultant marginal revenue curve is labeled MR.

The marginal cost curve (MC) intersects the marginal revenue curve at a rate of output of Q_m which can be sold at a price of P_m. Now assume that the government sets a maximum price of P_{max}. How much will the monopolist produce at this price? We want to find out where marginal revenue = marginal cost. There is a new marginal revenue curve which is different from the old one. It is the heavily shaded line from P_{max} to point *A* on the demand curve, for at quantities from zero to

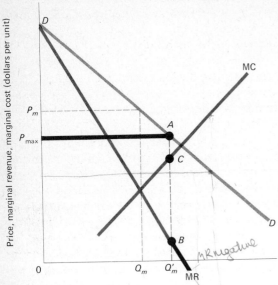

Figure 11-15: Price controls on a monopolist.
If the maximum price is set at P_{max}, then the monopolist can sell all it wants at that price up to quantity Q'_m. Thus, the heavily shaded horizontal line now becomes marginal revenue up to quantity Q'_m. It then has a discontinuous portion from A down to B and is coincident with the old marginal revenue curve thereafter. Profit-maximization requires that MC = MR. This occurs at quantity Q'_m in the discontinuous portion of the new marginal revenue curve. The monopolist's output will have increased (from Q_m to Q'_m) as a result of the price control.

Q'_m they can all be sold at a price of P_{max}, which is the legal maximum price. After point A (quantity Q'_m), however, the monopolist faces the remainder of the downward-sloping demand curve; then the regular marginal revenue curve becomes relevant. We have shown a new marginal revenue curve, then, which is $P_{max}ABMR$; it is discontinuous at quantity Q'_m. The heavily shaded portion on the old marginal revenue curve coincides with the new marginal revenue curve. Marginal cost intersects the discontinuous part of the marginal revenue curve at point C. Thus, for marginal revenue to "equal" marginal cost, the quantity to be sold would be Q'_m at price P_{max}. We find that an effective price control on the monopolist can, in principle, lead to a higher quantity sold with no "shortages."

Shortages would result if the legal maximum price were set below the intersection of the marginal cost curve and the original demand curve. (Can you show why on Figure 11-15?) Moreover, the diagram that we have worked with does not show what the rate of return is to the monopolist. If the price control were set at a price ($P <$ ATC) that results in economic losses, the monopolist would go out of business in the long run.

Do public utilities price discriminate?

It is often asserted that public utilities engage in price discrimination. It turns out that we can, indeed, analyze some of their pricing policies in terms of second-degree price discrimination. Public utilities do use multipart pricing, or what they call declining-block pricing.

Consider Figure 11-16. If the electrical utility wanted to sell the quantity Q_3, it could do so by charging the uniform price of P_3. Its total revenues would be represented by the rectangle $0P_3CQ_3$. However, if it engages in multipart pricing, or second-degree price discrimination, it might charge P_1 for the first Q_1 of kilowatts sold per month. It could charge P_2 for kilowatts sold between Q_1 and Q_2, and then finally it could charge P_3 for kilowatts sold between Q_2 and Q_3. The revenues it would receive would be the sum of the rectangle of $0P_1AQ_1$ plus Q_1DBQ_2 plus Q_2ECQ_3 or $0P_1ADBECQ_3$. The sum of these three rectangles exceeds the rectangle given by uniform pricing of P_3 times the quantity sold, Q_3. (Moreover, multipart pricing yields more revenue than charging the weighted average price.)

The economics of youth fares

Many airlines at different periods have offered youth fares. Those who were under a certain age, usually age twenty-two, were allowed to purchase youth-fare tickets, which were sold at a price lower than the price of the full-fare tickets that adults had to pay. However, the youth-fare-ticket

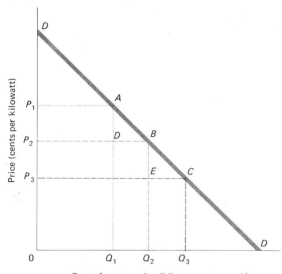

Figure 11-16: Declining block pricing.
Public utilities often use declining block pricing in which separate "blocks" of electricity can be purchased at declining prices. If the electric utility charges a uniform price of P_3, its revenues will be $0P_3CQ_3$. If, however, it charges a price of P_1 for the first Q_1 kilowatts used and then P_2 for the next "block" used up to quantity Q_2 and then price P_3 for the next "block" up to Q_3, its total revenues will equal $0P_1AQ_1 + Q_1DBQ_2 + Q_2ECO_3 = 0P_1ADBECQ_3$.

holder was not guaranteed a seat on a particular flight. Rather, the youth-fare-ticket holder had to accept seating on a standby basis, i.e., show up at the gate prior to the plane's departure and stand by until 10 minutes before flight time. If at that time there were empty seats available, then the ticket was accepted and the youth could board the plane.

This is a form of third-degree price discrimination (although we are referring to different-quality products, because youth-fare tickets involved uncertainty). There is probably a difference in the relative elasticity of demand of young adults and that of, say, business people. The demand of young adults is more elastic than the demand of business people. However, the analysis does not end there. Young adults have more elastic demand curves because their time is usually less valuable than that of business people.

That is to say, the opportunity cost of waiting in a standby system is less for most young adults than for business people. The total price of a trip by airplane is the money price of the ticket plus the opportunity cost of going to the airport, waiting in line, boarding the plane, sitting in the plane, and so on. The lower the opportunity cost, the greater the percentage of the total price of airplane travel is accounted for by the money price. Say that the money price of a plane flight is $100 and that the total time involved in waiting, boarding the plane, flying, etc., is 5 hours. If a young person's opportunity cost is $3 per hour, then the total price to the young adult for the plane flight is $100 + (5 · $3) = $115. Thus, the money price as a fraction of the total price is equal to $100/$115, or 87 percent. Now take the case of a person in business whose opportunity cost is, say, $20 per hour. The total price to this person is then $100 + (5 · $20) = $200. The money price of the plane flight expressed as a fraction of the total price is equal to $100/$200, or 50 percent. Thus, for those with a low opportunity cost, the observed demand curve for air travel in terms of the money price of the ticket may be more elastic. Hence, it makes sense to charge a lower price for youths than for adults. Their relative differences in opportunity cost leads to differences in the relative money price elasticities of demand.

On not making the punishment fit the crime

Crime is a large business in the United States. Individuals enter the crime industry for many reasons. One can identify at least two classes of criminals: professionals who can be treated as if they made rational cost-benefit calculations of the profitability of entering the illegal-activity industry (as opposed to a legal-activity industry); and those who become criminals either because of insanity or for emotional reasons.

If we assume, then, that the supply curve for illegal activities is less elastic for the insane and those who commit unpremeditated crimes than for other criminals, we can perhaps justify a differential set of penalties (costs) for the two different types of criminals who are convicted of the same illegal conduct. In other words, we wish to discriminate in setting penalties for criminal activity by making the penalty depend on whether the criminal was insane or not.

In fact, insane and unpremeditating criminals are generally punished less severely for a particular crime than someone who commits exactly the same crime but who is considered a rational and calculating criminal. Looked at in a slightly different manner, the imposition of a given punishment will have less effect on the quantity supplied by the insane than on the quantity supplied by the rational and calculating. Price discrimination involves not bothering too much about reducing the rate of return to criminal activity for the insane, where the elasticity of supply with respect to punishment is lower than for the sane.

We may be able to explain why judges are given fairly wide discretion in sentencing. The judge is allowed to decide if the person who committed the crime was insane or mentally incompetent and to mete out a lower sentence. However, we have to realize that resources will be spect *after the fact* trying to prove that the alleged guilty party is mentally incompetent. Our economic model helps us predict that criminals, actual and potential, will respond differently to changes in the "price" of engaging in criminal activity. But then, the same model will predict that if "insane" individuals get lighter sentences, those on trial will attempt to prove, *ex post*, their "insanity" at the time of the violation.

The pricing of textbooks: Is there a conflict between publisher and author

You are reading a textbook that I wrote. The publisher, the McGraw-Hill Book Company, decided on the price. It used a complicated formula which included such expected costs as the price of paper, printing and binding, art work, and so on. The price at which it arrived is most likely close to the prices of other competing books for intermediate price theory courses. The publisher knows,

after all, that it cannot set the price significantly above competing books without reducing its potential sales significantly (the price elasticity of demand is not zero).

It would seem that the publisher and the author would be working jointly toward the same goal. After all, they both want to make the highest rate of return possible; it turns out, however, that there is a conflict between the best interests of the publisher and those of the author. Whatever the price at which this book is selling when you buy it, I as an author would be better-off if it were sold at a lower price.

Two profit-maximizing prices

Authors are typically paid a royalty which is a fixed percentage of the total revenues or receipts of sales obtained by the publisher. Authors want to have total sales revenues as high as possible because this will maximize their royalties. The cost to the author *once the book has been written* is zero. In other words, the marginal cost to the author is equal to zero. Profit maximization from the author's point of view means maximizing total sales revenues. This is shown in Figure 11-17. Profit maximization occurs at the level of sales at which the marginal revenue curve intersects the horizontal axis (the author's marginal cost curve and is so labeled), or where marginal revenue equals zero. This level of sales would be obtained if the price were set at P_{author}. At that price, the elasticity of demand is equal to -1.[5]

However, consider the fact that the publisher does not have a marginal cost equal to 0. Rather, the publisher incurs, at the very minimum, additional paper, printing, and binding costs to produce one more unit of output. Thus, if we draw in the marginal cost curve $MC_{\text{McGraw-Hill}}$ in Figure 11-17 for the publisher, we find that the publisher's profit-maximizing price $P_{\text{McGraw-Hill}}$ is neces-

---

[5]Remember the formula $MR = P[1 + (1/\eta)]$. When $MR = 0$, $0 = P[1 + (1/\eta)]$; divide by P to get $0 = 1 + (1/\eta)$ or $-1 = 1/\eta$; multiply by $-\eta$ to get $\eta = -1$.

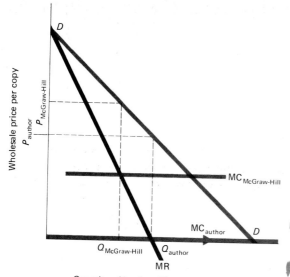

Figure 11-17: The conflict between publisher and author.
McGraw-Hill faces a marginal revenue curve MR and a
marginal cost curve $MC_{McGraw-Hill}$. It would like to set the
quantity produced of the textbook at $Q_{McGraw-Hill}$ and sell
that quantity at a price of $P_{McGraw-Hill}$. The author, however is paid a royalty based on a fixed percentage of total
revenues from the book. The author's marginal cost curve
is coincident with the horizontal axis because the author
has no marginal cost *once the book has been written.* We
know that total revenues are greater when the price
elasticity of demand equals minus unity or at that rate
of output at which marginal revenue equals zero. Thus,
the author would prefer the larger output Q_{author} to be
sold at the lower per unit price of P_{author}. That is also
where $MR = MC_{author} = 0$.

sarily higher than the author's profit-maximizing
price, which is labeled P_{author}. The textbook author is therefore constantly in conflict with his or
her publisher. It is not surprising, then, that when
queried, publishers often indicate that their authors frequently argue for a lower price. One observer of the publishing scene many years ago
argued that this was because authors overes-
timate the price elasticity of demand and underestimate the cost of production. The latter point is
irrelevant, however, to the author. Those costs
are irrelevent because the author does not incur
them. As long as the author believes that the publisher has set the price in the elastic region of the

demand curve, the author will always find it in his
or her best interests to argue for a lower price.[6]

Pricing books that are not equally successful

One often finds even within the same textbook
company that the same price is charged for books
that are differentially successful. Some have
argued that this is inconsistent with the maximization of the firm's profits. We can show in
Figure 11-18 that this is not the case. Consider
two intermediate price theory books published by
McGraw-Hill. One sells twice as many copies at
each and every price as the other, i.e., its demand
curve DD is twice the other's demand curve
$\frac{1}{2}D\frac{1}{2}D$. If the elasticity of demand is the same
for both intermediate price theory books at each
and every price (and it is in this case), then the
profit-maximizing price for the firm will be the
same.

Note that DD and $\frac{1}{2}D\frac{1}{2}D$ start from the same
point on the vertical axis. Using the vertical
formula for price elasticity of demand, we know
that at each and every price, both of these demand curves will have exactly the same price
elasticity of demand.

We assume that marginal costs are constant
and draw in a marginal cost curve MC which is
horizontal. (This is not an unreasonable assumption in textbook publishing.) We need two more
curves in order to find the profit-maximizing rate
of output and price to be charged for each book.
The curves we must draw in are the marginal reve-
nue curves that are marginal to DD and $\frac{1}{2}D\frac{1}{2}D$.
They are labeled MR_1 and $\frac{1}{2}MR$. Note that the demand curve for the less successful textbook,
$\frac{1}{2}D\frac{1}{2}D$, is coincident with the marginal revenue
curve MR_1 for the more successful textbook,
because we have assumed that the demand curve
for the latter is twice the demand curve for the
former. (Remember that the marginal revenue
curve for a straight-line demand curve always

---

[6]See Stanley Unwin, *The Truth about Publishing* (New
York: Macmillan, 1960).

bisects the distance between the demand curve and the origin on the horizontal axis. See page 117.)

We see in Figure 11-18 that at the profit-maximizing rate of output for the more successful book (where MC = MR at quantity Q_1) the profit-maximizing price is P. However, at the profit-maximizing rate of output for the less successful book found at quantity Q_2, we see that the profit-maximizing price is also P. Thus, it is not inconsistent with profit maximization for a textbook publisher to charge exactly the same price for two books when one is decidedly more successful than the other. Otherwise stated, so long as the demand curves intersect the vertical axis at the same point, there is no incentive to price discriminate.

Same elasticity

IBM machines and IBM Cards

International Business Machines Corporation has been the leader in the computer field since that industry began. For many years, IBM would only rent its computing and tabulating machines to users; it would not sell them. The rental agreement was generally expressed as a fee per shift per unit time period (a month, for example). Until recently, IBM required that the users buy tabulating cards only from IBM. If the machines broke down and IBM's technicians found that the renting firms were using someone else's cards, IBM imposed a penalty by imposing a charge for repairs. This is the method that the company used to police its requirement that no one else's cards be purchased.

At first glance, one may not immediately understand why IBM bothered to require that its own cards be purchased and, secondly, why it bothered to police such an agreement. However, if we think in terms of IBM as a monopolist, then we can come up with a prediction from a price-discriminating monopoly model that is consistent with past IBM pricing practices. We know from the theory in this chapter that higher profits can be obtained by price discrimination; however, it is

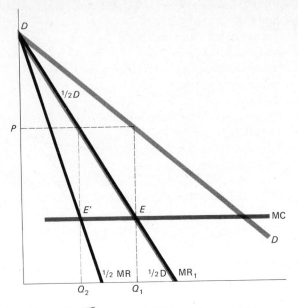

Figure 11-18: The pricing of differentially successful books.
Assume that there are two intermediate price theory books. One has a demand that is twice the demand for the other. The more successful book's demand curve is DD; the less successful book's is $\frac{1}{2}D\frac{1}{2}D$. Assume marginal cost is constant and equal to MC. The quantity to be produced for the more successful book will be Q_1, and it will be sold at price P. The quantity produced of the unsuccessful book will be Q_2, and it also will be sold at price P. The reason the price is the same is that at any price the elasticity of DD and $\frac{1}{2}D\frac{1}{2}D$ is the same. (Why?)

necessary to have information on the different price elasticities of demand for different classes of users. One way that IBM could approximate its users' price elasticity of demand is by *intensity of use*—those who use their machines more presumably had a relatively lower price elasticity of demand for computing services. One of the ways to monitor intensity of use is by the number of tabulating cards used. That is exactly why IBM required that only its cards be used. They provided an index of use intensity and, hence, relative elasticity of demand.

Now this argument would make little sense if IBM had not charged those who used more cards a higher price per unit of computing services than those who used fewer cards, and the company did just that. It charged a price for cards that was in excess of their marginal cost. Its price per unit of computing services was effectively higher to those with the lower elasticity of demand, i.e., those who used more cards. It chose this method of price discrimination rather than overtly charging a higher rental fee to different users. Perhaps this latter pricing technique was deemed too overt a form of price discrimination and therefore subject to antitrust prosecution.

Nonetheless, various antitrust actions against IBM have resulted in the discontinuation of this particular pricing practice. Under Justice Department pressure, IBM agreed to "cease and desist" its dual practice of renting only hardware and requiring the purchase of its own cards.

Glossary

Monopolist Single seller or supplier of a well-defined commodity for which there are no close substitutes.

Nondiscriminating monopoly A monopolist that charges a uniform price to all buyers.

Discriminating monopoly A monopolist that charges different buyers different prices for an identical product.

Price searcher A firm that does not take as given the price at which it can sell its product; rather, it searches out the profit-maximizing price-output combination; to be contrasted with price taker.

Concentration ratio The percentage of total sales or shipments in an industry accounted for by a specified number of firms, such as the top four or the top eight.

Lerner Index of monopoly power A measure of supposed monopoly power given by the ratio $(P - MC)/P$, where $P = $ price and $MC = $ marginal cost.

Price discrimination Charging different classes of buyers a different price for an identical product; or alternatively, charging the same price for products that have different marginal costs.

Price differentiation Price differences which reflect differences in marginal cost.

Third-degree price discrimination Different classes of demanders are distinguished by their relative price elasticities of demand; those with relatively inelastic demands pay a higher price than those with relatively more elastic demands.

Second-degree price discrimination Discrimination on the basis of quantity purchased. A declining rate schedule embodying quantity discounts is an example.

Multipart pricing A type of second-degree price discrimination in which the customer is charged a successively lower price for each marginal unit as more is purchased.

First-degree, or perfect, price discrimination A combination of first- and second-degree price discrimination in which every bit of consumer surplus is extracted from each consumer.

Markup pricing A type of business practice in which a profit margin of some specified amount (20 or 40 percent, for example) is added on to the unit cost of production to determine the price.

Summary

1. A pure monopolist is the only firm in the industry and faces the industry demand curve, which is, by necessity, downward-sloping. The demand curve facing a monopolist will be more elastic the more numerous, better, and cheaper are the substitutes. However, there is a trade-off between closeness of substitutes and number; a large number of imperfect substitutes will lead to an elastic demand curve in the same manner that a few good substitutes will do so.
2. Since price elasticity of demand for the monopolist's product is numerically greater than 0 and less than $-\infty$, marginal revenue is less than price.
3. The monopolist will never willingly operate on the inelastic portion of the demand curve.
4. Monopoly marginal revenue is greater in the long run than in the short run because it takes time for buyers to respond to price changes.
5. The profit maximizing price-output combination is found by discovering that rate of output at which $MR = MC$ and then determining the

maximum price at which that quantity can be sold.

6. A monopolist does not have a supply curve (defined as the locus of points showing the minimum prices at which given quantities will be offered for sale). Any particular monopoly price can result in a wide variety of rates of output; and the output produced will depend on the shape and position of the demand curve.

7. Monopoly profit occurs when average total cost is less than price. Monopoly should not, however, be equated with profits; many monopolists go out of business or never go into business because average total costs are everywhere above their demand curve.

8. Anyone wishing to purchase a monopoly can expect to pay the fully discounted present value of future monopoly profits. Thus, the expected rate of return will be the normal rate of return corrected for risk, rather than the monopoly rate of return.

9. A monopolist will operate several plants so that $MR = MC = MC_1 = MC_2 = \cdots$.

10. There are a number of measures of monopoly power, such as the concentration ratio and the Lerner Index. All of them have deficiencies. The concentration ratio, for example, does not take account of potential suppliers.

11. In general, we can predict that a monopoly will produce at a lower rate of output and sell at a higher price than a competitive industry, *ceteris paribus*. Moreover, the monopolist will generally not operate at a rate of output at which long-run average costs are at a minimum.

12. A monopolist can usually make a higher profit by engaging in price discrimination; this, however, requires that consumer classes be identifiable and separable, and that those who purchase the product at a lower price be effectively prevented from reselling it to those who would have to purchase it at a higher price.

13. The discriminating monopolist who engages in third-degree price discrimination will charge those with more-elastic demands a price lower than the price it charges to those with less-elastic demands.

14. Quantity discounts are a common type of multipart pricing in which the price of the last unit purchased is less than the price of previous units; however, in many cases, this may be a form of price differentiation, because transactions costs per unit typically fall as larger quantities are purchased.

15. Price discrimination is necessary for an industry to come into existence or to continue to exist when the long-run average cost curve is everywhere above the industry demand curve.

Selected references

Dewey, D., *Monopoly in Economics and Law* (Chicago: Rand McNally, 1959).

Harrod, R. F., "Doctrines of Imperfect Competition," *Quarterly Journal of Economics*, vol. 48, May 1934, pp. 442–470.

Hicks, J. R., "Annual Survey of Economic Theory: The Theory of Monopoly," *Econometrica*, vol. 3, January 1935, pp. 1–20; also in George J. Stigler and Kenneth E. Boulding (eds.), *Readings in Price Theory*, American Economic Association (Chicago: Irwin, 1952).

Machlup, Fritz, *The Political Economy of Monopoly* (Baltimore: Johns Hopkins, 1952).

Mansfield, Edwin, *Monopoly Power and Economic Performance*, 3d ed. (New York: Norton, 1974).

Marshall, Alfred, *Principles of Economics*, 8th ed. (London: Macmillan, 1920), book 5, chap. 14.

Robinson, E. A. G., *Monopoly* (London: James Nisbet & Company, Ltd., 1941).

Robinson, Joan, *The Economics of Imperfect Competition* (London: Macmillan, 1933), chaps. 2, 3, 15, and 16.

Questions

(Answers to even-numbered questions are at back of book.)

1. "Since a monopolist is the only supplier of a well-defined product, there is no limit to the price he or she may charge." Is this statement true or false? Explain.

2. Explain why a monopolist will never set a price (and produce the corresponding output) at which the demand is price inelastic.

3. If you were the monopoly owner of a perishable good, the demand for which was linear, would it be in your interest to let some of the good "perish" rather than sell it all? Assume

that you charge a single unit price for the good (i.e., there is no price discrimination). Also, how would you decide how much to charge?

4. Summarize the relationship between price elasticity of demand and marginal revenue.

5. Why should a monopolist's long-run marginal revenue (and elasticity) be greater than its short-run marginal revenue (and elasticity)?

6. Explain how a non-price-discriminating monopolist determines the profit-maximizing output and the price to charge per unit, and what the resultant economic profits, if any, will be.

7. Will a non-price-discriminating monopolist whose total revenue (TR) is less than total cost (TC) go out of business? Explain.

8. Explain how monopoly profits or losses are capitalized into the market value of a firm.

9. Why is it impossible to construct a monopolist's supply curve?

10. Why in the world would a monopolist making economic profits want to "rock the boat" by making long-run changes in his or her scale of operations? Why tinker with a good thing?

11. "The ultimate monopoly product would be one whose cross-elasticity of demand, with respect to any and all other products, was zero." Comment.

12. Contrast the long-run equilibrium of a non-price-discriminating monopolist with that of a perfectly competitive firm. Assume constant returns to scale.

13. What type (degree) of price discrimination might a doctor practice with respect to vasectomies, and what might limit his or her power to do so? What problem might a shoe shop owner have, in discriminating, that the above doctor wouldn't have?

14. In what way is first-degree price discrimination merely a special case of second-degree (multipart) price discrimination?

15. "The reason movie theaters charge youngsters and oldsters less than the rest of us is because theater owners want to help these two poor groups." Comment.

12

THE CREATION, DESTRUCTION, AND REGULATION OF MONOPOLIES

In the last chapter on monopoly pricing, we devoted very little space to explaining how monopolies might arise, the forces that would tend to reduce monopoly power, and the ways in which certain types of monopolies are regulated. Those are the tasks of this chapter. It is appropriate, therefore, to start out by discussing the ways in which **barriers to entry** allow firms within an industry to receive monopoly profits in the long run.

Barriers to entry

For monopoly power to continue to exist in the long run, there has to be some way in which the market is closed to entry. Either legal means or certain aspects of the industry's technical or cost structure would prevent entry. Below we will discuss several of the barriers to entry that have allowed firms to reap monopoly profits in the long run.

Ownership of resources without close substitutes

Preventing a newcomer from entering an industry is often difficult. Indeed, there are some economists who contend that no monopoly acting without government support has been able to prevent entry into the industry unless that monopoly had the control of some "essential" natural resource. Consider the possibility of one firm owning the entire supply of a raw material that is essential in the production of a particular commodity. The exclusive ownership of a vital resource serves as a barrier to entry until an alternative source of the raw material is found or an alternative technology not requiring the raw material in question is developed. A good example of this was the Aluminum Company of America (Alcoa), a firm that, prior to WW II, controlled the world's bauxite, the essential raw material in the production of aluminum. (We'll look more closely at the Alcoa experience in this chapter's Issues and Applications section.)

The essential resource required in the production process need not be a raw material; it can be a person such as a manager. A manager with a superior talent for directing a firm may enable the firm to obtain long-run monopoly profits. The monopoly, however, is not in the selling of the commodity, but rather in the possession by the manager of the superior talents. The manager will be paid according to his or her superior ability. Further, if someone were to take over that firm without the services of that manager, no more than the normal rate of return would be available.

Problem in raising adequate capital

It is often contended that certain industries require a large initial capital investment and that the firms already in the industry can obtain monopoly profits in the long run because no competitors can raise the large amount of capital needed to enter the industry. This is the so-called imperfect capital market argument employed to explain long-run, relatively high rates of return in certain industries. These generally are industries where large fixed costs must be incurred in order to merely start production. These fixed costs generally are for expensive machines necessary in the production process.

Certainly, it is more difficult, for any given

level of risk, to raise a larger amount of capital than a smaller amount of capital. But a sufficiently high-risk premium can presumably be added to the anticipated rate of return from investing in the risky industry to enable a newcomer to raise the needed capital. It may be, of course, that the anticipated rate of return offered to investors in such an industry would have to be so high that it would not be profitable for an entrepreneur to undertake entry into the industry. It is not clear why such a situation is called an imperfect capital market or why it should be considered a barrier to entry any more than any other higher-risk venture, but it often is.

Moreover, one must realize that it is not necessary to purchase all of the capital equipment required to enter an industry. Equipment can be leased, and numerous parts of the commodity to be sold can be purchased from outside suppliers. A few years ago, the Bricklin two-seater sports car venture did just that. Many of the components of the automobile were purchased from other automobile manufacturers. The company ultimately went into receivership after only a few thousand Bricklins were sold. Nonetheless, it had been able to raise sufficient amounts of capital to enter the industry but, as it turned out, not enough to sustain the initial production year's losses.

Licenses, franchises, and certificates of convenience

In many industries it is illegal to enter without a governmentally provided license of "certificate of convenience and public necessity." Specifically, you could not form an electrical utility to compete with the electrical utility operating in your area. You would first have to obtain a certificate of convenience and public necessity from the appropriate authority, which is usually the state's public utility commission. However, public utility commissions rarely, if ever, issue a certificate to a group of investors who want to compete directly in the same geographic area with an existing electrical utility; hence, entry into the industry in a particular geographic area is prohibited, and long-run monopoly profits could conceivably be earned by the electrical utility already serving the area.

In order to enter interstate (and also many intrastate) markets for pipelines, airlines, trucking, television and radio signals, the production of natural gas, and so on, it is necessary to obtain the equivalent of a certificate of convenience and public necessity. Since these franchises or licenses aren't given very often, long-run monopoly profits might be earned by those firms already in the industry. The logic behind issuing few certificates of convenience has to do with supposed economies of scale in the industries where they are required. If those industries do indeed experience large economies of scale, then allowing a large number of firms to compete would, it is reasoned, prevent consumers from benefiting from one firm being able to sell a large output with significantly reduced average costs.

Patents

Closely related to the franchise required for entry is a patent. A patent is issued to an inventor to protect him or her from having the invention copied for a period of 17 years. Suppose I discover a new film for super-8 movie cameras that develops itself instantaneously so that the roll is ready for projection as soon as it is exposed. If I am successful (or my attorneys are) in obtaining a patent on this discovery, I can prevent other individuals from copying me. Note, however, that I must expend resources to prevent them from imitating me even if I do have a watertight patent. Many resources are devoted by patent owners to enforcing the exclusive right. Indeed, I can have a patent on a particular commodity or production process and end up having no monopoly profits at all, because the costs of policing are so high that I don't bother to protect my patent or, if I do, I end up spending so much on policing costs that I eat up all of my monopoly profits.

It is contended that patents are necessary for defining and enforcing property rights in ideas. However, there is little theoretical justification for a patent's extending to 17 years. Why not 10, 20, or 50 years, or infinity? Economists don't have any generally accepted answers. There is a trade-off involved when the patent is made longer. The longer an individual can anticipate having a property right or monopoly in a specific invention, the more resources will presumably go into inventing patentable items. However, the longer a patent exists, the longer the monopoly exists and presumably the longer the price will remain at a monopoly level rather than a competitive one. To find the socially optimal length of a patent, we must weigh the benefits of inducing more research and creative efforts going into patentable products against the higher price tags that those products will carry during the length of the patent. There are some economists who even believe that the optimal length of patent rights should be 0 years.

Economies of scale

Sometimes it is not profitable for more than one or two firms to exist in an industry. This would occur when the industry demand curve's relation to the long-run average cost curve is such that several firms sharing the market could not each individually cover average total costs. Only when one or two firms engage in the production of the product can these firms take advantage of the economies of scale and average total cost be covered.

Consider the situation depicted in Figure 12-1. Here the industry demand curve is *DD*, and the long-run average total cost curve is LATC. Notice that average total costs are fall-

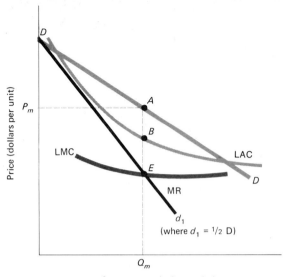

Output per unit time period

Figure 12-1: Economies of scale and monopoly.
Assume that the industry demand curve is DD. A single monopolist has a long-run average total cost curve LATC. It produces where long-run marginal cost LMC intersects marginal revenue MR, or at point E, which is quantity Q_m. It can sell this quantity at price P_m. It makes a profit per unit of the vertical distance between points A and B. Now, if two firms enter the industry and each shares the market equally, each firm's demand curve would be equal to d_1, which is equal to $1/2$ DD. d_1 coincides with the original marginal revenue curve facing the monopolist. However, with two firms in the industry, each would suffer economic losses because the average total cost curve ATC is everywhere above the proportionate demand curve facing each of the two firms in that industry. Only one firm will survive.

ing over a wide range of outputs. Indeed, over the entire range of output for which the average total cost curve lies below the industry demand curve, average total costs are falling. One firm can successfully operate in this industry at a rate of output of Q_m and make a profit per unit equal to the vertical distance between points A and B. The profit-maximizing output rate Q_m is determined by the intersection of the monopolist's marginal cost curve LMC and its marginal revenue curve MR. That intersection occurs at point E. Now consider what would happen if the industry were

split evenly between two firms, firm 1 and firm 2. Each firm's demand curve would look like the demand curve d_1.[1] (Demand curve d_1 is identical with the single monopolist's marginal revenue curve MR.) Notice that the duopolist's demand or average revenue curve is everywhere below the average total cost curve. Thus it would not be profitable for even a second firm to enter this industry and share the sales. Thus, we have a situation where economies of scale are so great that the long-run average total cost curve falls over such a large range that only one firm can successfully exist in this market. This is called the **natural monopoly**, which we will discuss later in this chapter.

Excess capacity

There are situations in which excess capacity in an industry can be an effective barrier to the entry of new firms. Assume that there are a large number of firms making, for example, quadraphonic high fidelity equipment. Rave reviews have come out telling all who are interested about the virtues of switching from stereo to "quad." The existing number of firms start tooling up for an anticipated boom in the quad industry. They purchase new plants, buy new machinery to make components, and generally expand in all dimensions. A year later, however, the public has not reacted with as much enthusiasm as was originally anticipated. The rate of sales of quad equipment is not what the firms expected it would be. All in the industry are faced with excess capacity since they do not find it profitable to continue the high rates of production that they had in the past.

Now, all firms in the industry are in a position to cut price dramatically should would-be

---
[1] They both have identical price elasticities of demand at any given price because they intersect the vertical axis at the same point.

competitors attempt to enter the industry. The existing firms are sitting with large amounts of capital equipment specialized to the product that they are selling. Much of that capital equipment represents a sunk cost. The existing firms are therefore in a position to meet all and any new competition. Thus, they can effectively keep out new entrants for some time.

Creation and destruction of monopoly profits

We have just listed a number of ways in which a monopoly profit can be created. When a legal barrier to entry can be erected, then, a monopoly profit is possible. It is not unreasonable to predict that resources will be spent on efforts to create monopoly profits. Resources will be allocated, for example, for seeking legislation to set up legal barriers to entry into an industry. Those already in the industry will spend the resources to create and/or maintain such barriers. We can say, then, that there is a market for the creation of monopoly profits or for the creation of barriers to entry in an industry.

Although we speak in this section of a market which is defined in the political sense (because *legal* barriers are constructed by legislation), we could consider the much broader market for barriers to entry. This would include, among other things, the ways of obtaining an essential resource and cornering the market in it. In any event, there is competition among net worth–maximizing entrepreneurs to set up legal barriers to entry so that they, rather than someone else, will obtain the resulting monopoly profits. Thus, we know at the outset that even if an individual firm obtains a legal barrier which will generate monopoly profits, those profits will not be as great as they might appear. This is because resources had to have been expended in order to erect the legal barrier and additional resources will likely be required to maintain the barrier. Thus, monopoly profits calculated *dis*regarding these costs are overstated.

Additionally, once a legal barrier is firmly established, there is competition to be allowed to operate within the umbrella of that barrier. Consider the competition among entrepreneurs to obtain licenses for radio and television broadcasting. This competition takes on many forms. It may take the form of demonstrating to the Federal Communications Commission that the proposed candidate for a license will operate "in the public interest." Or it may take on the form of a potential licensee using resources in a legal or illegal manner to influence the authorities ruling on the proposed license.

Customers are the losers in the case of successful monopolization. Therefore, they also have an incentive to spend resources; they wish to *stop* the barrier from being set up. Nonetheless, we predict that consumers will spend relatively few resources for the purpose of preventing monopolization. After all, organization costs are relatively much higher for customers—a diffuse group—than for suppliers, who are relatively few.

Dissipation of monopoly profits

Given that there is competition for the creation of monopoly profits and competition for the rights to those monopoly profits once they are created, some economists contend that this competition effectively dissipates any monopoly profits that arise through artificial barriers to entry. Take, as an example, the offering of a new television station license in a particular city. According to a competitive or a rivalry model, potential licensees will expend resources up to the point where the rate of return from obtaining the monopoly license will be no greater than the rate of return from entry in any other business. Thus, one would predict that monopoly profits, once created, will be competed away and that this competition will entail an expenditure of resources that is socially wasteful. However, it is not necessary to go this far in the analysis. The competitive model will predict that monopoly profits, once created, will be competed away *on the margin*. Certain individuals or firms may have specialized talents for obtaining monopoly profits through the political process. For example, there may be a firm that has worked out a way to obtain FCC licenses more cheaply than any other firm. This firm will receive the monopoly profit for obtaining a broadcasting license for its client.

We can extend this analysis to the political process. Politicians and their supporters generally expend many times what the politician will earn once elected. Clearly, the benefits of being in office are not measured correctly by looking at the money salary obtained by the elected official. But politicians are in a position to generate income for themselves and their supporters in many different ways. (This income does not necessarily have to be pecuniary.) At any rate, the competitive model would not predict that competition in the political arena would result in the dissipation of all monopoly profits to political office holders. Some politicians may have and indeed do have specialized talents and will be able to obtain monopoly profits in the long run because of those specialized talents.

Cartels and collusion

We have yet to talk about how monopoly profits can be created by the formation of a **cartel** or, more specifically, by collusion among an industry's members. In this section we will discuss the desire on the part of individual firms to collude and also the reasons why collusive agreements often tend to break down.

When a collusive agreement is legal and open, it is generally called a cartel. However, you must realize that economists often talk in terms of cartels even for illegal collusive agreements among firms that are in the same industry. A cartel can be thought of as a group of firms in the same industry that have banded together in order to increase the net worth position of their owners. This can be done by price fixing and restriction of output, as was accomplished by the Organization of Petroleum Exporting Countries (OPEC), or by jointly expending resources on advertising,[2] on getting legislation passed to prevent entry into the industry, and on policing the prevention of entry into the industry.

Increase in profits through cartelization

We can demonstrate the effects of cartelizing an industry on the rate of profit to each individual firm. In the simplest of all cases, each firm in the industry has identical average and marginal cost curves. Otherwise stated, each firm is equally efficient.

To start the analysis, consider a competitive situation. Assume that there are 100 firms in the industry. Assume further that we are in a situation of perfect competition. Thus, the price at which each individual firm sells its output is equal to its perceived marginal revenue. Each firm's output is the output at which $P = MC$. This price P_c is set by the interaction of the industry supply curve, which is the horizontal summation of 100 MC curves, and the industry demand curve. The individual firm, of course, does not observe the industry demand curve; rather, it responds to its horizontal demand curve at price P_c. In any event, it will produce an output q_c which is one one-hundredth of total industry output Q_c.

Now let us see what happens when the industry is cartelized. A cartel is formed with a

---

[2]"Every body needs milk."

central agency assigning production quotas. It assigns a production quota of one one-hundredth of the industry's total output to each individual firm. Assuming now that all firms obey these quotas, they will all produce the same output. Thus, we know that if each firm increases output by one unit, the industry will increase output by 100 units. It is no longer true that the individual firm can sell all it wants at the market-clearing price. Price now depends on the rate of output of the firm, because they are all acting in unison. We can now draw a demand curve ($= 1/100DD$) that faces the individual firm which is labeled dd in Figure 12-2. The reader should note that dd is based on two assumptions: (1) equal shares for each firm, and (2) no cheating, i.e., costless monitoring and policing of the cartel agreement by the central agency. Since this demand curve is downward-sloping, we draw a marginal revenue curve mr ($= 1/100$ MR) that is below dd.

The profit-maximizing rate of output for each firm is given by q_m and the profit-maximizing price for the firm and the industry is P_m. For the cartel, total industry output is 100 times q_m. The cartelized industry output is less than it was when the firms were in perfect competition; however, each individual firm in the cartel is now making economic profits. In the competitive situation, price was equal to marginal cost; in the cartel situation, price exceeds marginal cost and there is clearly a higher rate of profit for each firm (assuming they were profitable to start with). Thus, we can see the incentives for cartelization of an industry. Cartelization does not have to be thought of as being desired for "evil" purposes, but rather as a natural phenomenon consistent with our profit-maximizing assumptions. But these assumptions should hold throughout the analysis, and therefore, you should be skeptical about the long-run stability of the situation depicted in Figure 12-2. There will be forces preventing the successful formation of a cartel, and even if one is

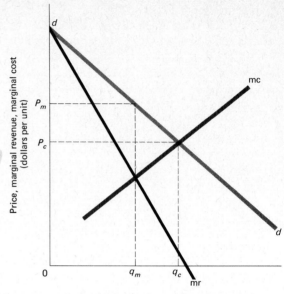

Individual firm's output per unit time period

Figure 12-2: Increasing profits via perfect cartelization. We assume that all firms are of equal size and are equally efficient. The proportional demand curve facing each firm is given as dd. The curve marginal to it is mr. For the individual firm in this industry, if it is competitive, profit maximization will be at an output where price P_c will be equal to marginal cost mc. Each firm will produce q_c. If there are 100 firms in the industry, then total industry output will be $100 \times q_c$. Now assume that output is allocated by a single agency directing the entire industry. If there is no cheating, each firm will be assigned output q_m and will sell its output at price P_m. Profits will increase so that monopoly profits are being made.

in fact initiated, there will be difficulty in the successful continuation of that cartel.

The incentive to cheat

The incentive to cheat in a cartel arrangement is great. The incentive not to join an existing cartel is also great. We can see this in Figure 12-3. In panel (b), the industry demand curve is DD. The curve marginal to that is MR. We assume a large number of equally efficient individual firms that are operated by a cartel manager. The summation of their individual

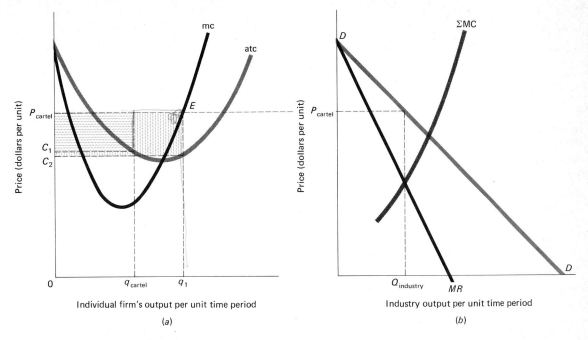

Figure 12-3: The incentive to cheat in a cartel.
The industry demand curve is DD in panel (b). Its marginal curve is MR. The summation of the individual firm's marginal cost curves is labeled ΣMC. A perfect cartel would set industry output at $Q_{industry}$. The cartel price would then be P_{cartel}. Assume that the individual firm's allotted output shown in panel (a) is q_{cartel}. It sells that output P_{cartel}. Its average total costs are C_1; therefore, its profit is the horizontally lined area. However, if the individual firm believes that no one else will cheat, it will take P_{cartel} as given and therefore equal to marginal revenue. It will move out to point E, where mc = P_{cartel} = mr. It will produce at output rate q_1. If indeed no other firm does cheat on the cartel, this firm's profit will increase to the entire horizontally shaded and vertically shaded area, since its cost at output rate q_1 per unit will be C_2, but the price will remain the same as before.

marginal cost curves above their average variable cost curves is labeled ΣMC in panel (b). The profit-maximizing rate of output for the cartel is $Q_{industry}$ and the profit-maximizing price is P_{cartel}.

The relevant curves concerning the individual firm are given in panel (a). Note that the horizontal axes in panels (a) and (b) are using vastly different scales. In panel (b), we are representing the industry output; in panel (a), we are representing the output of an individual firm. We assume now that the cartel manager has assigned an equal share of total industry output to each of the firms and it is represented by q_{cartel} in panel (b). At that rate of output, the individual firm's average total cost

is C_1. The profit that each firm in the cartel makes is therefore the difference between total revenues and total costs, or $(P_{cartel} \cdot q_{cartel}) - (C_1 \cdot q_{cartel})$.

If a disobedient firm attempts to cheat in the cartel, it might assume that the output rate of all other firms will remain constant. It can take, therefore, as a first approximation the cartel price as its demand curve and also as its marginal revenue curve. It will, therefore, profit maximize by expanding output until marginal revenue equals marginal cost, or out to point E. At output rate q_1, it will make total revenues of $(P_{cartel} \cdot q_1)$. Its cost will be $(C_2 \cdot q_1)$ because at the new output rate q_1, the average total cost is equal to the vertical distance $0C_2$. Therefore, its profits will equal the sum of all the horizontally and vertically crosshatched area. The increased profit by either not joining the cartel or by being a disobedient firm once in the cartel is equal to the vertically crosshatched area.[3]

Different firm efficiencies

When we initially discussed the possibility of cartelization, we assumed that all firms were equally efficient. The quota for each firm would clearly be an aliquot share of industry's output. If firms have different cost curves, however, there is a problem of determining the appropriate quota for each firm.

This is similar to how a multiplant monopoly should operate. It should operate where marginal revenue equals marginal cost of plant 1 = marginal cost of plant 2. The cartel should operate where industry marginal revenue = marginal cost of firm 1 = marginal cost of firm 2 = $\cdots$ = marginal cost of firm n, where there are n firms. This means that profit maximization for the industry cartel as a whole can only occur if quotas are inversely proportional to marginal costs. That is, those firms that are relatively less efficient will be given a quota to produce relatively less of total industry output; the more efficient firms will be given larger quotas. We identify the former by the fact that they have higher marginal cost curves; the latter have relatively lower marginal cost curves.

Cartels and policing costs

Throughout our discussion of the instability of cartels, the notion of policing or enforcement costs has been implicitly included. For any cartel to work, there has to be a manner in which the cartel arrangement is successfully

policed. We could actually consider the whole cartel-collusion problem in terms of crime and punishment. Any firm that violates a collusive agreement commits a "crime" against the cartel members. The cartel members, on the other hand, will try to detect and deter such crimes by punishing the "criminals." An "ideal," or "perfect," cartel results when the punishments are sufficient to deter all violations. On the other hand, the anarchistic competitive solution results when punishments and the cartel itself become ineffective.

The costs of policing any given collusive agreement will be lower the smaller the number of firms and customers in the industry. It is not surprising, then, that the degree of industry concentration is often used as a measure of the degree of monopoly power. However, the relationship is clearly not exact, and much must be inferred from industry data in order to come up with a notion of monopoly power using industry concentration ratios. As we pointed out in Chapter 11, such a measure tells us nothing about the likelihood of potential entrants.

Understanding the nature of enforcement costs for collusive agreements helps us understand the great electrical equipment conspiracy of the 1960s. A number of electrical firms in the United States got together regularly to determine prices and market shares for electrical equipment. This cartel had its greatest successes with electrical equipment that was sold to publicly owned electrical utilities. The reason was not hard to find. Public utilities purchased electrical equipment through "competitive" sealed bids. In such a situation, potential suppliers of a particular piece of equipment submit sealed bids to the public utility. At a specified hour on a specified date, all of the sealed bids are opened. Generally, the lowest bid is awarded the contract. The reason sealed bids are beneficial to any cartel is that all of the sealed bids are opened and made available for public inspection at the same time. Late bids are disallowed. Thus, if

---

[3]Strictly speaking, the cheater would have to lower price a slight amount to get the extra sales. So, we are really overstating the potential increased profits from cheating.

a collusive agreement were reached beforehand and a particular firm in the cartel had been chosen to get the job, that firm would put in the "lowest" bid. All the other firms in the cartel would deliberately submit higher bids. If any one of them attempted to cheat, it would be known immediately because the sealed bid would be opened and the knowledge would become public.

We might point out that the electrical equipment cartel broke up. The individual firms engaged in implicit price "shading" by discounting tied-in equipment in other than sealed-bid-type negotiations. In other words, the cartel member firm would sell a particular piece of equipment that was covered by the cartel agreement at the stipulated cartel price; however, if another piece of equipment had to be used and it was not covered by the cartel agreement, the cheating firm would offer a discount on it. It might sell a switch at the cartel price and give (at zero price) a transformer to the buyer in order to take away business from some other cartel member.

Mergers to enhance monopoly power

All the analysis above has been in terms of collusion or cartelization in an industry. There is an alternative way to obtain monopoly power. This is by **merger,** which is the joining of two or more firms under a single ownership or control. There are two types of mergers that concern us. One involves **horizontal integration** and the other, **vertical integration**.

Horizontal integration

Horizontal integration involves mergers among firms selling a similar commodity. In other words, it takes place across a given commodity space. If two shoe manufacturing firms merge, that is horizontal integration. If a group of firms, all producing steel, merge into one, that also is horizontal integration. Most all the cartel analysis presented above also applies to horizontal integration. But none of the enforcement costs are incurred where there is a single owner. Therefore, it might be stated that whatever monopoly power and monopoly profits can be obtained by way of collusion, they can better be obtained by merger as long as this latter process is not "too" costly. Mergers which result in "unreasonable" restraint of trade are, however, usually prevented or prosecuted by the Justice Department and/or the Federal Trade Commission under existing antitrust statutes.

Vertical integration

Vertical integration occurs when one firm merges with either a firm from which it purchases an input or a firm to which it sells its output. Vertical integration occurs, for example, when a coal-using electrical utility purchases a coal mining firm or when a shoe manufacturer purchases retail shoe outlets.

It turns out that there are few instances in which our analysis can explain vertical integration in terms of increasing monopoly power. Consider the simplest case where the purchaser of an input is a monopolist in selling the output but purchases its inputs in a competitive market.

BUYING A COMPETITIVE SUPPLIER. The price that the monopolist pays for its input, by assumption, has been a competitive price. This means that the monopolist is but one of many firms purchasing the output of the input supplier. That input is then used in the monopolist's product. The question is, How much will the monopolist benefit by this "backward" integration? Assume that it purchases the input-supplying company. What is the appropriate **internal transfer price** that should be built into the cost of producing the final product and, hence, into the marginal cost curve for the monopolist? The internal transfer price of an input is the price that is carried on the company's books when it computes its costs of production. From these costs, a marginal cost curve can be derived. If anything other than the full opportunity cost of the input is built into the monopolist's marginal cost curve, then a non-profit-maximizing price and rate of output will result. In other words, it makes no difference to the monopolist whether the input supplier is independent or part of the firm. The price of the input will remain the same, whether it be implicit or explicit. Consider the case where an automobile manufacturer purchases mufflers from an outside supplier for $20 apiece. In that situation, the automobile firm considers the $20 a cost. Assume that the automobile manufacturer then purchases outright a supplier of mufflers. I will continue to charge itself $20 per muffler even though the muffler firm was making, say, $5 profit on each muffler. It would be a mistake to consider for cost calculations that the price of the muffler was only $15, just because the automobile manufacturer now owned that supplier. This is exactly the same reasoning behind the incorrectness of the notion that funds generated internally within the firm are less expensive than funds that must be borrowed or raised by selling additional shares in the company. Funds that are obtained by corporate saving (retained earnings and depreciation allowances) have an opportunity cost of whatever they could earn if they were loaned to someone else.[4] If the firm does not charge itself this opportunity cost (at least implicitly) in making its investment decisions, it will not be maximizing the net worth of the shareholders. That is to say, the firm might make more money for its shareholders if it sold some of its output at a higher price after it took account of the true higher opportunity cost of its inputs.

---

[4]Some economists do point out, however, that funds generated within a firm assure that firm a source of supply with first priority and without the transactions costs associated with searching for the best outside source of financing.

ON FORECLOSING THE MARKET. American law discourages vertical integration. Somehow it is assumed that such mergers "foreclose one part of the market for rivals." The purchase of retail tire outlets by a tire manufacturer is supposed to prevent rival tire manufacturers from being able to sell tires to these retail outlets. But if we think about it, the ability of rivals to sell tires is only impaired if the *retail* chain of stores had monopolistic powers in the retail market when the tire manufacturer purchased it. And if this were true, we would know that the monopolistic chain of retail outlets would be sold to the tire manufacturer at a price that capitalized the future stream of monopoly profits and that the tire manufacturer would not capture any of those profits.

The point to be made is that monopoly power at one particular place in the production and distribution chain in no way confers monopoly power to any other point in that chain. If you own the only supply of a critical raw material in the production of record albums, then all you need do is set the monopoly profit-maximizing price on that critical input that you own. You will only hope to make a competitive rate of return on the additional investment needed to purchase record manufacturing companies and/or retail record outlets. They will not yield you any additional profits. (However, integration will occur, just as an organization of the firm did in the first place, whenever the benefits outweigh the cost of a larger collective unit or to forestall monopolization by some other firm or firms.)

Some arguments in favor of vertical integration to enhance monopoly power

The above discussion should not be taken to indicate that there is no situation in which vertical integration will not increase monopoly profits. There are, in fact, a number of situations that might result in a higher profit through vertical integration. We give some of them below.

THE SQUEEZE PLAY. In some instances, it is alleged that a "powerful" firm will be able to squeeze out independent and nonintegrated firms. Assume, for example, that the integrated firm has a monopoly at an early stage in the production of a final product. It can raise the price it charges the nonintegrated firm for this input, it is argued, and use its position at a later stage to lower the price of the final product. The independent fabricator has to buy the unfinished input at the "monopoly" price, but must sell at the relatively low price for final output. Independents can be forced out of business by this "squeeze." As logical as this may seem, it is not a costless ploy on the part of a vertically integrated firm. The vertically integrated firm must forego monopoly profits during the period in which the price of the final product is kept lower than it would be otherwise. This is sometimes known as cutthroat competition. Its rationality in terms of net worth maximization of the owners is certainly not without questions. It can be shown that it's cheaper to buy rivals outright (but that may be illegal).[5]

PRICE DISCRIMINATION. Vertical integration can sometimes allow a monopolist to practice more price discrimination than would be possible without such integration. The fabricator of an intermediate product may perceive that the final product is being sold to classes of individuals who have different price elasticities of demand. Perhaps the manufacturer of the intermediate product can more easily exploit these differences if that manufacturer is also the manufacturer of the final product. An example might be aluminum. The producer of aluminum cannot discriminate in the price of

[5]See Lester Telser, "Abusive Trade Practices: An Economic Analysis," *Law and Contemporary Problems*, vol. 30, Summer 1965, no. 3, pp. 465–477; and John S. McGee, "Predatory Price Cutting: The Standard Oil (N.J.) Case," *Journal of Law and Economics*, vol. 1, October 1958, pp. 137–169.

aluminum ingots for the different final products, like pots, pans, and car grilles, unless that aluminum producer is also the producer of those final products. Otherwise stated, if I am a buyer of an intermediate product that I use in the manufacture of my product, I might be able to buy out the producer of that intermediate product and discriminate perfectly in favor of myself. I would charge myself the true marginal value of that intermediate product; I would charge others monopoly prices on a discriminating basis. In other words, I would engage in third-degree price discrimination as the owner of the input supply.

PREVENTING ENTRY. Vertical integration may be used as a way in which entry into the industry can be prevented. The manufacturer of aluminum products may prevent entry into that industry if that manufacturer buys up the entire supply of all the ingredients that go into making aluminum.

The natural monopoly

We have already mentioned that one barrier to entry may be (industry) economies of scale. If economies of scale are so great that the long-run average total cost curve is downward-sloping over the relevant range, then only one firm can survive. That firm will be the one that expands output the most and, hence, enjoys the greatest decrease in average total cost. It is able to "undersell" rivals and eventually drive them out of business. A natural monopoly situation is depicted in Figure 12-4.

There we see that the LAC curve is downward-sloping over a relevant range of outputs. Now assume that the market demand curve is DD. The monopolist's profit-maximizing rate of output is where MR = LMC, or at output rate Q_m. The profit maximizing monopolist would then charge price P_m. Clearly, a competitive solution to the price-output decision could not

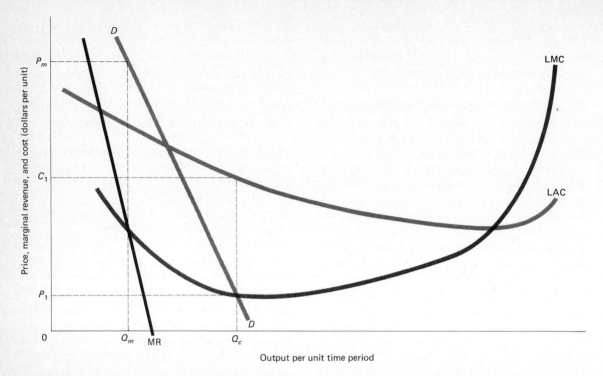

Figure 12-4: The natural monopoly situation.
The long-run average cost curve LAC is downward-sloping over the entire relevant range of outputs. In a competitive solution, price is equal to long-run marginal cost. If this natural monopolist were forced to sell at price P_1 and to produce output rate Q_c, it would incur a loss per unit equal to the difference between C_1 and P_1. Unrestrained, the monopolist would produce where marginal revenue equals marginal cost, or at output rate Q_m. It would charge a price equal to P_m.

prevail in this industry. A competitive solution requires that price equal marginal cost; but if price were equal to marginal cost P_1, the firm in this industry (i.e., the natural monopolist) would suffer a loss on every unit sold because the LAC curve is above the DD curve at the rate of output Q_c. The loss on each unit sold would be the vertical difference between C_1 and P_1 in Figure 12-4. Some theorists, in their desire to have price equal to marginal cost, have suggested that a subsidy be given equal to the distance between C_1 and P_1 per unit of output sold in this natural monopoly situation. It may be true that, with the subsidy, each consumer pays a retail price for the product equal to (long-run) marginal cost. However, taken together,

consumers of the product do not pay in total equal to the true social opportunity cost of the total quantity of this commodity consumed.

There are two alternatives which could be used in this natural monopoly situation.

Multipart pricing

Conceivably, the natural monopolist who would otherwise suffer a loss if the uniform price of P_1 were charged could engage in multipart pricing. Those demanders of the product with relatively inelastic demand curves would pay prices higher than P_1. The revenues in excess of the marginal cost of providing the units of output to these demanders with relatively inelastic demand curves could be used to cover some or all of the fixed costs.

Selling the rights to produce

In the absence of any regulation, the natural monopoly will set output at a rate at which marginal revenue equals marginal cost. In Figure 12-5, this is rate Q_m. The price that would be charged would be P_m, and the cost per unit would be C_m. Therefore, the monopoly profits will be the vertical distance between P_m and C_m times the quantity produced Q_m.

Consider the possibility of the government auctioning off the right to produce (on the basis of the price per constant quality unit to be charged the public). If the bidding is competitive, the end result will be a price charged that just equals long-run average cost (which includes a normal competitive rate of return

on investment). Thus we can see that the auctioning off of the right to produce will result in a price equal to P_1 (which is also equal to long-run average costs of C_1) and a quantity produced of Q_B. There would be no monopoly profits, only a normal rate of return. This is an alternative way of regulating natural monopolies if and when it is decided that they need regulation. (And note that the government appropriates the monopoly profits for "society" from the auction.)

The regulation of monopolies

The regulation of monopolies in the United States takes on basically two forms: antitrust legislation and regulatory activities of such agencies as the Federal Power Commission, the Civil Aeronautics Board, and so on. Presumably, antitrust legislation attacks the problem of monopoly at its root and therefore obviates the need for any other type of regulation. Monopolies are broken up or not allowed to form so that competitive pricing prevails. In what follows, we will discuss regulatory activities and omit any discussion of antitrust legislation.

Cost-of-service regulation

One type of regulation involves a regulatory commission attempting to ascertain what the cost of service is for the provision of some commodity, say, electricity. Cost of service regulation requires detailed knowledge of the costs of production and distribution of the commodity in question. Moreover, cost-of-service regulation requires that, in many instances, **common costs** be allocated to specific products. For example, the U.S. Postal Service has a truck that it uses to haul first-, second-, and third-class mail to various addresses. The cost of the truck constitutes a common cost for first-, second-, and third-class mail delivery. In what way can such a common cost be

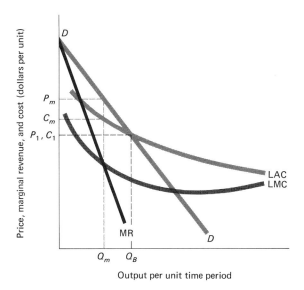

Figure 12-5: Selling the exclusive right to produce.
This is a natural monopoly. If no regulation restricts its activities, the monopolist will set output at Q_m and price at P_m. If the government sells the right to produce on the basis of price per constant-quality unit, competition for the franchise will result in price equal to P_1, which will equal long-run average costs C_1. The output rate will be Q_B.

allocated? It turns out that there is no way other than an arbitrary one that can be used. Thus, cost-of-service regulation faces the problem of arbitrarily allocating common costs.[6]

Moreover, cost-of-service regulation has to grapple with the problem of distinguishing between historical costs and opportunity costs. This is particularly relevant in the inflationary setting of the last decade. The historical cost of a steam generator may be very much lower than its opportunity cost because of inflation. Price based on historical cost will not then cover current opportunity costs.

Additionally, prices based on all costs rolled in together ignore the long-run marginal cost which may be many times greater than current average cost. This, again, is particularly true in an inflationary setting. An electrical utility that must expand in order to satisfy the demand at the current regulated price may have to incur costs that are many times greater than what it had to pay in the past for capital equipment. This is due in part to inflation and also in part to increased pollution-abatement equipment that must be purchased along with the "productive" capital equipment. In some instances, it has been shown that the long-run marginal cost of electricity is 5 to 10 times the price that is charged for it. If electricity consumers are not charged a price which reflects true long-run marginal costs of providing additional generation of that type of energy, then the quantity demanded by consumers will be greater than it would be otherwise. Thus, not allowing electrical utilities to "pass on" increased costs of expanding output leads to consumers *not* being faced with the true social opportunity cost of the electricity that they use. This causes an economically inefficient use of resources and potential problems with excess quantities of electricity demanded at regulated prices.

---

[6]See Marshall, *Principles of Economics*, 8th ed., book V, chapter VI, and mathematical appendix (New York: The Macmillan Company, 1949).

Rate-of-return regulation

Rate-of-return regulation involves a public utility commission, or some other commission, establishing a price that allows a "fair" rate of return on investors' equity in the regulated industry. Presumably, rate-of-return regulation prevents the monopoly, whether it be an electrical utility or telephone company, from reaping monopoly profits. In the simplest model of regulatory process, the company in question produces one output and uses two inputs, labor and capital, each of which is available to it in unlimited quantities at market-determined prices. The decisions of the firm are affected by regulation in only one way. No more than some fixed percentage of the value of its capital is allowed to be earned in any year. This fixed percentage is the fair rate of return computed on its so-called **rate base**, which is its capital stock. In the simplest of regulatory models, the management of the regulated firm is allowed to pursue its objective of maximizing profits exactly as it would in the absence of regulation, except for the establishment of prices. And for the model to make any sense, the fair rate of return and, therefore, the product price allowed by the regulatory agency is less than the rate of return that would be earned without constraints. In equation form, the regulated firm maximizes total profits subject to a regulatory constraint, or it maximizes

$$\text{Profit} = Pq - wL - rK \qquad (12\text{-}1)$$

where P = output price
q = output
L = labor
w = wage rate
K = capital stock
r = unit cost of capital (implicit rental rate/unit)

subject to

$$\frac{Pq - wL}{K} \leq z \qquad (12\text{-}2)$$

where

$$z = r + v = \text{rate of return allowed by}$$
$$\text{regulation and above the unit} \quad (12\text{-}3)$$
$$\text{cost of capital with } v \geq 0$$

The regulated firm is allowed to have a rate of return at least equal to the implicit rental value of the capital stock. The rate of return may be greater than r and depends on what v is. The regulators decide on v and hence on z. Presumably, z is less than the profit-maximizing rate of return since the regulators do not want to allow monopoly profits.

We know that with constraints, the way in which the profit-maximizing firm will act will be different from an unconstrained situation. Employing the simplified assumptions of the model above, it can be shown that the firm will overinvest in capital. This is called the **Averch-Johnson effect** because it was first noted by these two economists in a 1962 article.[7] The overinvestment occurs because when the percentage rate of return on investment is fixed at z and is less than the profit-maximizing rate, the regulated companies will have an incentive to "overinvest." The object of the game is to maximize total profits. If the rate of profit that can be earned on an investment is fixed, then why not increase capital investment to get higher absolute profits? The ratio of capital to labor in regulated industries is going to be higher than it would be without regulation. This is called an expansion of the rate base and it is inefficient.[8]

Problems with regulation

Regulation, even in principle, is not an easy job. In reality, it has proven to be extremely complicated. Below we examine only a few of the problems associated with regulation.

QUALITY OF SERVICE. For regulation to have any effect, the price per constant-quality unit must be regulated. If only the nominal price per nominal-quality unit is regulated, then a change in the quality of the commodity in question will alter the *real* price. So long as regulators are unable to regulate the quality of the commodity sold, the difficulty of effective regulation becomes relatively greater.

Consider regulating the price of a constant-quality unit of telephone service. Look at the many facets of the quality of telephone service. Getting a dial tone, hearing other voices clearly, getting the operator to answer quickly, having out-of-order telephones repaired rapidly, and putting through a long-distance call quickly are some of those facets. Regulation of the telephone company usually deals with the prices charged for telephone service. Regulators are concerned with the quality of service; but they can only regulate some of the dimensions of quality. If the telephone company wants to raise the price per constant-quality unit and the regulatory agency refuses a nominal price increase, it can cut down on the quality of the service and thereby implicitly raise the price per constant-quality unit. In many areas of the country, telephone companies are not allowed to charge a price for service to out-of-the-way rural areas which is significantly higher than the price charged for service to dense urban areas. In order to raise the price per constant-quality unit in the rural areas, telephone companies lower the quality of the service. In many rural communities, it may take months or even years before a private line can be obtained; but in the city, this is usually not a problem at all. Obviously, if you are charged a fee of $20 a month for phone service, it is one thing to have a private line and quite another to have three other peo-

[7]H. Averch and L. L. Johnson, "Behavior of the Firm under Regulatory Constraint," *American Economic Review*, vol. 52, December 1962, pp. 1053–1069.

[8]When the model becomes more complicated, however, it is not clear that the A–J effect works the way it is sup-

posed to work. See, for example, William J. Baumol and Alvin K. Klevorich, "Input Choices and the Rate of Return Regulation: An Overview of the Discussion," *The Bell Journal of Economics and Management Science*, vol. 1, no. 2, Autumn 1970, pp. 162–190.

ple share your party line. You have to wait if one of them is on the phone before you make your own call, you constantly get interrupted by others lifting up their phones in order to make calls when you are on the line, and in some cases, you hear their special ring on your phone when anyone calls them.

PRICING POLICIES AND "EXCESS" PROFITS. Regulatory commissions are presumably in the business of preventing higher than "fair" rates of return. It is not surprising, therefore, that regulatory agencies are reluctant to allow long-run marginal cost pricing or peak-load pricing. The former often results in higher than "fair" profits if long-run marginal costs exceed average costs by a great amount. LMC does exceed SAC for electricity in many areas of the country because of the increased costs of building plants, adding pollution equipment, and financing capital expenditures. Prices which are based on average costs, therefore, are much lower than prices based on long-run marginal costs. A regulatory agency presumably does not like the idea of allowing a firm to charge long-run marginal costs, even if that is the most efficient pricing solution, because "excess" profits may result.

Peak-load pricing involves the same problem. The demand for electricity has peaks in it during different times of the day and different times of the year, and storage is "too" costly. Regulatory agencies have been reluctant to require, or allow when requested, electrical utilities to charge higher rates for peak-load

times than for non-peak-load times. If higher rates were charged for peak-load times, electrical utilities would again find themselves with "excess" profits, and this would presumably serve as an embarrassment to the regulatory commissioners. Even though peak-load pricing leads to an allocation of scarce resources in such a way that require those who purchase the scarce resources to pay the full social opportunity cost, we have seen very little peak-load pricing in regulated industries. The Environmental Defense Fund (EDF) developed the arguments and the records that led to an order by the Wisonsin Public Service Commission in 1974 to the Madison Gas & Electric Company to inaugurate a system of peak-load pricing. Higher rates were set for summer months when air conditioning puts greater stress on the system. In addition to calling for a winter-summer price differential, the company was directed to differentiate between daytime and nighttime rates for large industrial users. However, it seemed that the cost of metering was too high to institute a time-of-day pricing system for all users.

In 1975 an experiment was started in the state of Vermont by Central Vermont Public Service Corporation. From 8 A.M. to 11 A.M. and from 5 P.M. to 9 P.M., the families in the experiment were charged a higher rate for electricity; the rest of the day they were charged a lower rate. Some families started running the dishwasher and cooking their dinners before 5 P.M. Others did their laundry before 8 A.M. in order to save on electrical bills.

Issues and applications

Barriers to entry and effective cartels: Aluminum and diamonds

A case in which a monopoly was maintained because a firm owned an essential raw material is found in the history of the Aluminum Company of America (Alcoa). It was the sole manufacturer of

aluminum ingots in the United States from the late nineteenth century until World War II. The monopoly position of the firm was at first maintained by the many patents that it had obtained for the different phases of the aluminum ingot production process. For example, the first person who discovered a process by which oxygen could be eliminated from bauxite assigned the patent to Alcoa. This patent, however, expired on April 2, 1906. Another process was invented permitting the smelting to be carried on without the use of external heat. This patent was assigned to Alcoa in 1903 but expired on February 2, 1909. Essentially, Alcoa had had either a monopoly on the manufacture of virgin aluminum ingot or a monopoly on the cheapest production process, and this eliminated all competition. After that date, one of the major ways in which Alcoa kept its monopoly position was by cornering sources of bauxite, the raw material. It did this by signing long-term contracts with the companies owning rights to this essential raw material; the contract specified that those companies could not sell the essential ore to any other company. As early as 1895, Alcoa obtained electric energy from three power companies and signed with each of them contracts prohibiting these companies from selling or leasing power to anyone else for the manufacture of aluminum. Unfortunately for Alcoa, in 1912 the courts invalidated these agreements.

In order to maintain its monopoly position in the industry after 1912, Alcoa expanded its productive capacity as fast as necessary to meet the increase in demand at the going price for aluminum. Indeed, it lowered prices in many markets in order to increase the quantity demanded for aluminum. In its defense against an antitrust suit, Alcoa contended that its dominance in the "virgin" ingot market in the United States did not give it a monopoly in that market. It was subject to the competition of imported virgin ingot and to the competition of secondary ingot, which is scrap aluminum. It is true that since aluminum does not deteriorate very quickly, the supply of secondary aluminum over time will become sufficiently large to provide competition for virgin aluminum. This is exactly the same problem facing the owners of the supply of "new" diamonds.

In terms of an actual cartel, which Alcoa was not (it was a single-firm monopoly), the owners of diamond mines in South Africa have been successful for many years. They have operated a cartel which has been able to keep the world price of

diamonds higher than a competitive price. This was done by regulating the export of diamonds. This has been possible because the owners of diamond mines in South Africa control over three-fourths of the world's diamond production. The first ingredient in this successful monopoly was the control of an essential resource. Secondly, the diamond mine owners used a single firm as their sole export agent. That firm is DeBeers. Most of the world's diamonds come out of the mines that use DeBeers as their sole export agent. Thus, it is possible to set a monopoly price on diamonds and not have any individual mine owner be able to cheat by offering diamonds at a lower price unless that diamond owner somehow goes around the DeBeers export agency. And lastly, no close substitute for diamonds has as yet been developed.

The creation of monopoly profits—
The case of taxicabs

One way to obtain monopoly profits is to foreclose entry into the market by legal means. If a law can be passed that requires a license be obtained in order to do business in a particular industry, those in the industry prior to the licensing restriction (and assuming a **grandfather clause**[9] in the law) will obtain monopoly profits. A clearcut case can be seen if we examine the market for taxi services throughout the United States. In many, if not most, cities, in order to operate a taxi, a license must be obtained. In New York City, this license is called a medallion. Before 1937 in New York, the taxicab industry had free entry. The price of taxi medallions was near zero, since they were given to anyone who wanted to operate a taxi. Little by little, the city began to restrict its issuance of new medallions. And little by little, anyone wishing to buy a medallion from the then-cur-

---

[9]Under such clauses, everyone in the industry is "grandfathered in" automatically when licensing is required. That is, existing firms obtain a license by virtue of already being in the industry.

rent owner had to pay a higher and higher price to purchase it. As the market price went up, those who obtained the medallions at lower than the market price were treated to increases in their net worth. By the end of the 1960s, the market price of a medallion reached $30,000.

What does that price represent? It represents the fully discounted present value of the expected stream of monopoly profits that can be obtained by having a legal taxicab in New York City.

Medallion owners who purchased or received them in the late 1930s and early 1940s obtained "monopoly" profits. However, owners today receive no more than a competitive rate of return on their labor and capital. Why? Because they have typically paid the market price for their medallions and this cost has been added to their other costs. An elimination of the restrictions on entry into the New York taxicab market would immediately subject all the present owners of medallions a large windfall loss. The emergence of "gypsy" cabs (whose owners don't have medallions) in New York City has already partially eroded the market value of medallions. Gypsies are cabs which have no *legal* right to pick up passengers for hire. Nonetheless, New York authorities have, for the most part, allowed these illegal cabs to operate in the city in recent years.

We can understand this situation by looking at Figure 12-6. Here we show that the city of New York has issued a fixed number of medallions equal to Q_1. The supply curve of medallions is thus completely price-inelastic at Q_1, and is represented by SS. As the city has grown and real income has increased, the demand curve for taxi services and, hence, for medallions has increased from DD to $D'D'$. The price of medallions has risen from P_1 to P_2. If free entry were allowed into the taxicab industry, the supply curve of medallions would shift to the right so as to always intersect the demand curve at a price of zero. (This is a point not lost on current owners!) In other words, the authorities would issue medallions to anyone who wanted them at a zero price. Whatever the quantity demanded at that zero price, the quantity supplied be equal—it would merely mean printing

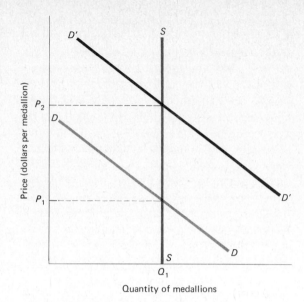

Figure 12-6: The rise in value of medallions.
If the city of New York sets the number of medallions at Q_1, then the supply curve is vertical, SS. If the demand curve a number of years ago was DD, then the going price was P_1. As population and real incomes rise, however, the demand curve shifts outward to the right to $D'D'$. The price or value of a medallion rises to P_2 because the quantity supplied is fixed.

up some more pieces of paper that authorized the bearer to operate a taxi in New York City.

Another case of foreclosing the market: Tobacco

More than three decades ago, owners of tobacco-producing land got Congress to pass legislation which allotted to the then-current half million growers of tobacco the right to grow tobacco on lands that were *then* in use. Since that time, there has been no new land put into tobacco production; and this is for a very good reason. Any tobacco that is grown on unlicensed land is taxed at 75 percent of its value. This tax is prohibitive. No potential tobacco farmers could hope to make any money if they had to pay this tax, because they would be in competition with the tobacco growers who do not have to pay it.

Who are the beneficiaries of restricting the supply of tobacco? Certainly not anyone who today purchases land that is licensed for tobacco growing. The price of licensed land was long ago bid up to levels that yielded new owners only a competitive rate of return. The ones who benefited from the monopoly position granted by Congress were the owners who had the land at the time the legislation was passed. To be more accurate, it is the original owners who had the land at the time it was generally known that the legislation was going to be passed. They reaped monopoly profits to the tune of $1,500 to $3,000 an acre because they could sell their land for more than they could prior to the acreage allotments.[10]

Glossary

Barriers to entry Such impediments to entry into an industry as legal franchises and large capital requirements; allow for monopolization.

Natural monopoly A monopoly that comes into existence when the minimum average cost of production occurs at a rate of output that is sufficient to supply the entire market at a price covering all costs.

Cartel A legal organization of firms in an industry that coordinates output and pricing decisions. The term is sometimes also applied to illegal collusive arrangements among firms in an industry.

Merger The joining of two or more firms together under a single ownership.

Horizontal integration Merger activity which involves firms selling the same commodity, e.g., two tennis racket manufacturers merging into one firm.

Vertical integration Merger activity which involves one firm buying either a seller of one of its inputs or a purchaser of its outputs, e.g., an electrical utility buying out its supplier of fuel.

Internal transfer price The cost figure used within

---

[10]See F. H. Maier, J. L. Hedrick, and W. L. Gibson, Jr., *The Sale of Flue-cured Tobacco Allotments*, Agricultural Experiment Station, Virginia Polytechnic Institute Technical Bulletin No. 148, April 1960.

one firm for the output of one part of the firm "bought" by another part of the firm, e.g., the price that the nuts and bolts division of General Motors Corporation charges the Cadillac division for nuts and bolts.

Common costs Costs which are common to the production of more than one output. For example, one building may be used for the production of many products. Its cost is common to all of those products.

Rate base The net worth or capital stock base upon which a "fair" rate of return can be earned by a regulated utility; it includes purchase price of buildings and equipment, for example.

Averch-Johnson effect A fixed rate of profit on investment will lead to a higher capital-to-labor ratio than in an unregulated situation. Sometimes called an inefficient expansion of the rate base.

Peak-load pricing A pricing system in which consumers are charged a higher price during peak demand periods than they are charged during off-peak periods. A toll bridge, for example, could charge a higher price during rush hours than it charges during all other hours.

Grandfather clause A legal device which allows individuals already engaged in an industry or occupation to avoid being subjected to the new law. A law requiring the licensing of water-sprinkler installers might have a grandfather clause which automatically gives a license to all those who were in the industry when the law was passed.

Summary

1. Barriers to entry include the following: ownership of "essential" resources that have no close substitutes, large capital requirements, government franchises and licenses, patents, and economies of scale.

2. Resources will be spent to obtain monopoly positions. These resources may be spent in the political arena. Further expenditures of resources will be required to keep the monopoly privilege.

3. Monopoly profits will be reduced by competition for them. However, some firms may still

be capable of obtaining long-run monopoly profits from their specialized resources.

4. One form of monopolization is cartelization.

5. If firms can be assigned output quotas so that the marginal cost for each firm is equal to the industry marginal revenue, then profits can be maximized for the cartelized industry. However, it is difficult to prevent cheating, and if firms are of unequal efficiencies, some will be unhappy with their allocations.

6. The cheating firm in a cartel or a collusive arrangement believes that the established cartel price will be its "going" price, even if it expands output. When it does expand output, it can increase profits, provided that other firms do not also cheat. Since each cartel member sees the same possibility, every cartel that is not policed by the government is inherently unstable.

7. The smaller the number of firms and customers in the industry, the lower is the cost of policing any collusive agreement.

8. Sealed bidding allows illegal colluders to monitor the price and output of member firms.

9. Mergers may involve either horizontal integration or vertical integration. Antitrust laws apply to both.

10. Backward vertical integration does not necessarily mean increased profitability, because the opportunity costs of all inputs are the same whether or not the input supplier is owned by the firm purchasing the input.

11. Forward vertical integration does not necessarily foreclose the market. Moreover, even if one firm merged with the monopoly seller of its products, the purchase price of that retail outlet would include the discounted value of all future monopoly profits. The purchasing firm would therefore only make a normal rate of return on that investment.

12. Arguments in favor of vertical integration to enhance monopoly power include: (1) being able to squeeze out independent, nonintegrated firms; (2) price discrimination; (3) prevention of entry by controlling a critical resource; and (4) forestalling monopolization by others.

13. When economies of scale are so great that the long-run average total cost curve is downward-sloping over a large range of outputs in relation to the industry demand, a natural monopoly

exists. The monopolist will be the firm which is able to enjoy the economies of scale first and thereby undercut its competitors.

14. If a natural monopolist is forced to charge a price equal to marginal cost, the monopolist will suffer a loss because it is producing in the downward-sloping portion of its LAC.

15. A natural monopolist cannot, therefore, merely be "instructed" to charge a price equal to marginal cost, for to obtain this price, the monopoly would have to be covered for its losses in the form of a subsidy. It could also be allowed to engage in multipart pricing, or price discrimination. Finally, the government could sell the rights to produce to the highest bidder. In this case, the price charged would be equal to the LAC of the firm, including the opportunity cost of the capital paid out to acquire the franchise.

16. Regulation has two forms. Both cost of service and rate of return regulation require intimate knowledge of regulated firms' cost curves.

17. In both types of regulation, it is impossible to allocate common costs. Moreover, it is virtually impossible to regulate the price per constant-quality unit because it is impossible to regulate all the aspects of quality.

18. When the rate of return on the capital stock is regulated, the regulated firms have an incentive to expand the capital stock or rate base as long as the rate of return permitted exceeds the marginal cost of capital, and the ratio of capital to labor in regulated industries will be higher than it would be without regulation.

19. Efficient use of resources would require that higher prices be charged during peak periods. However, regulatory commissions have generally not favored this type of pricing by public utilities because these utilities would earn higher than a "fair" rate of return in the short run and embarrass the commission regulating them. Also, a simpler rate structure is easier to administer.

Selected references

Bain, J. S., *Barriers to New Competition* (Cambridge, Mass.: Harvard University Press, 1956).

Kahn, Alfred E., *The Economics of Regulation*, vols. 1 and 2 (New York: Wiley, 1970).

McGee, John S., "Predatory Price Cutting: The Standard Oil (N.J.) Case," *The Journal of Law and Economics,* vol. 1, October 1958, pp. 137–169.

Phillips, Almarin (ed.), *Promoting Competition in Regulated Markets* (Washington, D.C.: The Brookings Institution, 1975).

Posner, Richard A., "Taxation by Regulation," *The Bell Journal of Economics and Management Science,* vol. 2, no. 1, Spring 1971, pp. 22–50.

Solomon, Ezra, "Alternative Rate of Return Concepts and Their Implications for Utility Regulation," *The Bell Journal of Economics and Management Science,* vol. 1, no. 1, Spring 1970, pp. 65–81.

Stigler, George J., "The Theory of Economic Regulation," *The Bell Journal of Economics and Management Science,* vol. 2, no. 1, Spring 1971, pp. 3–21.

Questions

(Answers to even-numbered questions are at back of text.)

1. Of the barriers to entry discussed in the text, which are government-created and which arise in the absence of government action?

2. "The elimination of all tariffs would dissipate more monopoly power than any other single governmental action." What do tariffs have to do with monopoly power?

3. Suppose you own the only mineral springs in your state. Why would we *not* expect to see the state government regulating the price you charge?

4. "Whenever a government entity creates a new monopoly right, there will be competition for its award." Having created the right, how might the government determine who gets it? What criteria might it use?

5. Would you expect to find more or less corruption of governmental officials in a regulatory agency which auctioned "certificates of convenience" or in one which rationed them according to nonpecuniary criteria? Why?

6. "All we milk producers need do is persuade the government to set a legal minimum on the price of milk, say 20 percent above the open-market price, and we'll all be set for life." What's wrong with this argument?

7. "Philosophically, I am vehemently opposed to government interference in the market place; however, as the owner of a liquor store, I can tell you that deregulation would be very bad for the citizenry. You wouldn't want a liquor store on every corner, would you?" Why would you predict a liquor store owner to defend regulation of his or her industry?

8. Distinguish between a cartel and other collusive agreements restraining competition.

9. Why might the existing firms in a cartelized industry prefer to be regulated by the government?

10. Is the ABA (American Bar Association) a cartel? What factors would you look for in attempting to make an informed judgment?

11. Why is the incentive so great for an individual firm to cheat on a cartel agreement?

12. Explain what a "natural monopoly" is. Why is the right of free entry insufficient here to prevent sustained monopoly rents?

13. "If a governmental regulatory agency ordered a public utility to price all of its output at marginal cost, the firm would lose money unless subsidy payments were made by the government." Is this statement true, false, or uncertain? Why?

14. Suppose your monopoly is regulated by the government. You are allowed to price your product at an average cost which includes a 10 percent per year rate of return on the fair market value of your investment. Does it matter to you whether "investment" is defined as your firm's net worth or by the value of its assets? Why or why not?

15. Rate of return regulation requires that a firm's investment (rate base) be established. What would be wrong with adding up the market value of all the firm's common stock and using that figure? Isn't that the best indicator of the fair market value of the firm?

13

PRICING AND OUTPUT UNDER MONOPOLISTIC COMPETITION

The models of perfect competition and pure monopoly represent two extreme forms of market structure. In the perfectly competitive model, we assume that there are numerous firms which produce a homogeneous product and which have no influence over price—they are price takers. In the pure monopoly model, we assume that the firm is a single seller of a good—the firm is a price maker. There are, however, market situations which seem to fall in between these two extremes. After all, many firms have some control over price, i.e., do not face a perfectly elastic demand curve, but are not really pure monopolists. In the 1930s, economists searched for a model that somehow bridged the gap between perfect competition and pure monopoly. It was, therefore, with great expectations that the economic world received models that had the qualities of both perfect competition and pure monopoly. These were the models of **monopolistic competition**, developed by Harvard's Edward Chamberlin and Cambridge's Joan Robinson. Chamberlin's book was *The Theory of Monopolistic Competition* and Robinson's was *The Economics of Imperfect Competition*. Both appeared in 1933. The theory that we outline in this chapter will be taken mainly from Chamberlin's work.

Characteristics of monopolistically competitive industries

In his work, Chamberlin presented some of the key characteristics of monopolistically competitive industries. We outline them below.

Product differentiation

Perhaps the most important feature of the monopolistically competitive market is product differentiation. The products, though similar, are not identical. Remember that in a perfectly competitive market we talked about homogeneous products, and in a monopoly we also referred to a homogeneous product that the firm sold. Now we are in a situation where each individual manufacturer of a product has an absolute monopoly over a product which is slightly differentiated from other similar products. There are numerous examples of such product differentiation—cigarettes, toothpaste, soap, and so on. Indeed, it appears that product differentiation characterizes most, if not all, American markets. We are not able to buy just one type of television set, just one type of pantsuit, or just one type of automobile. There are usually a number of similar but differentiated products to choose from in each product classification.

Actually, monopolistic competition is only one instance of this differentiation which is sometimes called **variation of production.** Each firm has to decide on an optimal product assortment; each firm has to decide on the appropriate level of quality for each product. But when viewed in this light, product variation can be found in market structures other than monopolistic competition.

Some economists like to differentiate between product differentiation that is "real" and that which is "artificial." Real product differentiation involves variations in physical characteristics, such as an actual chemical dif-

ference between two brands of washing machine detergent. Artificial product differentiation would involve different packaging materials, brand names, and advertising outlays. The above types of product differentiation, of course, represent only the tip of an iceberg. Firms can differentiate their products on the basis of location and service provided with the product sold.

The point to be made here is that in a monopolistically competitive market, each individual producer has an absolute monopoly in the production and sale of a differentiated product, but there are many close substitutes for that product.

Sales promotion—Advertising

Monopolistic competition differs with respect to perfect competition in that in the latter there is no sales promotion. No individual firm in a perfectly competitive market will advertise. After all, if the firm can sell all that it wants at the going market price, it has no incentive to incur advertising costs because the gains would be distributed across *all* firms in the industry. But such is not the case for the monopolistic competitor. Since the monopolistic competitor has at least some monopoly power, advertising may result in increased profits. How much advertising should be undertaken? As much as is profitable. It should be carried to the point where the marginal revenue from one more dollar of advertising just equals one dollar of marginal cost.

Often it is stated that the goal of the advertiser is to make the demand curve more inelastic for his or her product. However, this is an incorrect assessment of the goal of advertising. Consider Figure 13-1. We have drawn two demand curves, DD and $D'D'$. Using the vertical axis formula for price elasticity of demand, it is clear that $D'D'$ is more elastic than DD. Does that necessarily mean that a firm would like to have advertising cause the de-

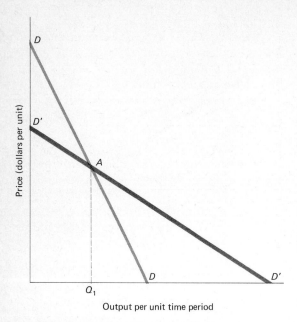

Figure 13-1: Advertising and the price elasticity of demand.

It is often asserted that advertising is undertaken in an attempt to make demand more inelastic. However, consider demand curves *DD* and *D'D'*. The latter is more elastic than the former; however, *D'D'* would be preferable at output rates in excess of Q_1 because it is to the right of *DD*, even though *DD* is relatively less elastic.

mand curve to rotate around point *A* from *D'D'* to the more inelastic *DD*? That depends on the profit-maximizing rate of output. At rates of output in excess of Q_1, the demand curve *D'D'* is more profitable, because any given quantity greater than Q_1 can be sold for a higher price.

The goal of advertising is to shift the demand curve to the right. A monopolistic competitor who advertises will always prefer a demand curve more to the right to a demand curve more to the left, whether or not the former is more or less elastic.

In the strictest model of monopolistic competition, advertising by one monopolistic competitor does not induce retaliatory action by others. That is to say, advertising is not undertaken as a reaction to encroachments of other firms on the particular market in question.[1] Nonetheless, we generally observe advertising by all of the firms in a monopolistically competitive industry. Sometimes this advertising is called competitive or defensive in the sense that it has no effect on *increasing* sales; rather, it is necessary for *keeping* sales at what they are and for preventing other firms from taking business away. **Competitive advertising** is sometimes contrasted with **informative advertising**, which actually imparts information that can be used by the consumer in deciding which product to buy. The distinction between competitive and informative advertising is a murky one; no operationally meaningful modus operandi has been offered to make that distinction.

Product groups

Up until now we have defined an industry as a collection of firms producing a homogeneous commodity. However, it is difficult to maintain this definition of an industry when we talk in terms of differentiated products. Each firm has a distinct product and thus is itself an industry, and we could describe each industry as the differentiated product and the firm that produces it. Chamberlin sought to solve this problem by lumping together firms producing very closely related products. These are called **product groups.** Some product groups that

---

[1]Which at first blush is a strange assumption, since shifting one's own demand curve outward means shifting someone else's inward. However, if there are a large number of firms, a perceptible shift in one firm's demand curve will be matched by imperceptible shifts in the demand curves of all other firms. Actually, in the purest model of monopolistic competition, there are a large number of firms; this model conforms to the competitive one in terms of the nonreaction by other firms. It is only when we move toward a situation where there are *not* a large number of monopolistically competitive firms that the assumption appears "strange."

come to mind are breakfast cereals, automobiles, toilet paper, and hand soap.

Demand for the monopolistically competitive firm

The monopolistically competitive firm perceives that it has some small amount of monopoly power. Hence, it does not consider that its demand curve is perfectly horizontal at the going market price for the product.

We can best analyze the individual firm in a monopolistically competitive industry (product group) in terms of each firm facing a **proportional demand curve**. This is, in fact, what Chamberlin used as his definition, for expositional purposes, of the demand curve facing the individual monopolistic competitor. "Such a curve will, in fact, be a fractional part of the demand curve for the general class of product, and will be of the same elasticity."[2] If there are 50 sellers, then the demand curve for the individual seller will show at each price one-fiftieth of the total quantity demanded at that price. We are implicitly assuming, then, that all firms are of equal size. We will make the further assumption that all firms have identical costs.

Look at Figure 13-2. Here we show the *proportional* demand curve $d_p d_p$. It represents the amount of demand going to a typical firm when all firms are charging the same price. In other words, it is constructed by taking one-fiftieth of total market quantity demanded at each price when we assume that there are 50 equal-sized firms. In general, when there are n equal-sized firms, it is constructed by taking $1/n$ of the total market quantity demanded at each price. Let us start out at a price of P_1. We assume that each firm is charging P_1. Each would therefore sell q_1 units of output per unit

---

[2]Edward H. Chamberlin, *Theory of Monopolistic Competition*, 5th ed. Cambridge, Mass.: Harvard, 1948, p. 90.

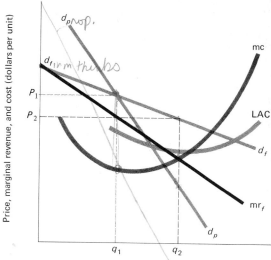

Individual firm's output per unit time period

Figure 13-2: Monopolistic competition—the firm and the industry.
The proportional demand curve $d_p d_p$ is drawn by assuming that all firms charge the same price and that all firms are of equal size. At a price of P_1, the firm will be producing at q_1. It perceives a firm demand curve of $d_f d_f$, which is drawn by assuming that all other firms will keep their prices at P_1. At price P_1, however, marginal revenue does not equal marginal cost. This occurs at output rate q_2. The individual firm believes that it can sell this quantity at price P_2. Such an output rate is not attainable at that price, however, because all firms acting together will individually face $d_p d_p$.

time period. However, the individual firm, according to Chamberlin's assumption, will act as if all other firms keep their price at P_1. Thus we assume with Chamberlin that the individual firm *perceives* a firm demand curve of $d_f d_f$ at price P_1. Notice that this firm demand curve has more elasticity to it at price P_1. It has more elasticity to it at every price than the proportional demand curve $d_p d_p$, because the individual firm in this model does not think that other firms will react to changes in its price. Therefore, if the individual firm lowers its price in order to capture a larger share of the market, it perceives that it will be able to take away business from other firms because they will keep the higher price on their products. If this were a perfectly competitive case (and indeed we can analyze perfect competition in this way also), then $d_f d_f$ would be perfectly horizontal at price P_1. In this instance it is not a perfectly competitive case, and therefore $d_f d_f$ has a marginal revenue curve that is everywhere below it. This marginal revenue curve is labeled mr_f. To repeat, the individual monopolistic competitor perceives its demand curve to be $d_f d_f$, the one that obtains if it changes its price while all other firms leave their price unchanged.

Under the above assumptions, P_1 is not a price that the individual monopolistically competitive firm will charge. It will increase output until marginal revenue equals marginal cost, or to output q_2. It perceives that it can sell this quantity at price P_2.

However, q_2 is unattainable at price P_2. Figure 13-2 is drawn for a typical firm. All firms acting together in their attempt to increase output *cannot* move along an individual demand curve $d_f d_f$. Rather, they must move along their respective proportional demand curve $d_p d_p$. Price P_2 and quantity q_2 is not an equilibrium combination. Each firm must find itself not only on its own firm demand curve $d_f d_f$, but also on the proportional demand curve $d_p d_p$.

Short-run equilibrium in monopolistic competition

Short-run equilibrium is defined as a situation in which the going market price is such that no firm has an incentive to change its own price or output. This can only occur where marginal revenue equals marginal cost. Further, the price must be such that the quantity demanded at marginal revenue equals marginal cost ($mr_f = mc$) is also at a point where the proportional demand curve $d_p d_p$ intersects the firm demand curve $d_f d_f$. Only at

this point is the firm not frustrated in its attempts to set whatever price and quantity at which the intersection occurs. Look at Figure 13-3. Here we show such a situation. At price P_e, the firm demand curve $d_f d_f$ intersects the proportional demand curve $d_p d_p$. The firm is operating both on its own perceived demand curve and simultaneously on the proportional demand curve. Moreover, this is a profit-maximizing rate of output because it occurs where the marginal cost curve intersects the firm's perceived marginal revenue curve mr_f.

Notice that in this short-run example of equilibrium, positive economic profits are being made by each individual firm. This can be seen by the position of the long-run average cost curve LAC. It intersects the quantity line below the price line. Economic profits are shown in Figure 13-3 by the shaded rectangle, $(P_e \cdot q_e) - (C_1 \cdot q_e)$

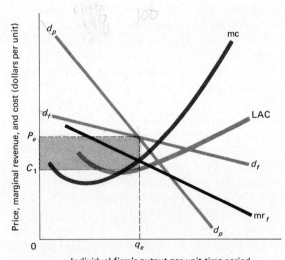

Figure 13-3: **Short-run equilibrium in a monopolistic competition.**
Eventually an output rate q_e will be found where $mr_f = mc$ and where the firm's perceived demand curve $d_f d_f$ intersects its proportional demand curve $d_p d_p$. It will sell its output at price P_e; its average total costs are C_1; and its profits are the shaded area.

Long-run equilibrium

Figure 13-3 could also represent the long-run equilibrium for the individual firm in a monopolistically competitive industry if entry into the industry were blocked. We say this because if entry is not blocked, the existence of positive economic profits will attract new firms into that industry, competing these positive economic profits away.

The long-run equilibrium will be defined in exactly the same way as the short-run equilibrium, but economic profits will be zero. They will be competed away by entry of new firms into the industry where they exist, just as they are competed away in the perfectly competitive industry in the short run. In other words, the long-run average cost curve must be tangent to the firm's demand curve at the short-run equilibrium price.

This can be seen in Figure 13-4. The profit-maximizing quantity produced per unit time period is perceived by the individual firm as q_e, for this is where marginal revenue equals marginal cost. The price that can be obtained for that quantity is P_e and is the price at which the perceived firm demand curve intersects the proportional firm demand curve. The long-run average cost curve is also tangent to the perceived firm demand curve $d_f d_f$ at the rate of output q_e and price P_e, or at point E. Thus at price P_e no economic profits are being received by any individual firm in the monopolistically competitive industry. The reason that this occurred is because positive economic profits, as represented in Figure 13-3, created a situation where other firms wanted to enter the industry to reap those positive economic profits. With a stable market demand curve, the proportional demand curve $d_p d_p$ would shift toward the origin, as n increased by new firm entry, until economic profits were driven to zero. That is what competition is all about.

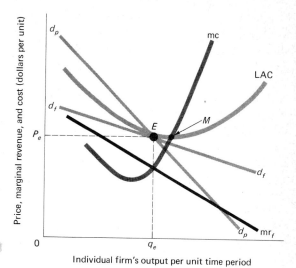

Figure 13-4: **Long-run equilibrium of firm, monopolistic competition.**
Positive economic profits will cause entry into the industry. The proportional demand curve $d_p d_p$ will eventually shift leftward until, at the equilibrium price, each individual monopolistic competitor will be earning zero economic profits. At point E, price P_e is just equal to long-run average costs.

The LAC tangency point and "excess" capacity

Remember back in Chapter 10 when we showed the long-run equilibrium for a perfectly competitive industry, where each firm produced at the minimum on its long-run average cost curve and its short-run average cost curve? This was because the horizontal demand curve facing any individual firm shifted until the price line or individual demand curve just touched or was tangent to the bottom of the long-run average cost curve. Then entry or exit would cease in the perfectly competitive industry. The same kind of analysis applies to monopolistic competition. However, since the demand curve perceived by the firm is downward-sloping because of the monopoly given it by product differentiation, the tangency point must be to the left of the minimum point on the long-run average cost curve. This can be seen in Figure 13-4, and it is exaggerated for the purpose of illustration in Figure 13-5. The minimum point M is where marginal cost intersects LAC. This is to the right of rate of output q_e.

Productive efficiency of resources occurs where long-run average costs are minimized. In Figure 13-5, the productive efficient rate of output q_c occurs at the minimum point on LAC, or at point M, where the marginal cost curve intersects LAC. The long-run equilibrium rate of output for the monopolistically competitive firm is q_e. The distance between these two outputs, q_c and q_e, has been labeled "excess" capacity. Note that excesss capacity in this particular case is negative. That means

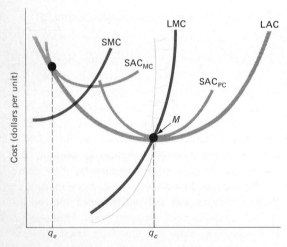

Figure 13-5: "Excess" capacity.
In perfect competition, LAC = LMC = SAC at the minimum point M. However, given the downward slope of the demand curve facing a monopolistic competitor, the long-run equilibrium occurs at an output to the left of M and at a price above M. The equilibrium rate of output for a monopolistic competitor might be q_e, where short-run average costs equal long-run average costs, but neither is at a minimum. The horizontal difference between q_e and q_c is one measure of excess capacity.

that each firm is too small to most efficiently utilize resources.

Why "excess" capacity?

There are two reasons why excess capacity or a rate of output that is not "ideal" exists in the monopolistically competitive firm. One is attributable to an inefficient utilization of society's resources; it occurs whenever $P > $ MC. The other is attributed to the fact that the monopolistically competitive firm does not produce enough and employ enough of society's resources to attain minimum average costs.

Why really not "excess"?

Note that as long as there is any slope whatsoever (greater than 0) to the individual demand curve $d_f d_f$, there is no way that the individual firm can operate at the *minimum* point on a long-run average cost curve or a short-run average cost curve and still cover those costs. Chamberlin contended that the difference between the actual long-run average cost of production for a monopolistically competitive firm in an open market and minimum long-run average cost represented the "cost" of producing "differentness." In other words, Chamberlin did not label this difference in unit cost a measure of excess capacity; that was an idea of economists who took up the model after him.[3]

Indeed Chamberlin argued that it is rational for consumers to have a taste for differentiation; consumers willingly accept the resultant increased production cost in return for choice and variety of output. We know that the so-

[3]J. M. Cassels, "Excess Capacity and Monopolistic Competition," *Quarterly Journal of Economics*, vol. 51, 1936–1937, pp. 426–433; R. F. Harrod, "Doctrines of Imperfect Competition," *Quarterly Journal of Economics*, vol. 49, 1934–1935, pp. 442–470; and R. F. Kahn, "Some Notes of Ideal Output," *Economic Journal*, vol. 45, 1935, pp. 1–35.

called excess capacity situation is a result of heterogeneity in the product; if there were no heterogeneity and all other assumptions in the model were retained, the firm would operate at the minimum point on its long-run average cost curve and its short-run average cost curve. Output would be ideal.

Proponents of the excess capacity argument cite casual evidence such as the proliferation of gasoline stations. Technologically speaking, each of those station pumps fewer gallons than it "could." Is this an indication of "excess" capacity?[4] The answer is not at all

obvious. There is such a thing as an optimal inventory of unused capacity. Barber chairs are not always filled. Neither are bathrooms in a home. Individuals have guest rooms that are unused most of the time added to their houses. In what sense can we call these inventories of unused capacity "excess"? We would somehow have to come up with an argument that product differentiation, and hence excess capacity, was unwanted by the consumer and its additional costs were in some way "forced" on him or her.

Issues and applications

Why do food stores give trading stamps?

The retail food business is a highly competitive one. There are literally hundreds of thousands of retail food outlets in the United States. They range from giant food chains like A&P and Safeway to small "mom and pop" corner stores in your neighborhood. If these stores are so competitive, why do we observe them using multipart pricing—a monopoly device—to extract higher profits? Why do we see them using trading stamps as gimmicks to attract customers? These two practices are not consistent with a purely competitive model. However, they are consistent with a monopolistic competition model which allows for slight degrees of monopoly power by individual sellers. We have already treated the case of quantity discounts or multipart pricing in supermarkets before. Here we will discover how

the use of trading stamps is consistent with price discrimination.

The price of the product includes shopping time

The full price of the product includes not only the monetary price but also the implicit opportunity cost of the time that went into searching out the product and purchasing it (and the time needed to consume it). We can assume that, *ceteris paribus*, the higher one values time released from shopping, the less one will engage in seeking out lower-cost shopping arrangements. In other words, a person who values time more relative to money income will substitute more money income in order to save shopping time. That person will use less time to discover lower prices. Therefore, the person who values time highly will

---

[4]The monopolistic competition tangency solution at output rate q_e just outlined has serious defects. For example, any two firms would seem to have an incentive to merge and thus produce more cheaply and more profitably the combined output suitably differentiated. They could share much of the production equipment and thereby use it a larger percentage of the time. Presumably, the product differentiation is relatively slight so that only a small

percentage of the production facilities have to be altered to produce the differentiated products. It would thus appear that the pressure toward combination, or merger, would destroy the tangency solution. Further, the conclusion that firms in monopolistic competition necessarily produce on the decreasing sections—to the left of "ideal" output q_e—of their long-run average cost curves would also be put in serious doubt.

exhibit a less elastic demand curve in a given store than the person who does not value time so highly.

Charging more to the "richer" person

Let us assume that there is a strong correlation between the value of time and the relative wealth of a person. We are assuming that richer people place a higher value on time than do poorer people. It follows, therefore, that in a particular store, the richer person's relative price elasticity of demand will be less than a poorer person's. Now the retailer is confronted with two classes of consumers. There are those with relatively less elastic demands and those with relatively more elastic demands. The retailer's problem is to separate these two classes and charge the richer customers a higher price than the poorer customers. One way that this can be and is done is to offer a rebate only to those customers who are willing to incur a time cost to obtain that rebate. The rebate is in the form of real goods that are obtainable in exchange for trading stamps—blue, green, or gold. However, the person who wants the rebate must collect the stamps, preserve them, and redeem them at a redemption station. All of these activities require time. Thus, poorer people, whom we are assuming can be used as a proxy for the relatively more elastic demanders, effectively pay a lower price for their food because they obtain goods when they redeem their trading stamps. The richer customers, with a relatively less elastic demand, refuse the stamps because of the time cost involved. They get no discount at all. Thus, the gross money price of groceries is the same to both classes of buyers, but the poor get a rebate equal to the value of the trading stamps' redemption exchange rate.

SOME IMPLICATIONS. If the above trading stamp model is useful, it presents us with some testable implications.[5]

1. We predict that trading stamps will be used relatively less often in cases where the total value of a single purchase is large. In such instances the receiver of the stamps from a large purchase incurs a small time cost in redeeming a large quantity of stamps to make the redemption worthwhile. In other words, not enough differential time costs are imposed to discourage relative low elasticity demanders from collecting the stamps.

This implication is consistent with the fact that trading stamps are almost exclusively used by grocery stores. One does not usually obtain them when purchasing an automobile or a home.

2. We predict that in cases where the commodity is personal service, relatively fewer trading stamps will be used. The differentiation of quality of services rendered is used as a substitute for the price discounting implicit in the trading stamp system. This implication is consistent with beauty shops and barbershops that do not use trading stamps.

3. We predict that owner-operated stores will use relatively fewer trading stamps than stores employing a large number of sales personnel. In the case of owner-operated stores, the owner can attempt to figure out relative price elasticities and alter the service given to the customers accordingly. Employees, on the other hand, have less incentive to figure out customer characteristics and therefore won't treat customers according to their relative price elasticities. Therefore, we predict more trading stamp use in large grocery stores than in small "mom and pop" stores. This, too, seems to be consistent with casual observation.

The optimal rate of advertising

The monopolistic competitor, like any other firm that advertises, must decide on the quantity of advertising to undertake. Advertising expenditures can be for newspaper ads, billboards, radio, television, or any other media spots. We hypothesize

---

[5]These are from A. A. Alchian and B. Klein, "Trading Stamps," 1976. (Unpublished mimeograph.)

that the quantity of a product sold is a function not only of its price but the level of advertising expenditures.[6]

Diminishing marginal returns

Let's start off our discussion by assuming that advertising expenditures have diminishing marginal returns. This would seem to make sense; the firm would exploit its best potential markets first, and exploitation of successive markets with advertising will be less productive. Within any particular market, successive increments of advertising should be less productive, since some of the advertising messages will fall on those who have already seen the advertising.

The optimal level to maximize profits

As always, we will invoke our familiar marginal-benefit-equals-marginal-cost rule to find the profit-maximizing rate of advertising. When the firm increases its expenditures on advertising, that increment will be marginal cost. The benefit will be the increase (if any) in profit. We assume for the moment that neither the price of the final product nor the marginal production cost of the good changes as we increase advertising expenditures by a small amount. The increase in profit resulting from a small increase in advertising expenditures will be equal to the increase in quantity sold times the per unit profits. Algebraically, then, the profit-maximizing firm should increase advertising expenditures up to the point where

$$\Delta A = \Delta q(P - MC_{production}) \qquad (13\text{-}1)$$

The left-hand side of Eq. (13-1) is the marginal cost of increasing advertising expenditures; the right-hand side is equal to the per unit profit $(P - MC_{production})$ times the increased quantity Δq sold as a result of ΔA additional advertising.

If we divide both sides of Eq. (13-1) by Δq, we

---

[6]We assume that any level of expenditures is optimally allocated.

obtain

$$\frac{\Delta A}{\Delta q} = P - MC_{production} \qquad (13\text{-}2)$$

Now if we take the reciprocal of this equation and multiply through by P, we obtain

$$\frac{P \, \Delta q}{\Delta A} = \frac{P}{P - MC_{production}} \qquad (13\text{-}3)$$

The numerator of the left-hand side of Eq. (13-3) is equal to the revenues obtained from the additional sales when advertising expenditures are increased; therefore, the left-hand side of Eq. (13-3) is equal to the marginal revenue resulting from an additional dollar spent on advertising. The right-hand side of Eq. (13-3) is equal to the numerical value (absolute value) of the price elasticity of demand. This follows from the relationship between marginal cost, price, and price elasticity of demand given in Chapter 5. There we saw that

$$MR = P\left(1 + \frac{1}{\eta}\right) \qquad (13\text{-}4)$$

But now we wish to deal with the absolute value of the price elasticity of demand so that this becomes

$$MR = P\left(1 - \frac{1}{|\eta|}\right) \qquad (13\text{-}5)$$

Finally, after rearranging Eq. (13-5), we obtain

$$|\eta| = \frac{P}{P - MR} \qquad (13\text{-}6)$$

Substituting $MC_{production}$ for MR (the profit-maximizing condition) we obtain

$$MC = P - \frac{P}{|\eta|}$$

$$\frac{P}{|\eta|} = P - MC$$

$$\frac{|\eta|}{P} = P - MC$$

$$|\eta| = \frac{P}{P - MC} \qquad (13\text{-}7)$$

Thus, we have the profit-maximizing optimum

for the individual firm, which is

$$\frac{\text{MR from last dollar}}{\text{spent on advertising}} = \frac{P}{P - MC} = |\eta| \quad (13\text{-}8)$$

We can interpret this rule as follows: Numerically low price elasticities of demand invite higher advertising outlays; numerically high elasticities of demand invite smaller amounts of advertising. This is true because we are operating in the region of diminishing marginal returns to advertising. The marginal revenue due to an additional dollar spent on advertising is declining; thus, the firm will increase advertising expenditures more when the ratio $P/(P - MC)$ and the absolute price elasticity of demand are both smaller.[7]

Glossary

Monopolistic competition A model of industrial organization in which there are numerous firms producing slightly differentiated products and each firm has some monopoly power. However, there is enough competition among firms that economic profits are eliminated in the long run by entry.

Variation of production The array of product assortments and levels of quality that each firm produces.

Competitive advertising Advertising which is used only to keep a firm's market share intact rather than to inform the consumer about real qualities of the product; sometimes called defensive advertising, to be contrasted with informative advertising.

Informative advertising Advertising which gives information about the product; to be contrasted with competitive advertising.

Product groups Groups of products that a supposedly well-defined set of firms are making, e.g., breakfast cereals, automobiles, and hand soap.

Proportional demand curve A proportional demand curve is drawn under the assumption that all firms charge the same price and that each firm faces $1/n$th of total demand when there are n firms.

Summary

1. Monopolistic competition is characterized by product differentiation and sales promotion.
2. Some investigators have attempted to differentiate between "real" and "artificial" product differentiation. The task, however, is not easy.
3. The goal of advertising is not to make the demand curve more inelastic but rather to shift it to the right.
4. Some investigators have attempted to differentiate between competitive advertising and informative advertising. However, the distinction is virtually impossible to make operationally meaningful.
5. In long-run equilibrium, no firm in a monopolistically competitive industry will make economic profits.
6. In long-run equilibrium, each monopolistic competitor will be operating on the downward-sloping portion of its long-run average cost curve and will not operate at the minimum point on that curve as do firms in a perfectly competitive industry.
7. It has been argued that monopolistic competition leads to "excess" capacity. However, Chamberlin contended that that was the "price" consumers had to pay for variety in the goods they bought. In this sense, excess capacity is no different than having any asset that is not utilized 100 percent of the time. We all own such assets, e.g., bathrooms, guest rooms, automobiles, etc.

Selected references

Chamberlin, Edward H., *The Theory of Monopolistic Competition*, 8th ed. (Cambridge, Mass.: Harvard, 1962), chaps. 4 and 5.

Dewey, Donald, *The Theory of Imperfect Competition* (New York: Columbia, 1969).

---

[7]This analysis is based on Robert Dorfman and Peter O. Steiner, "Optimal Advertising and Optimal Quality," *American Economic Review*, vol. 44, December 1954, pp. 826–836.

Machlup, Fritz, *The Economics of Seller's Competition* (Baltimore: Johns Hopkins, 1952), chaps. 5–7 and 10.

Samuelson, Paul, "The Monopolistic Competition Revolution," in Robert Quenne (ed.), *Monopolistic Competition Theory* (New York: Wiley, 1967).

Scherer, Frederic M., *Industrial Market Structure and Economic Performance* (Chicago: Rand McNally, 1971), chap. XIV.

"The Theory of Monopolistic Competition after Thirty Years," *American Economic Review, Papers and Proceedings*, vol. 54, no. 3, May 1964, pp. 28–57; papers by Joe S. Bain, Robert L. Bishop, and William J. Baumol; discussants: Jesse W. Markham and Peter O. Steiner.

Questions

(Answers to even-numbered questions are at back of text.)

1. Compare the assumptions underlying the perfectly competitive market with those of the monopolistically competitive market. How are they similar and how do they differ?

2. Assuming that all firms are faced with identical cost curves, compare the long-run equilibrium result (the relationship between the various cost and revenue variables) of a perfectly competitive industry with that of a monopolistically competitive industry.

3. What are some of the ways in which gas stations differentiate their products?

4. Which of the product variations in question 3 are "real" differences and which are merely "artificial"?

5. Service stations at or near freeway entrances and exits typically charge a few cents a gallon more than do other stations. How do they get away with it?

6. In what sense does the "marginal revenue" resulting from advertising differ from the marginal revenue concept we have been dealing with up to this point?

7. Suppose your monopolistically competitive firm "Fine-Tune" is presently selling 100 tune-ups per week at a price of $25 each. As the owner-operator, you initiate an ad campaign on an acid rock FM radio station, promising to "mellow-out any machine for two bits" ($25 in this context). As a result,

you find yourself fine-tuning 140 cars per week instead of 100. What is the "marginal revenue" of the ad campaign? What additional information do you need to determine whether or not your profits have risen?

8. Assuming that the advertising in question 7 in fact increased your profits, should you advertise even more? If so, at what point should you cease increasing your weekly outlay on advertising?

9. Distinguish between the motives underlying advertising by your state Dairyowners' Association and advertising by one of the individual dairies.

10. Are most toothpaste advertisements competitive or informative? How about the advertising of vacation spots? Typewriters? Mercedes Benz automobiles?

11. How is a proportional demand curve derived? Can you think of any objection(s) to this technique?

12. What is the implication of Chamberlin's assumption that each firm will act as though others will not react?

13. Describe the short-run equilibrium situation in a monopolistically competitive industry.

14. Explain how, in the long run, any economic profits will be competed away in a monopolistically competitive industry.

15. If people don't prefer differentiated products to standardized products, then why would a business expend resources seeking to destandardize its particular product? Is a "Chiquita Banana" "really" just a banana? If so, according to whom?

14

PRICING AND OUTPUT UNDER DUOPOLY AND OLIGOPOLY

We have studied price and output decision making in competition, monopoly, and monopolistic competition. In both competition and monopolistic competition, it was assumed that each individual firm did not take account of the reactions of other firms and that its pricing and output decisions were independent of other firms' behavior. In this chapter, we will study a market structure in which it is explicitly recognized that firms take account of and react to other firms' pricing and output decisions. Each of the few sellers is aware that the other sellers of the same product may take retaliatory actions to offset or hinder aggressive pricing and output behavior. When there are only two firms in an industry, we call it a **duopoly**. When there are more than two but not enough to make the industry perfectly or monopolistically competitive, we call such an industry an **oligopoly**. There is rivalry among a few.

In a duopoly or oligopoly, rivals may spend much of their time trying to second-guess each other. Their rivalry may include such forms of nonprice competition as advertising and product modification rather than the use of price competition. The number of possible ways in which oligopolists can act and react is large. Because of the many forms which rivalry can take, we do not have a single theory of oligopoly behavior. In this chapter, we start with a very simple model of oligopoly and then present some classical solutions to duopoly situations. Discussions of price rigidity, price leadership, and nonprice competition follow.

The simplest oligopoly model

Assumptions

To begin this discussion of oligopoly on its most general level, we make five assumptions.

THE INDUSTRY CAN SUPPORT ONLY A SMALL NUMBER OF FIRMS. The position and shape of the LAC curve relative to the industry demand curve is such that the industry can support only a small number of efficient plants and firms.

THE FIRM (AND PLANT) LAC IS UPWARD-SLOPING OVER THE RELEVANT RANGE OF OUTPUTS. The total cost curve of each firm is continuous and normal in the sense that marginal costs will always be positive and above LAC.

SINGLE-PLANT FIRMS ARE THE ONLY POSSIBILITY. Single-plant firms are the only possibility because of large diseconomies at the firm level, the possibility of antitrust action, etc. In other words, the cost of combining plants under common ownership and control is prohibitive.

FREE ENTRY. There are no barriers to enter into or exit from the industry.

HOMOGENEOUS PRODUCT. The firms produce similar products.

The oligopolist's demand curve

Now we are faced with the difficult task of drawing the demand curve for an oligopolist. We cannot use the industry demand curve because the oligopolist is not a monopolist.

We cannot use a horizontal demand curve at the market-clearing price because the oligopolist is, by definition, not a perfect competitor. We can say nothing about the demand curve of an oligopolist until we make an assumption about the interaction among oligopolists. We have to know something about the *reaction function* that we are looking at. Does each oligopolist believe that others will not react to changes in its price and/or output? If the typical oligopolist believes that they will react, then we must specify the manner in which the oligopolist expects them to react. In a perfectly competitive model, each firm ignores the reactions of other firms because each firm can sell all that it wants at the going market price. In the pure monopoly model, the monopolist does not have to worry about the reaction of rivals, since there are none by definition. This interdependence lies at the heart of every single oligopoly model, and as you might imagine, every time a new assumption about interaction among oligopolists is made, a new oligopoly model is born. For this simplest of oligopoly models, we will assume the following:

> Each firm expects and indeed knows that any change in price will be matched by all other firms in the industry.

We can see in Figure 14-1 the result of this assumption. The industry demand curve is DD. If the industry has only two firms, then each firm will believe that its demand curve is equal to the one labeled $\frac{1}{2}D\frac{1}{2}D$. This follows from our assumption that whatever price it chooses will be matched by its rivals. If we go to three firms in the industry, then each individual demand curve, as perceived by the individual oligopolist, will be $\frac{1}{3}D\frac{1}{3}D$.

The equilibrium number of firms

Since we have assumed unrestricted entry and exit, and further, since we assume that all firms have cost curves exactly alike, we can de-

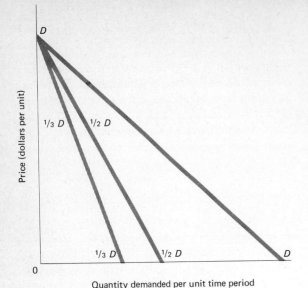

Figure 14-1: Proportionate demand curves.
If each firm expects that any change in price will be matched by all other firms in the industry, and if there are two firms in the industry, each will face a demand curve that is $1/2D1/2D$. If there are three firms in the industry, each will face a demand curve that is $1/3D1/3D$.

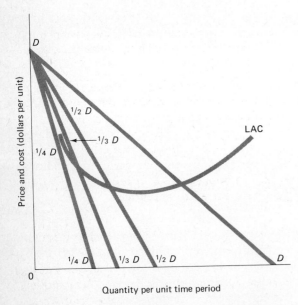

Figure 14-2: Establishing the equilibrium number of firms.
If the long-run average cost curve for the industry is LAC, then only three firms can be supported in this industry. If a fourth firm enters, each will face a demand curve equal to $1/4D1/4D$. The LAC curve is everywhere above that proportionate demand curve.

termine the number of firms that will be in the industry by adding the long-run average cost curve. It is shown in Figure 14-2. If there were one firm in the industry, other firms would be attracted because the long-run cost curve lies below the industry demand curve DD for a large range of outputs. If there were two firms in the industry, there would still be an incentive to enter. Finally, if three firms were in the industry, a fourth firm would not desire to enter because the LAC curve is everywhere above the proportionate demand curve $1/4D1/4D$. If four firms were in the industry, by our assumptions, none could cover long-run average costs. They would all suffer economic losses.

LONG-RUN ECONOMIC PROFITS. It is possible in this simple model that in the long run, economic profits will be obtained. This can be seen by transferring the proportionate demand curve for an individual oligopolist when there are three firms to Figure 14-3. The demand curve facing each of the three individual firms is $1/3D1/3D$. The long-run average cost curve is given as LAC, and the long-run marginal cost curve is LMC. The profit-maximizing rate of output for each individual oligopolist is at the intersection of marginal revenue and long-run marginal cost, or at a rate of output q_1. The price that the product will sell for is identically equal for each firm at P_1. Unit cost, given LAC, is C_1. Economic profits per unit time period are equal to the shaded area in Figure 14-3.

Given the assumptions in this model, this is the long-run equilibrium.

Interdependence and uncertainty

Now we change our assumptions. Firms now recognize their interdependence, but they are still not completely certain how interdependent they are. In other words, pricing and output decisions are made on the basis of in-

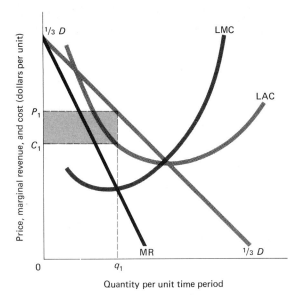

Figure 14-3: Long-run economic profits.
We have assumed that three firms will exist in this industry. Each faces a proportionate demand curve $\frac{1}{3}D\frac{1}{3}D$. The marginal revenue curve facing each firm is MR, the output for each firm is q_1, and the price is P_1. Costs are equal to C_1, and, thus, profit is the shaded area.

accurate or incomplete information about rivals' reactions. Again, it is difficult to proceed with model building unless we make specific assumptions about how firms *think* other firms will react. What we do in what follows is consider several so-called classic solutions to a situation in which there are only two firms, that is, a situation of duopoly.

The Cournot duopoly situation

Well over a century ago, Antoine Augustin Cournot, a Frenchman, published a theory of duopoly.[1] Unfortunately for Cournot, this

---

[1]Augustin Cournot, *Recherches sur les principes mathématiques de la théorie des richesses* (Paris, 1838). English translation by N. T. Bacon, *Researches into the Mathematical Principles of the Theory of Wealth* (N. V., Macmillan & Co., 1897, reprinted 1927).

theory did not become widely known or discussed until the 1930s. Although the model is intrinsically interesting and used as a basis of departure for further analysis, it does embody some rather restrictive assumptions.

Assumptions

The assumptions are similar to the simplified model presented above. The producers produce identical products at identical costs. We assume that costs are constant and that the two producers know exactly what the market demand curve is. They have perfect information about every point on *DD* in Figures 14-1 and 14-2. Further, both producers behave in exactly the same way. We are further assuming that buyers have perfect information. Therefore, each duopolist will always sell the product at exactly the same price.

Now we come to the behavioral rule that Cournot specified:

> Each duopolist, in selecting its own rate of output, assumes that the other duopolist's output will remain constant.

Of course, this assumption involves self-delusion. Each duopolist assumes that he or she can act without provoking an output reaction from the other. This is, in essence, a no-learning-by-doing model. Nonetheless, Cournot was able to show that, given his assumptions, the duopolist will approach an equilibrium rate of output and price.

The Cournot approach toward equilibrium

In order to understand how the model works, we start with an industry demand function for the commodity. To keep the flavor of Cournot's original publication, we will use mineral water as the commodity. We assume for simplicity that marginal cost is equal to zero.

Look at Figure 14-4. The industry demand curve is *DD*, and the marginal revenue curve

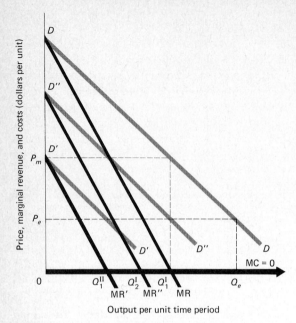

Figure 14-4: The Cournot duopoly model.
Marginal cost is equal to zero and, therefore, coincides with the horizontal axis. We start with demand curve DD. Duopolist I maximizes profit by setting output rate at Q_1^I because this is where MR = MC. Firm II now believes that its demand curve is $D'D'$, which is derived by subtracting the rate of output Q_1^I from demand curve DD. Duopolist II therefore maximizes profit by setting output at Q_1^{II}. Now firm I has the next move. It assumes that firm II will keep its rate of output at Q_1^{II}. It therefore perceives demand curve $D''D''$, which is drawn by subtracting output rate Q_1^{II} from demand curve DD. Duopolist I now sets its profit-maximizing rate of output at the new intersection of MR'' with MC, or at rate Q_2^I. This process continues. A determinate equilibrium will be reached where price is P_e, total output is Q_e, and each firm's profit-maximizing rate of output is $1/2\,Q_e$. If there were only one firm, the profit-maximizing output would be at Q_1^I sold at price P_m.

is MR. The two firms are I and II. Firm I starts the ball rolling, while firm II is temporarily inactive. Hence, DD is the demand curve facing firm I. It sets the rate of output where marginal revenue equals marginal cost. In this case, this is the output at which the marginal revenue curve intersects the horizontal axis. It

sets a rate of output of Q_1^I. The superscript refers to the firm and the subscript refers to the period, or "round." Thus Q_1^I indicates the output produced by duopolist I in the first round, or first period. It does this under the assumption that the second duopolist will keep its rate of output at 0.

Now firm II enters the market. It takes as given firm I's output rate of Q_1^I. Firm II believes that its demand curve is DD minus the rate of output Q_1^I. Its demand curve is $D'D'$, which is derived by subtracting from firm I's rate of output Q_1^I from DD. Firm II will maximize profit by setting its rate of output at where its new marginal revenue curve MR' intersects the horizontal axis, which is its marginal cost curve. Firm II will produce at rate Q_1^{II}. Firm I has the next move. It assumes that firm II will keep its rate of output at Q_1^{II}. Firm I perceives its new demand curve as the market demand curve minus the rate of output of firm II. This new demand curve is $D''D''$ in Figure 14-4. The curve marginal to this demand curve is labeled MR". Firm I will change its rate of output so that marginal revenue MR" equals marginal cost $= 0$. This is where MR" intersects the horizontal axis, or at a rate of output Q_2^I.

Each firm takes the other firm's output as given and then maximizes its profits by choosing the appropriate profit-maximizing rate of output. This process, however, will not go on indefinitely. Ultimately, the rate of output for each firm will tend toward an equilibrium amount equal to $1/2 Q_e$ in Figure 14-4 in the case of two firms. The price at which each firm sells its output is P_e. Notice that this differs from the perfectly competitive solution, which would require that price be equal to marginal cost which, in this case, would be zero. Thus, in the Cournot duopoly model, price exceeds marginal cost and the rate of output is less than it would be under perfect competition. However, in the Cournot model, the rate of output is greater than it would be in a pure monopoly. In a pure monopoly, the rate of output would be set at Q_1^I,[2] since there MR = MC. The monopoly price would be P_m in Figure 14-4.

The Edgeworth duopoly solution

There were and still are lots of criticisms of Cournot's model. One of the basic criticisms was that each firm assumed that the other firm's output was held constant. A French mathematician, Joseph Bertrand, suggested that a solution should be based on the assumption that the price charged by the other firm is constant. An English economist named Edgeworth, from whom the Edgeworth-Bowley box gets its name, took up this suggestion and developed a new duopoly solution.

Assumptions

In Edgeworth's model, there are two changes from Cournot's assumptions. The first is that the two suppliers of mineral water have a limited productive capacity. The quantity demanded at zero price exceeds what one single producer can supply. The second change is that in the very short run, two different prices for mineral water may be quoted in "the" market.

Most importantly, the assumption made by Edgeworth was that each duopolist selects the price that will maximize profit, and this price is selected on the assumption that the other duopolist will continue to charge the same price.

Moving toward equilibrium in the Edgeworth model

In the long run, Edgeworth assumes that the duopolists will charge the same price for the product and they will divide the market equally. Thus, we can use Figure 14-5. The rate of output for duopolist I is shown on the right-hand side, and the rate of output for duopolist II is shown on the left-hand side. The common vertical axis measures the price per unit. The demand curve for duopolist I is $d_1 d_1$, and the demand curve facing duopolist II is $d_{II} d_{II}$. *Both of these demand curves are constructed on the assumption that in the long run both sellers charge the same price.* These proportionate demand curves each equal one-half the market demand.

The maximum productive capacity for duopolists I and II are q_{max}^I and q_{max}^{II}, respectively. As in the Cournot model, the sellers persistently attempt to profit maximize and are incapable of learning. This, again, is a no-learning-by-doing model.

We start with duopolist I (who is temporarily a monopolist) setting a profit-maximizing price P_1. This is profit-maximizing because the corresponding rate of output q_1^I occurs where the marginal revenue curve intersects the horizontal axis, which is also the marginal cost curve in this example. For simplicity we have not drawn in the marginal revenue curve. (To check out the artist, see if q_1^I lies equidistant between point 0 and where the demand curve hits the horizontal axis.)

But duopolist II sees price P_1 charged by duopolist I and believes that by setting its price just below P_1, customers can be taken

---

[2]It can be shown that the Cournot solution applies for more than two sellers. Mathematically, if we assume a linear demand curve given by $P = a - bQ$, then the equilibrium rate of output for each firm is equal to $a/[2b + b(n - 1)]$ or $a/b(n - 1)$, where a/b is the quantity intercept of the demand curve and n is the number of firms in the industry. In our simple duopoly model, $n = 2$; in a monopoly solution, $n = 1$; and in a perfectly competitive solution, n approaches ∞. See Roy J. Ruffin, "Cournot Oligopoly and Competitive Behavior," *The Review of Economic Studies*, vol. 38, 1971, pp. 493–502.

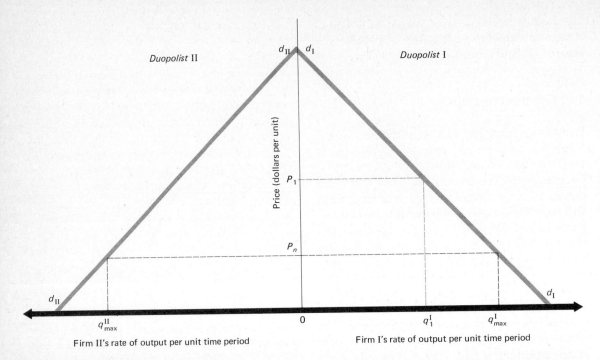

Figure 14-5: The Edgeworth duopoly model.
The proportionate demand curves are marked as $d_I d_I$ and $d_{II} d_{II}$. The assumed maximum rate of output for each firm is q_{max}^I and q_{max}^{II}, respectively. Duopolist I sets a profit-maximizing price of P_1. (Remember that the horizontal axis in these models is equal to marginal cost because MC = 0.) However, duopolist II will set price below P_1 and attempt to take customers away from duopolist I. This process will continue until price P_n is reached. At this price, each firm will start increasing price toward the profit-maximizing P_1. There is no unique equilibrium output or equilibrium price. (Without an effective output constraint, price would fall to zero—the competitive solution.)

away from duopolist I, who will continue to charge P_1.

However, when this is done, duopolist I sees that customers can be taken away from duopolist II if an even smaller price is charged. This price-warring continues until price P_n is reached. At this price neither firm can increase its output, because its output is equal to its capacity production. At price P_n, both duopolist I and duopolist II are producing at their respective maximum, q_{max}^I and q_{max}^{II}. Now what will happen? Clearly, if P_1 is a profit-maximizing price, then one duopolist will see that by raising the price above P_n, he or she can increase total profits. The other duopolist will follow suit and price will rise.

Thus, the Edgeworth model does not yield a solution at all. It merely gives the limits on the price and rate of output that will be seen in the duopoly market. The maximum price to be charged will be P_1, and the minimum price will be P_n. There is no unique equilibrium price; there is no unique equilibrium output. But there is a range of possible prices and outputs.

Before going on to other oligopoly models, we note here that the Cournot and Edgeworth models are not presented because of their relevance or realism. Rather, we show them to demonstrate the difficulties inherent in theorizing about oligopoly. There are difficult problems in obtaining the demand curve facing the firm when there is mutual interdependence between the oligopolists. That is at the crux of all problems with oligopoly theory.

The Chamberlin model

Edward Chamberlin, of monopolistic competition fame, came up with perhaps a more useful model than those of Cournot and Edgeworth. Chamberlin assumes that after the initial round, firm I recognizes that firm II will react to firm I's actions. After this recognition takes place with firm I, it also takes place within firm II. In other words, the two firms jointly recognize that the best thing they can do is to share the monopoly profits. Chamberlin's solution is presented in Figure 14-6. The profit-maximizing rate of output for the two firms taken together is the output at which marginal revenue intersects the horizontal axis where marginal cost equals zero. This is at output rate Q_e. The profit-maximizing price for the shared monopoly would be P_e. Thus, each firm would produce exactly one-half Q_e and sell at a price P_e. This is a stable duopoly solution, in contrast to the Edgeworth solution that is unstable.

Implicit in the Chamberlin model is a system of stable prices charged by all firms without explicit collusion. No written or even verbal agreement is in evidence. This is a form of noncollusive behavior that leads to the same results that a perfectly operated cartel would have. The problem with such a model is that it implies joint profit-splitting with zero enforcement costs. If such a model could be used to describe a situation with two firms, why could it not be used to describe a situation with three firms, four firms, or five firms? In other words, at what point does the number of firms become so large that the incentive to cut price is so great that the implicit cartel breaks down? These models do not tell us the answer.

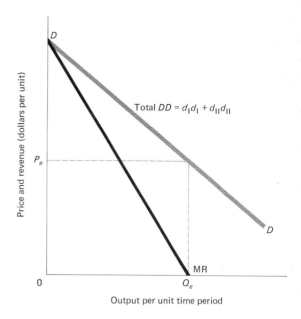

Figure 14-6: The Chamberlin model.
Chamberlin's model of duopoly assumes that the two firms jointly recognize that they want to share full monopoly profits; thus, total output is equal to Q_e and is sold at price P_e. Each firm produces one-half of that output. The demand curve is the summation of two proportionate demand curves.

Implicit collusion—The Stigler oligopoly model

All the so-called classic models of oligopoly include reaction functions. The results of such models have been shown to be rather inconclusive, the price-quantity solution varying from the monopoly to the competitive depending upon the conditions assumed. In fact, there are very few testable implications that one can derive from such models. George Stigler, in his model of oligopoly, eliminated reaction functions.[3] He accepts the hypothesis that oligopolists would like to collude to maximize joint profits. However, collusion is costly to undertake and even more costly to

[3]George Stigler, "A Theory of Oligopoly," *Journal of Political Economy*, vol. 72, February 1964, pp. 44–46.

police. It goes without saying that if all the firms in an industry acted together, they could set output and price to maximize total profits in the industry. Monopoly profits would therefore exist. Oligopoly, however, occurs in a world that is imperfect because transactions costs are not zero.

In the Stigler approach to oligopoly, the agreed-upon goal of the oligopolists is to collude; however, each recognizes that none can be restrained from cheating on any collusive agreement. There is some optimum amount of resources that will be used to detect trickery and cheating, but it is certainly not sufficient to allow the oligopolists to collude as if they were one. There will be some equilibrium quantity of deviation from any collusive solution that would represent a monopoly maximum for the oligopolists. Stigler treats oligopoly as an implicit or explicit cartel that is formed with full knowledge that the policing scheme used will be imperfectly, although tolerably, effective.

The testable implications of the Stigler collusive oligopolist model are as follows:

1. The fewer the number of firms involved, the more effective the cartel. A smaller number of firms means lower costs of policing a cartel arrangement.
2. Secret price cuts will be offered relatively more often to large than to small buyers. This is because the payoff from getting more business from the large buyer for any given price reduction is greater than from a small buyer.
3. The more homogeneous the product, the easier it is to enforce a collusive pricing agreement. When the product is heterogeneous, price cuts can take the form of quality improvements and are difficult to eliminate.
4. The more unstable the industry demand and/or cost conditions, the less likely it is that collusion will be successful. It is more difficult to enforce an agreement in

an industry that has to adapt to constantly changing circumstances of demand and supply.

Price rigidity and the kinked demand curve

The Chamberlin model implied stable prices without overt collusion. Another model, presented by economist Paul Sweezy, also implies price rigidity without collusion. Indeed, it is a more sophisticated model of price rigidity with independent action.[4]

Assumptions

In the Sweezy model, the assumption is made that the market consists of rivals who will quickly match price reductions but only incompletely and hesitantly follow price increases. This assumption allows us to postulate a demand curve facing an individual oligopolist.

The nature of the kinked demand curve

In Figure 14-7, we draw the **kinked demand curve** which is implicit in the Sweezy model. We start off at a given price of P_0 and assume that the quantity demanded at that price for this individual oligopolist is q_0. The oligopolist assumes that if its price is lowered, rivals will react by matching that reduction to avoid losing their respective shares of the market. Thus the quantity demanded for the oligopolist lowering the price will not increase greatly. This portion of its demand curve is relatively inelastic. This is shown by the demand curve to the right of point E in Figure

[4]Paul Sweezy, "Demand under Conditions of Oligopoly," *Journal of Political Economy*, vol. 47, August 1939, pp. 568–573. This model was advanced almost simultaneously by R. C. Hall and C. J. Hitch, "Price Theory and Business Behavior," *Oxford Economic Papers*, vol. 2, May 1939.

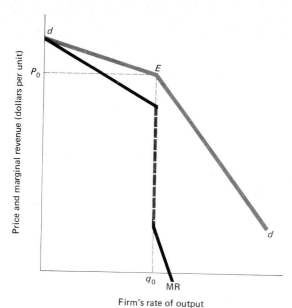

Figure 14-7: The kinked demand curve.
Start with the price of P_0. The firm assumes that if it raises prices, no firm (or at least only a few firms) will follow. Its demand is relatively elastic; however, if it lowers price, other oligopolists will follow. Its demand is relatively inelastic; thus, there is a kink at E. The kinked demand curve is dd; the marginal revenue curve is discontinuous at the output rate q_0 and is labeled MR.

14-7. On the other hand, if the oligopolist increases price, no rivals will follow suit. (If they do follow, they will follow incompletely.) Thus, the quantity demanded at the higher price for this oligopolist will fall off dramatically. The demand schedule to the left of point E will be relatively elastic. This is the flatter part of the curve to the left of point E. Consequently, the demand curve facing the oligopolist is dd, which has a kink at E.

The marginal revenue curve

To draw a marginal revenue curve for the kinked demand curve in Figure 14-7, we first draw a marginal revenue curve out from the vertical axis for the elastic portion of the demand curve (from the upper d to point E on the demand curve dd). At quantity q_0, howev-

er, the demand curve abruptly changes slope and becomes steeper. The marginal revenue curve therefore is discontinuous at the kink, or at quantity q_0. We see, therefore, that that discontinuous part is represented by the dashed line at quantity q_0 in Figure 14-7. The length of the discontinuity is proportional to the difference between the slopes of the upper and lower segments of the demand curve at the kink. [You can draw one in on any other kinked demand curve. Just remember that the MR curve always bisects any horizontal line (parallel to the horizontal axis) drawn from the vertical axis to the demand curve.]

Reactions to fluctuations in marginal cost

Over the discontinuous portion of the marginal revenue curve, the oligopolist does not react to relatively small changes in marginal cost. Look, for example, at Figure 14-8. Assume that marginal cost is represented by mc. The profit-maximizing rate of output is q_0, which can be sold at a price of p_0. Now assume that the marginal cost curve rises to mc'. What will happen to the profit-maximizing rate of output? Nothing. Both quantity and output will remain the same for this oligopolist. What will happen when marginal cost falls to mc"? Nothing. This oligopolist will continue to produce at a rate of output q_0 and charge a price of p_0. Thus, whenever the marginal cost curve cuts the discontinuous portion of the marginal revenue curve, fluctuations (within limits) in marginal cost will not affect output or price because the profit-maximizing condition MR = MC will hold.

Reactions to changes in demand

It also is possible to show situations in which a shift in demand will not affect the price charged by the oligopolist. It will, however, change the quantity produced.

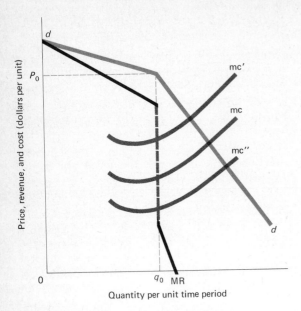

Figure 14-8: Changes in cost may not alter the profit-maximizing price and output.
So long as the marginal cost curve "intersects" the marginal revenue curve in the latter's discontinuous portion, the profit-maximizing rate of output q_0 and the profit-maximizing price P_0 will remain unchanged.

Consider panel (*a*) in Figure 14-9. The profit-maximizing rate of output for this oligopolist is q_0. The profit-maximizing price is p_0. The marginal cost curve intersects the marginal revenue curve in its discontinuous part.

Now there is a change in demand from DD in panel (*a*) to $d'd'$ in panel (*b*) of Figure 14-9. However, the kink stays at the same price P_0. We are assuming, therefore, that the shift in the demand curve dd to $d'd'$ is an exact outward shift with the slopes of the two different parts of the curve remaining the same. The cost curve does not change either. The marginal cost curve, mc, in panel (*b*) is the same as the marginal cost curve in panel (*a*). Clearly, the marginal cost curve intersects the new marginal revenue curve at a higher rate of output, and the profit-maximizing rate of output therefore increases from q_0 to q_1. So

long as the increase in demand is such that the marginal cost curve continues to "intersect" the discontinuous portion of the marginal revenue curve, the price will remain at P_0 even though output has changed. This example

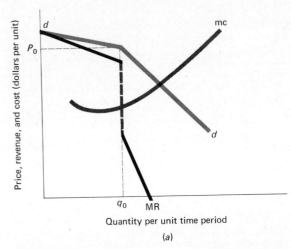

(*a*)

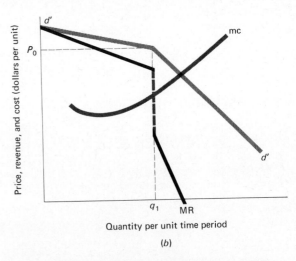

(*b*)

Figure 14-9: Changes in demand may not change profit-maximizing price.
In panel (*a*) we show demand curve dd with a kink at output rate q_0. The price that is charged is P_0. In panel (*b*) we show a shift or increase in demand to $d'd'$. However, if the kink remains at price P_0, that price will be maintained in the market, but output will increase for the oligopolist to q_1.

could be altered so that there would be a decrease in demand, and the results would be the same as long as the decrease in demand were sufficiently small to allow the marginal cost curve to continue "intersecting" the marginal revenue curve in its discontinuous portion. The price would remain the same with a decrease in demand, but the quantity provided by each oligopolist would fall.

The inverted kinked demand curve

Look at Figure 14-10. Here we show a kinked demand curve with the kink at point E. However, the upper portion is relatively steeper than the lower portion. This is just the reverse of the kinked demand curves we have been looking at. This reverse kink would be based on the individual oligopolist's expectation that all of its competitors will match any price increase that it initiates, but none will match a price cut. Presumably, such expectations would occur during an inflationary period.

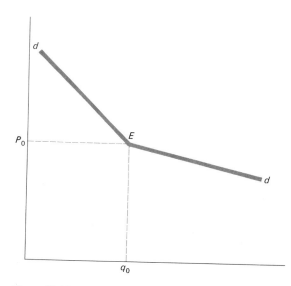

Figure 14-10: Inverted kinked demand curve.
If firms follow price increases but do not follow price decreases, the kinked demand is inverted. Presumably this applies to an inflationary situation.

Criticisms of the Sweezy model

After Sweezy's article first appeared, it was regarded by many economists as a definitive new general theory of oligopoly. Subsequent research and theoretical questioning have, however, cast some doubt on its general usefulness.

THEORETICAL PROBLEMS The theoretical problems are many. Not the least of them concerns how the initial price P_0 was determined in the first place. We start off the model with P_0 given. But if we do not know how P_0 was reached, then we do not have a general theory of oligopoly pricing and output decision making.

While it may be true that the kinked demand curve is accurate when interim knowledge about rivals' reactions is low, it is difficult to imagine that it is a long-run stable situation. Some economists contend that the kinked demand curve applies to a new industry in its early stages or to an industry in which new and previously unknown rivals enter the market.

Of course, the problem is that we still have a no-learning-by-doing model. The kink mentality is a barrier to changes in price that will increase profits, and this barrier is wholly of the oligopolist's own cerebral fabrication. It would seem that there are many ways in which the barrier could be circumvented. After all, that's what business is all about—a collection of devices for circumventing barriers to higher profits.

EMPIRICAL EVIDENCE The empirical evidence is not strong enough to support the existence of a kink. A study by George Stigler showed that in seven oligopolistic industries, price rises by one firm were met by price rises by other firms. Thus there seemed to be no asymmetry in the reaction of rivals to changes in price inherent in the kinked demand curve.[5] One empirical study does not disprove a theory, but it does cast doubt on the completeness of the Sweezy solution to the oligopoly pricing and output problem.

Implicit collusion models

There have been a number of implicit collusion models presented to try to explain oligopolistic industries. We will cover three of these theories. The first two are models of price leadership. The third deals with pricing to prevent entry. In all models there is no formal or explicit cartel arrangement.

Price leadership by the dominant firm

It is sometimes alleged that pricing in oligopolistic industries is controlled by the dominant firm, i.e., the largest firm in the industry. The basic assumption in this model is that the dominant firm sets the price and allows other firms to sell all they can at that price. The dominant firm then sells the rest. Given this assumption, a determinant solution for price and quantity can be derived.

The first thing we must do is derive the demand schedule for the dominant firm. This is done in Figure 14-11. First we draw the market demand schedule DD. Then we draw the supply schedule of the smaller firms. This is shown as Σmc_{small}. It is the horizontal summation of all the marginal cost curves of the smaller firms above their respective minimum average variable cost curves. To find the demand curve of the dominant firm, we need to find: (1) a point at which all the smaller firms supply the entire market demand and the dominant firm supplies zero demand, and (2) a point where the dominant firm supplies the

entire market and the small firms supply zero. In what follows, we add a third point in between.

Look at price P_1. At this price the small firms would supply the entire output for the industry. For at price P_1, the small firms would want to supply the total quantity that the market would purchase at that price, or the quantity from the vertical axis to point E on the demand curve DD. Remember that by

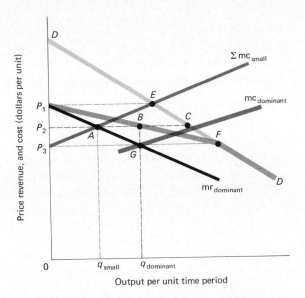

Figure 14-11: Price leadership by the dominant firm.
The market demand curve is DD. Assume that at price P_1 all the small firms taken together will provide the entire output; that is, the horizontal distance from P_1 to point E. At price P_2, the small firms will provide a quantity P_2A. The dominant firm would therefore provide the rest. Thus, we derive point B on the dominant firm's demand curve by subtracting the horizontal distance from P_2 to point A from the demand curve DD. In other words, $BC = P_2A$. At price P_3, the small firms will provide none of the output, for marginal cost exceeds that price. The dominant firm's demand curve becomes coincident with the industry demand curve. The dominant firm's demand curve is the heavy line P_1BFD. When we draw in the marginal revenue curve up to its discontinuous point, we find the profit-maximizing rate of output for the dominant firm at $q_{dominant}$ or at point G, where $mr_{dominant} = mc_{dominant}$. The profit-maximizing price is found on demand curve P_1FD; it is P_2.

[5] George J. Stigler, "The Kinky Oligopoly Demand Curve and Rigid Prices," *Journal of Political Economy*, vol. 55, no. 5, October 1947, pp. 432–449.

assumption, the dominant firm sets the price and *allows* other firms to sell all they can at that price. If the dominant firms set the price P_1 and followed this assumption, it would allow the small firms to supply everything; it would supply nothing at price P_1. This is therefore the vertical intercept of the dominant firm's demand curve. Now pick a price P_2 less than P_1. The smaller firms will provide output P_2A—the horizontal distance from the vertical axis to point A on the summed marginal cost curve. At price P_2, total quantity demanded is equal to P_2C, or the horizontal distance from the vertical axis to point C on the demand curve. We measure back from point C an amount equal to P_2A to find out how much is left over for the dominant firm. This gets up to point B. Thus, the dominant firm will supply output equal to the horizontal distance from P_2 to point B. Now we go to price P_3. At this price the small firms will provide nothing. Their costs are too high. The dominant firm will provide the entire market, or the horizontal distance from the vertical axis to point F on the market demand schedule. The dominant firm demand curve is the thick kinked demand curve that runs from the vertical axis at price P_1 through B to point F and then along the industry demand curve.

Given this demand curve, the dominant firm acts as a monopolist. We must now draw in a marginal revenue curve that is marginal to P_1FD. It is labeled $mr_{dominant}$. (For simplicity, on the diagram we have not drawn in the marginal revenue curve past the "kink" price F.)

The marginal cost curve for the dominant firm is labeled $mc_{dominant}$. It intersects the dominant firm's marginal revenue curve $mr_{dominant}$ at point G. The dominant firm's profit-maximizing rate of output is therefore given as $q_{dominant}$. The profit-maximizing price set by the dominant firm will be P_2.

The smaller firms, in the aggregate, will produce q_{small}.[6] At price P_2, total market demand is satisfied by the combined outputs $q_{dominant}$ and q_{small}. A price-quantity solution is obtained. It is stable because of our assumption that the small firms behaved passively as price takers. In other words, small firms are eliminated from consideration as rivals in the usual sense of the term.

Price leadership by the low-cost firm

An alternative price-leadership model involves leadership by the low-cost firm. We will simplify the analysis greatly by considering a duopoly situation in which there is a tacit agreement to share the market. This is merely an extension of the market-sharing cartel model we have talked about before. The two firms produce a homogeneous commodity. The market demand curve for this commodity is given in Figure 14-12 by the demand curve DD. Each firm faces a demand curve of dd, which is equal to one-half DD. This is a proportionate demand curve. The marginal revenue curve that is marginal to dd is labled mr.

The problem here is that the costs of the two firms are different; they are not identical. Firm 2 has higher cost curves than firm 1. Firm 2's average and marginal cost curves are given by AC_2 and MC_2, and firm 1's curves are given by AC_1 and MC_1. The lower-cost firm, firm 1, would, if given a choice, charge a price of P_1. The higher-cost firm, if given a choice, would charge a higher price P_2.

In this model, firm 2 has no choice but to follow the lower-cost firm, firm 1. If the firm does not follow and sets a price of P_2, its sales will be zero. All customers will go to firm 1,

---

[6] In order to simplify the diagram, $mc_{dominant}$ was drawn to intersect $mr_{dominant}$ at the quantity $q_{dominant}$, so that a new price line would not have to be drawn in.

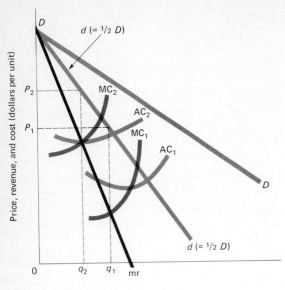

Figure 14-12: Price leadership by the low-cost firm.
Assume that two firms share the market such that each faces a proportionate demand curve $dd = \frac{1}{2}D\frac{1}{2}D$. The marginal revenue curve is mr. The lower-cost firm is represented by AC_1 and MC_1. It will produce at output rate q_1 and will charge price P_1. However, the higher-cost firm would like to produce at output rate q_2 and sell at price P_2. In this model, though, it has no choice but to follow the lower-cost firm. It will still receive profits because P_1 is higher than AC_2 at output rate q_1.

which is selling the product at price P_1. (We assume it can supply that larger quantity demanded.) The lower-cost firm becomes the price leader, and the price is set at P_1. Firm 2, even though the higher-cost firm, will still receive some profit. Firm 1, because of its lower costs, will make a much greater profit.

Problems with price-leadership models

There are a number of problems with price-leadership models that we could discuss. We mention just a few of them.

Unlikely nature of price leadership by low-cost firm

The price-leadership model presented in Figure 14-12 seems unlikely. Why would the lower-cost firm tacitly agree to share the market equally with the higher-cost firm? Assume for the moment that antitrust laws prevent the lower-cost firm from driving the higher-cost firm completely out of business. It would still seem reasonable that the lower-cost firm would not be willing to share the market equally but rather would set a price so that the higher-cost firm makes zero economic profits and gives up part of its share of the market to the lower-cost firm.

A theory of information

Information about future demands for a commodity, future alternative sources of supply, future production costs, and future changes in technology is not free. Information is a scarce resource and requires resources to obtain it. The information necessary for a firm to make a decision as to where to set output and price in order to maximize profits is costly. Thus, we might predict that in some instances some firms would prefer to allow other firms to generate that information. Firms would like, if they could, to be a free rider on the information obtained by other firms that would help each firm to set its profit-maximizing prices.

What better way to be a free rider than to allow the dominant, "richest" firm in the industry to do all of the market research to determine what the profit-maximizing price is? It is possible that price leadership by a dominant firm has nothing to do with collusion or shared markets, but rather with the fact that smaller firms are allowing the larger firm to spend all of the resources necessary to obtain the information for setting a profit-maximizing price. Price leadership by a dominant firm can be couched within the theory of information and the problem of the free rider.

Limit pricing

A model in which existing firms in the industry set prices in an attempt to discourage or prevent entry is called a limit-pricing oligopoly model. In all such models, the industry firms set prices so as to maximize the present value of their profit stream by retarding the entry of new firms; thus, a price is chosen that still allows some monopoly profits but not enough to attract new entrants.

The firm contemplating entry into a new market has to consider at least two possibilities: (1) entry will depress the market price if existing firms maintain their outputs, and (2) if the new firm contracts its output so as to reduce the price depression caused by its additional output, then this new firm may encounter higher average costs if it moves leftward and up its long-run average cost curve.

In Figure 14-13, we draw a hypothetical long-run average cost curve LAC and assume it is the same for all firms. The industry price is set at P_1; each firm's output is q_1. Assume further that existing firms will attempt to maintain that rate of output even with entry. Now consider the possibility that a new firm enters. Price must fall if this additional output is to be sold. Its additional output causes price to fall from P_1 to P_2. Clearly, all firms will now have losses which will be equal to the distance between the long-run average cost curve LAC and the price P_2, or the distance between E and F in Figure 14-13.

Now we know that the price-depressing effect of a new firm is directly related to its rate of output. If it reduces its rate of output, there will be a smaller reduction in the market price, but it will still suffer losses. Consider the possibility of the new entrant reducing output

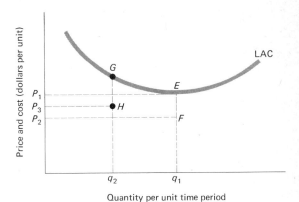

Figure 14-13: Limit pricing.
Assume that each existing firm produces at output rate q_1, and that each firm enjoys such cost advantages of large-scale production so that their average total costs are equal to $q_1 E$. Assume that price is P_1. If one firm enters with the same lowest-cost scale of operations and all other firms maintain their rate of output, the price will fall to P_2. Each firm that was in the industry will now suffer losses per unit of output equal to the vertical distance between E and F. If, on the other hand, the entering firm does not attempt to produce as much as the other firms, but adopts the scale of production q_2, price will fall only to P_3. The firms already in the industry will have smaller losses; but, the entering firm will not be able to enjoy lower average costs. It will suffer a greater loss, equal to the vertical distance between point H and point G.

from q_1 to q_2. The market price will now only fall to P_3 rather than P_2. However, the new firm will not be able to enjoy the lower per unit cost that the existing firms already enjoy, because they continue to produce at the same rate. Its cost will rise to G. It will make a loss per unit of output equal to the vertical difference between G and H. Other firms will incur a smaller loss per unit of output.

In this simplified example, any rate of output which a new entrant can produce will cause the market price to drop below the new entrant's long-run average cost. Entry is said to be blocked. If existing firms realize this, they may choose to raise prices above their long-run average cost. The degree to which they can raise their price above their minimum long-run average cost per unit depends on (1) the cost disadvantage the entrant realizes if it enters at a scale where LAC per unit is greater than that experienced by the existing firms, and (2) the price-depressing effect caused by the new entrant's output.[7]

Nonprice competition

By their very nature, oligopolistic markets do not exhibit active price competition. Price wars do erupt occasionally, but this is seen to be an implicit indication that communication channels among firms in oligopolistic markets are temporarily disrupted. With the exception of the Edgeworth model, the usual prediction for an oligopolistic market is stable prices. Competition, therefore, for an increased market share must take on some other form. The alternative form is what is generally called **nonprice competition**. Nonprice competition cannot be neatly subdivided into two or more categories because it can take on a large number of aspects. The only thing that we can say about nonprice competition is that it is an attempt by one oligopolistic firm to attract customers by some means other than a price differential. Product differentiation takes on many forms, but we will consider only advertising and quality differenials.

Advertising

As we pointed out in the last chapter, the primary purpose of advertising is to shift the demand curve to the right. This allows the seller to sell more at each and every price. Advertising may also have the effect of differentiating the product and of making the product's availability better known. To go into a

complete theory of advertising here would require us to get into the theory of information dissemination; we will not do this. Whatever can be said about advertising, its effects on the firm are certainly not completely predictable. Whether or not advertising in oligopolistic industries is beneficial to society as a whole is a question we cannot answer. It does exist, and hence, by assumption, it is perceived to be beneficial by each of the firms engaging in it.

Quality variations

Quality differentiation results in a division of one market into a number of submarkets. We talked earlier about product differentiation by quality differentials when we discussed monopolistic competition. A prime example of product differentiation is the automobile industry. There are specific, physically definable differences between different automobile models within one single firm. A General Motors Chevette and a General Motors Seville are certainly not the same animal. If we were to examine automobiles, we would see that competition among firms creates a continuous expansion and redefinition of the different models that are sold by any one company. There is competition to create new quality classes and thereby gain a competitive edge. Being the first in the market in a new-quality class has often meant higher profits. Witness the phenomenal success of the original Mustang. But also witness the dismal failure of Ford's Edsel a few years before the introduction of the successful Mustang.

Where are we in the theory of oligopoly?

If you found this chapter to be analytically somewhat less conclusive than the previous three, you are not alone. Most economists consider the theory of oligopoly to be the most perplexing of the models of industrial structure. It is particularly perplexing because

---

[7]See Joe S. Bain, "A Note on Pricing in Monopoly and Oligopoly," *American Economic Review*, vol. 39, March 1949, pp. 448–64.

oligopoly is so widespread and is especially common in manufacturing industries. We need only mention primary aluminum, primary copper, and automobiles to come up with clear cases of oligopoly. A very high concentration of total output is in the hands of the largest three or four firms, and there is a small number of firms within each industry.

Of course, the problem with oligopoly theory is that it is characterized by a recognized interdependency among sellers. We then must deal with what economists call conjectural variations in the firm's expectations about how other firms' outputs and/or prices will change as a result of its own changes in output and/or price. Depending on the specific assumptions we make, we come up with different models and different solutions. Unfortunately, economic theory does not suggest what assumptions to use. In any event, each of these theories must ultimately stand or fall on its predictive powers.

Issues and applications

Pricing in an allegedly oligopolistic industry: The case of automobiles

The automobile industry has been used as an example of an oligopoly for many years. What we would like to show in this application is that even though GM, for example, may appear to have a significant amount of monopoly or oligopoly power, that power is attenuated by the supply elasticity of the other automobile firms.

Deriving the relationship between one firm's demand and all other firms' supply

Let General Motors produce q_i. Then

$$Q_s = q_i + q_0 \qquad (14\text{-}1)$$

where Q_s = industry supply
q_0 = supply of all other firms

Both supply and demand are a function of price, and in equilibrium

$$Q_D(P) = Q_S(P) = q_i + q_0 \qquad (14\text{-}2)$$

where Q_D = market demand for autos.

Then $q_d = Q_D - q_0 \qquad (14\text{-}3)$

where q_d = demand for GM's cars.

The complete notation is then

$$
\begin{aligned}
Q_s &= \text{industry supply} \\
q_i &= \text{GM supply} \\
q_0 &= \text{all other supply} \\
Q_D &= \text{industry demand} \\
q_d &= \text{GM demand}
\end{aligned}
$$

In other words, what's left over is the demand for GM cars. Change each of the variables in Eq. (14-3) by a little bit, Δ,

$$\Delta q_d = \Delta Q_d - \Delta q_0 \qquad (14\text{-}4)$$

Divide Eq. (14-4) by $q_d \Delta P$ to get

$$\frac{\Delta q_d}{q_d \Delta P} = \frac{\Delta Q_D}{q_d \Delta P} - \frac{\Delta q_0}{q_d \Delta P} \qquad (14\text{-}5)$$

Now multiply Eq. (14-5) by P to get

$$\frac{\Delta q_d}{q_d} \cdot \frac{P}{\Delta P} = \left(\frac{\Delta Q_D}{q_d} \cdot \frac{P}{\Delta P}\right) - \left(\frac{\Delta q_0}{q_d} \cdot \frac{P}{\Delta P}\right) \qquad (14\text{-}6)$$

We rearrange Eq. (14-6). Multiply the first right-hand term by Q_D/Q_D and the second by q_0/q_0.

$$\frac{\Delta q_d}{\Delta P} \cdot \frac{P}{q_d} = \left(\frac{Q_D}{q_d}\right)\frac{\Delta Q_D}{Q_D} \cdot \frac{P}{\Delta P} - \left(\frac{q_0}{q_d}\right)\frac{\Delta q_0}{q_0} \cdot \frac{P}{\Delta P} \qquad (14\text{-}7)$$

But this equals

$$\eta_d = \left(\frac{Q_D}{q_d}\right)\eta_D - \left(\frac{q_0}{q_d}\right)\epsilon_o \qquad (14\text{-}8)$$

where ϵ_0 is the supply elasticity of the other auto manufacturers and η is price elasticity of demand.

From Eq. (14-8), we see that the price elasticity of demand for General Motors products, η_d, is a function of the market price elasticity of demand η_D and price elasticity of supply of other firms, and the (inverse of the) realtive share of industry output accounted for by the firm under study, Q_D/q_d. What is clear from Eq. (14-8) is the importance of ϵ_0. Since η is always negative, when we subtract ϵ_0, we always increase absolutely the price elasticity of demand facing the individual firm. In the short run, a demand curve for General Motors products might be inelastic. However, in the long run, if ϵ_0 is sufficiently large, that is no longer true. This analysis explains why a firm such as General Motors will sell in a market in which the demand is relatively inelastic and set a price lower than expected.

Some hypothetical numbers

Various estimates have been made of the price elasticity of demand for new automobiles. A good average is $\eta_D = -2$.

Remember that when the firm maximizes profits

$$MR = P\left(1 + \frac{1}{\eta_D}\right) = MC \qquad (14\text{-}9)$$

Thus, if we rearrange Eq. (14-9), we get

$$\frac{P - MC}{P} = -\frac{1}{\eta_D} \qquad (14\text{-}10)$$

Now, if we make the assumption that marginal cost is approximately equal to average cost (a not unreasonable assumption for firms selling millions of cars), then Eq. (14-10) becomes

$$\frac{P - AC}{P} = -\frac{1}{\eta_D} \qquad (14\text{-}11)$$

Then, if the industry price elasticity of demand is approximately equal to -2.0, we would expect that

$$\frac{P - AC}{P} = -\frac{1}{-2.00} = \frac{1}{2.0} \qquad (14\text{-}12)$$

This would indicate that 50¢ of each dollar would be a profit margin. However, if we look at the data relating to General Motors and other automobile companies, we do not find anything near a 50 percent profit margin on sales. What we find are figures much closer to 6 to 10 percent as the rate of return on sales. A 10 percent rate of return on sales is consistent with a price elasticity of demand facing an individual firm of about -10 when we use Eq. (14-10).

We can approximate, then, the price elasticity of supply facing, for example, General Motors, by using this information. Let us substitute for $\eta_d = -10$ and for $\eta_D = -2$ in Eq. (14-8). The share of industry output accounted for by General Motors is about 50 percent so that $Q_D/q_d = 2$, and $q_0/q_d = 1$. Thus, Eq. (14-8) becomes

$$-10 = (2)(-2) - (1)\epsilon_0 \qquad (14\text{-}13)$$

The price elasticity of supply of other firms, ϵ_0, is approximately equal to 6. A 1 percent increase in the price that General Motors charges for its cars will elicit a 6 percent increase in the quantity supplied from other companies. Thus, the monopoly or oligopoly power that General Motors has is limited by the supply of the other firms in the industry.

The court's view of oligopoly

Section I of the Sherman Antitrust Act states that "Every contract, combination in the form of trust or otherwise, or conspiracy, in restraint of trade or commerce among the several states, or with foreign nations, is hereby declared to be illegal." The Sherman Act, therefore, does not expressly prohibit oligopolies, because there is no explicit contract or combination in restraint of trade. When there is collusion, as occurred among the big electrical companies, then the violation of the law is clear.

In an oligopoly in which a few sellers supply most of the sales, the pricing practices of the sellers in such markets have been called **conscious**

parallelism. Such pricing policies are the result of the recognized interdependence of oligopolists. They know that there will be a reaction by the other oligopolists to a change in one's price. The result presumably is a tendency to avoid vigorous price competition. The question that has come before the courts is whether or not such "conscious parallelism" that is a result of oligopolistic interdependence can properly be viewed as a form of agreement to fix prices and in violation of section I of the Sherman Antitrust Act. In a famous case argued before the Supreme Court, *Theater Enterprises, Inc. v. Paramount Film Distributing Corporation*,[8] Supreme Court Justice Clark, speaking for the Court, noted

> ...but this court has never held that proof of parallel business behavior conclusively established agreement or, phrased differently, that such behavior itself constitutes a Sherman Act offense. Circumstantial evidence of consciously parallel behavior may have made heavy in-roads into the traditional judicial attitude toward conspiracy; but "conscious parallelism" has not yet read conspiracy out of the Sherman Act entirely.

In an important article, former Assistant U.S. Attorney General Donald F. Turner[9] contended that oligopolistic pricing behavior was similar in nature to competitive pricing behavior, but one other factor, rivals' responses, had to be taken into account. Moreover, Turner pointed out that there is no effective remedy for oligopolistic interdependence. A court injunction that "prohibited each defendant from taking into account the probable price decisions of his competitors in determining his own price or output would demand such irrational behavior that full compliance would be virtually impossible." Turner went on further to point out that a court injunction would have to require that the defendants reduce price to marginal cost and that the enforcement of such

a decree would involve the courts in public utility types of rate regulation for all oligopolists in the United States.

Turner, therefore, would eliminate the use of the Sherman Act to prosecute oligopolists. Rather, he suggested as an appropriate remedy breaking oligopolistic firms into smaller units either by special legislation or under section II of the Sherman Act, which prohibits monopolization or attempt to monopolize. Turner thought it was appropriate to charge oligopolists with jointly monopolizing their market.

Not all legal scholars agree with Turner's conclusions. Professor of Law Richard Posner, for example, points out that oligopoly is a necessary condition of successful price fixing, but not a sufficient condition. He contends that there is no vital difference between formal cartels and tacit collusive agreements; the latter are simply easier to conceal. If section I of the Sherman Act is to deter collusion by increasing the cost of colluding, then the tacit, as well as the overt, colluder should be, according to Posner, punished equally. After all, tacit collusion is not an unconscious state. Business people know what they are doing.

Posner does point out that the most serious problem with his proposal—applying section I against tacit collusion—is that of proving it.[10]

Glossary

Duopoly A market structure in which there are only two sellers.
Oligopoly A market structure in which there are several sellers and each takes account of the others' reactions.
Kinked demand curve A demand curve that has a kink, or abrupt change in slope, at some quantity; related to a theory developed by Paul Sweezy.

[8]345 U.S. 537, 74 S.Ct. 257, 98 LEd. 273 (1954).
[9]Donald F. Turner, "The Definition of Agreement under the Sherman Act: Conscious Parallelism and Refusals to Deal," *Harvard Law Review*, vol. 75, 1962, pp. 655ff.

[10]Richard A. Posner, "Oligopoly and the Antitrust Laws: A Suggested Approach," *Stanford Law Review*, vol. 21, 1969, pp. 1562–1576 and 1591–1592.

Nonprice competition Competition by means of quality changes, design changes, reliability, service, and so on; to be contrasted with price competition.

Conscious parallelism Pricing behavior by oligopolists in which each takes account of the other's potential reaction and therefore does not engage in vigorous price competition. No explicit collusive agreement is entered into, however.

Summary

1. In addition to competition, monopoly, and monopolistic competition, we study the market structures of duopoly and oligopoly in which each firm realizes that other firms will react to any changes in its price and/or output.

2. In the simplest oligopoly model, each firm assumes that any change in price will be matched by all other firms in the industry.

3. In the Cournot duopoly model, the two producers are identical and each selects its rate of output under the assumption that the other will continue to produce whatever it is presently producing. Although this is a no-learning-by-doing model, a determinate equilibrium can be reached.

4. In Edgeworth's model, each firm has a limited productive capacity and different prices for the product can temporarily prevail. Price is selected on the assumption that the other duopolist will continue to charge the same price presently charged. There is no determinate solution.

5. In the Chamberlin model of duopoly, each firm produces exactly one-half total industry output and they each sell at the joint profit-maximizing price (the price a monopolist would charge if it owned both firms).

6. In the Stigler model, the agreed-upon goal of the oligopolists is to collude, but each recognizes that none can be restrained completely from cheating. Oligopoly is an implicit cartel that is formed with full knowledge that the policing scheme used will be imperfectly, although tolerably, effective.

7. The implications of the Stigler model are (a) the fewer the firms, the more effective the cartel; (b) secret price cuts will be offered relatively more often to large as opposed to small buyers; (c) the more homogeneous the product, the easier it is to enforce a collusive price agreement; and (d) the more unstable the industry demand and/or cost conditions, the less likely the collusion will be successful.

8. In a kinked demand curve oligopoly model, the individual oligopolist assumes that if price is lowered, rivals will match the reduction, but if price is raised, rivals will not match the increase.

9. Marginal revenue for a kinked demand curve has a discontinuous portion at the kink.

10. It is possible that changes in cost and/or demand conditions will leave unchanged the price that the oligopolist will charge.

11. The kinked demand curve has been subject to criticisms. No indication is given as to how the initial price was arrived at, and the empirical evidence used to support the existence of a kink is weak at best.

12. Implicit collusion models include (a) price leadership by the dominant firm, (b) price leadership by the low-cost firm, and (c) limit pricing.

Selected references

Bork, Robert H., "Legislative Intent and the Policy of the Sherman Act," *The Journal of Law and Economics*, vol. 9, October 1966, pp. 7–48.

Fellner, William, *Competition among the Few: Oligopoly and Similar Market Structures* (New York: Knopf, 1949).

Machlup, Fritz, *The Economics of Sellers' Competition* (Baltimore: Johns Hopkins, 1952), chaps. 4 and 11–16.

Modigliani, Franco, "New Developments on the Oligopoly Front," *Journal of Political Economy*, vol. 66, June 1958, pp. 215–232.

Nutter, G. W., "Duopoly, Oligopoly, and Emerging Competition," *Southern Economic Journal*, vol. 30, April 1964, pp. 342–352.

Van Cise, Gerrold G., *The Federal Anti-Trust Laws*, 3d ed., rev. (Washington, D.C.: American Enterprise Institute for Public Policy Research, 1975).

Questions

(Answers to even-numbered questions are at back of text.)

1. What basic assumptions are common to most oligopoly models?

2. Under what circumstances would oligopoly models be appropriately applied to the retailing of gasoline?

3. Figure 14-1 presents a proportionate demand curve for an oligopolistic industry. What assumption underlies the use of these curves, and why is the assumption necessary?

4. Look at Figure 14-2. It appears that two firms could supply the industry demand more efficiently, from a cost standpoint, than could three. Why, then, does this model predict that three firms will emerge?

5. Figure 14-3 portrays long-run economic profits. How can that be the case if entry is unrestricted?

6. In Cournot's duopoly model: (*a*) What are his assumptions? (*b*) What is the long-run result predicted by the model?

7. How does Edgeworth's duopoly model differ from that of Cournot (*a*) in its assumptions and (*b*) in its solution?

8. Criticize the Cournot and Edgeworth models.

9. On what assumptions does Chamberlin's duopoly model rely? What result is obtained?

10. Explain why Paul Sweezy's kinked demand curve is kinked.

11. Under the kinked demand theory of Sweezy, why do shifts in the marginal cost curve often cause no change whatsoever in price or output?

12. If the dominant firm sets the price, what sort of behavior is assumed on the part of the rest of the oligopolists?

13. If the low-cost firm is the price leader, how could it run the other firms out of business? Why might it prefer *not* to do so?

14. Why do you think that advertising and minor changes in product design are so prevalent in many oligopolistic industries?

15. Suppose that oligopoly pricing and output policies were deemed to be a social evil. Can you imagine any problems that a government attorney, armed with the theories of this chapter, would have in prosecuting a case in which collusion had been alleged?

15

COMPETITIVE
RESOURCE
DEMAND

Some firms hire mostly skilled workers. The wages of skilled workers are, of course, relatively higher than those of unskilled workers. Some firms hire mostly unskilled workers.

At times, workers are laid off and later rehired. At other times, they are laid off and not rehired.

Wage rates and the amount of labor employed are indeed important topics to analyze because they affect the well-being of the approximately 95 million workers in the American labor force and their families. On a more general level, the pricing and employment of all inputs is a topic of concern because it has much to do with the distribution of income in the United States. We will restrict our discussion in this chapter to the pricing and employment of inputs purchased in perfectly competitive markets and lean heavily toward an analysis of the labor input. In the next chapter, we will undertake this same study when there is imperfect competition in both the output and the input markets. We will wait until Chapter 17 to undertake a discussion of income differentials. Right now, let's look at the firm's optimal employment of inputs.

Optimal input employment

We first dealt with the firm's optimal input combination when we undertook our study of the theory of the firm in Chapter 7. What we did there and in Chapter 8 was look at two variable inputs, capital and labor. We assumed that each could be purchased at a constant unit price. We further assumed that their quantities could be infinitesimally varied. This permitted us to draw a smooth isoquant curve convex to the origin. It was convex because of a diminishing marginal rate of technical substitution.

Starting out with a given dollar outlay, we asked the following question: What is the optimal or cost-minimizing combination of inputs? It was found to be where an isoquant curve was tangent to a given isocost or total outlay line. Given that the slope of the isocost line was equal to $-r/w$ and the slope at any point of the isoquant was $-MPP_K/MPP_L$, then we know that the optimal input combination was such that

$$\frac{r}{w} = \frac{MPP_K}{MPP_L} \quad \text{or} \quad \frac{MPP_K}{r} = \frac{MPP_L}{w} \quad (15\text{-}1)$$

where r = the implicit rental rate per unit of service flow from capital (capital-user charge) and w = the wage rate for a constant quality unit of labor. We can generalize Eq. (15-1) to more than two inputs. When there are n inputs,

$$\frac{MPP_x}{P_x} = \frac{MPP_y}{P_y} = \cdots = \frac{MPP_n}{P_n} \quad (15\text{-}2)$$

In other words, input cost minimization or output product maximization requires a combination of inputs such that the ratio of the marginal physical product of each input divided by its price is the same for all inputs.

Marginal cost and marginal revenue

Look at the reciprocal of any one of the terms in Eq. (15-2), e.g., P_x/MPP_x. The numerator is the price of a unit of the input.

Thus, an increase of one unit of an input such as x adds P_x to total cost, but it also adds to total product by the amount of MPP_x. The

fraction P_x/MPP_x is therefore the change in the firm's total cost per unit change in the product. But this is the same as our definition of the product's marginal cost. We know, then, that marginal cost equals P_i/MPP_i for the ith input, where output is expanded by increasing that particular input. Equation (15-2) can be rewritten as

$$\frac{MPP_x}{P_x} = \frac{MPP_y}{P_y} = \cdots = \frac{MPP_n}{P_n} = \frac{1}{MC} \quad (15\text{-}3)$$

Now consider the profit-maximizing firm selling its product in a perfectly competitive market. It will produce the output at which marginal revenue equals marginal cost and marginal revenue is equal to the price of the product. Thus we know that Eq. (15-3) can be written as

$$\frac{MPP_x}{P_x} = \frac{MPP_y}{P_y} = \cdots = \frac{MPP_n}{P_n} = \frac{1}{MC} = \frac{1}{MR} = \frac{1}{P}$$
$$(15\text{-}4)$$

$$\text{or} \quad \frac{P_x}{MPP_x} = \frac{P_y}{MPP_y} = \cdots = \frac{P_n}{MPP_n} = MC = P$$

where P (without a subscript) is the price of the product.

If the firm is to maximize profits, this equation must hold for all inputs. We can rearrange the terms of this equation to obtain the firm's profit-maximizing decision rule; it tells it how much of each input to employ. Let's do it for one input x.

We have from Eq. (15-4) that $MPP_x/P_x = 1/MR$. When we multiply this through by $(MR \cdot P_x)$, we obtain $MPP_x \cdot MR = P_x$. For the perfect competition $MR = P$, so this becomes $MPP_x \cdot P = P_x$. Thus for all inputs we have

$$MPP_x \cdot MR = P_x \quad \text{or} \quad MPP_x \cdot P = P_x$$
$$MPP_y \cdot MR = P_y \quad \text{or} \quad MPP_y \cdot P = P_y \quad (15\text{-}5)$$
$$MPP_n \cdot MR = P_n \quad \text{or} \quad MPP_n \cdot P = P_n$$

Thus firms selling and hiring in perfectly competitive markets will employ each input up to the quantity where the price per unit of input equals the marginal physical product of that input times the price of the output. This forms the basis for the firm's demand for an input. For example, consider a nursery that sells its planting services in a perfectly competitive market. Assume that it can purchase unskilled labor to dig holes at $4 an hour in a perfectly competitive labor market. It will hire workers at $4 an hour up to the point where the marginal physical product of its hole-digging labor force times the price it receives for that output from the customers is equal to $4.

The demand for one variable input

We will start our discussion of factor demand by considering the case of a single variable input in the same manner that we did back in Chapter 7. All inputs except labor we assume are fixed. Labor can be used in any discrete quantity. It is subject to the law of diminishing marginal physical returns.

We show the same table we used in Chapter 7 below; It has been relabeled Table 15-1. We have added two extra columns, however, which we will explain in a moment.

Value of marginal product

Marginal physical product is the increase in total physical product associated with a one-unit increase in the variable input. Remember that the marginal physical product of labor is not the amount of output produced by the additional unit of input per se. It is the additional output produced when an additional unit of labor is used in combination with a constant amount of all other inputs. The amount that an additional worker produces is his or her *average product*, or simply Q/L. After all, when an additional worker is hired, that worker produces some output, but more importantly, he or she alters the average amount of output that all other workers produce because they all work together. For a one-unit increase in labor ($\Delta L = 1$), this change is $MPP_L = APP_L + \Delta APP_L \cdot L$.[1]

If we multiply the marginal physical product times the price of the product, we come up with what is called the **value of marginal product** (VMP). In this case it is the value of marginal product of labor, or VMP_L. This is

---

[1]See pages 167–168 for the derivation of this equation.

Number of workers (1)	Total output (2)	Average physical product of labor [(2) ÷ (1)] (3)	Marginal physical product of labor* (Δtotal output/ Δlabor input) (4)	Price of product (5)	Value of marginal product [(4) × (5)] (6)
1	100	100	100	$9	$900
2	210	105	110	9	990
3	330	110	120	9	1080
4	405	101 1/4	75	9	675
5	475	95	70	9	630
6	500	83 1/3	20	9	180
7	490	70	−10	9	−90

Table 15-1
*All marginal figures refer to an interval between the indicated amount of whatever is in the denominator and one unit less than that indicated amount. This convention is used in all tables showing marginal quantities.

presented in column (6) of Table 15-1 where we see $VMP_L = MPP_L \cdot P$. We show the derivation of the value of marginal physical product curve in the two panels of Figure 15-1. Since we know that the firm will be operating only in stage II (somewhere between the two ridge lines in an isocost-isoquant diagram), we know that the firm will be operating only in the region of diminishing marginal returns. Hence, in panel (b) in Figure 15-1, we show only the downward-sloping portion of the marginal physical product curve. All we have to do to obtain the VMP curve in panel (a) in Figure 15-1 is find marginal physical product for a given rate of use of the input labor and then multiply it by the price of the output.

The short-run demand curve for labor, or the optimal employment of labor

We have already seen that a profit-maximizing firm will hire an input to the point where the price per unit of input equals the marginal physical product of the input times the price of the output. This was seen in Eq. (15-5). For example, if the price per unit input is $10 and the price per unit of output is $5, workers will be hired up to the point where marginal physical product is two units of output, such that $10 = 2 (= MPP) \cdot $5 (which is price per output unit). Now we have a name for output unit price times marginal physical product; that name is VMP, or value of marginal product. Thus, it turns out that value of marginal product curve is the firm's short-run demand curve for labor in a perfectly competitive market, *the quantity of all other inputs held constant*. For the perfectly competitive individual firm, the price of output remains constant no matter how much is sold. The price of the input, we will assume in this chapter, also remains constant; its supply is perfectly elastic to the individual firm. Thus we can see that the profit-maximizing quantity of labor will be obtained where the wage line (the "going" wage rate for the skill in question) intersects

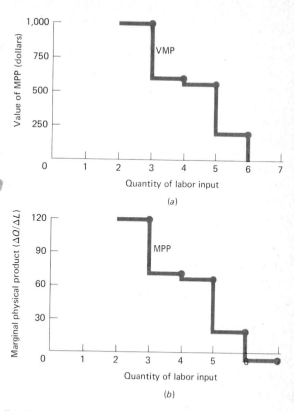

(a)

(b)

Figure 15-1 Deriving the VMP curve from the MPP curve. In panel (b), we show the MPP curve of column 4 of Table 15-1. We multiply that curve by the price of the product, $9, and obtain the value of marginal product curve, VMP, in panel (a). It is taken from column 6 in Table 15-1.

the firm's value of marginal product curve. This is presented in Figure 15-2. If the going wage rate per constant-quality unit of labor is w_0, the optimum quantity of labor demanded will be L_0. The line horizontal at w_0 represents the supply curve of labor to each firm when labor is purchased in a perfectly competitive labor market.

Input demand curve—Several variable inputs

We now complicate our analysis somewhat by varying more than one factor of production.

Short run

= demand for input in SR

Figure 15-2: **The profit-maximizing employment of labor.** We assume that labor can be obtained at wage rate w_0. The optimal quantity of labor demanded by the firm will be L_0, or where the wage line intersects the VMP_L curve.

In order to keep the problem manageable, however, we will confine our example to a situation in which there are only two variable factors of production. We will consider labor and capital. In a situation where there is more than one variable factor of production, the VMP curve no longer represents the demand curve for the input under study. The reason is because a change in the price of any one input will also result in a change in employment of the other variable inputs as the firm substitutes in the form of relatively cheaper inputs. But these changes will in turn then affect the quantity demanded of the original input whose price had changed. In other words, there is a feedback that we must take account of in deriving the demand curve for an input where other inputs are also variable.

A verbal explanation

When the price of labor falls, the quantity of labor demanded will increase because the new

lower wage line will intersect the VMP curve at a larger quantity of labor. However, as the quantity of labor used increases, the marginal physical product of the given of fixed capital stock, MPP_K, will increase because each unit of capital is now being operated by more laborers. If a die-stamp machine is operated by two workers instead of one, the marginal physical product of the die-stamp machine will be greater because the workers can take turns, thereby eliminating "downtime" and mistakes due to fatigue and boredom. In other words, each unit of the fixed amount of capital has more *complementary* input units with which to work.[2] We assume **complementarity** between capital and labor throughout.

From the expansion path to the demand curve for an input

Allowing for long-run changes in the capital stock, we can look at the above problems using isoquants and the expansion path.

In panel (*a*) of Figure 15-3, you see a typical input space with three isoquants drawn, Q_I, Q_{II}, and Q_{III}. The ratio of the wage rate w to the implicit rental cost of capital r, together with the isoquants, generates the two expansion paths labeled $0E$ and $0E'$. Remember the definition of an expansion path from page 202? That path shows how factor proportions change when output changes and input prices are constant. In other words, expansion path $0E$ would be generated as cost outlays increased and input prices remained constant. Thus the expansion path is the connection of the points of tangency between the changing isocost curve (that have constant slopes) with the higher and higher isoquants.[3] We start off

---

[2] It is possible, with K and L as *substitutes*, for the MPP_K to be reduced if the quantity of L rises. Then the firm will *reduce* the quantity of K and this in turn will increase the MPP_L.

[3] We use the simplified case here where the production function is linear homogeneous.

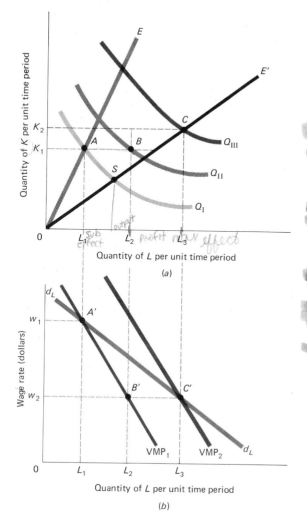

Quantity of K per unit time period

K_2
K_1

E
E'
C
A B Q_{III}
S Q_{II}
Q_I

0   L_1 L_2 L_3

Quantity of L per unit time period

(a)

Wage rate (dollars)

w_1 A'

w_2 B' C'

d_L

VMP$_1$ VMP$_2$ d_L

0   L_1 L_2 L_3

Quantity of L per unit time period

(b)

Figure 15-3: The demand curve for labor with two variable inputs.

Assume that capital and labor are complements. The starting wage rate is w_1; the quantity of labor demanded is L_1 in panels (a) and (b). L_1 is taken from the VMP$_1$ curve. Point A' in panel (b) corresponds to point A in panel (a). The amount of capital used with L_1 of labor is K_1. OE is the expansion path.

The wage rate falls to w_2. If there were no increase in the use of capital and no increase in the rate of output, the firm would slide down isoquant Q_1 from point A to point S. It would substitute labor for capital because labor is now relatively cheaper. This is the *substitution effect.*

However, at a lower wage rate and with the same cost outlay more labor can be bought while the firm continues to employ just as much capital. Thus, output would increase. The movement from point S to point B is, therefore, the *output effect.* The firm now operates on Q_{II}. Point B in panel (a) corresponds to point B' in panel (b) on the original VMP$_1$ curve. Point B in panel (a) is not on an expansion path. The firm will use more capital. This will cause the VMP curve to move out to VMP$_2$. The new optimum will be at point C'. If we connect A' and C' in panel (b), we obtain the firm's demand curve $d_L d_L$, for labor when capital is also varied. Point C' in panel (b) corresponds to point C in panel (a) where the firm operates on an expansion path OE.

in firm optimum in panel (b) with the wage rate equal to w_1. The quantity of labor demanded is at the intersection of the horizontal line at wage rate w_1 (which is the supply curve of labor) and the demand curve for labor VMP$_1$ when there is one variable factor of production. This intersection is labeled A'. The quantity of labor demanded is L_1. We know, however, that we must be somewhere on the expansion path OE drawn for a wage rate w_1 and an implicit user cost of capital r (that we do not show). Let us say that we start

out at point A on the expansion path OE. We are therefore going to be using L_1 of labor and K_1 of capital. Now the wage rate falls to w_2. In the first instance, holding K constant, the quantity of labor demanded would increase from L_1 to L_2. The firm would move down the value of marginal product curve VMP$_1$ from A' to B' in panel (b) of Figure 15-3. Clearly, this would move the firm to a higher isoquant because more labor and the same amount of capital is used. Thus, in panel (a) there would be a movement from point A to point B. There is an increase in output associated with the increased use of labor due to the reduction in the price of labor. This increased amount of output is represented by the movement from isoquant Q_I to the higher isoquant Q_{II}.

However, point B cannot be an optimal point. Note that the increased use of labor increases the marginal product of capital. Moreover, we know that the old expansion path $0E$ is no longer relevant because it was drawn for a relative wage rate of w_1/r. The new relative wage rate is lower; it is w_2/r. Thus, there is a new expansion path which is flatter than $0E$. It is labeled $0E'$. We know that the new equilibrium will require the use of more capital and also that the firm finds itself on a new expansion path. What happens is that the firm ends up at point C on the new expansion path $0E'$ in panel (a). What has happened in panel (b) is that the value of marginal product curve has shifted from VMP$_1$ to VMP$_2$ because more capital (K_2 instead of K_1) is being used. The optimal amount of labor will now be L_3. It is given in panel (b) by the intersection of the new lower wage rate w_2 with the new value of marginal product curve VMP$_2$, or point C'. In panel (b) of Figure 15-3, point A' gives the profit-maximizing quantity of labor demanded, L_1, at wage rate w_1. Point C' yields the profit-maximizing quantity of labor demanded, L_3, at lower wage rate w_2. If we connect such points A' and C', we obtain the demand curve for labor when there are two variable factors of production, capital and labor. This demand curve is labeled $d_L d_L$.

The three effects of a change in the wage rate

Implicit in the discussion just presented were the three effects resulting from a reduction in the wage rate. These three effects are called the substitution effect, the output effect, and the profit-maximizing effect.

THE SUBSTITUTION EFFECT. We have already discussed the substitution effect in Chapter 3; there we talked about the effect on quantity demanded of a product when there is a change in its relative price. The same analysis may be used here. The substitution effect can be seen in Figure 15-3 (a) as the movement from point A to point S. Remember, the expansion path $0E'$ is to the right of $0E$ when the wage rate falls and r is constant. Thus, if there were no increase in the use of capital and no increase in the rate of output, the firm would slide down the isoquant Q_I from A to S. It would substitute labor for capital because labor is now relatively cheaper. This portrays the substitution of labor for capital as a result of a decrease in the relative price of labor (an increase in the relative price of capital). In other words, this substitution effect, as measured by the movement from A to S in panel (a) of Figure 15-3, would occur if the entrepreneur were to produce the original level of output Q_I after the input price ratio had fallen.

OUTPUT EFFECT. Now consider that at a lower wage rate but with the same outlay, more labor could be bought while the firm continued to employ just as much capital. This would increase the firm's output. In panel (a) of Figure 15-3, the movement from point S to point B is the output effect. It is the increase in output (resulting from a reduction in the price of labor) after taking account of the substitution effect and holding total expenditures or costs constant. Point B in panel (a) of Figure 15-3 is a point showing the combination of the inputs, capital and labor, that would be employed if total expenditures on inputs remained unchanged.

THE PROFIT-MAXIMIZING EFFECT. The profit-maximizing firm does not, however, hold output constant when factor prices change; it does not hold total outlays constant either. In other words, neither point S nor point B in panel (a) of Figure 15-3 is the final optimal point for this firm. Remember from Eq. (15-1) that the profit-maximizing firm will always operate with a combination of inputs such that the ratio of the marginal physical product of each input divided by its price is equal for all inputs. But at point B in panel (a) of Figure 15-3 this is not the case. Only along the new expansion path $0E'$ is this equality found. Thus the movement from point B to point C is required for profit maximization. We call this increase from L_2 to L_3 in the quantity of labor demanded due to a reduction in its price the profit-maximizing effect of a decrease in the relative price of labor.

The slope of the input demand curve

Can we be guaranteed that when there is more than one variable factor of production the demand curve [such as the one labeled $d_L d_L$ in Figure 15-3(b)] will always be downward-sloping? After all, we did come up with the possibility of an upward-sloping demand curve for a product whenever the income effect for an inferior good was so strong that it overrode the pure substitution effect. This was the Giffen good case. It has been demonstrated by C. E. Ferguson that the factor demand curve must always be negatively sloped because, on balance, the three effects of an input price change must cause the quantity demanded to vary inversely with the price.[4]

The elasticity of substitution

When the price of labor fell in the last example, the quantity of labor demanded increased. With a given output level, there would have been a substitution effect and labor would have been substituted for capital. The responsiveness of the firm to a change in the price of an input can be measured by what

is called the **elasticity of substitution**. This measures the relative responsiveness of the capital-to-labor ratio to a relative change in the ratio of factor prices. The elasticity of substitution equals

$$\sigma = \left[\frac{\Delta(K/L)}{K/L} \middle/ \frac{\Delta(r/w)}{r/w} \right] \qquad (15\text{-}6)$$

where σ (*sigma*) is the Greek letter used for elasticity of substitution.[5] When $\sigma = -1$, a 1 percent decrease in the price of capital relative to the price of labor results in a 1 percent increase in the capital/labor proportion.

Numerous studies have been undertaken to estimate the elasticity of substitution of capital for labor. Quite a few have concluded that it is numerically close to 1; however, it varies from industry to industry and from short run to long run. Empirically, the firm can and does respond to changing relative input prices. The notion of fixed proportion production functions does not hold up in the real world.

The market demand curve

The market demand curve for any input is obtained by looking at all the individual firm's input demand curves. However, we cannot simply add together each firm's demand curve of the sort represented by $d_L d_L$ in panel (b) of Figure 15-3. The reason we cannot do this is because as the price of labor falls and more of it is hired, output will increase.[6] As the output of the entire industry increases, the price of the product must fall in order for the additional output to be sold. This results in a shift in VMP. Thus, we must take account of this reduction in the price of the output in deriving the market demand curve for input.

---

[4]C. E. Ferguson, "Production, Prices, and the Theory of Jointly Derived Input Demand Functions," *Economica*, new ser., vol. 33, 1966.

[5]The elasticity of substitution is equal to the responsiveness of the capital/labor ratio to changes in the marginal rate of technical substitution of capital for labor. However, we substitute for the marginal rate of technical

substitution the ratio of the two marginal products. We continue using the profit-maximizing rule given in Eq. (15-1) to get the ratio of the factor prices instead of the ratio of the marginal products.

[6]There are exceptions when there are several variable inputs.

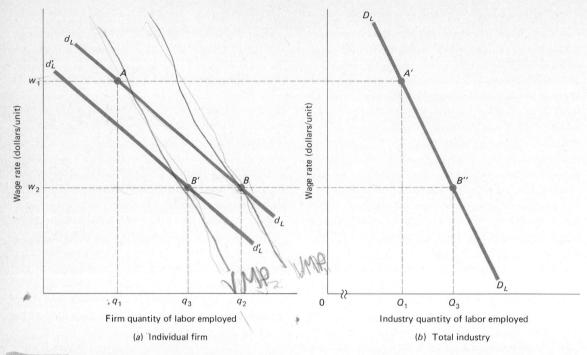

Figure 15-4: Deriving the industry demand curve for labor.

Assume a wage rate of w_1. The individual firm demand curve is $d_L d_L$ from Figure 15-3. This gives a point on the industry demand curve $D_L D_L$, which is point A' in panel (b). The quantity demanded is Q_1 for the industry, or q_1 for the firm. Now the wage rate falls to w_2. The firm increases quantity demanded to q_2; however, point B cannot be maintained for long. As all firms increase output, the price of the product must fall. The VMP curve shifts to the left to $d'_L d'_L$; the quantity of labor demanded falls from q_2 to q_3 in panel (a). Point B' gives us a new point in panel (b), point B''. Industry quantity demanded increases to Q_3. If we connect points A' and B'', we obtain the industry demand curve $D_L D_L$ for the input.

We do this in panels (a) and (b) of Figure 15-4. We start off with the assumption that each firm is identical and that its demand curve for labor is $d_L d_L$, as shown in panel (a) of Figure 15-4. The going wage rate for labor per constant-quality unit is w_1. This is the supply price of labor, the price per unit that the firm must pay. It intersects the firm's demand curve for labor at point A in panel (a). The quantity of labor demanded by the firm will be q_1. We multiply q_1 times the number of firms, and find that the quantity of labor demanded by the industry is Q_1. The wage rate w_1 and the quantity demanded in the industry, Q_1, give us one point on our industry demand curve, and that point is labeled A'.

Now assume that there is a reduction in the wage rate of workers to w_2. Each individual firm moves along its demand for labor curve. Thus, there is a movement from point A to point B on $d_L d_L$ in panel (a) of Figure 15-4. Each firm would like to hire q_2 of workers. However, if each firm were to hire q_2 of workers, they would end up producing more. When they produce more, the only way they can all sell this increased input is by reducing the price of the output.[7] But a reduction in the output's price will shift the value of marginal product curve. The firm's demand curve for labor will shift inward; each firm will see its own demand curve for labor shifting inward from $d_L d_L$ to $d_L' d_L'$. Rather than demanding quantity q_2, each firm will demand quantity q_3, where the firm's supply curve for labor (the horizontal line drawn from w_2) intersects the demand curve for labor at point B'. If we multiply quantity q_3 by the number of firms, we obtain the quantity Q_3 in panel (b). We now have another point for our industry demand curve for labor. It is at the intersection of the wage line with the new quantity demanded, or point B''. When we connect all such points, we get the industry demand curve $D_L D_L$ in panel (b).

We can see that the industry demand curve is steeper than the horizontal summation of the firms' demand curves. Consider the possibility that you work for a consulting firm that has been paid to predict what the increase in industry employment will be after a fall in the price of labor employed in that industry. If you make a prediction based on the present price of the product in that industry, you may be led astray. You would be looking at the summation of a set of individual demand curves such as $d_L d_L$ in panel (a) of Figure 15-4. You would be predicting that each firm would increase its quantity of labor demanded from q_1 to q_2, but you would be ignoring the fact that each firm will not be able to sell all that additional output unless the price of the output falls, thus moving each firm's demand curve for labor inward to $d_L' d_L'$. Hence you should instead discount the firm's intentions and make allowances for the fall in the prod-

uct price that will result when all firms expand their production.

The supply curve of the labor input

We have already talked about the supply curve of one variable input, labor, back in Chapter 3. What we did was use the indifference curve analysis to show how individuals would react to a change in the wage rate. Our analysis was based on the assumption that leisure was preferred to work. Rather than go through the analysis again, we will use that supply curve of labor which we derived in Chapter 3. Moreover, we will ignore for the moment its backward-bending portion. The supply of the labor input is therefore going to be upward-sloping (as it is in Figure 15-5). We use the supply curve to study pricing and employment of the labor input.

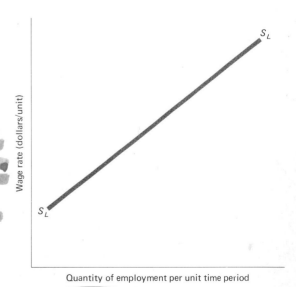

Figure 15-5: **The supply curve of labor.**
We assume an upward-sloping supply curve of labor $S_L S_L$.

---

[7]We ignore here problems that arise when several variable factors are used, for then we would have to account for changes in the prices of other inputs. See M. Friedman, *Price Theory: A Provisional Text* (Chicago: Aldine, 1962), pp. 180–183.

The determination of input price and employment

All we need do now is put together the market supply curve and the market demand curve to find the market-clearing price of a factor of production and the associated equilibrium quantity. This is shown in Figure 15-6 for labor. It could be drawn similarly for any other factor of production.

Note that Figure 15-6 has both a demand and a supply curve for labor that are drawn for constant-quality units. Further, the wage rate is an all-inclusive wage rate and includes the value of all fringe benefits. It is the implicit or alternative cost per unit of constant-quality employment that the employer incurs and that the employee receives.

The determinants of factor demand elasticity

We have not yet looked at what determines the price elasticity of a demand curve such as $D_L D_L$ presented in Figure 15-6. There are basically five determinants of an input's price elasticity of demand: (1) technological feasibility; (2) price elasticity of demand of final output; (3) supply elasticity of other inputs; (4) percentage of total cost accounted for by payment to the factor; and (5) length of time allowed for adjustment. We will treat these in that order here.

Technological feasibility

The price elasticity of demand for an input will clearly depend on the technical feasibility of substituting one input for another. In some cases, this technological feasibility is very limited; in others it is substantial. We measured technological feasibility by the elasticity of technical substitution, or σ, that we presented in Eq. (15-6) earlier. The coefficient is calculated with output held constant. In other

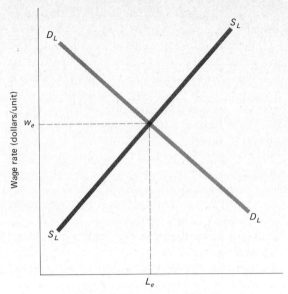

Figure 15-6: Equilibrium in the labor market.
We combine an industry demand curve $D_L D_L$ and an industry supply curve of labor $S_L S_L$. The equilibrium wage rate will be w_e. The equilibrium quantity of labor will be L_e.

words, it reflects a movement along an isoquant. The more sharply convex the isoquant is, the lower will be σ. The extreme is, of course, an isoquant that demonstrates fixed proportions. It is drawn perfectly horizontal and perfectly vertical from each point representing the required K/L ratio. (For a graphic illustration, refer back to Figure 7-10 on page 173.) This shows a σ equal to 0. In such a case, the price elasticity of demand for capital or for labor, all other things taken account of, would also be 0. The other extreme involves a $\sigma = -\infty$ and is represented by linear (straight-line) isoquants. We would then be dealing with perfect substitutes.

Price elasticity of demand of final output

Since the demand for any input is a **derived demand**, or derived from the demand for output, we would expect the price elasticity of demand of an input to be a direct function of the demand for final output. The more elastic the demand for the output, the more elastic will be the demand for each input, *ceteris paribus*. Think of this in terms of, say, a 10 percent increase in the relative price of an input. This will ultimately result in a certain increase in the price of the final product. The more elastic the demand for the final product, the greater will be the reduction in the quantity demanded, and hence the greater will be the reduction in the demand for the input required to produce this now smaller output. Consider as an example the price elasticity of demand for the labor input used in production of electricity. If the price elasticity of demand of the final output—electric energy—is close to 0, an increase in the price of the labor input (a higher wage rate) can be passed on to the consumer of electricity without the quantity of electricity demanded falling appreciably. Therefore, the reduction in the profit-maximizing rate of output will be very small, and hence, *ceteris paribus*, there will be little reduction in the quantity of labor demanded by electrical utilities.

The supply elasticity of other inputs

The greater the price elasticity of supply of other inputs, the greater the price elasticity of demand for the input under study. In other words, if firms in an industry can easily turn to a substitute input and obtain more of it by paying a very small increase in price, then the reduction in the quantity demanded of the input in question will be relatively great for any given increase in its price. Assume that aluminum and specialty steel (chrome) are close substitutes for use in automobile grilles. If the supply elasticity of aluminum is very high, i.e., increasing quantities can be purchased without affecting the unit price of aluminum, then whenever the price of specialty steel goes up, automobile manufacturers can easily switch to aluminum. This switch will be accomplished without a significant increase in the unit price of the input for making grilles, since the supply elasticity of aluminum is in this example very high. Thus, the price elasticity of the demand for the input called specialty steel by automobile manufacturers will, *ceteris paribus*, be high also.

Factor payments as a percentage of total costs

In many circumstances, the following proposition can be advanced: The smaller the percentage of total costs going to the variable input under study, the less the price elasticity of demand will be for that input. If the percentage of the total cost of some product going to the input in question is only 1 percent, a 100 percent increase in the price of that input will result only in one percentage point increase in total cost. It turns out that this proposition is usually correct, but it is not always true.[8]

Short versus long run

The price elasticity of demand for any input, just as the price elasticity of demand for any final product, will be greater the longer the time allowed for adjustment. The reasoning here is identical with the reasoning employed in looking at the demand for final output. The longer the time allowed for adjustment, the more adjustments can be made. For example, if the price of a certain type of machinery happens to increase, it may not be possible for plants to reduce appreciably the quantity of that machinery that they use in the short run; but in the long run, when they replace the machinery, they can substitute a different kind or employ more labor.

---

[8]See Martin Bronfenbrenner, "Note on the Elasticity of Derived Demand," *Oxford Economic Papers*, October, 1961.

Some extensions to short-run demand theory

Our profit-maximizing firm will, according to our theory, always hire workers up to the point where their wage rate just equals the value of their marginal product. However, such a theory ignores adjustment costs. It turns out that we can predict that, in the short run, firms may retain workers even though the value of their marginal product has fallen below their wage rate.[9]

This is sometimes called the theory of labor as a quasi-fixed factor of production,[10] or the reserve labor hypothesis.[11] Since there are costs to firing and hiring, such as payroll changes, training, and increased unemployment insurance levies, firms may keep on the payroll an inventory of workers or reserve labor force whose value of marginal product is lower than their wage rate, in anticipation of future increases in the rate of production. This would be particularly true when the prediction of changes in demand for final product could be done with a relatively high degree of certainty. Rather than fire workers when demand for final product diminishes, workers are kept on so that they are available without the entrepreneur having to incur rehiring and retraining costs when demand for final product increases.

An inventory of finished products can substitute for an inventory of workers. In other words, if there are ups and downs in final product demand, a firm can have a relatively smooth production schedule, thereby building up inventories during slack product demand periods. In this manner, it would have a smaller but steady labor force working all the time. Alternatively, it can have a larger labor force than necessary to meet current demand during slack periods. Rather than building up an inventory of finished goods, it merely holds the inventory of workers who are not fully utilized. When business starts booming again, this inventory of workers is again put back to work, i.e., is more fully utilized during the regular work week. Given this potential trade-off between inventories of finished goods and inventories of workers, we would expect the following: In industries where the relative cost of holding finished-goods inventories is higher, there will be relatively higher amounts of labor inventories, or reserve labor, during downswings in the business cycle. Empirically, this is what we find.[12]

Issues and applications

Can acreage restrictions work?

We saw the effects of price supports in the Issues and Applications section of Chapter 10. In a competitive industry, the supply curve is the horizontal summation of all the marginal cost curves above minimum average variable cost. Price will be set equal to marginal cost for the industry and for each firm. Using Eq. (15-4), we also know that the ratio of the price of each input to its marginal physical product will be equal to marginal cost which will be equal to output price. Consider an agricultural situation where the four factors of production are land, labor, equipment, and fertil-

---

[9]Walter Y. Oi, "Labor as a Quasi-fixed Factor of Production," *The Journal of Political Economy*, vol. 70, no. 6, December 1962, pp. 538–555; and Roger LeRoy Miller, "The Reserve Labor Hypothesis: Some Tests of Its Implications,"*The Economic Journal,*vol. 81, no. 321, March 1971, pp. 17–35.

[10]Oi, loc. cit.
[11]Miller, loc. cit.
[12]See, for example, Roger LeRoy Miller, "A Short-Term Econometric Model of Textile Industries," *American Economic Review*, vol. 61, no. 3, part 1, June 1971, pp. 279–289.

izer. The profit-maximizing firm in this industry will hire these four factors of production up to the point where

$$\frac{P_{\text{land}}}{\text{MPP}_{\text{land}}} = \frac{P_{\text{labor}}}{\text{MPP}_{\text{labor}}} = \frac{P_{\text{equipment}}}{\text{MPP}_{\text{equipment}}}$$

$$= \frac{P_{\text{fertilizer}}}{\text{MPP}_{\text{fertilizer}}} = \text{MC} = \text{MR} = P_{\text{product}}$$

(15-7)

When an effective price support (i.e., when the support price exceeds the market-clearing price, or $P_s > P_e$) is established for the output product, the use of all factors of production will be increased to lower each of their marginal physical products. (Remember, we are operating in the region of diminishing marginal physical returns.) This will increase each fraction in Eq. (15-7) until it is equal to the higher output price. This is portrayed by moving out *along* the given supply schedule SS in Figure 15-7. We see that if the support price is P_s, farmers will move from point E, the intersection of DD and SS, to point A on SS. The quantity supplied will therefore be Q_s. However, the quantity demanded will be where the new price line P_s intersects the demand curve at point B. The quantity demanded is now Q_D, less than Q_s.

When acreage restrictions are applied by the government, point A is no longer attainable. Indeed, almost all the supply curve SS is no longer feasible because it was obtained with *all* factors of production being variable including land. Assume that the limitation on land is such that it only affects decision making above point C on the supply schedule. In other words, at points below C on the supply curve SS, the amount of land is used less than the amount allowed under the acreage restriction provisions. Thus, there is no effect of such restrictions on the use of the smaller amount of land. We know that above point C, then, the only way that additional output can come forth is to use more labor, more equipment, and more fertilizer. Thus, the profit-maximizing farmer, given the restricted land inputs, will increase the use of labor, equipment, and fertilizer until the "common" marginal cost (MC) rises to equal the support price. In other words,

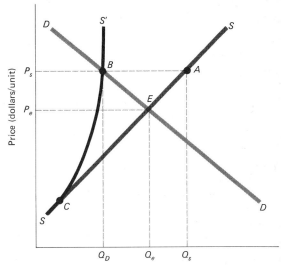

Figure 15-7: Price supports and soil banks.
If a price support is established at P_s, inputs will be increased so that the ratio of price input/marginal physical product of input rises and output will increase to Q_s. This will occur because we are in the region of diminishing marginal returns. If a soil bank is established, the new supply curve becomes SCS'. All inputs except the one fixed by law, land, are increased. Its price per unit used rises.

the new supply schedule is SCS'. We assume here that land is restricted by exactly the "right" amount so that the new supply schedule intersects the demand curve DD at point B and makes the quantity supplied equal to the quantity demanded at the support price P_s.

In this situation we note the implicit price per unit of land actually used in production rises. It is thus the owners of land who benefited from both the price support and the soil bank programs. A recent study of past farm programs reached just this conclusion. According to D. Gale Johnson, "Most of the benefit of the farm program has been capitalized into the value of farm land."[13]

---

[13]D. Gale Johnson, *Farm Commodity Programs: An Opportunity for Change* (Washington, D.C.: American Enterprise Institute for Public Policy Research), May 1973, p. 3.

Who is helped and who is harmed by minimum wages?

If you look at Figure 15-8, you can see that in an unrestricted labor market there will be an equilibrium wage rate at which equal quantities of labor are demanded and supplied. What if a legal minimum wage rate were set above the equilibrium wage rate? Who benefits and who loses from the imposition of a minimum rate above w_e?

We analyze the effects of a minimum wage in Figure 15-8. We start off in equilibrium with the equilibrium wage rate of w_e and the equilibrium quantity of labor demanded and supplied equal to Q_e. A minimum wage w_m, which is higher than w_e, is imposed. At w_m the quantity demanded for labor is reduced to Q_D and some workers now become unemployed. Note that the reduction in employment from Q_e to Q_D, or the distance from A to B, is less than the excess quantity of labor supplied at wage rate w_m. This excess quantity supplied is the distance between A and C, or the distance between Q_D and Q_s. The reason the reduction in employment is smaller than the excess supply of labor at the minimum wage is that the latter also includes a second component which consists of the additional workers who would like to work more hours at the new higher minimum wage. Some of these workers may be unemployed, but others may be employed elsewhere in the noncovered sectors of the economy at a lower wage.

In the long run, some of the reduction in labor demanded will result from a reduction in the number of firms and some from changes in the number of workers employed by each firm. The former cases occur when the firms affected by minimum wage legislation compete in the product market with other firms that somehow are unaffected or who manage to evade the law. Assume, for example, that other firms pay wages higher than w_m for superior quality labor. The minimum wage raises wages in the lower-wage market without causing any improvement in the quality of its labor. Thus, if the low-wage-paying

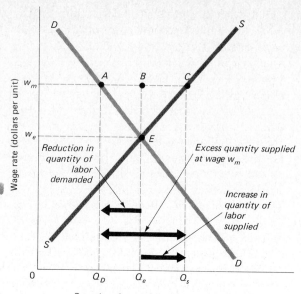

Figure 15-8: The effect of minimum wages.
The market-clearing wage rate is w_e. The market-clearing quantity of employment is Q_e and is determined by the intersection of supply and demand at point E. A minimum wage equal to w_m is established. The quantity of labor demanded is reduced to Q_D; the reduction of employment from Q_e to Q_D is equal to the distance between A and B. That distance is smaller than the excess quantity of labor supplied at wage rate w_m. The distance between B and C is the increase in the quantity of labor supplied that results from the higher minimum wage rate.

firms had been successfully competing with the high-wage-paying firms before the minimum wage law, they would now be at a competitive disadvantage and might have to move out of the local labor market or go out of business altogether.

Enforcement of the law

The effects of a minimum wage law depend crucially upon whether or not it is enforced. If the law is not enforced, it may have no effect whatsoever. The analysis of minimum wages is identical with the analysis of price controls. Although it is easier to see the effects of minimum wage legislation because the law will spell out specifically which kinds of labor are covered and what exemptions are allowed, it still does not always follow that the minimum wage is effective.

There are ways to get around minimum wage laws. In every instance where low-paid workers are receiving benefits in kind, such as below-cost lunches and free tickets to professional football games, there can be a substitution for benefits in kind by payment increases in money wages. For example, if a minimum wage forces money wages to go up, the employer can raise the price of lunches or charge for the professional football tickets to make up the difference between the new minimum wage and the former lower wage rate paid to the workers. Furthermore, firms may require kickbacks from employees, establish company stores, or require workers to live in company-owned housing. The price for company-store products or company-owned housing may exceed its market value. This is a way of paying a lower wage. Thus, if a minimum wage is forced on the employer, the actual wage can still be kept below the legal minimum by use of these devices. Another method to avoid the minimum wage loss is to hire relatives. In many cases, relatives of employers, particularly close relatives, are not covered under minimum wage laws and/or are not monitored closely by the Department of Labor. This particular way to avoid minimum wage laws may be a clue to understanding how small neighborhood grocery stores and restaurants can successfully compete with larger, presumably more efficient competing enterprises in their area. Dry-cleaning establishments that are owned by retired couples apparently are competing very effectively with dry-cleaning chains, presumably because of the former's ability to avoid minimum wave legislation, since the workers in the firm—the retired couple—don't have to pay themselves any particular wage rate.

We also must be careful to distinguish between the short run and the long run. It is a general proposition that short-run curves tend to be less elastic than long-run curves. Hence, we would expect that the minimum wage will have a much smaller effect in the short run than in the long run. What we would like to know (in order to assess its full impact on employment) is what happens in the long run.

The homogeneity assumption

All of the analysis so far has hinged on the common assumption that labor is homogeneous and that the minimum wage law applies to all labor. We know that this is not an accurate description of reality. There are many kinds of labor, and minimum wage laws are more explicit statements about which groups are to be affected and by how much. Therefore, we should not look at total employment but at employment of those groups affected.

This type of analysis, by the way, is consistent with the law's motivation. It is aimed at improving the living standards of lower-paid, lower-skilled workers. However, minimum wage laws appear to hurt exactly those groups they are intended to help. Minimum wage laws narrow the range of employment opportunities available to those at the lower end of the wage spectrum. This seems to be especially true for urban black teenagers. What happens is that there is substitution which works against the groups that are protected. Employers raise their skill standards[14] and become more capital-intensive whenever possible. Moreover, minimum wages prevent employers from offering apprenticeships and on-the-job training to low-skilled workers at relatively low wages.

Some empirical evidence

Quite a bit of empirical evidence has been gathered to demonstrate the unemployment effects of

---

[14]Workers may even overuse society's resources by obtaining useless education, etc., in order to quality for higher-paying jobs.

minimum wages on specific groups, such as teenagers. One study showed, for example, that there was a statistically significant reduction in the teenage/adult employment ratio associated with increased minimum wage level or coverage.[15] The investigator estimated that a 1 percent increase in the effective minimum wage reduces the teenage share of employment by 0.3 percent.

A report published by the Secretary of Labor in 1959 subsequent to the one-third increase in the minimum wage in 1956 from 75¢ to $1 per hour concluded "that there were significant declines in employment in most of the low-wage industries studied."

Casual evidence suggests that the effect on teenagers has been great. From 1950 to 1956 white teenage unemployment ranged between 7 and 11 percent. After the minimum wage was raised in 1956 to $1 per hour, white teenage unemployment shot up to almost 14 percent. It has remained in excess of 12 percent ever since then. There is an even more striking increase if we look at what happened to nonwhite teenagers. After 1956, their unemployment rate jumped from 13 percent to 24 percent. In a 1965 study by Dr. Arthur F. Burns, the conclusion was reached that "the ratio of the unemployment rate of teenagers to that of male adults was invariably higher during the six months following an increase in the minimum wage than it was in the preceding half-year."

Real as opposed to nominal minimum wages

A final note is in order. We live in an era of rising overall prices, i.e., inflation. It is important in determining the effects of a minimum wage to know how the minimum wage compares with other wages. It is not enough to say that the minimum wage in one year was $1 an hour and 20 years

later is $2.50 an hour. We have to know what happened to wages and prices in general during that time period. If the minimum wage is raised at a slower rate than the rate of inflation, it will lose some of its effect in destroying employment opportunities for low-skilled individuals.

The problem of labor market shortages

During the 1950s and the early 1960s, government officials proclaimed that a serious shortage of engineers existed in the United States. Ever since the end of World War II, there have been complaints of a shortage of professional nurses. No doubt we can discover at other times complaints of other labor market shortages. Is it possible for a shortage to persist in a labor market into which there is free entry? If we are willing to believe that specialized labor is in relatively fixed supply in the short run, then we can predict so-called shortages when there is an increase in the demand for a specific type of labor.

Let us consider what happened in the market for engineers and scientists in the 1950s and early 1960s. That was a period when universities, government, and private industry was hiring an increased number of scientists and engineers in order to "win the space race." This situation can be depicted in Figure 15-9. Here we show the supply curve of engineers as SS. The pre-space race demand curve is DD. The wage rate is w_1 and the equilibrium of quantity of engineers is Q_1.

Now, the demand curve shifts out in the late 1950s and early 1960s to $D'D'$. There would be no shortage if the wage rate increased to w_2, because at w_2 the new demand curve intercepts the stable supply curve at E'. The equilibrium quantity of engineers would be Q_2.

But the wage rate does not rise instantaneously to its equilibrium rate. It gradually moves up, and during this period of transition, shortages did indeed exist at the lower-than-equilibrium wage rates. Take, for example, the wage rate w_3. Here

[15]Finis Welch, "Minimum Wage Legislation in the United States," *Economic Inquiry*, vol. 12, no. 3, September 1974, p. 308.

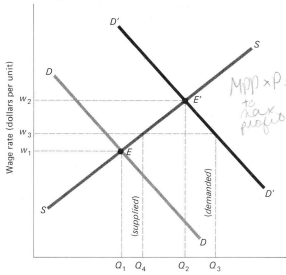

Figure 15-9: Adjustments to increases in demand.
We start out in equilibrium at point E, where the wage rate is w_1 and quantity of employment is Q_1. Assume demand shifts to $D'D'$. The new market-clearing equilibrium occurs at point E'. The new wage rate would be w_2, and the amount of employment would be Q_2. However, because of lags in adjustment, the wage rate rises to only w_3. At that wage rate, the quantity demanded will be Q_3, but the quantity supplied will be Q_4. Firms will experience a "shortage" of labor at that wage rate.

the quantity demanded will be Q_3, but the quantity supplied will only be Q_4. The difference will be a shortage at wage w_3. Those organizations desiring to hire engineers during this period will experience what they call a "shortage." They will not be able to hire all the engineers they want at the going wage rate. A shortage of this sort can take many years to be eliminated when the demand curve continues to shift to the right faster than the wage rate adjusts.[16]

---

[16]This analysis is taken from K. Arrow and W. Capron, "Dynamic Shortages and Price Rises: The Engineer-Scientist Case," *Quarterly Journal of Economics*, May 1959. See also Donald E. Yett, "The Chronic Shortage of Nurses," in H. Klarman (ed.), *Empirical Studies in Health Economics* (Baltimore: Johns Hopkins, 1970).

Glossary

Value of marginal product (VMP) of an input Marginal physical product of the input times the price per unit of output, or MPP · P. The market value of the marginal physical product of a factor of production.

Complementarity As applied to production inputs, we say that two factors are complementary if increased employment of one raises the marginal physical product of the other.

Elasticity of factor substitution A measure of the relative responsiveness of the capital/labor ratio to a relative change in the ratio of factor prices;

$$\sigma = -\left[\frac{\Delta(K/L)}{K/L} \bigg/ \frac{\Delta(r/w)}{r/w}\right]$$

Derived demand Demand that is derived from the demand for final output. The demand for production inputs is derived.

Summary

1. The firm's profit-maximizing combination of inputs will be such that

$$\frac{\text{MPP}_x}{P_x} = \frac{\text{MPP}_y}{P_y} = \cdots = \frac{\text{MPP}_n}{P_n} = \frac{1}{\text{MC}} = \frac{1}{\text{MR}} = \frac{1}{P}$$

or

$$\frac{P_x}{\text{MPP}_x} = \frac{P_y}{\text{MPP}_y} = \cdots = \frac{P_n}{\text{MPP}_n} = \text{MC} = \text{MR} = P$$

for the competitive firm buying inputs in a competitive market.

2. The profit-maximizing competitive firm's decision rule for input demand is to employ each input up to the point where the price per unit equals the value of marginal product.

3. The value of marginal product curve is derived by multiplying marginal physical product times the price per unit of the product.

4. The optimum quantity of labor hired by the competitive firm will be determined where the wage line, or supply curve of labor, intersects the VMP curve.

5. When capital and labor are complements, the demand curve for either will be less steeply sloping than the corresponding value of marginal product curve.

6. The three effects of a change in the wage rate are (a) the substitution effect, (b) the output effect, and (c) the profit-maximizing effect.

7. It can be proved that the factor demand curve will always be negatively sloped.

8. The total demand curve for an input is not the horizontal summation of an individual firm's demand curves because as each firm increases output, the output price must fall in order for them all to sell the increased output. The market demand curve for an input is more inelastic than the individual firm's demand curve for an input.

9. The equilibrium price and rate of employment of an input are determined by the intersection of the industry supply curve and the industry demand curve for the input.

10. Factor demand elasticity depends on (a) technological feasibility, (b) price elasticity of demand of final output, (c) the supply elasticity of other inputs, (d) the percentage of total costs accounted for by the factor's payment, and (e) the length of time allowed for adjustment.

11. When adjustment costs are taken into account, firms may retain labor even when the wage rate paid that labor exceeds the value of its marginal product. If labor is treated as a quasi-fixed factor or as an inventory, it may be retained during lulls in production to avoid the costs of hiring and retraining.

Selected references

Cartter, Allan M., *Theory of Wages and Employment* (Homewood, Ill.: Irwin, 1959), pp. 11–74.

Hicks, John R., *Value and Capital*, 2d ed. (Oxford: Clarendon, 1946), pp. 78–111.

Russell, R. R., "On the Demand Curve for a Factor of Production," *American Economic Review*, vol. 4, September 1964, pp. 726–733.

Scitovsky, Tibor, *Welfare and Competition*, rev. ed. (Homewood, Ill.: Irwin, 1971), chap. 7.

Questions

(Answers to even-numbered questions are at back of text.)

1. Most of the discussion in this chapter deals with examples in which labor is the variable input in the short run. Can you imagine a firm whose short-run fixed costs are labor and whose variable costs are capital?

2. "Capital and labor compete with one another. The workers of Flanders that sabotaged the machines of the early industrial era with their wooden shoes (sabots, thus the origin of the word 'sabotage'), knew well what the situation was." Comment critically.

3. What factors determine the amount of labor a perfectly competitive firm will hire in the short run if labor is the sole variable input?

4. Does a perfectly competitive firm have to worry about the impact of its own demand for labor on the local wage rate?

5. So long as the capital input of a firm is not fixed, and it generally is not, why is it not possible for a firm to simply "ride" its VMP curve up and down as the relative price of labor changes?

6. Explain the "substitution effect" of a fall in the relative price of labor.

7. Explain the "output effect" of a fall in the price of labor.

8. Explain the "profit-maximizing effect" of a fall in the price of labor.

9. Give the formula for the elasticity of substitution of capital for labor, and explain what it measures.

10. The price elasticity of demand for the final output product directly affects the elasticity of demand for the input factor. Why?

11. A chicken sexer is someone who is skilled at distinguishing male from female chicks. Often earning upward of $100 per day, a good chicken sexer can sex several thousand chicks in a single shift, with a high degree of accuracy. Which determinant of factor demand elasticity do you think would bear most heavily on the demand for sexers' services? Why?

12. Does the reserve labor hypothesis apply to a barbershop owner's demand for labor? Why or why not?

13. Why is it inaccurate to sum horizontally the labor demand curves of individual firms to arrive at the total industry demand for labor?

14. "I can see why the market supply curve of labor would be upward-sloping, at least in a free society where people aren't required to work. The supply of land, however, must be straight up and down (perfectly inelastic). After all, there's only so much land." Comment critically.

15. "The real exploitation of workers occurs in prisons. You talk about a captive market—there the government is the 'employer of *only* resort.' Since the supply curve for labor is vertical, at the number of inmates, the government can get away with paying even 5¢ per hour if it wants." Comment.

16

INPUT DEMAND
WITH IMPERFECT
COMPETITION

In the last chapter, we analyzed input demand when firms sold their products *and* purchased their inputs in perfectly competitive markets. In this chapter, we relax these assumptions. In the Issues and Applications section, we will examine the effects of minimum wages on an imperfectly competitive input market, the market for baseball players, and the economics of unions.

The demand for a resource by a monopolist

For the moment, let us continue to assume that the firm purchases inputs in a perfectly competitive market. That means that at the going price per unit of an input, the firm can purchase all it wishes. Thus, in the case of labor, the wage line represents the supply curve of labor for a firm. We alter the assumption, however, that the firm sells its product in a perfectly competitive market. We consider the case of a monopolistic seller. A monopolist, you will remember, faces a downward-sloping demand curve which is the industry demand curve. The monopolist cannot sell all he or she wants at a single going price. It is necessary to lower the price in order to sell more. We will consider only the case of a non-price-discriminating monopolist. The price at which the monopolist sells each unit of the product is the same to each buyer. In order to find the demand of a monopolist for an input, we must find out the value to the monopolist of increasing employment by one unit of the particular input in question.

Marginal revenue product

In the last chapter, we found the marginal physical product for a variable input and then multiplied it by the price of the output to obtain the value of marginal product. VMP (= MPP × price of output product) turned out to give us the labor demand curve for an individual perfectly competitive firm purchasing labor in a perfectly competitive market. We are now interested in finding out the demand curve for labor when the firm sells output in a noncompetitive market. In other words, what should we look at to find the labor demand curve for a monopolist? It would be inappropriate to do as we did in Chapter 15; we cannot merely multiply MPP times the price of the output. Why? Because the monopolist must take account of the fact that in order to sell an additional unit of output, it must reduce the price on all units sold (we are considering the case of a non-price-discriminating monopolist). If the monopolist wants to find out the change in total revenues that results from an increase in the use of a variable input, say, labor, the monopolist must look at the change in physical output due to the additional unit

of labor and the marginal revenue resulting from the sale of that additional output. Thus, to find the increase in total revenues due to a one-unit increase in labor, the monopolist will look at marginal physical product multiplied times the marginal revenue that results from the sale of that increased output. Thus, when we find MPP × MR, we obtain the increase in total revenues due to a one-unit increase in the variable input. This quantity is called **marginal revenue product (MRP).** MRP is similar to VMP except that it takes account of the necessity of lowering price in order for a monopolist to sell additional output. We show an example of the derivation of marginal revenue product in Table 16-1. We deal only with the case where the law of diminishing marginal physical returns is working. We see this in column (3), where we give the marginal physical product of labor; it is continuously declining. To find marginal revenue product in column (6), we obtain total revenues in column (5) for the various output rates obtainable by first two, then three, then four, up to seven workers per unit time period. MRP is then obtained by looking at the difference between total revenues each time we add one more worker.

In Figure 16-1, we plot the marginal physical product of labor MPP_L in panel (b) for two to seven workers. In panel (a), the resultant

Number of workers (1)	Total output (2)	$MPP_L =$ Δ total output/* Δ labor input (3)	Price of output (4)	Total revenues (5)	$MRP_L =$ Δ total revenue/ Δ labor input (6)
2	210	—	$9.00	$1,890.00	—
3	330	120	8.00	2,640.00	$750.00
4	405	75	7.50	3,037.50	397.50
5	475	70	7.00	3,325.00	287.50
6	500	25	6.80	3,400.00	75.00
7	490	−10	6.50	3,185.00	−215.00

Table 16-1
*All marginal figures refer to an interval between the indicated amount of whatever is in the denominator and one unit less than the indicated amount.

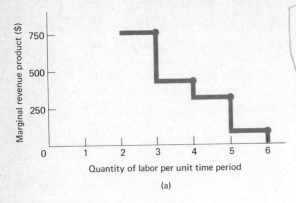

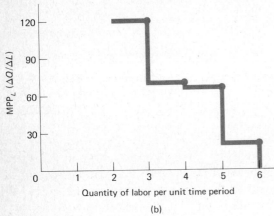

Figure 16-1: Deriving the MRP curve.
Panel (b) is the familiar marginal physical product curve taken from column 2 of Table 16-1. Panel (a) shows the marginal revenue product curve which represents the change in total revenues due to a one-unit change in labor input.

marginal revenue product curve is plotted (ignoring its negative portion). It is downward-sloping just as was the VMP curve in Chapter 15.

Monopoly demand for a single variable input

Assume now that there is only one variable input, and that is labor. Assume again that the monopolist purchases labor in a perfectly competitive input market. Therefore, the going wage rate per constant-quality unit of labor is given to the monopolist, and a line horizontal at that wage rate represents the perfectly elastic supply curve of labor to the monopolist.

In both competitive and monopoly profit maximization, optimal quantities of outputs and inputs are chosen such that marginal revenue equals marginal cost. This is a general optimization rule for any firm or any individual. What one has to do is determine the appropriate measures for marginal revenue and marginal cost in each new situation. In Chapter 15, we were dealing with input demand under perfect competition. Considering labor alone, the marginal cost of using one more unit of labor was identically equal to the going wage rate since, by definition, the firm could purchase all units of labor at a constant wage. Marginal revenue resulting from hiring one more unit of labor turned out to be equal to VMP, or MPP × price of final output. We now wish to look at the profit-maximizing optimal quantity of input demanded by a firm selling in a monopoly market. To do this, we change the formulas we used in Chapter 15 to reflect the fact that the monopolist cannot sell additional output at a constant price; rather, the monopolist faces a downward-sloping demand curve, and therefore, in order to sell the additional output due to an increase in the use of the variable input, the monopolist must lower the price on all units of the product sold. Go back to Eq. (15-4) on page 359. We now substitute marginal revenue for price and use

$$\frac{P_i}{MPP_i} = MC = MR \quad \text{[for all } i \text{ (inputs)]} \quad (16\text{-}1)$$

which means that

$$MPP_i \cdot MR = P_i \quad (16\text{-}2)$$

or for labor,

$$MRP_{labor} = P_{labor}$$

Profit maximization dictates that the monopolist hire labor up to the point where the marginal revenue product of labor equals the price of labor. We can find employment determination for a monopolist by looking at the price of labor and the monopolist's marginal revenue product curve. This is presented in Figure 16-2. Remember that we are still assuming that the firm can purchase its inputs in a perfectly competitive market. Thus, it faces a horizontal supply curve of the labor input at the going price of labor, or wage rate w_e. That wage rage equals the MRP at the intersection of the wage line with the MRP curve in Figure 16-2. The profit-maximizing monopolist facing the wage rate for the variable input labor at w_e will therefore purchase Q_e units of labor per unit time period.

Essentially, then, we have shown that the monopolist's demand curve for a *single* variable input, holding all others constant, is its marginal revenue product curve.[1] The monopolist faces a supply curve, if it buys the labor input in a perfectly competitive market, that is a horizontal line at the going market wage rate per unit of labor.

Comparison of input demand curves for a perfect competitor and a monopolist

We saw in Chapter 15 that the demand curve for labor for the firm purchasing such a variable input in a perfectly competitive market and selling its final product in a perfectly competitive market was the VMP curve. For the monopoly firm, the demand curve for labor was its MRP curve. Thus, both for the perfect competitor and the pure monopolist, their respective variable input demand curves are downward-sloping. In both cases, all or part of this downward slope is due to diminishing

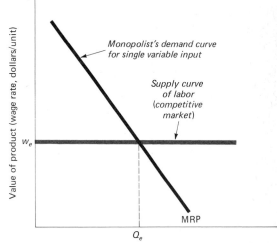

Figure 16-2: Monopoly employment determination.
If the going wage rate is w_e, the point at the intersection of that supply curve of labor with the marginal revenue product curve gives the optimal employment Q_e of the input.

marginal physical returns. However, the monopolist MRP curve has even more of a downward slope due to the fact that it must lower price as it attempts to sell additional output resulting from the use of additional units of the variable input. We expect, therefore, that when we make a comparison of a VMP curve with an MRP curve, the latter will be steeper and inside the former. This can be seen in Figure 16-3. The marginal revenue product curve must lie below the value of marginal product curve because marginal revenue is always below price for the monopolist. We assume that the underlying MPP curve is the same for both the monopolist and the perfect competitor in the product market.[2] At a wage rate of w_1, a monopolist would demand only Q_1 workers, but a perfect competitor

---

[1]Only that part of the MRP curve where total expenditures on the variable factor are equal to or less than total revenues is, strictly speaking, the firm's demand curve for that factor. This comment is similar to the stipulation

that the firm's supply curve is only that part of its marginal cost curve above average variable cost.
[2]Which implies that the production functions are the same.

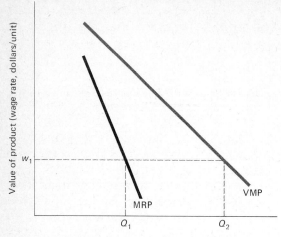

Figure 16-3: Comparing employment under monopoly and competition.

For any given wage rate, say w_1, the input demanded by a monopolist will be less than that demanded by a perfect competitor, because the demand curve for the monopolist for a single variable factor is MRP and that for the perfect competitor is VMP.

The monopolist's demand curve when several inputs are variable

What happens if the monopolist can vary more other inputs besides labor? We are back to the situation which we described in the last chapter when we had to consider that a change in the quantity of one variable input used also changes the marginal physical product of the other variable inputs used. Exactly

the same analysis applies to a monopolist as applies to a perfectly competitive producer. The only difference is that for the monopolist we show a marginal revenue product curve shifting instead of the VMP, which is the parallel construct for the competitor.

This can be seen in Figure 16-4. We start off with a wage rate of w_1. The firm can hire all it wants at w_1. This wage line intersects the marginal revenue product curve (MRP$_1$) at A. The quantity of labor demanded is Q_1. Now the wage rate falls to w_2. We move down the marginal revenue product curve (MRP$_1$) to point B. The new quantity of labor demanded is Q_2.

However, with this amount of labor used, the marginal physical product of capital will

would demand Q_2 workers. We can, therefore, state that a monopolist, *ceteris paribus*, demands less of a resource than a perfect competitor would. Take an example. Suppose there are a large number of shoe manufacturing firms in existence. At the going wage rate, say, $5 an hour, they demand, say, 300,000 workers. Now assume that all of the numerous firms are made into a monopoly with no change in the cost structure. At the same going wage rate of labor, the number of workers employed may fall to, say, 250,000.

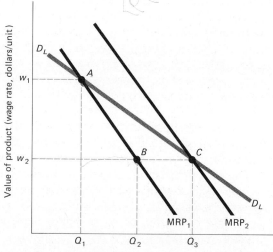

Figure 16-4: The monopolist demand curve when there are several variable factors.

We start out with wage rate w_1. The optimal employment of labor is Q_1 at point A on MRP$_1$. The wage rate falls to w_2. Optimal employment apparently increases to Q_2, where the w_2 line intersects MRP$_1$. However, the marginal physical product of capital will now rise because we are assuming complementarity. This will shift the marginal revenue product curve of labor to the right to MRP$_2$. The new intersection of the wage line (supply curve of labor) is at point C. The optimal employment will increase to Q_3. If we connect points such as A and C we have the demand curve for labor $D_L D_L$.

rise. Each unit of capital now has more units of labor working with it. Assuming that capital and labor are complementary factors of production, MPP_K will rise as more labor is used. By assumption, the price of a unit of capital services has not changed, but its marginal physical product has gone up. The profit-maximizing firm hires each input up to the point where its marginal revenue product equals its price. Since MPP_K has increased, the firm is no longer using the profit-maximizing optimal quantity of capital. In order to satisfy optimum condition [(Eq. (16-2)], the firm must now use more units of capital in order to lower MPP_K. (Remember that we are in the region of diminishing marginal physical returns.) However, when the firm increases the amount of capital that it uses, it will shift the MRP curve for labor to the right, since each unit of labor will now be working with more units of capital and we are assuming complementarity between capital and labor. The MRP curve shifts to MRP_2. The new wage rate w_2 intersects the new MRP curve at point C. The new quantity of labor demanded is Q_3. We connect points A and C to obtain the demand curve for labor when there is more than one variable factor of production. It is labeled $D_L D_L$.

The movement from Q_1 to Q_3 includes the substitution, output, and profit-maximizing effects discussed in the last chapter. On balance, however, the factor demand function must be negatively sloped.[3]

Equilibrium price and rate of employment

To determine the equilibrium price of an input and the level of input employment in a monopoly output situation, we put together a market demand curve and a market supply

---

[3]For a proof, see C. E. Ferguson, "Production, Prices, and the Theory of Jointly-derived Input Demand Functions", *Economica,* new ser., vol. 33, 1966, pp. 454–461.

curve for the factor of production in question. The analysis is exactly the same as it was in the last chapter. We therefore do not repeat it.

The demand for a resource in an imperfectly competitive input market

We now turn to the imperfectly competitive input market. Whenever a firm is unable to purchase all the inputs that it wants at the going market price, it is buying them in an imperfectly competitive market. In other words, this occurs whenever a firm faces a less than perfectly elastic supply curve for the input in question. We will again use the assumption that the purchaser of the input is a producer selling in a perfectly competitive market. Thus, we are looking at imperfect competition in the input market and not in the output market.

In its most extreme case, the situation just described in the last paragraph is one of **monopsony,** which means a single buyer. Several buyers might be called **oligopsony,** but this term is not often used. We will consider a monopsonist in the following section. We are talking about a monopoly in the purchase of an input. In Chapter 11, we talked about monopoly in the sale of an output.

Marginal factor cost curve

The monopsonist faces an upward-sloping supply curve of the input in question because, as the only buyer, it faces the entire SS curve. The monopsonist must pay a higher price for the last unit of the input, but in the case where no price discrimination in purchasing is possible, the monopsonist must also pay a higher price on all previous units purchased.

The supply curve of an input can be called the **average factor cost curve,** just as the demand curve for an output is often called the average revenue curve. We derived a curve marginal to the average revenue curve to rep-

Quantity of labor used by management (1)	Wage rate ($ per hour) (2)	Total wage bill [(1) × (2)] (3)	Marginal factor cost MFC = Δ wage bill/Δ labor = Δ (3)/Δ (1) (4)
0	—	—	—
1	$1.00	$1.00	$1.00
2	2.00	4.00	3.00
3	2.40	7.20	3.20
4	2.80	11.20	4.00
5	3.60	18.00	6.80
6	4.20	25.20	7.20

Table 16-2

resent the marginal revenue obtained by a monopolist from an extra unit of sales. Now we look at a curve marginal to the average factor cost curve; we will call it the **marginal factor cost curve.** It will give the increase in total factor cost that results from a one-unit increase in the purchase of the input under study.[1]

NUMERICAL EXAMPLE Consider the numerical example in Table 16-2. Here we show the quantity of labor purchased, the wage rate per hour, the total cost of the quantity of labor purchased per hour, and the marginal factor cost per hour for the additional labor bought.

We translate the columns from Table 16-2 to Figure 16-5. We show the supply curve as *SS*, which is taken from columns (1) and (2). The marginal factor cost curve is MFC and is taken from columns (1) and (4). The marginal factor cost curve must be above the supply curve whenever the supply curve is upward-sloping. If the supply curve is upward-sloping, the firm must pay a higher wage rate in order to attract a larger supply of labor. This higher wage rate must be paid to all workers; thus, the increase in total costs due to an increase in the labor input will exceed the wage rate.

Note that in a perfectly competitive input market, the supply curve is horizontal and the marginal factor cost curve is identical with the supply curve.

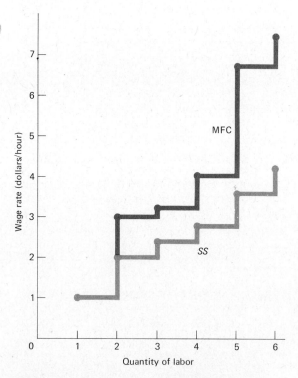

Figure 16-5: Derivation of a marginal factor cost curve. The supply curve is taken from columns 1 and 2 of Table 16-2. The marginal factor cost curve MFC is taken from column 4. It is the increase in the total wage bill resulting from a one-unit increase in labor input.

[1] Marginal factor cost has been called marginal expense of input, marginal expenditure for input, marginal resource (input) cost, and probably a dozen other names. They all refer to the same thing.

THE RELATIONSHIP BETWEEN MFC AND ELAS-
TICITY OF SUPPLY. Back in Chapter 5, we
showed the relationship between the price
elasticity of demand and marginal revenue.
We can use a similar technique to derive the
relationship between marginal factor cost and
the price elasticity of supply of the variable
factor.

If we ignore fixed costs, total costs will be
$TC = w \cdot L$. The increase in TC caused by an
increase in the labor input will be

$$TC + \Delta TC = (w + \Delta w)(L + \Delta L) \quad (16\text{-}4)$$

because the wage rate must change. Equation
(16-4) becomes, after carrying out the right-
hand side multiplication,

$$TC + \Delta TC = wL + w\Delta L + \Delta wL + \Delta w\Delta L \quad (16\text{-}5)$$

Let ΔL get smaller and smaller; as ΔL
approaches 0 ($\Delta L \to 0$), the $\Delta w \Delta L$ also approaches 0. Also, realizing that $TC = wL$, Eq.
(16-5) becomes

$$\Delta TC = w\Delta L + \Delta wL \quad (16\text{-}6)$$

Dividing through by ΔL, we get

$$\frac{\Delta TC}{\Delta L} = w + \frac{\Delta w}{\Delta L}L \quad (16\text{-}7)$$

But $\Delta TC/\Delta L$ is the change in total costs due
to a change in the variable input labor. This is
our definition of marginal factor cost, or MFC.
Then

$$MFC = w + \frac{\Delta w}{\Delta L} \cdot L \quad (16\text{-}8)$$

Now we multiply the last term on the right-
hand side of Eq. (16-8) by w/w:

$$MFC = w + \frac{\Delta w}{\Delta L} \cdot L\left(\frac{w}{w}\right)$$

or $\qquad MFC = w + w\left(\frac{\Delta w}{\Delta L} \cdot \frac{L}{w}\right) \quad (16\text{-}9)$

We can now factor out w:

$$MFC = w\left(1 + \frac{\Delta w}{\Delta L} \cdot \frac{L}{w}\right) \quad (16\text{-}10)$$

But the price elasticity of supply of labor is
defined as

$$\epsilon_L = \frac{\Delta L}{\Delta w} \cdot \frac{w}{L} \quad (16\text{-}11)$$

Therefore, our expression for marginal factor
cost becomes

$$MFC = w\left(1 + \frac{1}{\epsilon_L}\right) \quad (16\text{-}12)$$

Since for all upward-sloping supply curves
ϵ_L is positive, marginal factor cost will be
greater than the wage rate. If the elasticity of
supply of labor is 2.0 and the wage rate is $100
per week, then Eq. (16-12) tells us that
$MFC = 100(1 + \frac{1}{2}) = 100 \times 1.5 = \$150$. In the
case where the firm buys its inputs in a perfectly competitive market input market, ϵ_L is
equal to $+\infty$. Then, the second term in parentheses on the right-hand side of Eq. (16-12)
becomes 0 and marginal factor cost is therefore
equal to the wage rate.

Pricing and employment of a single variable input

The pure monopsonist is hypothesized to
maximize profit. We now have to alter Eq.
(16-1) because the price of the variable input is
no longer constant. Instead of the price of
input, we use marginal factor cost of input; Eq.
(16-1) becomes

$$\frac{MFC_i}{MPP_i} = MC = MR = P \text{ [for all } i \text{ (inputs)]} \quad (16\text{-}13)$$

Equation (16-9) represents the profit-maximizing combination of inputs for a firm
which is a perfect competitor in the output
market and a pure monopsonist in the input
market. Rearranging Eq. (16-13), we get

$$MPP_i \cdot P = MFC_i \quad (16\text{-}14)$$

or $\qquad VMP_i = MFC_i \quad (16\text{-}15)$

The output competitor who is a monopsonist in the input market will hire a resource

up to the point where the value of marginal product equals the marginal factor cost. We can see the pricing and employment of such an input by the profit-maximizing monopolist in Figure 16-6.

If labor is the only variable factor of production, we are looking at a VMP curve for labor. The profit-maximizing monopsonist will hire labor up to the point where MFC = VMP. This occurs at the intersection of the MFC curve with the VMP curve, or at point A. That gives the profit-maximizing rate of employment of labor, Q_L. Now, how much does the monopsonist have to pay per unit for that amount of labor? That is given by the supply curve SS. The intersection of the quantity desired, Q_L, with the supply curve SS is at point B. The wage rate that must be paid is w_1. We have, then, the wage and employment op-

timum for a monopsonist input user selling its output in a purely competitive market when there is only one variable factor of production which is purchased in an imperfectly competitive market.

Monopsonist pricing and employment with several variable inputs

With several variable inputs, we have the same analysis as we had in the last section. We take into account that there are many variable factors of production; Eq. (16-9) becomes

$$\frac{\text{MFC}_x}{\text{MPP}_x} = \frac{\text{MFC}_y}{\text{MPP}_y} = \cdots = \frac{\text{MFC}_n}{\text{MPP}_n} \quad \text{(16-16)}$$

for all n factors of production.

As the sole user of several variable productive inputs, a monopsonist will adjust the ratios of the inputs until the ratio of the marginal factor cost to the marginal physical product for each input is the same.[5]

When the monopsonist is also a monopolist

We can alter the analysis above to take account of the monopsonist input buyer who is also a monopolist in the output market. Instead of looking at the price of the product, we focus on its marginal revenue. Instead of using the value of marginal product curve, we want to use the marginal revenue product curve. The entire analysis above will be redone by utilizing the MRP curve rather than the VMP curve. Figure 16-6 becomes Figure 16-7. The profit-maximizing quantity of employment is obtained where the marginal factor cost curve intersects the marginal revenue product curve. This is at point A in Figure 16-7. The optimum quantity of input is therefore Q_1. This can be

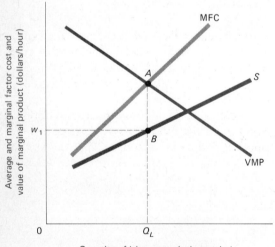

Figure 16-6: Price and employment of an input purchased by a pure monopsonist.

When we consider only a single variable input, the pure monopsonist will hire the input up to the point where MFC = VMP. This is point A. In order to obtain that quantity of labor Q_L, the pure monopsonist will have to pay only the wage rate w_1, which is read off the supply curve SS, where it intersects the quantity line at point B.

---

[5]Hence, the least-cost combination of inputs is obtained when the marginal rate of technical substitution equals the marginal factor cost ratio for any pair of inputs.

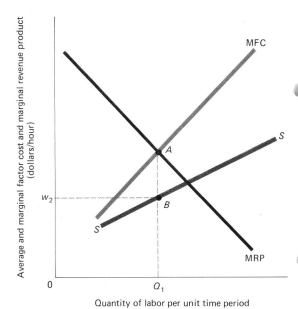

Figure 16-7: Pricing and employment of an input hired by the monopsonist-monopolist.
If the monopolist is also a monopsonist, it will hire the input up to the point where MFC = MRP at point A. This gives the optimal employment of Q_1. The wage rate that will have to be paid is given by the intersection of Q_1 with the supply curve SS at point B. It is wage rate w_2.

labor demanded, Q_1, will be smaller in Figure 16-7 than it was in Figure 16-6. Moreover, since we are at a point on the supply curve that is closer to the origin, the wage rate w_1 in Figure 16-7 will also be below the wage rate w_1 in Figure 16-6.

A summary of monopsony and monopoly situations

We have studied input factor pricing and employment with pure competition in the input and the output market and with monopoly in the input and the output markets. In Table 16-3, we present a summary of the various conditions under which output will be produced and the variable input, labor, will be demanded. Table 16-3 is presented graphically in panels (a) through (d) in Figure 16-8.

The notion of exploitation

Exploitation is defined as paying a resource less than its value. Otherwise stated, labor exploitation would be equal to the difference between the wage rate and the value of marginal product of labor. We consider the amount of exploitation that exists in a situation where a firm is both a monopolist and a monopsonist. This is depicted

obtained by paying a wage rate—if we are considering labor only—of w_2.
Notice that because marginal revenue is always less than output price, the quantity of

Input market structure	Output market structure	
	Pure competition	**Monopoly**
Pure competition	**(a)** $MC = MR = P$ $w = MFC_L = MRP_L = VMP_L$	**(b)** $MC = MR(< P)$ $w = MFC_L = MRP_L(< VMP_L)$
Monopsony	**(c)** $MC = MR = P$ $w < MFC_L = MRP_L = VMP_L$	**(d)** $MC = MR(< P)$ $w < MFC_L = MRP_L(< VMP_L)$

Table 16-3: A summary of monopsony and monopoly situations.
Optimal output and input employment; the case of labor

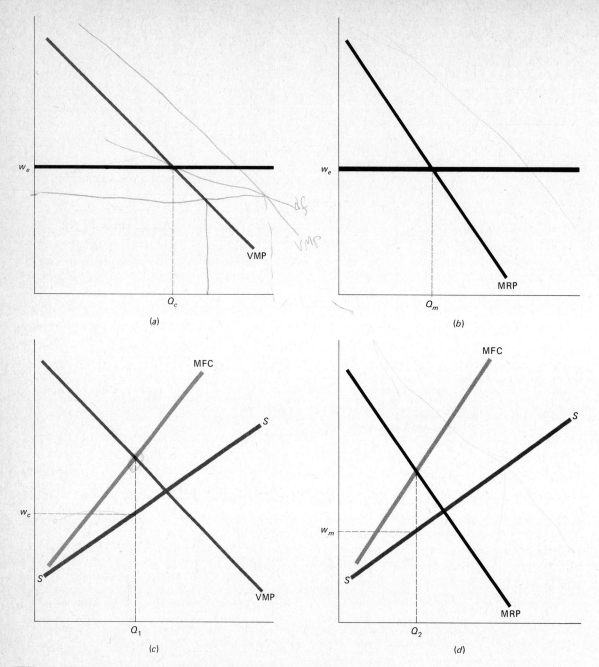

Figure 16-8: **Summary of pricing and employment under various market conditions.**
The panels in this diagram correspond to the sections marked (a), (b), (c), and (d) in Table 16-3. In panel (a) the firm
operates in perfect competition in both input and output markets. It purchases labor up to the point where the going
wage rate w_e is equal to VMP. It hires quantity Q_c of labor. In panel (b) the firm purchases the variable input labor
in a perfectly competitive market, but has a monopoly in the output market. It purchases labor up to the point where
the wage rate w_e is equal to MRP. It hires a smaller quantity of labor Q_m than in panel (a). In panel (c) and (d), the
firm is a monopsonist in the input market. In panel (c) it is a perfect competitor in the output market. It hires labor
up to the point where MFC = VMP. It will hire quantity Q_1 and pay a wage rate w_c. In panel (d) the monopsonist
is also a monopolist. It hires labor up to the point where MFC = MRP, which is quantity Q_2. It pays wage rate w_m.

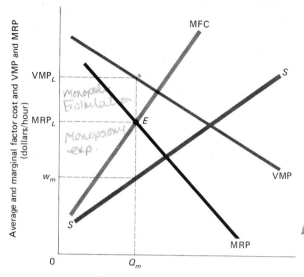

Figure 16-9: Exploitation.

Exploitation is defined as paying an input less than the value of its marginal product. In the situation depicted here, we have both monopoly and monopsony. The monopolist finds the profit-maximizing rate of employment of labor at the intersection of MFC and MRP, or point E. The profit-maximizing quantity of labor demanded will be Q_m which will be paid a wage rate w_m. Monopoly exploitation equals $(VMP_L - MRP_L)$. Monopsony exploitation equals $(MRP_L - w_m)$. Total exploitation equals $(VMP_L - w_m)$.

in Figure 16-9. The profit-maximizing monopolist/monopsonist will determine the quantity of labor demanded at the intersection of MFC and MRP, which is labeled E in Figure 16-9. It will pay a wage rate w_m for the quantity Q_m of labor. **Monopolistic exploitation** occurs because the monopolist looks at its MRP curve rather than its VMP curve which would be relevant for a perfect competitor. **Monopsonistic exploitation** occurs because the monopsonist looks at the MFC curve rather than the supply curve, as does the buyer of labor in a perfectly competitive market.

In a situation of both monopoly and monopsony, exploitation can be summarized as

follows:

$$VMP_L - MRP_L = \text{monopolistic exploitation}$$

$$MRP_L - w_m = \text{monopsonistic exploitation}$$

$$VMP_L - w_m = \text{total exploitation}$$

The price-discriminating monopsonist

We have considered only the situation in which the monopsonist was paying the same price to all units of the factor of production under study. In the situation shown in Figure 16-10, the monopsonist would purchase a

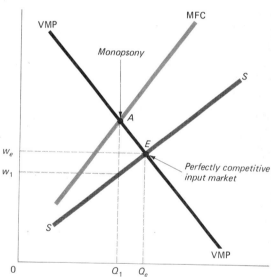

Figure 16-10: The price-discriminating monopsonist.

A nonprice-discriminating monopsonist will hire where MFC = VMP, which is at point A. Thus, the quantity demanded will be Q_1, and the wage rate paid will be w_1. In a perfectly competitive situation, the wage rate will be w_e, and the quantity of labor demanded will be Q_e. The perfectly price-discriminating monopsonist can, however, move up the supply curve by paying exactly the wage rate needed to get each additional worker without having to pay the previous workers a higher wage rate. The perfect price-discriminating monopsonist will increase quantity demanded to the competitive solution Q_e. However, only the last worker will receive a wage rate of w_e. All previous workers will receive progressively lower wages.

quantity of labor input Q_1 and pay a wage rate of w_1. In other words, at point A marginal factor cost would equal VMP if we assume that the monopsonist is a pure competitor in the product market.

We know that a competitive equilibrium would prevail at the intersection of SS and VMP. The quantity of labor demanded and supplied would be Q_e, and the wage rate would be w_e.

If there were perfect wage discrimination, the monopsonist would also end up at rate of input demand Q_e. This would occur because the perfectly discriminating monopsonist would move up the supply curve of labor and pay each individual worker exactly what was necessary to get that person to work. Only the marginal worker would be paid w_e; all other workers would be paid less. It is possible, then, that a perfectly discriminating monopsonist will hire the same amount of workers as a perfect competitor in the input market. The only difference will be that the workers will not all get the same wage rate and, indeed, all but one of the workers will receive a lower wage.

Given the heterogeneity of both the labor force and of job qualifications, we would expect that there would be some price discrimination for any given amount of monopsony power.

Conditions giving rise to monopsony power

Although it is difficult to imagine a situation in which monopsony power could be very great, it is certainly not difficult to imagine situations in which a firm faces an upward-sloping supply curve for labor. We discuss some of those situations now.

Specialized factors of production

The supply curve of highly specialized factors of production is probably upward-sloping to any individual firm. Some workers and professionals have highly specialized skills which cannot be obtained in large quantities at a constant wage rate, at least not in the short run. In order to get more of these people, the individual firm has to up the ante. This is necessary to bid them away from other firms. Note, however, that the longer the time allowed for adjustment, the more elastic will be the supply curve of any highly specialized factor of production. Thus we can come up with the notion that *monopsony power is less in the long run than in the short run.*

The company town

The most commonly cited case of monopsony is the so-called company town where there is only one employer. This situation was perhaps not uncommon in the past in the American textile and mining industries. The importance of such cases today is certainly diminishing if not already negligible. After all, it is now common for American workers to commute up to 50 miles to work. Thus the amount of monopsony power available to isolated employers has to be quite small; moreover, people do relocate. There has been very little empirical work on the amount of "labor market concentration" on the *hiring* side. But what has been done shows that there is little concentration in large cities; and for the United States as a whole, the fraction of counties where the 30 largest firms employed 50 percent of the labor force or more is quite small.

Collusive agreements

Just as there was an incentive for oligopolists to get together to collude to form, in effect, a monopoly, there is an incentive for oligopsonists to collude. A collusive monopsony might result from an agreement among employers not to raise wages individually or not to hire away each other's employees. One study did show that such agreements have existed.[6] We will examine one of the cases of this type in the Issues and Applications section of this chapter when we examine the market for professional baseball players.

However, we must indicate that the reasons why cartels tend to break down applies to employers who might engage in a collusive agreement. When the labor market becomes tight, the temptation for the colluding parties to cheat becomes very great. That is, once labor becomes "scarce," it is in the best interests of each employer to raise the wage rate of new employees relative to wage rates obtainable elsewhere. This wage-rate rise could be accomplished in ways which would make it extremely difficult to police such a monopsony collusive agreement. We therefore contend that the effects of monopsony collusive agreements are less than might be expected in the American labor market.

The demand curve for a monopsonist

Remember back in Chapter 11 when we studied the theory of a monopoly? We said that we could not derive a supply curve for a monopolist because there was no one schedule that gave a unique quantity of output forthcoming at any particular price. Output depended on an interaction of MC and MR. Indeed, we showed in Figure 11-4 that we could have two different quantities forthcoming at exactly the same price.

The same kind of analysis applies to a theory of monopsony. It turns out that there is no demand curve for a monopsonist. It is certainly not the VMP curve. The monopsonist has no demand curve for the variable input in the sense of a simple functional relation in which the quantity of the variable input depends on the price per unit of the variable input. For ex-

ample, the number of workers demanded depends not only on the supply schedule of workers but also on elasticity.

We can see all of this in Figure 16-11. We have drawn in a downward-sloping value of marginal product curve VMP. We start off with a supply curve of labor (SS) facing a monopsonist. The curve marginal to SS is MFC. The intersection of MFC with VMP is at point E. The quantity of labor demanded by the monopsonist will be Q_L. The monopsonist will pay wage rate w_1. Now, however, assume that there is a rotation in the supply curve to S'S'. The curve marginal to it is labeled MFC'. If, by chance, it intersects the VMP curve at point E, as we have drawn it, the monopsonist will still demand the same quantity of labor

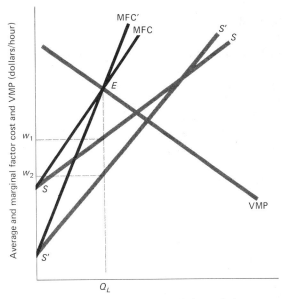

Quantity of labor per unit time period

Figure 16-11: **The monopsonist has no demand curve.** A demand curve is defined as a locus of points showing maximum prices at which given quantities will be demanded; however, we can show that the monopsonist will demand the same quantity of labor Q_L at two different wage rates w_1 and w_2, if the supply curve shifts so that the marginal factor cost curves intersect the VMP line at the same point E.

---

[6] Richard A. Lester, *Adjustments to Labor Shortages* (Princeton, N.J.: Industrial Relations Section, 1955), pp. 46–49.

Q_L but will pay only the wage rate w_2. Since a demand curve is defined as the maximum price for which a given quantity is demanded, VMP cannot be labeled a demand curve for labor by the monopsonist. For we have just shown a situation in which the same quantity of labor will be demanded at two different wage rates.

Issues and applications

A minimum wage in the face of monopsony hiring

One justification for a minimum wage has been the alleged existence of monopsony. Look at Figure 16-12. Here we show the monopsony pricing and employment of labor. The profit-maximizing monopsonist who sells its output in a perfectly competitive market will set the rate of employment at the intersection of MFC and VMP, or at point A. The quantity of the input employed is Q_1. The wage rate that must be paid to get that quantity of labor is w_1, which is determined by the intersection of the line drawn from A to Q_1 with the supply curve at point B.

Some economists have argued that a minimum wage can reduce this monopsonistic exploitation. If the minimum wage is set at w_m, the supply curve facing the monopsonist is now a horizontal line at the minimum wage rate w_m out to the old supply schedule, or point E. Then the supply curve becomes coincident with the old SS. In other words, there is a kink in it at quantity of labor Q_m. The new marginal factor cost curve facing the monopsonist becomes a horizontal line between the vertical axis and point E. There is a discontinuous part at Q_m between E and D. Beyond Q_m the marginal factor cost curve coincides with the old marginal factor cost curve. The profit-maximizing monopsonist will employ the input where marginal factor cost equals value of marginal product. This occurs at point E, at the start of the discontinuous part of the MFC curve, if the minimum wage is w_m. The profit-maximizing rate of employment will be Q_m, and this will be at wage

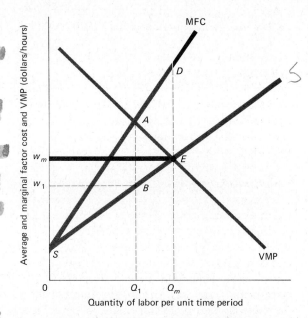

Figure 16-12: **The minimum wage and monopsony.** Assume that the monopsonist faces supply curve SS and marginal factor cost curve MFC. Now, MFC = VMP at the quantity of labor demanded Q_1 and the wage rate paid will be w_1. Assume a minimum wage is established at w_m. The monopsonist can hire up to Q_m of labor at that wage rate. Thus with the minimum wage its supply curve of labor is the horizontal line at w_m to point E on the old supply schedule. (Then the old supply curve becomes relevant.) The horizontal line which is heavily shaded is also equal to marginal factor cost. After the quantity of labor Q_m is hired, however, then the monopsonist must pay a higher wage and marginal factor cost then coincides with the original marginal factor cost curve. The profit-maximizing monopsonist faced with this minimum wage will hire where marginal factor cost equals value of marginal product. This is at point E. This monopsonist will increase employment to Q_m and pay a higher wage rate w_m.

rate w_m, which is the same at the wage rate in a perfectly competitive labor market.[7]

According to some critics of the minimum wage law, monopsony is the sole intellectual argument for minimum wages, and according to them, it is only in the discussion of minimum wages that the monopsony argument even comes up. Moreover, very little empirical work has been done to show the extent of monopsony. Even though the argument may be presented as a theoretical "justification" for minimum wages, we do not know if it is an empirically significant consideration. Earlier comments, however, suggest that it is not.

What do unions maximize?

Unions can also be looked upon as setters of minimum wages. Through collective bargaining, unions establish minimum wages below which no individual worker can offer his or her services. We can analyze the effects of a union in the face of a monopsony employer by using the same figure we used in the prior analysis. Figure 16-11 could be redone to show the possible effects of union minimum wage that exceeded the wage paid by a monopsonist. In such situations, it could be shown that a union setting a wage rate above those which would prevail in the monopsony labor market could actually increase employment and increase wages at the same time. However, we are again faced with the necessity of showing that monopsony is a significant factor in American labor markets (although we will show that it is important in professional sports).

When there is no monopsony

In a labor market where there is labor unionization but no monopsony, any wage rate set higher

than a competitive market-clearing wage rate will reduce total employment in that market. This can be seen in Figure 16-13. We have a competitive market for labor. The market demand curve is DD, and the market supply curve is SS. The market-clearing wage rate will be w_e; the equilibrium quantity demanded and supplied of labor will be Q_e. If the union establishes a minimum wage rate by collective bargaining that exceeds w_e, there will be an excess quantity of labor supplied. For example, if the minimum wage established by collective bargaining is w_u, the quantity supplied would be Q_S; the quantity demanded would be Q_D. The difference is the excess quantity supplied, or "surplus." We see that one of the major roles of a union which establishes a wage rate above the market-clearing price is to ration available jobs among the excessive number of workers who wish to work in unionized industries.

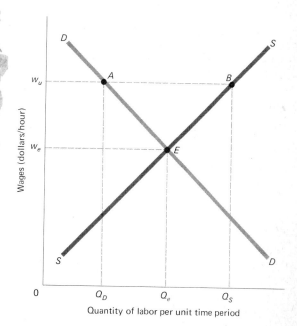

Figure 16-13: Unions must ration jobs.
If there is no monopsony, and if the union succeeds in obtaining a wage rate w_u, the quantity of labor demanded will be Q_D, but the quantity of labor supplied will be Q_S. The union must ration a limited number of jobs to a greater number of workers.

---

[7]This model is strictly correct only for the nondiscriminating monopsonist. The minimum wage would have no effect if it were set below w_1, and it would have its maximum employment effect if it were set at the intersection of SS and VMP, or at E.

We see that there is a trade-off here which must be faced by any union's leadership. Higher wages inevitably mean a reduction in total employment, as more persons are seeking a smaller number of positions.

Types of union behavior, or what do they maximize?

The analyses of union objectives have considered three possibilities. We view a union here as a monopoly seller of a service.

EMPLOYING ALL MEMBERS IN THE UNION. Assume that the union has Q_1 workers. If it faces a demand curve such as DD in Figure 16-14, the only way it can "sell" all of those workers is to accept a wage rate of w_1. This is a naive theory because unions could use some form of second-degree price discrimination to increase the average wage rate without reducing employment below Q_1.

MAXIMIZE TOTAL WAGES. If the union is interested in maximizing the gross income of its members, it will not want a membership of Q_1 members but will want to have Q_2 workers employed in Figure 16-14 and have them paid a wage rate of w_2. The marginal revenue curve intersects the horizontal axis at the quantity at which total revenues are maximized. Total revenues in this case represent the aggregate income of the union membership, $w_2 \cdot Q_2$.

Note that in this situation, if the union started out with Q_1 members, there would be $Q_1 - Q_2$ members who would be out of union work at the wage rate w_2.

MAXIMIZING WAGE RATES FOR A GIVEN NUMBER OF WORKERS. Assume that the union wants to maximize the wage rates for a part of the union's workers. This might be those with the most seniority. If it wanted to keep employed, say, Q_3 of workers, it would seek to obtain a wage rate of w_3. This would require deciding which workers should be unemployed and which workers should

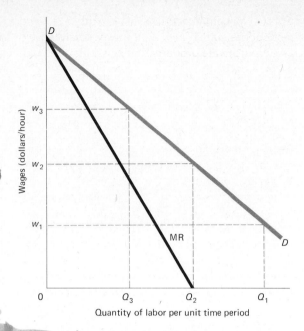

Figure 16-14: What do unions maximize?
Assume that the union wants to employ all its Q_1 members. It will attempt to get a wage rate w_1. If the union wants to maximize total wage receipts, it will do so at wage rate w_2, where the elasticity of demand is equal to -1. If the union wants to maximize the wage rate for a given number of workers, say Q_3, it will set wage rate w_3.

work and for how long each week they should be employed.

A PURE MONOPOLY APPROACH. We could analyze unions as pure monopolies. If business monopolies behave as if they maximize profits, why don't we analyze unions in a similar manner? In other words, why don't we assume that they behave as if they maximize the equivalent of monopoly profits or members' wealth? We could then say that unions would behave to maximize the difference between the total wage bill and the wage bill which is necessary to bid workers away from alternative employment. The problem with such an analysis is that it assumes that the union is proprietary, that is, that it is privately owned and the owners obtain all noncontractual income, or profits. Once we abandon this assumption, it is difficult to continue our analogy with business monopolies, which are, by the way, analyzed by assuming private property rights in the ownership of the monopoly.

A property rights approach to the economics of unions

Recently there have been a number of developments in the analysis of trade unions. One in particular that we will treat here examines the property rights structure within unions. This approach has been successfully used by Donald L. Martin.[8] Martin first points out that the theory of the profit-maximizing firm is based at a minimum on an implicit assumption of private property rights in resources and in the wealth increments arising from resource use. Models of union behavior cannot safely ignore the ownership characteristics of trade union organizations, because these characteristics define the alternative opportunities of unions.

LEGAL STRUCTURE OF UNIONS. Labor organizations are legally and structurally constituted to behave as collusive or monopolistic actors in the labor market. Legal, enforceable, and *exclusive* bargaining rights and the legal right to withhold production provide unions with the tools to generate monopoly profits for their members. Of particular importance is the fact that strikers are immune from antitrust laws. We cannot conclude, however, that unions will behave as if they were seeking to maximize the profits of union labor leaders simply because unions are capable of generating those profits. Here is where the institutional arrangements become relevant.

CAPTURABILITY OF RESULTS OF CURRENT ACTIONS ON PRESENT VALUE OF FUTURE WEALTH. Current actions of utility-maximizing individuals normally generate future consequences. However, unless

individuals can capitalize these future consequences into current transfer prices, they will not be as sensitive to all opportunities that would truly maximize their wealth. We note that with very few exceptions, private property in union membership is nonexistent. Unlike shareholders of a corporation, union members may not sell their membership rights to would-be unionists. Such sales are not legally enforceable and are almost universally prohibited in union constitutions; hence, the present value of future economic profits *cannot* be capitalized in the current value of membership to incumbents. Members must wait and hope that they will survive to claim such profits if and when they materialize.

Economic analysis suggests that the interests of utility-maximizing members, when confronted with the nonproprietary constraint, will generate union behavior inconsistent with the hypothesis that the organization is attempting to maximize its wealth. Whenever wealth-increasing opportunities cannot be captured in the immediate value of membership rights, union collective bargaining goals will be biased toward current versus future interests despite the obvious negative consequences for the organization and its members *in the long run.*

YOUNGER MEMBERS AND VACANCIES. We predict, then, that since current members cannot capture completely future wealth increases, younger members will attempt to bargain for more, i.e., higher wages now, despite the adverse future employment consequences for incumbents or potential additions to the firm's work force. We come up with another implication of the nonproprietary nature of unions. We expect them to practice nonprice rationing for vacant membership slots. That is, in the nonproprietary unions, the capitalized value of membership entry fees and dues payments will be lower than the present value of expected monopoly profits to would-be members. Entry into unions will be rationed, instead, on the basis of race, sex, nationality, and religion, as well as other personal characteristics.

---

[8]Donald Martin, *An Economic Theory of the Trade Union: A New Approach*, to be published.

STRIKES. The nonproprietary nature of most trade unions has an effect on the nature and characteristics of strike activity. Strikes impose immediate cost on strikers in the form of lost wages. They also impose future costs on union members, because in the future higher assessments will have to be made to build up a depleted strike fund. After all, when strikes occur, workers are often given money out of such a strike fund; the burden of rebuilding those depleted funds is only vaguely perceived in the present in nonproprietary unions, since they are unable to capitalize the value of membership rights. This suggests an explanation for strikes and strike lengths that often appear irrational to outside observers because the present value of the increments in wages is equal to or less than the present value of the total cost of the strike. But such strikes may be perfectly rational to the member of the nonproprietary union if a larger fraction of benefits may be captured earlier, while most strike costs are spread out over a longer period of time and incurred by future members.

UNION LEADERSHIP. The absence of private property in union membership rights lowers the returns to members from participating in efforts to police and change union management. As a result, the nonproprietary character of most unions provides greater opportunities for leaders, if they choose, to increase their own utility at the expense of rank and file members. This may take the form of (1) "sweetheart" contracts with employers; (2) collective bargaining packages that enrich union treasuries directly rather than increase the current wages and benefits of rank and file members; (3) diversion of union resources to prolong tenure and leadership; (4) the pursuit of local, regional, or national political interests at union expense; and (5) blatant corruption.

The demand for baseball players: A bilateral monopoly situation

We mentioned before that collusive agreements among potential monopsonists would be difficult

to enforce. It turns out that with the help of Congress and the Supreme Court, professional sports teams have for many years engaged in open collusive agreements to limit wages of their players. We will examine in this section only the market for baseball players.

We first assume that the players are unorganized and do not bargain collectively. The team owners, however, have formed a monopsony and agree that no team will attempt to bid away any other team's players. They further agree not to raise wages. This is the simplest model that can be applied to the baseball situation.

The marginal revenue product curve of the baseball team owner, taken as a group, is represented by MRP in Figure 16-15. The marginal factor cost curve facing the team owners, taken as a

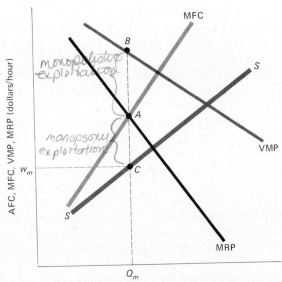

Figure 16-15: Monopsony and the demand for baseball players.

The baseball teams taken as a whole have an effective monopoly in the product market. Accordingly, they look to their MRP. They are also a monopsonist in the factor market. They hire workers to the point where MFC = MRP, which is at point A. They hire Q_m baseball players and pay a wage rate of w_m. The amount of monopolistic exploitation is the vertical distance between B and A; the amount of monopsonistic exploitation is the vertical distance between A and C.

whole, is MFC. The intersection of MRP and MFC is at *A*. The quantity demanded of baseball players is Q_m. The wage rate presented to baseball players is w_m. The amount of monopsony exploitation is the distance between *A* and *C*. The amount of monopolistic exploitation is the distance between *A* and *B*. Total exploitation is the vertical distance between *B* and *C*.

Now, what happens when the baseball players band together and form a monopoly in the sale of their services? This is the situation called **bilateral monopoly**; in this case its the factor market. We show it in Figure 16-16. The marginal revenue product curve of the baseball team owners, taken as a whole, is represented by MRP. We draw a curve that is *marginal* to MRP and label it MR. MR is, in effect, a marginal revenue curve, when we consider that MRP is the demand curve for baseball players' services by monopoly team owners. Thus, MR is no different from any other marginal revenue curve in a monopoly situation. The union of baseball players has a supply curve of *SS*. The curve marginal to that curve is called marginal factor cost curve, or MFC. The baseball team owners would like to set a wage rate of w_m, because this is where the team owners could obtain the profit-maximizing number of players and is determined by the intersection at point *A* of the marginal factor cost curve (MFC) and the marginal revenue product curve (MRP). However, the union, acting as the sole bargaining agent for all of the employees, would, if it were maximizing the equivalent of monopoly profits, want to set a wage rate of w_u. We determine the maximizing wage rate w_u by considering that the union is acting as a monopolist. Every monopolist will set output where MR = MC. What is marginal revenue in this case? It is the curve labeled MR, which is marginal to the demand curve for baseball players (MRP) by monopoly team owners. What is marginal cost? It is given by the supply curve of baseball players, or *SS*. MR and *SS* intersect at point *B*. That amount of baseball players' services can be sold to the team owners at a price of w_u given by the team owner's demand curve MRP. What we can say is that, in a situation of bilateral monopoly, the agreed-upon wage rate will be in

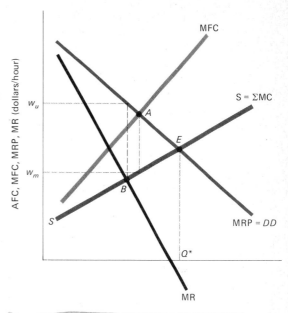

Figure 16-16: The players' union versus the team owners—bilateral monopoly in the factor market.
Baseball team owners would like to set up a wage rate where MFC = MRP; this occurs at point *A*. They would, therefore, want to set wage rate w_m. However, if the baseball players form a union, they want to sell the quantity of their product where MR = MC. Marginal revenue is given by the curve that is marginal to the MRP curve. This curve is labeled MR. The intersection, then, of marginal revenue and marginal cost, or *SS*, is at point *B*. Because the supply curve *SS* represents the summation of the individual marginal cost curves of the individual players, the players' union would like to set a wage rate of w_u. Joint profit maximization would dictate that the team owners and team players' union get together to offer quantity Q^*; then only the public would be exploited.

between w_m and w_u. If we were to assume that the union is proprietary, we would state that the union would attempt to attain w_u because that is the wage rate which maximizes the difference between total wages that are paid to employed baseball players and the minimum amount of wages required to bring this quantity of labor into the baseball playing market.

Joint wealth maximization

Actually, there is a determinant level of employment at which both the players and the team owners maximize their joint wealth. If we assume that transactions costs are zero, the two groups would agree to employ the number of players at which the supply curve intersects the marginal revenue product at point E. At this point the two groups are not attempting to exploit one another; rather, they are conspiring to exploit the spectators. There is a problem at point E, however, and that is how the wealth should be split between the group of players and the group of team owners.

Restricting competition for players

One of the ways that the team owners as a group have attempted to restrict the competition for players which would destroy the monopsony power that they have by acting in unison is the use of reserve clauses and drafts. A reserve clause, when in effect, has required any major league club wishing to acquire the services of another club's player to purchase his contract from the current owner. In this sense, once the player had signed a contract with a major league team, he had signed away part of the rights to his own baseball talent.

The reserve clause has in the past been coupled with the draft. With the draft system, the worst team in each league is given the first choice to select from ball players entering the profession. The next poorest team has the second choice. The third worse team has the third choice, and so on. The key provision of the past draft system has been that no team could bargain with a player who had been drafted by another team. Therefore, the draft system was used to eliminate the possibility that two or more teams would bid for the same athlete.

Does the reserve system alter the distribution of players?

Does the reserve clause actually change the distribution of good players among teams? If it doesn't, then we must seriously doubt the contention that the clause is necessary. We will find that

whether a player owns his contract or his team owns his contract, the distribution of players among teams will remain the same.

Consider two examples. Assume first that there is no reserve clause in existence. We have a player who is receiving a wage rate of $22,000 a year from the Yankees. The Giants decide to offer him $23,000 a year. If $23,000 a year is more than the value of this player to the Yankees, they will not increase his salary; they will allow the Giants to bid him away. If, on the other hand, his services to the Yankees are worth more than $23,000, he will be extended a counteroffer large enough to make him stay in New York. With no reserve clause, the player will end up playing for the club that most highly values his services.

Now let's take an example where the reserve clause is in effect. Assume the same player is working for the same $22,000 salary with the Yankees. The Giants decide to offer the Yankees $1,000 *a year* for this player's contract. If negotiations succeed, the Giants will end up paying $23,000 a year for the player. Of this amount, $22,000 is actually paid annually to the player under the original contract and $1,000 per year is paid to the Yankees. If the $1,000 per annum exceeds the player's net value to the Yankees after paying his $22,000-a-year salary, then it will be in the Yankees' best interest to sell his contract to the Giants. On the other hand, if this particular player is worth more to the Yankees than $23,000 (the $1,000 annuity offered by the Giants plus this player's $22,000 salary), it will refuse to sell his contract.

Surprisingly enough, under the reserve clause the circumstances under which this player will be transferred to the Giants are exactly the circumstances under which he will decide himself to transfer to the Giants when not subject to the reserve clause. He transfers to the Giants if the Giants find his services more valuable than the Yankees, *whether or not the reserve clause is effective.* We must conclude that the reserve clause does not cause a different distribution of players among teams than would obtain otherwise. This is a surprising result, indeed, but it does serve to discredit the allegations of baseball club owners. They want to keep the reserve clause because they, not the players, are the ones who reap any unexpected benefits of the services of exceptional players. (Note that if there is no reserve clause, the draft would be meaningless because it would not allocate property rights in players' contracts.)

Is there a monopsony in intercollegiate athletics?

In the preceding application we analyzed the monopsony in major league sports. It turns out that there is a similar, but less obvious, monopsony in big-time intercollegiate athletics. For many years now, the National Collegiate Athletic Association (NCAA) has functioned as a cartel that restricted the "salaries" that college athletes could earn. When we refer to the salaries of college athletes, we mean their implicit salaries, which may be composed of fellowships, jobs provided at higher than prevailing wages, and services sold to the college athlete at below market prices.

History of the NCAA

There are over 600 four-year colleges and universities that have memberships in the NCAA. The NCAA controls over 20 sports. It investigates and enforces all of the rules pertaining to these sports. Between the annual conventions of the NCAA, the NCAA Council operates this intercollegiate cartel. This council is dominated by those universities which operate big-time athletic programs.

Why the NCAA qualifies as a cartel

We can point to a number of reasons why the NCAA can be called a cartel with monopsony power.

1. It regulates the number of student athletes that universities can hire.

2. It often fixes the price that the university charges for intercollegiate sporting events.
3. It sets the prices, the wages, and the conditions under which the universities can hire student athletes.
4. It enforces its regulations and rules with sanctions and penalties.

The NCAA rules and regulations expressly prohibit bidding for college athletes in an overt manner. Rather, the NCAA requires that all athletes be paid the same for tuition, fees, room, board, and books. Moreover, the NCAA limits the number of athletic scholarships that can be given by a particular university. These rules are to prevent the richest universities from "hiring" the best student athletes.

Problems with enforcing the cartel agreements

Not surprisingly, from the very beginning of the NCAA, individual universities and colleges have attempted to cheat on the rules in order to attract better athletes. The original agreement among the colleges was to pay no wages. Almost immediately after this agreement was put into effect, colleges switched to athletic scholarships, jobs, "free" room and board, travel to college, and so on. It was not unusual for athletes to be paid $4 an hour to rake leaves, when the going wage rate for such work was only $2 an hour. Finally, the NCAA had to agree to permit wages up to a certain amount per year.

If all universities had to offer exactly the same money wages and fringe benefits, the less distinguished colleges in metropolitan areas would have the most inducement to engage in violation of the NCAA agreements. They would figure out all sorts of techniques to get the best student athletes. As evidence, we note that these schools cheated more than other universities and colleges, and their violations were detected and punished with a greater relative frequency than other colleges and universities.

The inducement to stay in the NCAA

One wonders why colleges and universities agreed to stay in the NCAA. Why would they agree to pay fines and accept punishments when they were caught engaging in "unethical" practices attempting to lure the best student athletes to their campuses? One reason that has been offered is that the NCAA had the power to impair the *academic* accreditation of any university or college that was caught violating the athletic code. Colleges and universities placed on probation or expelled from the NCAA thought that they would find it more difficult to recruit faculty. At one point, even Phi Beta Kappa would not authorize chapters at colleges and universities that provided "disproportionate" amounts of money for athletic scholarships even if that college or university had a superb, indeed superior, academic reputation.

In recent years, the NCAA has been subjected to a number of lawsuits by its own members. Such suits demonstrate the precarious nature of all cartel arrangements. In the meantime, whatever monopsony power remains in the cartel arrangement, it results in a lower implicit wage rate being paid to college athletes.

Glossary

Marginal revenue product (MRP) The change in total revenues that result from a unit change in the variable input ($\equiv$ MPP $\cdot$ MR).

Monopsony A single buyer.

Oligopsony Several buyers.

Average factor cost curve Another name for the supply curve, because at any point on the supply curve, the price given is equal to the average (per unit) factor cost.

Marginal factor cost curve A curve showing the increase in total factor cost due to a one-unit increase in use of that factor.

Exploitation Paying a resource unit less than its VMP in its *current* use.

Monopolistic exploitation Paying a resource its

marginal revenue product instead of its value of marginal product ($\equiv$ VMP $-$ MRP).

Monopsonistic exploitation Exploitation due to monopsony power. It leads to a unit factor price that is less than its MRP ($\equiv$ MRP $-$ w).

Bilateral monopoly A situation in which a monopolist sells to a monopsonist.

Summary

1. The pure monopolist's demand curve for a single variable factor of production, all other factors constant, is its marginal revenue product curve (if it purchases the input in a perfectly competitive market).
2. The marginal revenue product curve can be found by multiplying marginal physical product by marginal revenue.
3. For the monopolist purchasing inputs in a perfectly competitive market, the profit-maximizing combinations in inputs will be such that $P_i/\text{MPP}_i = \text{MC} = \text{MR}$ [for all i (inputs)], or marginal revenue product for each input should equal its unit price.
4. The marginal revenue product curve lies below the value of marginal product curve. A monopolist with the same production function as a perfect competitor will hire less of any input at any given input price.
5. When there are several variable inputs, the monopolist's demand curve is more elastic than any given marginal revenue product curve.
6. The equilibrium input price and rate of employment for the monopolist is at the intersection of its marginal revenue product curve and the supply curve of the input.
7. The marginal factor cost curve is everywhere above an upward-sloping supply curve.
8. The relationship between MFC and the elasticity of supply is MFC = $w \, [1 + (1/\epsilon_L)]$ when we look only at the labor input.
9. The monopsonist that sells its product competitively will hire inputs to the point where the value of marginal product of each input is equal to the marginal factor cost. If a monopsonist is also a monopolist, it will hire an input to the point where the marginal factor cost equals marginal revenue product. The factor price will

then be obtained from the supply curve for that quantity.

10. Exploitation can come about because of monopoly and/or monopsony. It occurs whenever an input is paid less than its VMP.
11. The price-discriminating monopsonist would pay different wages to different workers. He or she would hire an input to the point where the supply curve intersects the value of marginal product curve.
12. Monopsony power may come about because of (*a*) specialized factors of production, (*b*) a company town, and (*c*) collusive agreements.
13. Monopsony power is less in the long run than in the short run.
14. The monopsonist has no demand curve for an input, just as the monopolist has no supply curve.

Selected references

Cartter, Allan M., *Theory of Wages and Employment* (Homewood, Ill.: Irwin, 1959), pp. 77–133.
Fellner, William, *Modern Economic Analysis* (New York: McGraw-Hill, 1960), chap. 19.
Rees, Albert, *The Economics of Work and Pay* (New York: Harper & Row, 1973), pp. 75–80.
Robinson, Joan, *The Economics of Imperfect Competition* (London: Macmillan, 1933), pp. 218–228 and 281–304.

Questions

(Answers to even-numbered questions are at back of text.)

1. When there is only one variable input, how does a monopoly seller's demand for that input differ from that of a perfectly competitive seller?
2. Would the Whamo company's demand for Frisbee production workers be a good example of a monopoly seller hiring in a perfectly competitive labor market?
3. Why is it that, if an input is hired only by the monopolists, the horizontal summation of the individual firm's input demand curves is a valid derivation of the market demand curve, while in a perfectly competitive market this technique would overstate the demand for the factor?
4. "Just because sellers may be monopolists in the product market doesn't mean they are able to exploit nonunionized labor in a competitive labor market." Is this statement true or false, and why?
5. Under what circumstances can a firm selling in a perfectly competitive product market exploit workers?
6. Give examples of perfectly competitive sellers having monopsony power in the input market.
7. "Nonunion company towns epitomize the evils of economic power. If the worker doesn't like the wages offered, what can he or she do? In fact, the worker will surely be sacked if there are complaints or attempts to organize a union." Comment critically.
8. "People with highly specialized skills who are only employable by a handful of firms are often exploited. What few employers there are may agree, tacitly or otherwise, to keep those persons' wages down." Comment.
9. Can you give some examples of firms that are monopolists in their product market and also monopsonists in the input market?
10. Why will a monopsony hirer of labor who is able to price (wage)-discriminate "perfectly" hire the same amount of labor as a price (wage)-taking hirer of labor?
11. With a perfectly discriminating monopsonist, is there any exploitation?
12. Can economic theory explain the traditional reluctance of many individuals to discuss their earnings?
13. Is there a surplus of teachers and fire fighters? What information would help you to answer the question?
14. "She places such a high value on her time that we rarely get to even chat with her." What's wrong with this statement?
15. Does military conscription (a draft) result in economic exploitation in the sense in which that term is used in this chapter? Why is it misleading to look at the draft quota to determine the size of the labor shortage (excess quantity demanded) at the prevailing military wage rate?

17

WAGES, RENTS, AND INCOME DIFFERENCES

The difference between the annual income of a restaurant employee and that of the president of General Motors is immense. The difference between average wages in one industry and in another can be significant. Individuals who seemingly have the same qualifications and do the same job often appear to earn different money incomes.

In short, there are differences in both wage rates and money incomes. In this chapter we examine theories of wage structure and reasons why income differences arise.

Marginal productivity theory

The theory of pricing and employment of inputs in the last two chapters has generally been called the **marginal productivity theory** of the demand for factors of production. This theory has changed very little since the beginning of this century.

The marginal productivity theory has often been termed a theory of wages. However, marginal productivity only concerns itself with the demand side of labor. We pointed out, for example, that a competitive firm buying labor in a perfectly competitive market will employ workers up to the point where the wage rate equals VMP. In essence, then, the VMP curve was the individual firm's demand curve for labor. Certainly, then, marginal productivity is important when discussing employment and pricing of the labor input. However, we rarely are willing to speak of a demand theory of prices for other commodities. Rather, we talk in terms of demand and supply interacting to determine the relative price of the product in question. The same is true for labor. The demand side of the picture cannot be looked at in isolation.

Wages and employment are jointly determined by the interaction of supply and demand. To speak of the marginal productivity theory of wages is to speak of a demand theory of prices; and no one speaks of the demand theory of prices because price is determined by *both* demand and supply.

On being paid one's VMP

In the case of a firm selling its output in a perfectly competitive market and hiring inputs in a perfectly competitive market, marginal productivity theory indicates that workers are hired to the point where the wage rate equals the value of their marginal product. But if workers are paid just what they are worth, or the value of their marginal product, then how do entrepreneurs obtain any profits? To find the answer, we look at the MPP component of VMP. The marginal *physical* product of labor is *not* the amount of output produced by an additional unit of labor. Rather, it is the increase in total output when one more unit of labor is added. In other words, we cannot assign the quantity called marginal physical product to the *last* worker hired.

Consider Figure 17-1. Assume that the going market wage rate is w_1. The perfect competitor hiring workers in a perfectly competitive market will hire Q_1 of labor. Each worker will be paid w_1. However, the amount of revenue obtained by the employer is the price of the product times the *average* physical product of each worker, or $P \cdot APP$. This is given in Figure 17-1 by the curve labeled "Value of APP." With Q_1 workers, the vertical

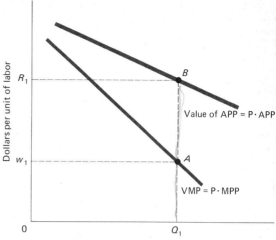

Figure 17-1: The distinction between the value of marginal product and the value of average product. When the quantity of labor employed per unit time period is Q_1, the worker is paid w_1, or the value of marginal product (equal to the price of the output times marginal physical product). The wage rate is equivalent to the reduction in total revenues that the firm would suffer if one worker quit, other inputs remaining constant. However, the "contribution" of any worker in conjunction with the nonlabor inputs is equivalent to that worker's average physical product times the price of the output; $APP \cdot P = R_1$. Thus, the firm can pay a wage rate equal to VMP and still have the vertical distance between A and B, or between w_1 and R_1, to pay the other factors of production.

distance between Q_1 and B (or between the origin and R_1) represents the revenue per worker received from selling the product of all the workers. On the vertical axis this is labeled R_1. We see that for each worker the employer pays a wage rate of w_1 but obtains a revenue of R_1. Consequently, the area of the rectangle $w_1 R_1 BA$ represents the amount of revenues available to pay the other factors of production.

If the workers are paid their VMP, by definition, they are each being paid an amount equal to the decrease in total revenues the firm would experience if one worker quit. The workers are not paid the value of what they produce in combination with other factors. Therefore, they are not paid R_1, for if that were so, there would be nothing left over to remunerate any other factors, like capital.

The process of wage equalization

Where all industries are identical, we would expect that wage rates of a given quality of labor would be the same in all industries. This is the process that we depict in Figure 17-2.

Assume that there are only two industries and that all resources are fully employed. We start out in equilibrium with a wage rate w_e, which is the same in industry I and in industry II. It is determined by the intersection of the respective demand and supply curves in those two industries: D_ID_I and S_IS_I in industry I and $D_{II}D_{II}$ and $S_{II}S_{II}$ in industry II. D_ID_I depends on wages in industry II; $D_{II}D_{II}$ depends on wages in industry I. (Why?)

Assume now that there is a shift in tastes and that the demand for the product produced in industry I increases. The demand for the output of industry II decreases. The demand curve for labor is derived from the demand for the final product. The demand curve for labor in industry I, represented in panel

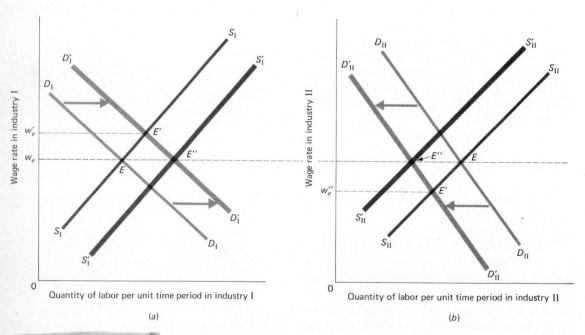

(a)

(b)

Figure 17-2: Wage adjustment.

Assume the economy consists of two industries. The demand and supply curves of labor are given for industry I in panel (a) and for industry II in panel (b). The initial equilibrium wage rate is w_e in both industry I and II. It is determined by the intersection of supply and demand in each industry [found at point E in panels (a) and (b)]. An increase in demand for industry I's output shifts the demand curve for workers rightward in that industry to $D_I'D_I'$. Initially the wage rate rises in industry I to w_e' (found at the intersection of the new demand curve with the old supply curve at point E'). The wage rate in sector II falls to w_e'' because the demand curve for its output and therefore labor has shifted leftward to $D_{II}'D_{II}'$. Assuming homogeneity of the labor force and perfect mobility, the supply curve of labor will now shift so that the wage rate in industry I depicted in panel (a) will fall back down to w_e; the wage rate in industry II depicted in panel (b) will rise back up to w_e. The new long-run equilibrium intersections are labeled E'' in both diagrams.

(*a*), shifts out to $D_I'D_I'$. On the other hand, the demand curve for labor in industry II shifts inward to $D_{II}'D_{II}'$ in response to the declining demand for that product. The new equilibrium wage rates are w_e' in industry I and w_e'' in industry II. The new intersections of supply and demand for labor are labeled E' in both panels (*a*) and (*b*). Given our assumptions, this is not a long-run equilibrium. The differential wage rate will attract workers from industry II into industry I. This will cause the supply curve of labor in industry I to shift outward to $S_I'S_I'$. Similarly, it will shift the supply curve of labor in industry II to $S_{II}'S_{II}'$. This process will continue until wages are equalized (assuming labor is homogeneous between industries and perfectly mobile). The new intersections of the demand and supply curves will be at E'' in both panels (*a*) and (*b*), and the long-run equilibrium wage rate will again be w_e in both industries. The only difference is that $E - E''$ of labor has shifted from industry II to industry I. The long-run industry labor supply curves are seen to be horizontal lines at wage rate w_e.

This analysis assumes a mobility of workers between industries. It also assumes, as we mentioned above, that the industries are equally desirable from the marginal workers' point of view.

Equalizing wage differences

When we realize that different workers attain different levels of satisfaction (or dissatisfaction) from the same type of work, then we open up our analysis to the possibility of wage differences which reflect varying tastes for different jobs. This is sometimes called the theory of equalizing wage differences. Individuals are willing to make a trade-off between less desirable occupations and increased income. The supply and demand in different industries, therefore, determines relative wages and the relative numbers of em-

ployees in different occupations. This is also considered a part of the theory of job choice.

Look at Figure 17-3. We assume that there are only two occupations. We plot the relative wage rate, w_I/w_{II}, in the two occupations on the vertical axis. The horizontal axis measures *relative* employment in the two occupations. It is labeled E_I/E_{II}.

The derived demand curve for labor is, as always, downward-sloping. As the relative wage in occupation I goes down, a larger quantity of that skill is demanded and a smaller quantity is demanded of the other skill, and vice versa.

The supply curve is upward-sloping. As the relative wage rate in occupation I increases, the number of individuals induced to leave occupation II to enter occupation I will in-

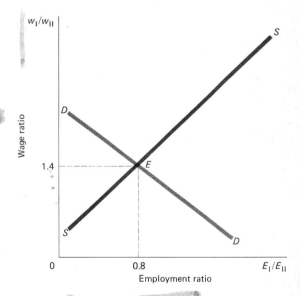

Figure 17-3: Equalizing wage differences.
The relative wage rate is shown on the vertical axis; the relative employment ratio on the horizontal axis. The supply curve *SS* is upward-sloping, indicating that workers have different preferences for the two jobs in question. If they didn't, the supply curve *SS* would be a horizontal line. The steeper the supply curve, the more individuals dislike occupation I relative to occupation II. The equalizing wage difference will be $w_I/w_{II} = 1.4$, for example. The relative employment ratio, E_I/E_{II} will be, say, 0.8.

crease. We assume in this analysis that all in-dividuals can do either job equally well. The reason the supply curve slopes up is that indi-viduals have different preferences for the two jobs in question. If individuals had equal preferences for these two jobs, the supply curve SS in Figure 17-3 would be a horizontal line. The steeper the supply curve, the more there are differences in worker preferences. In this situation, equilibrium occurs at the inter-section of DD and SS, or point E. This gives a relative wage rate of 1.4, for example, and a relative employment ratio of 0.8. That means that in equilibrium, the wage rate in occupa-tion I will be 40 percent higher than in occupa-tion II, and if there is a labor force of, say, 180,000 workers, 80,000 will be working in oc-cupation I and 100,000 will be working in oc-cupation II. (These ratios are purely hypothet-ical.)

The theory tells us that higher relative wages must be offered to get individuals to enter less desirable occupations. We do, how-ever, observe individuals making relatively low wages in what we might consider "less desirable" jobs. We have to take into account not only the tastes of the workers, but also the *supply* of workers relative to the quantities that employers desire. Washing dishes in a restaurant may be undesirable, but if there are a sufficient number of individuals who do not have the skills for other occupations, then the supply of applicants for the job of dishwasher will keep wages down.

Equalizing wage differences and geographical preferences

We can continue the analysis above by con-sidering the geographical preferences of indi-viduals. Real wage rates sometimes differ dramatically between less desirable and more desirable geographic locations. For example, secretarial wages in real terms in Honolulu may be quite a bit lower than in Chicago. Part of the difference can be explained by the dif-ferences in potential supplies of those persons seeking to work as secretaries in Hawaii and in Chicago.[1] The relatively larger potential supply of secretaries available in Hawaii is the result of its preferred climate. (One might say that the difference in real wages is the price that has to be paid for sunshine.) What we see is that the differences in real pecuniary incomes compensate for differences in the non-pecuniary aspects of employment. Figure 17-3 can be used for all such problems by redefin-ing the term "job" to include all its non-pecuniary aspects.

Qualitative difference in factors of production

Until now we have assumed that the factors of production under consideration are homoge-neous. Once we eliminate this assumption, we can account for some of the differences in wages we observe among individuals within the same occupation and among individuals working for the same firm. One worker may not be the duplicate of another because their skill levels are different. Remember that the profit-maximizing firm will hire an input up to the point where the price per unit of the input equals its marginal physical product times output price if we are talking about a perfect competitor, or MPP times marginal revenue if we are talking about a monopolist. If we have two groups of workers doing the same job but with unequal productivities, we will find that the profit-maximizing firm selling in a competitive market will hire each type of worker up to the point where

$$\text{MPP}_\text{I} \cdot P = w_\text{I} \qquad (17\text{-}1)$$

$$\text{MPP}_\text{II} \cdot P = w_\text{II} \qquad (17\text{-}2)$$

[1]We must, of course, normalize for population size. Also, geographical mobility is based on present value of wage differences over the life of a worker relative to the cost of migrating. See Larry Sjaastad, "The Cost and Returns of Human Migration," *Journal of Political Economy*, vol. LXX, no. 2, part 2, October 1962, pp. 80–93.

The two distinct marginal physical products are represented by the subscripts I and II and the corresponding unequal wage rates are represented by the same subscripts. The differential in wages between the more skilled and the less skilled will equal the differential in their respective marginal physical products. We can see this by multiplying Eq. (17-1) by $1/(P \cdot w_I)$ and then multiplying Eq. (17-2) by $1/(P \cdot w_{II})$. Then it is seen that Eqs. (17-1) and (17-2) are both equal to $1/P$. We can set them equal to each other, which yields

$$\frac{MPP_I}{w_I} = \frac{MPP_{II}}{w_{II}}$$

or $\qquad \dfrac{w_I}{w_{II}} = \dfrac{MPP_I}{MPP_{II}} \qquad (17\text{-}3)$

Long and short run

Occupational wage differentials can be expected to be greater in the short run than in the long run. The short-run supply curve of labor for a particular skill is going to be relatively inelastic compared with the equivalent long-run curve. In the immediate run it would be vertical, the number of people in the occupation being independent of the wage rate. However, given adequate time for training and/or the establishment of new training facilities, the number of qualified individuals in an occupation can and will be increased if wage differentials are sufficient to justify the costs of training and/or retraining. Thus in the long run, the supply curve of labor to an occupation will be very elastic, unless of course there are significant barriers to entry (e.g., professional licensing).

Rents to scarce natural talents

Another aspect of wage differentials that must be considered is explained by **economic rents** accruing to those possessing natural talents. Economic rent is defined as any payment over and above what is necessary to maintain a fac-

tor of production in its current activity. These natural talents of course will be more significant in some occupations than in others. They seem to be particularly important in athletics, acting, music, and other entertainment-type endeavors. In some cases, such economic rents can explain a great part of the difference between the earnings of successful musicians, for example, and the average musician. However, we must remember that such rents may be overstated. Remember that it is the *potential* gains that induce individuals to begin artistic careers. Such individuals have expectations about the probability of success (P) and about the potential gain if successful (V). We expect them, therefore, to spend up to the amount (PV) on "training" seeking to achieve success.[2] Moreover, the potential supply of singers, artists, and pianists is very great because of the nonpecuniary attractions of such careers. Many individuals will remain in these occupations in spite of their relatively low earnings. After all, sunk costs are forever sunk. Such low rates of pay and/or frequent periods of unemployment drive the average earnings of people in these occupations below those in the other skilled occupations in which native talent or ability is less important.

Furthermore, the supposed rents paid to very successful entertainers, for example, may in fact be necessary to induce all of the unsuccessful would-be entertainment stars to continue to enter and to remain in the occupation. (This is the V referred to above.) We are not, therefore, really dealing with a rent but rather a reward system in which the high rewards to those who "win" when multiplied by the probability of "winning" (becoming a star) just equals the average wage rate in other occupations where no such risk or possibility of hitting it big exists.

This discussion leads us to another factor that influences relative wage rates.

---

[2] If they are risk preferrers, then economic rents will be negative in the long run for the average person in, say, the entertainment field.

Uncertainty

The greater the amount of uncertainty about the stability of demand in an occupation, the greater will have to be the average wage rate for such an occupation compared with all other occupations that are similar but have less uncertainty. Such uncertainty about demand leads to uncertainty about the dispersion of income over a lifetime in a given occupation. We expect, then, that two occupations with equal average incomes but unequal dispersions will have different wage rates attached to them. The one with more dispersion of income will have a higher wage rate. This, of course, assumes that marginal individuals are averse to risk taking, i.e., that they prefer certainty.

Rents and quasi-rents

We talked earlier about rents to natural talents subject to a quantity supplied. Now we want to expand this discussion of rents to include rents to all factors of production. In general, we have looked at the pricing of variable resources. In the short run, however, there are fixed resources; and the shorter the period of time, the more fixed resources there will be.

The supply of land

One of the earlier writers on the topic of economic rent was David Ricardo. He assumed that the quantity of land in a country was fixed and that the country was a closed economy. The supply curve of land, then, is vertical; and the price elasticity of the supply of land is therefore 0. If the supply of land is represented by SS in Figure 17-4 and the demand curve is DD, then the price of land would be P_1. If the demand curve for some reason shifts out to $D'D'$, then price of land will rise to P_2.

Because David Ricardo considered the total demand for land, there were no alternative

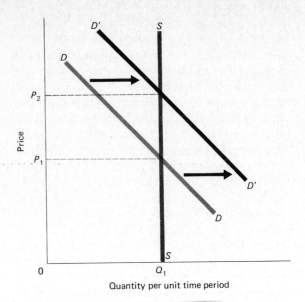

Figure 17-4: Pure economic (Ricardian) rent.
If indeed the supply curve of a factor of production were completely price inelastic in the long run, then it would be depicted by SS. At the quantity in existence Q_1, any and all revenues are pure rent. If demand is DD, the price will be P_1; if demand is $D'D'$, price will rise to P_2. Economic rent would be $P_1 \cdot Q_1$ and $P_2 \cdot Q_1$, respectively.

uses for land and no opportunity cost *to the economy* of using land. Pure economic rent was not considered a cost to the economy because cost includes only opportunity cost. It is equal to the outlay that could be avoided if output were not produced. The revenues derived from the ownership of land were considered by Ricardo (and also by Henry George) to be economic rent. Today it is called **Ricardian rent** and is defined as any surplus of revenue over and above the opportunity cost of production. In Figure 17-4, the demand curve is DD. Ricardian rent is equal to P_1 times Q_1. If the demand curve shifts to $D'D'$, economic rent increases to P_2 times Q_1. Economic rent is a long-run concept and is the amount of payment to a resource over and above what is necessary to keep the resource forever in existence in its current condition. There is some confusion between Ricardian rent and the earnings of entertainment super-stars. It is precisely those "outrageous" incomes that rock stars receive that induce individuals to enter the industry and work at very low wages in the hope of hitting it big. Sometimes economic rent of the nature just described is called a surplus because it does not influence the quantity of the good available. However, using the example of a well-known entertainment person, we can see that it is not a surplus. It serves a rationing or allocative function.

Consider folk singer Joan Baez. She has some particularly egalitarian ideas about how much tickets to her shows should cost. Consequently, when she gives a concert, all tickets are sold at the same price of, say, $5. Assume she will give five concerts a year, no matter how much she makes. Assume further that each concert hall has 20,000 seats and that number of tickets is available at a price of $5. Thus 100,000 individuals will be allowed to hear Ms. Baez per year. This is represented by point A in Figure 17-5. At $5 a ticket, however, the annual quantity of seats demanded is 150,000 and is represented by point B. The difference between A and B is the excess quantity of tickets demanded at the non-market-clearing price of $5 a seat. The additional economic rent that she could earn by charging the market-clearing price of, say, $15, would serve as the rationing device that would make the quantity demanded equal to the quantity supplied.

Part of the rent that she could have earned is dissipated—it is captured, for example, by radio stations in the form of promotional gains if they are allocated to give away a certain number of tickets on the air. Ticket scalpers also capture a part of the rents. Conceivably, Ms. Baez could charge the market-clearing price ($15 per ticket) and give away the portion of these rents ($10 per ticket) that are now being dissipated. In that manner, she could make sure that the recipients of the rents were "worthy" in her own estimation. Presumably, she has no special desire to increase the net

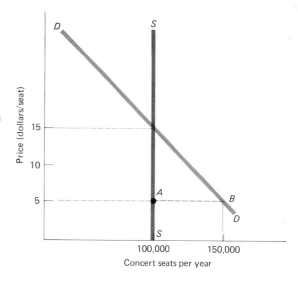

Figure 17-5: The allocative function of rent – the case of Joan Baez' Concerts.

If Joan Baez agrees to give five concerts a year at any price, and assuming that there are 20,000 seats in each concert hall, then her supply curve of concerts SS is vertical at 100,000 seats per year. The demand curve is given by DD. She wants only a price of $5 to be charged. At that price, the quantity of seats demanded per year is 150,000. The excess quantity demanded is equal to the horizontal distance between point A and point B, or 50,000 seats per year.

worth position of scalpers and corporations that own radio stations.[3]

Since economic rent is a long-run concept, it is now time to consider the short-run concept, which is a quasi-rent.

Quasi-rents

Any fixed factor earns an economic rent in the short run. This is because of the perfectly inelastic supply of such factors in the short run. We call the return to factors that are fixed

---

[3]It is interesting to note that Muhammed Ali understood this argument. In the beginning of his fighting career, he was interested in low-priced tickets so "his fans" could see him fight. They seldom did, however, since the actual price of a ticket exceeded the printed price. He then changed his behavior and started charging market-clearing prices and contributing enormous sums to hospitals and other charitable outlets.

in the short run a **quasi-rent**. Thus we can also define quasi-rent as the difference between total revenues and total variable costs. Quasi-rents are those revenues, if any, available for fixed factors and economic profits. The reason we call this a quasi-rent rather than an economic rent is that the factor is fixed only in the short run and not in the long run. The quasi-rent must be at least equal to the interest plus depreciation on a durable asset for that durable asset to be maintained. In other words, quasi-rents are payments to durable factors of production which do not influence the *current* quantity supplied of those factors of production but do influence the *future* quantity supplied.

In a competitive capital market, we know that rates of return (corrected for risk) tend to equality on the margin. Thus if the investment in a particular capital asset yields a long-run net rate of return that is below the yield on other investments, there will be in the future less investment in the relatively less profitable asset. The short-run gross return to a specialized capital good is indeed a quasi-rent, but if that gross return does not equal the long-run net return to all capital goods, the capital good in question will be allowed to depreciate and disappear.

We can illustrate quasi-rents by using the traditional cost curves of the firm. In Figure 17-6, we examine a firm in a perfectly competitive market receiving zero economic profits. The short-run average total cost curve is just tangent to the price line *dd*, which is the demand curve faced by a perfect competitor. The tangency occurs at the minimum point and is where marginal cost intersects average total costs. The profit-maximizing rate of output is q_1, but the firm's economic profits are zero. However, the return to the fixed factors of production is the rectangle $C_1 P_c EA$ and is equal to $AFC \cdot q_1 = (FC)$. This rectangle is also the quasi-rent, for it is payment to fixed factors of production which, by definition, in the short run have no alternative cost. They represent

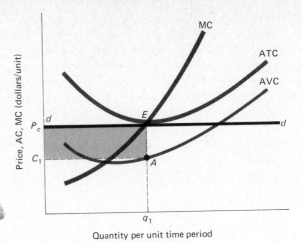

Figure 17-6: Measuring quasi-rents.
If output for the firm is q_1, the difference between average variable costs and price will be the quasi-rent per unit of output, since the firm will continue to produce in the short run as long as price exceeds minimum average variable costs. Its quasi-rents are equal to the rectangle $C_1 P_c EA$.

sent a sunk cost. If the firm obtained a price for its product that yielded just enough to cover average variable cost, the firm in the short run would remain in operation. The rate of return, however, to investment in that firm would be negative. In the long run, the firm would go out of business. Hence, any payment which more than covers average variable cost is considered a quasi-rent because it does not affect the current use of resources.

When quasi-rents are not enough

In some cases, quasi-rents fail to be sufficient to induce reinvestment in the capital asset in question. How can this arise? Simply because of mistaken expectations on the part of those who made the original investment. The investors failed to predict accurately the future course of the demand for and supply of the services of the durable capital good when it was built. This might occur, for example, if an investment were made in a machine that would become technically inefficient as the result of the invention of a superior machine the following year. Alternatively, the demand for the final output that the specialized machine helped produce may have declined because of a change in tastes or because of a fall in the price of its substitutes.

Prediction errors can rarely be eliminated. Moreover, they are more serious the more specialized the investment. A highly specialized machine that can only be used to make one specific product is much more at the mercy of the shifts in the supply of and the demand for the services of the machine that can be transferred only imperfectly to some alternative use. We say, then, that the demand for a machine is more stable the less specialized is the machine. We might predict, then, that we would find relatively more specialized machines in those industries with relatively more stable demand for their products.

The size distribution of money and nonmoney income

The share of national income going to labor accounts for about 75 percent of total national income. Much of the explanation of the distribution of money income can therefore be found in the explanations of wage differentials. However, there are other considerations that need to be examined. They are, in a sense, refinements on what we have just discussed. Before we go into them, let us take a look at the actual distribution of money income in the United States.

Money income differences

We present in Table 17-1 the percentage distribution of families by money income level in 1947, 1960, and 1973. In Table 17-2, we present percentage income shares for those same families in fifths (quintiles). We note from Table 17-1 that in 1973 almost 6 percent of families

Income class	1973*	1960	1947
Under $3,000	5.9	21.6	48.9
$3,000–$5,999	13.2	33.2	39.3
$6,000–$9,999	19.7	30.9	9.0
$10,000–$14,999	25.6	10.6	
$15,000–$24,999	26.2	2.8	2.8
Over $25,000	9.3	0.9	
Median income (dollars)	12,073	5,631	3,048
Median income (constant 1973 dollars)	12,073	8,436	6,032

Table 17-1: Percentage distribution of families by money income level.
*Total does not equal 100 percent because of rounding.
Source: U.S. Bureau of the Census, "Money Income in 1973 of Families and Persons in the United States," *Current Population Reports*, ser. P-60, no. 97 (1975), table 21, p. 60.

had reported money incomes of less than $3,000. This 6 percent of families had money incomes that were less than one-fourth of the median family income of approximately $12,000.

Nonetheless, there has been an improvement in the relative position of low-income families since the end of World War II. There has been a major decrease in the percentage of families with incomes below $3,000. Part of this is due to inflation. Between 1947 and 1973, prices rose by almost 100 percent. A $3,000 income in 1973 would be equivalent to a $1,500 income in 1947. In that latter year, about 20 percent of families had incomes below $1,500. This percentage had been cut by more than two-thirds by 1973. In terms of real income, the poor have made sizable gains over the period.

Another reason that the number of poor has been reduced is economic growth. All income classes increase their real incomes if the growth dividend is evenly distributed.

Such movement out of an income class, however, may not and in fact did not alter the relative shares of incomes earned by families.

Income group	1973	1960*	1947*
Lowest fifth	5.5	4.8	5.1
Second fifth	11.9	12.2	11.8
Third fifth	17.5	17.8	16.7
Fourth fifth	24.0	24.0	23.2
Highest fifth	41.1	41.3	43.3

Table 17-2: Percentage share of income for families before direct taxes.
*Total does not equal 100 percent due to rounding.
Source: U.S. Bureau of the Census, "Money Income in 1973 of Families and Persons in the United States," *Current Population Reports*, ser. P-60, no. 97 (1975), table 22.

This is seen in Table 17-2. That table groups families according to whether they are in the lowest 20 percent of the income distribution, the second lowest 20 percent, and so on. We see that in 1973, the lowest 20 had a combined money income of 5.5 percent of the total money income of the entire population. This is about the same that it had at the end of World War II. Accordingly, the conclusion has been drawn that there have only been slight changes in the distribution of money income. And, indeed, considering that the definition of money income used by the U.S. Bureau of the Census includes only wage and salary income, income from self-employment, interest and dividends, and such government cash-transfer payments as social security and un-employment compensation, we have to agree that the distribution of money income has not changed. Money income, though, is not total income for individuals who receive in-kind transfers from the government in the form of food stamps, public housing, and so on.

The distribution of total income

If we include in-kind transfers in estimating the distribution of total income, we find a very different picture of what has happened to the poor in the United States since World War II. In 1973 there were 23 million people officially

regarded as poor. However, those 23 million people received $18.8 billion of such in-kind transfers as food stamps, health care, and public housing. The lowest fifth income group in 1960 was estimated to have 4.8 percent of total money income. In terms of total income, it had 5 percent. In 1973 it was estimated, as given in Table 17-2, that this lowest fifth obtained only 5.5 percent of total money income. However, when in-kind transfers are added to the money income figures for 1973, the estimated share of the first quintile reaches about 12 percent.[4] Indeed, when these noncash forms of income are included, the relative position of the poorest fifth of families is improved by over 100 percent between 1960 and 1973.

Causes of income differences

We list below some of the causes of differences in incomes. A detailed discussion of these causes is beyond the scope of an intermediate price theory text.

AGE: Most workers follow a lifetime real income pattern that is typified in Figure 17-7. This figure is called an **age-earnings profile**. It shows how earnings rise with age, reach a peak around age 45 to age 55, and then fall. Note that this curve is drawn for a fixed level of nationwide productivity. Any change in national productivity would shift the curve.

Its shape is explained by a number of factors. First of all, younger workers typically have less training and experience. Their marginal physical products are lower on the average than those of older and more experienced workers. Secondly, the number of hours worked by the average worker goes up until around age 45 or 55. Then average hours worked per week go down; this explains to

---

[4] Edgar K. Browning, "How Much More Equality Can We Afford?" *The Public Interest*, Spring 1976, pp. 90–110.

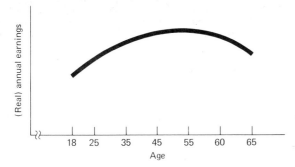

Figure 17-7: The age-earnings profile.
Real annual earnings (abstracting from changes in the national productivity) typically rise until they reach a peak between ages 45 and 55 and then fall.

some extent the downward slope of the age-earning profile to the right of the peak. Further, the age-earnings profile levels off and slopes down because of the effects of old age on marginal physical productivity. And lastly, the curve drops down abruptly to the horizontal axis at retirement. However, if we included the earnings from capital ownership, social security benefits, and other annuities, income would not drop to zero at retirement.

INHERITED CHARACTERISTICS. Many characteristics of entertainment stars are to a large extent inherited or innate. If one is born with a beautiful voice, one has an edge over someone who can't carry a tune. If one is born with an IQ of 160, all other things being equal, that person should have a higher income-earning potential than someone with half that IQ figure. There is currently a debate raging over the extent to which income-earning characteristics are actually innate or inherited and the extent to which they are determined by environment and society.

RISK TAKING. Those who work at more hazardous jobs will earn more, on the average, than those who do not. The relatively high salaries of those who walk steel beams on skyscrapers can be explained in large part by the increased

risk of injury or death. *Ceteris paribus,* we expect that the earnings of those with more safe jobs will average below those with less safe jobs.

UNCERTAINTY AND VARIANCE OF INCOME. As we pointed out before, if individuals on the margin are risk-averse, they require a larger expected income from a job which generates income in a less certain fashion with a higher variance than in other occupations. Thus, we would predict that individuals in jobs of the former type will have higher incomes, on average, than those with jobs of the latter type.

TRAINING. Given a set of individuals with exactly the same innate characteristics, those with more training will earn higher incomes. The training may be formal, obtained either by higher education or mail-order home study courses, or informal knowledge and training acquired on the job. Indeed, the role of on-the-job training is very important in explaining the variation of earnings with age. The reason training leads to higher income is because workers who are better trained have a higher marginal physical product than the less skilled. We will discuss this topic in more detail below under the general heading of investment in human capital.

INHERITED WEALTH. Those who inherit wealth can earn incomes which are higher than those with similar abilities and training who do not inherit wealth because the wealth will yield them an income. The degree to which inherited wealth affects the distribution of money income is quite small in the United States. It is more important in less developed countries where a smaller percentage of national income accrues to labor.

MARKET IMPERFECTIONS. Monopoly, monopsony, union policies, government-mandated minimum wages, licensing requirements, certification, and the like all lead to differences in money incomes among classes of workers. Those who benefit from these market imperfections receive higher money incomes at the expense of others.

DISCRIMINATION. In the labor market, discrimination by race, religion, or sex can explain certain income differences. Studies which attempt to correct for the differences in marginal physical productivities of different classes of workers grouped by race or sex generally show an unexplained "residual" that may be the result of discrimination. In other words, even after taking account of quantity and quality of schooling and other training, age, number of years in the labor force, and so on, when wage rates of men and women are compared, an unexplained differential still remains; likewise, when wage rates of whites and blacks are compared, a differential persists. This differential is attributed by some to discrimination. What is at issue, of course, is how much of that differential is truly because of discrimination on the basis of sex and/or race. The extent of discrimination cannot be measured by the difference between the median earnings of the one group and the other, because these medians take no account of differences in marginal productivity.

Investment in human capital

Much of the explanation of differences in labor incomes can be explained by the individual worker's **investment in human capital**. This is a term that has taken on a very broad meaning. In general, it is any activity on the part of a worker or potential worker that raises that worker's present or future marginal productivity. Thus, activities which come under the heading "investment in human capital" include the following:

1. On-the-job training
2. Formal education
3. Informal education

4. Health maintenance and improvement activities
5. Migration

There are other activities which could not be classified with the above. The activity that has received the most attention from economists is formal education.

The private rate of return to formal schooling

Look at Figure 17-8. Here we show two age-earnings profiles. One is for a high school graduate and the other is for a college graduate. Note that the latter's profile is below the former's for a number of years and then eventually rises above it. It turns out that to assess properly the investment in formal schooling, we must discount the higher future earnings that the college graduate typically makes. We also have to subtract the out-of-pocket costs and the foregone earnings incurred while remaining in school rather than going to work. Note that we do not subtract food and lodging

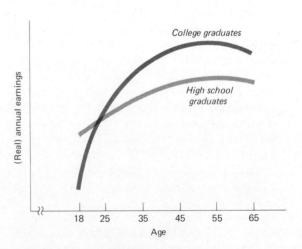

Figure 17-8: Comparing age-earnings profiles of high school and college graduates.
A college graduate's age-earnings profile is below a high school graduate's between the ages of 18 and about 25. Thereafter, however, the college graduate has a higher age-earnings profile that is a reflection of increased productivity.

as a cost of going to college because this cost would be incurred anyway and does not constitute a cost by our definition. As you might expect, it turns out that the largest cost of formal education is foregone earnings.

When all of these calculations are completed, we find that the annual rate of return to a college education is somewhere between 9 and 15 percent. This is a rate of return that is roughly equivalent to what could be earned in the *non*human capital markets. These figures may be biased, however; they don't attempt to assess the nonpecuniary benefits of going to college, and the data are only for those who *complete* college. Those who drop out may have been forced to do so, and some of the rate of return from going to college is a reflection of differential abilities.

Issues and applications

Quasi-rents and unionization

We noted that the earnings of a sunk investment are not costs to an industry. When no factor substitution is possible,[5] unions can raise wages to the point where all the quasi-rent that might go to the owners of the sunk investment is absorbed by labor without reducing employment or raising prices. However, we are dealing with a quasi-rent and in this situation the employment level could not be maintained in the long run. The income earned by the sunk investment is a quasi-rent because additional purchases of capital would be required to maintain (or increase) the capital stock in question. In the long run, that income is a cost because additional capital would be purchased only if investors expect to earn at least the risk-corrected market rate of return. As the capital stock depreciates, employment and output will fall. This has allegedly happened to many newspapers that have blamed unions for their demise.

Industries with large sunk investments and highly durable assets make excellent targets for labor monopolies because it is possible to transfer the quasi-rents of sunk investment to wage income.[6] In industries with little sunk in-

vestment, the short-run demand for labor would tend to be more elastic. Capital investments in those industries could be transferred quickly to other sectors or geographic regions of the economy. Also, the shorter the expected life of the asset, the more rapidly sunk investments can be depreciated if investment is not profitable.

We expect that investors in industries with highly durable fixed assets will recognize even a potential threat of high-wage policies by labor unions. This would decrease the rate of investment; and a higher expected rate of return on new investment in industries with large fixed durable assets is necessary to compensate for the risks associated with labor-union monopoly power, expropriation by taxation, new pollution equipment requirements, or outright confiscation.

We predict that unions would attempt to make greater relative wage gains and to exercise more monopoly power in those industries with a higher percentage of highly specialized, long-lived fixed assets. Thus we would expect exactly the kind of behavior we have seen with the railroad union. In principle, that union could have over time appropriated all the quasi-rent to the investment in track and rolling stock for itself.

Does education make people work harder?

A number of studies have shown that such professionals as physicians, dentists, and lawyers work

---

[5]That is, the elasticity of factor substitution, $\sigma = 0$, or fixed proportions.

[6]It is also true that these industries are highly capital-intensive. Thus labor's share is very small. The effects of union wage policies on prices would, hence, also be relatively small.

longer hours than nonprofessionals. For example, C. M. Lindsay reported that medical doctors worked an average of 62 hours a week.[7] That means that they enjoy less leisure than other individuals.

It turns out that there may be a relationship between the amount of leisure consumed, i.e., the work effort, and the returns to the investment in human capital.

Consider an individual who has not gone to college and who has both labor income and property income. This individual's labor-leisure choice is depicted in Figure 17-9. On the horizontal axis we measure leisure; on the vertical axis we measure income. The maximum amount of leisure attainable per unit time period is given as L_{max}. We assume that the individual has property equal to M_p. The budget constraint facing this individual before going to college is $L_B L_B$. The negative of the slope of that budget line is the wage rate. The optimum position for this individual is found at the tangency of indifference curve I with the budget line, or at point E. The individual consumes L_1 of leisure and enjoys a total income of M_T, of which M_p is income from property.

Now assume that in order to invest in human capital—to pay for going to college—the individual must give up all of his or her property endowment. After obtaining a college education, the wage rate for this individual has increased and his or her budget line after education becomes $L_A L_A$. The new consumption optimum is at point E', assuming that this person's tastes have not changed because of the additional education. The quantity of leisure consumed will fall from L_1 to L_2. This individual will earn a higher income M_T', but will work longer hours. In other words, after investing so much in acquiring more human capital, the individual chooses an optimum with relatively little leisure and relatively high money income.

Perhaps this explains Lindsay's reported fact

[7]C. M. Lindsay, "Real Returns to Medical Education," *Journal of Human Resources*, vol. 8, Summer, 1972.

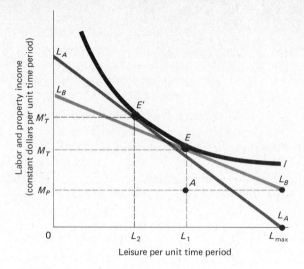

Figure 17-9: Investment in human capital and the labor-leisure choice.

Assume the individual has property income equal to M_p. The budget line facing this person before higher education is $L_B L_B$. The highest indifference curve I is tangent to the budget line at point E. This individual will consume L_1 of leisure, have M_p property income, and have labor income equal to the vertical distance between A and E. His or her total income will equal M_T. This individual liquidates and consumes all property in order to purchase a higher education. The new budget line after higher education is steeper because of increased productivity. It is $L_A L_A$ (which by construction is tangent to I). The new consumption optimum is at point E', assuming no changes in tastes. Total income rises to M_T', but leisure consumed falls from L_1 to L_2.

that medical doctors worked more than "mere" college graduates.

Can unemployment be considered an investment in human capital?

Unemployment is generally believed to be something that is unproductive and therefore not desired by the individual. After all, it usually means not earning income. The unemployment rate receives much media and political attention as an indicator of the hardship experienced by out-of-work working individuals. In reality, however, much of that period of unemployment consists of investment in a search for a better job. In the United States there are constant shifts in the supply of and the demand for workers in particular industries, and all these shifts necessitate changes in either relative wages or employment or both. Permanent shifts in relative demand away from a particular industry's product cause either cuts in wage demands or the movement of workers to other jobs in other industries. Which adjustment occurs depends on how the worker assesses his or her alternative employment opportunities.

Charles Holt described unemployment and the flow of workers into the unemployed category in 1969 in the following way:

> In the United States currently there are about 80 million employed workers, 3 million unemployed workers, and probably a comparable number of vacancies, but data on this are inadequate. Employment durations for all accessions average roughly 2.7 years. Unemployed workers and vacancies wait roughly a month on the average before finding work or employees. The total flow of quits and lay-offs amounts to 30 million per year. Some workers even travel the quit or lay-off loop several times in a year. Turnover rates of the order of 3 or 4 percent a month account for this tremendous flow. The stock of unemployed workers is replaced every month on average. Offsetting this flow from the stock of employed workers is a roughly equal flow of accessions. Employers have to recruit continually in order to hold a constant work force. The probability that an unemployed worker will find a job is roughly 20 percent per week.[8]

These data indicate the part that unemployment plays in the search for a new job. Much of this unemployment includes workers who voluntarily seek better job opportunities. In the process, they move from lower to higher productivity jobs, thereby contributing to economic growth.

---

[8]Charles C. Holt, "Improving the Labor Market Tradeoff between Inflation and Unemployment," *American Economic Review,* May 1969, p. 137.

A model of search unemployment

It is possible to analyze unemployment in terms of a rational choice in order to devote time to the search for a new job. For the purpose of the discussion here, firms are always assumed to have job vacancies.

Once a worker becomes unemployed, the duration of his or her unemployment depends on the costs of and the returns to obtaining *information* on alternative employment possibilities. If a worker is willing to accept a low enough wage, he or she can find a job almost immediately. But the worker usually isn't going to accept just any wage rate—and for very good reasons. The worker may be making a mistake by accepting a job at a wage rate below what he or she could receive by waiting. The worker has to wait because he or she does not have perfect information about the demand for his or her labor services. The worker must search for information about alternative employment opportunities. A worker, of course, does not have to become unemployed in order to search.

Obtaining information has a cost and there are various ways to obtain information. A worker who decides to remain unemployed in order to do this is specializing in this economic endeavor. He or she then becomes self-employed in the task of information collection. The information that is sought is the wages and job environments obtainable.

The more one specializes, the more efficient one can become. Therefore, the unemployed worker is more efficient at obtaining information about alternative job prospects than the employed worker. However, the cost of obtaining that efficiency is wages foregone. Another cost is that an unemployed worker may be perceived to be less desirable by a new employer than an employed worker. In other words, employment itself may be a recommendation and unemployment may give an undesirable signal to prospective employers. For an already employed worker, the decision-making process involves a comparison of the potential marginal benefits from full-time searching with the known costs of foregoing wages.

The reservation wage rate

The worker in this model will set a reservation wage rate below which, when unemployed, the worker will reject all wage offers and remain unemployed. That reservation wage rate is set so as to maximize the expected wealth position of the unemployed worker. We know that the optimal reservation wage rate will be higher the higher unemployment compensation is and the greater are all other such benefits available to the unemployed worker, such as food stamps, medical care, and welfare payments.

The reservation wage rate will usually not be set so as to cause the individual to accept the first job offer. Individuals can always find a job if they are willing to work for a low enough wage rate. What individuals do when they are unemployed is look for job *offers* from which they choose the best one. Unemployment in this model has the nature of investment. Voluntary unemployment represents the deliberate choice of lower current income in exchange for a higher expected future income.

Setting the wrong reservation wage rate

The reservation wage rate set by individuals is based on incomplete information about potential wage offers in the economy. When there are errors in forecasting, the unemployed workers may remain unemployed either too long or too little.

Let us take an example in which the individual worker has full knowledge of the *distribution* of relevant real wage offers but does not know exactly the nominal wage rates corresponding to appropriate real wages. If the worker predicts or estimates correctly, he or she will clearly invest the optimum amount of time in search unemployment. However, if the worker's estimate of the nominal wage rate is too high, he or she will set the reservation wage rate too high and will invest too much time in search unemployment. That is to say, the average duration of unemployment will be too long. On the other hand, when the worker's estimate of the nominal wage rate is too low, he or she will set the reservation wage rate below the optimal level and therefore invest a suboptimum amount of time in search unemployment. That is, the average duration of unemployment will be too short.[9]

Glossary

Marginal productivity theory A theory which relates the demand for an input to its marginal productivity. According to this theory, individuals are paid the value of their marginal product.

Ricardian rent Another name for pure (or economic) rent; a payment to a factor of production over and above what is necessary to keep that factor of production forever in existence in its current employment.   Long term

Quasi-rent A payment over and above what is necessary to keep a factor of production in existence in the short run in its current quality; however, in the long run if the quasi-rent is inadequate, the factor of production will be allowed to depreciate and not be replaced. To be contrasted with a pure, or Ricardian, rent.

Age-earning profile Income related to age; shows how real earnings rise with age, reach a peak around age 45–55, and then fall; in real terms and disregarding changes in national productivity.

Investment in human capital Any activity that raises a worker's present or future marginal

[9]For more complete analyses, see A. A. Alchian, "Information Costs, Pricing, and Resource Unemployment," *Western Economic Journal,* vol. 7, June 1969, pp. 107–128; Donald F. Gordon and John Allan Hynes, "On the Theory of Price Dynamics," Phelps, E. S. et al., *Microeconomic Foundation of Employment and Inflation Theory,* (New York: Norton, 1970) pp. 369–393; and Donald F. Gordon, "A Neoclassical Theory of Keynesian Unemployment," *Economic Inquiry,* vol. 12, no. 4, December 1974, pp. 431–459.

productivity—schooling, on-the-job training, etc.

Summary

1. The marginal productivity theory of factor prices indicates that individuals are paid the value of their marginal product; this is only, however, the demand side. The wage rate is determined not only by the value of marginal product (or marginal revenue product) but also by the supply schedule of labor.
2. A worker gets paid an amount equivalent to the reduction in the firm's revenues if the worker quits. The value of the output that the worker generates, however, is equal to the price of the output times each worker's average physical product, which exceeds the value of marginal product. The difference is available to remunerate other factors of production.
3. *Ceteris paribus*, wages will be higher in occupations that are less preferred. This is called equalizing wage differences.
4. Wages can be expected to differ in proportion to relative marginal physical productivities.
5. The longer the time period for adjustment, the greater the elasticity of supply of any particular type of labor.
6. Apparent economic rents often are not rents at all, but rather the necessary inducement to get individuals to enter an industry in hope of "striking it rich."
7. David Ricardo aggregated all uses of land and, therefore, assumed that land had no alternative use or opportunity cost; hence, all payment to land was considered by Ricardo to be a pure (economic) rent and which is now called a Ricardian rent.
8. Ricardian rent is price determined in the economy.
9. In the long run, if the factor of production is not paid its full opportunity cost, it will not be repaired or replaced.
10. The distribution of money income has not changed dramatically since World War II; if however such in-kind transfers as food stamps are included, the lowest fifth of income earners have improved their relative share by some 60 percent.
11. Income differences result from differences in (a) age, (b) inherited characteristics, (c) risk taking, (d) uncertainty and variance of income, (e) training, (f) inherited wealth, (g) market imperfections, and (h) discrimination.
12. Investment in human capital takes on such forms as: (a) on-the-job training, (b) formal education, (c) informal education, (d) health maintenance and improvement activities, and (e) migration.

Selected references

Carter, Allan M., *Theory of Wages and Employment* (Homewood, Ill.: Irwin, 1959).

Dalton, Hugh, *The Inequality of Income,* 2d ed. (London: Routledge, 1925), part 4, pp. 239–353.

Dunlop, J. T., *The Theory of Wage Determination* (London: Macmillan, 1957).

Marshall, Alfred, *Principles of Economics,* 8th ed. (New York: Macmillan, 1949), book 5, chap. 10.

Pigou, A. C., *The Economics of Welfare,* 4th ed. (London: Macmillan, 1932), part 6, chap. 5.

Ricardo, David, *The Principles of Political Economy and Taxation,* (New York: Dutton, 1962), especially chaps. 1–5.

Thurow, Lester C., *Poverty and Discrimination* (Washington, D. C.: The Brookings Institution, 1969).

Tobin, James, "On Limiting the Domain of Inequality," *The Journal of Law and Economics,* vol. 13, no. 2, October 1970, pp. 263–277.

Questions

(Answers to even-numbered questions are at back of text.)

1. According to the marginal productivity theory of factor pricing, how is a factor's price determined?
2. "If employers paid the VMP to each of their inputs, there would be no profits left over." Is this statement true or false, and why?
3. "Since all workers are not completely mobile, we should not expect to see wage differentials among firms or different regions of the country completely eliminated." Do you agree or disagree, and why?

4. Why do you think that many bank clerks earn less than many blue-collar workers having the same set of abilities? Assume in your answer that neither group is unionized.

5. Other things being equal, what might be the effect on regional wage differentials of rising energy costs?

6. Assuming that the work of a certified public accountant is no more or less pleasant than that of a supermarket checker and that neither group is organized, why would we expect to see the CPA's real wages higher in the long run?

7. What is the definition of economic rent? What is the difficulty in applying the concept to living resources?

8. "All revenue obtained by the Italian government from Renaissance art museums is economic rent." Is this statement true or false, and why?

9. What social function, if any, is served by economic rent?

10. How does a quasi-rent differ from pure economic rent?

11. Why must quasi-rents cover at least depreciation and the opportunity cost of the capital "tied up" in an asset, if the asset is to remain intact?

12. Why might we expect to find less sexual discrimination against employees in factories than in barber shops or restaurants?

13. If a proprietor is a racist and his or her customers are not, why will these preferences lower the earnings of the business?

14. "I know that racial discrimination in hiring is widespread. For that reason, if I ever open a light manufacturing business, I'm going to hire black teenaged women exclusively." What does the speaker have in mind?

15. "It would be inconsistent for a profit-maximizing entrepreneur whose customers and current employees carry no prejudices to discriminate in hiring on any basis other than that of productivity." Comment.

18

GENERAL EQUILIBRIUM ANALYSIS

Except for a few occasions, we have discussed individual markets as though they were completely isolated from the other markets in the economy. That is, we have only taken into account what happens in one particular market when, for example, a relative price changes, a tax is levied, a new law is passed, and so on. However, we are all aware that there are interrelationships among the microeconomic units in our economy. At the very minimum, there are interrelationships between the household sector and the business sector. In Figure 18-1, we portray schematically the interrelationships among the household sector, the credit sector, and the production sector. This is the so-called circular flow of income presented in Chapter 1. We have treated in some detail consumer decision making in Chapters 2 through 5. We briefly looked into the credit market in Chapter 6 and then spent some time analyzing firm decision making in Chapters 7 through 14. Finally, household decision making with respect to supplying factors of production was taken care of in Chapters 15 and 16. What we would like to do in this and the following chapter is put all these sectors together into what is called a **general equilibrium analysis**.

Partial versus general equilibrium analysis

You have been presented almost exclusively with what is called **partial equilibrium analy-**

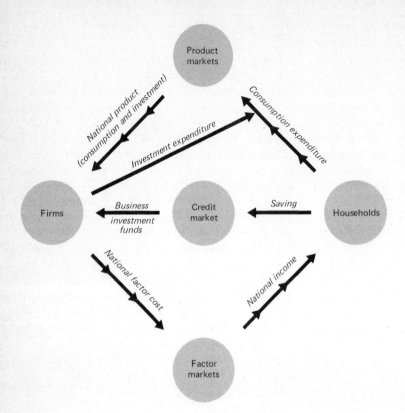

Figure 18-1: The circular flow of income.

Here we show a general equilibrium system which includes saving and investment. In addition to the product and factor markets, we therefore show a credit market. A more complete general equilibrium system would include the government sector and the foreign sector. Note that only the money flows have been depicted; the "real" flows have been omitted for clarity.

sis. Partial equilibrium analysis can best be characterized by the Latin expression *ceteris paribus*, meaning "other things being equal." In such an analysis, it is assumed that just about everything else is held constant. Not *all* other things are constant, because then there would be no change possible. In essence, partial equilibrium analysis allows us to focus on a single market and view it in isolation. For analytical purposes, the market is viewed as independent and self-contained; that is, it is independent of all other markets. We know, however, that markets interact. When we attempt to take account of these interactions among markets, we enter the realm of general equilibrium analysis.

General equilibrium analysis takes account of the interrelationships among prices and quantities of various goods and services. Just

as partial equilibrium analysis does not require that *all* other things be held constant, general equilibrium analysis does not allow *all* other things to vary. Something must be exogenous (outside the system) or "given" for us to start the analysis. General equilibrium analysis has been used to answer the question that has puzzled economists for some time: In a system of perfectly competitive markets, is there a set of prices that would allow all markets to be in equilibrium at the same time? Modern work by mathematical economists has resulted in an affirmative answer to this question. There does exist a set of relative prices that allows all markets to clear simultaneously if all markets are perfectly competitive. In this chapter, however, we will not analyze this question. Rather, we will present the rudiments of general equilibrium analysis in geometric form. By graphical necessity we are limited to two dimensions; we are therefore going to deal with a world in which there are two commodities and two factors of production. In order to generalize any further, we would have to employ a system of simultaneous equations. However, the following analysis does give the flavor of a larger model.

A note of warning: The distinction between general and partial equilibrium analysis is, in reality, only one of degree. After all, there is a limit to how many markets can be taken into account in any analysis. That limit is reached either by the cerebral limits of the economist doing the analysis or by the capacity of the computer that he or she is utilizing. True general equilibrium analysis would require the setting up of an almost infinite set of simultaneous equations, and this is a task no one has yet undertaken. When economists talk of general equilibrium analysis when dealing with practical problems, they are referring to taking account of several markets and the relationships between them. If the goal of the economist is to predict what will happen when the economic environment changes, his or her choice of partial or general equilibrium analysis depends on (1) the question being asked and (2) the degree to which the answer will change if more than one market is considered. Basically, it is a matter of what things can be "held" constant without destroying the experiment.

We have already introduced the theory of exchange between two consumers in Chapter 4 (pages 80–83). In that section we constructed an Edgeworth-Bowley box to illustrate the interaction between two individuals with given initial endowments of two commodities. We will recreate Figure 4-4 here as Figure 18-2. Since the derivation of the Edgeworth-Bowley box was explained in detail in Chapter 4, we do not spend time on it here. However, you should probably go back to Chapter 4 and reread the section on equilibrium in exchange.

The consumption problem

We have what is called a consumption problem. There are two consumption goods, x and y. These goods are available in fixed amounts. We have two consumers (or two households) that will together consume all of x and all of y together. We start off with each consumer in possession of a certain amount of x and a certain amount of y. The amount of x possessed by consumer 1 is represented by the distance from 0_1 to x_1 in Figure 18-2. Notice that consumer 1's endowments are measured from the southwest corner of the diagram. By assumption, consumer 2 has an initial endowment of x represented by the distance 0_2 to x_2, which is equal to the amount of x not consumed by consumer 1. This is seen as measured from the northeast corner of the diagram.

Similarly, the initial endowment of consumption good y for consumer 1 is represented by the distance from 0_1 to y_1. Consumer 2 has initial endowment of good y equal to $0_2 y_2$.

Consumer 1's preferences are given by indifference curves I_1, II_1, and III_1, consumer 2's preferences by I_2, II_2, and III_2.

Initial utility levels

Given the initial endowment, consumer 1 is situated on indifference curve II_1. Consumer 2 finds that indifference curve I_2 is being attained.

There is clearly a basis for exchange in this situation. The marginal rate of substitution of x for y for consumer 1 differs from the marginal rate of substitution of x for y for consumer 2. The two MRSs are given by the two tangents to the two respective indifference curves at the initial endowment point E. Those tangents are labeled $T_1 T_1$ and $T_2 T_2$. In other words, consumer 1 values x differently, on the margin, than does consumer 2.

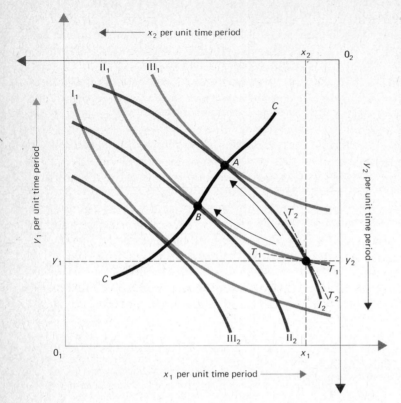

x_2 per unit time period

y_1 per unit time period

x_1 per unit time period

y_2 per unit time period

Figure 18-2: Equilibrium in exchange. Initial endowments are 0_1x_1, 0_1y_1, 0_2x_2, and 0_2y_2. At the initial endowment, however, the marginal rates of substitution given by the slopes of the tangents to indifference curves II_2 and I_1, T_1T_1 and T_2T_2, respectively, are not equal. Through exchange the consumers will move somewhere between points A and B. That is, they will move to a point on the contract curve CC where their marginal rates of substitution are equal.

Equilibrium exchange

As long as these two individuals are free to trade, they will do so. Trade could either move the individuals to point A or point B or to any point on the contract curve between A and B. If trade moved them to point A, individual 1 would move to a higher indifference curve and individual 2 would remain on the same one. If they moved to point B, individual 2 is the one who moved to a higher indifference curve and individual 1 would remain at the same level of satisfaction. Between A and B they are *both* on higher indifference curves. Where they move depends on their relative bargaining abilities. We know, however, that they will move to somewhere between points A and B before they cease

exchanging. The points between A and B are all points at which the marginal rates of substitution are equal for both individuals, or $MRS^1_{xy} = MRS^2_{xy}$. When we connect all such points by the line CC, we have a contract (or conflict) curve. It is the locus of points where the two individuals' sets of indifference curves just touch each other. General equilibrium of exchange will always occur on the contract curve, for that is where the marginal rate of substitution for all parties consuming both goods is equal. Note that the general equilibrium is not unique; it can occur at any point along the contract curve.[1]

Now that we have looked at general equilib-

---

[1]When we are dealing with more than two individuals, this would be called a contract hypersurface.

rium in exchange, let us go to the general equilibrium in production.

Production general equilibrium

We assume that consumer goods x and y are produced by inputs, capital (K) and labor (L). For the purpose of this discussion, the total quantities of capital and labor available are both fixed; and we also assume that they are always fully employed.

Initial employment

In Figure 18-3, we show the initial employments of the inputs, capital and labor, in the production of goods x and y. Good x's use of capital and labor is measured from the origin labeled 0_x (southwest corner of the diagram). Good y's use of capital and labor is measured from the origin 0_y (northeast corner). By assumption, the use of capital in industry x and in industry y must equal the total amount of capital available; the same is true for labor. Thus, given an initial use of capital and labor represented by point E' in Figure 18-3, we know that industry x uses k_x, industry y uses k_y, and $k_x + k_y = K$. With respect to labor, at point E' industry uses l_x of labor, industry y uses l_y and $l_x + l_y = L$.

This is an Edgeworth-Bowley box diagram, but we are now using it to depict production.

Adding the production function

We assume that the production functions for both x and y are given and do not change.

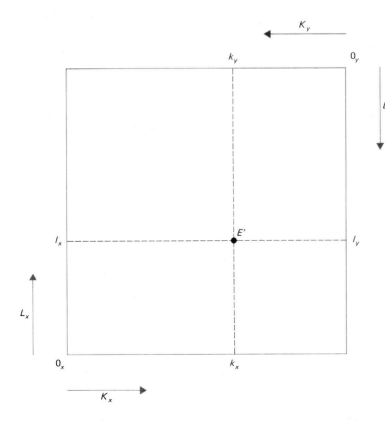

Figure 18-3: A production Edgeworth-Bowley box.

This diagram is similar to the ones we have used, but we are now looking at an input space rather than a commodity space. If the two industries produce x and y, and initially employ capital and labor at E', then the x industry will employ $0_x k_x$ of capital plus $0_x l_x$ of labor. The y industry will employ $0_y k_y$ and $0_y l_y$.

From these production functions, we construct normally shaped isoquants, represented in Figure 18-4 as Q_I^x through Q_{IV}^x for x, and Q_I^y through Q_{IV}^y for y. The initial allocation of inputs between the production of x and y is given by point E'. The highest isoquant on which point E' lies is Q_{II}^x for industry x and Q_{II}^y for industry y. The marginal rates of technical substitution in the two industries at point E' are the respective slopes of the tangents to the two isoquants intersecting at that point. In other words, the marginal rate of technical substitution in industry x equals the slope of ZZ measured with respect to the origin 0_x, and the marginal rate of technical substitution in industry y is equal to the slope of $Z'Z'$ measured with respect to the origin 0_y. These slopes differ and the marginal rates of technical substitution differ in the two industries. Recall that $MRTS_{KL} = MPP_L/MPP_K$. The dia-

gram shows that $MRTS_{KL}^x > MRTS_{KL}^y$. Thus, in industry x, the marginal product of capital is low relative to the marginal product of labor. Production rate Q_{II}^x could be maintained by substituting a relatively small amount of labor for a relatively larger amount of capital. In other words, the marginal rate of technical substitution of capital for labor in producing x is relatively high. The opposite is true in industry y. There the marginal rate of technical substitution of capital for labor in producing y is relatively low.

Consider the possibility of the producer of x substituting one more unit of labor in exchange for several units less of capital. At the same time, the producer of y could take the several units of capital released from x's production and maintain output by substituting them for several units of labor. In other words, operating at point E', there could be

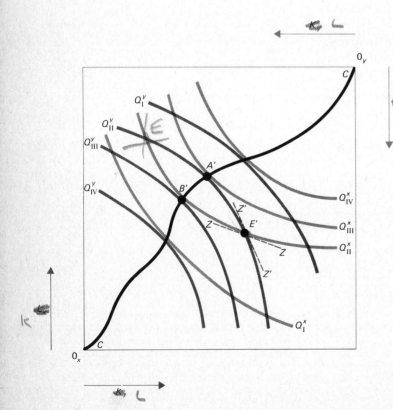

Figure 18-4: Equilibrium in production.

If the initial input allocations are such that the x industry and the y industry find themselves at point E', then the marginal rates of technical substitution as given by the slopes of the tangents ZZ and $Z'Z'$ will not be equal. The interindustry resource allocation will change so that the industries move to some point on the production contract curve CC, between and including points A' and B'.

input substitution by producers which would enable them to move either to point A' or to point B'. In either of these two cases, the output of one good would remain constant and the output of the other would increase. At point A' or point B' the marginal rate of technical substitution of capital for labor is the same in industry x and industry y. The locus of points like A' and B' is represented by the heavily shaded line CC. This is also called the contract (or conflict) curve. It shows all input combinations that equalize the marginal rates of technical substitution. Along CC, $MRTS^x_{K;L} = MRTS^y_{K;L}$.

General equilibrium of production

General equilibrium of production will occur whenever the marginal rate of technical substitution between each pair of inputs is the same for all producers who make use of those inputs. Just as the exchange equilibrium was not unique, this production equilibrium is not unique. It can occur anywhere along the contract or conflict curve.[2]

Note that the analysis of production equilibrium is analogous to exchange equilibrium analysis.

The production possibility frontier

Isoquants are drawn in an input space. The general equilibrium of production yielded a contract curve that represents the locus of points in an input space where the marginal rates of technical substitution are the same for the production of two goods. What we do now is translate the production exchange represented by the contract curve CC to an output space which will show us the **production possibility frontier**. The production possibility frontier is

also called a **transformation curve**. The production possibility frontier, or transformation curve, is defined as a curve showing the maximum attainable output combinations of two commodities when the initial endowments of the resources used in producing those commodities are given.

Mapping the contract curve

The way we obtain a transformation curve is to transfer the contract curve from the factor input space into a commodity output space. We look at the maximum combinations of x and y that can be obtainable from a given set of capital and labor inputs. When we transfer these combinations from Figure 18-4, we arrive at Figure 18-5.

Two points, A' and B', are taken from Figure

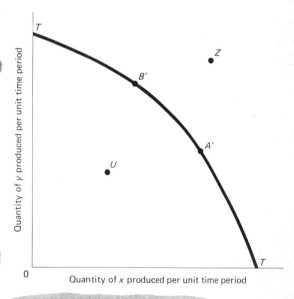

Figure 18-5: The transformation curve.
Transformation curve TT shows the maximum combinations of good x and good y that can be produced per unit time period with given resources and technology. Points A' and B' are taken from Figure 18-4. Point U represents underemployment of resources and is ruled out by assumption. Z is unattainable.

---

[2]Again, when more than two goods are involved, this would be called a contract hypersurface.

18-4. A' represents more production of x than B'. In other words, so long as resources remain fully employed, in order to obtain more of y, we must give up some x. The **marginal rate of transformation (MRT)** is the slope on the transformation curve TT.

Notice the concave-to-the-origin nature of the transformation curve. It is concave because the opportunity cost of shifting production from one good to another is increasing. If TT were a straight line, then the marginal rate of transformation would be constant. Were that the case, it would not matter if society were already using all its resources producing x or very few producing x. To produce one more unit of y would require the same sacrifice in each case.

Underemployment

We rule out point U in Figure 18-5 because it is inside the transformation curve. Points inside the transformation curve indicate that society's resources are not being fully utilized. We are assuming full employment in this analysis, however.

A point such as point Z is outside the transformation curve. It is outside the production possibility frontier, and hence it is physically unattainable at present. The maximum rate of production is represented by points such as A' and B'. There is no way at this time for this economy to attain point Z. Only if its endowments of factors of production were increased, or technological change enabled them to be more effectively combined, could Z be attained.

General equilibrium for both production and exchange

We now put together the two previous sections. We deal with a world of two consumers, two commodities, and two factors of production. The input base is given by the initial available quantities of capital and labor shown in Figures 18-3 and 18-4. The utility functions of the consumers are given in Figure 18-2. They are represented by each of their indifference maps. The question now is, What will be the final equilibrium? How much will each consumer consume of each good? How much of each good will be produced?

Maximizing consumer satisfaction

Before we can come up with the final equilibrium of production and exchange, we have to find out how consumer satisfaction can be maximized. It turns out that it is not maximized unless the marginal rate of transformation (MRT) in production (the slope of the transformation curve TT in Figure 18-5) is equal to the marginal rate of substitution in consumption between the two commodities. To begin with, we know that for maximum satisfaction to be obtained, the two consumers must have equal marginal rates of substitution. We know that for maximum production, the marginal rates of technical substitution between the inputs used to produce the commodities must be equal. To demonstrate that maximum consumer satisfaction requires that MRS = MRT, we take an example. Assume now that MRS and MRT are *not* equal. Consider the case:

$$\text{MRS}_{xy} = 1:1$$
$$\text{MRT}_{xy} = 1:2 \qquad (18-1)$$

Now assume that industry x wishes to reduce production by one unit, and also assume that individual 1 wishes to reduce the consumption of x by one unit. For individual 1 to maintain the same level of satisfaction, an additional unit of y must be consumed in order to offset the loss of one unit of x. Assume, then, that the production sector gives consumer 1 this extra unit of y. How does it do this? By reducing the production of x. But notice that the production sector can give up one unit of x, shift resources to the production of y, and produce *two* more units of y. Therefore, the production sector could satisfy consumer 1 by producing one less of x and giving consumer 1 one more of y, but there would also be one unit of y "left over". This one unit of y could be given to consumer 2. Consumer 2 could be made better off without making consumer 1 worse off. Consumer satisfaction is not maximized if the marginal rate of substitution between x and y is not exactly equal to the marginal rate of transformation between x and y.

You should be able to work through an example opposite to the one given above and reach the same conclusion.

Now we are ready to put together production and exchange.

Production and exchange on one diagram

We transfer the transformation curve TT from Figure 18-5 to Figure 18-6 and start off at point R with that combination of good x and good y being produced. We then transfer the Edgeworth-Bowley box diagram from Figure 18-2 to Figure 18-6. The initial productions are $0x_0$ and $0y_0$. The question is, What will be the optimal distribution of x and y between consumers 1 and 2? We know that we will be somewhere on the contract curve CC. But where on CC is the question? We can find out where by realizing that for maximum con-

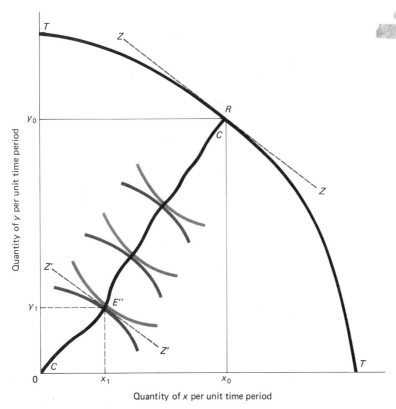

Figure 18-6: Equilibrium in production and exchange.

Assume that we have an Edgeworth-Bowley box of the size $0y_0$ and $0x_0$. Equilibrium will occur when both persons' marginal rates of substitution are equal to the marginal rate of transformation. This will happen when the tangent drawn to the point of equilibrium in exchange E'' is parallel to the tangent drawn to point R on the transformation curve TT. To have a simultaneous equilibrium in both exchange and production, ZZ and $Z'Z'$ must be parallel.

Quantity of y per unit time period

Quantity of x per unit time period

sumer satisfaction the marginal rate of product transformation between x and y must be equal to the marginal rate of substitution in consumption between x and y. We therefore draw a tangent to point R on the product transformation curve. The slope of the tangent ZZ is the MRT_{xy} at point R. Now we go into the Edgeworth diagram and find a point along the contract curve where the tangency line drawn between the two tangent indifference curves has exactly the same slope as ZZ. This occurs at point E''. The slope of $Z'Z'$ is equal to the slope of ZZ. At point E'', then, $\mathrm{MRS}_{xy} = \mathrm{MRT}_{xy}$. In final equilibrium, given that we started out at point R on TT, consumer 1 will consume $0y_1$ of y and consumer 2 will consume the rest, or the vertical distance between y_1 and y_0. Consumer 1 will consume $0x_1$ of x and consumer 2 will consume the rest.

In terms of determining the amounts of capital and labor that are allocated to the production of each commodity, we return to the Edgeworth-Bowley box diagram in Figure 18-4, which underlies the transformation curve in Figure 18-5 and Figure 18-6.

We have answered several questions: Given the amount of each good that is produced, we have shown how the output will be distributed between consumers. We also have shown how the available inputs would be distributed between industries when we assume maximum production and maximum consumer satisfaction. In the following chapter, we will relax the assumption that the amount of each commodity produced is given. What we will do is study welfare economics. Note that the conditions given by point E'', ZZ being parallel to $Z'Z'$, do not represent a unique solution. We still do not know how real income is distributed between individual 1 and individual 2, because $Z'Z'$ can be parallel to ZZ at any number of points on the contract curve. Basically, then, we have shown that at equilibrium $\mathrm{MRS}_{xy} = \mathrm{MRT}_{xy}$. We say nothing about what the distribution of income will actually be.

Issues and applications

A case study in economic interdependence—Input-output analysis

In the nineteenth century, a French economist named Leon Walras[3] was apparently the first to construct a general equilibrium model of an economy. In subsequent years that model was modified, but the formulation remains much the same as it was more than 100 years ago. Improvements have been made and the model has been extended. One of the major applications of general equilibrium analysis was first developed by Harvard's Nobel laureate Wassily Leontief.[4]

Input-output analysis is an empirical study of the interdependence among the various sectors in an economy. We know that the sectors are interdependent rather than independent, because production in one sector utilizes inputs which other sectors produce. The manufacture of a bicycle requires the inputs from such industries as fabricated metal, machinery, rubber products, chemical products, and the like. A change in the output of the bicycle industry therefore will require a change in the output of related industries. These changes may in turn require other changes in the outputs of still other industries.

Statisticians and economists have applied input-output analysis to a variety of problems. If one has a final output target, for example, input-output analysis can help determine the production of the various sectors of the economy required to obtain that one final output. The anal-

---

[3]Leon Walras, *Elements of Pure Economics* (translated by William Jaffé) (Homewood, Ill.: Irwin, 1954). The original French version was published in 1874.
[4]Wassily Leontief, *The Structure of the American Economy* (New York: Oxford, 1951).

	Sector purchasing				
Sector producing	Service	Manufacturing	Agriculture	Household sector	Total sales
Service	104.8	478.7	100.1	350	1,033.6
Manufacturing	500.9	704.8	310.7	400	1,916.4
Agriculture	120.0	190.3	94.1	200	604.4
Household sector	307.9	542.6	99.5	—	950.0
Total production	1,033.6	1,916.4	604.4	950	4,504.4

Table 18-1: The annual plan of input and output (in billions of dollars).

ysis has also been used to predict what employment, demand, and investment in a region or a country will be in the future. Economists have used it extensively in planning economic development. Indeed, its uses have been many in the last $2^1/_2$ decades.

Assumptions

In order to employ general equilibrium analysis, input-output analysis must make a number of simplifying assumptions. The first assumption is that the variables are the *total* quantities of particular goods demanded or supplied. Looking at totals reduces the number of variables and equations that must be included in the analysis.

A second assumption is that consumer demand is given. In other words, there is no need for demand theory in input-output analysis,[5] because input-output analysis generally ignores price as a factor determining the quantity demanded.

The third assumption is that inputs are used in fixed proportions and that there are constant returns to scale. This last assumption is crucial to Leontief's input-output system. This is known as the **linearity assumption.** From it we know that a given change in the output of a sector will require a proportionate change in all inputs used by that sector.

---

[5]Strictly speaking, this statement is only true in Leontief's open model which we use as our example here. In what he calls a closed model, the determinants of demand must be looked at. See Wassily Leontief, *Input-Output Economics* (New York: Oxford, 1966).

A SIMPLE INPUT-OUTPUT MODEL. We consider a hypothetical economy composed of manufacturing, service, and agricultural sectors plus the household sector. The annual flow of input and output in billions of dollars among these sectors is presented in Table 18-1.

The columns show which sector is a purchaser of output from other sectors or from itself. For example, if we read down the service column, we find that the service sector purchased $104.8 billion of output from its own sector, $500.9 billion from the manufacturing sector, $120 billion from the agricultural sector, and $307.9 billion from the household sector (capital and labor). Reading across the service sector row, we find that the sector produced $1,033.6 billion of total output. Note that the next to the last column represents purchases by the household sector.

The rows show what each sector does as a supplier or producer. For example, the first row shows that the service industry provided $104.8 billion of output to itself, $478.7 of output to the manufacturing sector, and $350 of output to the household sector.

The total sales column, which is the last one in Table 18-1, gives us the sum of the purchases by the three intermediate sectors, as well as the purchases by the household sector. As can be seen in input-output analysis, all outputs are imputed to some inputs. The difference between total sales and total intermediate purchases represents each of the first three sectors' payments to households for their capital and labor services. For example, the difference between the service sector's total output of $1,033.6 billion and total intermediate purchases of $725.7 billion is $307.9 billion, which represents payments to the household sector.

Technical coefficients

We now show Table 18-2, which is called a structural matrix. It is a listing of the **technical coefficients** which are derived from the data in Table 18-1. These are sometimes called **production coefficients** or **input coefficients**. In order to understand how we derive the coefficients in Table 18-2, look at the service column in Table 18-1. Total production for the service sector is $1,033.6 billion. To obtain the technical coefficients for the service sector, we divide all the entries in that column by the value of total gross service output, or

$$\frac{104.8}{1033.6} = .1014$$

$$\frac{500.9}{1033.6} = .4846$$

$$\frac{120.0}{1033.6} = .1161$$

$$\frac{307.9}{1033.6} = .2979$$

Each column entry in Table 18-2 lends itself to an economic interpretation. The technical coefficients give us the dollar value of input used in producing a dollar's value of output from each sector. For example, in the service sector column, we can state that in order to produce a dollar's worth of service output, 10.14¢ of service inputs, 48.46¢ of manufacturing inputs, 11.61¢ of agricultural inputs, and 29.79¢ of capital and labor inputs must be used.

We can also see by viewing the structural matrix, Table 18-2, which sectors are relatively more important in the production of any particular output. We can also determine the total amount of output required from each sector to accommodate a particular final demand "requirement." We would do this by solving a system of simultaneous equations.

Empirical estimates of the input-output structure

The U.S. Department of Commerce has available estimates of technical coefficients for the United States economy for the years 1947, 1958, and 1963. The November 1969 issue of the *Survey of Current Business* presents estimates for almost 370 separate industries. The interested student can look at pages 16–47 in that periodical for the results of the aggregated 1963 study in which the 370 separate categories have been reduced to 86. It can be readily seen by viewing the table that the task involved in constructing a large-scale input-output table is not simple.

CRITICISMS OF INPUT-OUTPUT ANALYSIS. One of the major criticisms of input-output analysis, particularly when it is used in order to predict "requirements" far into the future, is that the

	Sector purchasing			
Sector producing	Service	Manufacturing	Agriculture	Household
Service	.1014	.2498	.1656	.3684
Manufacturing	.4846	.3678	.5141	.4211
Agriculture	.1161	.0993	.1557	.2105
Household	.2979	.2831	.1646	
Total	1.0000	1.0000	1.0000	1.0000

Table 18-2: The structural matrix.

technical or production coefficients are constant. In the future, technology may change and reduce the technical coefficients if fewer of certain inputs are required. Moreover, changes in relative prices in inputs will result in changes in production processes and, hence, in technical or production coefficients. Cheaper inputs will be substituted for more expensive ones.

In spite of these telling criticisms, input-output analysis continues to be used as a predictive device to guide policy making. For example, the Department of Commerce used an input-output estimate done by Anne Carter of Brandeis University and Clopper Almon of the University of Maryland in order to estimate the effect of increases in oil prices on industrial and consumer prices. The input-output analysis done by the investigators was used in order to estimate the effect of the Arab oil embargo of 1973–74 on the level of employment in certain industries.

Glossary

General equilibrium analysis Economic analysis which takes account of the interrelationships between markets; to be contrasted with partial equilibrium analysis.

Partial equilibrium analysis A way of analyzing a market in isolation and without taking account of the interrelationships among markets.

Production possibility frontier The locus of points showing the maximum technologically feasible rates of output of x and y with a given endowment of inputs.

Transformation curve Another name for a production possibility frontier. A curve showing the maximum attainable output from given initial endowments of inputs. Otherwise stated, the transformation curve shows the rate of transformation of good x into good y when there is full employment of the initial endowment of inputs.

Marginal rate of transformation (MRT) The slope on the transformation curve (production possibility curve). MRT gives the rate at which one good can be transformed into another.

Input-output analysis The empirical study of the interdependence among the various sectors in the economy; generally involves assuming fixed proportions in production.

Linearity assumption An assumption used in input-output analysis in which inputs are used in fixed proportions; if output is to increase by 100 percent, all inputs must be increased by 100 percent.

Technical coefficients Coefficients in input-output analysis which indicate the dollar value of inputs used in producing a dollar's value of output from a particular industry or sector. Also called production or input coefficients.

Summary

1. Partial equilibrium analysis uses the *ceteris paribus* assumption. However, it is not true that *all* other things are held constant, because if they were, then no change would be possible.
2. General equilibrium analysis takes into account interrelationships among markets. Not all other things, however, are allowed to vary; something must be given or exogenous for us to start such an analysis.
3. The choice of how many interrelationships should be taken into account depends on the question being asked and the degree to which things can be assumed constant without invalidating the analysis.
4. Equilibrium in exchange requires that marginal rates of substitution between the same goods be equal for all individuals.
5. Equilibrium in production requires that the marginal rate of transformation between each pair of inputs be the same for all users of those inputs.
6. General equilibrium in both production and exchange requires that the common marginal rate of substitution for all consumers be equal to the common marginal rate of transformation for all producers. In a two-good, two-person, two-factor model, this would occur when the tangent drawn to the exchange equilibrium point on the contract curve has the same slope, i.e., is parallel to, the tangent drawn to the output combination point on the transformation curve.

Selected references

Barrett, Nancy Smith, *The Theory of Microeconomic Policy*, (Lexington, Mass.: Heath, 1974).

Baumol, William J., *Economic Theory and Operations Analysis*, 3d ed. (Englewood Cliffs, N.J.: Prentice-Hall, 1972), chaps. 15 and 20

Knight, Frank H., "A Suggestion for Simplifying the Statement of the General Theory of Price," *Journal of Political Economy*, vol. 36, June 1928, pp. 353–370.

Miernyk, W. H., *The Elements of Input-Output Analysis* (New York: Random House, 1965).

Walras, Leon, *Elements of Pure Economics*, translated by William Jaffé (Homewood, Ill.: Irwin, 1954).

Zeuthen, F., *Economic Theory and Method* (Cambridge, Mass.: Harvard, 1955), chap. 11.

Questions

(Answers to even-numbered questions are at back of text.)

1. How does general equilibrium analysis differ from partial equilibrium analysis?

2. On the one hand, general equilibrium is said to encompass all (*n*) markets; on the other hand, the analysis is typically presented for a world of two persons, two factors, and two goods. How can this be?

3. When would general equilibrium analysis be more appropriate than partial equilibrium analysis?

4. In a two-person, two-good world, what condition must exist for there to be a general equilibrium in exchange?

5. What is the "contract curve" and how is it related to general equilibrium in exchange?

6. "Given an initial distribution of the two goods, we can only say that exchanges will eventually redistribute the goods until some point on the contract curve is reached." Is the statement true or false, and why?

7. Suppose we did not know the initial distribution of the two goods between the two people. Can we say anything about those final distributions which will satisfy the conditions of general equilibrium in exchange?

8. Assume that the distribution of goods has reached a point on the contract curve. Now one or both of the persons' preferences change, for whatever reason. What must then occur?

9. In considering general equilibrium in production, are the initial endowments of productive resources stock or flows? Explain.

10. Figure 18-3's rectangular dimensions represent the endowments of the two productive resources. What, then, is represented by *E*'?

11. Could idleness of some labor or capital be shown on a diagram such as Figure 18-5? Explain.

12. What condition must be satisfied if there is to be a general equilibrium of production?

13. Point *E*' in Figure 18-4 is clearly inefficient because the MRTs for goods *x* and *y* are unequal. What are the maximum gains to be realized from resource reallocation: (*a*) measured in terms of additional output of good *x*? (*b*) measured in terms of additional output of good *y*?

14. Why must MRS and MRT be equal for all consumers and production processes to achieve a general equilibrium in both consumption and production?

15. "The integration of general equilibrium in exchange with general equilibrium in production yields a unique distribution (satisfying the criterion of MRS equal to MRT) for any given output combination." Is the statement true or false, and why?

19

WELFARE ECONOMICS

When the word "welfare" is mentioned, people generally think of programs to aid individuals with low incomes; also, some notion of well-being is implied. In economics, however, the term "welfare" has a specific meaning. Welfare refers simply to the level of utility, and **welfare economics** is that part of the study of economics that explains how to identify and arrive at what are called socially efficient allocations of resources. The study of welfare economics concerns itself only with that subset of options open to society that contains possible "best" solutions for resource allocation. The logical next step, then, is to choose the "best" or "optimum" among the alternatives in this reduced set. Of course, the term "best" is subjective. It is, therefore, not within the province of scientific analysis to call one type of resource allocation "better" than another. Even the term "optimal" is value-laden, and hence we must be careful when talking about the optimal allocation of resources not to infer that we are talking about the "best" or preferred allocation of resources. Whenever the term "optimal" is used in this and the following chapter, it does not carry with it this connotation; rather, it refers to maximizing the economic value of a given set of resources.

Assumptions used in welfare analysis

In order to make welfare analysis operative and value-free, some assumptions must be made at the onset. These assumptions are closely related to those used as the foundation for the theory of consumer behavior. Basically, there are three:[1]

1. The individual is the best judge of his or her own welfare.
2. If the individual prefers a to b, his or her welfare is greater with situation a than with situation b—the individual is "better off" with situation a than with situation b.
3. The individual acts in accordance with his or her own preferences.

In a sense, for welfare analysis to be meaningful, we must accept these assumptions which, in themselves, could be considered as value judgments. Few economists will accept these value judgments without attaching a few of their own qualifications. For example, assumption 1 is generally not considered to be applicable to young children. Moreover, the state acts "in the best interests of the public" by preventing individuals from purchasing and consuming drugs for which future consequences are not known.

Interpersonal utility comparisons

When we attempt to measure or establish levels of social welfare for groups of individuals, we immediately run into problems. If individual I is better-off with situation a than with b, but individual II is better-off with situation b rather than situation a, how do we measure the social welfare of individuals I and II? In order to do so requires interpersonal welfare comparisons, but there is no scientifically meaningful way to compare the utility levels of various individuals. Rather, all we are able to do is talk of either marginal utility rankings by individuals (but not between indi-

viduals) or rankings of marginal personal evaluations of an individual.

If we cannot compare utility levels interpersonally, then we cannot say very much about one distribution of income as compared with another. If, for some reason, I receive 10 times more income than you, there is no way to say that this is a worse distribution of income than if you receive 10 times more than I.

Faced with this problem, economists have approached welfare analysis in several different ways. Some have considered pricing and allocation policies without taking into account any resultant income distribution effects. A subsidy or a tax affects different income groups differently. Others have assumed that the existing distribution of income is in some sense "optimal." Still others have made the implicit or explicit assumption that any movement toward a more nearly equal distribution of income is, *ceteris paribus*, a "preferred" movement. A final and value-free approach has simply been to show the consequences of various changes, including how they affect both the size of the pie—total income—and the distribution of income. This approach has been considered primarily by those economists interested in the incentive changes resulting from various policy prescriptions. (We talked about this when we considered the work disincentive effect of high marginal tax rates in Chapter 3.)

Efficiency and the Pareto condition

Since economists are uncomfortable with interpersonal utility comparisons, in modern welfare analysis they go as far as they can without making such interpersonal comparisons. This is done by focusing on the notion of economic efficiency. You remember that we made the distinction between technical efficiency and economic efficiency. The former referred to the comparison of physical output

---

[1] All basically are variations on the axiom of consumer sovereignty, or competence.

to physical input; the latter, on the other hand, related the value of product output to input resource value. The measurement of economic efficiency then requires that values be placed on commodities. In welfare analysis, the values placed on commodities are those that the market presents to us.

The Pareto condition

The Italian economist Vilfredo Pareto specified for us a condition of optimal or efficient resource allocation, referred to as the **Pareto condition**. He applied it to a market situation. When the condition is satisfied, it is impossible for one individual to gain without another incurring a loss. Thus, when the Pareto condition is satisfied, it is impossible for all individuals to gain by further exchange. When the Pareto condition is not satisfied, it is possible (in principle) for at least one individual to gain without causing loss to any other; consequently all individuals can gain by further exchange.

We will see that any economic organization that leads to all individuals in a society being at a point on the contract curve is a Pareto-optimal organization. The term "Pareto optimality" is more in use than the term "Pareto criterion" or Pareto condition"; they all mean the same thing.

When we make welfare statements based on the Pareto condition, we cannot state that a change which leads to the Pareto condition makes society "better-off." Rather, it improves social welfare judged by the Pareto condition, but not necessarily by any other. It turns out that the Pareto condition is the common core of social welfare functions, but it is indeed a weak core. It tells us only that a change that makes at least one individual better-off and no one worse off is an "improvement" in social welfare. Conversely, a change that makes no one better-off and someone worse off results in a reduction in social welfare. Nothing can be said about a change that makes some better-off and others worse off; that would require comparing the increased satisfaction of the gainers with the lost satisfaction of the losers. Because most policy changes are of the latter kind, the Pareto condition or criterion is a weak one. We assume that policy changes which make everyone worse off will soon be altered.

Pareto versus efficiency criteria

It turns out that while the Pareto condition can be applied only to an economy with at least two individuals, the notion of economic efficiency can be applied to a one-person economy where there are no property rights and no interaction problems. For most problems, though, the fulfillment of the Pareto condition or the Pareto criterion coincides with maximum economic efficiency. In other words, for most purposes they are the same thing. Thus, failure to attain the Pareto criterion generally implies economic inefficiency.

Marginal conditions for optimal allocation of resources for social welfare

We already have the tools for understanding the marginal conditions for social welfare or Pareto optimality or optimal resource allocation. All you need remember is the definition of either equilibrium in exchange or equilibrium in production. Equilibrium in the preceding chapter occurred somewhere on the contract curve. On the contract curve, it was impossible to make one trading partner better-off without harming the other. However, off the contract curve, it was possible to either make one person better-off without harming the other, or make both of them better-off simultaneously. We know then that at any point on the contract curve, the Pareto condition is satisfied. This gives us the first marginal condition for social welfare.

Exchange

The marginal condition for the efficient allocation of goods is simply stated as follows: The Pareto condition requires that the marginal rate of substitution between any two consumer goods must be the same for all individuals who consume both goods, or $MRS_{xy}^1 = MRS_{xy}^2 = \cdots = MRS_{xy}^n$. The marginal condition for exchange must be satisfied or at least one individual would benefit from further exchange.[2]

A second and similar marginal condition relates to the use of factors of production.

Factor usage

The attainment of the Pareto criterion requires that the marginal rate of technical substitution between any pair of factors must be the same for all producers who use both factors, or $MRTS_{KL}^x = MRTS_{KL}^y$. If this condition did not hold, a reallocation of at least one input factor from one producer to another would increase total production without requiring the use of any additional input factors.

The final condition required for Pareto optimality involves the product market.

The product market

The Pareto condition is only satisfied when the marginal rate of transformation in production equals the marginal rate of substitution in consumption for every pair of commodities and for every individual, or $MRT_{xy} = MRS_{xy}$ for all individuals.

This can be most easily seen in a simplified example where there is only one individual in the economy.[3] The product transformation curve for the economy is given by TT in Figure 19-1. A tangent drawn to any point along that curve gives the marginal rate of product transformation between commodity x and commodity y. We now envision a set of indifference curves for goods x and y for our single consumer. The highest indifference curve that can be attained is labeled I. It is tangent to TT at point E. At point E, then, the marginal rate of product transformation (MRT) is just equal to the marginal rate of substitution (MRS) of x and y for this consumer. The optimal quantities of production and consumption are x_1 and y_1. We can extend this analysis to more than one individual. In the following sections we extend it to two individuals and examine the theory of welfare economics in more detail.

Welfare analysis in more detail

Using the tools we have already examined, we can develop a model for welfare comparisons.[4] We have already developed an Edgeworth-Bowley box for exchange and an Edgeworth-Bowley box for production, and we have derived the production possibilities frontier, or transformation curve, from the production version of the Edgeworth-Bowley box. Finally, we have shown in the previous chapter that optimum conditions of exchange require that the marginal rate of transformation between x and y be equal to the marginal rate of substitution. We will begin our analysis by assuming that the reader has reviewed pages 80–83. Now we derive a utility possibility frontier from the contract curve of the Edgeworth-Bowley production box.

---

[2]Note that Pareto optimality in exchange can occur with one person starving because he or she has so few resources with which to begin.

[3]This example cannot be used to talk of Pareto optimality but rather only of maximum economic efficiency.

[4]The presentation will largely follow Francis Bator, "The Simple Analytics of Welfare Maximization," *American Economic Review*, vol. 47, 1957, pp. 22–59, especially pp. 22–31.

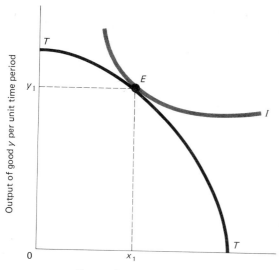

Figure 19-1: Satisfying economic efficiency.
We show a one-person economy. That person's highest
indifference curve I is tangent to the transformation curve
TT at E. Economic efficiency requires output rates of
$0x_1$ and $0y_1$ where the marginal rate of transformation
is equal to the marginal rate of substitution.

number attached to lower indifference curves.
We know that as we move from the left-hand
side of the box to the right-hand side of the
box along the contract curve, we are moving to
higher indifference curves for individual 1
and to lower indifference curves for individual
2. At each point, then, along the contract
curve we have utilities for each of the two
consumers. We translate these points to Figure 19-2. In that figure, consumer 1's utility is
measured on the horizontal axis and consumer
2's utility is measured on the vertical axis. The
resultant curve is a line such as UU. All the
points on that curve are points on the contract
curve. Note the similarity between the derivation of this utility possibility frontier to the
derivation of the product transformation curve,
or production possibility frontier.

The transfer of the contract curve to the utility possibilities curve is a transformation from

A utility possibility frontier

Note that the contract curve in any exchange
(Edgeworth-Bowley box) diagram, such as
those given in Figures 4-4, 18-2, and 18-6,
represents the Pareto-optimal locus of exchange points. In other words, when we are
on the contract curve, the Pareto criterion is
satisfied. On the contract curve, the marginal
rate of substitution is equal for both consumers under study. We can transform this
locus of equilibrium points from the commodity space to a utility space to obtain a **utility
possibility frontier.**

Assume that each indifference curve in the
Edgeworth-Bowley box represents a certain
level of utility for each of the two individuals.
We can pick any ordinal scale we want so long
as higher indifference curves have a number
attached to them that is higher than the

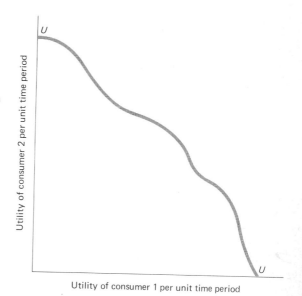

Figure 19-2: Utility possibility frontier.
The curve UU is the utility possibility frontier and is
derived from Figure 18-2. It is a transformation of the
contract curve from the output space to a utility space.
We have to assign arbitrary ordinal rankings to the
different indifference curves to obtain UU.

the output space to the utility space. For production we had a transformation of the input space to the output space.

The curve *UU* in Figure 19-2 corresponds to only one Edgeworth-Bowley box. It might correspond, for example, to the Edgeworth-Bowley box that would fit in the rectangle with vertical height $0y_1$ and horizontal with $0x_1$ in Figure 19-1. We know, then, that there are very large numbers of utility possibility frontiers. There is one for each of the very large number of contract curves within the equally large number of Edgeworth-Bowley boxes that could be traced out within the product transformation curve *TT*. Each point along the product transformation curve results in a new utility possibilities frontier. In Figure 19-3, we draw a number of utility possibilities frontiers. Each is associated with a different point along the product transformation curve or the production possibilities frontier. These are labeled U_1U_1 through U_4U_4. Note that each utility possibilities frontier has a negative slope throughout. That is all we can say about its shape. What can we do with this essentially infinite set of utility possibility frontiers? We can construct what is called a grand utility possibilities frontier.

A grand utility possibility frontier

If we only consider those points on utility possibility frontiers that are not inferior to any other point, we obtain a **grand utility possibility frontier**. This is the heavily shaded "envelope" of all of the utility possibility frontiers, each of which is associated with a point on the production possibilities frontier. This makes sense because any point *within* the heavily grand utility possibility frontier is inferior to any point on the grand utility possibility frontier. Interior points are inferior because the frontier points always yield higher utility for *both* consumer 1 and consumer 2.

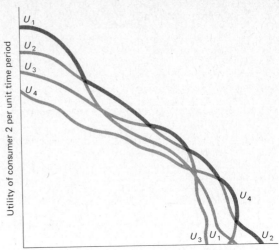

Figure 19-3: Grand utility possibility frontier.
There are an infinite number of utility possibilities curves, such as U_1U_1 through U_4U_4, and each corresponds to different-sized Edgeworth-Bowley boxes drawn to different points on the production possibilities frontier. When we take the envelope of all such utility possibility frontiers, we obtain the heavily shaded line which is called the *grand utility possibility frontier*.

To go further, we must be willing to assume or simply posit a social welfare function that depends exclusively on the positions of consumer 1 and consumer 2 on their own preference scales. As we will see in the following section, the construction of a social utility function, even theoretically, is a difficult conceptual task. Nonetheless, we will assume that it is possible to derive such a social welfare function.

We have drawn the grand utility possibility frontier as the heavily shaded, wavy line in Figure 19-4. It is taken from Figure 19-3. We have added four social welfare functions that are not dissimilar to individual indifference levels. Maximum achievable welfare is attained at the tangency of the grand utility possibility frontier and the highest attainable social welfare function. This is welfare function W_3W_3 in the figure. The tangency is at point E.

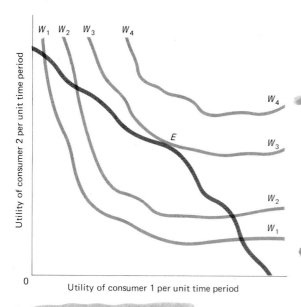

Figure 19-4: A constrained bliss point.

If we draw a set of social welfare functions such as W_1W_1 through W_4W_4, we can obtain a constrained bliss point at which the highest social welfare function just touches the grand utility possibilities frontier at point E.

What we have done, then, is reduce a very large number of possible equilibria to a single equilibrium point. The point E is called a **constrained bliss** point because it represents the organization of exchange, production, and distribution that leads to maximum attainable social welfare. Society would, of course, be better off if it could attain W_4W_4, but that is impossible with its current resources and state of technology. Bliss point E is constrained by the available resources and the state of the arts.

Perfect competition and economic efficiency

It turns out that the perfectly competitive price system examined in Chapter 10 has a very special quality. There is a correspondence between an allocation of resources that satisfies the Pareto condition and the allocation results

from a perfectly competitive price system. Indeed, this correspondence is exact. Every perfectly competitive allocation in long-run equilibrium satisfies the Pareto criterion, and every allocation that satisfies the Pareto criterion has associated with it a perfectly competitive set of prices.

Some caveats about the analysis

Before we show the equivalence of a perfectly competitive price system and an economically efficient system (one that satisfies the Pareto criterion), we must give a few warnings. The first one is that not every allocation that satisfies the Pareto condition is a social welfare optimum because the social welfare optimum depends on the social welfare function. In the example above, there was only *one* social welfare maximum, even though there was a large number of possible allocations of resources that satisfied the Pareto condition. Second, when we talk about distributional criteria (the distribution on income) with which to judge the performance of an economic system, we could find that a competitive system satisfying the Pareto condition leads to an "inappropriate" efficient allocation. For example, large numbers of individuals may be starving.

Third, just because we can show that a perfectly competitive system results in the satisfaction of the Pareto criterion, the real world does not provide us with a perfectly competitive price system. Indeed, the last chapter of this book will show the many ways in which the competitive model is different from the real world.

The meaning of a perfectly competitive price system

To refresh the reader's memory, we will specify what is meant by a perfectly competitive price system. We assume that there are n well-defined homogeneous goods. These goods include producer capital goods, intermediate goods, and consumption goods. Each of the goods has an equilibrium price which is established by the interaction of supply and demand. (The price to which we are referring is, of course, the *relative* price. *Absolute* prices are of little concern when dealing with the allocation of resources.) The equilibrium prices clear each market; the quantities demanded and supplied of each good are equal. We further assume that transactions costs are zero and that firms and consumers have perfect information. Thus, each good has one and only one price; that is, the price per constant quality unit is uniform throughout the market.

Consumers will take the prices of final goods and their budget constraints as given and adjust their behavior to maximize utility. In terms of firm behavior, we assume that there is a large number of firms and that each firm operates to maximize profits.

Now we are ready to show the relationship between perfect competition and the satisfaction of the Pareto condition.

The equivalence between perfect competition and satisfaction of the Pareto Criterion

All we need to do is show that the marginal conditions for optimal resource allocation are satisfied in a perfectly competitive price system. We examine each of the three marginal conditions separately.

EXCHANGE. To attain Pareto maximum it is necessary that the marginal rate of substitution between any pair of consumer goods is the same for all individuals who consume both goods. In a perfectly competitive system, each consumer takes the prices of goods as given. For utility maximization, each consumer must equate his or her marginal rate of substitution of x for y to the price ratio P_x/P_y. This was seen in the discussion of consumer behavior in Chapter 2. In equilibrium, then, the consumer equates the rate at which he or she is willing to trade x for y to the rate at which x and y can in fact be traded in a competitive market. In other words, the point at which an indifference curve is tangent to the budget constraint is the point of optimum allocation for the consumer. In perfect competition, each individual has an MRS equal to P_x/P_y; and, therefore, the marginal condition for exchange is satisfied. Otherwise stated, if $MRS_{xy}^1 = P_x/P_y$ and $MRS_{xy}^2 = P_x/P_y$, then $MRS_{xy}^1 = MRS_{xy}^2$.

FACTOR SUBSTITUTION. To attain a Pareto optimum, the marginal rate of technical substitution (MRTS) between any two inputs must be the same for all producers who use both inputs. Again, this is seen to be the case in a perfectly competitive system. Producers take the prices of factor inputs as given. To maximize profits, subject to a budget constraint, they must operate where an isoquant is tangent to the isocost line. But the slope of the isocost line is the ratio of the prices of the two inputs. Hence, if all producers face the same input prices, they will all choose that combination of inputs at which the marginal rate of technical substitution between every pair of inputs is the same. In other words, if $MRTS_{KL}^x = P_K/P_L$ and $MRTS_{KL}^y = P_K/P_L$, therefore $MRTS_{KL}^x = MRTS_{KL}^y$.

PRODUCT SUBSTITUTION. A Pareto maximum requires that the marginal rate of transformation in production be equal to the marginal rate of substitution in consumption for each pair of commodities and for each individual who consumes both of those commodities. In other words, MRT must equal MRS. This can be shown to be satisfied in a perfectly competitive situation. The MRT is the slope of the transformation curve and is equal to the ratio of the marginal cost of x to that of y. We know, though, that each profit-maximizing firm in a perfectly competitive system will choose a rate of output at which marginal cost is equal to price. Therefore, for every firm, price equals marginal cost and hence $MC_x/MC_y = P_x/P_y$ for all firms, but P_x/P_y is also equal to the consumer's marginal rate of substitution of x for y. Hence, this third condition for a Pareto optimum is satisfied. Competitive markets, therefore, satisfy all the marginal conditions for the attainment of a Pareto maximum. An important question is now brought to the fore. Given the equivalence of a perfect competition and Pareto maximum, has anything been said that is important for policy purposes? Should the government be guided by this "equivalence theorem" and attempt to, say, break up monopolies? We will, briefly, examine this thorny issue in later sections of this chapter and in the last chapter of the book.

Distributional criteria

The discussion of attaining Pareto maximum is one way to evaluate the performance of an economy. There are others, however, and we have hinted at them when we discussed construction of the social welfare function. The criterion for the "best" distribution of income has taken on much importance in recent years. In fact, many economists argue that any welfare criteria that ignore distribution of income involve a contradiction in terms. After all, resource allocation involves, in addition to questions of what is produced and how it is produced, the question of to whom the product is distributed. Looking only at efficiency ignores the matter of income distribution. To be sure, the reason that economists have felt most comfortable with efficiency arguments is that value judgments are presumably eliminated from the discussion. Lately, however, distribution problems have been interjected into all economic policy questions. Discussions of income redistribution programs, in particular, implicitly assume that welfare of society is increased when income is redistributed from the relatively well-to-do to the relatively poor.

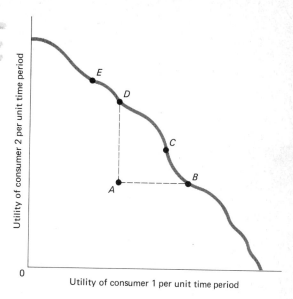

Figure 19-5: Kaldor-Hicks Criterion.
We draw in a utility possibilities frontier. If the economy is at point A, any move to any point between B and D is preferred, since no one is made worse off and someone is made better off; however, a movement to a point such as E would make consumer 2 better off, and consumer 1 worse off. According to the Kaldor-Hicks Criterion, since the gainer could and would be willing to compensate the loser for his or her loss, this would be a preferred move.

The Kaldor-Hicks criteria

In the 1930s a number of economists attempted to derive distributive welfare criteria which would hopefully not be based on value judgment considerations. In other words, value judgments of the relative importance of different individual's welfare was to be removed from the argument. The first attempt was made by two economists in England, Nicholas Kaldor and John Hicks.[5]

We demonstrate the Kaldor-Hicks welfare criterion in Figure 19-5. We have drawn a standard utility possibility frontier. All points

[5]Nicholas Kaldor, "Welfare Propositions in Economics and Interpersonal Comparisons of Utility," *Economic Journal*, vol. 49, September 1939, pp. 549–552; and J. R. Hicks, "The Foundations of Welfare Economics," *Economic Journal*, vol. 49, December 1939, pp. 696–712.

on the frontier, of course, satisfy the Pareto condition. Any movement along the frontier involves a redistribution of welfare. A movement from point E, for example, to point C requires that consumer 2 lose and consumer 1 gain. In other words, along the utility possibilities frontier, any improvement in one consumer's welfare necessarily requires a reduction in the other consumer's welfare. Both Kaldor and Hicks assume that such redistributions can be affected by either lump sum transfers of wealth or redirection of income flows.

Now assume the economy is at point A. A move to point E would not be an improvement according to the Pareto condition because it would involve a reduction in the welfare of consumer 1. However, a movement to point B, C, or D would be a welfare improvement for either consumer 1 or consumer 2 or both consumers. In fact, a movement to any point in the section bounded by AD, AB, and the utility possibilities frontier *between* points B and D would improve welfare for both. Everyone could be made better-off by such a change. Kaldor further argues that a move from A to E could also be labeled an improvement, because when point E has been reached, we could redistribute income or wealth to move the economy to a point such as C at which everyone would be better-off.

In a world without transactions costs, points A would never be a stable equilibrium. For example, consumer 2 should be willing to "bribe" consumer 1 to move to point D. The bribe must be large enough to move consumer 1 somewhere below point D on the utility possibility frontier. And as long as the bribe does not move consumer 1 below point B, consumer 2 will be willing to pay that bribe rather than stay at point A.

Thus, by the Kaldor-Hicks criterion, any point on the utility possibilities frontier is preferred to any point below the frontier. The only assumption in the Kaldor-Hicks criterion is that consumer 2 can compensate consumer 1

for a loss in welfare by direct money payment. We should note, however, that both Hicks and Kaldor talked only of *potential* compensations. Hicks asked whether we could possibly get an agreement among consumers to go from A to E. Kaldor asked the question, If we are at E, could we ever get agreement to go back to A? Both researchers assume that policymakers have knowledge of the utility functions and act as if to satisfy the Pareto condition.

The theory of social choice

We talked earlier about how to derive a social welfare function, but we really didn't indicate the full extent of the difficulties in deriving even the simplest welfare function. Work by Nobel prize–winner Kenneth Arrow has shown that a social welfare function can not always be derived by allowing citizens to vote for different allocation outcomes. His main point was that the social welfare function could not be obtained even if individual preferences are consistent.[6]

In investigating the formulation of social preferences, Arrow stated five axioms which he believes that social preference structures must satisfy to be minimally acceptable to the population. They are as follows:

Complete ordering. Social preferences must, like individual preferences, be completely ordered. They must satisfy the condition of transitivity. Thus, if a is preferred to b, then b is not preferred to a. Further, if a is preferred to b, and b is preferred to c, then a is preferred to c.

Responsiveness to individual preferences. If situation a is socially preferred to situation b by a given set of individuals and if individual rankings change so that one or more individuals raise situation a to an

---

[6]See Kenneth Arrow, *Social Choice and Individual Values* (New York: Wiley, 1951).

even higher rank and no one lowers situation *a* in rank, then situation *a* must remain socially preferred to situation *b*.

Nonimposition. Social preferences cannot be imposed independently of individual preferences.

Nondictatorship. Society must not prefer situation *a* to situation *b* just because one individual prefers *a* to *b*.

Independence of irrelevant alternatives. Assume that there are three situations available, *a, b,* and *c*. Society prefers *a* to *b* and *b* to *c*. Consider the possibility of *c* disappearing. Society must still consider *a* preferable to *b*.

The reason that we have the term **Arrow Impossibility Theorem** is that no voting system allows all these five axioms to be satisfied. In fact, a simple model can show that the first axiom will not be satisfied even if individuals have consistent preferences. Consider three individuals. They are asked to rank situations *a, b,* and *c*. They vote by writing in the number 1 for their first choice, 2 for their second choice, and 3 for their third choice. Consider that the voting went as presented in Table 19-1. Each individual has consistent preferences. Two individuals, I and III, prefer *a* to *b*. Two individuals, I and II, prefer *b* to *c*. Nonetheless, the majority prefers *c* to *a* (individuals II and III). Thus, majority voting would choose situation *c* over *a*, and this preference of the majority is inconsistent with those of the individuals composing that majority. Arrow's work thus indicates that the use of the democratic process of voting in an attempt to formulate a social welfare function can produce contradictory welfare criteria.

Note that an important aspect of the Arrow Impossibility Theorem is the assumption of a majority voting system. He did not take up the possibility, for example, of a voting system that required unanimity and permitted the buying and selling of votes. This is a topic into which we will not enter here.

Individual	Economic situation		
	a	*b*	*c*
I	1	2	3
II	3	1	2
III	2	3	1

Table 19-1: Voting for *a, b,* or *c*.

The theory of second best

We have shown that satisfaction of the Pareto criterion results in an efficient allocation of resources. We showed in Figure 19-5, for example, that a movement from point *A* to a point on the utility possibilities frontier between *B* and *D* would improve social welfare measured by the efficiency or Pareto criterion. However, it could occur that one or more of the Pareto conditions cannot be satisfied because of such institutional restrictions as monopoly, indivisibility of the product, or other restraints which are the result of "externalities" (with which we will deal in the following chapter). If it is the case that the best or highest welfare position is unattainable, it then becomes relevant to ask whether or not a "second-best" position can be attained by satisfying the remaining Pareto marginal conditions. The so-called **theory of the second best** says no. If one or more of the necessary conditions for the Pareto maximum (i.e., the marginal conditions for optimal resource allocation) cannot, for whatever reason, be satisfied, then in general, it is neither necessary nor is it desirable to satisfy the remaining marginal conditions.

The formal proof of the second-best theorem is rather complicated.[7] We can demonstrate it on a much less technical level by using Figure 19-6. Here we show a product transformation

---

[7]See Kelvin Lancaster and R. G. Lipsey, "The General Theory of Second Best," *Review of Economic Studies*, vol. 24, 1956–57, pp. 11–32.

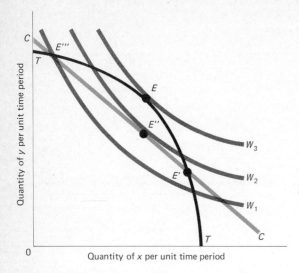

Figure 19-6: Theory of second best.
TT is a product transformation curve. W_1, W_2, and W_3 are social welfare functions. The welfare maximum occurs at point E. Assume, however, that only points on the line CC are attainable. The Pareto condition would require that we move to E' or E''' because that would put us back on the transformation curve TT. However, a move to point E'' would put us on a higher social welfare curve W_2 than we would be on if we were either at E''' or at E'.

curve TT. We know that a welfare maximum occurs when the social welfare function W_3 is tangent to the product transformation curve. This occurs at point E. (Note that we've drawn our social welfare function in the product space instead of in the utility space as we did before.) Assume for the moment that E is unattainable. Some institutional restraint or some natural impediment occurs and only combinations along the line CC are attainable. If we wanted to satisfy the Pareto criterion, we might automatically say that a movement from the curve CC to point E''' were called for because that would put us on the product transformation curve. However, that would put us on social welfare function W_1. If, instead, we move to point E'', we could attain a higher social welfare function W_2. Thus, in accordance with the theory of second best, it

may be better when one of the marginal conditions for Pareto maximum is unattainable to violate some of the other marginal conditions in order to attain welfare maximum.

The theory of second best has been used to question the desirability of economic policies that attempt to attain the Pareto conditions by considering an isolated situation. Proponents of such piecemeal policies to achieve the Pareto conditions in one market contend that so long as the markets in question are relatively unrelated, it does not matter that in the other markets some of the conditions for the attainment of Pareto maximum are unsatisfied. Economic policy for the steel industry, for example, should not be influenced by imperfect competition in the toothpick industry.

Measuring welfare costs

A topic related to the theory of welfare economics deals with the actual measurement of what is called the welfare cost of market imperfections. In order to understand the concept of welfare cost, we must be willing to make a number of assumptions and to employ a measure which is called consumer surplus and which we covered briefly in Chapter 4.

Consumer surplus

When you go into the store to buy a loaf of bread, the price you pay is, by definition, the market-clearing price. But the market-clearing price does not necessarily indicate the value that you place on the loaf of bread (unless you're indifferent between buying and not buying). We know that if you buy the loaf of bread, the value you place on it cannot be less than the price of the loaf. If the value you place on it were less than its value, you would not buy it. However, the value you place on it could be and, indeed, many times is higher than its price.

An experiment could be made to show how

much higher than its price the value of that loaf of bread is to you. It would be an *all or nothing* experiment. Say you normally purchase 10 loaves of bread per month. You would enter the store and the store owner would say, "How much will you pay for all 10 loaves of bread rather than do without them?" The maximum you would pay would be the dollar value of the satisfaction you receive from having 10 loaves of bread rather than having no bread at all. The difference between the maximum you are willing to pay for the 10 loaves of bread and what you would have to pay for them is consumer surplus. It is the amount over and above the market value of the commodity that consumers would pay rather than do without a specified quantity of that commodity. Another way of looking at consumer surplus is that it is the difference between total evaluation for a specified quantity of the good in question and the market value of that commodity (price times quantity). We looked in detail at this topic in Chapter 4.

Graphically, consumer surplus can be represented in Figure 19-7 as the area between the price line and the demand curve. If this diagram does not seem familiar to you, go back and reread pages 83–85.[8]

Consumer surplus is a real part of economic welfare. It is not some fiction that we make up. Consider its definition. It is the amount of money income that you would pay over and above what you have to pay rather than do without the quantity of the commodity that you consume or actually purchase for consumption. Thus, if you were pressed, you would indeed give up more money in order to have that quantity of that commodity. You would have to sacrifice the consumption of other less desired goods and services, and

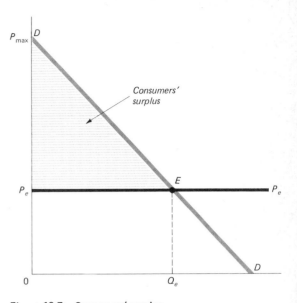

Figure 19-7: Consumers' surplus.
Consumers' surplus is the area between the demand curve and the price line and equal to the triangle $P_e P_{max} E$. It represents the difference between total evaluation and market value.

therefore, consumer surplus is an actual increase in welfare because it allows you to consume more of other commodities.

The producer's side

A similar analysis can be made on the producer's side. In Figure 19-8, we show a typical upward-sloping supply curve *SS*. We assume an equilibrium price of P_e. The quantity produced will be Q_e. Remember that the supply curve represents the locus of minimum prices at which different quantities will be forthcoming. Thus, for example, for quantity Q_1, producers would be willing to supply that quantity at price P_1. However, the market-clearing price is P_e, which is higher than P_1. The difference, then, between the prices at which producers would be willing to sell their products and the prices they actually receive is an economic rent. This particular economic rent is also called **producers' surplus** (to be

---

[8]Also remember that for the analysis to be correct, commodities must be independent and the marginal utility of income must be constant.

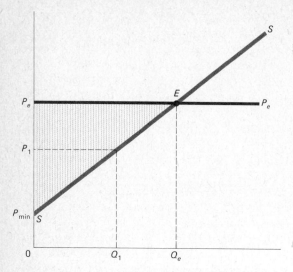

Figure 19-8: Producers' surplus or quasi-rents.

The supply curve SS shows the minimum price at which a given quantity will be forthcoming; and, therefore, the amount of resources necessary to obtain a given quantity. However, if price is P_e, the market value of quantity Q_e is equal to the entire rectangle $0P_eEQ_e$. The difference is the triangle $P_{min}P_eE$. The shaded triangle is producers' surplus; it equals the revenues received in excess of what is necessary to keep resources producing the quantity Q_e per unit time period.

symmetric with the terminology for consumers). Actually, this economic rent is more a short-run quasi-rent as explained in Chapter 17.

The shaded area in Figure 19-8 is our measure of economic rent. It is the quantity of money income over and above what is necessary to keep resources in the industry sufficient to produce quantity Q_e. Thus, the triangle $P_{min}P_eE$ is similar in nature to the shaded area in Figure 19-7.[9]

Putting producers and consumers together

When we put the supply and demand curve together, we can see that at any market-clear-

[9]E. J. Mishan, "What Is Producers' Surplus?" *American Economic Review*, vol. 58, no. 5, December 1968, pp. 1269–1282.

ing price there is a consumer surplus enjoyed by consumers and a quasi-rent enjoyed by producers. These are the two shaded triangles in Figure 19-9.

WELFARE COSTS. We can obtain a geometric measure of the magnitude of the reduction in welfare that results from a market imperfection—taxes, subsidies, monopoly, etc.—by comparing the diagram in Figure 19-9 with a situation in which there is such imperfection. What we do is look at the reductions in consumer surplus and in quasi-rents caused by the imperfection. We do this for a hypothetical output restriction in Figure 19-10; and in the Issues and Applications section we look at the application of welfare cost analysis to the measure of the social cost of monopoly and to distortions from price controls.

First consider Figure 19-10. In competitive equilibrium, the intersection of DD and SS is

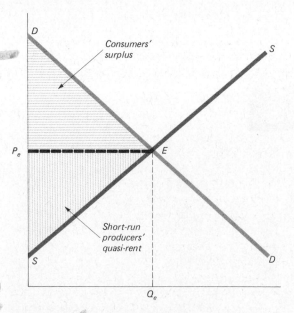

Figure 19-9: Putting consumers' and producers' surpluses together.

At any given market-clearing price P_e, consumers' and producers' surpluses are the shaded triangles.

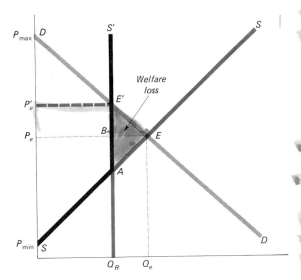

Figure 19-10: The welfare cost of output restriction.
If output is restricted to a maximum of Q_R, the supply
curve becomes SAS'. (We assume that output allotments
are given to the most efficient producers, so that we keep
the same supply curve through the portion S to A.) The
new equilibrium is at point E'; the new market-clearing
price is P'_e. The welfare loss will be the triangle $AE'E$.

at E. The market-clearing price is P_e. The
market-clearing quantity is Q_e. The consumer's surplus is the triangle $P_e P_{max} E$. The

quasi-rent is represented by the triangle
$P_e P_{min} E$. Now, a government authority imposes
an output restriction that limits firms to
producing no more than Q_R. Assume for simplicity that the output quota is passed out to
the most efficient firms so that the original
supply schedule up to the restricted quantity
is a part of the new supply schedule. The new
supply schedule now becomes S up to point A
and then vertical to S'. The intersection of the
new supply curve with the old demand curve
is at point E'. The price at which Q_R will be
sold is P'_e. Note that there has been a reduction in consumer surplus and in quasi-rent.
The reduction in consumer surplus is equal to
$P_e P'_e E' E$. The change in producer surplus, or
quasi-rents, is equal to the reduction given by
the triangle ABE, *plus* an increase transferred
from consumers to producers equal to the
rectangle $P_e P'_e E' B$. Thus, not all the reduction
in consumer surplus was lost. The rectangle
was transferred to the producer. That which
was lost completely was the triangle left over,
or $BE'E$. When we add this to the producer
surplus loss, or ABE, we obtain the welfare
loss triangle, or $AE'E$, due to an output restriction at Q_R. This **welfare loss** is also called
welfare cost or deadweight loss.

Issues and applications

The welfare cost of monopoly

We are now in a position to estimate the social
welfare cost of monopoly. Consider a hypothetical situation. We have a choice of either pure monopoly or pure competition. The cost curves are
exactly the same in both cases. This is presented
in Figure 19-11.

Assume for simplicity that marginal cost is constant. In a perfectly competitive situation, the
curve labeled MC is also the supply curve and is
the horizontal summation of all the individual
firms' marginal cost curves. The competitive
solution is at the intersection of MC and DD, at

point E. The competitive quantity would be Q_e
and the competitive price would be P_e, because
we assumed constant marginal costs. The
amount of quasi-rent is zero. However, the
amount of consumer surplus at price P_e is the triangle $P_e P_{max} E$.

Now assume that the industry is monopolized
and the cost curve remains exactly the same. The
monopoly firm looks at the marginal revenue
curve MR. It chooses the profit-maximizing quantity at the intersection of MR and MC at point E''. It
then finds the price at which it can sell this quantity Q_m by consulting the demand curve DD. The
product is sold at price P_m. Monopolization of the

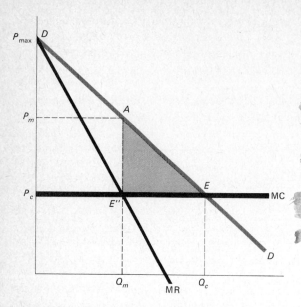

Figure 19-11: The welfare cost of monopoly.
Assume a constant marginal cost MC. Perfectly competitive equilibrium is found where the industry supply
curve MC intersects the industry demand curve DD.
Output would be Q_c; the price would be P_c. Assume
now that a monopolist takes over and that there is no
change in marginal costs. The monopolist sets output
where marginal revenue equals marginal cost at point E''.
The quantity sold will be Q_m. Price will be P_m. The
reduction in consumer surplus is equal to P_cP_mAE.
However, part of that reduction in consumer surplus is
transferred to producers. This transfer or increase in
producer surplus is equal to P_cP_mAE''. What is left is
the shaded triangle $E''AE$, which is our measure of the
welfare loss of monopoly.

industry results in a higher price and a lower
quantity produced and consumed. It also results
in a reduction in consumer surplus equal to
P_cP_mAE. But the rectangle P_cP_mAE'' is transferred
from consumers to the monopolist leaving a
deadweight loss equal to the triangle $E''AE$. Note
that we must further assume that the resources
released from the monopolized industry go into
other industries where they are fully employed
and where they generate benefits just equal to
their total cost of $Q_mE''EQ_c$. Then the welfare loss
is the triangle $E''AE$.

Measuring monopoly power

On page 284 we offered indexes of monopoly
power. One often used is the Lerner Index, which
is $P - MC/P$. We will see from Figure 19-12, however, that the Lerner Index is not a reliable
measure of the severity of monopoly effects.

Consider two single firm monopolies, I and II.
Assume that the demand curve facing firm II is
equal to one-half the demand curve facing firm I.
They are selling in different markets, but they are
both monopolies. The demand curve for the first
monopolist is D_ID_I. The demand curve for the
second monopolist is $D_{II}D_{II}$, which, it turns out, is
also the marginal revenue curve for the first mo-

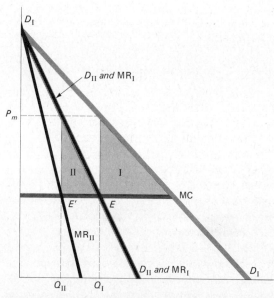

**Figure 19-12: The welfare cost of two monopolies with
equal Lerner Indexes.**
The two monopolists have the same marginal cost curves
MC. One has one-half the demand of the other. They
both sell at the same price P_m. The welfare cost of
monopoly in the first case is the shaded triangle I; in the
second case, it is the shaded triangle II. The former has
a larger welfare cost than the latter, but they both have
the same Lerner Index of monopoly power because the
marginal cost and the price are the same.

nopolist because it is one-half of $D_I D_I$.[10] The marginal revenue curve for the second monopolist is the dashed line MR_{II}. Both monopolists face demand curves which have identical price elasticites. (Why?)

Each firm will produce at MR equals MC. We assume a common and constant MC. The first firm will produce quantity Q_I at the intersection of MR_I and MC, or at point E. The second firm will produce quantity Q_{II}, where the marginal revenue curve MR_{II} intersects MC at point E'. Both firms will charge the identical price P_m. Their Lerner monopoly power indexes will be equal because $(P_I - MC_I)/P_I = (P_{II} - MC_{II})/P_{II}$. However the respective welfare costs, as represented by the shaded triangles I and II, are quite different. The welfare loss or cost (sometimes referred to as deadweight loss), is much greater from monopoly I than from monopoly II. Thus, the Lerner monopoly power index is seriously deficient in measuring the severity of the social welfare costs.

Fighting to keep a monopoly

If a monopoly has been achieved, the monopolist may have incurred costs to obtain the monopoly. Moreover, in order to retain the monopoly profits, the monopolist will incur further costs. On the other hand, consumers may, and indeed do in certain cases, spend resources in order to eliminate the monopoly. For example, if the monopoly arises because a law has been passed allowing only a limited number of companies to produce a product, consumers might band together to have legislation enacted which could rescind this policy.

Other producers will attempt to interfere or infringe upon any monopoly that generates positive monopoly profits. Those profits are represented by the rectangle in Figure 19-11 (page 279, labeled $P_c P_m AE$). In the limit, that rectangle will be dissipated by the resources that go into

maintaining and fighting the contrived monopoly. Thus, in a sense, the welfare rectangle of monopoly is an underestimate of the deadweight loss associated with monopoly.

Empirical estimates of monopoly efficiency loss

One of the first studies undertaken to estimate the actual welfare loss associated with monopoly in the United States was done by Professor Arnold C. Harberger. He looked at the period from 1924 to 1928. His assumptions were heroic: Marginal cost was assumed constant and the price elasticity of demand was assumed to be -1 in all industries. He identified monopolized industries by their relatively high average rates of return on assets. As can be seen from Table 19-2, he estimated the welfare loss to be 0.1 percent of national income.

Criticisms of Harberger's assumptions and analysis have been numerous. George J. Stigler[11] pointed out that the rational monopolist would

Investigator	Demand elasticity	Estimated welfare loss as a percentage of national income
Harberger*	−1.0	0.1
Kamerschen†	Various, averaging −2 to −3	6
Worcester‡	−2	0.5

Table 19-2

*A. C. Harberger, "Monopoly and Resource Allocation," *American Economic Review*, vol. 54, May 1954.

†D. R. Kamerschen, "An Estimation of the Welfare Losses for Monopoly in the American Economy," *Western Economic Journal*, vol. 4, December 1966.

‡D. A. Worcester, Jr., "New Estimates of the Welfare Loss to Monopoly, United States, 1956–1969," *Southern Economic Journal*, vol. 40, October 1973.

---

[10]See pages 115–117.

[11]George J. Stigler, "The Statistics of Monopoly and Merger," *Journal of Political Economy*, vol. 64, February 1956.

only operate in the range where elasticity is equal to −1 if marginal cost were 0. Moreover, monopolists' reported profit rates omit implicit monopoly returns and patent royalties. Finally, Stigler pointed out that such intangible items as goodwill are often counted as assets by monopoly firms so that their reported profit is shown to be a relatively small percent of total assets. This criticism, if relevant, would indicate that Harberger defined too few firms as monopolists.

Stigler's objections were taken into account by other researchers. We find in Table 19-2 the results obtained by Kamerschen and Worcester. The former's estimate is a relatively high 6 percent of national income. The latter's estimate, however, based on firm rather than industry data, is 0.5 percent of national income and not much greater than Harberger's original estimate.

Even if these figures are accurate estimates of the welfare triangles or deadweight losses, they do not take account of the welfare losses associated with the dissipation of monopoly rents when resources are used to obtain, maintain, and protect those monopoly positions.

Welfare costs/price controls

Consider Figure 19-13. SS is the aggregate supply schedule in an industry of price takers. DD shows the consumers' marginal evaluations, or the economic value of varying quantities of output. We assume in this analysis that any income redistribution which results from price controls has no effect on the DD schedule. Without controls, equilibrium is at P_e and Q_e. A lower maximum price of P_c is legislated. At P_c manufacturers will provide Q_c and consumers will demand Q_d. The distance Q_dQ_c is unsatisfied demand. The rectangle P_cABP_e is the transfer from producers to consumers that results from the lower price paid for Q_c units of output at the controlled price.

The size of the economic welfare losses de-

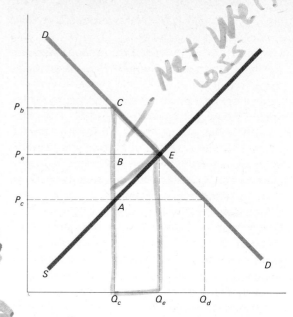

Figure 19-13: The welfare cost of price controls.
Without price controls, the market-clearing price is P_e; the equilibrium quantity is Q_e, which is found at the intersection of SS and DD, point E. At the maximum price allowable P_c, the distance between Q_d and Q_c represents unsatisfied demand. If the price control is effective, there will be a transfer of producers' surplus to consumers' surplus equal to the rectangle P_cP_eBA. If there is an efficient black market, the welfare cost will be the triangle ACE; and, if there is *not* an efficient black market, the welfare loss will exceed ACE.

pends on the system by which output is distributed among consumers. If efficient black markets operate, the economic value of output at the margin will be the same for all consumers. Consequently, the area Q_cCEQ_e is the economic value to consumers of the output which is no longer produced because the price ceiling discourages production. If marginal cost equals price in other sectors of the economy, the area under the supply schedule Q_cAEQ_e is the economic value of other goods sacrificed by using resources to produce the output Q_cQ_e because the market value of the additional resources used in increasing output reflects the value of their marginal product in other sectors of the economy.[12] *ACE* is the net welfare loss to society that results from the price ceiling. This welfare loss means that the economic loss to those who are harmed by the price ceiling exceeds the economic gain to those who benefit. Since *ACE* represents a net welfare or deadweight loss, the price ceiling would not be politically feasible if compensation had to be made to those who are harmed. Under a system of majority rule, however, such an economically inefficient rationing scheme would be feasible if the majority coalition consists of the net beneficiaries.

Moreover, if black markets are not efficient, the net economic welfare loss will exceed *ACE*. Because the economic value of output at the margin may not be the same for all consumers, all the gains from voluntary exchange among consumers will not be realized. For example, consider Figures 19-14 and 19-15. Assume consumer A is allowed to purchase $\overline{X}_A$ units at the legal ceiling price P_c. At P_c this consumer wants to consume only X_A^0 and so he or she is able to purchase *more* than he or she wants to consume. But consumer B, we assume, is allowed to purchase $\overline{X}_B$, which is *less* than the X_B^0 he or she would like to consume at a price of P_c. If there are efficient black markets, consumer A would sell $\overline{X}_A - X_A^0$ on the black market and consumer B would purchase $X_B^0 - \overline{X}_B$. The shaded triangles represent the economic gains to each consumer realized from exchanges on the black market. However, if efficient black markets are wholly or partially suppressed by the government, the gains from exchange between consumers represented by the shaded areas will not be realized. Consequently, the net welfare loss will exceed ACE.

When price controls create shortages which are not rationed through black markets, some buyers

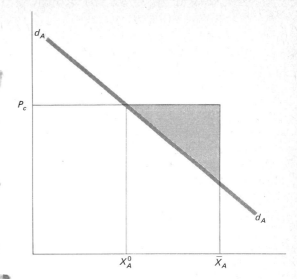

Figure 19-14: The gains from selling in the black market.

If this consumer has demand $d_A d_A$ and holds quantity $\overline{X}_A$, he or she would sell the quantity equal to the distance between $\overline{X}_A$ and X_A^0. The gain from exchange for this consumer would equal the shaded area.

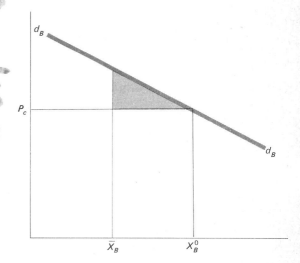

Figure 19-15: The gains from buying in the black market.

This consumer has demand $d_B d_B$ and holds quantity $\overline{X}_B$. If allowed to trade in the black market, he or she will purchase the quantity equal to the horizontal distance between $\overline{X}_B$ and X_B^0 from the consumer in Figure 19-14. The gain from exchange is equal to the shaded triangle.

---

[12]If monopoly power and/or taxes distort prices so that they no longer reflect the marginal rate of transformation between goods, this analysis of welfare losses breaks down. In such situations, any statement about welfare losses or gains must specifically consider the sectors to which resources are transferred.

prefer to pay higher prices rather than do without additional consumption. Those buyers who cannot obtain the goods in short supply at the official ceiling price will form black-market coalitions with sellers, who obviously prefer higher prices. The greater the excess demand for goods and services, the larger the proportion of buyers who will join sellers in coalitions to raise prices.

Glossary

Welfare economics The study of socially efficient solutions to the problem of resource allocation; involves eliminating solutions which can be shown to be "inferior" to other feasible solutions without the use of normative economics.

Pareto condition A situation in which it is impossible for all individuals to gain from further exchange. In other words, if one individual is made better-off, another must be made worse off. Also called the Pareto optimal allocation of resources, Pareto optimality, Pareto maximum, and Pareto criterion.

Utility-possibility frontier The transformation of the contract curve from an output space to utility space; derived in a fashion similar to the derivation of the product transformation curve; gives the maximum combinations of utilities for consumer I and consumer II from given endowments of goods.

Grand utility possibility frontier The envelope of the highest segments of all feasible utility possibility frontiers. Each possible utility frontier is associated with a different point on the production possibilities frontier.

Constrained bliss An organization of exchange, production, and distribution that leads to maximum attainable social welfare. The point on the grand utility possibilities frontier that is tangent to the highest social welfare function possible.

Arrow Impossibility Theorem No democratic voting system can be used to obtain a social welfare function which satisfies the five minimal axioms Arrow specifies. In fact, the axiom of transitivity cannot be satisfied even if all individual preferences are transitive.

Theory of the second best If one (or more) of the marginal conditions necessary for optimal resource allocation is not satisfied, it does not follow that welfare is improved if the remaining marginal conditions are satisfied.

Producers' surplus The amount of revenues received by producers in excess of what is necessary to induce them to provide a specified quantity of a good.

Welfare loss The reduction in consumer and/or producer surplus from a distortion in the economy; also called welfare cost or deadweight loss.

Summary

1. In welfare economics we assume that: (*a*) individuals are the best judges of their own welfare; (*b*) individuals who prefer situation *a* to *b* receive greater welfare from situation *a* than from situation *b*; and (*c*) individuals' choices reveal their preferences and, hence, their welfares.

2. Welfare economics attempts to carry on analysis without interpersonal utility comparisons.

3. The Pareto condition or Pareto optimality is generally synonymous with the economically efficient organization of resources.

4. The Pareto condition requires that marginal rates of substitution between goods be equal for all consumers, that the marginal rate of technical substitution between any pair of inputs be the same in all industries, and that the marginal rate of transformation for any two goods be equal to the marginal rate of substitution for those two goods.

5. We can derive the utility possibility frontier by transforming the output space to a utility space. When we map all possible utility frontiers and obtain the envelope of the segments of the highest utility possibility frontiers, we get a grand utility possibility frontier.

6. If we had a social welfare function, we would find the constrained bliss point where it is tangent to the grand utility possibility frontier.

7. The marginal conditions that satisfy the Pareto criterion are achieved when there is perfect competition and vice versa. In other words,

there is an equivalence between perfect competition and the achievement of Pareto optimality.

8. The Kaldor-Hicks welfare criterion assumes that any movement from a point inside the utility possibility frontier to a point on the utility possibility frontier is an improvement because the consumer who is made worse off could be bribed by the consumer made better-off. The Kaldor-Hicks criterion is based on potential and not on actual compensations.

9. In his theory of social choice, Kenneth Arrow presented five axioms he believes the social preference structure must satisfy to be minimally acceptable to the population: (*a*) complete ordering, (*b*) responsiveness to individual preferences, (*c*) nonimposition, (*d*) nondictatorship, and (*e*) independence of irrelevant alternatives.

10. Arrow showed that not even the first axiom would necessarily be satisfied in a majority rule democratic voting situation. Thus we have the Arrow Impossibility Theorem which states that no voting system can satisfy the five axioms.

11. In situations where not all the marginal conditions for Pareto optimality can be satisfied, the attempt to satisfy the remaining conditions will not necessarily improve social welfare. This is the theory of second best.

12. By using the concepts of consumer surplus and producer surplus, we can measure the welfare cost of such distortions in the economy as monopoly, taxes, subsidies, and output restrictions.

13. An important welfare cost in monopoly is the waste of the resources that are used to obtain, police, maintain, and fight monopolies.

Selected references

Bahm, Peter, *Social Efficiency: A Concise Introduction to Welfare Economics* (New York: Wiley, 1973).

Baumol, William J., *Economic Theory and Operations Analysis*, 3d ed. (Englewood Cliffs, N.J.: Prentice-Hall, 1972), chap. 16.

Graff, J. de V., *Theoretical Welfare Economics* (London: Cambridge, 1957).

Little, I. M. D., *A Critique of Welfare Economics*, 2d ed. (Oxford: Oxford, 1957).

Scitovsky, T., *Welfare and Competition: The Theory of a Fully Employed Economy* (Homewood, Ill.: Irwin, 1951), chap. 7.

Questions

(Answers to even-numbered questions are at back of text.)

1. With what does welfare economics deal?
2. Is the optimal allocation of resources any "better" than any other? Explain.
3. What are the three basic assumptions of welfare analysis?
4. "Clearly a redistribution of $1 of Elizabeth Taylor's income or wealth to a very poor person would increase that person's well-being (utility) more than it would decrease hers. Consequently, the net effect of such a coerced transfer would be to increase social welfare." Is this statement demonstrably true or false? Explain.
5. "To the extent that it lessens incentives to produce, a government program which redistributes income through the coercion of taxation will decrease the nation's annual output from what it otherwise would have been." Is this statement demonstrably true or false? Explain.
6. What criterion was laid down by Vilfredo Pareto for an efficient allocation of resources?
7. What are some of the limitations of Pareto's condition?
8. Demonstrate graphically for a single-person economy the MRS equal to MRT condition required for optimal allocation of resources.
9. In Figures 19-2 and 19-3, what is measured on the *x* and *y* axes? What are the units?
10. From what diagram is a utility possibilities frontier derived? How?
11. What is the "grand utility possibility frontier" and how is it derived?
12. If a perfectly competitive economy will satisfy the Pareto criterion, does it follow that any

move from a nation's existing market structures toward a perfectly competitive structure
will necessarily increase social welfare?

13. According to the Kaldor-Hicks welfare criterion, any point on the utility possibility
frontier is preferred to any point below it.
Why?

14. What does the Arrow Impossibility Theorem
assert?

15. What is consumers' surplus and what does it
have to do with economic welfare?

16. What is producers' surplus (short-run economic quasi-rent) and why does it not persist
over time as consumers' surplus does?

20

EXTERNALITIES, PUBLIC GOODS, AND MARKET FAILURE

We observed in the previous chapter that a system of perfectly competitive markets would lead to attainment of the Pareto optimum. But perfect competition is not so "perfect" as it at first seems. Unless demand and supply reflect *all* the benefits and *all* the costs of producing and consuming a product, the prices that result from perfect competition are not the "right" ones. If this be the case, then maximum welfare will not be achieved. This is the result of externalities about which we briefly talked earlier. This entire discussion falls under the rubric of **market failure**. When the organizational costs of institutional barriers prevent markets from operating fully, a situation often described somewhat loosely as market failure exists and another approach to welfare maximation is required. In order to understand more clearly the concept of externality, we must first examine the concepts of social benefits and social costs.

Social benefits and social costs

We dealt with true (opportunity) costs in Chapter 8 and made the distinction there between the explicit and the implicit costs of a private firm. We pointed out that individual behavior is based on true—explicit plus implicit—costs. What we were talking about there was the concept of private cost or the costs to private individuals and firms.

But there is another concept that we must not overlook and that is **social** or full economic **costs**. Social costs include all private costs incurred by the parties to a transaction, whether they be explicit or implicit, plus any additional costs visited on other individuals. It is both impossible and unlikely that the individual entrepreneurs will take account of social costs. This is particularly so in a competitive market where, unless they set price equal to marginal private costs, they will not maximize profits and will eventually go out of business.

If society's welfare is also to be at a maximum, however, marginal private costs must be equal to marginal social costs. To maximize profits, all activities of the individual firm must be carried to the point where marginal private revenue equals marginal private cost, or where private marginal benefits and costs are equated. But to maximize welfare, marginal social benefits and costs are taken into account. Only then can we consider that a welfare maximum is being approached.

It is in the context of this terminology that the notion of external economies and diseconomies is discussed. An external economy is found when the marginal social cost of an activity is *less than* its marginal social benefit. An external diseconomy occurs when marginal social cost is *greater than* marginal social benefit. If either exists, the Pareto condition is not satisfied. One of the earlier articles[1] on "market failure" due to externalities distinguished between **technical, ownership,** and **public good externalities**. We will now examine each of these three externalities in some detail.

Technical externalities

There are two technical externalities which can, in theory, lead to market failure. These are the result of production functions which exhibit indivisibilities and production functions which exhibit increasing returns to scale.

Indivisibilities

Consider a production process that requires constant input proportions and yields constant returns to scale. Two persons and two shovels can do twice as much as one person with one shovel; but we cannot have half a person with half a shovel; consequently, we have an indivisibility in the production process.

It turns out that **indivisibilities** become important only when there exist production processes whose utilization requires a relatively high rate of output. Consider the example where there is a small-scale process where one unit of output requires one machine and one person. Together, the machine and the person can produce 1 ton of output per unit time period. Contrast this with a large-scale process that requires 50 machines and 50 persons to produce 100 tons of output per unit time period.

The large-scale process cannot be operated at a rate of less than 100 tons of output per unit time period, but it can be operated at any higher level and we will assume that it displays constant returns to scale.[2] In other words, we can use 51 machines and 51 persons to produce 102 tons of output per unit time period; or we can obtain 2 tons of output from the use of one person and one machine.

Note that both the small- and large-scale processes use capital and labor in the same one-for-one ratio. The input combination in both processes is a dose of one machine and one person. However, for anything less than 50 input "doses," the large-scale production process cannot be employed. We must use the small-scale process. When we do this, howev-

---

[1]Francis M. Bator, "The Anatomy of Market Failure," *Quarterly Journal of Economics*, vol. 72, 1958, pp. 351–379.

[2]See pages 204–207.

er, we obtain only 1 ton of output per input dose. We see, then, that there is a discontinuity in output per unit of input when we jump from 49 tons with 49 doses to 100 tons with 50 doses of the inputs. The large-scale process will clearly be used for all outputs of 100 tons or greater but cannot be used for outputs of less than 100 tons. We get, then, a discontinuity in the returns to scale. In other words, we obtain increasing returns to scale when we have indivisible alternative processes and increase the rate of output up to or beyond the output required for the employment of the more efficient process. Hence, indivisibilities lead to increasing returns to scale even though each production process taken by itself shows constant returns to scale. This has been termed a technical externality by some economists. We will see why when we examine what happens if increasing returns to scale exist.

Increasing returns to scale

We looked into the cause of natural monopoly in Chapter 12. There we showed that if long-run average costs fall over the relevant range due to increasing returns to scale, a natural monopoly will result. The natural monopolist, however, will produce the output at which marginal revenue equals marginal cost and charge a price which exceeds marginal cost. Therefore, even where externalities are absent, this monopoly behavior does not bring about the equality of marginal social costs and marginal social benefits. If, for some reason, the falling long-run average cost curve did not lead to a natural monopoly, two or more firms could not continue to exist in the same industry; if they set a price equal to marginal cost, it would be less than average cost. Each firm selling at marginal cost would thus incur a pure loss.

In some markets, then, a technical externality that results from increasing returns to scale causes market failure because it leads to

monopoly, and price will exceed marginal cost. Monopoly arises because a freely competitive market cannot exist when the price equals marginal cost, because at that price firms would suffer pure economic losses.

Ownership externalities

Often private costs differ from social costs because a resource that is being used or abused is not owned by the person inflicting damage on the resource. The classic cases of ownership externalities are pollution of air and publicly owned bodies of water.

When private costs differ from social costs, we usually term the situation a problem of externalities because individual decision makers do not bear all the costs borne by society. Rather, some of these costs are external to the decision-making process. We might want to review the problem in Figure 20-1. Here we have drawn a supply curve for product x. The supply curve, however, is equivalent to the horizontal summation of all the individual marginal cost curves and includes only internal or private costs. The intersection of the demand and supply curves will be at price P_e and quantity Q_e. However, we will assume that the production of good x involves external costs which private businesses do not take into account. Those externalities could be air pollution, water pollution, scenery destruction, or anything else of that nature.

In any event, we know that the social costs of producing x exceed the private costs. We can show this by drawing the supply curve $S'S'$, which is above the original supply curve SS. It is above that original curve because it includes both the externalities and the internal or private costs, or the full economic costs of producing the product. Now the "correct" market equilibrium price would be P_1 and the quantity supplied and demanded would be Q_1. We see that the inclusion of external costs in the decision-making process would lead to

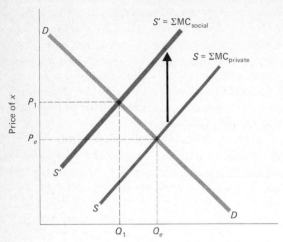

Figure 20-1: Making private costs equal social costs.
If firms take account of only private costs, the supply curve is SS. The quantity demanded and sold will be Q_e at a price P_e. However, if social costs are taken into account, the supply curve becomes $S'S'$. If a tax (equal to the external costs per unit of output) were imposed so that the price facing the consumer was P_1, then the quantity demanded and sold would be Q_1. Consumers would then be paying for the full social cost of their actions.

a higher price and a smaller quantity of the product produced and consumed. We can say, therefore, that where economic costs are not being fully borne by the creators of those costs, the price is "too low" and the quantity produced is "excessive."

Correcting the signals

We can see here an "easy" method of reducing the amount of pollution and environmental degradation. Somehow the signals in the economy must be changed so that decision makers will take into account all of the costs of their actions. In the case of automobile pollution, we might want to devise some method whereby motorists either were taxed according to the amount of pollution they generated or were compensated for not generating it,

depending on who owns the rights to "clean" air. In the case of a firm, we might want to devise some system whereby businesses were taxed for the amount of pollution for which they were responsible or were compensated *not* to pollute. In both cases, they would have an incentive to install pollution-abatement equipment.

When you think about it, however, it may not be appropriate to levy a uniform tax on the physical quantities of pollution created. After all, we're talking about social costs. The social costs of some action are not necessarily the same everywhere in the United States. If you drive your smelly, belching car in the middle of the Mojave Desert, you will probably not inflict any significant damage on anyone. (We are notorious for ignoring the "preferences" of natural flora and fauna.) No one is there to complain; the natural cleansing action of the large body of air around you will eliminate the pollution you generate to such an extent that it results in little or no economic harm.

Essentially, we must measure the economic damages rather than the physical amount of pollution. This point cannot be overemphasized. A coal-fed steam electric generator in New York City will cause more damage than the same equipment in, say, Helena, Montana. This is so because the concentration of people in New York City is much higher than in Helena. In addition, there are already heavy demands on the air in New York City, and additional pollution will not be naturally cleansed. There are millions of people who will breathe that smelly, sooty air and thereby incur the costs of sore throats, sickness, emphysema, and even premature death. There are many, many buildings which will become dirtier; cars and clothes will also become dirtier much more quickly. A given quantity of pollution will cause more harm in concentrated urban environments than it will in less densely populated rural environments. If we were to establish some form of taxation to align social costs with private costs and force people to internalize externalities, we would need to have a measure of economic costs instead of merely physical quantities. Moreover, we would want to make sure that those who can decrease pollution at least cost do so; i.e., we want to minimize the cost of reducing pollution by any given amount.

Property rights

Now let's find out why there will be a difference between social costs and private costs. Why do certain situations create externalities, while others do not? Consider, for example, some of the things you own. Suppose you own a bicycle. If someone slashes the tires or bends the spokes, you can, in principle, press civil charges to recover damages. The damages you recover would be equal at least to the reduction in the market value of your bike. The same is true for a car. Anyone damaging your car is liable for those damages. The court will uphold your right to compensation (although obtaining compensation is not costless).

Common property

What if you live next to a stinky steel factory? The air around you, something that you use continuously, is altered. You may also be "altered" by breathing it. However, you more than likely have no right to stop the air pollution or to obtain compensation for the destruction of the air around you. This is so because you do not have property rights in the air surrounding you; neither does anyone else. Air happens to be what is called a **common property** resource. Herein lies the crux of the problem. Whenever property rights are indefinite or nonexistent, social costs will differ from private costs. This is as you would expect. When no one owns a particular resource, its users have no incentive to consider their particular despoliation of that resource. In

fact, a person would be wrong to assume that an individual decision not to damage that resource will produce a significant effect on the total level of pollution. When one person decides not to pollute the ocean, there will still be about the same amount of ocean pollution, since the individual is a small part of the total number of polluters.

When property rights exist, individuals have legal recourse for any damages sustained through the unsanctioned use of their property. When property rights are well defined, the use of property—that is, the use of resources —will generally involve contracting by the owners of those resources with those potential users. If you owned land, you might contract with another person so that your land could be used for grazing cattle. The contract would most likely be written in the form of a rental agreement. We can predict that whenever contracting and/or enforcement of such agreements becomes exceedingly expensive or difficult, social and private costs will diverge. Whenever contracting and enforcement of property rights are relatively costless, social costs and private costs will tend to be one and the same. In fact, this is why externalities are problems only in certain areas of activity of our society. We don't worry about social and private costs in the majority of the activities that go on in our economy, because almost all of what goes on involves contracting among individuals and the transference of property rights.

When property rights do not exist

Surprisingly enough, even when property rights do not exist, private costs can equal social costs; and this is particularly true when transaction costs are minimal. In such situations, there is no misallocation of resources. Let's take a simple example. Suppose you live in a house with a nice view of a lake. The person living below you plants a tree. Over the years the tree grows larger and larger and eventually it cuts off your view of the lake. In most areas, nobody has property rights to views, and therefore, you usually cannot go to the courts for relief. You cannot file suit against your downhill neighbor for obstructing your view. That neighbor has the property right to grow a tree, and you have no right to your view.

Contracting

You do have an alternative, however. You can, as it were, contract with your next-door neighbor to top the tree (to make it shorter). How much of a "bribe" would you offer? You could start out with a small money figure and increase the size of the offer either until he agrees or until you reach your limit. Your limit will be equal to the value you place on having an unobstructed view of the lake. The neighbor will be willing to top the tree if the payment is at least equal to the reduction in his or her property value due to a shorter tree. In this manner, you make your neighbor aware of the social cost of such action; you make explicit the social cost of growing a large tree which blocks your view and lowers the value of your property. But you do this in a rather odd way—by attempting to use bribery. Your neighbor is informed of the true cost of his actions. Alternatively, your neighbor could come to you and ask how much you would be willing to pay to have the tree topped.

Let's see if things would be different when property rights were actually vested in views rather than in tree growing. Let's say that the property rights to a view were vested in you. Therefore, anybody destroying the view would have to pay damages to you. In this particular case, the downhill landowner would have to bribe you for permission to block your view. The bribe to you would have to be at least equal to the reduction in the value of

your property because of the obstructed view. (This bribe will also be a measure of the value of the view itself.) If the downhill landowner doesn't offer a sufficient bribe, you will not accept and the tree will have to be topped. The allocation of resource outcome is the same regardless of who owns the rights.

Opportunity costs

Now let's change the situation. Assume that your neighbor has the property rights in *your* view. This is a strange situation indeed, but it is equivalent to the example in which no one had the view property right. If your neighbor has the property right in your view, will things be different than they were when you had the property right? If you think so, you're wrong. Just because your neighbor now owns "your" view does not mean he or she will ignore the cost of its obstruction. After all, your neighbor would be giving up the opportunity of making some money in a deal with you by asking you how much you would be willing to pay to have the tree topped. If you were willing to pay enough, your neighbor would top it. If not, it would be left as is.

In other words, your neighbor would take account of the opportunity cost. This is the key to understanding why private costs will equal social costs in all three of the above situations. In the first instance, there were no property rights; in the second case, property rights were given to the uphill land owner and in the third case, property rights were given to the downhill landowner. In each and every situation, opportunity costs exist and will be taken into account. The contracting involved is relatively simple. Only two parties are concerned, and verbal agreements could be made relatively easily. This particular example leads us to a strange, but nonetheless valid, conclusion.

When transaction costs are minimal, it does not matter who has the property rights in the resource under study, as long as somebody does. The resource will be used in exactly the same way regardless of the property right structure. Otherwise stated, if transaction costs are small, the allocation of resources does not depend on who has property rights in those resources.

The above statement is generally called the **Coase Theorem,** named after Ronald R. Coase. He demonstrated that in a world of zero transaction costs, the wealth-maximizing behavior of individuals takes account of external effects.[3]

Wealth distribution

Note that in reducing "externalities," the distribution of wealth will be affected and will depend on who, if anyone, has the property rights initially. The person who gets the property rights to some resource that was formerly common property will clearly be better-off; the wealth of this individual will be increased. In the above example, if a large untopped tree is more valuable to its (downhill) owner than is the view to the uphill landowner, the tree will not be topped. Think about this. In the case where the uphill landowner had the property right of the view, he or she will accept a bribe from the downhill tree owner that is at least equal to the reduction in the uphill property value due to the obstructing tree. The downhill landowner will offer a sum that does not exceed the increase in his or her property value due to an untouched tree. If the view is more valuable than the untouched tree, the downhill owner will not succeed in bribing the uphill landowner but will have to top the tree.

On the other hand, if the downhill landowner has the property rights in the view, he or she will have to be bribed to top the tree. If the increased value of the unobstructed view leads the uphill landowner to offer a sum which is greater than the value of an untouched tree to the downhill landowner, the downhill landowner will accept the bribe and top the tree. In either case, the resources—the view and the tree—will be used so that they generate the highest economic value.[4]

When transaction costs are high

Our example so far is pretty simple. It involves only two people and the contracting or transactions costs are small. What about cases where the transactions costs aren't so small? Take the example of a factory polluting a city of several million people. It would be difficult for the several million people to get together to bribe the factory to reduce its pollution or for the factory to contract with them to acquire the right to pollute. The transactions costs here would be extremely high.[5] Therefore, we cannot predict that private costs will equal social costs for the factory. This is probably the case with many environmental problems.

Note that indefinite property rights in and of themselves are not always a problem if contracting can be done cheaply. However, when large numbers of people are involved, contracting is difficult, and in many instances, the actual costs are difficult to measure and/or the creators of those costs are difficult to identify. If ships are spilling oil into the ocean, how do you find out which ones are doing it? The costs of finding out may be too high to justify probable benefits of the undertaking. This

---

[3] Ronald R. Coase, "The Problem of Social Costs," *Journal of Law and Economics,* October 1960, pp. 1–45.

[4] We ignore income effects on the demand curves for trees and for views.

[5] It should be noted that the evolution of class action lawsuits in recent years has substantially lowered the transactions costs of legal proceedings in the environmental area.

discussion of property rights leads us to another possible solution to our environmental problems.

Pinpointing property rights

Instead of attempting to tax polluters in proportion to the economic damages caused by their pollution, we could define property rights more precisely; contracting would then have to take place between potential polluters and those being polluted. In the case of the obstructing tree, it did not really matter who was endowed with property rights in the view. In fact, indefinite property rights really were inconsequential to the outcome of the situation except, of course, for the wealth positions of the individuals. This is not the case with other environmental problems. For example, we might want to make factories liable for the pollution that they create. When we do that, we are implicitly vesting the citizens of that community with the rights in the common property resources of water and air surrounding the factories; individuals living there will implicitly be the owners of the "public" air and water. The factory will therefore be liable for uses of water and air which impose costs on those persons.

In a sense, this is not really "fair." Customers and employees of and stockholders in that factory are made to bear the costs of pollution. After all, a common property resource is, by definition, owned by everyone. The problem is that when it is "owned by everyone," it is actually owned by no one. It would be arbitrary to assign rights in a common property resource to the local homeowners; it would be just as arbitrary to assign the property rights to the factory owners. But because it is less costly, administratively, to make the individual factory owners pay, we still might want to go ahead with this arbitrary assignment of property rights, to the local homeowners, that is. In essence, government decision makers will be acting on behalf of the homeowners when dealing with the polluting factory. Government decision makers will somehow have to determine the value of the economic damages that the factory's pollution is causing and require that the factory either make full compensation, install pollution-abatement equipment, or do some combination of the two. Any compensation would be distributed to the homeowners in a manner that approximated the economic cost sustained by each of them. That, of course, is a difficult problem, particularly since government decision makers are themselves unable to capture any increased benefits from "correctly" distributing the compensation. It might be simpler to use the "bribe" money to clean up some of the pollution caused by the factory instead of trying to compensate the losers (the individual homeowners). Note that here, as elsewhere, the optimal level of pollution is not zero. *The optimal level is that level at which the social benefits of further reducing pollution just equal the social costs of doing so.* If the benefit to society is 90¢ for $1 more of pollution abatement, then we've already gone too far.

Public good externalities

We treated the concept of a public good back in Chapter 4. There we showed that the way to derive a market demand curve for a public good was to sum the individual demand curves vertically rather than horizontally. This was because the marginal cost of providing the services of a public good to one more consumer is zero once the public good has been produced. We must be careful to distinguish between the positive cost of *producing* the public good from the zero cost of using the public good.

The externality comes into play if the marginal social cost of sharing one more unit of consumption of the public good is zero and a price above zero is being charged; then we have violated the welfare maximizing criterion of equating marginal social benefits and marginal social costs. Another way of looking at this is that in a system of perfect competition, there is an equality between the marginal rate of transformation of good x into good y and the marginal rates of substitution of good x for good y of, say, consumer I and consumer II. In the public situation, however, consumer I's consumption of good x does not restrict consumer II's consumption. Thus, the marginal rate of transformation should equal the *sum* of the two marginal rates of substitution. Perfect competition and perfectly competitive prices may lead, therefore, to underproduction and underconsumption of public goods.

With public goods, transactions costs are usually sufficiently high that it is difficult to monitor the intensity of consumer demands and charge for them. We run into what is known as the **free** or cheap **rider problem**. Since it is difficult or impossible to exclude those who have not paid for the use of the public good, it is hard to get a sufficient number of individuals to reveal their true demand and then voluntarily to agree to pay for the production of the public good. Bargaining between potential users and the potential suppliers of the public good is often costly. Take the example of national defense. If everyone were asked to contribute voluntarily to national defense, we would probably devote a relatively small amount of resources to national defense. Each individual thinks that his or her contribution is an insignificant part of the total amount needed for national defense, and therefore, it won't make any difference if he or she does not contribute very much or any at all. That person may choose to be a free rider. This problem is not always insurmountable with public goods. Many voluntary associations continue to exist even though the free rider problem plagues them. Homeowners in a certain area may band together into a homeowners' association in which individuals voluntarily contribute dues each year in order to provide for trees on the perimeter of the development, special lights, and so on. Not everyone joins, and yet the association will continue to exist because a sufficient number of persons will voluntarily pay their annual dues. Educational TV "subscriptions" would be another example.

Public goods that become private

We must be careful here, however, because the private market has a long history of entrepreneurs' attempts at converting public goods into private goods. This is exactly what putting a wall around a baseball field or a room around a movie screen is all about. In this manner, private entrepreneurs can in fact provide what would otherwise not be provided if consumers were not charged for the right to see a baseball game or a movie. Indeed, even the history of the classic example of a public good that seemingly cannot be provided by the private sector shows how ingenious entrepreneurs can be. The classic case of a public good is the lighthouse. Once a lighthouse is built, the marginal cost of providing the land-demarcating services to ships during storms is very close to zero, and it seems literally impossible to make ships pay for the use of the lighthouse because of the problems of identifying which ships go by it and of enforcing payment. A little historical investigation, however reveals that in England lighthouses were for many years private. Lighthouse owners apparently were making profits on their lighthouses, because the number of private lighthouses increased from 1700 to 1834. They obtained payment from shipowners by assessing the shipowners at the docks according to the tonnage of the ship. While it may seem that enforcement costs were high, apparently they were not high enough to prevent private entrepreneurs from collecting enough revenues to continue building more lighthouses. Usually only one ship was in sight of the lighthouse at any one time. If the ship (which displayed its flag) had not prearranged (prepaid) for the light, the light would not be shown.[6]

Public good benefits

Public goods are often seen as goods which generate positive externalities for which individuals "should" not have to pay because the marginal cost of providing those externalities is zero after the public good has been produced. The problem with this type of analysis is that it does not allow the individual members of the consuming public to be faced with their share of the total cost of producing the public good. Individuals react to signals. If the signal is nonexistent, i.e., if the price of consuming more of a public good is zero, the consumers will individually not take account of their combined actions. It is possible in these circumstances that "too many" rather than too few public goods will be provided.

[6]See Ronald R. Coase, "The Lighthouse in Economics," *Journal of Law and Economics*, vol. 18 no. 2, October 1974, pp. 357–376.

Issues and applications

Honey bees and externalities

The classic case of ownership externalities is in the production of honey and apples. It turns out that this example, like that of the lighthouse, never fit reality; this can be seen if we examine it more carefully.[7]

You can buy apple blossom honey, blueberry blossom honey, cranberry blossom honey, alfalfa honey, red clover honey, fireweed honey, mint honey, sage honey, orange honey, and even cabbage honey. We all know how honey is made. Bees extract the nectar of various blossoms and transform it, via one of nature's mysterious processes, into the honey you buy in the store. In many states there are large bee farms, with hives generally consisting of one or two brood chambers, a queen excluder, and from zero to six supers. A brood chamber is a wooden box large enough to contain eight or ten movable frames. Each frame will have a wax honeycomb built by the bees. It is in the hexagonal cells of this comb that the queen will lay her eggs and the young bees, or brood, will be raised. The

bees store the nectar and pollen which they use for food. Honey is usually not extracted from this chamber but from the frames of a more shallow box, called a super, placed above the brood chamber. The queen excluder is placed between the super, which is used only for honey, and the brood chamber, which is used only for raising young bees. The excluder prevents the queen from laying eggs in the upper section of the hive.

Beekeepers and bees work throughout the year. During part of the year, usually from spring to fall, the colonies of bees hatch continuously. The infants are raised on pollen, and they remain in the brood for about 3 weeks of their working life helping to clean and repair the wax cells in the brood. For the remainder of their lives, usually 2 or 3 more weeks, they look for pollen and nectar.

Bees are at their busiest in the spring when they are pollinating fruit trees and the infants must be fed with nectar and pollen. Fruit tree owners benefit from having honeybees nearby: they will enjoy a larger yield per acre because of the pollination services the bees provide. Here we have a classic situation that in the economic literature has been labeled as an external benefit. In 1952 the economist J. E. Meade pointed out that applying more labor, land, and capital to

[7]Steven N. S. Cheung, "The Fable of the Bees: An Economic Investigation," *Journal of Law and Economics*, April 1973.

apple farming will not only increase the output of apples, but will also provide more food for the bees. Meade called this a case "of an unpaid factor, because the situation is due simply and solely to the fact that the apple farmer cannot charge the beekeeper for the bees' food."[8]

We can look at the situation from the other side of the coin. The apple trees may provide food for the bees, but the bees also fertilize the apple blossoms. If the beekeeper in the vicinity of the apple trees increases the size of the colony, he or she presumably foresees the increased benefit as the additional revenues that will be received from selling a larger quantity of honey. At the same time, though, the apple farmer will receive a benefit in the form of a higher pollination rate of his apple blossoms and, hence, a higher quantity of apples at the end of the season. Again we appear to have a situation of an unpaid factor or an externality. There are benefits external to both the decision made by the apple farmer and the decision made by the beekeeper.

In economic analysis, an externality is associated with market failure. That is, the private market fails to allocate resources in an efficient manner. The apple and bee example has been used in economics for many years now to demonstrate an externality in which the government should step in and correct the relative prices by appropriate taxes and subsidies in order to take account of benefits that the apple farmer and the beekeeper apparently do not perceive, or at least, cannot charge for.

Only recently has someone taken the time to find out if the quaint apple farmer–beekeeper example is real. Besides the fact that apple blossoms yield little or no honey, apparently both beekeepers and fruit growers do understand that bees provide valuable pollination services. Moreover, beekeepers and fruit growers realize that plants will provide valuable honey crops. Once it is understood by at least one of the parties in question that a valuable external benefit occurs as a result of his or the other's action, we would expect that some attempt would be made to take advantage of this knowledge. That attempt would translate itself into a contractual arrangement between the fruit grower and the beekeeper. Contracts are not a new invention; they have existed since the beginning of social relations among humans. We all know of certain types of contracts, e.g., the kind made with a bank in order to borrow money. But contracts are not limited to such obvious endeavors. In fact, contracts exist, either explicitly or implicitly, for an incredibly large number of economic and even noneconomic transactions. We can cite a marriage contract, an employment contract, and an educational contract; there are contracts for just about every action known. The beekeeepers and the fruit and plant growers, therefore, might be expected to reach an agreement that would take account of the so-called externalities involved in each one's behavior.

We find conclusive evidence that both nectar and pollination services are indeed bought and sold in the marketplace. In many cases, all we have to do is look in the Yellow Pages. We find there an entry for "pollination services." Economists for many years thought that "the apple farmer cannot charge the beekeeper for the bees' food and the beekeeper cannot charge the apple farmer for the bees' pollination services," but this is not the case. Not only can the parties charge for the services they render each other, they actually do so; and some of them make a very good business of it. In a study in the state of Washington,[9] it was found that about 60 beekeeepers each owned 100 or more colonies. During the peak season, the colonies' total strength was about 90,000 bees. Beekeepers would relocate hives from farm to farm by truck. Beekeepers not only rendered pollination services to different fruit and plant owners at different times of the year, but extracted different types of honey at different times

---

[8]J. E. Meade, "External Economies and Diseconomies in a Competitive Situation," *Economic Journal,* March 1952, pp. 56–57.

[9]Steven N. S. Cheung, op. cit.

of the year as well. On the average, the Washington hives took care of $2^1/_2$ crops a year. The accompanying Table 20-1 shows that beekeepers sometimes provided pollination services and sometimes didn't; sometimes plant owners provided honey services and sometimes they didn't.

When we look at what beekeepers charge for pollination services, we find an interesting but not wholly unexpected phenomenon. The greater the expected honey yield, the smaller the pollination fee. Essentially then, the beekeeper is paid partly in honey for the pollination services that are rendered to the plant owner. Moreover, the more effort per pint of honey yield the beekeeper puts into dispersing hives throughout the orchard, the more charged for this service, because pollination improves with increased dispersal of hives.

So here we have a situation where a seemingly elusive resource, a flying insect, renders services to the owner of another resource. A very specific type of contract has been drawn up for these circumstances in order to take account of any benefits obtained. These contracts take both oral and written forms. In the state of Washington, a printed one is issued by the Association of Beekeepers. A contract need not be in writing, however, to be enforceable in a court of law. In any event, oral contracts are not generally broken when information about who broke one travels quickly. This is exactly the situation in the world of beekeepers and farmers in which everyone knows everyone else's reputation. A glance at the written pollination contracts reveals stipulations concerning the number and strength of the colonies, the time of delivery of the hives and the time of their removal, what will be done to protect the

Plants	Number of beekeepers	Pollination services rendered	Surplus honey expected	Approximate season	Number of hives per acre (range)
Fruits and nuts					
Apple and soft fruits*	7	Yes	No	Mid-April–Mid-May	0.4–2
Blueberry (with maple)	1	Yes	Yes	May	2
Cherry (early)	1	Yes	No	March–Early April	0.5–2
Cherry	2	Yes	No	April	0.5–2
Cranberry	2	Yes	Negligible	June	1.5
Almond (Calif.)	2	Yes	No	February–March	2
Legumes					
Alfalfa	5	Yes and no†	Yes	June–September	0.3–3
Red clover	4	Yes and no	Yes	June–September	0.5–5
Sweet clover	1	No‡	Yes	June–September	0.5–1
Pasture§	4	No	Yes	Late May–September	0.3–1
Other Plants					
Cabbage	1	Yes	Yes	Early April–May	1
Fireweed	2	No	Yes	July–September	n.a.
Mint	3	No	Yes	July–September	0.4–1

Table 20-1: Bee-related plants investigated in the state of Washington, 1971.

*Soft fruits include pears, apricots, and peaches.
†Pollination services are rendered for alfalfa and the clovers if their seeds are intended to be harvested; when they are grown only for hay, hives will still be employed for nectar extraction.
‡Sweet clover may also require pollination services, but such a case is not covered by this investigation.
§Pasture includes a mixture of plants, notably the legumes and other wild flowers such as dandelions.
Source: S. N. S. Cheung, "The Fable of the Bees: An Economic Investigation," *Journal of Law and Economics*, April 1973, Table 1.

bees from pesticides, how the hives should be placed, and the cost of the hives' services.

Whenever there are expected gains to be made from contracting among different parties in an economic system, and as long as the cost of making and enforcing the contract is less than the expected gains, we generally observe the making of written or oral contracts. This is true even where natural resources are concerned. Thus the economist's classic example of an externality turns out to have been largely internalized. It does provide us, though, with valuable clues to when and where externalities will exist. In the case of the bees, contracting was profitable for the parties concerned; in the cases of automobile pollution, destruction of scenic beauty, and over fishing, the costs of negotiating and enforcing contracts clearly exceed the potential gains. This is so because we do not yet have any cheap (efficient) way to define, measure, and enforce property rights to the clean air, scenic beauty, and the fish swimming in the ocean.

Glossary

Market failure A situation in which the market solution does not lead to a Pareto optimum.

Social cost All private costs of an action, plus costs which are incurred by "innocent" third parties.

Technical externalities Externalities which occur because of indivisibilities in the production process or returns to scale.

Ownership externalities Externalities which occur because of ill-defined or nonexistent property rights—common property problems.

Public good externalities Externalities which arise because of the nature of public goods; the cost of monitoring and charging for marginal units of the product are prohibitively high.

Indivisibilities Situations in which the production process is such that a relatively small rate of output with the existing equipment is not feasible.

Common property Property that is owned by all and therefore owned by no one.

Coase Theorem When transactions costs are zero, the assignment of property rights will not alter the allocation of resources.

Free rider problem Individuals may attempt to get a "free ride" on a commonly provided good by indicating that they do not want that good and therefore will not pay for it. They believe that enough others will indeed pay for the good so that it will be provided to them anyway. This is also known as the cheap rider problem, because nothing is free.

Summary

1. Whenever an unrestrained market leads to a violation of the marginal conditions for Pareto optimality, we have a market failure.
2. For a welfare maximum to be obtained, marginal social costs must equal marginal social benefits for all resource-using activities.
3. This maximum may not be achieved if there are technical, ownership, or public good externalities.
4. Technical externalities are the result of production functions which exhibit indivisibilities and increasing returns to scale.
5. Ownership externalities result from the absence of well-defined ownership rights. In some cases, private costs can be made equal to social costs by taxation or subsidization.
6. It is necessary to estimate the economic damages rather than the physical damages of pollution-creating activities. The former will differ from the latter and depend on the number of individuals affected by the same amount of physical damages.
7. We predict that common property will not be treated in the same way as property with well-defined rights assigned to someone or some group. In the case of common property, individuals will treat it as if they do not own it and the result is pollution of air, water, etc.
8. In a world of zero transactions costs, the Coase Theorem indicates that a change in the property rights will not alter the allocation of resources. However, it will alter the distribution of wealth.
9. The key to understanding the Coase Theorem is to understand that an opportunity cost exists even when property rights do not exist. If my

train emits sparks which set your corn on fire, I am suffering an opportunity cost equal to the amount of money you would give me to install spark arresters on the train (assuming, of course, that you would pay me more than the mere cost of the arresters).

10. The optimal level of pollution abatement is at that point at which marginal social benefits equal marginal social costs.

11. Public goods have marginal costs of zero only after they are produced. Prior to the production of the good, the production costs themselves represent a marginal cost to society.

12. Individual wealth maximizers expend resources in order to change public goods into private goods.

Selected references

Bator, F. M., "The Anatomy of Market Failure," *Quarterly Journal of Economics*, vol. 72, August 1958, pp. 351–379.

Baumol, William, *Economic Theory and Operations Analysis* (Englewood Cliffs, N.J.: Prentice-Hall, 1965), pp. 368–371 and 375–380.

Buchanan, James M., and W. C. Stubblebine, "Externality," *Economica*, vol. 29, November 1962, pp. 371–384.

Chamberlin, E. H., "Proportionality, Divisibility and Economies of Scale," *Quarterly Journal of Economics*, vol. 62, February 1948, pp. 229–262.

Questions

(Answers to even-numbered questions are at back of text.)

1. Why do you think that economic discussions of external economies and diseconomies focus on *marginal* social costs and *marginal* social benefits rather than *total* social costs and *total* social benefits.

2. What is meant by the expression "market failure"?

3. How does a homeowner determine what quantity of resources to allocate improving the outward appearance of his or her property? From a social point of view, in an urban or suburban area is the "right" amount of resources allocated to this task? Explain.

4. From a social standpoint, are too few, just the right amount, or too many resources allocated to the production and consumption of rooftop television antennas? Why?

5. In a given geographic area, might there exist technical externalities in the provision of fire-fighting services? If so, why might there be an inefficient allocation of resources?

6. Construct a standard supply-demand diagram and show the initial equilibrium price and quantity. Assume that the good visits external costs on third parties (persons not involved in the transaction), and adjust the diagram to compensate for that fact. How does the "adjusted" situation compare with the original?

7. Now construct a second supply-demand diagram for any good and show the equilibrium price and quantity. Assuming that the good generates external benefits, modify the diagram to allow for them and show the new equilibrium price and quantity. How does the "adjusted" situation compare with the original?

8. What is the problem with common property resources?

9. Suppose you own a large piece of property in the center of which lies a lake. You locate a feedlot on the edge of the lake and begin fattening cattle. The feedlot runoff pollutes the lake and kills many of the fish. Are there any externalities here? Explain.

10. Do plants and animals have property rights?

11. Suppose you were contemplating a use of your property which would generate substantial external benefits for the property owners in the surrounding area. How might you go about capturing (internalizing) these benefits for yourself?

12. "Blockbusting" is a term used in recent years to describe the alleged profitability of certain techniques of racially integrating residential neighborhoods. Here is how it is supposed to work. A speculator places a family of a different race in a racially homogeneous neighborhood. This, it is argued, causes a panic on the part of the other residents fearing that their property values will drop substantially on account of the integration. Re-enter the speculator (blockbuster) who placed the orig-

inal family. He or she now approaches the other owners and offers to buy their homes at rather low prices which many accept because they think that the bottom is yet to come. After buying most or all of the homes in the neighborhood, the speculator proceeds to sell the homes at nondepressed prices to members of the new racial or ethnic group who have wanted to live in the neighborhood for years but had somehow been unable to do so in the past. Analyze critically this "racism for fun and profit" theory with particular reference to externalities.

13. "Abate or compensate? That is the question." What does this statement have to do with external costs?

14. How much of an external diseconomy is socially optimal from the standpoint of an efficient allocation of resources? To what extent should society utilize its scarce resources in abating the nuisance?

15. Summarize the dilemma presented by public goods.

ANSWERS TO CHAPTER QUESTIONS

Chapter 1

2. No, it doesn't matter; what does matter is whether or not the model, taken as a whole, predicts well.

4. It went down; whereas a quart of tequilla "cost" 10 liters of beer in 1970, by 1978 it could be "bought" for only 9 liters of beer.

6. Such a change in relative prices would make gas appliances somewhat less attractive in comparison with their electric counterparts because the former would have become relatively more expensive to operate. We would expect appliance manufacturers to adjust production accordingly.

8. What is important, you should point out to him, is that when the price of something rises, *some* of the users of the product decide to consume less than they had previously and this results in a decreased quantity demanded. (One must make the distinction between marginal and average.)

10. It is meaningless to talk of the quantities that buyers would be willing to buy and sellers would be willing to sell, unless we have defined, at least conceptually, the product we have in mind. Unless consumers are indifferent between Pintos and Vegas, and the relative successes of the two cars strongly suggests that they are not, we cannot meaningfully aggregate the two into something called the demand for "subcompact cars." Note that what is important is that potential buyers *perceive* the two products to be interchangeable; they need not actually be identical.

12. (*a*) Expected future clothes-washing services per year for *n* years, (*b*) expected future hours of sailing per year for *n* years, (*c*) expected future meals per unit time period for *n* time periods, (*d*) expected future dividends per year for *n* years, and (*e*) expected future consumption of goods and services per unit time period for *n* time periods.

14. It does matter, particularly if you are desirous of bringing about a change in one of them. This lesson was learned, at immense cost, during the Great Depression of the 1930s. The Roosevelt administration felt that falling prices were causing the fall in production. On the basis of that theory, the National Recovery Administration (NRA) was created for the purpose of stopping wage and price competition. This, it was reasoned, would stop the fall in production and corresponding layoffs. Its unconstitutionality aside, the program was an economic disaster; if anything, it aggravated the unemployment situation. The falling wages and prices were not the *cause* but rather, at least in part, the *effect* of declining production. The Congress had the two reversed, and consequently, their NRA program was a dismal failure. (*b*) If changes in C are inducing changes in both A and B, then any effort to affect A via B, or vice versa, will be of no consequence.

Chapter 2

2. An indifference curve represents all of the possible combinations of two goods which the consumer in question finds to be equally satisfying.

4. The difficulty is that such preferences are inconsistent. Since A is preferred to B, which is preferred to C, then it should follow that A is also preferred to C. To assert the reverse is to be inconsistent. Note that the existence of some consumers who may in fact hold such preference patterns does not invalidate the theory. One does not empirically test the validity of a scientific model by examining the behavior of a single individual.

6. The MRS of *f* for *d* is 1:3 between 1*f* and 2*f*. Between 2*f* and 3*f*, the MRS of *f* for *d* is 1:5. Yes, the third *f* involved a greater sacrifice of *d* (5*d*) than did the second *f* (3*d*).

8. Since B is on both I and II, it would follow that all points on both I and II are equally satisfying. Comparing D with C, though, we note that both represent the same number of movies, but that D represents more novels than C. This cannot be so unless the consumer finds both quantities of novels equally satisfying, which violates our assumption that more is preferred to less. Therefore, the curves cannot cross.

10. Budget lines don't show levels of satisfaction, but merely attainable combinations of goods. Therefore, given the above information, there is no way of saying whether a consumer was made better-off or worse off by the price changes. The addition of the indifference map of a particular consumer will enable us to answer the question. Draw two or three indifference curves on your diagram and you will see.

12. When more of a good is consumed, *total* utility derived from it increases (at least it does so until one has reached the point of "saturation," beyond which additional consumption actually decreases total utility). *Marginal* utility, on the other hand, decreases as more is consumed (it actually becomes negative beyond the point of saturation). Therefore, the only way to cause a good's marginal utility to increase is to cut down on its consumption. If this is still not clear, review Figure 2-6.

14. If we could measure levels of satisfaction in discrete units ("utils"), then we could say, for instance, that I represented 55 utils and II represented 65 utils, and that the latter was 10 utils higher than the former. However, as the ordinalists have demonstrated, such "cardinal" measures of utility do not exist; consequently, we can only say that a consumer prefers those combinations of goods represented by II over those portrayed by I. We cannot say (nor can the consumer, for that matter) *how much* better-off he or she is at the higher level of indifference represented by II.

Chapter 3

2. An inferior good is defined as one of which an individual purchases less when his or her income rises and more when his or her income falls. A superior good is defined as one of which an individual purchases more when his or her income increases and less when his

or her income falls. Yes, the same good can be both. In fact, most goods are superior up to some level of income beyond which they become inferior. See the "backward-bending" Engel curve in Figure 3-5.

4. The price-consumption curve shows the different amounts of a good which a consumer will buy when faced with alternative prices for that good. One need only transfer the price and quantity combinations to a new graph where price is measured vertically and quantity horizontally.

6. In order to isolate the effect of a change in real income on the respective quantities of x and y demanded, the relative prices of the two goods must remain constant. If the relative prices are allowed to change, it is impossible to obtain an unambiguous measure of the change in income.

8. You would try to find a business that produced an inferior good. Why? Because when real incomes fall, the quantity of inferior goods demanded actually rises, because their income elasticity of demand is negative.

10. If the good is a very small proportion of one's budget (shoelaces, for example), the income effect can be set aside as insignificant. Even a doubling of the price of an item like shoelaces or toothpicks would have only a negligible effect on one's real income.

12. Unless the movie star really enjoys negotiating with merchants, we would expect him or her to spend less time searching. The time of a movie star is likely much more valuable than that of a police officer. Consequently, the "cost" of going from dealer to dealer, or even phoning them, is higher. If the cost is higher, we would expect less of it (information) to be consumed.

14. Both indexes have the problem of ascertaining the price of the product in the earlier period (P_1), because the product didn't exist at that time. Of course it could be estimated, but this gets very tricky. The Laspeyres index has the further problem of assigning a weight (Q_1) to a product that was nonexistant in the earlier period and therefore not part of anyone's budget at that time. Technically, the weight should be zero because the good was previously absent from the market basket.

Chapter 4

2. Consumer surplus is the amount over and above the price actually paid for a commodity which the consumer would have been just willing to pay rather than do without it. In a two-person world, an owner of Cokes who *knew* the other person's marginal valuation of successive units of the drink would sell it on a sliding scale. For example, the owner could charge $1 for the first Coke, 75¢ for the second, 50¢ for the third, etc.; alternatively, an all-or-nothing offer could be made that would just induce trade. Our analysis of exchange in this chapter has implicitly assumed that exchanges were made at a single unit price. Note also that in a competitive world where there are several owners and buyers of Coke and/or substitute products, such an appropriation of another's consumer surplus is much less likely to occur.

4. Legally, in an auction which is advertised to be "without reserve," once the auctioneer puts an item on the auction block (starts taking bids), the item must be sold to the highest bidder. In other words, the owner's reservation price is zero. On the contrary, in an ordinary auction the auctioneer reserves the right to reject any or all bids prior to banging the gavel. In this case the owner has a positive reservation price in mind which may or may not be disclosed at the start of the bidding.

6. In their exchanges, both will benefit by moving northwest until arriving at the contract curve somewhere between E' and E'', at which point trading will cease. This means that individual 1 will be offering good x for good y, and individual 2 will be offering good y for good x.

8. Understanding Figure 4-6 is the key to this question. At price P_1, the consumer purchases 2 cokes per day. The shaded area

shows that for any quantity less than 2, he or she would have been willing to pay a higher unit price. Since both the cokes were bought at price P_1, consumer surplus was realized on all units of Coke except the last one. Also note that since Cokes are assumed in Figure 4-6 to be minutely divisible, the "last unit" can represent the smallest quantity of Coke of which you can conceive.

10. It does and it doesn't. It doesn't in the sense that the final allocation of the Coke will be the same irrespective of the initial Coke endowments. It does make a difference, though, because the wealth positions of the individuals, which include the money that changed hands in the Coke swap, will clearly be affected by the initial ownership of the commodity.

12. If one person's consumption does not decrease the amount available for others, the good is a public one. Because Alaska and Hawaii are distinct geographic entities, the allocation of national defense resources to their protection would lessen somewhat the amount of resources available for defense of the continental United States. On the same reasoning, local police protection is clearly not a public good. The quantity of law enforcement resources is fixed at any moment in time. On Saturday nights, for example, police departments must forego certain activities in order to focus on others deemed to be more important. For example, while writing a traffic citation, a motorcycle officer may be interrupted by a more urgent call on his or her radio.

14. There are a whole range of prices which will leave both you and the dealer better off by exchanging money for car(s). The dealer would like to acquire all or some of your consumer surplus. For this reason, it is in the interest of the dealer to know as much as possible about your preferences, as revealed by the maximum amount of money you are willing to pay for the car. Consequently, knowledge of any private deliberations between, say, spouses while the salesperson has stepped out of the cubicle, is extremely valuable to the dealer.

Chapter 5

2. We know that the $\Delta q/\Delta P$ term must remain constant, because it is merely the inverse of the slope, and a straight line's slope is by definition constant. However, looking at the other term, because P and q are inversely related, we know that the ratio P/q will never be the same for two different prices; hence the product $(\Delta q/\Delta P)(P/q)$ must also change with every change in price (quantity).

4. At any given price, the steeper demand curve is less elastic (or more inelastic) than the other one. However, at any given quantity, their elasticities are identical.

6. No, it cannot. The household demand for salt and the diabetic demand for insulin may have price elasticities near zero at their current prices. However, at sufficiently high prices, their respective demands must of necessity become elastic. After all, at any moment there is only a finite amount of real income with which to buy things.

8. The formula is $(\Delta q/\Delta P) \cdot (P/q)$. The second term is easy. You know the price P. Just "pick off" the corresponding quantity demanded, q, and you've got P/q. As for $\Delta q/\Delta P$, merely construct a tangent to the demand curve at point (q,P) and measure its slope, $\Delta P/\Delta q$. Invert it and you have $\Delta q/\Delta P$. Now find the product of the two terms and you've got the point elasticity of demand at price P (quantity q).

10. (a) Negative (complements), (b) positive (substitutes), (c) positive (substitutes), (d) negative (complements), (e) negative (complements), (f) positive (assuming that they are substitutes, but they well may be complements, at least for some people).

12. The problem is with the denominator, percentage change in P. Since the initial price was 0, any increase in price is of infinite percentage. However, if the arc-elasticity formula is used there will be no problem. The denominator of the denominator, P, will become the average of $P_1 (= 0)$ and $P_2 (= 10)$, or $(P_1 + P_2)/2 (= 5)$.

14. The statement is false. Economic theory makes no such prediction. The person mak-

ing the statement is probably confusing the notion of search costs or transactions costs with elasticity. (See Chapter 4.) For example, we would expect persons whose time is less valuable to spend more of their time seeking bargains in the marketplace and looking for a longer time before deciding to buy. This does not prove, however, that their demand is more elastic, because we must include the value of their time spent shopping (search costs) in the prices they "pay." Note also that wealthier individuals often find it in their interest to hire others (agents, brokers, etc.) to examine the marketplace and maybe even make decisions on their behalf.

Chapter 6

2. The total price of golfing is the money price (clubs, green fees, etc.) *plus* the opportunity cost of time "consumed" playing and getting to and from the course. Consequently, as one's after-tax wages rise, it becomes more expensive to golf. Of course, this does not necessarily mean that you will golf less, because golfing may be a superior good (service) to you.

4. The person's preferences are consistent with a positive personal rate of discount. Our theory suggests that most persons are willing to pay more to consume something now rather than later. *How much* more they are willing to pay will determine when, if ever, they see the movie in question. Note that watching a movie on TV is not free; it takes time, more time, in fact, because one must suffer through the commercials as well.

6. The present value of a future dollar is less than a dollar in hand, as long as there exists a positive interest rate. Put another way, a sum smaller than a dollar, invested today, will grow until it becomes a dollar (or more) at some time in the future.

8. Originally, you would be willing to pay $20 for it because $1 per year is the "interest" on $20 at 5 percent per year. If the interest rate then fell to 2 percent per year, your perpetuity would be worth $50, because $1 per year interest on a $50 investment would yield 2 percent per year to its buyer.

10. For a 10 percent per year rate of return, the answer is $1,000. To earn 12 percent on your investment, you must pay no more than $887; to earn 8 percent per year, the bond must be bought for no more than $1,134.

12. The annual premium would equal the expected annual claims divided by the number of participants, or 15 pregnancies × $1,000 per pregnancy equals $15,000, divided by 100 women equals $150 per person per year. The first problem is that even though 15 pregnancies per 100 women may be the annual average, the figure could easily fluctuate from, say, 5 to 25 pregnancies and cause their $15,000 per year to bring in a surplus during some years and a deficit during other years. Second, and potentially much more disruptive of their scheme, is the probability of what insurance people call "adverse selection." The demand for the services of obstetricians and gynecologists slopes downward like any other demand curve; at a lower price, more will be demanded. Consequently, the quantity of deliveries demanded annually is greater at $150 per year than it is at $1,000 per year. Those women voluntarily joining this league are likely to conceive at well above the average rate of 15 per 100 per year.

14. A futures market "processes" information, both good and bad, affecting the future supply and demand for particular commodities. One way to make money trading in futures (some would say the only way to do so consistently) is to have better information than the other traders. In deciding how much to spend on weather information, one must weigh the present value of expected future benefits against the present value of expected future costs (review Eq. 6-22). It is unlikely that many speculators have their own weather service. The cost of producing reports which are better than those already available is, no doubt, very high.

Chapter 7

2. It is indeed difficult to come up with any. While examples of "labor intensive" pursuits (being a strawberry picker or bootblack) are numerous examples of "labor exclusive"

production are far more difficult to think of. Perhaps personal services, the "oldest profession" being the most notorious, come the closest. Even there, however, some capital generally accompanies the labor input.

4. It is not only possible, but not that uncommon. Many metropolitan transit companies don't own their own buses. Some taxi companies don't own the very tires their sedans roll on. This is accomplished by *leasing* the item (trucks, buses, tires) in question from a subcontractor of sorts (lessor). Why would a firm "job out" a task like the supplying of equipment? The entrepreneur has determined it (leasing) to be less costly than owning the equipment in question.

6. The ability to negotiate is critical. The contract curve stresses the point that there are many different outcomes realizable by exchanging with another person; that person may be a potential employee, supplier, customer, lender, or other business party. As will be seen later, since we do not live in a two-person world, competition will set limits on the range of prices at which goods and services will be exchanged. However, since information is a scarce commodity, the phenomenon of negotiation will always be with us. In each and every transaction, there are greater or smaller gains from voluntary exchange to be had by each party. Other things equal, the larger gains will accrue to, and hence increase the wealth of, the better bargainer.

8. The problem, as was pointed out in the chapter, is one of cost. There is nearly always a trade-off between cost and time (or more accurately, expedience). At a higher cost one can get, say, a piece of equipment installed more quickly. How much a firm can justify spending to expedite a change in one of its "fixed" inputs will depend upon the present value of the contemplated additional input to the firm. Suffice it to say that, *ceteris paribus*, the lower the present-value cost of a change in a "fixed" input, the sooner "the" short run will end and "the" long run begin.

10. You need to know the relative prices of the inputs you are using. A production function merely states the relationship between various combinations of inputs and output,

in physical terms. In determining the cost-minimizing combination of labor and capital that will fill the orders, you need to know the relative price of labor and capital. *Note:* As you will learn in Chapter 10, an efficiently run firm does *not* allow the marketing department to make output decisions without also considering production cost information. In that sense, this situation is highly artificial.

12. Stage III is dispensed with most easily. Since total physical product actually declines as more of the variable input is added, it would clearly not be in a firm's interest to use more of that input, even if its marginal cost were zero. Stage I is equally unattractive because, over that range of outputs, the average physical product of the variable input is rising and causing the average variable cost (assuming the input can be hired at a constant unit price) to fall. For this reason, expansion of output beyond stage I is in order.

14. A sufficient increase in total cost would shift tt' outward (upward) until Q_3 was attainable. Also, a sufficient decrease in either the price of capital (r) or the price of labor (w), or both, would rotate and/or shift tt' outward making output Q_3 attainable. Note that we have assumed no change in technology. Such an improvement would shift Q_3 (and all other isoquants) toward the origin and make Q_3 attainable (if the advances were of sufficient magnitude) without any change in TC, r, or w.

Chapter 8

2. Despite the fact that the machine has long since been written off for tax-accounting purposes, it may still have a positive market value, which will be realized when the machine is sold or scrapped. The firm is still losing the interest that could be earned by selling the asset and investing the proceeds. Furthermore, even if the present scrap value is zero, there is an implicit cost of keeping it, equal to the rental value of the space it is taking up in the plant.

4. It is both. Pornography, like beauty, is in the eye of the beholder. Whether passersby find the video to be offensive (an external cost) or

attractive (an external benefit) is a matter of individual preferences. No doubt most communities would contain individuals holding both views.

6. Certainly most accountants would consider an existing long-term lease obligation to be a fixed cost. However, it is usually possible, through negotiations and possibly a lump-sum settlement, to get out of a lease. Consequently, your short run may be terminable, at a cost, on fairly short notice.

8. You are not minimizing costs for output Q because, given the relative prices of capital and labor, you are using too much capital and not enough labor. By using less capital, its marginal physical product will rise; by using more labor, its marginal product will fall. This substitution of labor for capital should continue until the ratio of their marginal products is the same as that of their relative prices, or 10 to 1.

10. The "planning" or "envelope" (LAC) curve represents the locus of points that give the least unit cost of producing any given rate of output. The concept is important when one must decide which scale of operations to adopt. Such a decision usually takes the form of deciding what size "plant" to construct.

12. You should increase output at plants 2 and 3, thereby raising MC at both, and decrease plant 1's output so as to decrease its MC. This should be continued until the MCs are all equal and will occur at a MC greater than $8 and less than $10.

14. The authors of our Constitution may well have had something akin to our LAC concept in mind when they drafted the commerce clause. The effect of sufficiently high duties (taxes) levied by any state on the "exports" of another state would have been to limit to one state the extent of the market in which any one firm could sell. This in turn would have prevented the realization of lower unit costs in those industries exhibiting substantial economies of scale, and would consequently have kept prices from being as low as they would have otherwise been. Note that those consumers in the states with the smallest populations would have had the most to lose.

Chapter 9

2.

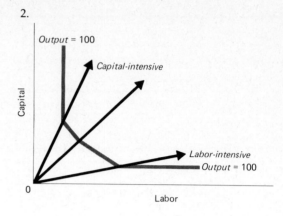

4.

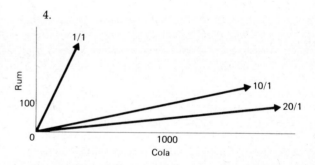

6. $Z = 5X_1 + 2X_2$ is the objective function. All other equations are constraints because they define limitations on the values of the variables.

8. Maximize $Z =$ $5X_1 + 2X_2$
   subject to $3X_1 + 2X_2 \leq 10$
                  $6X_1 + X_2 \leq 8 \quad (-2)$
   then $3X_1 + 2X_2 = 10$

$$\frac{-12X_1 - 2X_2 = -16}{-9X_1 \qquad = -6}$$

$$X_1 \qquad = 2/3$$

Substituting $6(2/3) + X_2 = 8$, then $X_2 = 4$.
Hence, $X_1 = 2/3$, $X_2 = 4$ is the maximum point in the feasible region. Solving the objective function yields $Z = 5(2/3) + 2(4) = 10/3 + 8 = 11^1/_3$.

10.

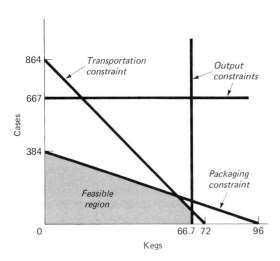

Chapter 10

2. The industry demand curve is negatively sloped; it is relevant in so far as its interaction with the industry supply curve (ΣMC) determines the product price. The demand facing the individual firm, however, is infinitely elastic (horizontal) at the current market price.

4. There is no limit to the number of criteria one can dream up. Here are five which may or may not resemble the ones you selected:
   (a) Queuing ("First come, first served.")
   (b) By sex ("Ladies first.")
   (c) By age ("Age before beauty.")
   (d) By physical strength ("I'll fight you for it!")
   (e) By income and/or wealth (a "means" test)

6. Sometimes profit maximization involves loss minimization—making the best out of a bad situation, so to speak. Since fixed costs are invariant in the short run, the decision whether or not to produce is based entirely on variable costs. As long as the going price is above average variable cost, it is better not to cease production entirely. The excess of revenues over variable costs can be used to defray part of the fixed costs which will have to be paid in any event.

8. Assuming that the business is not a corporation and that the year's profits included any salary that she drew for her own labor, the firm is actually suffering an economic loss of $2,000 per year. Aside from the explicit accounting costs which have been deducted from revenues ("sales") in arriving at "profit," we must deduct the implicit costs of both the equity capital ($8,000 per year) and the owner's labors ($10,000 per year). Subtracting both of these from the $16,000 accounting profit yields an economic loss of $2,000 per year. Like many self-employed individuals, this person has "paid a price" to work for herself. Two other qualifications should be noted. In light of the risk involved in an ordinary business, an 8 percent per year opportunity cost of capital (that earned on a government-backed certificate of deposit) was far too low. Twelve to fifteeen percent per year would likely have been more appropriate. Second, since most self-employed persons work very long hours, the $10,000 per year opportunity cost of her labor was also probably on the low side.

10. Equilibrium price means that the amount supplied equals the amount demanded. The competitive sellers would prefer a higher price, while buyers would prefer a lower one. Everybody is "happy" only in the sense that, given the price, each is able to buy or sell all he or she wishes. The problem with disequilibrium prices is that they cause frustration in the market. If the price is "too high" (greater than P_e), the amount supplied exceeds the amount demanded and causes frustration on the part of at least some of the sellers because they are unable to "move" all the merchandise they would like to at that price. If the price is "too low," buyers are frustrated by their inability to buy all they would like at that price. If that price were not permitted to rise, sellers would be forced to use some other rationing criterion or criteria besides money to decide who would get their desired amount of goods. The first situation ($P > P_e$) is often called a "buyers' market" and the second situation ($P < P_e$) a "sellers' market."

12. A nonscarce ("free") good is one of which at a price of zero the quantity demanded is less

than or equal to the quantity supplied. Consequently, your graph should show a demand curve intercepting the horizontal (Q/t) axis at or to the left of where the corresponding supply curve intercepts that axis.

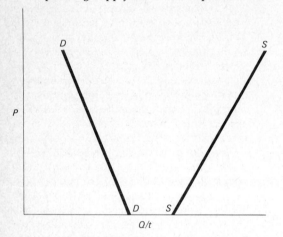

14. Apparently your friend, superentrepreneur, has a unique ability to combine resources more efficiently than others. One way to "handle" this is simply to assert that his or her opportunity cost is understated. Clearly, a sufficiently high opportunity cost assigned to a proprietor's time will shift up the firm's SAC until economic profits disappear.

Chapter 11

2. If, at the price charged, the demand were inelastic, that would mean that total revenues could be increased and total costs decreased by raising the price and selling fewer units. Consequently, the profit-maximizing price must be a higher one. Trial and error would lead to further price increases until an elastic portion of the demand curve was reached. Even further increases in price (decreases in output) would be in order as long as marginal cost exceeded marginal revenue.

4. If η is numerically greater than 1 (elastic), marginal revenue is positive; a decrease in price will result in more total revenues. If η is numerically equal to 1 (unitary elastic), marginal revenue is 0; a change in price will

not affect total revenues at all. If η is numerically less than 1 (inelastic), marginal revenue is negative; a decrease in price will result in less total revenues.

6. Output Q is set at the level where MC = MR. The price charged is the maximum price at which that output Q can be sold, and can be "read" off the demand curve. Economic profits will exist if TR exceeds TC (where TR is equal to $P \times Q$ and TC is equal to ATC $\times Q$). If the TC exceeds TR, the monopoly is "reaping" economic losses.

8. To the extent that TR exceeds TC (economic costs, of course), the firm's market value will be higher by a multiple of those annual economic profits. The multiple is the inverse of the opportunity cost of capital. In effect, the stream of expected future economic profits is discounted to its present value as presented in Chapter 6, and that figure is included in the firm's market price.

10. There are many possible reasons. Just because economic profits are being made doesn't necessarily mean that even higher profits aren't attainable. The demand schedule may have shifted since the last plant was set up. Technology may have changed. Relative input prices may have changed. Any one of these would alter the optimum scale of operations. Note how rare it is that firms ever purchase new equipment which is identical with that which is being phased out.

12. A perfectly competitive firm, in long-run equilibrium, exhibits the following per unit cost and revenue relationships: $P = MR = SMC = LMC = SAC = LAC$. For the monopolist, the result is a bit different: $SAC = LAC < P > MR = SMC = LMC$. Note that if the monopoly profits are capitalized into the firm's value, SAC and LAC will *equal P*.

14. In both cases a sliding scale of prices is charged which results, in effect, in quantity discounts (lower unit prices when more is purchased). The difference is that, while multipart pricing implies discrete variations in unit price according to quantity purchased, perfect price discrimination would capture all consumer surplus from the buyers. Total revenues become the entire

area under the demand curve up to the output being sold; and the last unit is sold for a price just equal to its MC. Note that the amount of information required to even approach perfect price discrimination is astronomical.

Chapter 12

2. The effect of tariffs is to penalize foreign producers when they sell in "our" market. This is, in effect, a barrier to those firms entering the United States market for goods. The reduction or elimination of tariffs increases competition and decreases any monopoly power that might have existed as a result of those tariffs. Note, though, that, even with a tariff American producers must still compete. The tariff just means that they will produce at a higher MC which causes a misallocation of resources on a global scale.

4. The possible criteria are many. The most obvious is money: auction the rights to the highest bidder. Note that the form of competition will be directly related to the criterion or criteria established by the issuing authority. The "tune" of the bidding will be effectively "called" by the government. Whenever something of value is distributed, rivalry among potential recipients is bound to result.

6. The first problem is that, unless the government somehow controls production, an excess supply (a "glut" or surplus) will result. The quantity supplied will exceed the quantity demanded at the above-market-clearing price. Unless the government stands ready to buy unlimited quantities at that price, effectively pegging it at that level, a lower (black-market) price will develop. At this lower price, producers will be able to sell all their production, and this was not possible at the pegged price. Any program which attempts to subsidize producers by outlawing "low" prices, without getting a handle on supply, is doomed to failure. For this reason, "price support" programs are inevitably followed by maximum production quotas of one kind or another.

8. Cartel agreements are generally aboveboard. OPEC (The Organization of Petroleum Exporting Countries) holds periodic publicized meetings after which it typically announces what "the" price of crude oil will be. There is little pretense of secrecy. Other collusive agreements, executed in violation of the law, are typically characterized by secrecy and clandestine behavior in direct proportion to the penalties for being caught.

10. Is entry restricted? Yes. State bar examinations accomplish that. Is competition discouraged? Yes. "Recommended" minimum fee schedules discourage price cutting. In addition, advertising, perhaps the most common form of rivalry, is severely regulated by the state bars. Are there sanctions for violating the "code of ethics"? Yes. In all states it is illegal to practice law without a license. Furthermore, transgressions of the rules by licensed attorneys (members of the bar) subject them to the possible loss of their license as a result of so-called disbarment proceedings.

12. A natural monopoly occurs in industries where there are substantial economies of scale in relation to the market demand for the product. The relationship between LAC and *DD* is such that one firm can supply the entire market at lower unit costs than could two or more firms. For this reason, once one firm establishes a plant of sufficient size to take advantage of the economies of scale, there is no incentive whatsoever for another firm to duplicate those facilities.

14. Yes, it does. For a firm that was highly "leveraged" (financed with borrowed money) the second method would be far more advantageous. Since the tax laws permit the deduction of interest payments as a cost of operation, chargeable against sales in arriving at profit, there would be a great incentive for a firm not only to buy new equipment frequently, but to do so with borrowed money, even if it had to pay an interest rate greater than 10 percent per year! Note that this argument presupposes a demand of sufficient strength to generate revenues adequate to cover all these "costs" including the "permissible" rate of return on "investment."

Chapter 13

2. Recall that in a perfectly competitive market, in long-run equilibrium, $P = MR = SMC = SAC = LMC = LAC$. This outcome is shown graphically in Figure 10-16(b). In a monopolistically competitive market, the result is that $P = SAC = LAC > MR = LMC = SMC$. There exists "excess capacity" which, in Chamberlin's definition, is the price consumers pay for differentiated products.

4. The burden of proof rests on the person who seeks to demonstrate that a product difference is merely "artificial" or "superficial." Does the addition of carburetor-cleaning additives to gasoline amount to an "artificial" differentiation of the product? How about "service with a smile"? Is that not preferable to service with a frown? A better product, like beauty, is in the eye of the beholder. The fact that every day millions of people fork over the additional cost of these "mere frills" suggests that at least some consumers find them to be product-enhancing.

6. Marginal revenue in its usual sense refers to the change in total revenue attributable to a change in price of sufficient magnitude (a zero price change being sufficient in the case of an infinitely elastic demand schedule) to cause the quantity demanded to change by one unit. This involves a movement along a given demand schedule. In the case of advertising, however, "marginal revenue" results from a shift in the demand schedule which is the result of an advertising effort that enables (hopefully) more to be sold at each and every possible price.

8. If "MR" > MC, increased, advertising outlays will further increase profits. Advertising outlays would be increased until "MR" = MC. More specifically, when $MC_{advertising}$ plus $MC_{production}$ equals "MR," advertising outlays are optimal from the standpoint of maximizing profits.

10. The distinction is not clear. Toothpaste, mouthwash, and deodorant ads are often informative only in the sense that they remind us of our inherent biological condition. Photographs of the Taj Mahal or Machu Picchu, which give potential tourists a glimpse of these tourist attractions, seem to be more informative. When the British Tourist Board beckons us to "Come home, America (to the United Kingdom), all is forgiven," we are reminded of our Anglo-Saxon heritage and, in some historical sense, are "informed" by the ad. Typewriter and car ads that focus on the product's performance would be classified as "informative" by nearly everyone.

12. The result is that each firm consistently overestimates the elasticity of its demand curve and makes decisions based upon an imaginary demand curve $d_f d_f$ and its associated marginal revenue curve mr_f.

14. If entry of new firms is not prevented, entry will occur in response to the existence of economic profits. As the number of firms, "n," increases, the proportional demand curve $d_p' d_p'$ will shift leftward (actually it will rotate clockwise about its price or vertical axis intercept). Eventually, economic profits will be completely dissipated by such entry and price will be equal to LAC. At this point, there are no economic profits and entry will cease.

Chapter 14

2. Only in an isolated area where there are but a handful of stations within, say, a 50 or 100 mile radius would an oligopoly model be expected to predict well. In most areas of the United States, there are just too many gas stations competing in any given locale to warrant the use of the oligopoly model. The monopolistic competition models might better explain gasoline retailing in most markets.

4. Since entry is unrestricted, the potential for economic profits will result in entry, according to this simple model, so long as some segment of one of the proportionate demand curves lies above the LAC curve. Output can be more efficiently (cheaply) produced, in this case, by two firms rather than three.

6. (a) Cournot assumed that perfect information would keep both firms' prices identical. He further assumed that each firm would behave as if the other would not change its output in

response to any change in the other's output. (b) The long-run result was a price greater than MC (the competitive price) but less than the monopoly price.

8. In both models, both duopolists are assumed to continue to behave on the basis of assumptions about their rival's behavior that are repeatedly demonstrated to be false. They don't learn from their experiences. It is difficult to conceive of entrepreneurs so stubborn in their beliefs that they refuse to recognize overwhelming evidence that their reaction-function assumptions are inaccurate.

10. The kink arises from the assumptions of the model. Sweezy assumes that if any one firm raises its price, none of the others will follow. Consequently, a maverick firm's price increase will result in a drastic decrease in its total revenue. Conversely, the model assumes that any price decrease will be matched by all rivals.   For this reason, the quantity demanded will probably not increase enough to cover increased costs and profit will likely be less. Under these assumptions, it is in no individual firm's interest to "rock the boat."

12. They are presumed to be completely passive and to behave as price takers. They act as though their individual demand curves were perfectly elastic at the price set by the dominant firm, and they set their individual outputs at a level equating marginal cost with that price.

14. The consequences of an overt price war can be disastrous for oligopolistic firms. For that reason there are strong group pressures not to disturb the industry price structure. More subtle and less easily detectible means like advertising and minor design variations are commonly used in an attempt to increase revenues and/or share of the market.   Such revenue-increasing techniques are perceived by other firms to be less threatening and therefore more acceptable forms of competition.

Chapter 15

2. Their behavior was tantamount to killing the goose that laid the golden egg. Labor and capital are complementary inputs; each enhances the marginal productivity of the other. The higher-paid workers are the ones who work with such sophisticated equipment as giant punch presses, welding rigs, etc. Janitors, on the other hand, typically do their work with such relatively unsophisticated tools as brooms and mops; their substantially lower productivity is reflected in their lower wages.

4. By assumption, it does not. Generally, the quantity of labor hired by a single firm is insignificant in relation to the overall demand for labor. However, the next chapter will deal with labor markets in which a firm *is* sufficiently large to affect prevailing wages by its own hiring and firing.

6. Just as a fall in the relative price of a commodity will induce consumers to substitute more of it for other products in their consumption, entrepreneurs will make similar substitutions in response to a change in the relative price of an input. A movement from A to S on Figure 15-3(a) demonstrates how, if the identical output is still to be produced, it will now be done with less capital and more labor in response to a fall in the relative price of labor.

8. In response to a fall in the price of labor, a firm will do more than just substitute labor for capital. It will also go beyond merely increasing its labor purchases with the cost savings realized from a fall in the price of labor. Since the marginal product of capital has risen with the increased input of labor, the firm will actually increase its use of capital in attaining the new optimal input combination. This increase is shown by the differential K_2 minus K_1 in Figure 15-3(a).

10. Suppose the demand for the output product is highly elastic.   Even a relatively small increase in the price of the input factor, which correspondingly raises the price of the output product, will cause a large decrease in its quantity demanded and therefore in employment.

12. The theory is not well suited to service industries because it is just not possible for an entrepreneur to keep an inventory of, say, razor cuts. Services, by their very nature, are con-

sumed as they are produced and are therefore nonstockpileable. This is no doubt one of the reasons that barbershops seldom employ barbers on a straight salary. Part of the risk of idleness (and the corresponding reward of busyness) is thereby borne by the employee.

14. Two points need be made. First, the quantity of land *is* augmentable. The Dutch, by building elaborate systems of dikes and canals, have been pushing the ocean back for decades. Secondly, at sufficiently low rental rates, some land will be withdrawn from the land use market because the owner prefers to use it for hunting or picnics or just for the scenic beauty of its idleness.

Chapter 16

2. It depends. If (*a*) Frisbees are manufactured in an area having a large labor force in relation to Whamo's employment demands, and (*b*) Whamo is not unionized, then the example is OK. This assumes, of course, that you accept the characterization of Whamo as the monopoly seller of Frisbees.

4. The statement is false. It is true that in a competitive labor market the monopoly seller has no power to affect the wage it pays. However, exploitation refers to paying a worker less than his or her VMP. Monopolists don't hire enough of the resource in question; they cease hiring when the MRP equals the going wage. Since VMP always exceeds MRP for a monopolist, it must also exceed the going wage at the monopolist's profit-maximizing output. Consequently, there is exploitation, by definition.

6. Some examples would be Coors beer in Golden, Colorado; Bethlehem Steel in Bethlehem, Pennsylvania; Winnebago Corporation in Forest City, Iowa; and many a coal mining town in West Virginia. As long as your example is one of a dominant employer (dominant in its local labor market, that is) selling its product(s) in fairly competitive markets, you're OK.

8. This monopsony argument is not unlike the one in question 7. In the long run, if the wage level is unsatisfactory, some of these

"specialists" will retrain. Similarly, students will choose not to go into the field; they will acquire other skills. In the long run, the supply of labor faced by these monopsonists will be pretty flat.

10. The perfect price discriminator never pays more than the opportunity cost of any unit of labor he or she hires. Under these circumstances, the MFC curve is the *SS* curve and there is no reason for the firm to restrict its hiring. By assumption there is no problem of bidding up wages of existing employees in order to get an additional employee to come on board. If this is unclear, look again at Figure 16-9.

12. The nondiscussion of wages is consistent with price (wage) discrimination by employers. Keeping one's employees "in the dark" regarding each other's earnings facilitates the practice of unequal pay for equal work. It is also in the interest of those employes who are better paid to stifle the flow of information on pay levels.

14. If a person's time is very valuable, it is because *others* have placed a high value on it. It isn't Elizabeth Taylor herself but rather movie afficionados that place a high value on her time. John Denver's time is valuable because music listeners feel that it is. The same holds true for physicians and circus freaks. Lacking a demand, "skills" and "resources" are absolutely worthless in the market sense of the word.

Chapter 17

2. The statement is false. Because a firm utilizes an input only to the point that the input's VMP or MRP is equal to its price, and marginal product is declining, it follows that all the inframarginal (up to the marginal) units are producing more value than they are being paid. This differential is used to compensate other factor inputs. The residual, if any, would be profits.

4. It is the nonpecuniary aspects of clerical and blue-collar jobs that account for much of the spread in pay. Aside from differences in "status," clerical workers typically don't have

to dirty their hands or work around fumes and noise or out of doors. The probability of being killed or injured is much lower in an office than on a factory floor or construction site, and job security may also be greater as well.

6. Not only is a higher level of innate ability required, but the training of a CPA is substantially greater than that of a retail clerk. In the long run, CPA wages must reflect the costs of their training in order that there be an incentive for additional workers to continue to train for that field.

8. The statement is false. Some of the revenue may indeed be rent. However, the buildings housing the art have to be maintained, guards have to be hired, ticket takers paid, etc. Occasionally, ransoms on stolen paintings even have to be paid. All of these costs are part of the cost of keeping the art objects intact, and these costs must be subtracted from revenues in calculating economic rent.

10. Quasi-rent is a short-run concept. By definition, in the short run some inputs are fixed. In defining them as fixed, we are implying that their short-run opportunity cost is zero. Consequently, their supply to the firm is perfectly inelastic. The quasi-rent concept is applied primarily to specialized equipment which is costly to relocate. Bridges and hydroelectric dams would be good examples.

12. The consumers of factory products rarely meet or are even aware of the people who make the product. In service industries, however, the consumer typically meets the producer face to face. Those preferring to be served by a "this" or a "that" would presumably be willing to pay more to have that preference satisfied. Consequently, the incentives for the proprietor to discriminate in hiring are greater and more direct.

14. If the discrimination is noneconomic (not based upon productivity differences), then the group being discriminated against ought to represent a bargain-basement pool of cheap labor. A manufacturer hiring that labor would have lower production costs than those of discriminating competitors. Note that if enough firms caught on to this idea, their actions would cause the in-

tergroup wage differentials to vanish. (Apply Figure 17-2 here.)

Chapter 18

2. Through the use of mathematics, general equilibrium analysis can handle multimarket economies. However, in order to present the concepts in two-dimensional (plane) geometry, we must restrict the number of consumers, inputs, and outputs to two each. Note that all the concepts developed are applicable to a multimarket reality.

4. The goods must be distributed in such a manner that the marginal rate of substitution between good x and good y is equal for both parties. If it were not equal, further exchange would be necessary in order to bring about the equality.

6. The statement is false because it is too broad. We can say a bit more about the final distribution once we know the initial allotments. Figure 18-2 shows that, while it is true that trade will occur until the contract curve is reached, the final distribution will be limited to that portion of it which is between points A and B. Study Figure 18-2 until you have satisfied yourself that, in the absence of coercion, it would be irrational for one of the consumers to arrive at a point on the contract curve outside of segment AB.

8. A change in their preferences will necessitate a reconstruction of their respective indifference maps. This will generate an entirely new contract curve. Now additional exchanges will be necessary in order to enhance the well-being of both parties. These exchanges will cease when the new contract curve has been reached.

10. E' portrays an initial allocation of the two resources to the production of goods x and y. In order to determine the respective outputs of goods x and y when resources are so allocated, we must look to the production isoquants for each good. These are shown in Figure 18-4. Q_{II}^x and Q_{II}^y correspond to specific rates of output for each good.

12. The marginal rate of technical substitution (MRTS) between each pair of inputs must be

the same for all producers who make use of those inputs.

14. If the MRTSs were not equal, resources could be reallocated in such a manner as to increase the production and consumption of one good without decreasing the production or consumption of the other. This would clearly increase the level of utility of either or both consumers (depending upon the distribution of the new output mix) without decreasing the satisfaction of either one. If the MRSs of two or more consumers were unequal, additional utility could be generated for one or both by moving toward the contract curve (voluntary exchange). If this is not clear, review the example discussed under the heading "Maximizing Consumer Satisfaction" on page 428.

Chapter 19

2. Positive economics is not intended to answer questions of good, bad, better, or worse. When we speak of an optimal allocation of resources, we are referring to an allocation which is socially efficient in the sense that no further voluntary exchange will occur.

4. Since interpersonal utility comparisons are impossible, there is no known way of proving or disproving such a statement. A "utilometer" device, cardinally quantifying persons' perceived utilities, has yet to be developed.

6. If the existing allocation of resources is such that no person can gain without another incurring a loss, the condition has been satisfied. This is just another way of saying that no further voluntary exchange will occur; the contract curve has been reached.

8. Your graph should look like the one in Figure 19-1. The highest attainable level of indifference is represented by the indifference curve which is tangent to the product transformation curve. The point of tangency shows the respective rates of production and consumption of the two goods; and the MRS is equal to MRTS.

10. A utility possibilities frontier is another way

of looking at a contract (or conflict) curve. Any movement along a contract curve will result in higher utility for one person and lower utility for the other (thus the notion of "conflict"). A number of those levels of indifference are ranked for each consumer. Those rankings become the ordinal units on the utility possibilities frontier.

12. No, it does not necessarily follow. The theory of second best suggests that such a partial movement toward perfect markets may actually lessen social welfare. This point has important implications for economic policy.

14. Arrow starts with five axioms which he believes that social preference structures must satisfy to be minimally acceptable to the population. He has found no majority voting system which satisfies all five criteria. This theorem has stimulated much critical reflection on the democratic process.

16. The producers' surplus obtained from producing and selling any particular unit of a good is the difference between what the producer would have been barely *willing* to accept for that unit and what he or she actually *did* receive for it. Free entry into an industry and/or expansion of existing firms will compete away short-run quasi-rents. In contrast, in the absence of perfect price discrimination, consumers' surplus will persist.

Chapter 20

2. Market failure refers to situations in which perfectly competitive markets fail to allocate resources in a welfare-maximizing manner. By implication, some modification of the market outcome might succeed in improving the allocation of resources.

4. If we are in agreement that rooftop TV antennas detract from the appearance of a home and impose an eyesore cost (not to be confused with isocost) on neighbors and passersby, then our nation overallocates resources to production of such antennas. This is a situation of external diseconomies, because marginal social cost exceeds marginal social benefits.

6. Since the new supply schedule is to the left of

the old (external costs have now been included) and the demand schedule remains
unchanged, the new equilibrium quantity is
smaller. Economic welfare would be increased by such a contraction of output and
the associated increase in price.

8. Everyone owns them and nobody owns
   them. Consequently, there is no incentive for
   any user to be concerned with the future
   value of the resource in question. This is
   perhaps most clearly observable in the behavior of fishing boat owners. The goal of
   each boat owner is to harvest fish as long as
   marginal private cost is less than the going
   price of such fish. The opportunity cost of
   depleting the stock of fish does not affect the
   decisions of the proprietor. Any single boat
   operator would be foolish to behave otherwise in light of the nonownership of the fish.

10. In effect, much conservation legislation at-
    tempts to assign "rights" to plants and wild
    animals. Judges as well have been asked to
    define ecological rights. Historically, howev-
    er, wild plants and animals have been "fair
    game" for Homo sapiens.

12. There is an implied assumption that some
    people would prefer to live in a racially and
    ethnically homogeneous neighborhood or, at
    least, that they think others hold such prefer-
    ences. The whole notion of a "panic" rests
    upon such an assumption. More devastating
    to the theory, however, is the implied as-
    sumption that information costs are very
    high, at least in the short run. Even if the
    alleged decline in property values does occur,
    Mr. or Ms. Blockbuster will not be the only
    person seeking to buy on the downswing. To
    the extent that home-seeking persons,
    brokers, and speculators perceive the tempo-
    rary nature of the decline, their bidding for
    homes will lessen, if not prevent entirely (in
    the case of perfect information), the decline
    in property values. This would remove
    Blockbuster's incentive for such an undertak-
    ing and prevent it from occurring. The
    theory fails.

14. Pollution should be further reduced as long
    as the marginal social benefit from such
    reduction exceeds the marginal social cost of
    doing so.

INDEXES

NAME INDEX

INDEX TO GLOSSARY TERMS

SUBJECT INDEX

Optimal input combination

When there are n inputs,

$$\frac{\text{MPP}_x}{P_x} = \frac{\text{MPP}_y}{P_y} = \cdots = \frac{\text{MPP}_n}{P_n}$$

In other words, input cost minimization or output product maximization requires a combination of inputs such that the ratio of the marginal physical product of each input divided by its price is the same for all inputs.

$$\frac{\text{MPP}_x}{P_x} = \frac{\text{MPP}_y}{P_y} = \cdots = \frac{\text{MPP}_n}{P_n} = \frac{1}{\text{MC}} = \frac{1}{\text{MR}} = \frac{1}{P}$$

or $\quad \dfrac{P_x}{\text{MPP}_x} = \dfrac{P_y}{\text{MPP}_y} = \cdots = \dfrac{P_n}{\text{MPP}_n} = \text{MC} = P$

$$\text{MPP}_x \cdot \text{MR} = P_x \quad \text{MRP} \quad \text{or} \quad \text{MPP}_x \cdot P = P_x \quad \text{VMP}$$

$$\text{MPP}_y \cdot \text{MR} = P_y \quad \text{or} \quad \text{MPP}_y \cdot P = P_y$$

$$\text{MPP}_n \cdot \text{MR} = P_n \quad \text{or} \quad \text{MPP}_n \cdot P = P_n$$

Long-run equilibrium of a perfectly competitive firm

$$\text{SMC} = \text{SAC} = \text{LAC} = \text{LMC} = P$$

Price elasticity of supply

$$\epsilon = \frac{\Delta Q/Q}{\Delta P/P} = \frac{\Delta Q}{\Delta P} \cdot \frac{P}{Q}$$

Lerner Index of monopoly power

$$\frac{P - \text{MC}}{P}$$

The elasticity of substitution

$$\sigma = \mp\left[\frac{\Delta(K/L)}{K/L} \bigg/ \frac{\Delta(w/r)}{r/w} \right]$$

Marginal factor cost

$$\text{MFC} = w\left(1 + \frac{1}{\epsilon_L}\right)$$

Monopsonist pricing and employment with several variable inputs

$$\frac{\text{MFC}_x}{\text{MPP}_x} = \frac{\text{MFC}_y}{\text{MPP}_y} = \cdots = \frac{\text{MFC}_n}{\text{MPP}_n}$$

for all n factors of production

NOTES

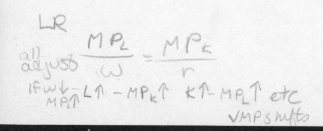

In PC $\quad MC = \dfrac{P_x}{MP_x} = \dfrac{P_y}{MP_y} = MR = P$

$$P \times MP_L = P_L$$
$$VMP = VMP$$

LR

all adjust $\dfrac{MP_L}{w} = \dfrac{MP_K}{r}$

if $w\downarrow - L\uparrow - MP_K\uparrow \quad K\uparrow - MP_L\uparrow$ etc
$MP_L\uparrow$
VMP shifts

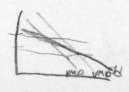